The Genealogist's Companion and Sourcebook

2ND EDITION

 Published by Betterway Books, an imprint of F&W Publications, Inc., 4700 East Galbraith Road, Cincinnati, Ohio 45236. (800) 289-0963. Second edition.

Other fine Betterway Books are available from your local bookstore or on our Web site at www.family treemagazine.com.

07 06 05 04 5 4 3 2

Library of Congress Cataloging-in-Publication Data

Croom, Emily Anne
The genealogist's companion and sourcebook / by Emily Anne Croom.—2nd ed.
p. cm.
Includes bibliographical references and index.
ISBN 1-55870-651-8 (alk. paper)
1. United States—Genealogy—Handbooks, manuals, etc. I. Title.

CS47.C75 2003
929'.1'072073—dc21

2003050017
CIP

Editor: Sharon DeBartolo Carmack, CG
Associate editor: Erin Nevius
Production Coordinator: Michelle Ruberg
Design: Sandy Conopeotis Kent
Interior design/cover design: Sandy Conopeotis Kent

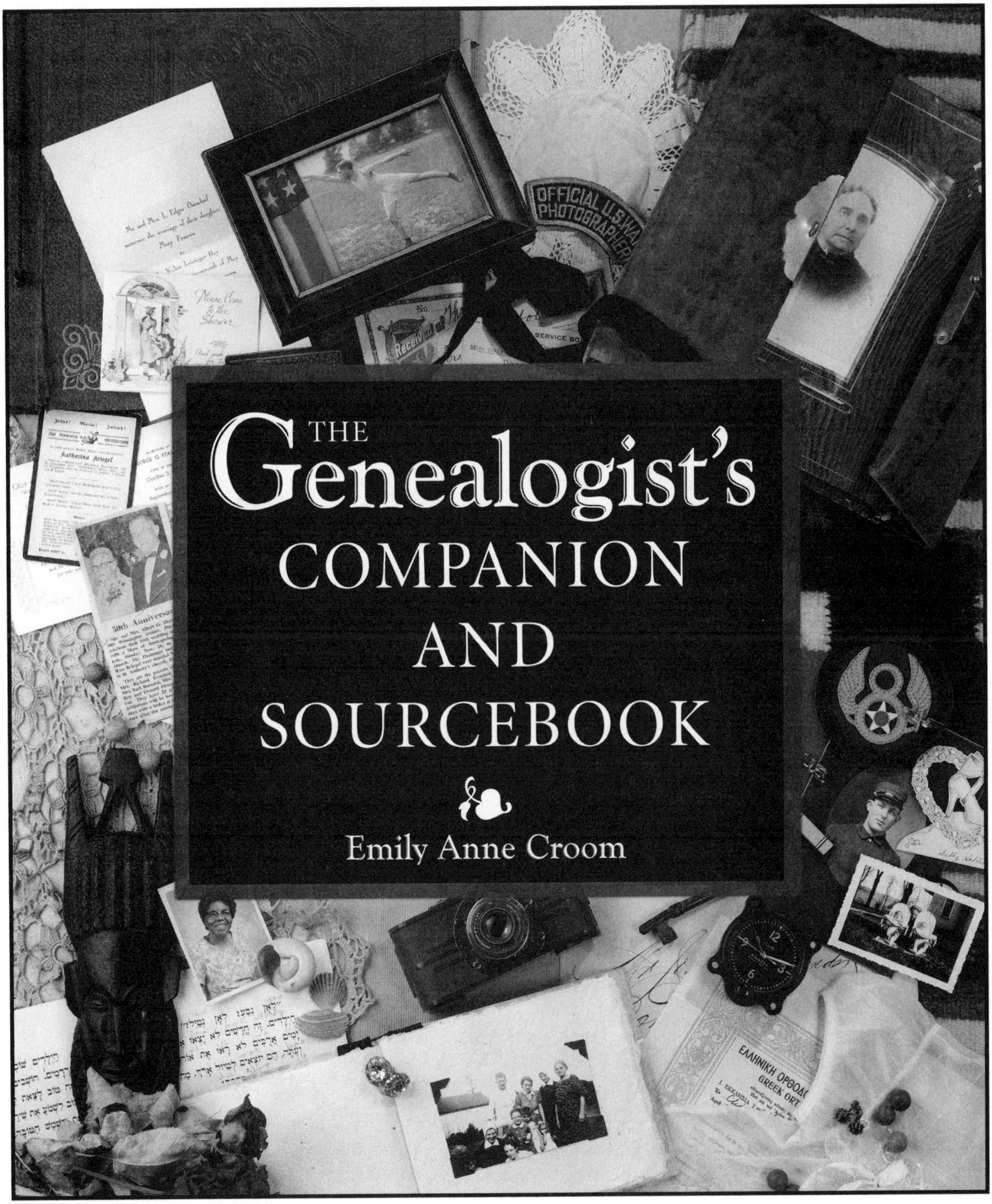

The Genealogist's Companion and Sourcebook

Emily Anne Croom

BETTERWAY BOOKS
CINCINNATI, OHIO
www.familytreemagazine.com

About the Author

Emily Anne Croom is an active genealogy researcher, writer, speaker, and teacher with a master's degree in history. She writes for several periodicals, and her other Betterway books are *Unpuzzling Your Past*, 4th ed.; *The Unpuzzling Your Past Workbook*; *A Genealogist's Guide to Discovering Your African-American Ancestors*, with Franklin Smith; and *The Sleuth Book for Genealogists*. Visit her Web site at <www.unpuzzling.com>.

Dedication

In memory of three among many who still influence my life and work in positive ways:

—Mama, the teacher and writer, who encouraged me to teach and write, applauded my achievements, forgave my shortcomings, and taught me to observe details.

—Daddy, the engineer, who taught me to worry and to keep my nose to the grindstone; who, when he saw the first edition of this book (1994), tried to make me promise never to write another one. . . because "I chewed off all my fingernails worrying about this one."

—Charlotte Metcalf Loomis, my dear friend, who taught me not to worry but to "let" and laugh; whom I would have chosen for a big sister, given the opportunity; who gave me all her ancestors to study; and whose spirit still nudges me in all I attempt to do.

Acknowledgments

Authors seldom work entirely alone, and a comprehensive book is often the product of an author's vision, encouraged and aided by family, friends, and colleagues. Singled out from among all these, I want to express my appreciation to my students for many good experiences and all that I learn from them. Thank you to the numerous librarians and archivists nationwide who contributed information about their collections and their states. Several were especially accommodating, including Sheran Johle of Southwestern University, Georgetown, Texas; Rebecca Preece of the New Jersey State Archives; Constance Potter of the National Archives; staff and volunteers at the Kansas City regional branch of the National Archives; the volunteer librarians at the Bering Family History Center, Houston; and the entire staff of Clayton Library Center for Genealogical Research, Houston.

Sixteen dedicated genealogists shared their success stories and/or documents for inclusion in this second edition: Lona Dee Boudreaux, Gay E. Carter, A.G. Conlon, Alice Ellis, Marilyn Finer-Collins, Charlie A. Gardes, Jo Anne Gulliver, Cary Hall, Marjorie Lowe, Pat Metcalfe, Lugenia Parham-Evans, Aryl-Jeanne Reed, Alexander Perry Scott, Karen F. Stanley, Virginia Simms Toney, and Charlene Wilson.

Another important contributor to this effort has been my personal computer guru, Robert A. Shelby, who kept the technology working and even made a midnight house-call when the computer died. The four genealogists to whom I am most indebted for countless hours of discussion, manuscript reading, and sharing of ideas and expertise are my friend Charlie A. Gardes; my friend Gay E. Carter, reference librarian at the University of Houston-Clear Lake; my friend Franklin Smith, who shared in the research for the case study in chapter nine and is my co-author in *A Genealogist's Guide to Discovering Your African-American Ancestors*; and my patient husband, Robert T. Shelby.

—Emily Anne Croom, Bellaire, Texas, 2003

Table of Contents at a Glance

Table of Contents

Your Genealogy Companion

This sourcebook is your companion for U.S. research, focusing on resources outside the family. The book's two primary goals are (1) to describe the genealogical contents and benefits of numerous sources and encourage you to use them and (2) to let you know how you can get your hands on them in order to use them. Thus, it provides how-to information and is a reference book. You can read it straight through or consult chapters as they become pertinent to your research.

For a review of the use of family sources—family Bibles, letters, interviews, and others—and basic research methods and sources, consult *Unpuzzling Your Past*. Techniques for solving genealogical problems and scaling brick walls are the focus of *The Sleuth Book for Genealogists*.

YES, THERE IS HOPE

"Where do I go from here? What do I do now?" Have you ever asked these questions when you have run into a stumbling block or a genuine "brick wall" in your research? Although we have to admit that all lineages come to a research halt before we are ready to give them up, we can solve many genealogical problems and identify many ancestors.

Usually the key is finding the right records. Numerous records are waiting to be found; we need to know where to look. Recorders in the past—clerks, ship captains, census takers, newspaper editors, clergymen, immigration authorities, and perhaps even neighbors—may have recorded exactly what we want to know. Our challenge is finding what they wrote. Of course, some of these now-valuable records have been thrown out as trash, washed away in floods, or gone up in flames. These losses are a real obstacle to research, and we must think creatively to find alternate sources for the answers they may have contained. For example, a marriage record may not exist in the marriage registers at the courthouse, but a military pension application for the husband, his widow, or even their son may contain an affidavit confirming the marriage date and place.

So, don't declare a brick wall until you have tried many records contemporary with your ancestors—records that are the subject of this book. Every state and every county have unique records in addition to the "standard" ones. Look for both kinds. What helps you solve a problem in one place may not exist in another place. Helping you find out what is available is one purpose of this book.

Finding the Records

It is one thing to know about a source but another to know how or where to find it. Thus, this book guides you in finding the record: where it is available for use, for purchase, or for rent. Many materials are also available through interlibrary loan at local public libraries or through photoduplication services of archives and libraries.

Part of this book concentrates on special *places* for research, such as courthouses and libraries, the kinds of genealogical sources available there, and how to use them. The book also discusses *sources*, such as maps, newspapers, census records, military records, passenger lists, and others available for use in many libraries and archives or on microfilm or CD-ROM.

At this time, relatively few original records are digitized on the Internet, but some are abstracted or described there. The Internet is a valuable tool for identifying and locating both family and public records; use search engines and links from Cyndi's List (see bulleted list below) and other Web sites as tools to aid your research. Although this book mentions a number of Web sites that contain reference information or articles for furthering your knowledge, Internet "research" is not the focus or purpose of this book. The Internet can provide you with good clues and suggestions, but most of the documents that help answer tough genealogical questions are not available online.

Important

Throughout this book are certain names, abbreviations, or acronyms related to finding records:

- **Ancestry.com**—Orem, Utah; (800) 262-3787; <www.ancestry.com>. Some non-subscription databases; subscription access to digitized census records, newspapers, and other resources. Check for databases on ethnic groups as well.
- **Archives I**—the primary National Archives facility at 700 Pennsylvania Avenue, Washington, DC.
- **Archives II**—the National Archives facility in College Park, Maryland.
- **Cyndi's List**—<www.cyndislist.com>; a major reference site with links to thousands of Web sites for reference, research, and connecting with other genealogists.
- **FHL**—Family History Library, Salt Lake City; (800) 537-5971 (customer service); <www.familysearch.org>. Records are available for use in Salt Lake City or, for a small rental fee, through the Family History Centers worldwide; for locations see the Web site and your local telephone directory under Church of Jesus Christ of Latter-day Saints.
- **Genealogy.com**—(800) 548-1806; <www.genealogy.com>. Subscription access especially to family and local histories and digitized census records; free access to numerous surname forums at <www.genforum.genealogy.com>.
- **Heritage Quest Online**—part of ProQuest; (800) 760-2455. Access to digitized census images and books if you hold a library card from or visit a subscribing library; individual subscriptions not available at this time.
- **Interlibrary loan**—Consult your local public or academic librarian.
- **NARA**—National Archives and Records Administration, Washington, DC; <www.archives.gov> (see Appendix A). Numerous articles pertinent to genealogy and National Archives records are in the quarterly *Prologue*. From <www.archives.gov/publications/prologue/genealogy_notes.html> you can access archived issues, the current issue, and indexes to articles.

- **National Archives Microfilm Rental Program**—a private company renting census and selected military records only; P.O. Box 30, Annapolis Junction, MD 20701-0030; (301) 604-3699; <www.archives.gov/publications/microfilm_catalogs/how_to_rent_microfilm.html>.
- **PERSI**—*Periodical Source Index*, from Allen County Public Library, Fort Wayne, Indiana. Indexes hundreds of genealogy and history periodicals; available in print, on CD-ROM, and by subscription online; not an every-name index. (See chapter eight for more about this resource.)
- **Scholarly Resources**—distributor of National Archives and other microfilm and CD-ROMs; 104 Greenhill Avenue, Wilmington, DE 19805-1897; (800) 772-8937; <www.scholarly.com>.
- **WorldCat**—a huge bibliographic database of OCLC (Online Computer Library Center) that helps librarians and researchers locate materials in libraries worldwide. Usually you can access the database from (1) local public or academic libraries or (2) from home using your library card number. Such a search is especially helpful when you are looking for published materials, but it includes some microform and archival materials as well.

To learn which National Archives facilities hold a certain microfilm publication, go to <www.archives.gov/research_room/alic/research_tools/search_microfilm_catalog.html/>, click on "microfilm publications catalog," type in the micropublication number (such as M1301 or T526) under "enter microfilm ID," submit your search, then click on "display search results," then click on "full record." After the description of the publication is a list of the National Archives facilities holding that series of microfilm and information about purchasing rolls. (M and T numbers are available in the National Archives microfilm catalogs and in the descriptions of National Archives records discussed throughout this book.) This process does not include public or academic libraries or historical societies that may hold the publication; check with them individually. Be aware that not all online library catalogs include the library's microprint holdings. Also be aware that as Web sites change, specific pages and instructions listed in this book may change.

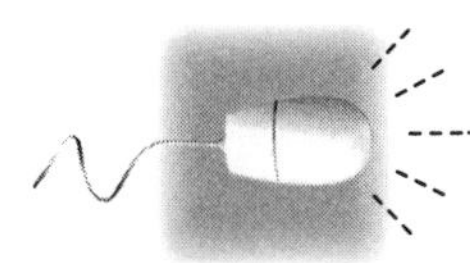

Internet Source

All Internet addresses provided in this book were current when the book went to press.

Because of the constantly changing nature of the Internet, no book can list all current Web sites that may contain abstracted, transcribed, or digitized records of the kinds discussed in this book, but a number of helpful Web sites are listed throughout this book. Visit these and use your favorite search engines to locate the records, either on no-charge or subscription sites. Remember, you should consider any abstracted or transcribed record as a finding aid to lead you to the original records, or the earliest extant copies, or microfilm of them. Credible and accurate genealogy cannot rely only on the Internet and library books. Helping you find and use the originals (or records closest in time to the ancestors) is the focus of this book.

Online subscriptions for censuses and other records can be beneficial but do not fit into everyone's budget. Access to many records online, free of charge, or in a library is possible, and new materials become available every month. However, genealogical research costs some money, whether for online subscriptions, reference books such as this one, document copies, journal subscriptions, microfilm rental, or travel. Consider your budget, your goals, and your priorities. Doing good-quality genealogy, even on a budget, is a much worthier goal than freely downloading generations of undocumented names that may not belong to your ancestors after all.

An Invitation

Some of us need encouragement to try new avenues of research, and real-life examples often make sources inviting. One way we become interested in a new source is to hear about someone else's success in using it. That is why this book includes numerous research examples and case studies. These come from my research and that of other genealogists. All the contributors, including me, are everyday, motivated genealogists who focus on doing legitimate, quality research. If we can do it, so can you. The examples are your invitation to try these and similar sources in your research.

Reminder

The endnotes (beginning on page 439) may also give you ideas for sources to try and may answer questions you have when reading. Successful genealogists have learned the importance of reading the notes along with the text in any work. Not only does source documentation, either in the notes or in the text, tell you where the information was found, it suggests that you look for the same kind of record when it seems applicable to one of your ancestors.

In our rushed lives, we tend to want instant rewards and immediate success. Sometimes, we are lucky enough to experience those quick results and unexpected discoveries in genealogy. However, the case studies and success stories presented in the book did not all happen with a snap of the fingers or a look in one record. Most involved using multiple sources over a period of months or years.

I constantly remind myself of my favorite Shakespeare quotation: "Though patience be a tired mare, yet she will plod on." By the same token, if we plod around in circles, without direction or focus, we limit our success. Thus, it is important to concentrate on a "tough," "elusive," or "brick-wall" ancestral problem with dedicated attention instead of spreading research efforts too thin by trying to work on too many lineages at once. For example, instead of trying to research all sixteen great-great-grandparents at the same time, you will have more success and less frustration by focusing your effort on one great-great-grandmother, along with her children and siblings, to try to identify her parents. The other fifteen will wait.

In the bibliographies throughout the text, you will find resources for further reading, or indexes and guides to help you find materials, or examples of published genealogical abstracts and compilations. You will not find in this book numerous lists of printed sources that genealogists use to get clues about specific ancestors—abstracted deed records, published family histories, and the like. This book invites you to go beyond those resources to the records themselves. However, the bibliographies are a sampling from many subject areas. Their purpose is to show you some of the materials that are available and invite you to look in library catalogs to find materials pertinent to your research and your ancestral locales.

GENEALOGY: A CONTINUAL LEARNING PROCESS

This book is an important component of the continuing learning process in which all genealogists participate. We all begin as newcomers to the discipline of genealogy, and we gain knowledge and experience as we research. I do not like the terms *intermediate* and *advanced* when referring to levels of research experience. Researchers with predominantly New England ancestors may have become highly skilled in using New England research materials but have little knowledge of Southern research when they discover a Southern ancestor, and vice versa. Those with twentieth-century immigrant ancestors will learn about and skillfully use resources different from those needed to research seventeenth-century colonial ancestors. These differences do not make one person advanced and another intermediate.

Important

Successful genealogists continually learn about new sources and techniques and use them in research. No one is an expert in everything. A local researcher focusing on only one county can become the expert in the history, genealogy, and records of that one county but have little experience with research extending beyond it. As our research broadens over several centuries and several regions or nations, our success depends on our continuing education and the availability of records.

This continuing education takes place in at least several settings: societies, published materials, seminars and classes, and online.

Societies

Some genealogists ask, "Why should I join a local historical or genealogical society when my ancestors lived halfway across the country?" The following are some of the reasons for and benefits of local, state, surname, or lineage-based society membership:

- Meeting other genealogists with whom you can share questions, research, transportation, and friendship. Some have even met their future spouses in such a society.
- Participating in genealogical and social functions.
- Attending meetings and seminars featuring speakers and interesting programs. Even if you live in Oregon and your ancestors lived mostly in the Ohio Valley, your society may present programs on general genealogical methods and on research in Ohio Valley states because other members' ancestors lived there too.
- Receiving the society's journal which contains more tips and information.
- Receiving the society's list of members' ancestral surnames. From such surname lists, you may identify distant relatives with whom to share research.
- Volunteering to help with society projects, such as recording county cemeteries or indexing a local newspaper. Through the efforts of genealogists in the Ohio Valley, you may have benefited from a cemetery transcription book; here is an opportunity to reciprocate.
- Contributing to the local genealogy library as the society sponsors fund-raising to buy such things as census records, the state vital records index, or another special collection.
- Working with special interest groups focusing on topics such as Polish ancestry or Native American research.

Even if you don't live nearby, joining a regional, ethnic, surname, or national society and/or one in your ancestral location can be beneficial as you

- receive the society's journals and newsletters, often with articles about research in your ancestral area or native land, case studies by successful researchers, abstracted records, or membership surname lists that may lead you to distant cousins
- learn of historical or genealogical publications of the society and, sometimes, acquire them at member discounts
- have access to book-loan programs and the society library
- help sponsor projects such as indexing and library acquisitions
- share your research with the society's members, library, or journal
- make contact with other researchers around the country whose ancestors were from the same location or had the same surname as your ancestors
- post queries about your ancestors in society publications or on the society Web site
- gain a great excuse for a vacation to visit ancestral ground where you've already made contacts
- attend society-sponsored seminars and reunions

Learn about the National Genealogical Society at its Web site <www.ngsgenealogy.org>.

Identify local, county, state, regional, international, surname, and ethnic societies through such sources as these:

1. Cyndi's List www.cyndislist.com
2. the Federation of Genealogical Societies www.fgs.org or www.familyhistory.com/societyhall/main.asp
3. society journals
4. Internet search engines
5. Rootsweb and USGenWeb pages, www.rootsweb.com and www.usgenweb.com
6. *Everton's Family History Magazine* (July/August issues) and *The Handybook for Genealogists* (Draper, Utah: Everton Publishers, latest edition)

Books and Articles

Reminder

Another avenue of continual learning is reading articles in society journals, in genealogical magazines, and online. The National Archives site provides a number of good articles and links to other articles, serials, and publications at <www.archives.gov/publications> and <www.archives.gov/research_room/alic/index.html>.

Several genealogical journals offer high-quality, in-depth, often scholarly articles and well-researched case studies. Among the best journals are

- *The American Genealogist*, published in Demorest, Georgia
- *National Genealogical Society Quarterly*, published by the society, Arlington, Virginia
- *The New England Historical and Genealogical Register*, published by the New England Historic Genealogical Society, Boston, Massachusetts
- *The New York Genealogical and Biographical Record*, published by the New York Genealogical and Biographical Society, New York City
- *The Virginia Genealogist*, published by John Frederick Dorman, Falmouth, Virginia

In addition to these are interesting and often well prepared journals of state and local genealogical and historical societies. Also, several popular magazines attract the general reader with basic but informative articles on many genealogical subjects. These publications include:

- *Ancestry*, from Ancestry.com
- *Everton's Family History Magazine*, from Everton Publishers; a successor to *Everton's Genealogical Helper*
- *Family Chronicle*, published in Toronto, Canada, for Canadian and U.S. readers
- *Family Tree Magazine*, from F&W Publications, Cincinnati

Genealogists also can benefit from having a personal library of books. As you study your research notes, your ancestors, or history late at night, on holidays, or at other times when you cannot be at a local library, you may well have questions in need of immediate answers. Some of these answers may be available online if you know where to look, but reference books at home may provide answers more quickly.

The core of a personal library includes:

- books and articles on research in your ancestral state(s) (see page 186) or country of origin
- a detailed atlas of your ancestral state(s) and maps of ancestral counties
- a general U.S. history reference book and a U.S. atlas and/or historical atlas
- your favorite genealogical how-to and reference books
- an atlas of your ancestral country or region outside the United States
- general and genealogical dictionaries
- published county or family histories (to be used with caution)

Economical place-specific materials in your personal library could include research outlines on states, other countries, and various languages; these are available from the Family History Library, (800) 537-5971 (customer service) and online at <www.familysearch.org/Eng/Search/Rg/frameset_rhelps.asp>. Many genealogists also collect CD-ROMs of journals, reference books, indexes, census records, and reference materials, some of which are mentioned throughout this book. Even on a limited budget, you can gradually acquire some of these materials, sometimes secondhand, and put others on your birthday and holiday gift lists.

REMINDERS FOR RESEARCH

1. Begin with yourself and work backward in time, one generation at a time.
2. A valuable tool in studying any ancestor is a chronology or timeline of events in the ancestor's life; include the ancestor's interaction with the cluster of relatives, friends, and associates.
3. Documenting each piece of information you find validates your research efforts.
4. Evaluate your data carefully for accuracy and for planning further research.
5. Investigate multiple sources, such as the ones in this book, to learn as much as you can about your ancestors.

CLUSTER GENEALOGY: WHAT AND WHY?

Technique

Before delving into U.S. public sources, let's consider a concept that will play a role throughout this book and in many successful genealogical research efforts—cluster genealogy. **Even when you focus your research on one ancestor, you probably will benefit from studying his or her spouse, children, and siblings at the same time.** This group, along with other relatives, friends, and neighbors, becomes a cluster of people who interacted with the ancestor and whose records may tell you more about the ancestor.

In one case study in chapter eleven, the search for one ancestor in immigration records led to the discovery of previously unknown relatives, whose immigration records in turn identified other family members and helped create a family group for study. In these records, the target ancestor was a child; the adults named in the immigration records became the targets of research because adults generally created more public records than children.

As basic as this concept may seem, many genealogists fail to realize the significance of the cluster approach until they are well into their research. Then they have to backtrack to look for key relatives or neighbors whom they had missed or ignored. Thus, to make your research more effective and more efficient, remember this approach when you study a newly discovered ancestor, tackle an elusive one, or use a source for the first time. The cluster not only gives a broader, more thorough picture of the family and the community as the ancestor knew it, but it is also a technique of research that often produces positive results.

Studying the cluster also helps you evaluate and/or confirm information you find in research. You may not find one specific source that provides a long-sought name, relationship, date, or place. You may find discrepancies in several sources. In such instances, you

CLUSTER GENEALOGY FOR THE TWENTY-FIRST CENTURY

Cluster genealogy is fantastic! I was recently contacted by a Shockley family genealogist (Beverly) in response to a message I had posted on the Van Buren County, Tennessee, Rootsweb page. She is a descendant of the white Shockley family who owned my black Shockley family. She also put me in contact with another black Shockley descendant (Mary, my second cousin twice removed) and another white Shockley descendant (Jim). The four of us started sharing information; each of us had pieces of the puzzle. Beverly sent a link to a Web site listing some of our family members who were buried in a particular cemetery. The two men (Hoyte and Wayne) who run that Web site added two more researchers and started sharing both stories and photos of my family! We created a Myfamily.com secure Web site so all eight of us can post in one place the data we have gathered. This way, each of us can record our documentation in a secure place before we update our Web sites, books, etc. In less than thirty days, I have gained three pictures from the late 1890s or early 1900s; learned the names of my fourth-great-grandparents, my third-great-grandfather's siblings and their spouses, my third-great-grandfather's children and their spouses and his grandchildren and their spouses; spoken to three distant cousins either by phone or e-mail; been invited to a Shockley family reunion; become the designated black Shockley family historian; and become part of a wonderful network of Shockley family researchers. Since very little about this line was passed down in my side of the family, this network is a great aid to research. I can hardly wait to visit some of the family elders with whom I've made contact through this network. *Lugenia R. Parham-Evans*

can often get a better indication of the "truth" by studying a group of relatives. This strategy can help in many ways by

- identifying an ancestor's parents or maiden name
- establishing birth, marriage, migration, or death dates
- sorting several people of the same name
- determining places of origin or residence
- identifying naming patterns and middle names that could be clues to ancestral names

YOU NEVER KNOW UNTIL YOU LOOK

For More Info

For in-depth information on long-distance research, see Christine Crawford-Oppenheimer's *Long-Distance Genealogy* (Cincinnati: Betterway Books, 2000).

The subtitle for this book should be "You never know until you look." The following chapters address U.S. sources created or found in local, county, state, and federal jurisdictions. Each chapter describes sources that genealogists find useful, and yet no book can address every possible source. Thus, let your imagination soar. When a chapter or case study mentions a type of source, consider whether this could help your research and how you might find similar records from your ancestral location. Even if you cannot travel to the ancestral locale, you probably can find pertinent sources and documents in the ways described throughout this book.

Your target ancestor will not be named in every source you consult, but a source may provide clues in the form of other names, dates, locations, relationships, or other sources to consider. Remember, every ancestral life was unique; therefore, let each ancestor's life and records guide your efforts.

Because we cannot know ahead of time what we will find in a given record group or document, this book includes some examples and case studies that illustrate unusual or out-of-the-ordinary information that is tucked into these sources. You may or may not find the same information on your favorite ancestor, but you may find something totally unexpected that gives a sagging research project a jump-start or enlivens the story. Although I have refrained from ending every chapter with the motto I've assigned to this book, it is true: You never know until you look.

Federal Census Records

Censuses can be taken for many reasons. For the federal censuses, which began in 1790, the primary motivation was, and is, counting the population every ten years to determine representation in the House of Representatives, as provided in the Constitution, Article I. (This article also allows enumerations to help Congress apportion direct taxes, and such taxes were collected several times before 1900. The sixteenth amendment, ratified in 1913, allowed for income taxes, without regard to apportionment among the states or to any census.) Over the years, census inquiries have added wide-ranging demographic questions that provide valuable details about our ancestors.

After gathering information from family sources, many people turn to census records to begin their research in public records. All the censuses contain valuable clues and information. A sizable portion of this data lies beyond the basic census in the supplemental schedules. Although some of these are not strictly genealogical, they are certainly historical and deserve attention.

Warning

It is common knowledge that the censuses are not perfect or complete. People were missed in every census; some were counted twice. Omissions may be due to the loss of the original schedule or part of it, mistakes in copying the pages, isolation of the family in a hard-to-reach location, absence of the family when the enumerator arrived at their house (with no neighbors around to provide information), accidental omission by the census taker, or inclement weather that prevented the census taker from reaching the family. If the family was on the road, moving to a new home, they may have been missed or counted in both the old and new locations.

Like nearly all sources, census records may contain discrepancies and therefore call for caution in their use. Names, ages, and birthplaces for some individuals differ from census to census; females are sometimes reported as males, and vice versa. However, despite their imperfections, census records can benefit your research in many ways if you know what information they contain and how to use it.

To form the most complete picture of each ancestral family, look for family members in each census—federal, state, or other—taken during their lifetimes. In research, *family* includes the parents and children in a nuclear family as well as the collateral lines of brothers, sisters, and cousins in each generation, and the families of spouses. The more you learn about this extended family cluster, the more you are likely to learn and understand about the ancestral lineage you are researching.

In cases where family, courthouse, or archive records have been destroyed by fire, flood, or neglect, the census data on a specific family may be the best or the only readily available source for a given time period. Of course, the genealogist must not only gather the information but must also sort, thoroughly study, and carefully evaluate the findings before drawing conclusions. In many cases, corroborating evidence needs to be drawn from other sources.

For your convenience in using this chapter for reference, after the sections on census availability and census day, the records are discussed in the following order and in rough chronological order within each section:

- Population and Slave Schedules, 1790–1870, pages 14–32
- Soundex, pages 32–38
- Censuses, 1880–1890, pages 38–46
- Population Schedules, 1900–1930, page 46–49
- Other Finding Aids, pages 49–64
- Censuses after 1930, page 64
- Federal Decennial Censuses for the Territories, pages 64–66
- Using the Population Schedules of the Census, pages 66–70

AVAILABILITY OF CENSUS RECORDS

It is great to know about pertinent sources, but locating them for use is another matter. Fortunately, microfilm, CD-ROM, online, or printed copies of the population schedules are readily available. In this book, *availability* means one of three options: (1) where you can use the material in original, microfilm, digitized, electronic, or printed form; (2) where you can purchase copies; and (3) from whom you can rent copies. (See pages 2–3 for contact information.)

Use of census and related records is possible at many public, academic, and special libraries nationwide and at state archives or historical societies. Numerous such libraries have census microfilm and/or CD-ROM collections or access to censuses online through subscription sites, such as Ancestry.com, Genealogy.com, and Heritage Quest Online (available through subscribing libraries). The National Archives and its regional branches have extensive census collections, including Soundex and other finding aids. Contact the libraries and archives in your area for information on their holdings.

Many abstracted and some digitized censuses are online at such sites as USGenWeb <www.usgenweb.com> or <www.us-census.org/>, Rootsweb <www.rootsweb.com>, and Afrigeneas <www.afrigeneas.com/aacensus> (for African-American census records). Non-subscription online links to census records include Genswap <www.genswap.com/census.html>, Census Online <www.census-online.com/links/index.html>, and Cyndi's List <www.cyndislist.com>.

If you find abstracted or transcribed censuses online or in books, consult the census records themselves—the microfilm, a photocopy of the original, or a copy of a digitized image—to check for accuracy.

Purchase of National Archives microfilm is possible through its Web site or through Scholarly Resources. Heritage Quest has produced digitized census records on CD-ROM. You can obtain photocopies of specific census pages from the National Archives by using NATF Form 82 and providing the necessary finding information. You can request the required form from the Reference Services Branch (NNRS), National Archives, Washington, DC 20408, or online at <www.archives.gov/global_pages/inquire_form.html>.

Rental of census microfilm (population and slave schedules, Soundex, and other finding aids) is possible from (1) the Family History Library through its Family History Centers and (2) the National Archives Microfilm Rental Program, which offers both library and individual memberships.

In order to rent census microfilm, you need to know which roll(s) to request. Contents and roll numbers for the censuses of 1790 through 1930 are online at <www.censusmicrofilm.com/fedcens.htm>. In addition, the microfilm catalogs for 1790 through 1920, which include roll numbers for each state, are online at <www.archives.gov/publications/genealogy_microfilm_catalogs.html#census>. You can use the catalogs for all the censuses, including 1930, at many libraries or purchase them from the National Archives (see <www.archives.gov/publications/how_to_obtain_publications.html> for ordering information).

CENSUS DAY

In each census year, Congress designated one day as census day. The information given to the census taker was to be correct as of that day, which was not necessarily the day when the enumerator actually visited each house. Persons who died after census day were to be included because they were alive on census day. Babies born after census day were to be omitted because they were not yet members of the household on census day. Of course, these instructions were not always followed to the letter, but we must be aware of them and study the information with the rules in mind. **Be sure to record the date of the actual enumeration when it is given at the top of the census page.** It shows each family as residents of a given place on *that* day and may help you interpret the information furnished in the report. We should not assume that an entry contains errors or omissions before we have studied it and compared it with data from other sources.

Tip

CENSUS DAY 1790–1960

1790, 1800, 1810, 1820	First Monday in August— 2 August 1790, 4 August 1800 6 August 1810, 7 August 1820
1830, 1840, 1850, 1860, 1870, 1880, 1890, 1900	June 1
1910	April 15
1920	January 1
1930, 1940, 1950, 1960	April 1

Using the Census-Day Rule

How can you know whether a given family was observing the "census-day rule"? Perhaps you cannot know for certain, but these reports on infants illustrate how the rule works. In 1870, census day was June 1. In Milam County, Texas, enumerated in August, the Ben Duckworth family reported a son Benjamin F. Jr., age 1/12, or one month. This census asked for the month of birth if the child was born within the census year and reports that this baby was born in April. Thus, the family evidently followed the census-day rule; the baby was not yet two months old on June 1.

Likewise, in 1900 the Joseph M. Martin family of Smith County, Mississippi, listed son Clifton Martin as five months old, born in December 1899. In other words, the baby had not yet reached six months of age by June 1. Because these two families apparently observed the census-day rule in part of their interview, we hope they reported the rest of their information with the same care and accuracy.

The example of Clifton Martin introduces another caution for genealogists in figuring birth dates based on the ages reported in the census. The census asks for each person's age as of the most recent birthday, prior to census day. Genealogists must be careful in subtracting the reported age from the census year and assigning a birth year. We must *estimate* birth years until we have corroborating evidence from other sources.

For example, consider a fifteen-year-old in 1910. Subtracting fifteen from 1910 may imply an 1895 birth date, which may not be correct. Based on the 1910 census day, the census suggests the teen was born between 15 April 1894 and 14 April 1895. Especially when using censuses other than that of 1900 (the only one that reports a month and year of birth for everyone), genealogists sometimes say the child was born *circa* ("about," abbreviated *c* or *ca*) 1895, or *circa* 1894–1895.

With the varying census days, you may be able to narrow (but not necessarily confirm) the period of an ancestor's birth by comparing the reported age and the census day over several censuses. An example is that of Cora Greenapple's age as reported in five censuses:

Age 10 in 1880 suggests birth between 1 June 1869 and 31 May 1870.
Age 30 in 1900 suggests birth between 1 June 1869 and 31 May 1870.
  Her birth date was reported in 1900 as October 1869.
Age 40 in 1910 suggests birth between 15 April 1869 and 14 April 1870.
Age 50 in 1920 suggests birth between 1 January 1869 and 31 December 1869.
Age 60 in 1930 suggests birth between 1 April 1869 and 31 March 1870.

The consistency of the reported ages is helpful to the researcher and may indicate (but does not guarantee) a greater chance of accuracy than if the ages varied from census to census. The combined information from five censuses suggests Cora's birth between 1 June 1869 (the earliest possible) and 31 December 1869 (the latest possible, with Cora turning fifty before 1 January 1920, or by 31 December 1919). Compare the 1900 census, reporting her birth in October 1869, with the others, and they are consistent. A family Bible, birth certificate (if she was born in the few locations that recorded births in 1869), baptism record, marriage record, passport, death certificate, tombstone, obituary, or other documents could provide further corroboration of an October 1869 birth. However, be alert for evidence of a different birth date.

The researcher's curiosity is naturally aroused in the case of the James Blakeney family of Tippah County, Mississippi, who talked to the enumerator on 26 October 1850 (census day was 1 June 1850) and reported the youngest member of the family, Nancy C., as age 1/365 (one day old). Was she born on October 24 or 25 or on May 30 or 31? The census alone does not answer the question but considerably narrows the choices.

Not "Taken Elsewhere"?

Of course, the enumerator was to explain the rules to the families. The St. Joseph County, Michigan, enumerator in 1830 was Elias Taylor, who seemed to take his job seriously. In the attempt to follow his instructions precisely, he wanted to include all those who fell within his frontier jurisdiction on June 1 but did not want to count anyone who might have been reported in another place of residence on that day. Thus, on his census pages, he marked eight families with an asterisk. On the last page he explained: "Those Families marked Thus * are Such as were mooving [*sic*] on the 1st day of June and Could not as they verily believed be taken [enumerated] else where."

As an aside, the records of the assistant marshals who took the 1830 census (see Figure 2-5, on page 52) show that Elias Taylor enumerated 1,313 people in his assigned county and was compensated with $167.56, a goodly sum in 1830.[1]

On the other hand, some families were actually "taken elsewhere" and recorded twice in the census. We cannot know whether the census takers overlapped their jurisdictions by mistake, or the family moved, or some other factor caused a duplicate entry. The Perry Reel family was enumerated twice, with only slight differences in details, in 1880 in Pottawattamie County, Iowa; both entries were dated June 30:

In census research, "e.d." is the abbreviation for "enumeration district."

E.D. 179, SHEET 25, FAMILY 225	E.D. 192, SHEET 49, FAMILY 520
Perry Reel, 41, born IN, father b VA, mother b MD; farmer, Hazel Dell township	Perry Reel, 42, b IN, father b VA, mother b MD; sheriff in Council Bluff
Millie Reel, 35, wife, b IN, father b TN	Millie Reel, 35, b IN, parents' bpl unknown
Dora Reel, 16, dau, b IA, parents b IN	Dora E. Reel, 16, dau, b IA, parents b IN
Emma Reel, 14, dau, b IA, parents b IN	Emma Reel, 14, dau, b IA, parents b IN
Clay Reel, 12, son, b IA, parents b IN	Clay Reel, 12, son, b IA, parents b IN
Rosa Reel, 9, dau, b IA, parents b IN	Rosa Reel, 10, dau, b IA, parents b IN
William Reel, 9/12, son, b IA, parents b IN	William Reel, 1, son, b IA, parents b IN

POPULATION AND SLAVE SCHEDULES, 1790–1870

Census content varies from year to year. Censuses from 1790 to 1840 named only heads of households, with family members and slaves listed in age brackets or as total numbers. (See the chart "Age Brackets Used in the 1790–1840 Federal Censuses" on page 15.) After 1790, each census requested more detailed information from the populace. The specifics are listed in the chart "Which federal census reports . . . ?" on page 22. Beginning in 1850, every free person in each household was listed by name, age, gender, race, birthplace, and occupation. This wealth of information makes the federal census not only one of the most useful and rewarding genealogical sources but an essential tool for researchers.

1790 Federal Census and Substitutes

The first federal count of the population to determine each state's representation in the House of Representatives took place in 1790. Territories were included in the counts as well, probably with territorial growth and eventual statehood in mind. Once a territory achieved a population of at least five thousand free white adult males and thus qualified for one non-voting representative in Congress, its representation did not depend on census numbers.

Notes

The 1790 census was a fairly simple report. **Although some of these first schedules have been lost, eleven of them are extant, published, and indexed:** Connecticut, Maine (although still part of Massachusetts), Maryland (except Allegany, Calvert, and Somerset counties), Massachusetts, New Hampshire, New York, North Carolina (except Caswell, Granville, and Orange counties), Pennsylvania, Rhode Island, South Carolina, and Vermont. Congress extended the census law to Vermont when it became the fourteenth state in 1791, while the enumeration process was still underway.[2]

AGE BRACKETS USED IN THE 1790–1840 FEDERAL CENSUSES				
Year	**White Males, including heads of household**	**White Females, including heads of household**	**Slave/"Free Colored" Males**	**Slave/"Free Colored" Females**
1790	16 and upwards under 16	total number, regardless of age	total number of slaves; total number of "all other free persons," primarily free blacks and some Indians, other than heads of household who were named	
1800, 1810	under 10 of 10 & under 16 of 16 & under 26 of 26 & under 45 of 45 & over	under 10 of 10 & under 16 of 16 & under 26 of 26 & under 45 of 45 & over	total number of slaves; total number of "all other free persons except Indians not taxed." Basically the same as 1790.	
1820	same as 1800 and 1810, with an additional column for males 16 to 18 (also reported in the 16 to 26 column but not to be counted twice)	same as 1800 and 1810	under 14 of 14 & under 26 of 26 & under 45 of 45 & over	under 14 of 14 & under 26 of 26 & under 45 of 45 & over
1830, 1840	under 5 of 5 & under 10 of 10 & under 15 of 15 & under 20 of 20 & under 30 of 30 & under 40 of 40 & under 50 of 50 & under 60 of 60 & under 70 of 70 & under 80 of 80 & under 90 of 90 & under 100 of 100 & over	under 5 of 5 & under 10 of 10 & under 15 of 15 & under 20 of 20 & under 30 of 30 & under 40 of 40 & under 50 of 50 & under 60 of 60 & under 70 of 70 & under 80 of 80 & under 90 of 90 & under 100 of 100 & over	under 10 of 10 & under 24 of 24 & under 36 of 36 & under 55 of 55 & under 100 of 100 & over	under 10 of 10 & under 24 of 24 & under 36 of 36 & under 55 of 55 & under 100 of 100 & over

Genealogists debate the definition of a census and the use of other kinds of records to create a substitute when an original was destroyed. Understandably, some argue that a census is a census and nothing else substitutes for it, for lists of heads of household cannot provide the missing information on family members and their ages that the original census may have given. Others acknowledge that a lost census cannot be completely duplicated from noncensus sources but try to identify as many as possible of the heads of household in a community at a given time. Such information can be valuable even if it is not complete. Most researchers prefer to have some information rather than none and appreciate the substitutes. Texas researcher Gifford E. White has provided a compromise in his book, *1830 Citizens of Texas* (Austin, Tex.: Eakin Press, 1983). He includes some actual census material with evidence from other sources to create a body of information about who was in the area in that year, but he does not call it a census.

For the 1790 federal census, it is easier to accept the compiled substitutes since the original census provided little information about family members and reports varied somewhat from place to place. Substitutes exist for a number of the early states.

Delaware. To compile *The Reconstructed Seventeen Ninety Census of Delaware* (Arlington, Va.: National Genealogical Society, 1954), Leon De Valinger Jr. used tax lists, although these show only property owners.

Georgia. *The Reconstructed 1790 Census of Georgia: Substitutes for Georgia's Lost 1790 Census*, by Marie DeLamar and Elisabeth Rothstein (Baltimore: Genealogical Publishing Co., 1989 reprint of 1976 edition), includes names from a number of sources, including wills, deeds, tax records, court minutes, voter lists, newspapers, and jury lists in an attempt to identify more people.

Maryland. Helping to offset the loss of its 1790 census, Somerset County, established in 1666, has a number of county records, including wills and estate records, land and marriage records, a 1783 tax list, and the 1778 oaths of fidelity to Maryland. These oaths were published by Richard S. Uhrbrock in the *National Genealogical Society Quarterly*, Vol. 59 (1971): 103–104. Allegany County, created in 1789 from Washington County, has records from its early years, some beginning in 1791 or 1792. Washington County records may also aid in an Allegany County search. For Calvert County, which dates from 1654, only a few eighteenth-century records still exist, due to a courthouse fire in 1882. Records such as the partial 1783 tax list and the oaths of fidelity of 1778 may be the best substitutes available.

New Jersey. *New Jersey in 1793: An Abstract Index to the 1793 Militia Census of the State of New Jersey*, abstracted by James S. Norton (Salt Lake City: Institute of Family Research, 1973), serves as one substitute source for that state.

North Carolina. Tax lists for Caswell, Granville, and Orange counties, North Carolina, were published with the 1790 census schedules that the Government Printing Office issued in 1908. Period tax lists for Caswell (1777, 1780, 1784) and Orange (1784–1793) have also been published by T.L.C. Genealogy Books of Miami, Florida.

Kentucky

Kentucky was part of Virginia until July 1790, and the census enumeration began in August. Although Kentucky was not yet a state, it was a separate district from Virginia when the census was taken. Returns submitted from Kentucky no longer survive.

The First Census of Kentucky 1790, a substitute compiled by Charles B. Heinemann (reprint, Baltimore: Genealogical Publishing Co., 1981), used tax lists of Kentucky counties existing at the time of the 1790 census: Bourbon, Fayette, Jefferson, Lincoln, Madison, Mason, Mercer, Nelson, and Woodford. However, these are not necessarily 1790 lists.

Another Kentucky source is *The 1787 Census of Virginia* (Netti Schreiner-Yantis and Florene Speakman Love, compilers, 3 vols., Springfield, Va.: Genealogical Books in Print, 1987). Although compiled from tax lists, these volumes contain more information than some of the 1790 census returns because this particular tax enumeration named free males over twenty-one, not just heads of household. The 1787 Kentucky counties of Bourbon, Fayette, Lincoln, Madison, Nelson, and part of Mercer are included in these Virginia returns. To try to fill in the blanks left by the loss of the Jefferson and part of the Mercer county lists, the compilers added names from other Mercer County records and used 1789 tax lists from Mercer and Jefferson Counties. (See further discussion under "Virginia and West Virginia.")

Virginia and West Virginia

Virginia's 1790 census also has been lost. The substitutes have been created largely from annual state tax rolls dating from 1782. If you do not have access to the books discussed below, you can look for your ancestors in these records by studying the microfilmed tax rolls (personal property and/or land taxes), available at the Library of Virginia, Clayton Library in Houston, the Family History Library, and on loan through Family History Centers.

Heads of Families at the First Census 1790—Virginia, the Virginia substitute schedule published by the Census Bureau (Washington, D.C.: 1908), was compiled from state tax records of 1782 to 1785, housed in the state library. These records included only thirty-nine counties:

Albemarle	Gloucester	Middlesex	Princess Anne
Amelia	Greenbrier (WV)	Monongalia (WV)	Richmond
Amherst	Greensville	Nansemond	Rockingham
Charlotte	Halifax	New Kent	Shenandoah
Chesterfield	Hampshire (WV)	Norfolk	Stafford
Cumberland	Hanover	Northumberland	Sussex
Essex	Harrison (WV)	Orange	Surry
Fairfax	Isle of Wight	Pittsylvania	Warwick
Fluvanna	Lancaster	Powhatan	Williamsburg town
Frederick	Mecklenburg	Prince Edward	

Reminder

Remember, present West Virginia was part of Virginia until 1863.

Forty counties were missing from this compilation. *Virginia Tax Payers, 1782–1787: Other Than Those Published by the United States Census Bureau* (Augusta B. Fothergill and John Mark Naugle, compilers, Baltimore: Genealogical Publishing Co., 1978) makes up for many of those omissions, using personal property tax lists for the following counties:

Accomack	Culpepper	King and Queen	Prince William
Augusta	Dinwiddie	King George	Rockbridge
Bedford	Elizabeth City	King William	Southampton
Berkeley (WV)	Fauquier	Lincoln (KY)	Spotsylvania
Botetourt	Fayette (KY)	Louisa	Washington
Brunswick	Goochland	Londoun	Westmoreland
Buckingham	Hardy (WV)	Lunenberg	York
Campbell	Henrico	Montgomery	
Caroline	Henry	Northampton	
Charles City	James City	Prince George	

Franklin and Russell counties, formed in 1785, are not included in these lists, but researchers should consult the lists or other records of the parent counties of Bedford, Henry and Patrick (for Franklin) and Washington (for Russell). Ohio County, in present West Virginia, was formed in 1776 and has early land and probate records which may help make up for the loss of 1790 census information. The counties of Pendleton and Randolph, also now in West Virginia, were formed in 1787; lists for their parent counties may reveal many of their residents: Augusta, Hardy, and Rockingham for Pendleton County; and Harrison, for Randolph County. A number of these Virginia and West Virginia counties have early records of other kinds, which can help researchers locate and identify ancestors.

These two books cover most of the states of Virginia and present West Virginia but concentrate on the earlier dates of 1782–1785. Since Kentucky and Virginia were focal points of migration in the years before and after the Revolutionary War, thousands of people moved to, from, and through those regions every year. *The 1787 Census of Virginia* (Netti Schreiner-Yantis and Florene Speakman Love, compilers), therefore, is a major source of information, if not a true census, from a very fluid population area. In one way, the tax lists that form these volumes are a better census than the 1790 census—they name not only heads of household but also other white men over twenty-one.

For example, Elliott Coleman of Cumberland County, Virginia, was listed just below William Coleman, to whom his tax was charged. This William was likely his father, rather than his brother by the same name. Elliott was apparently still living at home; he did not marry until two years later. In addition, the report indicates no young men in William's household between sixteen and twenty-one. Other records suggest that Elliott was twenty-two at this time.

In the same county, a Henry Coleman was apparently living with Samuel Allen, to whom his tax was charged. In some cases, though probably not this one, a young man living with a family of a different surname could provide a clue to a son-in-law relationship—a young man married to one of the daughters of the household.

In some of the lists, white males between sixteen and twenty-one were named, not just listed by number. Females were usually excluded from the lists unless they were heads of household, in which case they were not subject to taxes.

These two volumes of 1787 tax lists include all the counties and towns listed above, in addition to the following:

Alexandria	Jefferson (KY)	Nelson (KY)	Randolph (WV)
Bourbon (KY)	Madison (KY)	Ohio (WV)	Richmond city
Franklin	Mercer (KY)	Petersburg town	Winchester city
Fredericksburg town			

Northwest Territory

The Northwest Ordinance of July 1787 set in place the procedures for governing the region north of the Ohio River and became the model for the creation of new states. The states of Illinois, Indiana, Michigan, Ohio, and Wisconsin eventually came from this Northwest Territory. In 1790 the area was sparsely settled, with most inhabitants in Washington, Marietta, and Hamilton (Cincinnati) counties, Point Garrison, and Ft. Harmar in what became Ohio; Kaskaskia, Prairie du Pont, and Cahokia in the Illinois area; Petite Cote (Michigan); and Knox County (Indiana).

Congress did not include this area in the law that provided for the 1790 census.[3] However, volumes II and III of the published *Territorial Papers of the United States* contain some census returns and other useful lists of early inhabitants, as shown below. Each published volume of the *Territorial Papers* is indexed. (See chapter three for more discussion of the *Territorial Papers*.) See the following references:

VOLUME II

p. 252–253, a May 1790 petition from forty-six inhabitants of the Illinois country
p. 253–257, lands claimed by forty-two Kaskaskia inhabitants from governor's February 1791 report
p. 257–258, Kaskaskia inhabitants before and after 1783
p. 259, census of Cahokia, 1790–91 (heads of household)
p. 260–261, census of Prairie du Pont, 1790–91 (heads of household)
p. 263 ff, more than one hundred individuals with land claims in the District of Cahokia in or before 1783
p. 278–279, inhabitants of Prairie du Rocher, 1790
p. 281–282, inhabitants of Kaskaskia, Cahokia, and Prairie du Rocher, 1790
p. 285–287, heads of family of Post Vincennes in Knox County, 1783
p. 422, a petition of about 120 French inhabitants of Gallipolis, 1792
p. 470, a 1793 estimate of the numbers of people in the settlements of the whole Territory

VOLUME III (See this volume for dates before or after 1790.)
p. 291–293, civil and militia appointments for Washington County (Ohio), December 1789
p. 295, civil and militia appointments for Hamilton County (Ohio), January 1790
p. 304–305, civil and militia appointments for St. Clair County (Illinois), April 1790
p. 333, militia orders, Hamilton and Washington counties (Ohio), September through December 1790

Any publication that claims to be a census or substitute census for this area but does not provide the source of its information is of little use. Consult the *Territorial Papers*, county and state records, and other period records for evidence of early inhabitants.

Tennessee

Tennessee was part of North Carolina until May 1790, when it was organized as the Territory Southwest of the River Ohio. Like the Northwest Territory, the Southwest Territory was not included in the law providing for the first census. Apparently Secretary of State Thomas Jefferson suggested to Governor Blount of the Southwest Territory that an enumeration of his rapidly growing jurisdiction would be of value. The governor followed through on the request and sent the returns to Washington.[4] Apparently these returns have not survived, but various sources, in addition to some county records, are available to help researchers identify Tennessee residents of the 1790 period. Published sources include these:

1. *Index to Early Tennessee Tax Lists* (Byron and Barbara Sistler, compilers and publishers, Nashville, Tenn.). These tax lists span the years from 1783 to 1825, but not all counties have existing lists from all those years.

2. *Early Tennessee Tax Lists* (Mary Barnett Curtis, comp., Ft. Worth, Tex.: Arrow Printing Co., 1964) contains tax lists for twenty-two East Tennessee counties for which no census exists before 1830. The lists are alphabetical by county, with no master index.

3. *1770–1790 Census of the Cumberland Settlements: Davidson, Sumner, and Tennessee Counties* (Richard C. Fulcher, comp., Baltimore: Genealogical Publishing Co., 1987). This record is compiled from deed and land records, court minutes, marriage records, wills and inventories, tax rolls, territorial papers, newspapers, and other sources from these early middle-Tennessee counties.

4. *The Territorial Papers of the United States*, Volume IV, pages 431–442, list appointments by Governor Blount between October and December 1790 for militia officers, sheriffs and constables, justices of the peace, civil officers, and attorneys licensed to practice law in the territory. These and other such documents identify some of the heads of household in the territory during the census year.

5. *Commission Book of Governor John Sevier, 1796–1801* (Nashville: Tennessee Historical Commission, 1957) includes civil and military appointments and licenses and is indexed.

6. *Tennessee Marriages: Early to 1800* (Jordan R. Dodd, editor, Bountiful, Utah: Precision Indexing, 1990) is alphabetical by brides and grooms and gives the marriage date and the county in which the marriage is recorded.

Other Regions

The scattered residents of the Indian lands that became Alabama and Mississippi were not covered by the 1790 census. Some of the land was still claimed by Georgia but was not organized into counties of the state of Georgia. Therefore, any American residents in those Indian lands are probably not included in the substitute for the 1790 Georgia census. Land west of the Mississippi, as well as Florida, Spanish West Florida, and eastern Louisiana were, of course, not yet parts of the United States; other sources have to be consulted for evidence of 1790 residents.

1800–1840 Censuses

Between 1800 and 1840, and even more so for the next hundred years, the government increased the questions on the census form. Between 1810 and 1840, census takers queried the population on a number of subjects dealing with occupations, immigration or citizenship, military service, and disabilities, although the information did not mention individual names. The chart "Which federal census reports . . . ?" on page 22 lists the subjects covered in these questions and the censuses in which the questions appear. Also see page 15 for the list of column headings for these censuses.

In these census years, the government wanted more specific information on ages for the population. (For an 1840 example, see Figure 2-1, on page 21). In 1820, a separate column counted only free white males between sixteen and eighteen. These young men were also enumerated in the sixteen-to-twenty-six age bracket, where they were to be counted. The reason for this extra column is unclear. In some states, young men of that age were newly eligible for state militia service, but there was no national draft and no imminent threat of war. Some men were taxable at age sixteen, and some may have been eligible to vote at that age. Nevertheless, **when studying your families in this census, don't count the sixteen- to eighteen-year-olds twice.**

Important

In the early censuses, some enumerators had pre-printed forms; others used handwritten forms. On the handwritten forms, column heads may appear only on the first page of the district, town, or other civil division. In extracting ancestral information from these censuses, make or use pre-printed extraction forms, readily available in such sources as *Unpuzzling Your Past*, 4th ed. (Cincinnati: Betterway Books, 2001; forms through 1930) and *The Unpuzzling Your Past Workbook* (Cincinnati: Betterway Books, 1996; forms through 1920). These help you record family members in the correct columns. However, you may find that in different states, the various sections of these early censuses may be arranged in different orders; so check carefully the headings on the pages you read.

Figure 2-1 illustrates a sheet from the 1840 census of Marion County, Kentucky. It is only the left-hand sheet of two pages; the second page includes slave enumerations, the questions pertaining to certain occupations, and the column for naming military pensioners. The page shown illustrates several common occurrences that researchers find in these records:

- The top row of numbers represents the totals brought forward from previous pages of the county enumeration.
- Names of heads of household in this county show given names first; some lists may use last names first.
- Lines 1 and 5 list two free black families—McEroy [*sic*] and Dyer. (Several white McElroy families lived in the county.)
- Several same-surname clusters are enumerated on the page: Bickett, Price, Thomas, Beauchamp, four Abells (one of whom may be the enumerator), and five Spauldings. Several of these appear to be single young men living near households that may be their parents; one young Bickett appears to be a widower with a daughter under age five.
- At least three heads of household appear to be widows.

Another page of the same county enumerated the students and faculty of St. Mary's College: six boys "of five and under ten", forty boys between ten and fourteen, sixty-eight

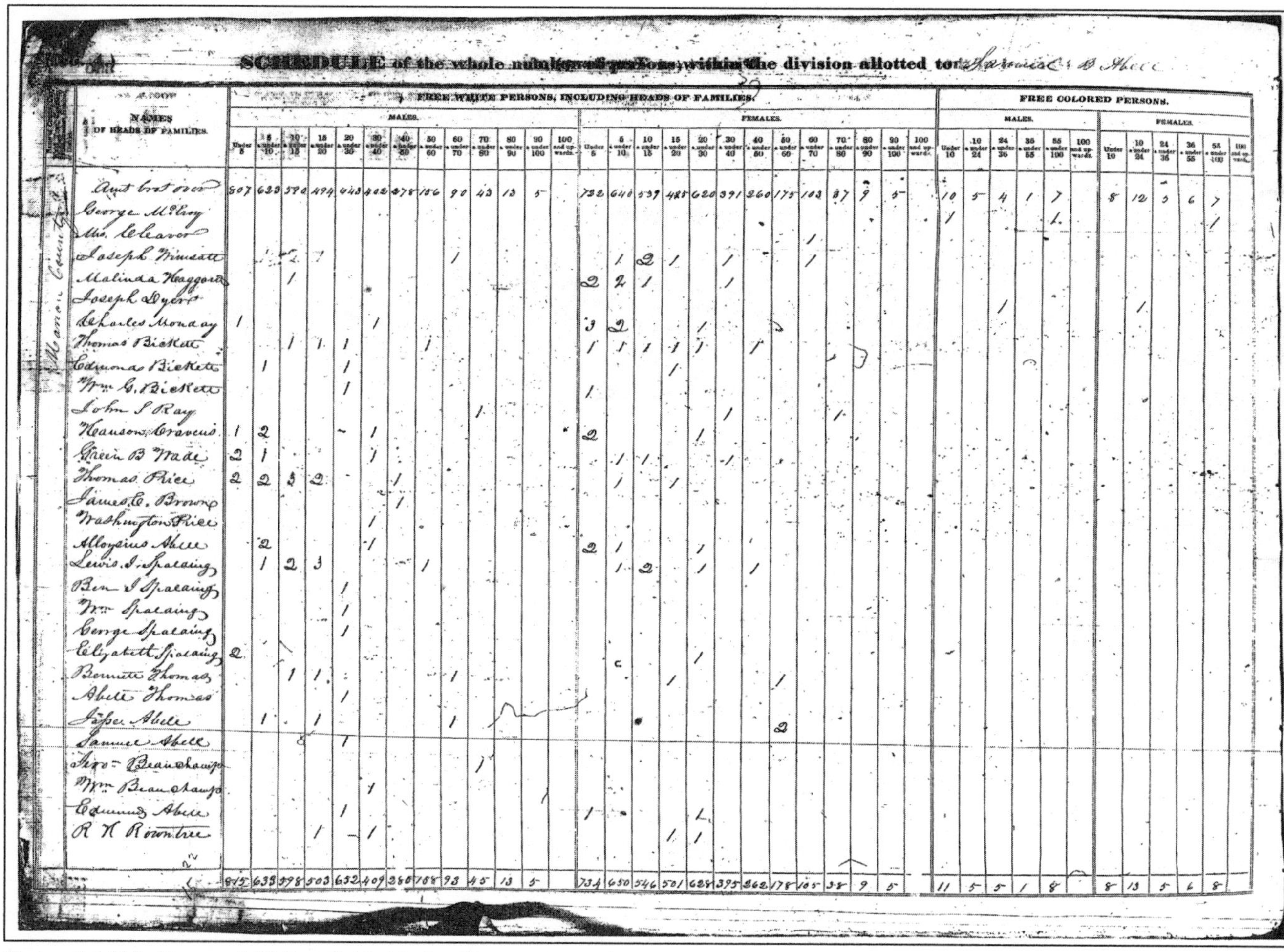
SCHEDULE of the whole number of persons within the division allotted to

FREE WHITE PERSONS, INCLUDING HEADS OF FAMILIES.

MALES. FEMALES.

FREE COLORED PERSONS.

NAMES OF HEADS OF FAMILIES.

George McElroy
Mrs. Cleaver
Joseph Wimsatt
Malinda Haggard
Joseph Dyer
Charles Monday
Thomas Bickett
Edmund Bickett
Wm. G. Bickett
John S. Ray
Hanson Graves
Green B. Wade
Thomas Price
James C. Brown
Washington Price
Alloysius Abell
Lewis I. Spalding
Ben I. Spalding
Wm. Spalding
George Spalding
Elizabeth Spalding
Bennett Thomas
Abell Thomas
Jasper Abell
Samuel Abell
Geo. Beauchamp
Wm. Beauchamp
Edmund Abell
R. H. Rowntree

Figure 2-1 U.S. Census of 1840, roll 18, Marion County, Kentucky, 351.

teens between fifteen and nineteen, thirteen men in their twenties, sixteen men in their thirties, five men in their forties, and four men in their fifties. They were counted in the totals of their age columns. Many county residents attended the school, but some students and faculty may have boarded at or near the campus. In situations like this, the researcher has questions to study: (1) whether their families also included them in their households, or (2) whether a hole in a family's enumeration where a certain son should be counted may be due to his attendance at such a school.

1840 Revolutionary/Military Pensioners

The 1840 federal census form included a space to list "Pensioners for Revolutionary or Military Services" and their ages. The column appears on the second page of the schedule after the slave columns. **Each pensioner was to be included in the census tally of the household in which he or she lived, but not all were actually included.** A number of these pensioners, such as James Browne (age ninety-one) and John Walker (eighty-five) of Wake County, North Carolina, were still the heads of their own households, as is clear from reading the entries. One Wake County head of household was pensioner Jesse Harris (eighty), a free black man. Other Wake County veterans were living with relatives of the same name, such as William Wood (eighty-two), living with Marcum Wood, and John Green (eighty-eight), living with Samuel Green.

Reminder

WHICH FEDERAL CENSUS REPORTS . . . ?

age, sex, race of each individual in free households	1850 forward
agricultural schedules	1850–1880
alien (*see also* foreigners; male; naturalized citizen)	1900–1930
attendance in school	1850 forward
months attending school	1900
highest grade of school completed	1940
birth date (month/year) of each person	1900
month of birth if born within the census year	1870, 1880
birthplace of each person	1850 forward
of each person's parents	1880–1930
blind	1830, 1850–1890, 1910
citizenship, *see* male; naturalized citizen	
citizenship of the foreign born	1940
convict	1850, 1860, 1890
crippled, maimed, deformed	1890
deaf and dumb	1830, 1850–1890, 1910
In 1830, the questions asked for free or slave persons who were deaf and dumb under age 14, between age 14 and 24, and over age 25.	
defective, dependent, delinquent schedules (DDD)	1880
disabled: crippled, maimed, bedridden, or other disability	1880
education, *see* attendance in school; reading and writing	
employment/occupation information	
duration of unemployment this year	1940
employer, self-employed, or wage earner	1910–1930
months unemployed	1880–1900
number in household employed in agriculture	1820, 1840
number in household employed in commerce	1820, 1840
number in household employed in manufacturing	1820
in manufacturing and trades	1840
number in household employed in mining	1840
number in household employed in ocean navigation	1840
number in household employed in canal, lake, and river navigation	1840
number in household employed in learned professions or as engineers	1840
number of hours worked last week	1940
number of weeks out of work in 1909	1910
number of weeks worked in 1939	1940
occupation of each individual	1850 forward
whether person worked yesterday	1930
whether person worked last week	1940
seeking work	1940
working in public emergency work (WPA, etc.)	1940
home housework or unable to work	1940
foreigners not naturalized (*see also* alien)	1820, 1830
home or farm as residence	1890–1910, 1930, 1940
home owned or rented	1890–1940
home owned free of mortgage	1890–1920
farm owned or rented	1890
farm owned free of mortgage	1890
value of home or monthly rent	1930, 1940
homeless child	1890
illness, current, or temporary disability	1880
chronic or acute illness, length of time afflicted	1890
immigration year	1900–1930
number of years in United States	1890, 1900
income during 1939	1940

industry/manufacturing schedules	1810, 1820, 1850–1880
insane, idiot	1850–1880
defective in mind	1890
language, native	1890, 1910–1930
native language of parents	1920
speaks English	1890–1930
male, eligible/not eligible to vote	1870
manufacturing, *see* industry	
marital status	1880 forward
age at first marriage	1930
married once or more than once	1910
married within the [census] year	1850–1890
month of marriage, within the [census] year	1870
number of years of present marriage	1900, 1910
mortality schedules	1850–1880
mother of how many children, number living	1890–1910
mother tongue, *see* language	
name of each individual in free households	1850 forward
name of head of household only	1790–1840
name of person furnishing information	1940
naturalized citizen ("Na") or first papers ("Pa")	1890–1930
year of naturalization	1920
number of household in order of visitation	1850 forward
occupation of each person (*see also* employment)	1850 forward
parents, whether foreign born	1870
birthplace of parents	1880–1930
pauper	1850, 1860, 1890
persons temporarily absent from household	1940
prisoner	1890
radio set in home	1930
reading and writing, whether able to read or write	1890–1930
persons unable to read and/or write	1850–1880
relationship to head of household	1880 forward
residence of each person on 1 April 1935	1940
school, *see* attendance in school; reading and writing	
slaves by age and gender	1820–1860
number of slaves in household	1790–1860
social statistics schedules	1850–1880
Soundex	beginning 1880
street address of family	1880 forward
value of real estate owned	1850–1870
value of home or monthly rent	1930
value of personal estate	1860, 1870
veterans	
pensioners	1840
Union veterans and widows, special schedule	1890
Civil War veteran, Union or Confederate, or widow	1890
Civil War veteran, Union or Confederate	1910
veteran of U.S. military or naval forces, which war	1930

Additional questions asked of random persons in 1940 concerned birthplaces of parents, language spoken in home, veterans and their survivors, Social Security participation, and marriage and childbearing of women.

Still other pensioners were living in households of a different surname, and the genealogist usually hopes that this situation may lead to identifying a married daughter, a sister, or another relative. Examples from Wake County, North Carolina, include Thomas Holland (eighty-four), living with Lewis Barkers, and Joseph Shaw (eighty-three), in the household of Drury King. Each of these veterans was the oldest person listed in the family, and the head of household was considerably younger.

The genealogist, therefore, needs to remember that (1) the head of household was not always the oldest person in the family, (2) pensioners who were not heads of household will probably not appear in indexes that cover heads of household only, and (3) pensioners who were heads of household are not indicated as pensioners in most census indexes. In addition, these pensioners were not limited to Revolutionary soldiers, sailors, and widows. It is clear that Thomas T. Doty (forty-four) and Robert Rains (fifty-six), listed as pensioners in Madison County, Alabama, were not Revolutionary veterans. Both were born after the Revolution. Their military service came later, perhaps in the War of 1812 or the Indian wars.

To check for ancestral pensioners, you have several choices:

- Consult the 1841 government publication *A Census of Pensioners for Revolutionary or Military Service* or the 1989 reprint by Genealogical Publishing Co. The latter reproduces the census (the names and ages of pensioners and the heads of household with whom they were living) and includes an index.
- Search abstracts of the pensioners' entries for all thirty states and territories online at <www.usgennet.org/usa/topic/colonial/census/1840>.
- Read the entire census for the county where the pensioner was thought to be living, especially since indexes sometimes contain errors or omissions.

In addition, some published indexes to the 1840 heads of household also include pensioners:

1. Alabama. (Betty Drake, comp., originally 1973, reissued by Reprint Company Publishers, Spartanburg, S.C.) For twelve counties formed from the Creek and Cherokee Cessions of the 1830s.
2. Iowa. (Bettylou Headlee, comp., Fullerton, Calif.: Mrs. Beverly Stercula, 1968.) There were six pensioners in Iowa in 1840.
3. Michigan. (Estelle A. McGlynn, comp., ed., Detroit Society for Genealogical Research, Inc., 1977.)
4. Mississippi. (Thomas E. and Berniece D. Coyle, comp., Lewisville, Tex.: Coyle Data Co., 1990.)
5. North Carolina. (Gerald M. Petty, comp. and publisher, Columbus, Ohio, 1974.)

1850, 1860, and 1870 Censuses

Beginning in 1850, federal censuses named each free individual in each free household, including free blacks and Indians living among the general population; they did not mention each person's relationship to the head of household. However, in 1850, 1860, and 1870, census takers were instructed to list, in a typical household, first the head of household, then the wife, the children in descending age order, and last other household members, related or not. (Figure 9-4, on page 335, shows an 1870 census page.) Households were to be listed and numbered in the order the census taker visited them. Residential institutions such as boarding schools, jails, and poorhouses were counted as households; often the nature of the dwelling was written perpendicularly in the margin. If more than one family resided in a household, they were to be designated with the same dwelling number and different family numbers.

Reminder

For the 1800–1870 censuses, numerous printed and online indexes list heads of household and individuals in a household of a different surname. Remember to check for spelling variations of your surnames.

The persons named within each household were to be those "whose usual place of abode" on June 1 was in that household. Those who were temporarily away and were expected to

CENSUS PAGE COLUMN HEADINGS, 1850–1870

1850–1870

1. dwelling number, in order of visitation
2. family number, in order of visitation
3. name of every person whose usual place of abode was with this family on June 1
4. age of every person as of his or her last birthday prior to June 1, or estimate thereof (see page 26 for more details)
5. sex of every person named
6. color of every person named (see page 28 for details)
7. profession, occupation, or trade of every person over age 15; 1870 schedule asked enumerators to be very specific in reporting this information
8. value of real estate owned

1850

9. birthplace: state, territory, or country other than United States
10. mark for each person who married within census year (1 June 1849–31 May 1850)
11. mark for each person who attended school within the past year, other than Sunday school
12. persons over 20 who cannot read and write
13. as applicable, write *deaf, dumb, blind, insane, idiotic, pauper, convict*

1860

9. value of personal estate owned
10. birthplace: state, territory, country other than United States
11. mark for each person married within census year (1 June 1859–31 May 1860)
12. mark for each person who attended school within the past year
13. persons over 20 who cannot read and write
14. as applicable, *deaf, dumb, blind, insane, idiotic, pauper, convict*

1870

9. value of personal estate owned
10. birthplace: state, territory, country other than United States
11. mark if father was foreign-born
12. mark if mother was foreign-born
13. if born within census year*, name of month
14. if married within census year*, give month
15. mark if attended school within the census year*
16. mark if person cannot read
17. mark if person cannot write
18. as applicable, *deaf, dumb, blind, insane, idiotic*
19. male citizen of United States, 21 or older
20. citizen with right to vote denied other than for crime or rebellion

*Census year: 1 June 1869–31 May 1870

return were to be included with their permanent family. Students away at school were to be listed with the household where they regularly lodged, as of census day. Resident employees of shops, hotels, and eating establishments who regularly slept at their place of work were to be enumerated there, as long as they were not counted elsewhere. Those who were employed in navigation of internal U.S. rivers and canals and returned home periodically were to be enumerated at their home. Such persons who lived on the vessel where they were employed were to be "taken" (enumerated) as a family group with the vessel as their place of abode. These rules could have been confusing to the assistant marshals taking the census and to the population; this confusion could help explain why persons were "missed" or enumerated twice.

Chapter nine discusses the importance of the 1870 census in African-American genealogy. This was the first federal census after the Civil War, which ended in 1865, and thus the first to name the former slaves who had become free at the end of the war. Studying the families and their neighbors in this census is very important in finding pre-war African-American ancestors.

Many households included additional residents—parents or in-laws, siblings and their children, employees or business associates, or servants. The extra people ranged from infants to the elderly. For extra income, many families also took in boarders—children and youth working away from home in a household of neighbors or relatives; students in a local academy or college; or single young adults, such as school teachers, clerks, and lawyers. Some boarders were related to their host family, but even in the later censuses where relationships were requested, they were not always recorded or accurate.

Children in the household, especially those with a different surname, may have been

- offspring of the wife/mother by a former marriage
- cousins, nieces or nephews, or grandchildren
- adopted or foster children living with relatives other than their parents or with an unrelated family
- young apprentices, employees, or wards of the head of household

Research Tip

Genealogists must consider the extra people in the household. Studying them is sometimes critical to research. The chart "Identifying Extra Members of Households" on page 27 shows four typical situations of extra and related people in households from the 1850 to 1870 censuses; the chart gives age and birthplace for each person. Test yourself. What are the most likely possibilities for a relationship? Think about how you would search for an answer. Since relationships were not stated in these three censuses, researchers must consider the most logical and likely situations in conjunction with evidence found on the family in other sources.

Reporting Name, Age, Gender, Birthplace

The census taker was to list each free person by name, last name first. Researchers probably cannot learn whether some marshals tried to save time by listing everyone with initials only or simply used initials in the copies they made. Nevertheless, some censuses available for research give only the persons' initials. Everyone was to be labeled M (male) or F (female). Birthplace meant state, territory, or other country. If the reporting family did not know someone's birthplace, the census taker was to list "unknown."

The age reported for each person was to be the age as of their most recent birthday prior to census day. Some of the population apparently rounded off their ages to the nearest zero or five. Those who did not know their exact age were to estimate it. Infants under one year of age were listed as a fractional age: e.g., 3/12 for three months.

Occasionally, census takers recorded more specific information on ages and birthplaces, as did enumerator Charles J. White in Chatham County, Georgia, in 1860. Although the parents' information for one Schwencke family followed the instructions, the enumerator was meticulous about recording vital information for the children. The parents, John and Louisa Schwencke (both thirty-nine, both born in Prussia) had three children. The eldest son, John, was born in New York City and in June 1860 was ten years and ten months of age: written *10 10/12*. The second son, Charles, was born in Philadelphia and was seven years, four months of age. The youngest child was daughter Louisa, born in Savannah, reported as age three years and eleven months.

If these parents gave accurate ages for their children, the birth dates can be figured fairly closely. John had already passed his tenth birthday by June 1 (census day) and completed ten months of his eleventh year. We could estimate his birth date as July 1849. Charles had turned seven earlier in 1860 and had completed four months of his eighth year. We could therefore estimate his birth date as January 1853. Louisa had completed eleven months of her fourth year by 1 June, 1860. This suggests that she would have turned four in June

IDENTIFYING EXTRA MEMBERS OF HOUSEHOLDS

Example 1: 1860 San Augustine Co., Tx.

A. Huston	61	Pa.
Elizabeth "	55	Oh.
J.N. "	18	Tx.
Henry "	15	Tx.
Priscilla "	14	Tx.
Alla "	10	Tx.
Mary M. Kyle	20	Tx.
Ella "	2	Tx

Example 2: 1850 Hardeman Co., Tn.

Elliott G. Coleman	27	Va.
Catherine "	19	S.C.
Mary "	2	Tn.
Lucy "	2/12	Tn.
William "	19	Va.

Example 3: 1870 Cherokee Co., Tx.

Moses Cummings	44	Tn.
Cordelia "	35	Tx.
James "	20	Tn.
Martha "	16	Tn.
John A. "	14	Tx.
Mary "	12	Tx.
Columbus "	4	Tx.
Ella "	2	Tx.
Elizabeth Everett	16	Tx.
Almanza "	14	Tx.

Example 4: 1860 Smith Co., Ms.

Joseph Martin	60	Ga.
Nancy "	54	Ga.
Oquin C. "	29	Ms.
James T. "	27	Ms.
William S. "	24	Ms.
Nancy H. "	17	Ms.
Karen V. "	14	Ms.
Robert J. W. "	12	Ms.
Mary C. "	9	Ms.
William R. "	4	Ms.
Terra A. "	3	Ms.
Harriet A. "	1	Ms.

Answers to the identity of the extra person(s) in the household:

1. Married to A.S. Kyle in 1857, Mary Huston was now a young widow coming home with her daughter to live with her parents and siblings. County marriage and land records and family records confirm these facts.
2. Husband's younger brother, William, lived with the family, as shown in family letters.
3. The two Everetts were Cordelia's children by her first husband, as shown in county probate records of their father. The four eldest children are Moses's by his first wife, shown in the previous census and family records. The age gap between Mary and Columbus signals a possible change in wives, which is confirmed in the county marriage record for Moses and Cordelia. The two youngest children were from the current marriage, as confirmed in vital records and family records.
4. The researcher must ask whether a fifty-four-year-old woman would have been the mother of the three youngest children. The eldest son, Oquin, had recently lost his wife; he and his three children (the three youngest in the household) had moved home to live with his father and probable stepmother. The 1850 census had shown him as a single young man in this family. Later census records and his wife's obituary confirmed the situation. Because this is a "burned" county, marriage and probate records are not available for further confirmation.

1860 and implies a June 1856 birth date. Not only do we get more precise birth date possibilities from this census entry, we get more precise information on when and where to look for the family as they became established in their new country: New York City in the summer of 1849, Philadelphia in January 1853, and Savannah in June 1856. Perhaps this information could help narrow a search for naturalization papers.

Another Savannah resident, Patience R. Pleasants (fifty-six) was a "lady of leisure" born in Petersburg, Virginia. Living with her was an apparent daughter, Eloise (thirty-two), born in Richmond, Virginia. Eloise's husband, Alexander Campbell, a thirty-two-year-old wharf clerk, was from Argyleshire, Scotland. What a boon to researchers to get this immigrant's birthplace, especially since Campbell is such a common name in the U.S. and in Scotland.

Also in Chatham County, in the county jail, were I. Egbert Farnum (thirty-four), an adventurer from Charleston, South Carolina, in jail for piracy; John Lawson (fifty), a merchant from Sevier County, Tennessee, in jail for bank robbery; Louis W. Wells (forty-five), a commission merchant from Hartford County, Connecticut, locked up for swindling; and Betty C. McLean (thirty), a prostitute from Kilkenny, Ireland, in jail for vagrancy.

Reporting Race

In 1850 and 1860, the "color" choices on the census form were white (space to be left blank), black (B), and mulatto (M). On the slave schedules, the choices were black (B) and mulatto (M). In 1870, the column for color was to be filled in for every person—white (W), black (B), mulatto (M), Chinese (C), and American Indian (I).

Reporting Occupations

One helpful piece of information added to the censuses beginning in 1850 was the occupations of those in the family over age fifteen who were considered to have an occupation or profession. The census takers were to give specific denominations for clergy—"Meth." (Methodist), "R.C." (Roman Catholic), "O.S.P." (Old School Presbyterian), and others. However, many are listed simply as minister, clergyman, or preacher. Most employed persons were listed simply as farmer, planter, overseer, blacksmith, laborer, printer, clerk, attorney at law, physician, barber, hotel keeper, and the like, without more specific information.

In addition to occupation, the form in all three of these censuses asked for the value of one's real estate. In rural areas, this sometimes helps researchers determine the relative size of the farm or plantation, especially in combination with county land and tax records. In 1860 and 1870, the form also asked for the value of the personal estate. Large numbers in that column could be a clue to a large business or, in 1860, a large number of slaves.

Instructions in 1870 asked census takers to be particularly careful and specific in reporting occupation information—the exact kind of work and in what kind of establishment. Instead of the generic "factory hand," they were to specify the kind of factory where the person worked. Instead of "mason," they were to distinguish between stone masons and brick masons. Also, children who were gainfully employed and helping with family support were to be listed. Some teenagers were reported as "assisting on farm." Many children, teenagers, and other household members, even when assisting with the household chores, were properly listed as "at home" or "at school" or "attending school." These details add more to your knowledge of your ancestor's family and life.

"Farmers" were men or women who farmed land on their own; a "farm hand" or "farm laborer" worked for wages for someone else. A "day laborer" was considered someone who worked at odd jobs in a town or city, not someone working on a farm.

Beginning in 1870, women who did not work outside the home were to be listed as "keeping house" because "housekeeper" meant a person receiving wages from someone else for these duties. Sometimes, a housewife's occupation was listed as "domestic," which probably meant "keeping house" unless other remarks indicated she was a "domestic servant" in someone else's home. By 1900, family members, including wives, who worked on the family farm were listed as "farm labor—home farm." By 1910, housewives were to be listed with no occupation.

Tip

If you come across an occupation you don't understand, look for similar entries in that location. Study the history of the area at that time to learn more about economic activity in the county, and study the other people with the same occupation. Also try to find out more through other sources, such as the local newspaper, county history, exhibits at a local museum, or county courthouse records.

1870 Duplications

In 1870, at least three cities were enumerated twice: Indianapolis, New York City, and Philadelphia. The two enumerations for each city are microfilmed together in the 1870 census microfilm M593. The first enumerations were made during the summer, as were those for most of the country; the second ones, during January and February 1871. Apparently, someone felt the residents were undercounted or misreported the first time and wanted to try to get a better record the second time.

In some of the neighborhoods, the information is more complete on the second set of schedules, and some residents probably were missed in one or both. The published indexes from Heritage Quest include entries from both lists. However, duplicate entries appear only when the surname spelling differed in the two lists. In the fifth ward of Indianapolis, for example, Matthew Fox and George Rouser were enumerated twice but indexed once—for their entry on the August schedule. Their neighbor John Doneley (February list) or Donnely (August list) was indexed for both entries.

Their neighborhood showed some differences in the two lists, in both families and individuals, but people could have moved in the six months between censuses. (Regardless of the census-day rule, the February census taker could not enumerate people who were no longer living there, and he may have enumerated newcomers who had lived elsewhere in the city in August.) We must wonder whether the families listed below were aware of the census-day rule and whether family members celebrated birthdays between August and February. Matthew Fox's family entry was almost identical in the August and February enumerations, but the information differed considerably for some families, as shown in these examples:

- George and Mary Rouser had five children, most of whose ages were different in the two schedules. Josephine was reportedly six in August and seven in February; George, four in August and five in February. William was age three in both lists. The August enumeration showed Peter as nine months old with an October 1869 birth date; here, either the math or the memory was inaccurate. The February 1871 schedule reported him as six months old, born in November 1869; this age was possible if they observed the June census day. Mary's birthplace was reported as Prussia in August and Baden in February. In the occupation column, George and Mary both were reported as bakers in February; Mary was "keeping house" in the August schedule.
- Edward Hart/Heart and his wife, Rosa (name different and unclear on the February list), were age thirty-one and twenty-seven, respectively, in the August schedule but twenty-nine and twenty-eight in February. Their child Agnes was reported as three and four. The August enumeration showed infant Margaret as ten months old, with an October 1869 birth date. The February 1871 report of her as Abbey, five months old, with a December 1869 birth date, was possible if they observed the census-day rule. Edward's birthplace changed from Ireland in August to Scotland in February.
- John and Catherine Donnely/Doneley in the August entry were listed as fifty-six and fifty-eight years old, respectively, with a sixteen-year-old Martha Patterson (no occupation) living in their home. In February, the schedule did not list Martha with them and showed their ages as fifty-two and thirty-seven.

The implication for genealogists is clear: Whether or not your ancestral head of household is shown in a printed 1870 index or in one of these enumerations, read both schedules, study the reports carefully, and seek further evidence in other sources.

Many of the Minnesota 1870 schedules were casualties of fire. Thus, the four rolls of

Minnesota schedules in M593, the 1870 federal schedules, represent only the surviving pages, not complete coverage. The copy kept in the state has been microfilmed as T132, which also includes some mortality schedules.

1870 Omissions

Many researchers find the 1870 census troublesome. However, consider some reasons for the numerous omissions and mistakes. Everywhere immigration was increasing, and these newcomers were on the move to new homes. Many Civil War widows were remarried and starting new families. Railroads all over the country were rebuilding or expanding, and people saw economic opportunity along the routes. Boom towns along the railroads thrived, some only momentarily; and every day saw new arrivals and departures, especially in the town at the end of the line. It is a wonder that in such areas a census was taken at all. Especially in the South, this was a period of depression and great transition. Older families were moving out in droves to new lives farther west, and new families were moving in from the North and Europe. The census of 1870 was the first after the Civil War, and some areas of the South were still under military rule. Perhaps bitter memories and feelings in these areas caused families to evade the enumerator's visit and simply "go fishing."

Things to Remember

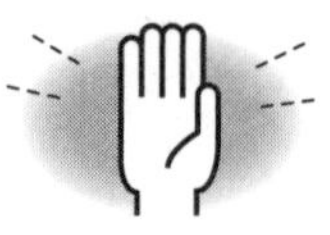

Warning

Genealogists must be cautious in using and studying the 1850 to 1870 censuses. **Being aware of the following tips may prevent false assumptions:**

1. A wife was to be listed after her husband. However, if a male head of household was single, the female listed after his name may have been an unmarried sister or daughter, a sister-in-law, or another relative. His mother or grandmother, of course, would be of an older generation, as shown in the age column.
2. The apparent wife of the head of household may not have been the mother of all the children. She may have been a second or third wife; she may not have been the mother of any of the children.
3. Sometimes, a man's second wife had the same given name as his first wife.
4. Without further study, we cannot assume that the "wife" named in 1850 was the "wife" enumerated, unnamed, in the 1840 census.
5. Sometimes, the wife's children by a previous marriage were listed with the same surname as the head of household instead of their actual surname.
6. Elders in the household may have been parents, grandparents, or other relatives.
7. Censuses sometimes showed an adult son as head of the household, even if he was single and living in the household of his father, mother, or both parents.
8. Families, even those with different surnames, listed next to or within a few entries of each other were often related—cousins, parents and their married children, married sisters, etc.
9. Reported birthplaces and ages often vary from census to census. Study each census available for family members, and seek confirmation in other records.
10. We cannot know who reported the information to the census taker and how accurate their knowledge was.
11. Census takers usually wrote what they heard or thought they heard; they may or may not have asked the family to spell names. Enumerators often spelled phonetically. Thus spelling variations are common in census records. These variations do not mean that the census takers or the families were illiterate; standardized spelling was not the issue that it is today.

Sometimes, census takers provided additional information not requested on the forms. This information can be as short and simple as notes to identify twins or grandchildren. In Madison County, Mississippi, in 1860, the enumerator bracketed the names of eight children and identified them as "minor heirs of Jas. S. Pritchard." (*Jas.* is a common abbreviation for *James.*) In Jasper County, Mississippi, the 1870 enumerator listed Molly Parker's occupation as "living with son." Many enumerators listed the county or town of birth instead of the state or country. In 1850 and 1860, enumerators were to identify couples who had married within the previous twelve months. However, some recorded the year when every couple married. The possibility of finding such gems is reason enough to look for ancestors and their cluster of relatives in every available census—you never know what's there until you look.

Slave Schedules

The slave schedules of 1850 and 1860 can be helpful but do not contain a great amount of genealogical information for either black or white ancestors. As sometimes happens in the general population schedules, many pages are faded or damaged. The schedules usually named slaveholders or their agents, although in some cases slaveholding women were identified simply as *Mrs.* or *Widow* and their surname. The pages listed slaves individually by gender and age but not by name. One rare instance where slaves were named was in Bowie County, Texas, in 1850. Figure 9-5, on page 336, is an example of a slave schedule.

See Also

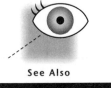

See chapter nine for more on slave research.

Slave schedules were made for Alabama, Arkansas, Delaware, District of Columbia, Florida, Georgia, Kentucky, Louisiana, Maryland, Mississippi, Missouri, New Jersey (1850 only), North Carolina, South Carolina, Tennessee, Texas, Virginia, and the Indian lands west of Arkansas (1860 only). The 1850 Delaware slave schedule is included at the end of the Sussex County returns, roll 55 of M432 of the National Archives microfilm. The 1850 District of Columbia slave schedule is likewise at the end of the free population returns, on roll 57 of M432.

No 1850 census was taken for the unorganized territory that became Oklahoma. However, the 1860 general population census for Arkansas included white residents in "Indian lands west of Arkansas," i.e., the Indian nations of the Five Civilized Tribes. The 1860 slave schedule for Arkansas also included slaveholders and 7,393 slaves in the Indian nations. Slaveholders included whites, Indians, and residents of mixed blood. In the Creek nation, one slave owner was named as "Hope a Negro."

Black researchers often use these schedules to look in a given household for a group of slaves that matches their ancestral family members in gender and age. The schedules thus become a finding aid in the identification of the slave family in a potential slaveholder's household. This identification is a preliminary step in tracing the black family through the slaveholding family's records. (See chapter nine.)

Researchers sometimes find that the slave schedules name widows, heirs, and executors in a way that the free schedules do not and thus yield important clues for further research in land and probate records. In addition, white researchers use the slave schedules to determine whether their ancestors or extended family members held slaves and how the slave population changed over the years.

The details sometimes surprise modern genealogists who may have preconceived notions about how their ancestors fit into their society. Some may assume their ancestors were large plantation owners, but the slave schedules show only one or two slaves, or none. On the other hand, others think of their ancestors as people who would find slaveholding repugnant; yet, the schedules may show twenty or thirty slaves. Although we in the twenty-first century view the subject of slavery differently from the way many ancestors viewed it, the facts are part of the family history of both white and black families. Our role is to report what we find even though we cannot know exactly what our ancestors thought and felt.

SOUNDEX

Numerous printed and online indexes exist for the censuses prior to 1880; a few have been created for the 1880 census. However, an important index for censuses of 1880 and after is the Soundex.

Soundex is an index based on the sounds in the surname and is a useful finding aid for some of the 1880 through 1930 censuses. The reason for Soundexing certain censuses in the 1930s and 1940s was the Census Bureau's large and increasing number of requests for age verification, especially from government agencies and from individuals born before their states began recording births. Not only did retirees need to prove their ages for Social Security benefits, which began 1 January 1937, but individuals and the government needed age verification for state old-age pensions, passports, and national defense reasons (probably including ages of draftees and enlistees during World War II).

Notes

For more, see "The WPA Census Soundexing Projects" by Claire Prechtel-Kluskens in *Prologue*, vol. 34 (Spring 2002), online at <www.archives.gov/publications/prologue/spring_2002_soundex_projects.html>. Robert C. Russell of Pittsburgh developed and first patented the Soundexing system in 1916.

In 1935, the Bureau of the Census requested funding to give more than 2,500 people jobs through the newly-created Works Progress Administration (WPA) to index the 1900 census in anticipation of Congress passing a program for old-age assistance. (The Social Security Act passed in August 1935; the application process began in 1936.) Next, the Census Bureau indexed the 1920 census and part of the 1880 census. An effort was made to index the 1930 census, but the project was terminated in 1943, before that indexing was complete.

By 1940 when the bureau received funding for the partial index of the 1880 schedules (only households with children age ten and under), it was thought that the index would be useful for the bureau's needs for only a few more years. (Remember, genealogy was not the reason for the indexing.) After all, children ten and under in 1880 (born in 1869 and after) were near or at retirement age by 1940; they were the ones from the 1880 census most likely to need age verification. However, the 1900 and 1920 censuses had already been indexed; perhaps part of the thinking was that many of these 1880 children could be verified from later censuses already indexed.

WPA employees first created census extraction cards for families and for individuals living in institutions or households of a different surname. Then the cards were assigned Soundex codes before being microfilmed. The Soundex coding system sorts names by their sounds. You need the code number, discussed below, in order to use the index.

Soundex is usually available as microfilm of the original card file, and its value is enormous. It abstracts not only the members of the household and their ages but also the family's location on the census (enumeration district, sheet number, line number). This tool is especially valuable when you do not know where in a given state a family was living. The film is arranged by state, then alphabetically by the first letter of the surname, then by Soundex code number: A000, A100, A106, A235, A356, and so forth. Within each code, given names are alphabetical. If several people have the same name, they are listed in the alphabetical order of birthplace, i.e., state or country.

Soundex Code

Since the Soundex code is based on sounds in the surname, letters with similar sounds are given the same code. Use these steps to form the code for most names:

- Begin with the initial letter of the surname and set it aside as the first part of the code.
- Strike out all vowels (*a*, *e*, *i*, *o*, *u*) and *y*. Most of us have been taught to strike out *w* and *h* and treat them the same way as the vowels. However, they were not always handled the same way. (See below.)
- Change the remaining consonants into numbers according to the chart below.
- Double letters, or consecutive letters with the same code number, are coded as only one digit. (This applies to the initial letter of the code as well as to the code's numbers.)
- If you run out of key letters before you have a three-digit code, simply add zeros.
- If you complete the code before you have gone through the entire name, disregard the remaining consonants.

Code Number	*Key Letters*
1	b, p, f, v
2	c, s, k, g, j, q, x, z
3	d, t
4	l
5	m, n
6	r

Examples of Soundex Coding

WILLOUGHBY	SCHMIDT	MACKAY
W 4 2 1	S 5 3 0	M 2 00
W421 is the code.	S530 is the code.	M200 is the code.
GLASSCOCK	ADCOCK	LEA (or LEE)
G 4 2 2	A 3 2 2	L 000
G422 is the code.	A322 is the code.	L000 is the code.

H and W Rule. Based on rules actually used by many or most employees who prepared the census Soundexes (and others), the letters *h* and *w* were to be disregarded as if they were not present in the name, unless one of them was the initial letter. Differing or alternate codes occur only when the *h* or *w* falls between two letters that have the same code number, in such combinations as *chs* (Sachse, Ochs, Ochsner), *chk* (Wichkoski), *schk* (Blaschke, Mitschke, Peschke), *shc* (Ashcroft), and *thd* or *tht* (Rothdeutsch, Smithton). In such cases, disregarding the *h* or *w* would cause the like-coded letters to be pushed together and translated as one digit.

The following are examples of the application of this rule as shown on 1900 Soundex cards:

- Sochse and Sachse—S200 (coding S-cs-0-0) instead of S220 (coding S-c-s-0)
- Schsekoweske—S220 (coding Scs-k-sk) instead of S222 (coding Sc-s-k-sk)
- Ochs—O200 (coding O-cs-0-0) instead of O220 (coding O-c-s-0)
- Smithton—S535 (coding S-m-tt-n) instead of S533 (coding S-m-t-t)
- Ashcroft—A261 (coding A-sc-r-f) instead of A226 (coding A-s-c-r)

By the same method, Mitschke would have a code of M320 (coding M-t-sck-0), rather than M322 (coding M-t-sc-k). Rothdeutsch would be coded R332 (R-td-t-sc), not R333 (R-t-d-t). In some of these situations, the names could be grouped as mixed codes so that finding them would not be too lengthy a process, regardless of which code is used. If you don't find such names under one code, try the other possibility in case it was Soundexed differently.

For More Info

For more history and explanation of the "H&W" rule, see *The Complete Soundex Guide* by Willis I. Else (Apollo, Penn.: Closson Press, 2002) and "The Original Soundex Instructions" by Tony Burroughs in the *National Genealogical Society Quarterly* 89 (December 2001): 287–298.

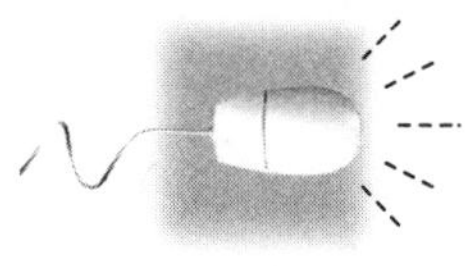

Internet Source

Some Web sites provide Soundex coding for you; at this writing some do not use the rediscovered "H&W" rule and some do. If you learn the system yourself, you can evaluate codes provided on these sites. Four sites which in November 2002 were using the "H&W" rule were these:

- http://1930census.archives.gov/beginSearch.asp, using the Soundex search
- http://resources.rootsweb.com/cgi-bin/soundexconverter
- http://gatons.com/~teaser/javascript/soundex.html
- www.bradandkathy.com/cgi-bin/yasc.cgi

Figure 2-2, below, shows four Soundex cards. The 1900 card for Gusta Ochs of Pennsylvania illustrates the "H&W" rule with the code O200. Anto Maria Archuleta's 1880 card from New Mexico Territory shows that the enumerator listed the town of birth for each family member: Los Cañones, Collote [Coyote], and Abiquiu in Rio Arriba County. George Apodaca's 1880 family included infant son Hipolito, age 15/30 (fifteen days old) instead of 0/12 (less than one month old). Anton Schsekoweske's card illustrates the "H&W" rule and an individual card for a person in a household or in an institution whose surname was different from that of the head of household. He was a pauper living in the county poor house. His birth month and citizenship are marked "NR," not reported.

Family Cards and Individual Cards. In creating the Soundex and Miracode cards (see page 36), indexers grouped family members together on "family cards." These usually show

A 132 NEW MEXICO TERRITORY
Apodaca, George (HEAD OF FAMILY) VOL. 2 E.D. 20 SHEET 20 LINE 16
W (COLOR) M (SEX) 25 (AGE) N. Mex (BIRTHPLACE)
Mora (COUNTY) Santiago (M. C. D.)
(CITY) (STREET) (HOUSE NO.)
OTHER MEMBERS OF FAMILY

NAME	RELATION-SHIP	AGE	BIRTHPLACE
Apodaca, Manuela	W	20	N. Mex
— Hipolito	S	15/30	N. Mex

1880 CENSUS–INDEX DEPARTMENT OF COMMERCE BUREAU OF THE CENSUS A-1a

PENNSYLVANIA
Ochs, Gusta (HEAD OF FAMILY) VOL. 164 E.D. 328 SHEET 6 LINE 56
W (COLOR) Nov (MONTH) 1857 (YEAR) 42 (AGE) Penna (BIRTHPLACE)
Phila (COUNTY)
Philadelphia (CITY) Leithgow (STREET) 1240 (HOUSE NO.)
OTHER MEMBERS OF FAMILY

NAME	RELATION-SHIP	BIRTH MONTH	BIRTH YEAR	AGE	BIRTHPLACE
Ochs, Clara D.	W	July	1855	45	Penna

1900 CENSUS–INDEX DEPARTMENT OF COMMERCE BUREAU OF THE CENSUS A-1a

Schsekoweske, Anton VOL. 31 E.D. 75 SHEET 6 LINE 57
W (COLOR) NR (MONTH) 1819 (YEAR) 81 (AGE) Germany (BIRTHPLACE) NR (CITIZENSHIP)
Juneau (COUNTY) Fountain Town (M. C. D.)
(CITY) (STREET) (HOUSE NO.)
ENUMERATED WITH Juneau County Poor House
RELATIONSHIP TO ABOVE Pauper
REMARKS
A-3

A624 NEW MEXICO TERRITORY
Archuleta, Anto Maria (HEAD OF FAMILY) VOL. 2 E.D. 29 SHEET 28 LINE 44
W (COLOR) M (SEX) 28 (AGE) Los Cañones (BIRTHPLACE)
Rio Arriba (COUNTY) Cañones (M. C. D.)
(CITY) (STREET) (HOUSE NO.)
OTHER MEMBERS OF FAMILY

NAME	RELATION-SHIP	AGE	BIRTHPLACE
Archuleta, Telesfora	W	24	Abiquiu
✓ Plasido	S	5	Collote
✓ Clodoveo	S	2	Collote

1880 CENSUS–INDEX DEPARTMENT OF COMMERCE BUREAU OF THE CENSUS A-1a

Figure 2-2 Sample Soundex cards.

the names of the nuclear family and other relatives along with an indication of non-relatives living in the house, such as "+2 boarders."

Individual cards show persons with a different surname from the head of household; persons in the household not related to the family; or people living in an institution, hotel, or other mostly unrelated group (see Figure 2-2). The head of the institution or owner of the facility was considered the head.

For 1880, 1900, and 1920, the individual cards showed the name of the head of household with whom the individual was enumerated and a blank where the census taker could write in the individual's relationship to the head. The 1910 and 1930 Soundex cards contain a printed list of the most common relationships or reasons for the individual being in the household, with a blank in which the enumerator could specify any other relationship or reason. The individual cards are a major tool for finding orphans, foster children, in-laws, employees, and others not living with a spouse, siblings, or parents.

Spelling Variations. Of course, names were sometimes spelled in different ways in public records or were misread when being indexed. It may be necessary to search several Soundex codes before you find the family you want. For example, the names Thomas, Thompson, and Thomason can sound similar when spoken. Thus, families with one of these names could be enumerated under any of the three. However, the Soundex codes are different—T520, T512, and T525—and thus could require research in several parts of the Soundex. Closely related codes are sometimes mixed together on the microfilm, especially when each contains relatively few names.

Prefixes. Prefixes such as *van*, *de*, *de la*, and *le*, were to be considered part of the surname but were sometimes omitted in coding. However, I have found the name DelHomme under D450 and have not had to search under *H*. Prefixes in Hispanic surnames, such as de la Fuente, may or may not have been encoded. Thus, this name could be Soundexed under D415 or F530.

Compound Names. To find households with compound surnames, you may have to check various possibilities. American Indian and Chinese names may be coded under the name that appears in the surname position on the census. If they are compound names, such as Mary Red Blanket, figure the codes for Red Blanket, for Blanket, and for Red. You may find the name coded different ways. A name such as St. Vincent was supposed to be coded as if *St.* were spelled out and the two words were one: Saint Vincent or S531, but check S315 as well (coded as if *St.* were not spelled out).

Important

Soundex coding was also used for indexing a number of immigration and naturalization records.

Compound names of Hispanic origin, showing both father's surname and mother's maiden name, were to be coded using only the father's surname. For example, the name Cruz y Cortez or Cruz-Cortez was to be encoded using only the patrilineal name, Cruz (C620). If the parilineal surname was de la Cruz, the prefix may or may not have been used in the coding process. However, the matrilineal name, Cortez, was not to have been used for Soundex purposes.

Religious Orders. Those members of religious orders whose names begin with *Sister* or *Brother* usually are Soundexed under S236 and B636, with *Sister* and *Brother* considered their surnames for indexing purposes. The same applies to *Mother* (M360) and *Father* (F360), although any of these listed by surnames would be Soundexed by that name. In the Soundex lists, these persons are not always in alphabetical order. For example, the 1900 Louisiana Soundex for S236 lists Sister Roserio first, before the names beginning with *A*. In addition, the top of this list includes three females whose names were not designated *Sister* but whose relationship was given as Sister of Charity, Sacred Heart Convent, St. James Parish. Their names were given as A. Higgins, A. Schernaildre, and A. Stanard; yet they were coded under S236. Several professors at the St. Vincent Academy in Baton Rouge were listed separately under B636: Brother Adelard, Brother David, and Brother Justinian. However, Brother Jerome of Alexandria, Rapides Parish, was named as head of household with Brothers Humbert, Theodore, and Calestine living in the house. The latter three were *not* entered in the Soundex under their own names.

The inconsistencies are clear, but researchers seeking these people have one Soundex code with which to begin. Of course, some members of religious orders do not retain their family surnames; therefore, researchers should not expect to see these names in the census or Soundex. In cases where several members of the same religious house have the same given name, you may be able to distinguish among them by the birth dates and birthplaces given in the census.

In summary, for most ancestral surnames, the Soundex rules are fairly straightforward. The greatest number of difficulties arise from

- spelling variations, which may necessitate trying several codes.
- prefixes, which may or may not have been coded.
- compound names—whether the name was considered one word (WhiteFox—W312) or two (White Fox) with only one name encoded (W300 or F200).
- abbreviations of Saint, Mount, Sister, or Brother—whether the name was coded as abbreviated or as if it were spelled out (Saint Clair—S532 or St. Clair—S324).

Soundex Availability

The Soundex is available for many 1880 and 1900 through 1930 census schedules:

- 1880 only for households containing children age ten and under. Part of the 1880 Illinois Soundex was omitted in the filming. Those names in the O200–O240 codes have been privately printed by Nancy Gubb Frederick of Evanston, Illinois and are available on microfiche from the Family History Library, catalog number 6100258.
- 1900, 1920 for all households.
- 1910, partial. Refer to the chart "Soundex Availability" on page 37. For 1910, see separate rolls of Soundex microfilm for these cities: Alabama—Birmingham, Mobile, Montgomery; Georgia—Atlanta, Augusta, Macon, Savannah; Louisiana—(Miracode) New Orleans, and Shreveport; and Tennessee—Chattanooga, Knoxville, Memphis, Nashville.
- 1930, partial. Refer to the chart "Soundex Availability."

To find availability and film numbers of specific census and Soundex rolls for the general population schedules, refer to the catalogs published by the National Archives Trust Fund Board. One covers 1790–1890. Each of the 1900 through 1930 censuses has its own booklet. These publications are available from the National Archives and can be found in most libraries with census collections. See the Web site <www.archives.gov/publications/microfilm_catalogs.html> for the online catalogs.

1910 Miracode

Partial indexes for the 1910 census were created in the 1960s. As the chart on page 37 shows, Soundex is available for some states. For others, a similar system—Miracode—was used. The codes are, or should be, generated using the same rules as Soundex. As Willis Else pointed out in his study, if 1910 religious-order names were abbreviated Sr. (sister) or Br. (brother) in the Miracoding process, they received a code of S600 or B600.

SOUNDEX AVAILABILITY

1910 Soundex available for	1910 Miracode available for	
Alabama	Arkansas	Michigan
Georgia	California	Missouri
Louisiana (except New Orleans and Shreveport)	Florida	North Carolina
Mississippi	Illinois	Ohio
South Carolina	Kansas	Oklahoma
Tennessee	Kentucky	Pennsyvlania
Texas	Louisiana (New Orleans, Shreveport)	Virginia
		West Virginia
(Soundex gives enumeration district and page number.)	(Miracode gives enumeration district and family or visitation number, and uses the same coding system as Soundex.)	

No 1910 Soundex available for*

Alaska	Indiana	Nebraska	Puerto Rico
Arizona	Iowa	Nevada	Rhode Island
Colorado	Maine	New Hampshire	South Dakota
Connecticut	Maryland	New Jersey	Utah
Delaware	Massachusetts	New Mexico	Vermont
District of Columbia	Military Installations	New York	Washington
Hawaii	Minnesota	North Dakota	Wisconsin
Idaho	Montana	Oregon	Wyoming

*At this writing, Heritage Quest CD-ROM indexes for 1910 heads of household are available for all fifty states and military installations.

1930 Soundex availability

Alabama	Kentucky (Bell, Floyd, Harlan, Kenton, Muhlenberg, Perry, and Pike counties)	Louisiana	West Virginia (Fayette, Harrison, Kanawha, Logan, McDowell, Mercer, and Raleigh counties)
Arkansas		Mississippi	
Florida		North Carolina	
Georgia		South Carolina	
		Tennessee	
		Virginia	

Figure 2-3, on page 38, shows a Miracode individual card and family card. The individual card for Arthur Mallett contains this information:

- The top line contains the finding information, left to right: his residence in San Joaquin County; the town name, which was not reported on this card; volume number 102, which you don't need if you will be looking at the microfilm; enumeration district number 126 and the family or visitation number 59, both of which are very important to locating the individual or household on microfilm.
- The second line shows, left to right, the Miracode (Soundex) number M430, surname Mallett, given name Arthur, his relationship to the head of household ("BO," boarder), his race ("W," white), age (22), birthplace (Utah), and state of residence (California).
- On the third line, "enumerated with" prepares you for the fourth line.
- The fourth line indicates that Arthur lived with a white (W) head of household (H) named Myrteloh A. Weaver.

The family card in Figure 2-3 shows the following:

- The top line shows that the family was in Alameda County, the town of Alameda, in an enumeration in volume 1, enumeration district 16, and identified as family 128.
- The second line gives the Soundex code M430 and surname Melotte. The head of the

household (H) was August Mellotte, white (W), age 45, born in Belgium, living in California.

- The third line identifies his wife (W) Magdeline, age 42, born in Belgium.
- The fourth line identifies his daughter (D) Gustavine King, age 20, born in Belgium.
- The fifth line shows that his son (S) Henry Melotte, age 18, was born in Belgium.
- The sixth line identifies his son-in-law (SL) Leo King (the husband of Gustavine), age 21, born in California.
- The last line indicates that his grandson (GS) Leo (King) was living in the household but his age was not reported (NR); Leo was born in California.

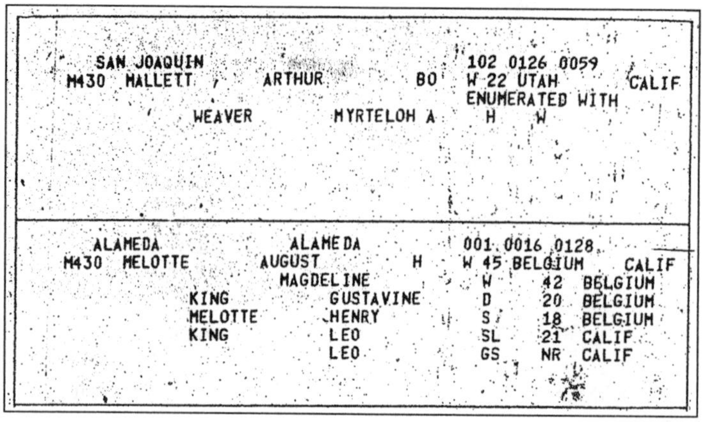
SAN JOAQUIN 102 0126 0059
M430 MALLETT ARTHUR BO W 22 UTAH CALIF
ENUMERATED WITH
WEAVER MYRTELOH A H W

ALAMEDA ALAMEDA 001 0016 0128
M430 MELOTTE AUGUST H W 45 BELGIUM CALIF
MAGDELINE W 42 BELGIUM
KING GUSTAVINE D 20 BELGIUM
MELOTTE HENRY S 18 BELGIUM
KING LEO SL 21 CALIF
LEO GS NR CALIF

Figure 2-3 Sample Miracode cards.

Neither the Soundex cards nor the Miracode cards contain all the information shown in the census. Thus, you should use the finding information—state, county, enumeration district number, and family number—to locate the household on microfilm to check for accuracy and further information.

1880–1890 CENSUSES

For researchers, the greatest difference between the pre-1880 censuses and those of 1880 to 1940 is that the census form, beginning in 1880, requested the relationship of each household member to the head. Family members who appeared in previous censuses to be spouses, children, and in-laws or parents were now to be identified as such. Thus, the 1880 census is a very important record for every family. The demographic questions asked between 1880 and 1940 are shown in the chart "Which federal census reports . . . ?" on page 22. Column headings in numerical order are shown in the chart "Census Page Column Headings, 1880–1890" on page 39.

True, not all relationships were reported or reported accurately, at least in the copies which genealogists have available to read. In some cases, stepchildren were reported as children; cousins were reported as boarders; some relationships were not reported; and other errors or omissions occurred. However, on the whole, the new information is welcome and helpful. The chart "Abbreviations Used to Show Relationships" on page 47 shows the most common terms and abbreviations used to describe relationships in the censuses from 1880 forward. Some enumerators wrote out the words; others used abbreviations, either standardized or their own, using capital or lowercase letters. More abbreviations can be found on the National Archives Web site at <www.archives.gov/publications/microfilm_catalogs/census/schedules/1910_federal_population_census.html>.

In 1880, the categories for reporting race were the same as those used in 1870: white

CENSUS PAGE COLUMN HEADINGS, 1880 AND 1890

1880 column headings (Census year 1 June 1879–31 May 1880)

1. dwelling number in order of visitation
2. family number in order of visitation
3. name of every person whose usual place of abode on June 1 was with this family
4. color (see page 38 for details)
5. sex
6. age as of last birthday before 1 June 1880
7. if born in census year, name of month
8. relationship of each person to head of household (See chart on page 47 for details.)
9. mark if person is single
10. mark if person is married
11. mark if person is widowed; *D*, if divorced
12. mark if married within census year
13. profession, occupation, or trade of each person age 10 or older
14. number of months unemployed during census year
15. name of illness or disability if person is ill or disabled on day of enumerator's visit
16. mark if blind
17. mark if deaf and dumb
18. mark if idiotic
19. mark if insane
20. mark if maimed, crippled, bedridden, or otherwise disabled
21. mark if attended school within census year
22. mark if person cannot read
23. mark if cannot write
24. place of birth: state, territory, country other than United States
25. place of birth of person's father
26. place of birth of person's mother

1890 row headings (Census year 1 June 1889–31 May 1890)

1. given name, middle initial, surname
2. whether Civil War veteran or widow
3. relationship to head of household
4. color (see below for details)
5. sex
6. age at most recent birthday
7. single, married, widowed, divorced
8. whether married during census year
9. mother of how many children and number of these children living
10. birthplace

11., 12. birthplace of father, of mother

13. number of years in United States
14. whether naturalized
15. whether naturalization papers have been taken out (see page 49)
16. profession, trade, or occupation
17. months unemployed during census year
18. months in school during census year

19., 20. if able to read, if able to write

21. whether speaks English; if not, name of language the person speaks
22. if suffering from acute or chronic disease, name it and length of affliction
23. whether defective in sight, hearing, speech; whether crippled, maimed, deformed (name defect)
24. whether prisoner, convict, homeless child, pauper
25. supplemental schedule page
26. is the home hired (rented) or owned by head or member of family?
27. if owned, is it free of mortgage?
28. if head of household is farmer, is farm he cultivates hired (rented) or owned by head or member of family?
29. if owned, is it free of mortgage?
30. if home or farm is owned and mortgaged, give post-office address of owner

(W), black (B), mulatto (Mu), Chinese (C), and American Indian (I). For 1890, however, enumerators were to report the same groups, with the addition of Japanese, but were to distinguish between black (three-fourths or more black ancestry), mulatto (three-eighths to five-eighths black), quadroon (one-fourth black), and octoroon (one-eighth or less black ancestry, "any trace of black blood")

1880 Census and National Index

In 2001, the Church of Jesus Christ of Latter-day Saints (under the trademark FamilySearch) released a set of CD-ROMs called *1880 United States Census and National Index*. While it does not replace the microfilm or digitized images of the 1880 census, this set is a major reference tool. Many libraries and Family History Centers have this collection, and many researchers find the cost affordable enough to warrant having a set at home, especially for those late-night or weekend study sessions when the libraries are closed. (See page 2 for contact information.)

Because of its importance, this tool merits mention here. Researchers have two main options: a national index and a regional or statewide index that includes abstracts of the basic family information from the census microfilm.

Case Study: A Sample Search

Case Study

A search for one Kentucky-born couple, Sallie (or Sarah) R. and James Proctor Knott, illustrates the process. The national index was the first stage of this search because (1) it was not known under which name Mrs. Knott or her husband may have been enumerated; and (2) their residence was suspected but not confirmed. This search could have begun with the Kentucky CD, but the national index shows same-name individuals nationwide in case the target persons were living in a place the researcher did not expect.

The national index (twenty discs) allows you to search for an individual by name and other criteria: race, gender, birth year, birthplace, and residence. The results show all individuals in the country with the same or similar name and matching criteria. The regional and state indexes (thirty-five discs) are quicker to use if you know where the target ancestors were.

The first search—for white females named Sallie Knott—yielded nineteen names, including the similar surnames Knotts, Nott, Nodd, and McNott. Variant spellings of Sallie appeared, but no Sallie R. and no Sarah. (Sallie is a common nickname for Sarah.) None matched the target person's approximate age and birthplace.

The second attempt used her formal name, Sarah Knott, and added an approximate birth date of 1830; the database allows a search of five years on either side of the date you enter. This search yielded fifteen women of the same variant surnames, with first or middle names of Sarah and various middle initials. This time, the national index showed only one Sarah R. Knott, and she was the only one listed as born and living in Kentucky. She matched the criteria.

See Also

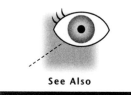

See page 288 for more on Mr. Knott.

With the same criteria as the national search, the Kentucky CD revealed one woman; the abstract showed Sarah R. Knott (age forty-seven) and her husband, J. Proctor Knott (age fifty), in Lebanon, Marion County, Kentucky. The puzzling item was his occupation, abstracted as "labor." However, the microfilm later showed his occupation as "Law." He was indeed a lawyer and a Congressman. Enumerated next to them were Mr. and Mrs. J.B. Chapman—J.B. and "Mitura," shown as "Kitura" in the microfilm and known from family records to be Sallie's sister Keturah. Sallie had been living in their household (shown as James B. and Catura) in 1870, and Mr. Knott has not yet been identified in that census.

A hunch based on these circumstances prompted a search of the 1880 national index for Mr. Knott. He was known by his middle name but was listed in various ways in other records. The national index search for males with the surname Knott and born about 1830 in Kentucky yielded eleven names, including two entries for J. Proctor Knott—the one already mentioned in Kentucky and one in Washington, DC. The "details" view on the District of Columbia CD showed Congressman Knott of Kentucky living in an apparent boarding house with several other government employees, in a neighborhood full of similar residences. The microfilm corroborated the information and showed the address as 1108 F Street North West, a few blocks from the White House.

The question then was the actual whereabouts of Congressman Knott. He probably was not in Kentucky (enumerated June 1) and Washington (enumerated on June 2) on consecutive days. The Web site for the Office of the Clerk of the House of Representatives provided the information that the second session of the Forty-sixth Congress was in session from

December 1879 to 16 June 1880. Since they recessed after the census taker visited Knott's boarding house, the next question will be finding evidence that he was still in attendance.

A Wild Card Search

Another useful feature of the regional and state index CDs is a wild card search. A photograph in my collection, labeled "Nancy Altaffer, Wilbur's mother," indicated that the woman was an adult in 1880 but gave no indication of residence or the photographer's name. Researching her would depend on knowing where to look.

The national index search for Altaffer yielded seventy-one individuals with that surname and two Altofer men; there were no matches for Wilbur or Nancy. Additional queries found no one named Altafer, Altaver, or Oltaffer. The residences of the Altaffers, mostly Pennsylvania and the greater Ohio valley, suggested moving to the regional CDs for a wild card search using the surname Alt*, meaning any name beginning with the letters *Alt*. This effort produced a result in Michigan—a Nancey Altoffer, age thirty-nine and wife of John F. Altoffer. The couple had two sons with middle initials *W*; they will be subjects of research along with the parents to try to identify Wilbur and his mother. It was surprising that the spelling variation Altoffer had not been listed along with Altaffer and Altofer in the national index. A separate search of Altoffer yielded a handful of adults but no other Nancys.

The wild card search also allows placing the asterisk first (e.g., "*fer") or in the middle of the name. In this case, "Al*fer" and "Al*ver" searches produced these additional spelling variations: Aldaffer, Aldefer, Alltoffer, Althofer, Altaver, Althaver, and Allver. No doubt, a number of these individuals were related and would have to be included in a serious study of the extended family.

Online Version of This Database

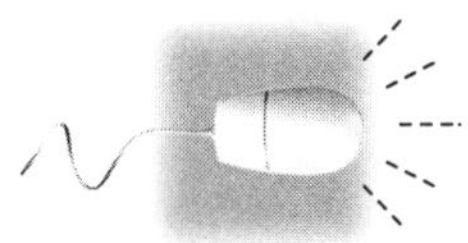

Internet Source

The information from this CD set is online at the Family History Library Web site <www.familysearch.org>, along with the 1881 Canadian and 1881 British censuses. The searching tools are similar to those for the CDs but not the same, and at this writing the wild card search is not possible. If you know exactly how an ancestor's name was listed in the census, you can request a search for that person and/or the head of the household. If you do not get a match and you are fairly certain the person was enumerated, try the spouse's name or the name of a child in the family. For a U.S. search, if you fill in the race, birthplace, and/or birth date of the person you are researching, you must supply both given name and surname in order to conduct the search. You cannot limit a search by gender. You can limit a general surname search, without a given name, by race or birth year range, but not both.

Although more time-consuming than a search for a specific name, another option is to conduct a general search for everyone by the surname who was listed in the census or in a given state. Then, you can read through the list to find those who may be the ones you are trying to find. I had to use this process in the search for a photographer named E. Poole since I did not know (1) his given name, (2) whether his name was listed by his initial or by his given name, (3) where he was born, (4) where he was living in 1880, or (5) the names of any family members.

First, a search using the initial instead of a given name yielded sixty-six names—only those of Poole and variant spellings who were enumerated by that initial. None of the abstracted census entries matched the criteria of the target white adult male who was a photographer. Then, a request for white heads of household named E. Poole reported a list of sixty-three names, obviously with some overlap of the previous search, but apparently they were individuals living in households headed by an E. Poole. None matched the necessary criteria.

The next search was for all white individuals with the surname Poole; the resulting list was five thousand names. The system would not allow this search to be narrowed by adding a birth date range because I could not supply a given name.

Out of curiosity, I requested individuals with the surname Poole, regardless of race, born on twenty years either side of 1843, because I suspected he was an adult by 1885, and probably by 1880. This search again yielded a pool of five thousand names, both black and white; perhaps that number is the limit of the search capacity. Finally, I asked for all Pooles regardless of race or birth date and got five thousand names. Note: If your results number more than two hundred, the screen does not tell you how many names are on your list. You learn that by scanning through pages of two hundred at a time.

The choice, then, was to scan through the five thousand Pooles and variant names and select for later viewing the males whose given name began with the letter *E* or whose middle initial was *E* and who were born between 1823 and 1863. This process narrowed the list to ninety-seven men. By reading each of these selected abstracts, I found one Emory E. Poole, photographer, of South Bend, Indiana, who matched the criteria of the person I was trying to identify and locate. Now, I have someone to study further in a specific location.

The CD-ROM set, for me, has been easier to use for such broad searches. However, if you don't have access to the CD set or want to try the Canadian or British censuses at the same search site, this online resource is a valuable tool.

1885 Census

In 1885 the federal government offered to help pay for a census for any state that wanted to take one between the decennial censuses. Only Colorado, Dakota Territory, Florida, Nebraska, and New Mexico Territory accepted the offer. These 1885 censuses included population schedules very much like the 1880 enumerations, with agriculture, industry, and mortality schedules attached. The New Mexico schedules include an enumeration of Civil War veterans, both Union and Confederate. Because of the loss of most of the 1890 census (see below), the 1885 schedules are important resources.

Microfilm of these censuses may be purchased from the National Archives or Scholarly Resources. National Archives film numbers are Colorado–M158, Florida–M845, Nebraska–M352, New Mexico Territory–M846. Schedules are available for use at the archives or historical society of each of these states and a number of other research libraries. The North Dakota part of the territorial census is available on microfilm on interlibrary loan from the Historical Society in Bismarck. The South Dakota originals of the territorial census, with the agriculture and mortality schedules, are at the state archives, from which microfilm copies are available on interlibrary loan. The Family History Library also rents the microfilm for Colorado, Florida, Nebraska, New Mexico, and the South Dakota portion of the Dakota Territorial schedules.

1890 Census

Most of the 1890 population schedules were destroyed in January 1921 by a fire at the Department of Commerce Building, where they were stored. (The National Archives had not yet been established.) However, the surviving pages reported over six thousand people and are indexed on two rolls of National Archives microfilm (M496)—roll 1, surnames A–J, and roll 2, surnames K–Z. The schedule fragments themselves are on three rolls of

National Archive microfilm (M407)—roll 1, Alabama, roll 2, Washington, DC, and roll 3, the rest of the country. The extent of the records is summarized in the list below.

Apart from the records in the National Archives, the Georgia State Archives has (1) three rolls of microfilm of the copy of the Washington County, Georgia, 1890 schedule that the county purchased from the government before the fire and (2) another volume of that county's schedules that is not microfilmed. The film cannot be borrowed on interlibrary loan from that repository but can be purchased. The microfilm can be rented from the Family History Library (film numbers 0295947–0295949).

The following are the surviving population schedules for 1890:

Alabama—Perry County, about three-fourths roll of microfilm, the largest unit surviving.

District of Columbia—about one-half roll of microfilm.

Georgia—Columbus in Muscogee County: only the households of James C. Denton and Catherine Davis. Washington County 1890 census available at and from the Georgia Archives (see above).

Illinois—Mound Township, including Grant Village, in McDonough County: about 240 households. Most of the entries are legible.

Minnesota—Rockford Township in Wright County: only the George Wolford family.

New Jersey—Jersey City in Hudson County: only the households of James Nelson, Samuel Cross, and Thomas Clooney.

New York—Eastchester in Westchester County: only the John Neormann (?) family. Brookhaven Township in Suffolk County: only the Joel H. Raynor family.

North Carolina—South Point Township in Gaston County: only the households of George Martin, Miles J. Slanes (?), Christopher Buff, and Able Linbarger, with whom Edgar Love lived. River Bend Township in Gaston County: about ninety-six households. Township 2 in Cleveland County: six households.

Ohio—Cincinnati in Hamilton County: only the Alexander Hay family and a young black widow, Amand(a)? Williams, who lived alone. Wayne Township in Clinton County: the households of Dempsey Sexton, Jeremiah Keith, and William W. Syferd.

South Dakota—Jefferson Township in Union County: only the James M. Lafferre family.

Texas—Justice Precinct 6 in Ellis County: about forty-three families. Mountain Peak town in Ellis County: fourteen families. Ovilla Precinct in Ellis County: only the households of Whitfield F. Bockett and Wilhering/Whithering W. Wood. Precinct 5 in Hood County: only the William Locklin/Lockley family (name spelled both ways on the same page). Justice Precinct 6 in Rusk County: only the Dallas Forman(?) family. Justice Precinct 7 in Rusk County: only the Joseph J. Wallace family. Trinity town in Trinity County: only the William T. Evans family. Precinct 2 of Trinity County: about twenty-six families. Kaufman town in Kaufman County: only Green S. Clark Sr. and his wife. (The place designation of this entry is illegible on the microfilm but must have been identified in some other way.)

The 1890 census form was different from those used before and after 1890. The column headings ran down the left side of the page, and the information itself ran across it in five columns per page, making room for five people to a page. The given names in a household read across the top row, with the surnames below. Civil War veterans had a space in which to give their type of service. Below were the spaces for relationship to head of household, age, race, marital status, length of marriage, birthplace, birthplaces of parents, occupation, language, and education information.

Idea Generator

Helping to fill in the gap of the missing 1890 schedules are various substitutes and compilations, including the following:

- City directories for many cities, found in libraries nationwide. Other directories for such groups as lawyers, doctors, professional and fraternal organizations, alumni, students (yearbooks), and others.
- 1885 censuses, discussed in the previous section, for Colorado, Dakota Territory, Florida, Nebraska, New Mexico Territory.
- First Territorial Census of Oklahoma, 1890. One roll of microfilm available for use at libraries, for purchase (National Archives publication M1811), and for rent from the Family History Library (film 227282).
- California 1890 Great Register of Voters, index available on CD. Also the book, *The California 1890 Great Register of Voters Index*, 3 vols., California State Genealogical Alliance, comps (North Salt Lake, Utah: Heritage Quest, 2001). These records include names, ages, birthplaces, occupations, addresses, and naturalization information for registered voters (white or Hispanic males age twenty-one or over) in California in 1890.
- Various state censuses taken in or near 1895, including Iowa, Kansas, Michigan (1894), Minnesota, New Jersey, New York City (1890 "police census," a city-generated enumeration), New York State (1892), Rhode Island (1885), South Dakota, Washington (odd-numbered years 1881–1891, 1892), and Wisconsin.
- Various territorial or local censuses and county records, especially tax rolls or voter lists.
- Various American Indian censuses between 1885 and 1898 (see chapter ten and National Archives subject catalog *American Indians*).
- <www.ancestry.com/search/rectype/census/1890sub/main.htm>
- 1890 Special Census of Union Veterans and Widows (see below).

1890 Union Veterans and Widows

A special 1890 census of Union veterans or their widows provides information about each man's service during the Civil War. It does not substitute for the lost 1890 population schedules because it provides different information, but it places veterans or their widows in a given place at a given time. Although it does not cover the entire population, it contains valuable data. Unfortunately, this census is not complete, but it does use 118 rolls of microfilm (M123).

The reports are organized by state, then numerically by supervisor district, then alphabetically by county. Returns are available for the District of Columbia (Lincoln Post No. 3), fragments of states alphabetically from California through Kansas, part of Kentucky, states alphabetically from Louisiana through Wyoming, Oklahoma Territory and Indian Territory, and veterans on naval vessels and in naval yards or their widows. The California–Kansas fragments cover about 220 servicemen from these localities:

California: Alcatraz military post at San Francisco

Connecticut: Ft. Trumbull at New London, the naval station at New London, Hartford County Hospital in Hartford

Delaware: State Hospital for the Insane at New Castle

Florida: Ft. Barrancas at Warrington in Escambia County, St. Francis Barracks in St. Johns County, part of Jefferson County

Idaho: Boise Barracks in Ada County and Ft. Sherman in Kootenai County

Illinois: part of Chicago in Cook County, and Henderson County

Indiana: Boonville in Warrick County, and four from Reynolds, White County

Kansas: Great Bend in Barton County

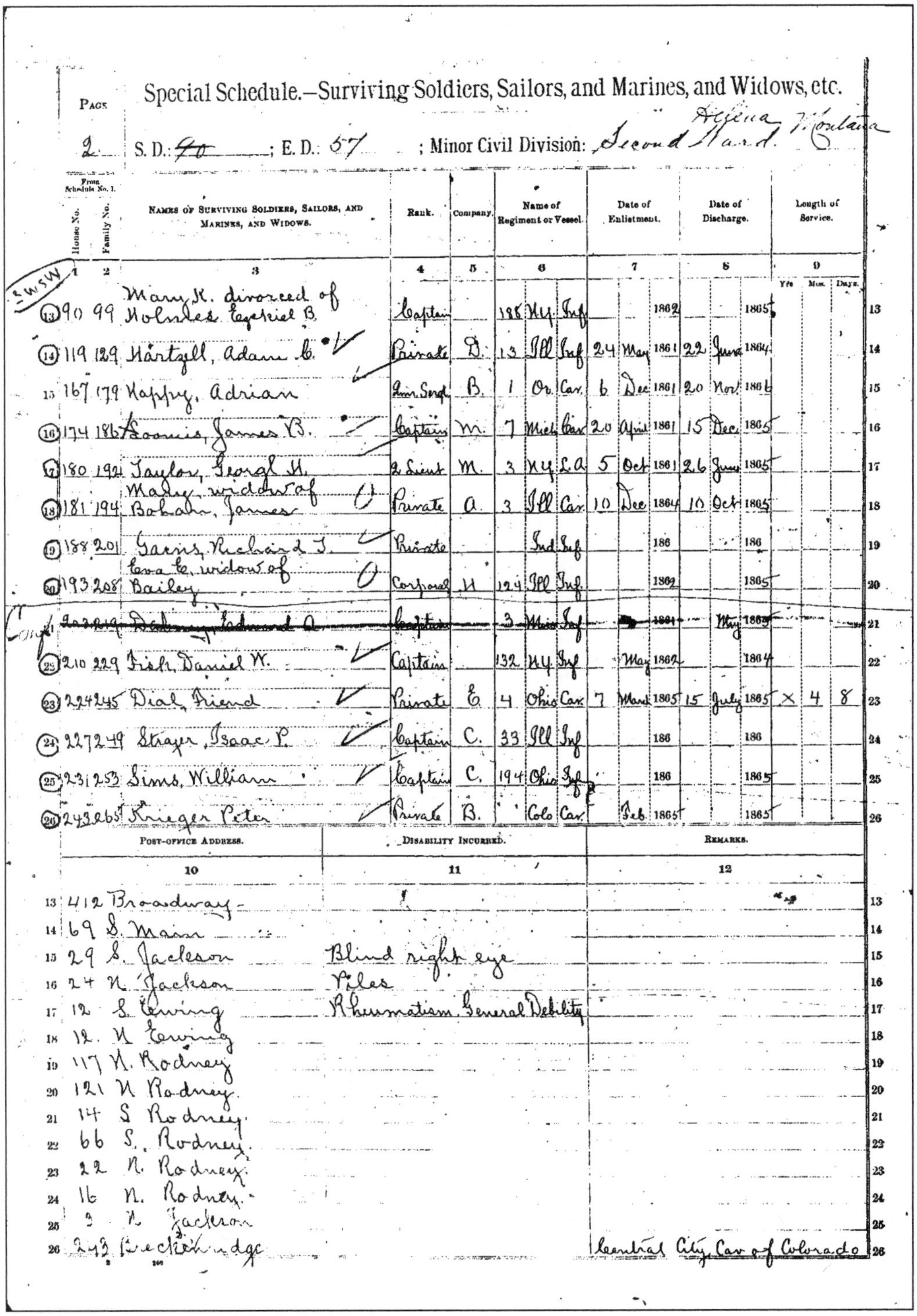

Special Schedule.—Surviving Soldiers, Sailors, and Marines, and Widows, etc.

Page 2 ; S. D.: 40 ; E. D.: 57 ; Minor Civil Division: Second Ward Helena Montana

Line	House No.	Family No.	Names of Surviving Soldiers, Sailors, and Marines, and Widows	Rank	Company	Name of Regiment or Vessel	Date of Enlistment	Date of Discharge	Length of Service (Yrs. Mos. Days)
13	90	99	Mary H. divorced of Holmes, Ezekiel B.	Captain		188 NY Inf	1862	1865	
14	119	129	Hartzell, Adam C.	Private	D.	13 Ill Inf	24 May 1861	22 June 1864	
15	167	179	Happy, Adrian	Com. Sergt	B.	1 Or. Cav.	6 Dec 1861	20 Nov 1864	
16	174	186	Loomis, James B.	Captain	M.	7 Mich Cav	20 April 1861	15 Dec 1865	
17	180	192	Taylor, George H.	2 Lieut	M.	3 NY L.A.	5 Oct 1861	26 June 1865	
18	181	194	Mary, widow of Bohahn, James	Private	A.	3 Ill Cav	10 Dec 1864	10 Oct 1865	
19	188	201	Garins, Richard T.	Private		Ind Inf	186	186	
20	193	208	Eva C. widow of Bailey	Corporal	H	124 Ill Inf	1862	1865	
21	[illegible]	[illegible]	[illegible] (struck out)	Captain		3 [illegible] Inf	1861	May 1865	
22	210	229	Fish, Daniel W.	Captain		132 NY Inf	May 1862	1864	
23	224	245	Dial, Friend	Private	E.	4 Ohio Cav	7 March 1865	15 July 1865	X 4 8
24	227	249	Strayer, Isaac P.	Captain	C.	33 Ill Inf	186	186	
25	231	253	Sims, William	Captain	C.	194 Ohio Inf	186	1865	
26	243	265	Krieger, Peter	Private	B.	Colo Cav	Feb 1865	1865	

Line	Post-Office Address (10)	Disability Incurred (11)	Remarks (12)
13	412 Broadway		
14	69 S. Main		
15	29 S. Jackson	Blind right eye	
16	24 N. Jackson	Piles	
17	12 S. Ewing	Rheumatism General Debility	
18	12 N Ewing		
19	117 N. Rodney		
20	121 N Rodney		
21	14 S Rodney		
22	66 S. Rodney		
23	22 N. Rodney		
24	16 N. Rodney		
25	3 N. Jackson		
26	243 Breckinridge		Central City Cav of Colorado

Figure 2-4 Schedules Enumerating Union Veterans and Widows . . . of the Civil War, 1890, NARA microfilm M123, roll 35, Helena, Montana, e.d. 57, p. 2.

New York: one soldier from a New York unit whose entry is mostly illegible and whose residence is not given

This special census furnishes a variety of information: name of veteran or widow, rank the veteran held while in service, and his unit and dates of service. Additional information varies with the enumerator but may include such items as these:

- Wounds received—"blind right eye," "shot in arm," or "kicked in the side by a horse."
- Remarks about the war—"participated in the capture of assassin Booth," "served

under Gen. Blunt," and "This man served both in Conf. and U.S. Army was wounded in Conf. Services."
- Date of death—"died of Pulmonary Disease 1884," "died Dec. 20, 1876," and "died Nov. 3, '62 Hospital, Newburn [*sic*], N.Car."
- Illness or disability in 1890—"Rheumatism. General Debility" and "weak lungs from exposure."
- Condition in 1890—"poor and needy" and "now in destitute circumstance."
- Post-office or street address—"412 Broadway" in Helena, Montana; "447 Thalia St." in New Orleans; or simply "Shreveport."
- Aliases—Henry Wills, alias Charles Wright, in Dillon, Montana; Sylvester Westbrook, alias Sylvester Brown, in Mississippi; Reuben Andrews, alias Green Johnson, in Mississippi.
- Veterans living near each other who served in the same unit and thus are part of a cluster of associates. If one is your ancestor, the others may be valuable subjects to study as you research your ancestor.
- Information on widows—remarriage; living condition or address in 1890; or, as shown in Figure 2-4, on page 45, "Mary K. divorced of" Ezekiel B. Holmes.
- Occasionally a Confederate soldier, such as Edward A. Dabney, crossed out in Figure 2-4. If such an entry pertains to your ancestor, double-check the information by looking for his name in the compiled service record indexes for C.S.A. (Confederate States of America) and U.S.A. units. Remember also that not all paperwork survived the war and storage over the years; in some cases, the census may be the only evidence of service that remains.

Although the schedules included some Confederates who were later crossed out, Southerners also joined units recruited locally to fight on the Union side. The Limestone County, Texas, census includes men who fought in the First Tennessee Cavalry and Second Florida Cavalry. Both were Union soldiers whose compiled service records match the information given in the census. Robertson County, Texas, includes at least one Union soldier from the First Alabama Cavalry, U.S.A., not C.S.A.

These schedules give a human touch to the statistics of the war and provide information helpful in getting copies of service records and pension files. In some cases, this census may be the only source of the information it provides.

POPULATION SCHEDULES, 1900–1930

See Also

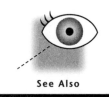

See the chart "Census Page Column Headings, 1900 and 1910" on page 48. See the chart "Census Page Column Headings, 1920 and 1930" on page 50.

Because the censuses from 1900 forward contain more information than the earlier enumerations, they are essential in genealogical research. The 1900 census requested three special pieces of information for which genealogists are grateful but which they must use cautiously:

- the month and year of birth for each individual
- the number of years each couple had been married
- the number of children each mother had borne and how many were living (reported in 1900 and 1910)

The information on the birth of children provided in these two censuses (1) helps you get a more complete picture of the family and (2) suggests that you look for evidence of children who had died young or who were living away from their parents.

Sometimes, this census is the only source of these particular details. Remember, however, that we do not know who reported the details to the census taker and how accurate the

ABBREVIATIONS USED TO SHOW RELATIONSHIPS

The National Archives list does not show "foster daughter," but it probably would be FD or FoD, based on the other foster relationships reported; likewise AdF probably would be used for adopted/adoptive father.

A—aunt
Ad—adopted
AdD—adopted daughter
AdM—adopted/adoptive mother
AdS—adopted son
AL—aunt-in-law
B—brother
BL, BiL—brother-in-law
Bo—boarder
C—cousin
CiL—cousin-in-law
Cl—child
D, dau—daughter
DL, DiL—daughter-in-law
Emp—employee
F—father
FB, FoB—foster brother
FF—foster father
FL—father-in-law
FoS—foster son
FoSi, Fsi—foster sister
GA—great aunt
Gcl—grandchild
GD, Gd—granddaughter
GF—grandfather
GGF—great-grandfather
GGM—great-grandmother
GM—grandmother
Gml—grandmother-in-law
GN—grandnephew, great-nephew
Gni—grandniece, great-niece
God Cl—godchild
GS—grandson
Gsl—grandson-in-law
GU—great-uncle
Gua—guardian
H, head—head of household
Hb—half brother
Hbl—half brother-in-law
Hsi—half sister
Hsil—half sister-in-law
Husband, Husb—husband
L—lodger
M—mother
ML—mother-in-law
N—nephew
Ni—niece
Nil—niece-in-law
NL, nl—nephew-in-law
NR—not reported
R—roomer
S—son
SB, Sb—stepbrother
Sbl—stepbrother-in-law
Scl—stepchild
SD—stepdaughter
SDL, Sdl—stepdaughter-in-law
Se, Ser—servant
SeCl—servant's child
SF—stepfather
Sfl—stepfather-in-law
Sgd—stepgranddaughter
Sgs—stepgrandson
Si, Sis—sister
SL—son-in-law
SiL—sister-in-law
SM—stepmother
Sml—stepmother-in-law
Ss—stepson
Ssi—stepsister
Ssil—stepsister-in-law
Ssl—stepson-in-law
U—uncle
Ul—uncle-in-law
Vi—visitor
W—wife

information was. Try to find other records that corroborate what the census provides. Very often, the birth dates in the 1900 census are inaccurate by several months or several years. Many families did not keep written records of vital events and had to estimate for the census.

The 1920 schedules were very similar to the previous two but did not include the years of marriage or the number of children born to mothers. The 1920 census is available, with Soundex, for all the states. This census includes the military and naval population living abroad. It does not include a separate Indian schedule, as do the 1900 and 1910 censuses.

In 1930, the census asked whether a family owned or rented their home, and requested the value of the home (if owned) or the monthly rent (if rented). Many of the renters paid between $9.50 and $70 rent in small Southern towns; no doubt the rent varied from place to place. The other interesting statistic in 1930 was whether the family owned a radio. [The first radio station began broadcasting in 1920. The period of the 1930s to the 1950s has been called the Golden Age of Radio. NBC and CBS began broadcasting in 1926 and 1927, respectively.]

Marriage Information

Learning how many years a 1900 couple had been married may help you (1) find a marriage record for them, (2) search for a death record for a previous spouse, or (3) determine which children were born to which wife. Sometimes, the husband and wife show a different number of years of marriage. Misunderstanding the instructions, they may have reported the total years of marriage, including previous marriages, during the lifetime of one or both partners.

CENSUS PAGE COLUMN HEADINGS, 1900 AND 1910

1900 (Census year 1 June 1899–31 May 1900)

street name down left margin, if in a town
house number of home (not always given)

1. dwelling number in order of visitation
2. family number in order of visitation
3. name of every person whose usual place of abode was with this family, 1 June 1900
4. relationship to head of household
5. color (see below)
6. sex
7. month of birth, year of birth
8. age at last birthday before 1 June 1900
9. marital status: *S, M, Wd, D*
10. number of years married (see page 47)
11. mother of how many children
12. number of children living
13. birthplace of named person

14., 15. birthplace of person's father, mother

16. year of immigration to United States
17. number of years in the United States
18. *Al*-alien; *Na*-naturalized; *Pa*-"first papers" (intent) filed for naturalization
19. occupation of every person 10 or older
20. number of months unemployed in census year
21. number of months in school in census year

22., 23., 24. can read, write, speak English

25. *O* if home is owned by head of family; *R* if home is rented
26. *M* if home is owned and mortgaged; *F* if owned free of mortgage
27. *F* if home is a farm; *H* if it is a house.
28. number of farm schedule (schedule no longer exists)

1910 (Census year 15 April 1909–14 April 1910)

street name down left margin, if in a town
house number of home (not always given)

1. dwelling number in order of visitation
2. family number in order of visitation
3. name of every person whose usual place of abode was with this family, 15 April 1910
4. relationship to head of household
5. sex
6. color (see page 49)
7. age at last birthday before 15 April 1910
8. marital status: *S, M, Wd, D* (see below)
9. number of years in present marriage
10. mother of how many children
11. number of children living
12. birthplace of named person

13., 14. birthplace of person's father, mother

15. year of immigration
16. *Na*-naturalized; *Al*-alien; *Pa*-"first papers" (intent) filed for naturalization
17. *English* or name of language spoken
18. trade or profession of child or adult
19. specific industry or work performed
20. *Emp*-employer; *W*-wage earner, *OA*-working on own account (self-employed)
21. whether out of work, 15 April 1910
22. number of weeks unemployed, 1909

23., 24. can read, can write any language

25. whether attended school any time since 1 September 1909
26. *O* if home is owned by head of family; *R* if home is rented
27. *M* if home is owned and mortgaged; *F* if owned free of mortgage
28. *F* if home is a farm; *H* if it is a house
29. number of farm schedule (not extant)
30. Veterans: *UA*-Union army; *UN*-Union navy; *CA*-Confederate army; *CN*-Confederate navy

31., 32. *Bl*-Blind; *DD*-both deaf and dumb

Some widows and widowers reported the number of years they had been married. Those married less than one year were to be reported as zero years.

The 1910 census asked specifically for the number of years in the present marriage. The column for "marital status" asked whether persons were single, divorced, widowed, or married. Those who had been married once were reported as "M1"; those married twice or more were listed as "M2." In 1930, the census asked for each person's age at the first marriage.

Reporting Race

To what extent census takers explained the instructions or the populace followed them, we cannot know. Nevertheless, these censuses used the following categories for reporting race:

- 1900—white (W), black (B), Chinese (Ch), Japanese (Jp), American Indian (In).

- 1910, 1920—white (W), black (B), mulatto (Mu), Chinese (Ch), Japanese (Jp), American Indian (In), other (Ot). In 1920, schedules for Puerto Rico were printed in Spanish.
- 1930—white (W); Negro (Neg) which included persons with any portion of Negro blood, unless Indian blood predominated and the person was accepted as Indian in the community; Indian (In), which included persons of mixed blood, unless the person was accepted as white or black in the community; Mexican (Mex), Chinese (Ch), Japanese (Jp), Filipino (Fil), Hindu (Hin), Korean (Kor), other (spell out in full). People of mixed white and other races were to be reported as the race of the non-white parent; persons of other mixtures were to be reported according to the race of the father, except in the cases of Negroes and Indians as previously mentioned.

Reporting Immigration and Citizenship

From 1890 forward, the censuses asked specific information of immigrants, besides questions on birthplace and birthplace of parents (see also the charts on pages 39, 48, 50):

- 1890—number of years in the United States, whether a person was naturalized, whether the naturalization process had begun ("whether naturalization papers have been taken out")
- 1900—year of immigration, number of years in the United States, and citizenship status: "Al" (alien) for those who had taken no steps toward naturalization, "Pa" for those who had taken out first papers in the naturalization process, "Na" for naturalized citizens
- 1910, 1930—year of immigration, and whether naturalized (Pa or Na) or alien (Al)
- 1920—same as 1910, plus year of naturalization

This information, compiled on an individual immigrant and combined with such data as the U.S. birthplaces of children, can help pinpoint the immigrant's location at the time of naturalization and help the researcher locate immigration and/or naturalization records.

OTHER FINDING AIDS

With the lack of Soundex for many 1880, 1910, and 1930 families, researchers are fortunate to have other finding aids available. In many cases, these considerably reduce the time involved in locating ancestral families in the censuses. Creative use of these aids often produces positive results. The finding aids discussed in this section are available for use at the National Archives and its regional branches, the Family History Library, and many libraries nationwide; on loan through Family History Centers (some are also available through the National Archives Microfilm Rental Program); and for purchase from the National Archives or Scholarly Resources.

1880–1930 Index to Institutions

This resource is a microfilm copy of a card index, organized by state and then alphabetically by the name of the institution. The entry gives the name of the institution; the city and/or county of location; the number of persons residing there; and the volume, enumeration district, and page number of its location on the census. The lists include such institutions as schools, universities, academies, college dormitories, hospitals, orphan homes, alms houses/poorhouses, jails, state penitentiaries, Masonic homes, homes for the aged, marine and army barracks, domestic military installations, industrial schools and homes, homes for ladies, ships and tugs in port, naval vessels, hotels, railroad and timber camps, mines, other com-

CENSUS PAGE COLUMN HEADINGS, 1920 AND 1930

1920 (Census year 1 January 1919–31 December 1919)

1. name of street
2. house number or farm
3. dwelling number in order of visitation
4. family number in order of visitation
5. name of every person whose usual place of abode was with the family, 1 January 1920
6. relationship to head of household
7. *O* if home is owned by head of family; *R* if home is rented
8. *M* if home is owned and mortgaged; *F* if home is owned free of morgage
9. sex
10. color or race (see page 49)
11. age at last birthday before 1 January 1920
12. marital status: *S, M, Wd, D*
13. year of immigration to United States
14. *Na*-naturalized; *Al*-alien; *Pa*-"papers" (intent) filed for naturalization
15. year of naturalization
16. in school since 1 September 1919?

17., 18. can read, can write any language

19. birthplace of named person
20. mother tongue, if foreign-born
21. birthplace of father
22. mother tongue of father, if foreign-born
23. birthplace of mother
24. mother tongue of mother, if foreign-born
25. *English* or name of language spoken
26. trade, profession, or specific work done
27. specific industry or type of work done
28. *Emp*-employer; *W*-wage earner; *OA*-working on own account (self-employed)
29. number of farm schedule (not extant)

1930 (Census year 1 April 1929–30 March 1930)

1., 2. street name, house number or farm

3. dwelling number in order of visitation
4. number of family in order of visitation
5. name of each person whose usual place of abode was with the family, 1 April 1930
6. relationship to head of household
7. *O* if home is owned; *R* if rented
8. value of home if owned, or monthly rent; no answer necessary for farm family
9. whether family owns a radio
10. whether family lives on a farm
11. sex
12. color (see page 49)
13. age at last birthday before 1 April 1930
14. marital status: *S, M, Wd, D*
15. age at first marriage
16. in school any time since 1 September 1929
17. whether able to read and write
18. birthplace of named person

19., 20. birthplace of father, mother

21. for foreign-born, language spoken in home before coming to United States
22. year of immigration to United States
23. *Na*-naturalized; *Al*-alien; *Pa*-"papers" (intent) filed for naturalization
24. whether able to speak English
25. trade, profession, or specific work done
26. specific industry or business
27. *E*-employer ;*W*-wage earner; *O*-working on own account; *NP*-unpaid, family member
28. worked yesterday?
29. (unemployment schedule not extant)

30., 31. veteran ? If so, *WW*-world war; *Sp*-Spanish-American; *Civ*-Civil War; *Phil*-Philippine insurrection; *Box*-Boxer rebellion; *Mex*-Mexican "expedition"

32. number of farm schedule (not extant)

mercial operations at which employees lived, Indian reservations, fire stations, life-saving stations, religious houses, and Shaker communities.

For 1880, the institutions are found at the end of the last roll of the Soundex set for each state. Institution indexes were not included for California or for Indian Territory (now Oklahoma), which had no census for that year.

The 1900 index (T1083) consists of eight rolls of microfilm that are alphabetical by state. In addition, institutions in the Philippines, Alaska, Hawaii, and Indian Territory are included, as well as all the U.S. military and naval installations outside the continental United States and ships in port or at sea.

Included before or after the institutions for each state in the 1900 list are the Soundex cards for people whose surnames were not reported (marked "N.R.") or were indecipherable, especially foreign and Indian names. In an attempt to help identify these persons, some of the "N.R." cards indicate surnames of other members of the same household or surnames listed before and after that name on the actual schedule. This list helps to account for some of the people who do not appear on the regular Soundex.

The 1910 institutions index is available only for Alabama, Louisiana, Mississippi, South Carolina, Tennessee, and Texas. The institutions are found at the end of the last Soundex roll for each of these states.

The 1920 institutions index is also filmed at the end of the last roll of Soundex for each state or territory. Such indexes were made for all states and territories except Arizona, Florida, Georgia, Rhode Island, South Carolina, South Dakota, Tennessee, and Guam.

For 1930, institutions are listed at the end of the Soundex for eleven of the Soundexed states (see the chart "Soundex Availability" on page 37); Georgia's institutions are not included. Many institutions are listed at the end of the enumeration district descriptions for their county (see below). In some locations, they had their own enumeration district numbers. The National Archives online enumeration district locator (see page 56) can also search for specific institutions that had their own enumeration district numbers (use a geographic search through "search places" and click on "search institutions").

Early Enumeration District Descriptions

Most of these volumes are what their title suggests—descriptions of the boundaries of the enumeration districts (E.D.) used in taking the censuses from 1830 forward. The National Archives microfilm series T1224, *Descriptions of Census Enumeration Districts, 1830–1950*, is 156 rolls of microfilm from Record Group 29, Records of the Bureau of the Census. When first filmed, all but the 1900 descriptions were part of National Archives microfilm T1224. The ten rolls for 1900 were on microfilm T1210. Although libraries that purchased the two series may still have them cataloged and filed as two publications, now the series T1224 includes the following:

- 1830 and 1840, roll 1.
- 1850 and 1860, roll 2.
- 1870, roll 3.
- 1880, rolls 4–6.
- 1890, rolls 7–17. These could be helpful in locating veterans on the 1890 special census of veterans and widows.
- 1900, rolls 18–27 (formerly T1210).
- 1910, rolls 28–40.
- 1920, rolls 41–60.
- 1930, rolls 61–90.
- 1940, rolls 91–118.
- 1950, rolls 119–156.

This microfilm is available for purchase from the National Archives or Scholarly Resources; for use at or loan from the Family History Library; and for use at the National Archives, its regional branches, and many libraries with census collections. The National Archives Microfilm Rental Program, at this writing, rents the 1910 and 1920 rolls of T1224 and the 1900 rolls under their previous number, T1210.

The first roll of T1224 is actually accounts of compensation paid to assistant U.S. marshals who were the census takers in 1830 and 1840. Most of these pages simply name each county, town, or other subdivision; the marshal who covered that area; and his pay, based

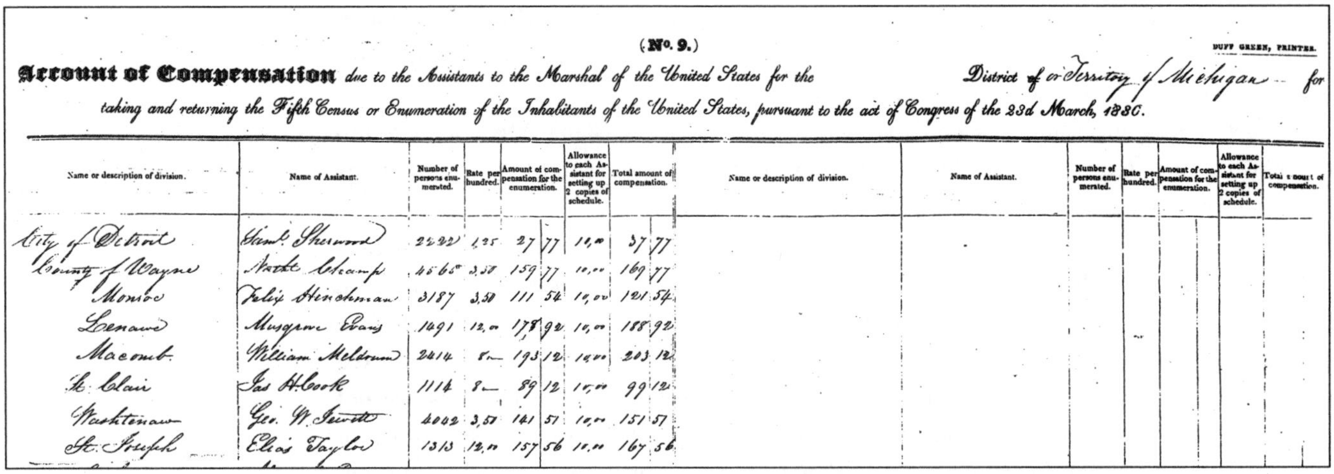

(No. 9.) DUFF GREEN, PRINTER.

Account of Compensation due to the Assistants to the Marshal of the United States for the District of or Territory of Michigan for taking and returning the Fifth Census or Enumeration of the Inhabitants of the United States, pursuant to the act of Congress of the 23d March, 1830.

Name or description of division.	Name of Assistant.	Number of persons enumerated.	Rate per hundred.	Amount of compensation for the enumeration.	Allowance to each Assistant for setting up 2 copies of schedule.	Total amount of compensation.
City of Detroit	Saml. Sherwood	2222	1,25	27 77	10,00	37 77
County of Wayne	Nathl. Champ	4565	3,50	159 77	10,00	169 77
Monroe	Felix Hinchman	3187	3,50	111 54	10,00	121 54
Lenawee	Musgrove Evans	1491	12,00	178 92	10,00	188 92
Macomb	William Meldrum	2414	8 —	193 12	10,00	203 12
St. Clair	Jas. H. Cook	1114	8 —	89 12	10,00	99 12
Washtenaw	Geo. W. Jewett	4042	3,50	141 51	10,00	151 57
St. Joseph	Elias Taylor	1313	12,00	157 56	10,00	167 56

Figure 2-5 Descriptions of Census Enumeration Districts, 1830–1950, NARA microfilm T1224, roll 1, 1830, Michigan.

on the number of people enumerated. Figure 2-5, above, shows the 1830 half page for the Territory of Michigan.

For 1850 to 1870 (microfilm rolls two and three), the descriptions show, for the most part, only the territory assigned to each marshal. Some show the enumerator's compensation. Many census takers covered their entire county. If the county was large, either in square miles or in population, two or more marshals split the county, covering specified townships, civil districts, precincts, or portions of the county identified by descriptions such as "north of Mill Creek" and "south of Mill Creek" or east and west of a main road through the county. The civil jurisdictions may or may not be the same today, but other landmarks, such as rivers and towns, probably are good reference points. In towns and cities, enumerators had assigned precincts, wards, or other civil jurisdictions, sometimes with a notation in 1870 that the district was mostly residential, industrial, commercial, or dedicated to mining.

The census schedules between 1830 and 1870 did not show enumeration district numbers. Thus, for rural and frontier parts of the country, these district descriptions are historical and interesting, especially if your ancestor was one of the marshals trudging through the elements to count the population. If your ancestor was in a city and the printed indexes do not include the head of household, comparing the family's address, a street map, and the enumeration district description may help you narrow your page-by-page search through the schedules.

1880–1920 Enumeration District Descriptions

These volumes are organized by census year, then state, and then supervisor's district; thus, the counties may not appear in alphabetical order. Within each supervisor's district, the enumeration districts are listed numerically, with the enumerator's name (through 1900), the county or town where the enumeration district was located, and a brief description of the boundaries of that district. Reading through enumeration district descriptions may be a quicker way to narrow a census search than reading page by page through the census of a populous town or county.

Important

For example, **the Soundex for 1880 included only households with children age ten and under.** Thus, if you have an address for an urban family and a street map, these enumeration district descriptions may save time in finding the family. It also may be possible to plot the enumerator's path in taking the census. The 1880 Washington, DC, enumeration district 54, where Congressman J. Proctor Knott lived, was described in a way that makes it easy to plot on a current city map because most of the streets are still there:

> West side of 11th and 'D' streets northwest to 'G' street northwest; south side of 'G' street to 14th street; east side of 14th street to 'D' street northwest and north side of 'D' street to 11th street northwest.

The enumeration district descriptions also include rural areas. They may be more difficult than city districts to outline on a map because some of the landmarks may have changed. The part of Clinton District, West Virginia, in enumeration district 80 in 1900 was described this way:

> all of the district west of a line beginning where the county road crosses Marion County line, at or near Ross' Mill on White Day Creek, thence with said road to the Morgantown and Bridgeport turnpike at Corother's Tannery, and thence with said turnpike to Morgan district line.

Case Study: Enumeration District Descriptions Circumvent Soundex Problems

Case Study

The enumeration district descriptions became useful in the following search because of 1900 Soundex problems. However, you could apply the process to any family who was missed or not identified in the Soundex or other index for 1880 to 1930. The process may be easier for the earlier years when towns were not as populous as they became after World War I.

The John A. Iiams family lived in Houston, Texas, but the 1900 Soundex for their code, I520, did not show the family. John and his wife, Mary, both died before 1910; John died first, by about 1902, leaving at least one son, Claxton, born about 1900–1901. Was John alive for the 1900 census? Were they Soundexed under a misread surname? The 1900 Soundex had not answered these questions under the appropriate code.

Because the capital letter *I* in older handwriting is sometimes confused with *J* or *S*, this surname is often misspelled or misread. Thus, alternative Soundex codes would probably begin with the initial letter *J* or *S*. The most likely would have been J520, which also includes all the Joneses, about a roll and a half of film. Browsing that much Soundex film or reading the entire city seemed an inefficient use of time and energy.

The 1900 city directory suggested that John was still living when the directory was compiled and showed the family residence as 1403 Johnson Street. This street is on a current city map, which shows modern thoroughfares (some of which were major streets in 1900), railroad tracks, bayous, the cemetery in the area, cross streets, and parallel streets. John and Mary Iiams had relatives in enumeration district 66 in 1900, probably in the same ward as the Iiamses, but the Iiams family was not in enumeration district 66. Perhaps Johnson Street was in a district numbered in the sixties and located in the same ward. Yet, reading all the districts between sixty and sixty-nine seemed too time-consuming when there was no indication of ward numbers on the census pages.

The enumeration district descriptions came to the rescue. The minor problem was that several of the potential districts used the city limits instead of streets or bayous for the boundaries; of course, the current city map does not show the 1900 city limits. Thus, it was difficult to determine exactly where these districts were. Districts that extended into the central business district, or north of White Oak Bayou, or south of Buffalo Bayou were eliminated from the search because they were not in the target area of the city. The choices then narrowed to two or three districts. From its description, enumeration district 63 seemed the most likely. Its description mentioned two streets and railroad tracks that were on the modern city map near Johnson Street:

> Begin at the junction of Houston Avenue and H.&.T.C.R.R. main line track, thence with the said railroad track to the western city limit, thence north with the line of the city limits to Spring street, thence east on Spring street to Houston Avenue, thence south on Houston Avenue to the place of beginning.

On the census microfilm, that district was easy to find, and the enumerator had written the street names down the left side of each page. Johnson Street appeared in the margin, with only three houses in the 1400 block. At 1403 the census taker found John A. and Mary Iiams, married for seven years, with their son Frank, age six, the only child born to the couple at that time (see Figure 2-6, below). The entire process from finding the address in the city directory, locating it on the city map, using a process of elimination on enumeration district descriptions, and locating the family in the record took less than an hour—much more efficient than searching rolls of other Soundex codes. In this case, it no longer matters how or whether they may have been Soundexed.

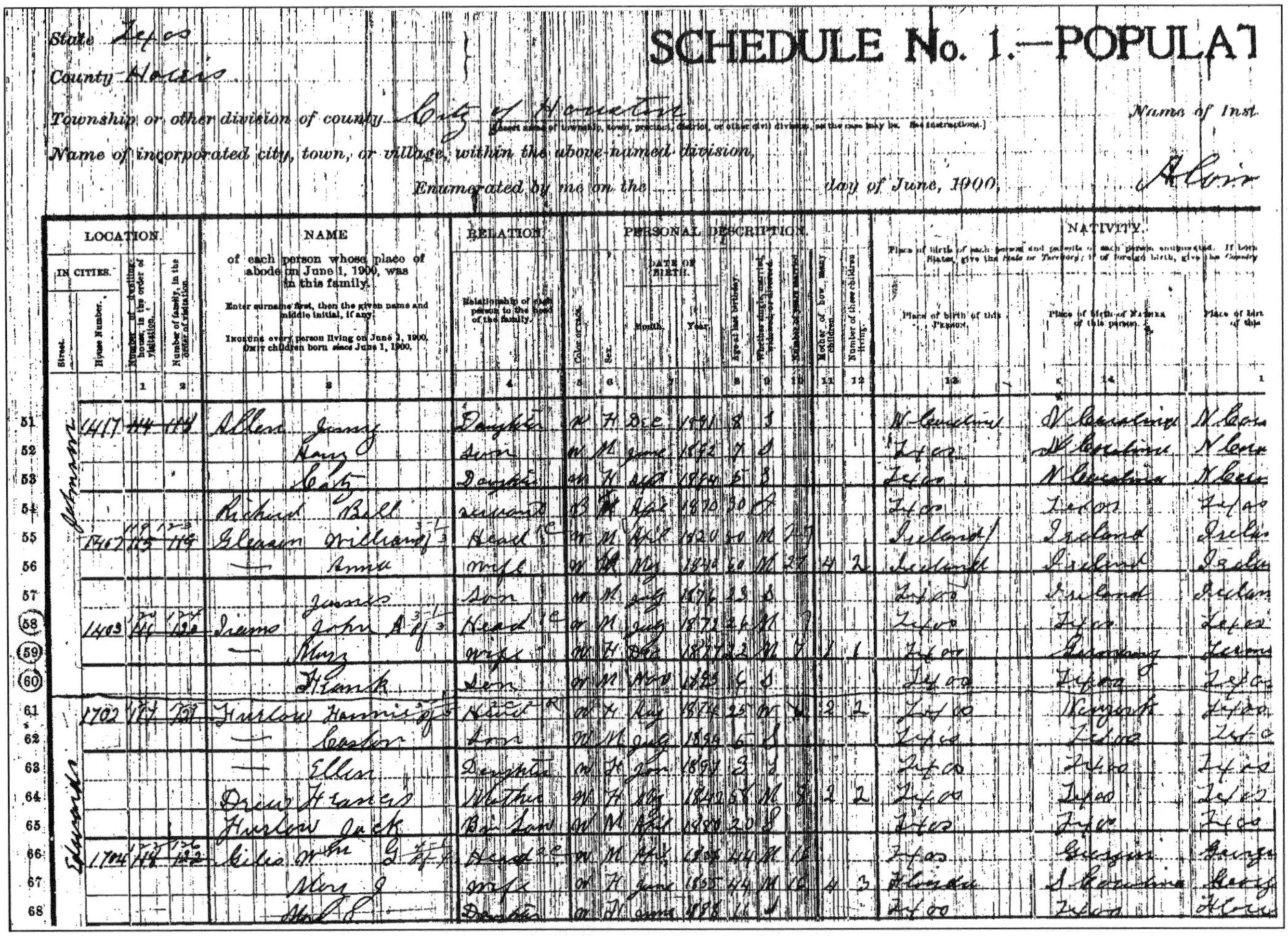
SCHEDULE No. 1.—POPULAT

Figure 2-6 U.S. Census of 1900, roll 1642, Harris County, Texas, e.d. 63, sheet 7, family 124, John A. Iiams family.

1930 Enumeration District Descriptions

Because only ten Southern states and parts of two others were Soundexed for the 1930 census, the enumeration district descriptions are a major resource for locating ancestral families in the census. The microfilm rolls of these district descriptions for 1930 include all the current states and Guam, Puerto Rico, the Virgin Islands, American Samoa, and the Panama Canal Zone.

One feature of the 1930 enumeration district descriptions is a new way of numbering the districts. Within each state, the counties were numbered, usually alphabetically. Thus, each enumeration district number begins with the county number. Angelina County, for example, is the third county listed alphabetically in Texas; its district numbers read 3-1, 3-2, 3-3, etc. Another new finding aid for 1930 is the inclusion of the corresponding enumeration district from 1920. If you have located the family in the 1920 census, use that year's district number to help locate the 1930 district number. Note that with population growth, many enumeration districts from 1920 had to be split into several for 1930, but the descriptions may help narrow the choices. The following illustrates the process for the 1930 census.

Case Study: When the Enumeration District Number Did Not Match

Case Study

As is the case for most states, Texas has no Soundex for 1930, so the enumeration district descriptions are important finding aids. This search began with knowledge that the A.S. Croom family of Lufkin, Angelina County, Texas, was in enumeration district 6 in the 1920 census. In the 1950s, their address was on North Raguet Street, but was it the same in 1930?

The enumeration district descriptions for 1930 showed nineteen districts for Angelina County; the first several districts were in the city of Lufkin. Enumeration district 6 from 1920 had been split into three districts for 1930, with city limits, railroad tracks, and several streets as boundaries. No city map was readily available to check these landmarks, and the city limits had probably changed since 1930.

With three district numbers as guides, the next step was reading the 1930 census micro-

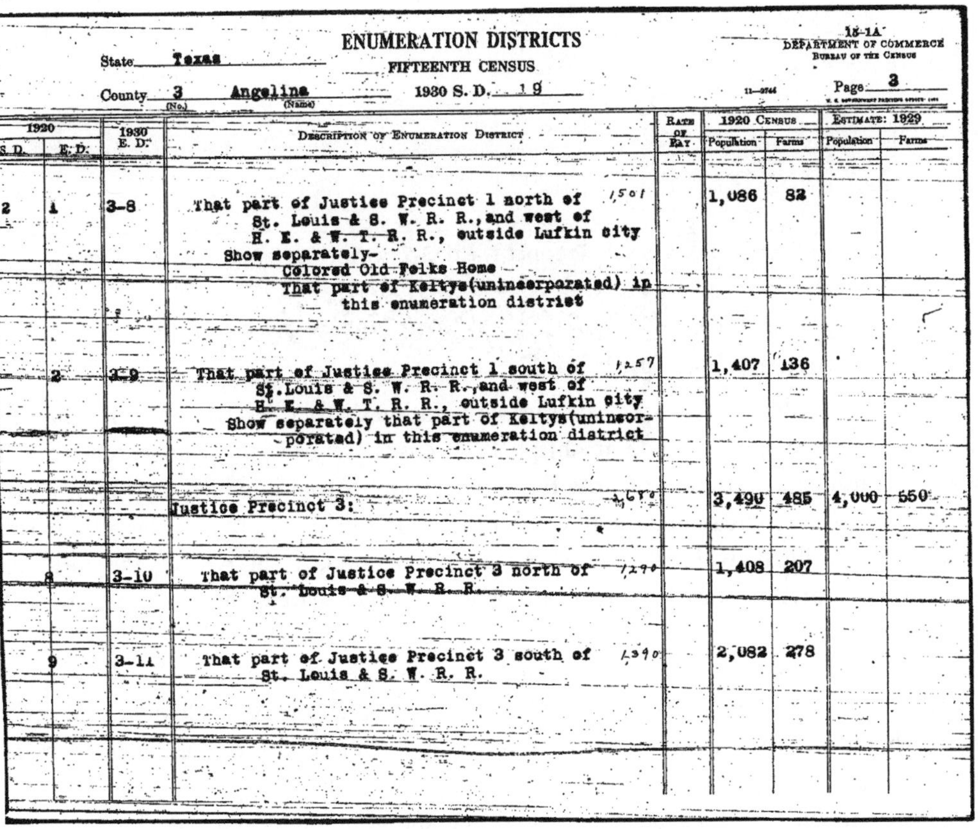

ENUMERATION DISTRICTS
FIFTEENTH CENSUS

15-1A
DEPARTMENT OF COMMERCE
BUREAU OF THE CENSUS

State Texas
County 3 (No.) Angelina (Name) 1930 S. D. 19
Page 3

1920 S.D.	1920 E.D.	1930 E.D.	Description of Enumeration District	Rate of Pay	1920 Census Population	1920 Census Farms	Estimate: 1929 Population	Estimate: 1929 Farms
2	1	3-8	That part of Justice Precinct 1 north of St. Louis & S. W. R. R., and west of H. E. & W. T. R. R., outside Lufkin city. Show separately- Colored Old Folks Home; That part of Keltys (unincorporated) in this enumeration district (1501)		1,086	82		
	2	3-9	That part of Justice Precinct 1 south of St. Louis & S. W. R. R., and west of H. E. & W. T. R. R., outside Lufkin city. Show separately that part of Keltys (unincorporated) in this enumeration district (1257)		1,407	136		
			Justice Precinct 3:		3,490	485	4,000	550
	8	3-10	That part of Justice Precinct 3 north of St. Louis & S. W. R. R.		1,408	207		
	9	3-11	That part of Justice Precinct 3 south of St. Louis & S. W. R. R.		2,082	278		

Figure 2-7 Enumeration District Descriptions, NARA microfilm T1224, roll 87, 1930-Texas, Angelina County, p. 3.

film for those districts. On the early pages of district 3-1 were families on North Raguet, but the census taker had written a note at the top of the first page saying "contains no farms." This should have been a warning sign because this Croom family lived on a farm. However, their street, and thus maybe their household, was enumerated on these pages. A page-by-page search of district 3-1, 3-2, and 3-5 did not reveal the family. It was time to return to the district descriptions instead of reading the other sixteen districts.

Scanning nineteen district descriptions did not take long, especially when family oral tradition suddenly became a clue. The description of district 3-9 (Figure 2-7, on page 55) indicated the inclusion of the community of Keltys, which had been in enumeration district 2 in 1920. The children of this family had talked about living near Keltys or going to school at Keltys. Thus, district 3-9 seemed the best district to try next. On the last page, with no street name in the margin, was the entry for A.S. Croom and the two youngest children. Croom appears to have first been enumerated as married, and the mark was corrected to read "W" (widowed). In fact, his wife died only two weeks before census day.

Apparently, those who established the county's districts for 1930 used the 1920 districts rather loosely and chose to separate the farms from the city itself. Although the Croom family's post office address was Lufkin, it appears they lived outside the city limits in 1930. This provides another question for the researcher to study. (See the enumeration in Figure 2-8, below.)

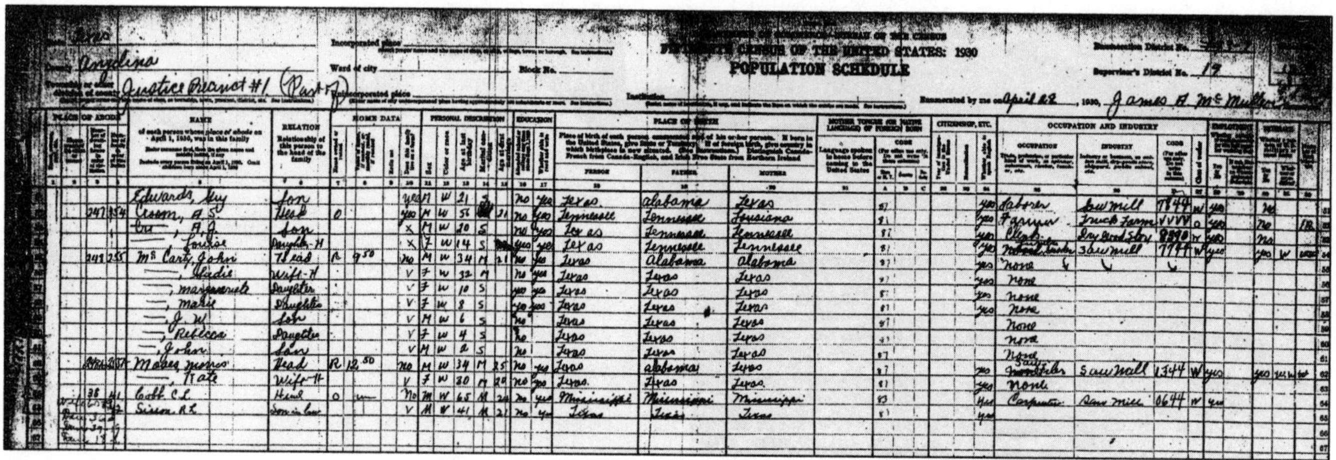
FIFTEENTH CENSUS OF THE UNITED STATES: 1930
POPULATION SCHEDULE

Figure 2-8 U.S. Census of 1930, roll 2288, Angelina County, Texas, Justice Precinct 1, e.d. 3-9, sheet 13B, family 254, A.S. Croom family.

Online Enumeration District Descriptions

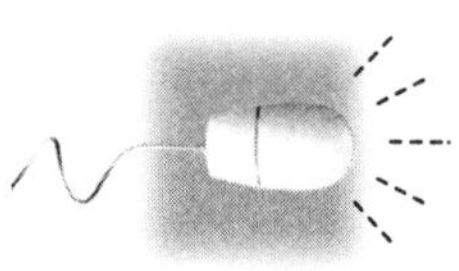

Internet Source

The National Archives Web site posts the enumeration district descriptions, including the twelve Soundexed states, online at <http://1930census.archives.gov/beginSearch.asp>. Its purpose is to help researchers identify the enumeration district in which their family lived in 1930 in order to streamline the research process and help researchers identify the rolls of census microfilm on which their families were enumerated. At this writing, the site allows two kinds of searches: Soundex and geographic. For either search, choose a state and click "continue."

For the Soundex search, supply a surname in a Soundexed state and receive the appropriate Soundex code, including codes with the rediscovered "H&W" rule discussed earlier in this chapter. The site then refers you to the Soundex microfilm to find the enumeration district number and the census microfilm to find your family.

The geographic search includes the Soundexed and non-Soundexed states. If you search by county (or Louisiana parish), the results give you a description of all the enumeration districts in the county. Reading these and comparing the boundaries or coverage with a county map can help you narrow the choices of a district to search for your family.

You can narrow the geographic search by choosing a city from a drop-down list or supplying a geographic place name, such as a town, institution, or street. The city list contains more cities than appear on the microfilmed index to selected city streets (see page 60). If you list a street, don't use *East*, *West*, *Street*, *Avenue*, or other qualifiers. A few differences exist between the online enumeration district identifier and the microfilmed enumeration district descriptions or the index to selected city streets:

1. An online query for Locust Street in San Antonio, Texas, provided four enumeration district numbers for which that street was a district boundary. The index to city streets (page 59) allowed a search for East Locust and provided one district number—the one where the target family lived.
2. An online request for Marfa, Presidio County, Texas, showed three district descriptions that included the town name:

Pub Nbr.	*Roll Number*	*County*	*ED*	*Enumeration District (ED) Descriptions*
T626	2385	Presidio	189-1	Marfa City (North Part)
T626	2385	Presidio	189-2	Marfa City (South Part)
T626	2385	Presidio	189-3	Justice Pct.1 Excluding Marfa City

However, the microfilmed district descriptions provided a specific dividing line—the G.H. and S.A. Railroad—between the northern and southern halves of town. Familiarity with the town and the location of these tracks immediately narrowed that search to enumeration district 189-1. In other cases, the online database provides the north, south, east, and west boundary lines of the district; the microfilmed descriptions may be less specific.

3. The online reference does not provide the corresponding 1920 enumeration district number as does the microfilm.
4. The Web site provides the census microfilm roll number for the enumeration district number; the microfilm of district descriptions, created before computer databases, does not. Clicking on the census roll number brings up the contents of the roll; this is helpful information if the district numbers are not sequential on the census microfilm or if the counties are not strictly alphabetical on the roll.
5. On the online county or city search, a separate set of results, after the district descriptions, is a list of institutions and the enumeration district in which each is found. On the microfilm, the institutions and named apartments are at the end of the county, but they also may be listed as part of the description of the district where they were located.

1930 Enumeration District Maps

Another finding aid available for 1930 census research is the National Archives microfilm M1930, *Enumeration District Maps for the Fifteenth Census of the United States, 1930*. Although few maps exist for the 1880 and 1890 districts, many more are available for twentieth-century censuses in the records of the Census Bureau, Record Group 29, at the Cartographic and Architectural Branch (NNSC), National Archives at College Park, 8601

Adelphi Road, College Park, MD 20740-6001. You can request copies of these maps, which are marked with the boundaries of the enumeration districts.

The microfilmed maps for 1930 vary greatly in size, scale, detail, and quality. The maps are arranged alphabetically by state, then alphabetically by county, then by town or other civil districts within the county. Maps of the territories and overseas possessions were filmed at the end of the states. The microfilm is available for use at various libraries, the National Archives and its regional branches, and the Family History Library; it is available for loan through the Family History Library.

Caution: Learn from my mistake. The first map I used on this microfilm showed a town divided into five areas, numbered one through five. Somewhat puzzled, I thought they were the enumeration district numbers and went to the census microfilm prepared to scan three of the districts for my ancestor. Although the ancestor was listed in the first district I read, I revisited the map and realized that those numbers must have indicated precincts, wards, or some other local division that had nothing to do with the census. The town's enumeration district numbers, though faded and less prominent than the others, were marked 246-1 and 246-2, using the county number as part of the district identification. It became very clear that the ancestor would have lived in district 246-1. Be aware that other numbers may appear on the maps, and look for the complete enumeration district numbers.

Case Study

Case Study: Contest of Finding Aids

My husband's grandparents lived in the rural community of Leander in Vernon Parish, Louisiana. The state is Soundexed for 1930, but the family name is a common one, whose Soundex code fills two microfilm rolls. If Grandpa was enumerated by his initials, "J.W.," he would be listed on the first roll. If he gave the census taker his given name (John) or the middle name he went by (Wes or Wesley), his Soundex card would be on the second roll. In order to locate their census entry, we first tried the online enumeration district descriptions, using the geographic search.

The negative results meant the town name was not part of an enumeration district description. A search using the parish name brought up nineteen enumeration districts. With a detailed Louisiana atlas, we checked off districts that were not candidates—Leesville, Fullerton, Rosepine, and other parts of the parish. This process of elimination left six districts as possibilities for research. All their descriptions were ward numbers, not post office names. Since ward numbers are not shown on current road maps and atlases, we could not determine which one included Leander.

The next step was a visit to Clayton Library (Houston). While my husband scrolled through the two rolls of Soundex microfilm, I looked at the microfilm enumeration district descriptions and crossed off one more district. The district description map (M1930) for Vernon Parish answered the question, showing all the enumeration districts, including Leander in district 58-18. As my husband began the second roll of Soundex microfilm, I went to the census microfilm and found the family quickly. Robert rewound the Soundex film without the need for finishing his search and claimed an unfair contest since he had forgotten his best reading glasses.

I claimed the exercise makes two valuable points: the finding aids work well, even for Soundexed states, and the lack of Soundex should not be a deterrent to 1930 census research.

1910 Cross Index to Selected City Streets

A valuable finding aid for the 1910 census is the street index for selected cities (M1283). To use this index, you need to know the street address of the target household. This index contains no surnames, only addresses. For example, in Atlanta, Georgia, 202 Lake Avenue was in enumeration district 113, but 282 Lake Avenue was in enumeration district 112. Even knowing a street name without the number would save time by narrowing down the districts in which to search. City directories for these communities often supply the needed addresses. This microfiche index can be purchased from the National Archives or Scholarly Resources, rented from the Family History Library, or used in many libraries.

Cities Available in the 1910 Cross Index to City Streets

Alabama—Birmingham, Mobile, Montgomery
Arizona—Phoenix
California—Long Beach, Los Angeles, San Diego, San Francisco
Colorado—Denver and its institutions
District of Columbia
Florida—Tampa
Georgia—Atlanta, Augusta, Macon, Savannah
Illinois—Chicago, Peoria
Indiana—Fort Wayne, Gary, Indianapolis, South Bend
Kansas—Kansas City, Wichita
Maryland—Baltimore
Michigan—Detroit, Grand Rapids
Nebraska—Omaha
New Jersey—Elizabeth, Newark, Patterson
New York—Brooklyn, Bronx, Manhattan, New York City, Richmond
North Carolina—Charlotte
Ohio—Akron, Canton, Cleveland, Dayton, Youngstown
Oklahoma—Oklahoma City, Tulsa
Pennsylvania—Erie, Philadelphia, Reading
Texas—San Antonio
Virginia—Richmond
Washington—Seattle

1930 Index to Selected City Streets

The *Index to Selected City Streets and Enumerations Districts, 1930 Census* (M1931) fills seven rolls of microfilm. Like its 1910 counterpart, the film is arranged by state and city. Within each city's pages, streets are alphabetical. Those designated as North, South, East, or West may be listed under the street name or the prefix. Numbered streets are listed in numerical order, regardless of any prefix. The pages of the index show the city's name at the bottom of the page. The list provides the enumeration district number for the street or for a range of house numbers on that street.

For locating urban residents, this process is efficient and fairly quick, even for those cities with Soundex. If the surname you need is common in the state, using the index to selected city streets and scanning one enumeration district may be quicker than scanning numerous Soundex cards.

A number of libraries, state archives, and state historical societies have city directory collections for their town, state, or region. (See page 143 for more on searching city directories.) Check with libraries for availability; the National Archives and its regional branches, the Family History Library, and the National Archives Microfilm Rental Program have this publication.

Case Study

Case Study: Using the 1930 Index to Selected City Streets

1. The first step was looking at the microfilm of Worley's San Antonio (Texas) City Directory of 1929–1930 for an address for Thomas M. and Mattie E. Metcalfe. Their home address was 418 East Locust. In many cases, family memory or family papers could supply the same information.
2. The second step was consulting roll seven of M1931 for the only Texas city in this index. In alphabetical order, Locust Street, both east and west, was listed as being in enumeration district 15-71. The number 15 is for Bexar County, the fifteenth alphabetically in Texas. Figure 2-9, below, shows this page of the index.
3. The last step was scrolling through roll 2294 of the 1930 census microfilm to Bexar County and district 15-71. Since the street names were written along the left margin of the page, it was easy to scan for East Locust and its house numbers. Sheet 7A of the district was dedicated mostly to residents in the 400 block of East Locust. At 418 were the Metcalfe couple, their adult son Thomas Jr., and three roomers—two men and one woman. Although Thomas Metcalfe Sr., at age seventy-six, had no occupation, his wife, Mattie, age sixty-five, was listed as a seamstress working at home; family tradition reports that she did not furnish meals to her roomers but did sew for several women in the city.

Figure 2-9 Index to Selected City Streets and Enumeration Districts, 1930 Census, NARA microfilm M1931, roll 7, San Antonio, Texas, p. 35.

Streets	House Nos.	E. D.
Leal	(1102 - 134?)	15 - 53
	(1407 - 2034)	15 - 54
	(2101 - 2602)	15 - 206
Leal Al.	----	15 - 2
Lecompte	**--	15 - 9, 15-199 csc
Lee (outside city)	-----	---
Lee Hall (Los Angeles Heights)		15 - 81
Leigh	(102 - 414)	15 - 115
	(501 - 658)	15 - 117
Lenard (Columbia Heights)(outside city)		---
Lannon (outside city)		---
Leona, N.	(111 - 119)	15 - 49
	(206 -620)	15 - 45, 46
Leona, S.	(105 - 427)	15 - 19
	(503 - 723)	15 - 22
	(800 - 1144)	15 - 24
Leopold	----	15 - 118
Leroux	----	15 - 39
Lester Ave. (fenfield Add.)(outside city)		15 - LU
Letitia Ave. (changed to Rosewood Ave.)		---
Lexington Ave.	----	15 - 68
Lexington Ave. (outside city)		15 - LU
Lewis	(88 - 98)	15 - 67
	(101 - 130)	15 - 67, 73
	(210 - 317)	15 - 74
	(411 - 721)	15 - 75
	(810 - 1020)	15 - 76
Lightfoot Ave.	----	15 - 40
Ligustrum Drive (outside city)		---
Linares Ave. (formerly Hood Ave.)	----	15 - 14, 197
Lincoln	----	15 - 210
Lincoln Place (California Gardens)(outside city)		---
Lindell Place (formerly Preston Pl.)		15 - 83
Linden	----	15 - 134
Linden Ace. (Columbia Heights)(outside city)		---
Lindeman Ave. (outside city)		---
Linn	----	15 - 216
Linwood Blvd. (See Lynwood Ave.)		---
Lipan	----	15 - 9
Lishon	----	15 - 12
Live Oak	----	15 - 88
Livingston (Harlandale)(outside City)		---
Llano (outside city)		---
Locke Ave.	----	15 - 104
Lockhart	----	15 - 110to 112
Lockwood	----	15 - 9
→ Locust, E.	----	15 - 71
Locust, W.	----	15 - 75, 76
Lodge Lane	----	15 - 84

Leal to Lodge Lane San Antonio Page 35

Cities in the 1930 Selected City Streets Index

Arizona—Phoenix

California—Berkeley, Long Beach, Los Angeles County (Los Angeles and forty-eight other cities, with institutions and apartments), San Diego, San Francisco

Colorado—Denver

District of Columbia

Florida—Miami (including Miami Beach and South Miami), Tampa

Georgia—Atlanta

Illinois—Chicago (with institutions and apartments), Peoria

Indiana—Fort Wayne, Gary, Indianapolis, South Bend

Kansas—Kansas City, Wichita

Maryland—Baltimore

Michigan—Detroit (including Hamtramck and Highland Park), Grand Rapids

Nebraska—Omaha

New Jersey—Elizabeth, Newark, Paterson

New York—Bronx and Manhattan, Brooklyn (with institutions and apartments), Queens (with institutions and apartments), Richmond

North Carolina—Towns with more than 10,000 population: Asheville, Charlotte, Concord, Durham, Elizabeth City, Fayetteville, Gastonia, Goldsboro, Greensboro, High Point, Kinston, Lexington, New Bern, Raleigh, Rocky Mount, Salisbury, Shelby, Statesville, Thomasville, Wilmington, Wilson, Winston-Salem. In addition, on roll 6, towns with fewer than 10,000 population are listed with their county, enumeration district number, and adjacent enumeration districts. Townships and institutions named on census pages are separately indexed by county and enumeration district number. County maps are also shown on roll 6.

Ohio—Akron, Canton, Cincinnati, Cleveland, Dayton, Youngstown

Oklahoma—Oklahoma City, Tulsa

Pennsylvania—Erie, Philadelphia (including streets and many neighborhood names, institutions, and named apartments), Reading

Tennessee—Memphis

Texas—San Antonio

Virginia—Richmond

Online Enumeration District Street Index

Thanks to Stephen P. Morse, a privately-created online index to selected city streets includes more cities than the microfilm index and is easy to use. The site is <www.stevemorse.org/census>. You can select a state, city, and street. If the street is short and was in only one enumeration district, the search result will give you the enumeration district number immediately. If the street fell into more than one district, the results will give you all the pertinent district numbers.

You can narrow the search by selecting cross streets from a list of streets in the city at the time. If you don't have a city map or knowledge of the city from which to choose cross streets, the site links to a current map showing the street. This process is especially helpful if you have a specific street address with which to choose the nearest cross streets.

The cities available on this site include those in Soundexed states as well as non-Soundexed states. In addition to those shown in the microfilm list above, at this writing, the following cities are included. More are being added.

Alabama—Birmingham, Mobile, Montgomery

Arkansas—Little Rock

California—Alameda, Bakersfield, Fresno, Oakland, Riverside, Sacramento, San Jose, Santa Ana, Santa Barbara, Stockton

Colorado—Colorado Springs, Pueblo

Connecticut—Bridgeport, Hartford, New Britain, New Haven, Stamford, Waterbury

Delaware—Wilmington

Florida—Jacksonville, Orlando, St. Petersburg

Georgia—Augusta, Columbus, Macon, Savannah

Hawaii—Hilo, Honolulu

Idaho—Boise, Pocatello

Illinois—Aurora, Berwyn, Cicero, Decatur, East St. Louis, Evanston, Oak Park, Rockford

Indiana—East Chicago, Evansville, Hammond, Muncie, Terre Haute

Iowa—Cedar Rapids, Davenport, Des Moines, Sioux City, Waterloo

Kansas—Topeka

Kentucky—Covington, Lexington, Louisville, Newport, and the seven Soundexed counties (see chart on page 37)

Louisiana—Baton Rouge, Monroe, New Orleans, Shreveport

Maine—Bangor, Lewiston, Portland

Massachusetts—Boston, Brockton, Brookline, Cambridge, Chelsea, Everett, Fall River, Haverhill, Holyoke, Lawrence, Lowell, Lynn, Malden, Medford, New Bedford, Newton, Pittsfield, Quincy, Salem, Somerville, Springfield, Waltham, Watertown, Worcester

Michigan—Bay City, Dearborn, Flint, Jackson, Kalamazoo, Lansing

Minnesota—Duluth, Minneapolis, St. Paul

Mississippi—Jackson

Missouri—Kansas City, Springfield, St. Joseph, St. Louis

Montana—Anaconda, Billings, Butte, Great Falls, Helena, Missoula

Nebraska—Lincoln

New Hampshire—Concord, Manchester, Nashua

New Jersey—Atlantic City, Bayonne, Camden, Clifton, East Orange, Hoboken, Irvington, Jersey City, Passaic, Trenton, Union City

New York—Albany, Binghamton, Buffalo, Elmira, Jamestown, Mt. Vernon, New Rochelle, Niagara Falls, Rochester, Schenectady, Staten Island, Syracuse, Troy, Utica, Yonkers

Ohio—Cleveland Heights, Columbus, Hamilton, Lakewood, Norwood, Springfield, Toledo, Warren, Zanesville, and others

Oklahoma—Enid

Oregon—Astoria, Eugene, Klamath Falls, Medford, Portland, Salem

Pennsylvania—Allentown, Altoona, Bethlehem, Chester, Harrisburg, Johnstown, Lancaster, McKeesport, New Castle, Pittsburgh, Scranton, Upper Darby, Wilkes-Barre, Williamsport, York

South Carolina—Charleston, Columbia, Spartanburg

Tennessee—Chattanooga, Knoxville, Nashville

Texas—Austin, Beaumont, Dallas, El Paso, Fort Worth, Galveston, Houston, Port Arthur, Waco, Wichita Falls, and others

Utah—Ogden, Salt Lake City

Virginia—Lynchburg, Newport News, Norfolk, Roanoke

Washington—Aberdeen, Bellingham, Bremerton, Everett, Hoquiam, Longview, Olympia, Port Angeles, Seattle, Spokane, Tacoma, Vancouver, Walla Walla, Wenatchee, Yakima

West Virginia—Charleston, Huntington, Wheeling, and the seven Soundexed counties (see chart on page 37)

Wisconsin—Kenosha, Madison, Manitowac, Milwaukee, Racine, Wauwatosa, West Allis

1900–1930 MILITARY, MERCHANT SEAMEN, CONSULAR CENSUSES

The 1900 census of military and naval installations outside the continental United States, including ships, is part of the T623 census microfilm series. The personnel in these schedules are Soundexed (in T1081) apart from the general population since they are enumerated separately from the general population returns that are organized by state. Use this military/naval Soundex if you are looking for a specific person or family. The names of overseas installations themselves are included in the T1083 *Index (Soundex) to the 1900 Federal Population Census Schedules for Institutions* under Military and Naval Institutions. Most of these installations were located in the Philippine Islands, Puerto Rico, or Cuba. Use the institutions index if you already know the name of the post, station, or ship you want to find.

Domestic military and naval installations and their personnel are included in the general 1900 population schedule for the county and state in which they were located. The individuals stationed at domestic installations are Soundexed according to their usual Soundex code, with the general population. The domestic installations themselves are indexed with other institutions in the state in which they were located.

The 1910 military/naval schedules (part of T624) are microfilmed but have not been Soundexed. The only installations appearing in the institution indexes would be those located in the states that have such indexes (see "1880–1930 Index to Institutions" on page 49). These schedules contain posts and stations in the Philippine Islands and Panama Canal Zone; ships stationed in U.S. ports or such other areas as Japan, Panama, Guam, and the Philippines; and the Naval Academy, military hospitals, and other such installations. Some of the pages, such as those from the USS *Louisiana* and the USS *Texas*, are even typewritten! The forms used are the same as the regular population schedule forms, and they often report the specific assignment and rank of each serviceman.

The 1920 military/naval/consular service census from overseas locations is Soundexed (M1600) and includes an institution index. The consular service enumerations include U.S. embassies abroad.[5] As in the other census years, domestic military and naval installations are part of the general population census and Soundex.

A 1910 example illustrates the value of searching these records. At Camp Eldridge, Laguna, Philippine Islands, First Lt. John J. Fulmer (age thirty-one, born in Pennsylvania) lived with his wife of one year, Viola J. (twenty-three, born in Louisiana). Living with them, or visiting, were Lena Brooks (forty-six, born in Louisiana) and Helen Brooks (ten, born in Michigan), John's mother-in-law and sister-in-law. Lena Brooks reported that she had been married for twenty-five years and that five of her six children were living. Somewhere, a genealogist may be scouring the countryside for these Brooks ladies without realizing that Viola Brooks had married an army officer who was stationed in the Philippines in 1910.

In 1930, military installations within the United States or enumerated territories and possessions were included in the institutions listed in the enumeration district descriptions and thus are usually identifiable in the institution results of a *county* search at <http://1930census.archives.gov/stateSearch.asp>. Using the name of the installation in a "geographic place" search often results in the message "Sorry, no records were found." However, enumeration district numbers for numerous domestic military and naval installations are listed by state in *The 1930 Census* (Thomas Jay Kemp, editor, North Salt Lake, Utah, HeritageQuest, 2002), pages 73–78. Apparently, overseas military installations and ships at sea were enumerated in 1930, but schedules have not been located.[6] It is possible that ships were enumerated in their home ports.

U.S. personnel in the consular service, including U.S. embassies abroad, in 1930 are enumerated by city name on two rolls of National Archives microfilm, 2630 and 2638, of series T626. At this time, no index is available for this part of the census.

The *1930 Census of Merchant Seamen* (M1932) is three rolls of microfilm for men serving on merchant vessels flying the U.S. flag. The questionnaire included personal information similar to that asked of the rest of the population. One additional piece of information was the address of the next of kin: wife, parents, or other near relative. The schedules list the vessels' names, owners, and home ports.

CENSUSES AFTER 1930

Reminder

Current law requires census records to be kept confidential for seventy-two years. Those who need information from their own family's closed census returns must contact the Census Bureau office in Jeffersonville, Indiana (Bureau of the Census, National Processing Center, 1201 East Tenth Street, Jeffersonville, Indiana 47132; phone: (812) 218-3046). This office was located in Pittsburg, Kansas, until 1991.

An individual may request his or her own record from the censuses of 1940 and after. The fee for a search, at this writing, is forty dollars, which covers the search of one census year for one person and a transcript of the information, if found. The transcript is a typed report with an official seal certifying that the information is a correct copy of what is on the original. Included is the applicant's name, age, birthplace, citizenship, relationship to the head of the household, and name of the head of household. This report does not include any other family members' names or census information. The primary purpose of this report is proof of age, citizenship, or parentage.

For all other information, such as occupation, education, or language on that one census entry, the applicant must request a *full schedule*, i.e., complete entry, and pay an additional ten-dollar fee. Full schedule searches are possible only for the censuses up to and including 1960.

The authorization required for release of information must come from the person or the legal guardian. If the person is deceased, a certified copy of the death certificate must accompany the release from the spouse, a parent, child, sibling, grandparent, estate administrator or executor, or legal beneficiary. In certain situations, legal evidence of the need for the information must be provided, for the records are considered confidential. The report will be sent only to the person to whom the information pertains or to the authorized representative in the immediate family, not to any collateral relatives, e.g., cousins, nephews, or aunts.

The necessary application, form BC-600, may be obtained online at <www.census.gov/genealogy/www/agesearch.html> or from the Jeffersonville office or regional Census Bureau offices located in Atlanta, Boston, Charlotte (North Carolina), Chicago, Dallas, Denver, Detroit, Kansas City, Los Angeles, New York, Philadelphia, or Seattle. The instructions and fee structure are explained on the application form. The search usually takes three to four weeks.

FEDERAL DECENNIAL CENSUSES FOR THE TERRITORIES

The states that once were territories often have population schedules for the period before they became organized territories or states. The list below shows the existing censuses (not substitutes or lost schedules) and, where applicable, the parent state or territory in whose census they were included. The date of statehood is given with the state name. For more information, see Territorial Papers, page 175 of this book; *Map Guide to the U.S. Federal Censuses, 1790–1920*, by William Thorndale and William Dollarhide (Baltimore: Genealogical Publishing Co., latest edition); atlases of historical county boundaries (see page 248); and state historical atlases. County boundary changes may have affected the jurisdiction in which some residents were enumerated.

Alabama (1819)—Federal censuses before statehood no longer exist; 1810 territorial census for Washington County exists.

Alaska (1959)—First federal enumeration, 1900.[7] See also page 164.

Arizona (1912)—1860, enumerated as Arizona County in New Mexico. 1870 as Arizona Territory; a few residents may be included with Pah-Ute County, Nevada, or Washington County, Utah. 1880–1910 as Arizona Territory.

Arkansas (1836)—1830 as Arkansas Territory.

Colorado (1876)—1860, Arapahoe County included in Kansas Territory, northeast Colorado towns included with Nebraska Territory. 1870 as Colorado Territory.

Florida (1845)—1830, 1840 as Florida Territory.

Hawaii (1959)—1900 forward as Hawaii Territory. See also page 165.

Idaho (1890)—1860, included as parts of Washington Territory and Utah Territory. 1870, 1880 as Idaho Territory.

Illinois (1818)—1810 as Illinois Territory. Randolph County schedule extant, covering much of southern Illinois and most of the non-Indian population.

Indiana (1816)—Pre-statehood censuses no longer exist.

Iowa (1846)—1840 as Iowa Territory.

Kansas (1861)—1860 as Kansas Territory.

Louisiana (1812)—1810 as Orleans Territory.

Michigan (1837)—1810 as Michigan Territory, but lost except part of Detroit and Michilimackinac. Fragments or handwritten copies are held at the Burton Historical Collection, Detroit Public Library; transcriptions are at many libraries. 1820, 1830 as Michigan Territory.

Minnesota (1858)—1830 included in Michigan Territory, probably as Chippewa and Crawford counties. 1840, any residents in northeastern part included with Wisconsin Territory; any in southern and western parts, with Iowa Territory. 1850 as Minnesota Territory.

Mississippi (1817)—1810 territorial census exists for Amite, Baldwin, Claiborne, Franklin, Jefferson, Warren (with Claiborne), and Washington counties. See page 167 for details.

Missouri (1821)—1830 as state of Missouri. (In 1820, Missouri was Louisiana Territory; the census has not survived.)

Montana (1889)—1860, eastern part included with unorganized part of Nebraska Territory; western part included in Washington Territory. Check also Dakota Territory. 1870, 1880 as Montana Territory.

Nebraska (1867)—1860 as Nebraska Territory.

Nevada (1864)—1860, most of present state included with Utah Territory.

New Mexico (1912)—1850–1910 as New Mexico Territory.

North Dakota (1889)—1850, Pembina County included as part of Minnesota. 1860, western part included with Nebraska Territory, eastern part as unorganized Dakota Territory. 1870, 1880 as part of Dakota Territory.

Ohio (1803)—1790, no census taken. 1800 census of Washington County, Northwest Territory, with 1803 Washington County territorial census on National Archives film M1804 (one roll) and Family History Library film 2155491.

Oklahoma (1907)—1860 with Arkansas, as Indian lands west of Arkansas. Has also been published: (1) *Federal Population Schedule of the United States Census, 1860: Indian Lands West of Arkansas*, Dorothy J. Tincup Mauldin, comp. (Tulsa, Okla.: Oklahoma Yesterday Publishers, 1990); (2) *Indian Lands West of Arkansas (Oklahoma): Population Schedule of the United States Census of 1860*, by Frances Jerome Woods (Fort Worth, Tex.: Arrow Printing Co., 1964); (3) *1860 Census of the Free Inhabitants of Indian Lands West of Arkansas (Oklahoma Indian Territory)*, Carole Ellsworth and Sue Emler, comps. (Gore, Okla.: Oklahoma Roots Research, 1984). 1890 territorial census (see pages 44 and 162). 1890 Cherokee Nation and Creek censuses. 1900 as Oklahoma Territory and Indian Territory. 1907 census extant only for Seminole County on National Archives microfilm M1814.

Oregon (1859)—1850 as Oregon Territory.

South Dakota (1889)—1860, western part included with Nebraska Territory, eastern part as unorganized Dakota Territory. 1870, 1880 as part of Dakota Territory.

Utah (1896)—1850 (1851)–1880 as Utah Territory.

Washington (1889)—1850 as part of Oregon Territory. 1860–1880 as Washington Territory. 1860, 1870 include some people in San Juan Islands as part of Whatcom County.

Wisconsin (1848)—1820, 1830 with Michigan Territory. 1840 as Wisconsin Territory.

Wyoming (1889)—1850 with Utah Territory. 1860, southwest corner with Utah Territory; southeastern portion with Nebraska Territory. 1870, 1880 as Wyoming Territory.

1900–1930 Censuses of Territories

The United States acquired overseas possessions in 1898 as a result of the Spanish-American War and the annexation of Hawaii. At this time, of course, Alaska (purchased in 1867), Arizona, Oklahoma, and New Mexico were still territories as well.

Censuses were taken in 1900 and 1910 for the territories of Alaska, Arizona, Hawaii, New Mexico, and Oklahoma/Indian Territory (statehood, 1907). For 1910, a census without a Soundex exists for Puerto Rico. American personnel attached to military and naval installations in overseas possessions would be found in the military/naval schedules. These are Soundexed for 1900 and 1920.

Territories and possessions covered by the 1920 and 1930 censuses and the 1920 Soundex are Alaska, American Samoa, Guam, Hawaii, Panama Canal Zone, Puerto Rico, and the Virgin Islands.

Reminder

USING THE POPULATION SCHEDULES OF THE CENSUS

Gathering census records that include ancestors and their siblings means more than just adding names and vital statistics to a database. By studying all available censuses for family members, you may find clues to origin, parents' names, maiden names, deviant behavior, migration patterns, medical history, occupational history, and explanations of other aspects of family history. These details, in turn, can lead you to investigate other sources to learn more.

Census records are also important tools in the practice of cluster genealogy. The cluster of people around an ancestor can provide valuable clues, suggestions, and answers. In the case of burned courthouses, especially in the South, census records are sometimes the only evidence for, if not confirmation of, relationships and vital data. Below are a few of many possible situations in which census records of the cluster aid in solving some of the problems common to genealogical research.

"Lost Relatives" May Not Be Lost

Some "lost" individuals or families are actually listed and waiting to be found. If you do not find the family in the index or Soundex, consider these options:

1. Use spelling variations and speech patterns when searching indexes and census returns. How might a census taker have written the name upon hearing it, especially if it was spoken with a local or foreign accent? Pronunciation is often the root of the problem, for in the English language, we do not always spell words as we pronounce them. Powell and Poole may both be pronounced as "pool," and Gloucester is pronounced "Gloster." Even harder for today's spelling-conscious researchers to accept are names that are often interchanged, such as these: (1) Barnett(e), Bernard, and Barnard and (2) Robertson, Robberson, Robinson, Robison, and Robson.

   Variations occur in given names as well. That's how Eva became Ever, Sarah became Sahry, and Arabella became R. Obella in records. Pronunciation or haste may explain why one Holmes family was recorded as Haynes in the 1850 census and why Williamson creeps into records as Willison, Williams, and Wilmson. The researcher must be alert to these realities. Keeping a written list of variations of your research names can help you make a more thorough search.
2. Use the finding aids described in this chapter to try to narrow the search.
3. Use other records to verify the family's location during the census year.
4. Read the census for the entire county where you believe the family was living at census time.
5. Read the census schedule for the nearest neighboring county, surrounding counties, parent county, or counties along a travel route from a previous home.
6. Look for siblings, in-laws, or other relatives in the index and census. Cousins, nieces, uncles, grandparents, or other relatives could have lived with a family of the same surname and not be indexed separately. Even people with different surnames in a household were not always indexed under their own names.
7. If you have reason to believe that the microfilm copy you have been studying is missing pages or households, ask if an original copy exists at the state archives and is accessible to researchers. Some people could have been missed in the copying process.
8. Remember that differing handwriting styles and unfamiliarity with names in a county may have caused surnames to be read incorrectly, even by careful transcribers or indexers. The 1820 census index for South Carolina did not list Evan Shelby, but a page-by-page search of the county's enumeration located his entry. Curiosity sent the genealogist back to the index to read the entire *S* listing to see whether the index had missed the name or used an alternate spelling. Indeed, Evan was indexed under Strelvy; the indexer had simply misread the handwriting. In the 1870 census, the indexed Frank Shelby was actually Isaak Shelby in a very scribbled census entry. It is easy to understand how the indexer made this mistake, but these examples should put researchers on guard to try alternative spellings and techniques for locating ancestors' records.

For More Info

For more case studies involving census records, see Kathleen Hinckley's *Your Guide to the Federal Census* and Franklin Smith and Emily Croom's *Genealogist's Guide to Discovering Your African-American Ancestors.*

Case Study

Case Study: Cluster to the Rescue

Although this study took place in Texas records, the process and the principles work in any state for which Soundex or other indexes exist.

Fletcher McKennon grew up in the home of her grandmother Susan R. Mood, a preacher's widow, in Georgetown, Texas. The 1900 and 1910 Soundexes showed neither Fletcher McKennon nor Mrs. Mood. The Texas Soundex contained cards for other Mood family members in Georgetown and Greenville, but neither the granddaughter nor the grandmother was enumerated with those families. The challenge was to find an alternative to reading the county enumeration page by page looking for the two "missing" females who unquestionably were living in the county.

The new effort called for a review of the family situation in 1910. Fletcher's widowed mother, Margaret McKennon, had lived in Mexico, where she taught in a mission school, in 1900 but had become the librarian at the local university in 1903. Would the Soundex show her on an individual card as a member of her mother's household? Indeed, it did. Another individual card showed Margaret's elder daughter, Kittie [*sic*] Mood McKennon, in the same household. This finding information led back to the census, where all four females were recorded where they were supposed to be. The original problem now had a solution. Fletcher had been enumerated and, as later was discovered, Soundexed under her middle name as Elizabeth Fletcher McKennon. Mrs. Mood was enumerated probably under the surname Wood; the handwriting could be interpreted either way. Curiosity led back to the Soundex, where she was indeed listed as Wood. No wonder the first two attempts to find her using the code M300 had not been successful.

The second challenge was finding Mrs. Mood and six-year-old Fletcher in 1900. Margaret and Kitty McKennon were in Mexico at that time. Given (1) the Mood-Wood problems of the 1910 census, (2) the failure to find Fletcher McKennon in a previous 1900 Soundex search, and (3) the lack of motivation to read through both Mood and Wood Soundex codes, a better, time-saving option was a cluster approach. On University Avenue near the Mood house in 1910 lived three other families of whom Fletcher later spoke whenever she recalled her childhood: Hughes, Cody, and Booty. Cody was chosen as the Soundex code (C300) that might have the fewest households to scan. Claud C. Cody was quickly identified in the Soundex and then in the census, listed on University Avenue.

The 1900 census taker did not go straight down University Avenue but interspersed cross streets between the blocks of University. Thus, six pages after the Cody entry was the Mood household. This time Mrs. Mood was enumerated as Mood, but Fletcher was enumerated as McKenno, which has the Soundex code M250 instead of M255 (for McKennon). The family's South Carolina pronunciation may have influenced the census taker's hearing and spelling, and thus later Soundexing, of the name. This variation explains the failed attempt to find the child in the Soundex. A curiosity check of the McKenno Soundex microfilm revealed Fletcher McKenno living in the household of Susan Wood. This revelation made a convincing argument that the cluster approach—looking for the neighbors—indeed was the quicker way of finding the family entry.

Case Study

Case Study: Clues to a Wife's Maiden Name

Have you ever read a census and been tempted to skip over persons of a different surname who were listed with your family? If so, it is time to reform your habits. Sometimes, these people were employees or boarders, but often they were relatives. Their presence may provide important clues; in this case, the clue led to the wife's maiden name.

In counties where marriage records exist, it is relatively easy to determine a wife's maiden name, but in "burned counties" a clue in the census may be vital to research. This case is from a group of families that lived in five different counties during a century of their history—Chesterfield in South Carolina and Jones, Covington, Jasper, and Smith in Mississippi. All five counties suffered courthouse fires after the families moved farther west. The loss of most early records makes finding the maiden names of wives in these counties a real challenge.

Evan Shelby moved his family from South Carolina to Mississippi about 1827. In 1850, Evan, his son Alfred, and their families lived in Jasper County in a cluster of Blakeney and Shelby families. These Blakeneys and Shelbys shared given names: William, John, Alfred, Alvin, Harriett, Louisa, and Matilda.

Evan's son John P. Shelby married about 1842 (at an unknown location), and the 1850 census enumerated him in neighboring Smith County with his wife, Matilda (twenty-eight, born in South Carolina), three young sons, and a Robert Blakeney (twenty-five, reportedly born in Mississippi). Nearby were three Blakeney families. Could Blakeney be Matilda's maiden name? Might Robert be her younger brother?

No Shelby family records aided in the search for Matilda's maiden name. However, one of John and Matilda's great-grandsons years ago asked his father about her name. The older man could not remember it but thought it started with *Bl.* None of the names they thought of sounded "right," but they did not think of Blakeney.

Pursuing these clues (census and vague recollection) involved following as many of the Blakeneys and Shelbys as possible and amassing many census records. Evan was the only Shelby identified in the 1820 South Carolina census, and five Blakeney families lived near him in Chesterfield County. These were the only Blakeneys in the state, according to the census, except for one family in a neighboring county. In the 1825 *Mills' Atlas* of South Carolina (Reprint, Easley, S.C.: Southern Historical Press, 1980), the Chesterfield County map, prepared in 1819, showed only one Shelby residence. Its closest neighbor was a Blakeney, and several other Blakeneys lived nearby.

By about 1827, when the Shelbys moved to Mississippi, son John P. was eight or nine years old, not of courting age. Matilda would have been only four or five at that time. Did her family move to Mississippi? The only Smith-Jasper area Blakeney couple of the age to be her parents had a Matilda in their family in the 1850 census. If her family stayed in South Carolina, how did she and John get together?

The National Union Catalog Pre-1956 Imprints showed that a John O. Blakeney in 1928 had written a family history about the Chesterfield County Blakeneys. Fortunately, it was available on interlibrary loan. Since the author was born in Jasper County, Mississippi, in 1852, no doubt he had known some of the Blakeney cluster listed in the 1850 census.

Although the author did not document the information he shared, he included many birth dates, as if from family Bibles, even when he had no marriage and death dates. In a cousin line to his own was John Blakeney of Chesterfield County, South Carolina, and his twenty (yes, *twenty*) children by three wives. Among the children of the first wife were James, who married Harriet Shelby, and Matilda, who married John Shelby. In 1850, James and Harriet Blakeney were enumerated next to John Shelby's brother Alfred and one house away from Evan Shelby. The census suggested that James and Harriet Blakeney had married about 1841 or 1842; their seven-year-old son John was born in Mississippi.

This Harriet Blakeney probably was a daughter of Evan Shelby and a sister of John and Alfred. The 1830 and 1840 censuses of Evan Shelby's household show one young female of Harriet's age who had not been identified up to this point of the research, and no other candidates had surfaced.

Because census records indicate that John Blakeney Sr. remained in South Carolina, Matilda Blakeney and John P. Shelby must not have grown up together. They may have renewed childhood acquaintance through the marriage of James Blakeney and Harriet Shelby; the two couples married within a year or two of each other.

One problem with the Blakeney book was a note printed with Matilda's entry: "born Sept. 24, 1822, m John Shelby, Hill County, Texas." The birth date agreed with the 1850 census (the only census to name Matilda), and the husband's name was encouraging evidence. However, John and Matilda did not live in Hill County. Deed records and John's signature on a legislative petition show that he was in Robertson County, Texas, in 1870 and thereafter. His and one son's Confederate pension applications indicate they came to Texas in 1868 or 1869. It is frustrating that this Shelby family is not enumerated in the microfilmed 1870 census or the handwritten copy in the Texas State Archives or in the Mississippi or Louisiana census. Nor is it known whether Matilda came to Texas. Family tradition suggests she may have died in Mississippi before the family moved.

Nevertheless, did any John and Matilda Shelby live in Hill County? Records indicate no Shelbys there before the 1870s. Enumerated only by initials, the J.T. and M.A. Shelby in Hill County's 1880 census were not born in South Carolina but in Arkansas and Georgia, respectively. Their ages were thirty-six and thirty-four, not even close to the John (sixty-one) and Matilda (who would have been fifty-eight) of this search, and the Hill County children had different names, ages, and birthplaces from John P. Shelby's children. This Hill County couple does not match the criteria necessary to be the daughter and son-in-law of John Blakeney of Chesterfield County.

A piece of positive evidence is this John Blakeney's 1875 will, which named his daughter Matilda Shelby. The will mentioned the children of his first two wives only to say that they had already "been advanced out of my estate heretofore as much as I designed that they should have." Probably because of this clause, the father made no statement to indicate whether any of them were deceased or had heirs. Research has identified no other John and Matilda Shelby in that era and no evidence to suggest that this Matilda was not John Blakeney's daughter.

The fact remains that in burned counties, early records are scarce. Therefore, census records have consistently been a principal source of evidence. The presence of Robert Blakeney in the household of John P. Shelby in 1850 was a red flag that required attention. From Blakeney records found so far, it seems that this Robert was not Matilda's brother but a cousin whose exact relationship has not been determined. In genealogy, answers always prompt more questions.

SUPPLEMENTAL SCHEDULES

Over the years, Congress has authorized the collection of supplemental information at the same time as the population censuses. **I call these the "AIMS" schedules: agriculture, industry/manufacturing, mortality, and social statistics.**

Notes

1810, 1820, and 1832 Censuses of Manufactures

In 1810, Congress asked census takers to gather information on certain manufacturing pursuits in their counties. Some of this information exists for a few counties on the population census microfilm for Delaware, Louisiana, Maine, Maryland, Massachusetts, New Hampshire, New York, North Carolina, Pennsylvania, Rhode Island, South Carolina, Vermont, and Virginia. For example, one Stokes County, North Carolina, page with clear headings (page 546) names owners of tanneries, cotton machines, shoe factories, paper mills, oil mills, and breweries and shows separate columns for the quantities and values of their products.

The New York manufacturing information contained in the 1810 census is also on one roll of microfilm (M1792). The details vary from county to county. For example, in Dutchess County, New York, the census taker simply added columns at the end of the population schedule to count horses, cattle, sheep, looms, and yards of cloth produced. The Broome County enumerator identified individuals and their occupations—for example, Samuel Seymour, operator of a lampblack factory; John Myers, a blacksmith; and Jonathan Crane, owner of a sawmill. Several enumerators simply summarized the livestock and the kinds of establishments in the county: Genesee County reported seven tanneries, eight distilleries, two saltworks, 385 looms, fourteen gristmills, twenty sawmills, and so forth. One of the most detailed reports came from Orange County, where the census taker itemized the operations of specific furnaces, forges, cut nail factories, and other businesses. These reports hold interesting historical information about somebody's ancestors.

1820 Manufacturing Schedules

In 1820 Congress authorized a more detailed census of manufacturers. Although it was meant to be a survey of those who made more than $500 a year, it includes many smaller operations. The schedules are not complete, but individuals who made more than $500 annually are indexed. The returns are microfilmed on National Archives series M279, available at the National Archives, some of its regional branches, and the Family History Library. Other libraries may hold the rolls pertaining to their states.

This census asked for information on raw materials, employees, machinery, expenses, kinds of articles made and their market value. If your ancestor is listed on these schedules, you may learn interesting family history. For example, David Patton of Shelbyville, Bedford County, Tennessee, was a cabinetmaker who used walnut, cherry, and poplar planks to make bureaus, "cabboards," and tables of all kinds with a set of cabinet tools that cost him about $100. He cleared about $200 annually and remarked, "this is tolerable good business but the sales is not fast." (See Patton's report in Figure 2-10, on page 72.)

In some counties, census takers recorded the information on schedules similar to the population schedules: names down the left column and details about the business operations written across the page. For a number of states, the reports include printed statistical summaries, or digests. The digests only—no schedules on individuals—are available for Alabama, Arkansas, Louisiana, Michigan, and Missouri.

1832 Manufacturing Schedules

A census of manufactures was taken again in 1832 in an effort to determine the effects of foreign competition and tariffs on domestic industry. The returns were published under the title *Documents Relative to the Manufactures in the United States, Collected and Transmitted to the House of Representatives, in Compliance With a Resolution of January 19, 1832, by the Secretary of the Treasury*. They were originally published in 1833 as House Document 308, of the twenty-second Congress, first session, Serial 222 and 223. (See chapter eight for information on the Serial Set.) The two volumes were reprinted in 1969 (New York: Burt Franklin, an affiliate of Lenox Hill Publishing and Distributing Corporation). The returns cover the following states, in the order listed:

- Volume I (Serial 222)—Maine, New Hampshire, Vermont, Rhode Island, Connecticut
- Volume II (Serial 223)—New York, New Jersey, Pennsylvania, Delaware, and Ohio

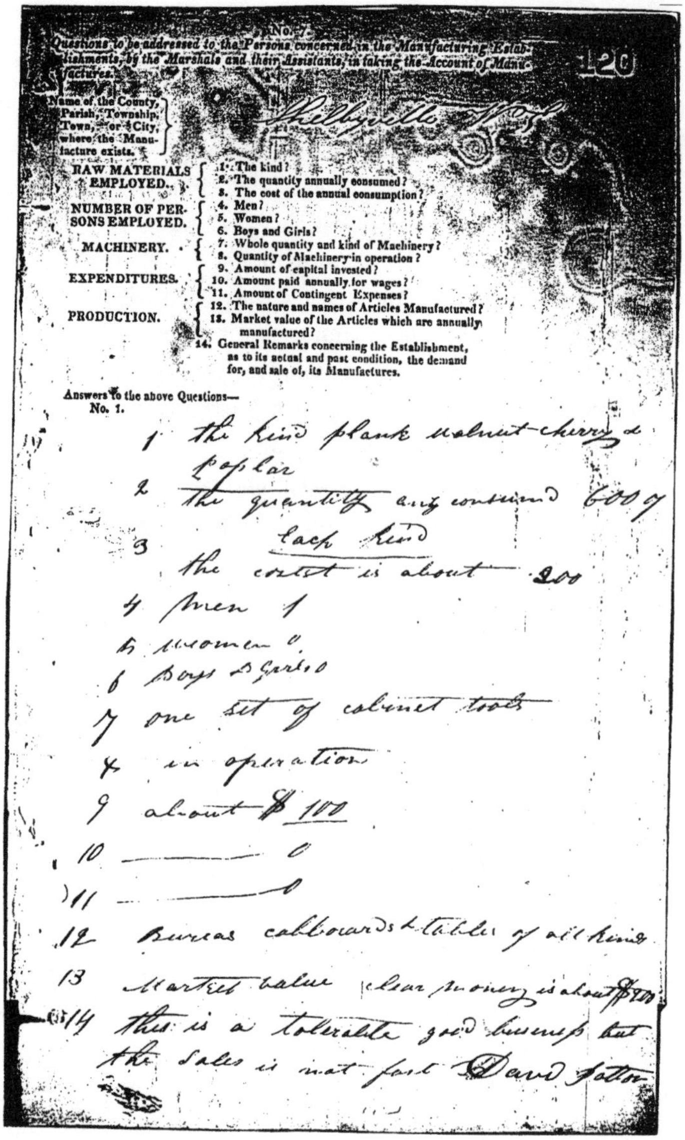
No. 7.

Questions to be addressed to the Persons concerned in the Manufacturing Establishments, by the Marshals and their Assistants, in taking the Account of Manufactures.

120

Name of the County, Parish, Township, Town, or City, where the Manufacture exists. Shelbyville No. 1

RAW MATERIALS EMPLOYED.
1. The kind?
2. The quantity annually consumed?
3. The cost of the annual consumption?

NUMBER OF PERSONS EMPLOYED.
4. Men?
5. Women?
6. Boys and Girls?

MACHINERY.
7. Whole quantity and kind of Machinery?
8. Quantity of Machinery in operation?

EXPENDITURES.
9. Amount of capital invested?
10. Amount paid annually for wages?
11. Amount of Contingent Expenses?

PRODUCTION.
12. The nature and names of Articles Manufactured?
13. Market value of the Articles which are annually manufactured?

14. General Remarks concerning the Establishment, as to its actual and past condition, the demand for, and sale of, its Manufactures.

Answers to the above Questions—
No. 1.

1 the kind plank walnut cherry & poplar
2 the quantity an[illegible] consumed 600 of each kind
3 the cost is about 200
4 men 1
5 women 0
6 Boys & Girls 0
7 one set of cabinet tools
8 in operation
9 about $ 100
10 ——— 0
11 ——— 0
12 Bureaus cubboards & tables of all kinds
13 Market value clear money is about $[illegible]
14 this is a tolerable good business but the sales is not fast David [illegible]

Figure 2-10 Records of the 1820 Census of Manufactures, NARA microfilm M279, roll 27, Bedford County, Tennessee, no. 120.

The text contains statistics and much information on individual manufacturers. For example, from Hamilton County, Ohio, tanner and currier Henry B. Funk reported that he employed ten men at an average wage of $22 per month. Using mostly domestic raw materials, he manufactured about $18,000 in articles during the year.

Special Enumerations

Especially in the twentieth century, the Census Bureau has taken a variety of special censuses. Between 1915 and 1938, about twenty-three municipalities or counties paid for Census Bureau enumerations of their rapidly growing populations between decennial censuses. The government compiled the statistics for city use. At this writing, according to the National Archives staff and Census Bureau staff, apparently none of the schedules have been located or microfilmed.

From 1935, special censuses of various businesses exist. Descriptions of the contents are on the microfilm rolls rather than in a descriptive pamphlet. At this writing, the following are available on microfilm; all titles begin with "1935 Census of Business."

- M1797—Schedules of Advertising Agencies, 1 roll.

- M2066—Schedules of Banking and Financial Institutions, 31 rolls.
- M2067—Schedules of Miscellaneous Enterprises, 43 rolls.
- M2068—Schedules of Motor Trucking for Hire, 103 rolls. Arranged by state, county, town; contains name and owner of business and other details.
- M2070—Schedules of Radio Broadcasting Stations, 1 roll. Business data, few names.

1850–1880 Non-Population Schedules

The four federal enumerations between 1850 and 1880 contain supplemental schedules that provide the family historian with interesting information on agriculture, industry, and society. These are not genealogical in that they do not contain relationships and vital statistics of individuals. However, the schedules are important glimpses into the past that add to our knowledge of our ancestors' lives and communities.

The agriculture schedules contain information valuable for many genealogists since the majority of the population lived in rural areas and a large percentage were farmers. In 1850, the schedule had forty-six columns of questions, including the name of the farm owner or agent; the number of acres of improved and unimproved land; cash value of the farm and its implements; cash value and numbers of livestock; and amount and value of produce, crops, and homemade manufactures. The information was to cover the year preceding the enumeration—1 June 1849 (or 1859, 1869, 1879) to 1 June 1850 (or 1860, 1870, but 31 May 1880, as printed on the forms).

In 1850, for instance, W.W. Chapman of Washington County, Oregon Territory, owned two horses, forty-five milch (milk) cows, and two oxen. During the preceding year, he had grown one hundred bushels of Irish potatoes and made two hundred pounds of butter. C.A. Welch of the same county valued his 105 acres of improved land at $3,000 and his livestock at $1,300. His stock included nine horses, three cows, ten oxen, four other cattle, twenty-four sheep, and fifteen swine. He reported that he had made eight hundred pounds of butter and two hundred pounds of cheese.

The 1860 agriculture schedule was virtually the same as that for 1850. The 1870 schedule had a few added questions, such as the value of forest products, giving fifty-two columns of categorized information. The 1880 schedule increased to one hundred columns of requested information. Most of the categories remained the same but asked for more detail, including the first questions about poultry and the number of eggs produced in the preceding year. Pertinent blanks were not always filled out. Sometimes, comparing these schedules with the population schedules can help researchers reconstruct the ancestral neighborhood and identify potential employers of those who worked as farm laborers or overseers.

The industry or manufacturing schedules asked for the same kind of information: name of company or individual; name and value of product made; quantities, kinds, and values of raw materials used; the kinds of motive power or machinery used; and the work force employed and their wages. One illustration from 1850 is William Williams of Polk County, Oregon Territory, who owned a sawmill valued at $1,200. He used water power to mill 2,880 logs valued at $3,500. He employed an average of four men, whose wages cost the owner $100 a month. In 1849, the mill produced 720,000 feet of lumber valued at $28,800. In 1869–1870 in Boise City, Idaho Territory, William Neily made 160 pairs of boots, and his neighbor Peter J. Pefly made fifty saddles.

The 1850 and 1860 schedules were the same. The 1870 form asked for the quantity of horsepower used, the number and kinds of machines, the number of children or youth employed, the number of months the business operated during that year, and annual wages of employees. The 1880 schedule had inquiries for special classes of manufacturing establishments: boot and shoe factories, cheese and butter factories, flour mills and gristmills, saltworks, lumber mills and sawmills, brickyards and tile works, paper mills, coal mines, quarries, and agricultural implement works. The enumerations asked for the amount of capital invested, number and daily wages of employees, length of operation or season, and specific information peculiar to each industry.

The 1880 manufacturing schedule showed W.J. Leatherwood of Baker County, Oregon, with $3,000 capital invested in a sawmill that worked eight months a year. He paid wages of $2.50 a day for ordinary laborers (as opposed to skilled laborers), who worked eight hours a day in winter and spring and ten hours a day in summer and fall. C.W. Bonham, a blacksmith of the same county, put in ten-hour days twelve months a year. When he had helpers, he paid $1.50 a day for ordinary labor and $3.50 for skilled.

The social statistics schedules from the same census years (1850–1880) do not name individuals but do give historically pertinent information about each town, township, or ward in the counties. The statistics include the number and kinds of schools, number of pupils and faculty members, the number and kinds of libraries, the nature and circulation of newspapers and periodicals, the seating capacity of churches and other places of worship, the number of paupers of U.S. and foreign birth and expenditures for their support, and information on wages. The 1850 statistics tell us that in Hillsborough County, Florida, the Indian corn crop that year was cut in half by drought. The 1870 Idaho statistics inform us that a carpenter in Ada County could make $6 a day without board, but at Rocky Bar in Alturas County, he could make $8 a day. Workers who received board from their employers usually earned $10 to $15 a week less than those paid without board.

A *Report on the Social Statistics of Cities* (George E. Waring Jr., compiler), using information gathered in the 1880 census, was published by the Government Printing Office in 1886. Each volume ends with an index.

- House Miscellaneous Document 42, part 18 (47th Congress, 2nd session) serial 2148 (New England and Middle States—New York, New Jersey, Pennsylvania, and Delaware).
- House Miscellaneous Document 42, part 19 (47th Congress, 2nd session) serial 2149 (Southern and Western states and territories).

These descriptions of 222 cities give details about location, history, and climate; transportation, streets, and navigation; markets, commerce, manufacturing; institutions, parks, and amusement places; burial and cemeteries, epidemics, pest houses, and prevention and treatment of infectious diseases; street cleaning, police and fire departments, sewage and garbage departments; drinking water; and recording of births, disease, and deaths. Not all cities reported on all subjects, but researchers can gain valuable historical information on each city. The report can be found in most libraries that have the U.S. Serial Set, and most federal depository libraries have the Serial Set.

See Also

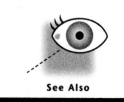

See page 292 for more on the Serial Set.

Figure 2-11, on page 75, is a partial page from part 18, serial 2148, describing Jersey City, New Jersey. Other pages reported such information as the following:

- The population in 1880 was 120,722: 119,351 whites; 1,340 blacks; 21 Chinese; and 10 Indians. Of these, 81,464 were native-born; 39,258, foreign-born. The city's population had exploded since 1840, when it was about 3,000. This kind of information helps genealogists understand the environments in which their ancestors lived.
- Forty-three miles of paved streets were paved with Belgian blocks, cobble-stones, or crushed stone. Wood had been found to be unsatisfactory for street paving; most streets remained unpaved. Most important streets had good sidewalks. No omnibus

lines ran in the city, but several "horse-railroads" operated. This information is local and social history, of interest when studying ancestors' lives in depth.

- The city required burial permits, issued upon receipt of a death certificate. The six cemeteries connected with the city were New York Bay Cemetery, Jersey City Cemetery, Hudson County Catholic Cemetery, Saint Peter's Cemetery, Bergen Reform Church Burial Ground, and Speers Cemetery. The sketch reported the location, size, and descriptive information on each one, noting that the New York Bay Cemetery was the burial site for many Revolutionary soldiers. This kind of information may help genealogists find additional sources for research.

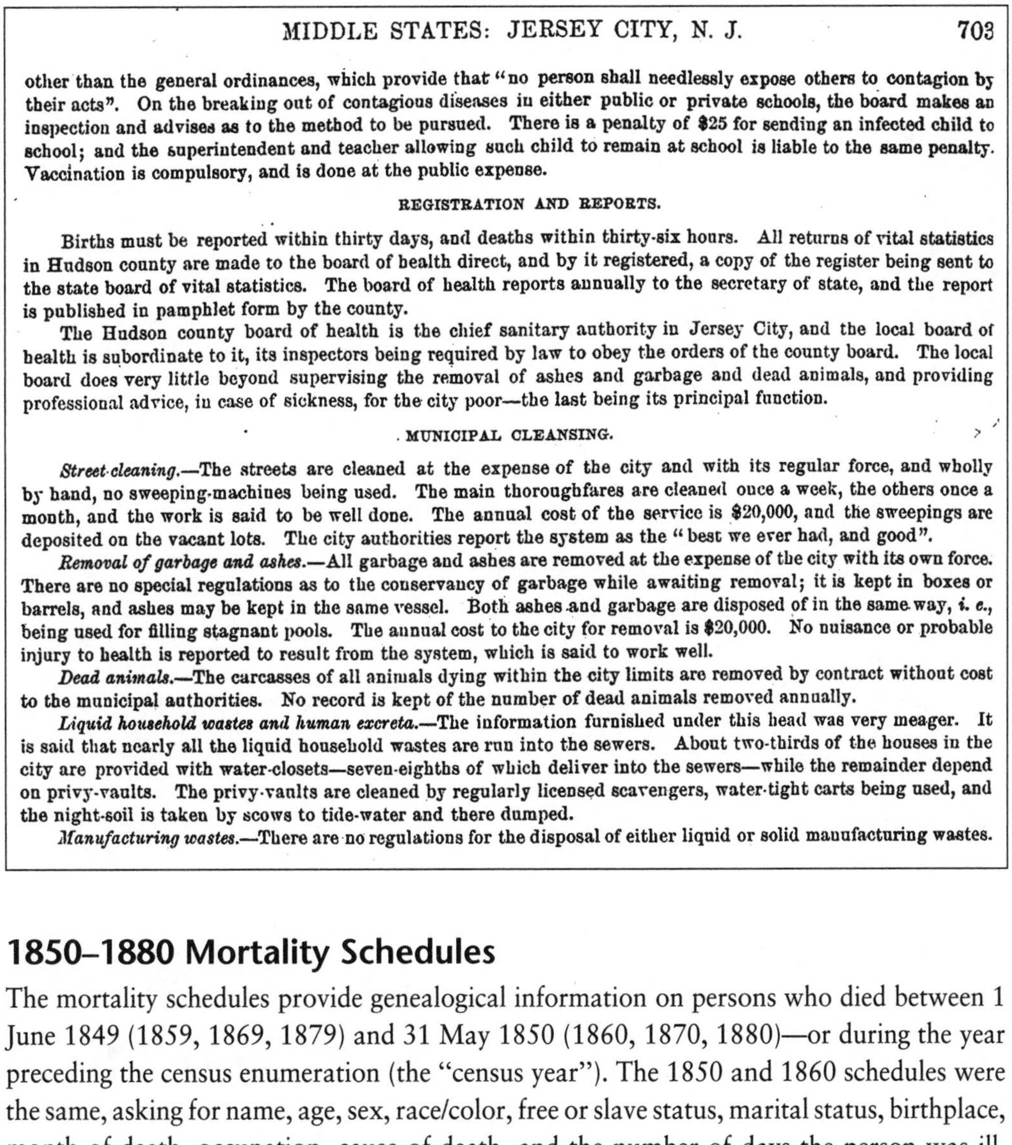

MIDDLE STATES: JERSEY CITY, N. J. 703

other than the general ordinances, which provide that "no person shall needlessly expose others to contagion by their acts". On the breaking out of contagious diseases in either public or private schools, the board makes an inspection and advises as to the method to be pursued. There is a penalty of $25 for sending an infected child to school; and the superintendent and teacher allowing such child to remain at school is liable to the same penalty. Vaccination is compulsory, and is done at the public expense.

REGISTRATION AND REPORTS.

Births must be reported within thirty days, and deaths within thirty-six hours. All returns of vital statistics in Hudson county are made to the board of health direct, and by it registered, a copy of the register being sent to the state board of vital statistics. The board of health reports annually to the secretary of state, and the report is published in pamphlet form by the county.

The Hudson county board of health is the chief sanitary authority in Jersey City, and the local board of health is subordinate to it, its inspectors being required by law to obey the orders of the county board. The local board does very little beyond supervising the removal of ashes and garbage and dead animals, and providing professional advice, in case of sickness, for the city poor—the last being its principal function.

MUNICIPAL CLEANSING.

Street-cleaning.—The streets are cleaned at the expense of the city and with its regular force, and wholly by hand, no sweeping-machines being used. The main thoroughfares are cleaned once a week, the others once a month, and the work is said to be well done. The annual cost of the service is $20,000, and the sweepings are deposited on the vacant lots. The city authorities report the system as the "best we ever had, and good".

Removal of garbage and ashes.—All garbage and ashes are removed at the expense of the city with its own force. There are no special regulations as to the conservancy of garbage while awaiting removal; it is kept in boxes or barrels, and ashes may be kept in the same vessel. Both ashes and garbage are disposed of in the same way, *i. e.*, being used for filling stagnant pools. The annual cost to the city for removal is $20,000. No nuisance or probable injury to health is reported to result from the system, which is said to work well.

Dead animals.—The carcasses of all animals dying within the city limits are removed by contract without cost to the municipal authorities. No record is kept of the number of dead animals removed annually.

Liquid household wastes and human excreta.—The information furnished under this head was very meager. It is said that nearly all the liquid household wastes are run into the sewers. About two-thirds of the houses in the city are provided with water-closets—seven-eighths of which deliver into the sewers—while the remainder depend on privy-vaults. The privy-vaults are cleaned by regularly licensed scavengers, water-tight carts being used, and the night-soil is taken by scows to tide-water and there dumped.

Manufacturing wastes.—There are no regulations for the disposal of either liquid or solid manufacturing wastes.

Figure 2-11 *Report of the Social Statistics of Cities*, George E. Waring Jr., comp. (Washington, D.C.: Government Printing Office, 1886), for Department of the Interior, Census Office, Part I—New England and Middle States, 703, Jersey City, N.J.

1850–1880 Mortality Schedules

The mortality schedules provide genealogical information on persons who died between 1 June 1849 (1859, 1869, 1879) and 31 May 1850 (1860, 1870, 1880)—or during the year preceding the census enumeration (the "census year"). The 1850 and 1860 schedules were the same, asking for name, age, sex, race/color, free or slave status, marital status, birthplace, month of death, occupation, cause of death, and the number of days the person was ill. Note that although slaves were named in these schedules, no surname or slaveholder's name was specified. If a slaveholder reported at the same time a death in his own family and any deaths among his slaves, the deceased persons could be listed on consecutive lines of the schedule page. Thus, the name just before or perhaps just after a slave's name could be a clue to the identification of the farm or plantation where the slave lived.

Figure 2-12, on page 76, is an 1850 mortality schedule from Chatham, Barnstable County, Massachusetts, where a number of deaths resulted from consumption, dysentery,

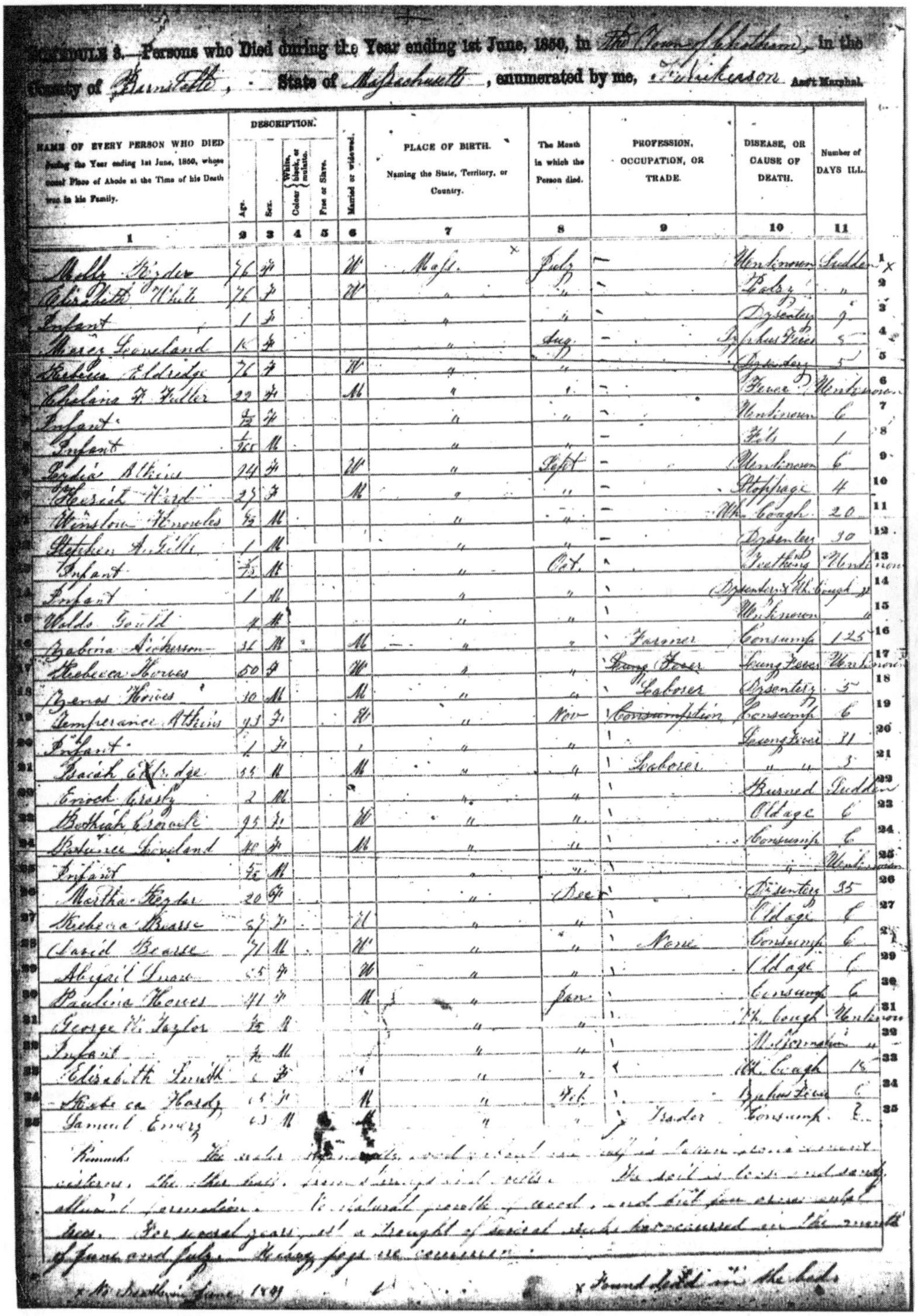

SCHEDULE 3.—Persons who Died during the Year ending 1st June, 1850, in The Town of Chatham, in the County of Barnstable, State of Massachusetts, enumerated by me, F. Nickerson Ass't Marshal.

NAME OF EVERY PERSON WHO DIED during the Year ending 1st June, 1850, whose usual Place of Abode at the Time of his Death was in his Family.	DESCRIPTION. Age.	Sex.	Colour (White, black, or mulatto).	Free or Slave.	Married or widowed.	PLACE OF BIRTH. Naming the State, Territory, or Country.	The Month in which the Person died.	PROFESSION, OCCUPATION, OR TRADE.	DISEASE, OR CAUSE OF DEATH.	Number of DAYS ILL.	
1	2	3	4	5	6	7	8	9	10	11	
Molly Ryder	76	F			W	Mass.	July	—	Unknown	Sudden	1
Elizabeth White	76	F			W	"	"	—	Palsy	"	2
Infant	1	F				"	"	—	Dysentery	9	3
Mercy Loveland	16	F				"	Aug.	—	Typhus Fever	5	4
Rebecca Eldridge	76	F			W	"	"		Dysentery	5	5
Chelana F. Fuller	22	F			M	"	"	—	Fever	Unknown	6
Infant	[illegible]	F				"	"	—	Unknown	6	7
Infant	[illegible]	M				"		—	Fits	1	8
Lydia Atkins	74	F			W	"	Sept	—	Unknown	6	9
Harriet Hird	27	F			M	"	"	—	Stoppage	4	10
Winslow Knowles	[illegible]	M				"	"	—	Wh. Cough	20	11
Stephen A. Gill	1	M					"	—	Dysentery	30	12
Infant	[illegible]	M				"	Oct.		Teething	Unknown	13
Infant	1	M				"	"		Dysentery & Wh. Cough	[illegible]	14
Waldo Gould	[illegible]	M				"	"		Unknown		15
Sabina Nickerson	31	M			M	"	"	Farmer	Consump.	125	16
Rebecca Howes	50	F			W	"	"	Lung Fever	Lung Fever	Unknown	17
Zenas Howes	10	M			M	"	"	Laborer	Dysentery	5	18
Temperance Atkins	43	F			W	"	Nov	Consumption	Consump.	6	19
Infant	1	F				"	"		Lung Fever	31	20
Isaiah Eldridge	55	M			M	"	"	Laborer	" "	3	21
Enoch Crosby	2	M				"	"		Burned	Sudden	22
Bethiah Crowell	95	F			W	"	"		Old age	6	23
Patience Loveland	40	F			M	"	"		Consump.	6	24
Infant	[illegible]	M				"	"		"	Unknown	25
Martha Ryder	20	F				"	Dec.		Dysentery	35	26
Rebecca Bearse	57	F			W	"	"		Old age	6	27
David Bearse	71	M			W	"	"	None	Consump.	6	28
Abigail Snow	55	F			W	"	"		Old age	6	29
Paulina Howes	41	F			M	"	Jan.		Wh. Cough	Unknown	30
George W. Taylor	[illegible]	M				"	"		Unknown	"	31
Infant	[illegible]	M				"	"		Wh. Cough	18	32
Elizabeth Smith	[illegible]	F				"	"		Typhus Fever	6	33
Rebecca Hardy	[illegible]	F			M	"	Feb.		Consump.	[illegible]	34
Samuel Emery	[illegible]	M				"	"	Trader	Consump.	[illegible]	35

Remarks [illegible]

Figure 2-12 1850 Mortality Schedule, Chatham, Barnstable County, Non-population Schedules for Massachusetts, 1850–1880, NARA microfilm T1204, roll 9.

and unknown causes. A one-day-old infant died of "fits"; an eight-month-old infant reportedly died from teething. These pages bring a deep sense of reality to research, emphasizing the frailty of life and the realities of loss that families experienced.

The 1870 schedules also asked if a parent of the deceased was of foreign birth. In addition, the 1880 form asked how long the person had been a resident of the county, where the person contracted the causal disease or condition, and the name of the attending physician. Of course, not all the blanks were always filled in, but each entry provides some information.

Reminder

Persons on the mortality schedule were not to be included in the general population schedule, which was to include only *living* persons in the household on census day. However, this instruction must have been confusing to some enumerators or families; persons on mortality schedules were sometimes named on the population schedule. One example is the two sons of Napoleon and Laura Shelby of Clarke County, Mississippi. Both boys were listed in the 1880 census, then crossed out with *dead* written beside both names. The mortality schedule shows each of the children: three-year-old Charles who died in June (no year indicated) and one-year-old Verne who died in April (1880). Technically, Charles should have been listed on the mortality schedule only if he died in June 1879, and, in that case, not at all on the population schedule. Since he appears on both lists, it may be that he died in June 1880, between June 1 and the date of the enumerator's visit.

It is interesting to read the terms used to list cause of death, such as "congestion of the brain" or "softening of the brain." Consider the entry for Hamburg native Charles Quail, a married thirty-two-year-old Clarke County, Washington, saloon keeper who died in May 1860, after "2 1/4 months" of illness. The cause of death was "mortification." The enumerator's remarks explain that Charles's wounds received during the Indian wars were the final "mortifying cause" of death. In these years, common causes of death were consumption, pneumonia, diarrhea and related conditions, fevers of various kinds (typhoid, malaria, etc.), drowning and other accidents, burns, childbirth, and various conditions thought to be related to the heart. Occasionally, the enumerators identified epidemics, such as occurred in McLennan County, Texas, in 1870 when thirty-nine children and eleven adults died of measles. The enumerator in Jasper County, Mississippi, reported that most of the deaths in his county in 1850 resulted from scarlet fever.

Benjamin Thigpen was an assistant marshal who took his job of enumeration seriously. He added these remarks to the mortality schedule of Jasper County, Mississippi, in 1860; spelling and punctuation are his:

> The most Fatal and prevailing Diseases are Typhoid Fever and Pneumonia the former mostly in the autumn and fall the latter in winter and spring. The Typhoid fever seems to prevail mostly in the hill country rather than in the Pararie and swamp lands. It Generally attacks Adult persons between the ages of fifteen and forty five years and in a good degree fatal. The diseases prevailing mostly among children are worms and measles. . . . Causes of Typhoid Fever said to be Atmospheric and that of Pneumonia the sudden changes pertaining to the Climate. The Character of the water in the Pararie soil is lime and in the Hills freestone The nature of the soil is principly lime and Lime is its only natural Fertilizer Some portion however is Sandy. The Rocks are Flint Pebbles and some small Lime Rocks The Natural Growth is Pine Oak Hickory Blackjack in the hill lands and in the swamps sweet and Black Gums Poplar Beech magnolia Ash &c &c. Springs late and cool. A Disease called Black Tonge prevailed among the cattle & deer to an alarming extent a part of the year ending June the 1st 1860 without any known Local or stensible cause.

Enumerators also added remarks about crops and productions in their county and about particular cases that they reported in the schedule. Erastus B. Johnson of Choctaw County, Mississippi, added a note to the 1870 report of the death of Bazel Willson, a sixty-eight-year-old farmer. The comment may indicate particular friendship with and respect for the deceased or may have been the request of the family member who gave the information: "He is not dead but sleeping in Jesus."

Many of the original mortality schedules are stored at the National Archives or in institutions of the state to which they pertain. Microfilm copies are available for use in many of the larger public and academic libraries and special libraries such as that of the Daughters of the American Revolution in Washington, DC. Many of the state libraries, archives, or historical societies have these schedules for their state and neighboring states; from some of these institutions, you can also purchase or rent microfilm copies. Microfilm is available for purchase from the National Archives and Scholarly Resources; for rent from the Family History Library for some states; and for use at the National Archives and some regional branches, the Family History Library and many other libraries nationwide. A number of the schedules have been abstracted and published. Consult the chart at the end of this chapter for more specific information.

1880 Defective, Dependent, Delinquent (DDD) Schedules

In 1880, the census schedules included a special enumeration of people who were residents of various asylums, such as prisons or poorhouses, or who had various afflictions that made them dependent on others for support. These dependent persons included homeless children, the indigent, the insane, the deaf, and the blind. The purpose of this special schedule was to identify people in these categories and to learn more specifically about their situations.

One William Douglas lived in Middleton in Ada County, Idaho. He was totally blind, yet partly self-supporting, and had lived for six years in an institution for the blind in Newton, Iowa, from which he was released in 1876. In Whiteville, Hardeman County, Tennessee, the names of Rufus Green and Calvin Hall were recorded on the schedule of "insane" persons. Before the schedules were sent off, Dr. A.P. Waddell, M.D., scratched out the names and wrote, "I have known Rufus Green and Cal Hall for many years—they are both colored and are both of sound mind. Some mistake has been made." In the same county, Ben Oppenheimer of Bolivar had been deaf since the age of three, due to scarlet fever. He had lived for three years at the Kentucky State Mute Asylum, from which he was discharged in 1855.

About William Burnette, listed as insane, the enumerator, J.R. Jones of Hardeman County, wrote

> I cannot learn any thing in reference to the above named person only that he was of sound mind up to the Shiloh Battle in April 1862 but soon after said battle he became insane and has been so ever since. He is in good health and lives with his brother George L. Burnette. He is a married man but his wife left him after he became insane. No physician has ever examined him; it is believed that he was so frightened that he became insane.

These DDD schedules were made in most states. Even in the states where they were not made or no longer exist, some of the information is available in the regular population schedules, columns sixteen to twenty, on which the DDD schedules were based. Microfilm copies are available from many of the same places as the mortality and supplemental schedules. Consult the list at the end of this chapter for more specific information on where you can use or rent these schedules.

Researchers who identify ancestors in prisons, poorhouses, or other asylums should use the information as clues to seek other documents in state, county, or city records pertaining to those ancestors or their relatives.

Where to Find AIMS Schedules, 1850–1880

The purpose of the list below is to help genealogists locate and use the records pertaining to a particular research locale. For obvious reasons, patrons may have limited access to fragile originals unless the microfilm is very faded or missing a page. Usually, the state archives, state library, or historical society holds the most complete collection of the supplemental schedules for a given state, whether originals or microfilm. However, many public, academic, and society libraries and archives have microfilm of their state's schedules; larger libraries hold the schedules for multiple states. Since online library and archive catalogs do not always include microfilm, check with the facilities in your area to learn about their holdings. Also consult the National Archives regional branch in your research area.

The Family History Library rents some schedules, mostly mortality, for a number of states. The National Archives Microfilm Rental Program handles general population census schedules only; it does not rent the nonpopulation schedules. Many mortality schedule abstracts have been published; consult library catalogs for availability. Some mortality schedules are transcribed or indexed online. Use the book and online transcriptions as finding aids for the originals/microfilm.

Library/Archive Source

Your local library will handle interlibrary loan requests for you. You may need to provide roll numbers or other information from the holding institution to facilitate the processing of your request.

For interlibrary loan availability and purchase information, contact the facility in the state. Some facilities have this information on their Web sites. A link to state archives Web sites is available at <www.coshrc.org/arc/states.htm>; for links to state archives, libraries, and historical societies, see <www.cyndislist.com> and <www.firstgov.gov>. (In some states, the umbrella organization is the state historical society, but each state is organized uniquely.) The current *American Library Directory* is another source of contact information.

Space limitations prevent detailing more than one facility per state that holds these records. **The list below indicates the schedules held in each state for the years indicated and reflects information supplied by these institutions.** Since library and archive collections are not static, these institutions may acquire additional schedules, and institutions not listed here may have the schedules for their state. Additional schedules may exist in other locations for these states. In addition, the federal government published statistical summaries for these schedules. If the schedules do not exist as originals or microfilm copies, you may still get some information (although not specific to individuals) in the published reports, often held at the state library or a federal depository library.

Important

AIMS Schedules by State

National Archives microfilm T655 contains mortality schedules and some indexes—formerly in the custody of the Daughters of the American Revolution—for Arizona, Colorado, District of Columbia, Georgia, Kentucky, Louisiana, and Tennessee. The list refers to other National Archives microfilm that includes some or all of the schedules for the state; ask the state facility or a National Archives regional branch for a roll list and availability of the microfilm.

How to Read the Chart

A = Agricultural   I = Industry/Manufacturing   M = Mortality   S = Social Statistics
DDD = 1880 Defective, Dependent, Delinquent Schedule
50, 60, 70, 80 = Years available
AIMS 50–80 means all schedules are available for 1850–1880.
AM 50–80 means agriculture and mortality are available for 1850–1880

Alabama Department of Archives and History—AIM 50–80 (limited use of I 80 original); S 50–70; DDD.

Alaska—purchased 1867; no federal censuses taken 1870, 1880; M1871 is a 1929 agriculture schedule for Alaska.

Arizona State Library, Archives and Public Records—M 70–80. See also microfilm T655, M 70 (Mohave through Yuma counties), M 80. Actually all four counties in 1870 fell alphabetically between Mohave and Yuma.

Arkansas History Commission—AIM 50–80; S 50–70; DDD.

California State Library—AIM 50–80; S 50–70; DDD. See also Bancroft Library, University of California, Berkeley.

Colorado, Denver Public Library—AIM 70–80. See also Colorado State Archives (AIM 1885); T655 for M 70–80; see also North Carolina, Duke University.

Connecticut State Library—AIM 50–80; S 50–70; DDD.

Delaware Public Archives—AIMS 50–80; DDD. See also Delaware Historical Society.

District of Columbia, National Archives—AIMS 50–70 on microfilm M1793; A 80 on M1794; I 80, DDD on M1795; M 50–80 on T655. NARA has schedules for many states on microfilm. See also North Carolina, Duke University.

Florida State Division of Libraries and Information Services, Bureau of Archives and Records Management, Florida State Archives—AIM 50–80; S 50; DDD. See also State Library of Florida within same division.

Georgia Department of Archives and History—AM 50–80 (A 50, Appling through Putnam counties); I 80; S 50–70 (50, Baker through Wilkinson counties); DDD. See also microfilm T1137; T655 (M 50–80); and North Carolina, Duke University.

Hawaii—not applicable, not part of United States until 1898.

Idaho State Historical Society, Historical Library and State Archives—AIM 70–80; S 70; DDD. AIMS 70 omit Alturas County.

Illinois, Newberry Library—AIM 50–80 (I 70, Cook through Lee counties; M 70, Ke through W counties); S 50–60. No DDD. Check Illinois State Archives for S 70 and DDD availability; see also microfilm T1133. (1865 agriculture schedules for Macoupin, McHenry, Montgomery, Ogle counties included with A 70 schedules)

Indiana State Archives—AIS 50–70; DDD. Indiana State Library, Genealogy Division has M 50–80.

Iowa, State Historical Society of Iowa, Des Moines and Iowa City—AIM 50–80; S 50–70; DDD. See also microfilm M1156.

Kansas State Historical Society, Library and Archives Division—A 70–80; IM 60–80; DDD. See also microfilm T1130.

Kentucky Department for Libraries and Archives, Archives Research Room—AIM 50–80. DDD. See also microfilm M1528; T655 for M 50 (Pendleton through Woodford counties), M 60–80; see also North Carolina, Duke University.

Louisiana Secretary of State, Louisiana State Archives, Research Library—A 50–80; M 50 (Ascension through Vermilion parishes); M 60–80; I 80; S 50–70; DDD. See also Louisiana State Library, Louisiana Section; Louisiana State University, Middleton Library, Baton Rouge; Family History Library catalog; microfilm T1136 (basically the same as what the state archives has); T655 (M 60–80).

Maine State Archives—AIM 50–80; S 50–70; DDD.

Maryland State Archives Library—AM 50–80; I 50–60, 80; S 50–70; DDD. See also microfilm M1793 for Worcester County, A 50. See M1799 for Baltimore City and County, A 50–60; I 50–60; S 50–60.

Massachusetts Archives—AIMS 50–70; I 80. National Archives, Northeast Region, Waltham, has microfilm T1204: AIM 50–80, S 50–70, DDD.

Michigan, Department of History, Arts, and Libraries, State Archives of Michigan—AI 50–80; M 60–80; S 50–70; DDD. Microfilm; limited use of originals. See also Library of Michigan within same department; microfilm T1164; T1163 for M 50.

Minnesota Historical Society—AIM 60–80; S 60–70; DDD. See also microfilm M1802 for A 60.

Mississippi Department of Archives and History—AIM 50–80; S 50–70; DDD.

Missouri Historical Society, St. Louis—AIM 50–80; S 70; DDD. See also Missouri Office of Secretary of State, Missouri State Archives (AM 50–80).

Montana Historical Society and Archives—AIMS 70; AIM 80; DDD. See also microfilm M1806; M1794 for A 80.

Nebraska State Historical Society, Library/Archives Division—AIM 50–80; S 60–70; DDD. AIM for 1885 census. See also microfilm T1128.

Nevada Historical Society, Reno—AIM 70; IM 80; probably DDD. See also Nevada State Library and Archives (A 80; M 70–80); microfilm M1794 for A 80.

New Hampshire State Library—AIM 50–80; S 50–70; DDD. See also New Hampshire Division of Records Management and Archives.

New Jersey Department of State, Division of Archives and Records Management—AIM 50–80; S 50–60; DDD (limited use of original). If writing for information, use P.O. Box 307, Trenton, NJ 08625-0307. See also New Jersey State Library (AIM 50–80; government-published compiled social statistics); Rutgers University, Alexander Library, Special Collections (AIM 50–80); microfilm M1810 for M 50–80.

New Mexico Commission of Public Records, New Mexico State Records Center and Archives—AIMS 70; AIM 85, including schedule of Civil War veterans, both Union and Confederate; part of the Territorial Archives of New Mexico Collection, also available at academic libraries in the state; limited use of originals, but available on microfilm at archives and state library.

New York State Library—AIM 50–80 (I 70 for Essex through Yates counties); S 50–70 (S 60, for Monroe through Yates counties); DDD. See also New York Genealogical and Biographical Society.

North Carolina Division of Archives and History—AIM 50–80; S 50–70; DDD. See also microfilm M1805.

North Carolina, Duke University—Originals held: Colorado (A 70–80; I 70–80; S 70; DDD); District of Columbia (all AI; S 50–70; DDD); Georgia (all A [50, Appling through Putnam]; I 80; S 50–70; DDD); Kentucky (all AI; S 50–70; DDD); Louisiana (all A; I 80; S 50–70; DDD); Montana (A 80); Nevada (A 80); Tennessee (all A; I 50, 80, 60 [Monroe through Wilson counties], 70 [Anderson through Lewis counties]; S 50–70; DDD); Virginia (1860 Halifax County, AIMS, Slave Schedule, Population Schedule); Wyoming (A 80).

North Dakota, State Historical Society of North Dakota, State Archives and Historical Research Library—M 80; state M 1885. See also South Dakota.

Ohio Historical Society, Archives/Library Division—A 50–80; I 50–80 (60, partial coverage); M 50 (counties H through W), 60 all, 80 (A through Geauga counties only); DDD (Fulton through Medina counties). See microfilm T1159. See also State Library of Ohio, mostly the published statistical reports.

Oklahoma—Apparently none taken. The only non-Indian census from these years is 1860.

Oregon Secretary of State, Oregon State Archives—A 50, 70–80; IM 50–80; S 50–70; DDD.

Pennsylvania State Library—AI 50–80; M 70–80; S 60–80, DDD. See also microfilm T1138 for A 50–80; T1157 for I 50–60; M1796 for I 70–80; M1838 for M 50–80; M597 for S 50–70 and DDD.

Rhode Island State Archives—AIM 50–80; S 50–70, 80 (one page fragment); no DDD.

South Carolina Department of Archives and History—AIM 50–80; S 50–70; DDD.

South Dakota Cultural Heritage Center, State Historical Society, State Archives—A 70–80, 1885 summary of agriculture schedule, no names; M 70–80 plus 1885; DDD.

Tennessee State Library and Archives—AI 50–80; M 50–60, 80; DDD. See North Carolina, Duke University, for the partial coverage of I 60–70; see also Family History Library catalog; microfilm T1135; T655 for M 50–60, 80.

Texas State Library and Archives—AIM 50–80; S 50–70; DDD. See also microfilm T1134.

Utah, Family History Library—AM 50–80; I 60–70; S 50–70. See also microfilm M1807 for M 70.

Vermont Department of Libraries, Reference and Law—AIM 50–80; S, only the statistics within Government Printing Office publications; not separated out by Vermont; ask at reference desk for specific locale. See also microfilm M1798 for AI 50–70; M1807 for M 70.

Virginia, Library of Virginia—AIM 50–80; S 50–70; DDD. See also microfilm T1132; M1808 for Northern District of Halifax County, 1860 AIMS plus free and slave schedules.

Washington State Office of Secretary of State, Division of Archives and Records Management, Archives—AIMS 60–70; AIM 80; DDD. See also microfilm A1154, formerly T1154 (AIMS 60–70; AIM 80; DDD).

Washington DC, see District of Columbia.

West Virginia Department of Culture and History, Archives and History Library—AIM 50–80; S 50–70; DDD. See also West Virginia University, Morgantown.

Wisconsin, State Historical Society of Wisconsin, Archives—AIM 50–80; S 50–70; DDD.

Wyoming—The state library and University of Wyoming have the published statistical compilations that the government produced after the census information was collected. The state archives reports that they hold no non-population schedules. See microfilm M1794 for A 80.

FOR FURTHER REFERENCE

The 1930 Census: A Reference and Research Guide. Thomas Jay Kemp, ed. North Salt Lake, Utah: HeritageQuest from ProQuest, 2002.

Map Guide to the U.S. Federal Censuses, 1790–1920. William Thorndale and William Dollarhide. Baltimore: Genealogical Publishing Co., 1993, paperback edition.

Unpuzzling Your Past. Emily Anne Croom. Cincinnati: Betterway Books, 2001. Census extraction forms 1790–1930.

Your Guide to the Federal Census. Kathleen W. Hinckley. Cincinnati: Betterway Books, 2002.

County and Courthouse Records

Many genealogists, after studying federal census records, turn to county records for research. Each state has its own county organization, but there are similarities that allow a general discussion of county (or New England town and Virginia independent city) records. Some states collect older county records into the state archives or historical society. Others leave old records in the counties.

Numerous, but not all, of these records have been microfilmed. In some places, filming stopped with records of about 1900; in others, records up to the mid-twentieth century are on film. Consult the Family History Library catalog for availability, and check with the state archives for interlibrary loan possibilities. Many such records have been abstracted and published, some even on the Internet. Use published resources as finding aids and clues, but follow up by looking at the original records at the holding facility or on microfilm. Regardless of where you find them, county records provide a gold mine of information for historians and genealogists.

Visiting county courthouses is a fascinating activity. Yet, some experiences in them are more fascinating than others. After visiting one courthouse that we placed at the head of our "pitiful" list, my husband and I developed this list of equipment (beyond the basic pencil and paper) for the intrepid genealogist who frequents these places. If you have done much courthouse research, you will understand why each item is listed; although the list is written somewhat tongue in cheek, it is not entirely "just for grins." If you have not visited courthouses, consider yourself forewarned.

1. Washable, perhaps dark, comfortable clothes and comfortable shoes. In many courthouses, you will be standing to look at the records. If you will be handling very old record books, carry a small clothes brush—for your clothes, not the books. However, I try not to wear shorts or jeans to courthouses; I prefer dressing up rather than down to look like the serious researcher that I am and not what courthouse personnel may consider "another bothersome genealogist."
2. Work gloves to protect your hands when moving stuff piled in front of basement shelves that may hold the exact book you need, if you could only get to it.
3. For basement work, hard hat, flashlight, dust mask, dust rag, perhaps flyswatter. In some courthouses, this is no joke.

4. Magnifying glass.
5. Quarters or other change for copy machines, snack machines, and parking meters.
6. Dollar bills for parking lots and copies of records.
7. Snack or lunch. Most of us don't work carefully or thoroughly when we're tired and hungry. Take a break for fresh air and a snack; ask about a snack room or nearby restaurant. The records will wait if you can, and some courthouses still close for the noon hour.
8. **Your best smile, tact, and patience.** Each courthouse office has its own rules and policies; we must be or appear to be cheerful about following them.
9. Your list of what you want to do at that courthouse, made out legibly ahead of time, and placed where you can get to it easily. Refer to it frequently.

Important

Most courthouse employees are pleasant and helpful, but most are not genealogists, cannot suggest a plan of research to you, and cannot research for you. We must take up a minimum of their time, for they have their own work to do. Thus, it is not necessary and sometimes not wise to tell them that you are a genealogist, and don't tell them your family history or ask for genealogical advice. Determine before you arrive what records you want to see, and ask where these records are kept. You can often browse among the records and find other items of interest. Some courthouses get so many visits and inquiries from genealogists that they are trying to limit accessibility and do not answer mail. Before you visit, call the office you need to visit to determine location and hours, especially for the day you want to do research.

Different counties hold their records in different offices, depending on state law, storage space, and the level of activity at the courthouse. If you cannot learn ahead of time where particular records are kept, ask when you arrive.

In New England, many of the records the rest of the country creates at county courthouses are created at the town hall. In Rhode Island, these records are all town hall records; in other New England states, some are town records and some are county records. Refer to books and articles about New England research, such as those listed on pages 187–190. One book helpful in locating New England records is Marcia D. Melnyk's *Genealogist's Handbook for New England Research* (Boston: New England Historic Genealogical Society, 1999, 4th edition, or later edition).

Likewise, Virginia's independent cities create and maintain their records. For a list of these cities and a brief history of the concept, see Carol McGinnis's *Virginia Genealogy: Sources & Resources* (Baltimore: Genealogical Publishing Co., 1993).

County Records on Microfilm

If you read the records on microfilm, you do not need to know in advance which office houses the records; the microfilm catalog will guide you to the film you need. To identify records to rent through a Family History Center, go to <www.familysearch.org> or the CD-ROM catalog, and choose Place Search. Here you have two choices. (1) Type in the name of your research state; then click on "Related Places," and choose the county name. (2) Type in the county name without the word *county*; type in the state name under "part of." These steps will get you to the list of materials available about that county, including records available on microfilm. Only the microprint materials circulate.

Using the microfiche catalog at a Family History Center, pull the fiche card that contains your state and county and read the all entries for the county. You may discover records you did not think to look for. The microfiche catalog is older than the CD-ROM and online versions and, thus, does not list newer materials but gives a good overview of county records.

Microfilm Source

Some state archives allow interlibrary loan of some county records on microfilm to libraries within the state; some participate in interlibrary loan out of state as well. Check state archives Web sites or call to ask about their interlibrary loan availability.

County Record Groups

County records can be arbitrarily divided into groups for discussion purposes. They are not necessarily cataloged or stored in these divisions. The following categories help group records and can act as a checklist for a search.

1. Vital records—birth, marriage, and death records. Divorce records are discussed under "Court Records" since they are generated as court records.
2. Records dealing with property, even if that is not the primary reason for the record's creation—land records, estate records (wills, inventories, settlements, etc.), property taxes, marks and brands, and slave records, since slaves were considered property. (See chapter nine for slave records.)
3. Court records—civil, criminal, justice of the peace, probate, and others. Records can include dockets, minutes, and case files. Cases of particular interest to genealogists are divorces and naturalizations. (See chapter eleven for naturalizations.)
4. Administrative and miscellaneous records—minutes of county commissioners (known in some places as county supervisors or police jury), county employee records, sheriff and jail records, professional licenses, business registration papers, automobile registration, voter registration, election returns, elected official bond books and records, records on roads and bridges, any other taxes or registrations, and other miscellaneous records.

VITAL RECORDS

Birth and death records have been kept in many forms. States began keeping these records at different times and have done so with varying consistency and with varying degrees of completeness. In many cases, the more recent the record, the more detailed is the information provided. In many areas, these events are recorded first at the town or city health department, and copies are sent to the county and state, or just to the state. Each state has its own procedures. States outside of New England were much slower than these in beginning civil registration of births and deaths.

In many states and on some USGenWeb sites and others are indexes to county or state vital records. Use these indexes when they are available, but let them guide you to the original record. Don't stop with the index if the original record is available, even on microfilm.

Connecticut set an example that genealogists wish all states had followed; they began creating vital records about the same time that each town was formed. A number of town records date from the seventeenth century, including Wethersfield from 1634 and Hartford and Saybrook from 1635. In the early twentieth century, Lucius Barnes Barbour led an effort to abstract and index the state's vital records from the first records in each town to about 1850 or a little later. Known as the Barbour Collection, these records are housed at the Connecticut State Library, and research libraries have microfilm copies. In 2002, Genealogical Publishing Company of Baltimore completed the publication of this valuable collection in fifty-five volumes, representing records of more than 125 towns. Be aware that some towns, including New Haven, are not included in the Barbour Collection, but New Haven birth, marriage, and death records through about 1901, with indexes, are available on microfilm through the Family History Library.

Birth Certificates

Bare basics appear in some early one-line registers: name, birth date, birthplace, gender and race of the child, and parents' names. This information is helpful, but some records contain much more detail. Although many forms request the mother's maiden name, it is not always given. Some certificates ask for the baby's full name, time of birth, and birth order within the family; name, nationality or birthplace, race, and age of each parent; length of parents' residence in the county or the local area; the specific street address of the family if in town; and the doctor's or midwife's name.

Warning

Birth or death records within one set of siblings may give different information on parents' names. Sometimes omissions or mistakes are due to haste in filing the record or lack of knowledge on the part of the doctor or other informant. Because of the discrepancies that often exist, it is advisable to collect these records for all the siblings. For older records, check for availability on microfilm and save money by making microprint copies from the film instead of ordering official copies from the county or state.

Figure 3-1, on page 87, illustrates a less-than-perfect birth certificate. All the information is provided except the baby's name. Comparing other birth certificates in the family with the 1920 and 1930 censuses has suggested which son's birth the certificate probably reports.

Delayed birth certificates are sometimes filed years after the event to clarify information, to add the baby's name, or to create a record that was not filed at the time of birth. These delayed certificates are usually filed in the county of birth, with the county probate court, county court clerk's office, or the office that normally records births and deaths. Documents allowed as evidence of the birth may vary from state to state, but basically they must confirm age and parentage. They may include affidavits from parents, relatives, or friends who were old enough to remember the birth of this particular child to these particular parents, a census record which states a person's age at a given date and parents' names, a school record which gives the birth date and/or parentage, an old voter registration card, or other such records. The registration office normally returns the supporting documents to the applicant but may record abstracts from the documents. Indexes may or may not include the delayed records.

Death Certificates

Like birth records, death certificates, can be sparse or full of details. The one-line entries of early records often show only basic information: name of decedent, death date and place, marital status, and cause of death. Some asked for no informant, next of kin, survivors, or parents' names.

Figure 3-2, on page 87, is the 1908 Minnesota death certificate for Mrs. Jennie L. Revell. The reported birth and death dates and the reported age at death agree with each other. In addition to birthplace and parents' names and birthplaces, this preprinted form called for other data valuable to genealogists, including the decedent's age at first marriage (Jennie was nineteen), the number of children born to that person (three), and how many of the children were living (one). Later death certificates in the same state did not request that information but asked for the name of the spouse. For Jennie Revell's certificate, the informant (her husband) could not supply her mother's name, and the form asked only for the

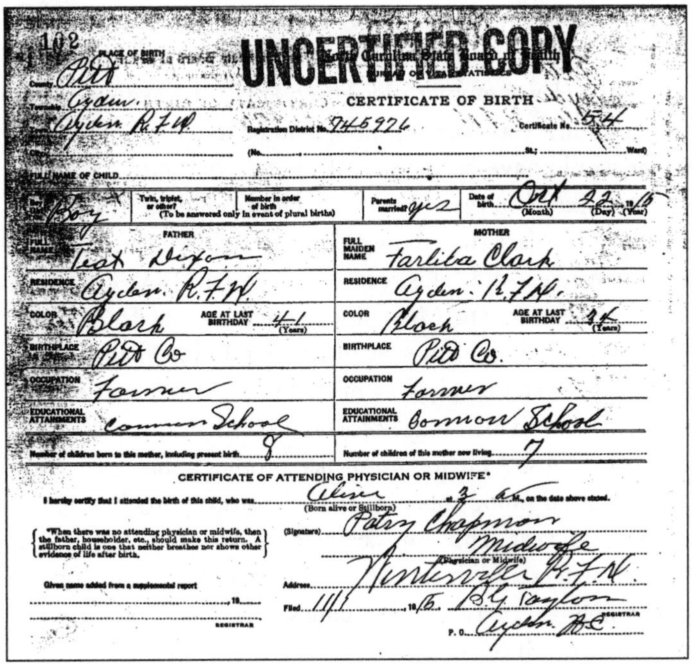

UNCERTIFIED COPY

CERTIFICATE OF BIRTH

County: Pitt
Township: Aydan
Ayden R.F.D.
Registration District No. 745976
Certificate No. 54

Sex: Boy
Parents married? yes
Date of birth: Oct 22 1915

FATHER
Full name: Teat Dixon
Residence: Ayden R.F.D.
Color: Black
Age at last birthday: 41 (Years)
Birthplace: Pitt Co
Occupation: Farmer
Educational attainments: common School
Number of children born to this mother, including present birth: 8

MOTHER
Full maiden name: Farlita Clark
Residence: Ayden R.F.D.
Color: Black
Age at last birthday: 36 (Years)
Birthplace: Pitt Co.
Occupation: Farmer
Educational attainments: Common School
Number of children of this mother now living: 7

CERTIFICATE OF ATTENDING PHYSICIAN OR MIDWIFE*

I hereby certify that I attended the birth of this child, who was Alive (Born alive or Stillborn) at 3 a.m., on the date above stated.

*When there was no attending physician or midwife, then the father, householder, etc., should make this return. A stillborn child is one that neither breathes nor shows other evidence of life after birth.

(Signature) Patsy Chapman
Midwife
(Physician or Midwife)
Address: Winterville R.F.D.

Given name added from a supplemental report ..., 19...

Filed 11/1, 1915. R.G. Taylor
Registrar
P.O. Ayden N.C.

Figure 3-1 Birth certificate for unnamed Dixon son, 22 October 1915, certificate 54, Pitt County, North Carolina, Register of Deeds-Vital Statistics, Courthouse, Greenville.

state or country of birth, nothing more specific. Forms vary from time to time and state to state but usually contain information or clues of value.

Death records are secondhand sources of birth information. As the researcher, therefore, you must be alert to the possibility that birth date, birthplace, or parents' names and birthplaces may be incorrect; you should corroborate this information with other sources whenever possible. Comparing death certificates of siblings may or may not clear up discrepancies or omissions in information about parents. However, other sources will have to be used to provide comparative information on the birth of the deceased. One case illustrates the process.

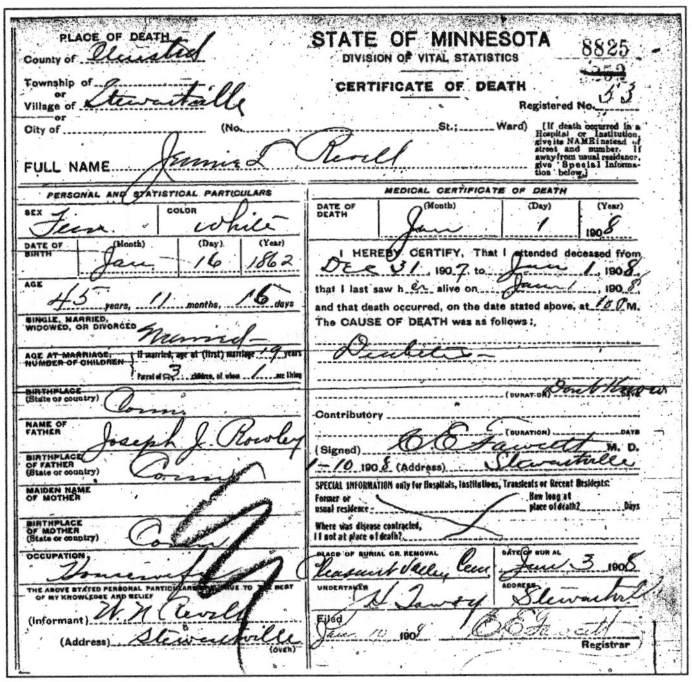

PLACE OF DEATH
County of Olmsted
Township of ... or Village of Stewartville or City of ... (No. ... St.; ... Ward) [If death occurred in a Hospital or Institution, give its NAME instead of street and number. If away from usual residence, give Special Information below.]

STATE OF MINNESOTA
DIVISION OF VITAL STATISTICS
CERTIFICATE OF DEATH
8825
Registered No. 53

FULL NAME Jennie L. Revell

PERSONAL AND STATISTICAL PARTICULARS
Sex: Fem.
Color: white
Date of birth: Jan (Month) 16 (Day) 1862 (Year)
Age: 45 years, 11 months, 16 days
Single, married, widowed, or divorced: Married
Age at marriage, number of children: If married, age at (first) marriage 19 years; Parent of 3 children, of whom 1 are living
Birthplace (State or country): Conn.
Name of father: Joseph J. Rowley
Birthplace of father (State or country): Conn
Maiden name of mother: [illegible]
Birthplace of mother (State or country): Conn
Occupation: Housewife
The above stated personal particulars are true to the best of my knowledge and belief
(Informant) W. H. Revell
(Address) Stewartville
(OVER)

MEDICAL CERTIFICATE OF DEATH
Date of death: Jan (Month) 1 (Day) 1908 (Year)
I HEREBY CERTIFY, That I attended deceased from Dec 31, 1907 to Jan 1, 1908, that I last saw her alive on Jan 1, 1908 and that death occurred, on the date stated above, at 10 a.M.
The CAUSE OF DEATH was as follows:
Diabetes
(Duration) Don't know
Contributory ... (Duration) ... days
(Signed) C. E. Fawcett M. D.
1-10, 1908 (Address) Stewartville
SPECIAL INFORMATION only for Hospitals, Institutions, Transients or Recent Residents:
Former or usual residence: ... How long at place of death? ... Days
Where was disease contracted, if not at place of death?
Place of burial or removal: Pleasant Valley Cem.
Date of burial: Jan 3 1908
Undertaker: H. Lawry
Address: Stewartville
Filed Jan 10 1908 C. E. Fawcett
Registrar

Figure 3-2 Death certificate of Jennie L. Revell, January 1908, Olmsted County, Minnesota, certificate 8825, Minnesota Division of Vital Statistics, St. Paul.

On the death certificate for Mississippi-born Mrs. Mary Liles, her son reported her birth date as 2 February 1863. At her death in January 1929, one week before her next birthday, she was said to be sixty-seven years and eleven months old. This points out one discrepancy on the certificate itself. If the reported age was correct, she would have turned sixty-eight the next week; thus her birth year would have been 1861. If the reported birth date was correct, she would have actually been sixty-five years and eleven months old when she died.

However, the larger discrepancy is the fact that she was enumerated with her parents and siblings in the 1860 census as a five-year-old. This record indicates an 1855 birth year if the age and the February date were correct. The Mississippi state census of 1866 places her in the "under-ten" category and suggests a birth year in or after 1856. These earliest two records seem to support each other. The family was missed in the 1870 census. The 1880 census reported her age as twenty-one, which suggests an 1859 birth year and conflicts with the more consistently documented 1859 birth date of her brother John. So far, no record of her 1900 census entry has been found, but the 1910 census reports her age as fifty-three, which indicates an 1857 birth year. Thus, the death certificate only complicated an already confused situation, which suggests birth years from 1855 to 1863. Based on the 1860s censuses and data about her siblings, an 1854–1858 date seems most likely, but the jury is still out. The point remains that death certificates may be, but are not always, accurate. Researchers need to corroborate the information with data from other sources, including records of siblings.

Reminder

Don't forget the 1850–1880 mortality schedules as evidence of deaths during census year. While not complete, they are the only records of many deaths.

FAMILY SECRET UNCOVERED

Family "memory" was that John Revell's third wife, Elizabeth, of Hamilton County, Nebraska, died before 1885. I realized this was in error when I discovered an entry in the 1885 census for John, Elizabeth, and the children. Two children had been born since the 1880 census, and Elizabeth was listed as "insane." While researching at the Nebraska State Historical Society in Lincoln in 2000, I used the card index to death records, looking for other members of the Revell family. One card indicated a death record for an Elizabeth Revell in 1931. Who was this? She turned out to be John's wife, who did not die in the 1880s but in 1931 in the Lincoln State Hospital; she was ninety-four years old. Finding the death certificate cleared up the question of why the older generations never spoke of Elizabeth but opened new questions for research. *Pat (Palmer) Metcalfe*

Finding Vital Records

Family papers often contain vital records or alternate sources of the information: family Bibles, obituaries, certificates of all kinds, letters, diaries, scrapbooks, and funeral programs and notices. Tombstones and religious records may also furnish this information.

In most states, recent birth and death registrations are centralized at the state bureau or division of vital records, vital statistics, or health; each state is organized uniquely. Privacy laws may affect accessibility, and the regulations change. A number of states now limit requests for vital record copies to the individual or a parent, child, spouse, sibling, or legal representative; some allow those with a legitimate and legal (meaning not illegal) reason to get copies for genealogical purposes. Web sites such as <www.vitalrec.com>, <www.usavital.com>, and the federal Center for Disease Control site listed on page 89 try to keep relatively current the information about regulations for getting copies. When in doubt, check the Web site of, or inquire of, the state archives, vital statistics office, or county holding the records you need.

When ordering copies, be prepared to wait from a week to six months. If you have a choice, try the town or county for copies and use the state as a last resort. Of course, fees for copies and searches vary from state to state. Genealogists find that copy requests by mail sometimes return with (1) information that no record was found, even when the researcher knows a record was created or (2) a record for a different individual who does not meet the requested criteria of name, date, place, etc. Sometimes better results occur when you go in person to the holding institution, hire someone who can go in person, or identify the record by certificate number or volume and page number so that you can request a specific document.

Microfilm Source

You may be able to identify or get copies of records on microfilm. Check the Family History Library catalog, other library catalogs, and the holding institutions for availability of indexes, transcriptions, or microfilmed original records. (A number of indexes are published or online.) Remember, abstracts or transcriptions may contain errors; even copies the towns and counties sent to the state may contain errors. Try to see or get a copy of the original record, or at least a first-generation copy.

References to help you find the records you need include these:

- *International Vital Records Handbook*, by Thomas J. Kemp. Baltimore: Genealogical Publishing Co., 2000 or later edition. Includes state by state listing of agency and address, cost, limitations or restrictions, and the necessary forms, which may be photocopied.
- *Where to Write for Vital Records: Births, Deaths, Marriages, and Divorces.* Hyattsville, Md.: U.S. Department of Health and Human Services, Public Health Service, 1999 or later edition. Gives agency, address, and availability of records for states and territories as well as records of citizens born "on the high seas" or in foreign countries. At this writing, online access to this publication is through the Center for Disease Control Web site at <www.cdc.gov/nchs/howto/w2w/w2welcom.htm>.
- Online: <www.vitalrec.com>; <www.usavital.com>; Web sites of state archives and vital statistics offices; USGenWeb pages for the county or state; links from Cyndi's List <www.cyndislist.com>.
- Recent books and articles on research in each state (see page 186).
- *Ancestry's Red Book: American State, County & Town Sources*, Alice Eichholz, ed. Salt Lake City: Ancestry, 3d ed. to be released in 2004. Contains state-by-state description of records of many kinds, including vital records.

Birth and death records, especially from the nineteenth century, are sometimes available for researchers at county courthouses or city halls. Some cities initiated birth and death registration before their states did and continue to maintain their own records. In a number of cities, births and deaths that occur within city limits are registered with the city rather than the county.

The list below is a general guideline for the beginning dates of most statewide civil birth and death registrations, with copies (sometimes originals) being filed at the state vital statistics or health department. Many legislatures passed the registration law in the year listed, but the population did not always comply in large numbers until later—sometimes twenty years later. For earlier records, check with the county clerk, county or town vital records office, and the state archives. A number of states periodically transfer state-held records to the state archives.

BEGINNING OF STATEWIDE VITAL REGISTRATION

State	Year	Notes
Alabama	1908	Birth records closed for 125 years and death records closed for 25 years except to immediate family or with the family's written permission.
Alaska	1890	Birth records closed 100 years except to the individual or parents.
	1912	Death records closed for 50 years.
Arizona	1909	
Arkansas	1914	Access limited to family members.
California	1905	From July 1905. For birth record copies, you must supply most of the information you are looking for—exact name, birthplace, date of birth, parents' full names—plus your reason for wanting the copy and your relationship to the named person.
Colorado	1910	Births.
	1900	Deaths.
Connecticut	1897	State-level registration; some town clerks began registering these events before 1650.
Delaware	c. 1913	Birth records closed 72 years; death records, 40 years.
District of Columbia	1874	Births.
	1855	Deaths.
Florida	1917	Copies of birth certificates available to the individual or parents or their legal representatives; check city health departments.
Georgia	1919	Copies of birth records limited to individual or immediate family member who can supply full name of individual and parents, birthplace, birth date, and reason for the request; check major cities for earlier records.
Hawaii	1853	
Idaho	1911	County recorder may have 1870–1911 records.
Illinois	1916	
Indiana	1907	Births.
	1900	Deaths.
Iowa	1880	County or state copies by mail for those who can demonstrate relationship to the individual and who can supply full name of individual and parents, birth date and birthplace; in person in the county clerk's offices, researchers can usually get copies.
Kansas	1911	Restrictions on access to death records (relationship to deceased, stated reason for the request, and ID).
Kentucky	1852	First attempt lasted about a decade, but some counties continued registration in the 1870s and 1890s. For details on what is available for each county, see *Inventory of Kentucky Birth, Marriage, and Death Records, 1852–1910*, by Jeffrey Michael Duff, comp., rev. ed. (Frankfort, Ky.: Archives Branch, Public Records Division, Dept. for Libraries and Archives, 1982.
	1911	Post-1911 records available from the state vital statistics office.
Louisiana	1914	Early-twentieth-century records at state archives; early New Orleans records at state archives (births from 1790, deaths from 1804).
Maine	1892	Original certificates to state vital statistics board; town clerks kept these records from the earliest years, most from the eighteenth century; state archives holds pre-1923 records.
Maryland	1898	City of Baltimore held its own records until 1975.
Massachusetts	1600s	From about 1841, town clerks were to begin sending copies to the secretary of the commonwealth (state); compliance from some was slow; from 1896, copies were sent to state registry of vital records, but now these records are transferred to state archives every five years; at this writing, pre-1911 records are in the state archives; most pre-1850 records are published.

Michigan	1867	
Minnesota	1900	Statewide births at state bureau of health; some counties and towns have records from the 1870s; some regulations on access.
	1908	Statewide deaths at state bureau of health; some regulations on access.
Mississippi	1912	
Missouri	1909	Pre–August 1909 records at county clerk's office or state archives; state records from 1910 forward available to immediate family.
Montana	late 1907	Birth records less than 30 years old accessible only to individual, parent, spouse, or child.
Nebraska	late 1904	County clerks may have early-1904 and pre-1904 records.
Nevada	1911	County recorders may have pre–July 1911 records.
New Hampshire	1640	Town clerk's offices; many published.
	1883	State bureau of vital records began.
New Jersey	1848	Scattered pre–May 1848 records exist; state archives holds 1848–1878; post-1878 records are at state health department. For copies, you must supply much of the information you are looking for—exact full name, place of birth (including hospital name), date, mother's maiden name—and you must be the individual or parent, child, spouse, sibling, or legal representative; and you must supply ID, and state reason and relationship in the request.
New Mexico	1920	
New York	1881	Births; genealogy copies available after 75 years, if individual is deceased.
	1880	Deaths; genealogy copies available after 50 years.
North Carolina	1913	State archives holds death records prior to 1955.
North Dakota	1923	Division of vital records also holds some records from earlier attempt in 1890s and some earlier records from 1870s and 1880s.
Ohio	1908	Law of 20 December 1908; at this writing, death records 1908–1944 are at state archives, Ohio Historical Society; pre-1908 records may be at state archives or county probate court.
Oklahoma	1908	Law of October 1908; birth certificate copies only to individual or parent.
Oregon	1903	Birth records closed 100 years; death records, 50 years.
Pennsylvania	1906	Pre-1906 records may be at register of wills, orphans court in the county; some city records available from earlier years.
Rhode Island	1853	Town records dating from the town's settlement are not complete, but those to 1850 are transcribed and published: *Vital Record of Rhode Island 1636–1850*, 21 vols., by James N. Arnold, comp. (Reprint, Boston: New England Historic Genealogical Society, 1980s); 1850–1853 records in town clerk's office; for post–1853 records, state archives holds birth records more than 100 years old, and death records more than 50 years old.
South Carolina	1915	
South Dakota	1905	Law of July 1905.
Tennessee	1914	Records of previous attempt, 1908–1912, at county or at state archives; major cities have earlier records; archives gets records more than 50 years old.
Texas	1903	Copies of birth certificates available after 50 years; death certificates, after 25 years; for more recent records, immediate family or legal representative may obtain copies, but must provide full name of subject, reason for request, and relationship.
Utah	1905	For earlier records, try county clerk's office; bureau of vital records holds death records 50 years before transferring them to state archives.

continued

Vermont	1857	Records kept in the towns; some have much earlier records; Public Records Division has copies more than 5 years old.
Virginia	1853	First law provided registration through 1896; some locales continued registration; these records are at the state archives, also on microfilm, and many have been published. Death records public after 50 years; birth records, after 100 years.
	1912	Second law providing for registration.
Washington	1891	From 1897 to law of 1 July 1907, requiring registration at state level, registration was a county function; many pre-1907 records are microfilmed; copies of post-1907 records can be obtained from state vital records office by providing fairly complete information.
West Virginia	1917	Records prior to 1917 may be at county clerk's office; before statehood in 1863, counties were under Virginia law, which provided for vital registration in 1853; many continued such registration after 1863, to or beyond 1900; state archives has many pre-1916 delayed birth records and twentieth-century death records.
Wisconsin	1907	Law of October 1907 required registration because 1852 and 1878 attempts got less than full compliance; existing pre-1907 records are usually at office of county register of deeds and/or state archives; microfiche indexes available for purchase; Web site for Department of Health and Family Services <www.dhfs.state.wi.us/vitalrecords/genereq.htm#G4> has list of all counties and the dates of their earliest filed vital records.
Wyoming	1909	Law of July 1909.

MARRIAGE RECORDS

Marriage records are usually found in county courthouses or town halls, with copies often in the state library, archives, or historical society. In some states, more recent records are also centralized in the state vital statistics or vital records office, but the county (the town in New England or independent incorporated town or city in Virginia) is the place where the license is issued and the record generated. The office in the county courthouse that keeps the records varies from county clerk to probate clerk, circuit court clerk, register of deeds, or town clerk. The vital statistics guides listed on page 89 and research guides to your state(s) of interest can give you the specific information you need to find marriage records. Most states required marriage registration before they required birth and death registration; many began registering marriages as soon as the county or town was organized.

Kinds of Marriage Records

Marriage records come in many varieties, some more helpful than others. One form, for which few records survive is marriage by banns, a practice dating back to the thirteenth-century Catholic Church. Until the mid-nineteenth century, especially in out-of-the-way rural areas where access to the county courthouse for a bond or license was difficult, couples in some colonies or states could post for three consecutive weeks in a public place, such as the church, their intent to marry. The clergymen who celebrated such marriages were supposed to record the events in the church register, but many did not. Sometimes, a civil official such as a justice of the peace was allowed to perform these weddings.

Until the late nineteenth century in many areas, grooms had to sign a bond at the county courthouse before being granted license to marry. The wording may have differed, but the intent was the same—ensuring that no lawful cause existed to prohibit a legal marriage. Usually this meant that neither party was underage and trying to marry without parental permission, and that neither party was already married to someone else. In some states, another requirement was that the bride be a resident of the county in which the bond was made. Although some bonds were handwritten, Figure 3-3, below, shows a 1789 bond on a preprinted form from Cumberland County, Virginia. The signatures are those of the groom and the surety, often the father, brother, or other relative of the bride.

Once the bond was executed, the couple received the marriage license, which they presented to the authorized clergyman or civil official who performed the marriage ceremony. State law often required that the wedding take place in the same county where the license was obtained. According to one family's tradition, a Tennessee couple married twice in the same day because the minister realized after the wedding that it had taken place just across the county line. Thus, he moved the wedding party back to the county where the license was issued and went through the ceremony a second time.

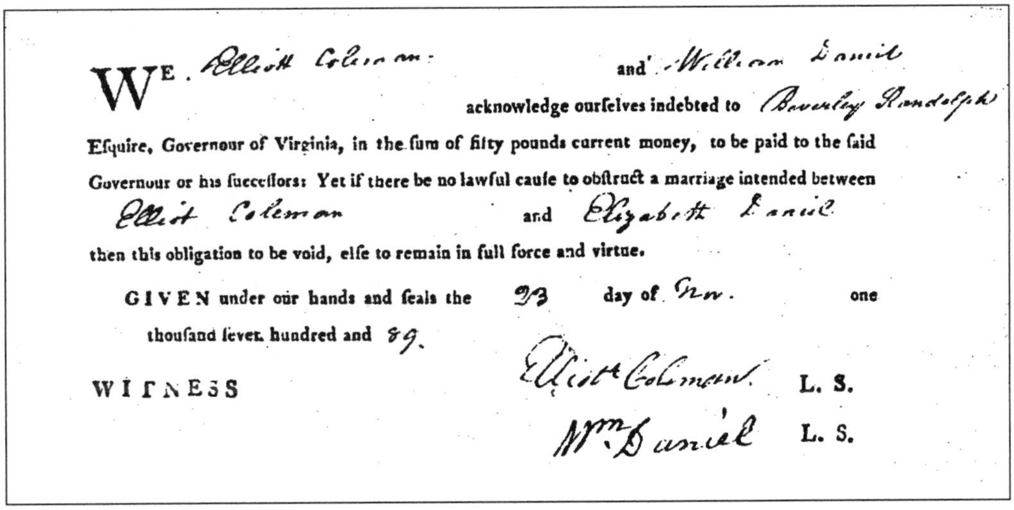
WE. Elliott Coleman and William Daniel acknowledge ourſelves indebted to Beverley Randolph Eſquire, Governour of Virginia, in the ſum of fifty pounds current money, to be paid to the ſaid Governour or his ſucceſſors: Yet if there be no lawful cauſe to obſtruct a marriage intended between Elliott Coleman and Elizabeth Daniel then this obligation to be void, elſe to remain in full force and virtue.

GIVEN under our hands and ſeals the 23 day of Nov. one thouſand ſeven hundred and 89.

WITNESS

Elliott Coleman L. S.

Wm. Daniel L. S.

Figure 3-3 Marriage bond for Elliott Coleman, Cumberland County, Virginia, file for 1789, no. 32, Library of Virginia, Richmond, photocopy of original.

Eventually, states dropped the bond as a separate step in the process, and the license became the sole permission to marry. At some point after the ceremony, the clergyman or authorized civil official—usually justice of the peace, county judge, or district judge—was supposed to complete his portion of the license, giving the date and place of marriage; sign his name to the document; and return it to the courthouse for filing and the conclusion of the process. If the clergyman identified his denomination or faith, that information is a clue to the possible religious preference of the bride or groom, or both.

Some clergymen were more diligent than others about returning the licenses, doing so in a timely fashion, while some waited weeks or months. In fact, some county marriage registers show the license being taken out but never returned and filed. Such an omission could mean either that the couple never married or that the minister never filed his return. In these cases, the genealogist must seek other confirmation of the marriage, or evidence that it did not take place.

Figure 3-4, on page 95, shows the 1903 New York City marriage record for Thomas W. Julian and Nora Herrington. Not only does the record give the wedding date and the names of the bride and groom, witnesses, and the clergyman, but it also provides the ages of the bride and groom, their parents' names, and the couple's places of birth. In this case, both were immigrants to the United States: the groom from Montreal, Canada, and the bride from County Cork, Ireland. Although the document lists the groom's mother simply as "Mary," it provides the bride's mother's maiden name: Mary Sullivan.

In addition to marriage licenses and returns, the marriage registers and original license files may contain related records, such as affidavits of the couple's ages or permission from

SOME ABBREVIATIONS USED ON MARRIAGE LICENSES

Men who performed marriages often used abbreviations to identify their credentials or affiliation. Common ones include these:

AME	African Methodist Episcopal
JCC	judge of the county court, circuit court
JP	justice of the peace
M of ME	minister of the Methodist Episcopal Church
MES, MEN	Methodist Episcopal Church South, or North. "*South*" and "*North*" were often written out.
MG	minister of the gospel
OMG	ordained minister of the gospel
PE	Protestant Episcopal Church
VDM	Latin *Verbi Domini Ministerium*, minister of the Word of God

a parent or guardian, especially for an underage person to marry. These documents may be filed with the returned license or in the marriage register.

One marriage license in the Gonzales County, Texas, County Clerk's office had no minister's return, but it provided an explanation. Young Martin V. McAnelly had obtained a marriage license on 11 November 1858 from the county clerk, F. Chenault. Two days later Martin wrote the following note on the back of the license and sent it back:

> November the 13 1858
> Mr Chenault Dear Sur I am sorry to inform you that I am defeated in my match [smeared through] weddin the girl got contrary I suppose that tha is sumthing els in [unreadable] but I am veary thankful to you for your kiendness and I hope that it is all right with us vary resspectfully [*sic*] yours M.W. McAnelly

A year and ten days later, Martin married a different girl in a neighboring county.

Most states had in the past and still have age requirements for marriage; even within one state, these requirements sometimes changed over time. In 1884, Richard Massie of Adair County, Kentucky, wrote a note authorizing the county clerk to issue a marriage license for his eighteen-year-old daughter, Jennie Massie, to marry Frank Vaughn. However, in 1897, George McNeil of Guadalupe County, Texas, filed an affidavit that he was at least twenty-one and his intended bride, Miss Carrie Mulky, was at least eighteen, the legal ages for marriage in Texas at the time. Figure 3-5, on page 96, shows two other notes attached to the same Texas county's marriage register. In one, Thomas Tyler's authority and point of view are clear: no one was to marry his fourteen-year-old daughter, Fannie. Apparently he believed someone entertained notions of marrying her, and he moved in to forestall any such efforts. The other note, from Mollie A. Sansom, tells the county clerk that her sister and the intended bride, Nancy A. Dollery, was of age. Of additional interest to genealogists is the mention that Nancy lived with her sister because, apparently, both their parents had died. With the

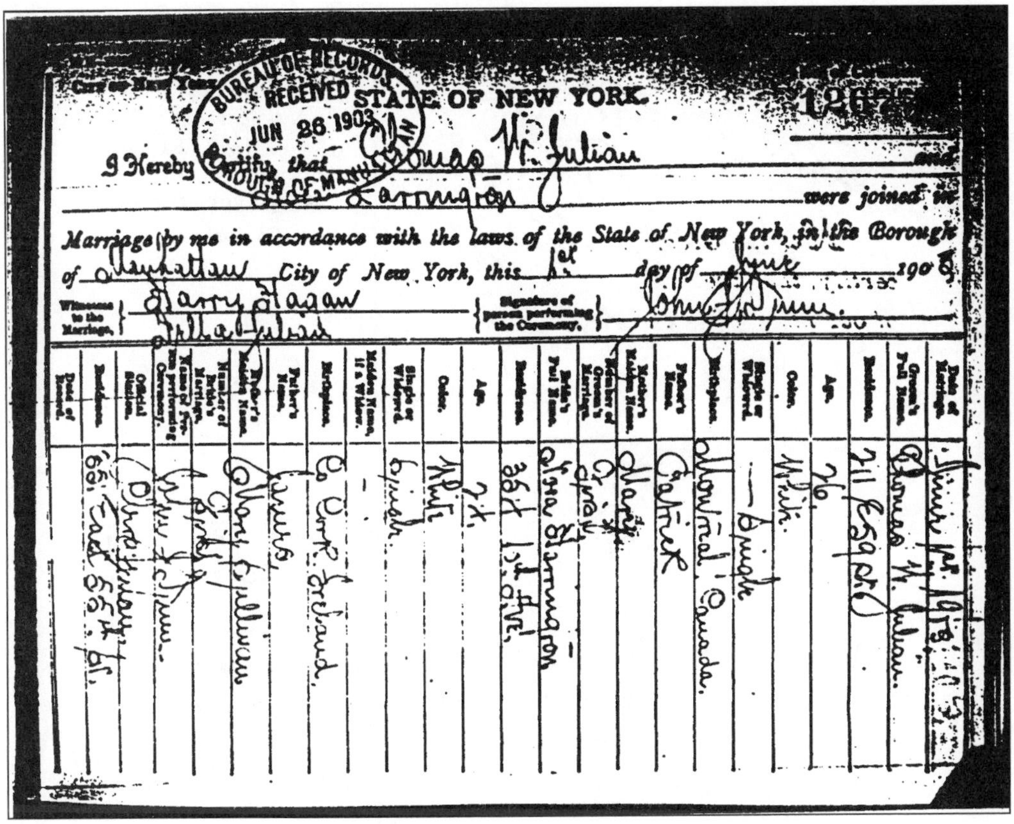
BUREAU OF RECORDS RECEIVED JUN 26 1903 BOROUGH OF MANHATTAN

STATE OF NEW YORK.

I Hereby Certify that Thomas W. Julian and Nora Harrington were joined in Marriage by me in accordance with the laws of the State of New York, in the Borough of Manhattan City of New York, this 1st day of June 1903.

Figure 3-4 Marriage license of Thomas W. Julian and Nora Harrington, certificate 12677, Manhattan Bureau of Records, "Manhattan Marriage Records, 1866–1937," Certificates 12001–13000 (1903), FHL microfilm 1570980.

advantage of readily available genealogical sources, it is easy to confirm part of the note in the 1880 census in a neighboring county where the two sisters and their two brothers lived with their parents, Sarah C. and David Dollery. The note and the census narrow the search for the parents' death dates and places.

Marriage and Death Notices in Other Sources

Sometimes, genealogists find evidence of births, marriages, and deaths in other records, especially military pension application files, homestead files, Indian tribal enrollment files, and newspapers. For example, when the widow Chig-ah-me-qua Mash-Kaw of Pent Water, Oceana County, Michigan applied in 1864 for a pension based on the service of her deceased husband, James Mash-Kaw, she had to supply evidence of their marriage. The justice of the peace who had married them made a handwritten copy of the record on file at the county clerk's office to include with her application. That record affirmed that they married on 6 August 1858 in the presence of two named witnesses and gave James's Indian name as Kah-kuh-ge-wa Mash-Kaw. Each piece of information becomes helpful as clues for further research. In some cases, the county record no longer exists; in others, descendants do not know where the marriage took place until they locate such a file.

Many marriage and death notices abstracted from newspapers have been published in genealogical journals and books. (Nineteenth-century newspapers carried very few birth announcements.) The following are examples of the numerous abstracts published as books. Use WorldCat (see page 3) and library catalogs to identify others from your ancestral areas.

Printed Source

Abstracts of Marriages and Deaths and Other Articles of Interest in the Newspapers of Frederick and Montgomery Counties, Maryland From 1831–1840, by L. Tilden Moore. Bowie, Md.: Heritage Books, 1991.

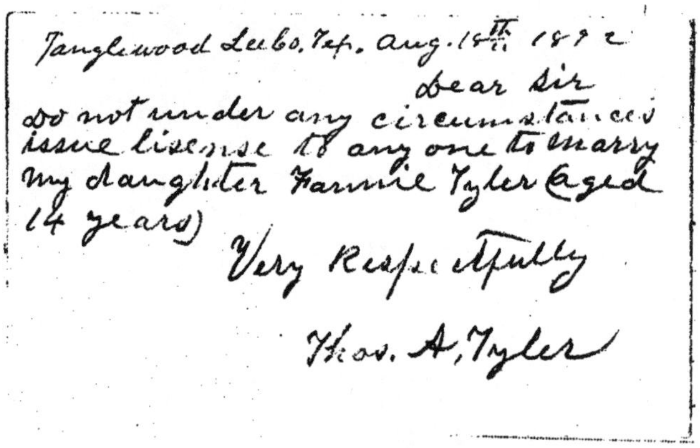
Tanglewood Lee Co. Tex. Aug. 18th 1892
Dear Sir
do not under any circumstances
issue lisense to any one to marry
my daughter Fannie Tyler (aged
14 years)
Very Respectfully
Thos. A. Tyler

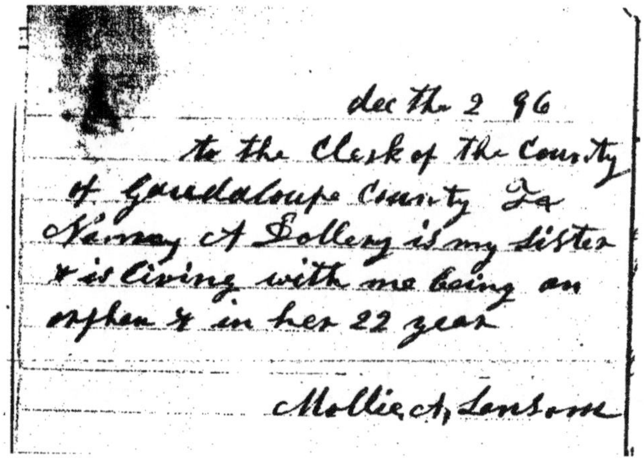
dec th 2 96
to the Clerk of the County
of Guadaloupe County Tx
Nancy A Solley is my sister
& is living with me being an
orphan & in her 22 year
Mollie A. Sansom

Figure 3-5 Notes added to marriage license book, Guadalupe County, Texas, Tyler note from Vol. 3:10 (August 1892), Sansom note from Vol. 4:72 (December 1896), FHL microfilm 1035074.

Births, Marriages and Deaths From "The Marin Journal," San Rafael, Marin County, California, January 2, 1873 to December 30, 1880, by Carolyn Schwab. Novato, Calif.: Marin County Genealogical Society, 1998.

Clark County, Ohio Newspaper Abstracts, by Anne Burgstaller Snodgrass. Springfield, Ohio: Clark County Genealogical Society, 1984–1986.

Delaware Genealogical Abstracts From Newspapers, by Mary Fallon Richards, John C. Richards, and Carolina M. Sparks. Wilmington: Delaware Genealogical Society, 1995.

Extracts From Havensville, Ks. Newspapers: Obituaries, Marriages and Miscellaneous Stuff, by Kay F. Sellers. Topeka, Kans.: K. Sellers, 1999.

Kent County, Michigan: Marriage and Death Newspaper Notices . . ., by Marguerite Novy Lambert and James N. Jackson. Detroit: Detroit Society for Genealogical Research, 2001.

Marriage and Death Notices From the Southern Christian Advocate . . ., by Brent Holcomb. Easley, S.C.: Southern Historical Press, 1979.

Marriage and Death Notices From Wilmington, North Carolina Newspapers, February 1847–December 1850, by Helen Moore Sammons. Wilmington, N.C.: Old New Hanover Genealogical Society, 1995.

Marriage and Obituaries From Early Georgia Newspapers, by Folks Huxford. Easley, S.C.: Southern Historical Press, 1989.

Marriage Notices From Washington County, New York, Newspapers, 1799–1880, by Mary Smith Jackson. Bowie, Md.: Heritage Books, 1995.

LOOSE MARRIAGE CONSENTS IDENTIFY A FAMILY

Passports of Southeastern Pioneers, 1770–1823, by Dorothy Williams Potter, contains an entry on page 292 from 23 November 1811 that ordered passports prepared for three families to travel through the Indian Nations to the Western Country—in this case, Louisiana. One family was Abner Glover, his wife, and seven children, from Edisto District, South Carolina. Identifying unnamed family members such as these, especially before the 1850 census, often requires research in numerous sources to find pieces of the family puzzle. In this case, the loose marriage consents at the St. Helena Parish, Louisiana, courthouse furnished the identities for most, if not all, of the 1811 travelers. (These consents are unbound documents, not part of a marriage record book; they are stored in boxes in a vault.)

On 23 November 1814, exactly three years after the passport application, Abner Glover consented for his daughter Sally to marry John Sullivan; the witness, William Glover, has been shown in further research to be a son of Abner Glover. On 13 June 1816, Abner Glover and his wife, Sary, gave consent for their daughter Mary to marry John Albritton. Then, Patrick Glover in February 1825 certified that his father, Abner Glover, was willing for his daughter Delila to marry William Zachary. These three documents identified five of Abner's seven children and his wife, who may or may not have been the mother of all seven children.

Abner's wife, Sary, apparently died between 1816 and 1826, and he remarried. In May 1826, Abner and his wife, Elizabeth, agreed that Isaac Zachary could marry "our daughter" Mary. The cover of the document first called her Mary Dawson, with the name Glover written below. This record suggests that Abner married a widow, Elizabeth Dawson, who had a daughter, Mary, by her previous husband.

The last two Glover siblings listed in the marriage consents were Rebecca and Ann. Abner consented for Rebecca to marry Abraham Pennington, and the couple's wedding took place on 27 November 1828. Unless Rebecca married under the age of seventeen, she was one of the 1811 travelers and married exactly seventeen years after the family's journey west began. In addition, her 1850 census record reports her birthplace as South Carolina.

The final daughter, Ann, married Jacob Pennington, with her father's consent, in October 1832, twenty-one years after the family's migration. Because she and Jacob have not yet been identified in succeeding census records, it is not clear when or where Ann was born. Abner's household in the 1820 census shows a female under ten who could well have been Ann, but the record, of course, does not identify names, specific ages, or birthplaces. Thus, we do not know yet whether Ann was the seventh child moving west with the family. Nevertheless, the marriage consents were a gold mine of information in identifying this family. *Charlene Wilson*

Marriages and Deaths From the Newspapers of Lancaster County, Pennsylvania, by F. Edward Wright. Westminster, Md.: Family Line Publications, 1988.

Tennessee Newspaper Extracts and Abstracts: Marriage, Death, and Other Items of Genealogical/Historical Interest: The Knoxville Press, by Pollyanna Creekmore. Knoxville: Clinchdale Press, 1995.

LAND AND PROPERTY RECORDS

Records that give information about property make up a sizable portion of any courthouse collection. People record evidence of their property, pay taxes on property, give away property, buy and sell property, and fight over property. Much of this property is land and the buildings on it but may also include livestock, crops, and natural resources. In slaveholding areas before 1865, property included slaves. **The genealogical importance of property records is tremendous, for they are much more than just evidence of property and residence.** They often contain information on clusters of relatives living in the area and provide valuable proof of relationships.

Important

Earmarks and/or brands on livestock may not provide much more genealogical information than evidence that a particular ancestor was in a given county at a given time, but the records are interesting bits of history. Besides in some deed books, they may be found in court minutes or separate books reserved for such registration. In the court minutes of Davidson County, Tennessee, on "Wensday," 7 January 1784, James Shaw recorded his stock earmarks and his brand, *IS*, created from his initials. (In his era, the letters *I* and *J* were often written the same.)

TAX RECORDS

Tax rolls are records of both real (land) and personal property on which the state, county, and/or city accessed taxes. Annual property taxes were sometimes combined with poll taxes (head taxes) in county records, and many counties no longer keep their tax records beyond a certain number of years. "Old tax records" in some counties means the 1960s or 1970s. In some cases, the older records have been microfilmed and placed at the state archives or historical society. Other counties have stashed their nineteenth-century tax books in old jails and basement storage areas that are impossible to reach. Many tax rolls are available on microfilm through the Family History Library.

Of course, not all residents of the county owned taxable property; therefore, not all residents are listed on the property tax rolls. However, these assessment lists give a good, if not complete, picture of residents and their taxable wealth. They also are valuable in identifying sons as they reached taxable age and were added to the list of family members who were present in a given year. Absence from the rolls may indicate that someone had died, moved away, had no taxable property, or for some reason was exempt from taxes.

Women were rarely listed as taxpayers unless they were widows or were unmarried. Laws in most states, some even into the twentieth century, did not allow married women to own property in their own name; thus, they were not taxpayers. However, widows who had taxable men in their household were sometimes listed on the rolls, as were women who were administrators or heirs of an estate or guardians of minors, even if a man was acting as their agent on the rolls.

Taxpayers who were guardians for others or were administrators or executors of estates were responsible for paying any taxes owed by the estates they oversaw. In 1841 and 1842 in Putnam County, Georgia, W.W. Arnold paid tax as guardian for William P., Sarah D., and Jno. E. Gholson, minors. By 1846, Arnold was guardian for William P. and John E. Gholson. The genealogist must ask (1) whether Arnold was related to the Gholson minors and what documents might provide more information and (2) what happened to Sarah D. Gholson between 1842 and 1846 (married? died? no longer a minor? moved?).

If a taxpayer, for various personal reasons, had an "agent" paying his tax, the genealogist needs to see a red flag waving. For example, in 1838, why was Elmore Callaway paying tax as agent for Joseph Mason and John Trippe paying tax as agent of William F. Trippe? The two with the same surname were likely related. The others may have been relatives, close friends, or business partners. The researcher may never learn exactly why Callaway was paying Mason's tax; Mason may have been out of the county or needed help in paying. Nevertheless, the connection of the names in the tax rolls is a clue that demands further investigation.

Defaulters or delinquent taxpayers were often listed at the end of the district or county list. Some states also attached a list to each county's roll for resident taxpayers who owned land in other counties, or taxpayers who owned land in the county and lived elsewhere. Read these lists as well.

If the rolls show taxpayers in rough alphabetical order, you can scan quickly for people of your focus surname. However, some are written in the order that the taxpayers paid their taxes or the tax collector visited them. This kind of record can be very useful in determining place of residence, neighbors, and, sometimes, relationships. An interesting article that compares census and tax records of a given year to identify a "missing" ancestor is "Finding 'Missing Men' on Early Census Records: The Example of Thomas Russell," by Ruth Land Hatten in the *National Genealogical Society Quarterly* 81 (March 1993): 46–50.

States varied their categories of taxable property from time to time. Although few, if any, taxpayers would have had property in all columns, the following were the taxable personal property items in Mississippi in 1842, as shown in the column headings on the Panola County form:

- Amount of sale of Merchandize [*sic*] Subsequent to 1 January 1841 and prior to 1 March 1942
- Number of Stallions and price of Season
- Jacks
- Number of Billiard Tables
- Amount of money loaned at interest
- Notes employed in notes, bonds, checks, or bills of credit of any description whatever, as Security for money advanced
- Amount of Bank Stock subscribed for in any incorporated Bank
- Amount of Merchandize [*sic*] Sold at auction
- Number and value of Pleasure Carriages
- Number and value of Watches
- Number and value of Clocks
- Number of Bowie knives
- Number of Cattle
- Number of white polls [white males of taxable age]
- Number of free coulored [*sic*] persons
- Number of Slaves above the age of 5 and under 60 Years
- Amount of State Tax due by each person

The real estate tax rolls of many states asked for information on the number of acres a taxpayer owned; the location of the land (county, watercourse, survey, township and range, or other designation); sometimes how many acres were improved or unimproved, planted or fallow; sometimes the original grantee; and sometimes an adjoining neighbor's name. Occasionally, states used "combined" rolls, reporting personal and real property on the

See Also

See page 333 for a case study that uses tax rolls to help trace slave ancestors.

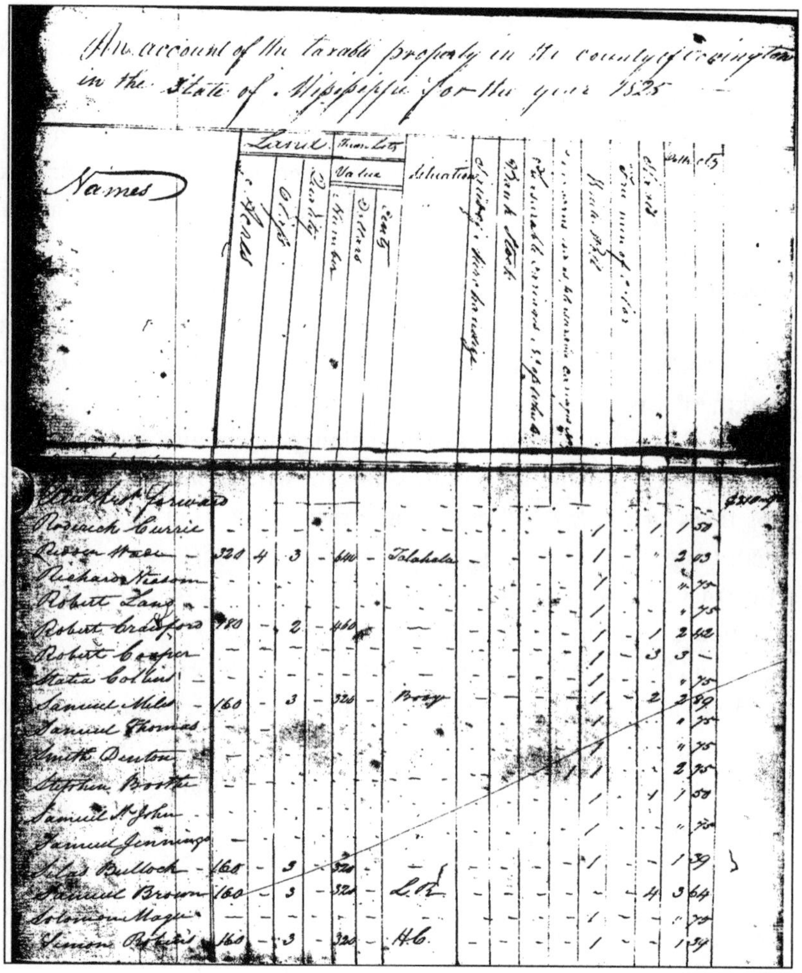
An account of the taxable property in the county of Covington in the State of Mississippi for the year 1825

Names

Amount Forward
Roderick Currie
Reuben Ware
Richard Nelson
Robert Lang
Robert Crawford
Robert Cooper
Statia Collins
Samuel Miles
Samuel Thomas
Smith Denton
Stephen Booth
Samuel McJohn
Samuel Jennings
Silas Bullock
Samuel Brown
Solomon Magee
Simon Roberts

Figure 3-6 Combined tax roll for 1825, Covington County, Mississippi, page listed alphabetically under *R*, microfilm from Mississippi Department of Archives and History.

same page. Figure 3-6, above, shows the Covington, Mississippi, combined tax roll for 1825, alphabetized mostly by first name!

Quit rents were colonial land taxes that residents in the North American colonies, except for New England, paid annually on patented or granted land. This practice was a carryover from English feudal customs. The surviving rolls are helpful in placing men and some women in a given place at a given time; sometimes they show information on land holdings. Some of these records exist in state archives or historical societies; some are on microfilm and available through a Family History Center. Check library catalogs and PERSI for those that have been published. One published source is *The Quit Rents of Virginia, 1704*, by Annie Laurie Wright Smith, comp. (Baltimore: Genealogical Publishing Co., 1980).

Other colonial taxes in some locations included parish levies (for the established church). County tithable, assessment, or rate lists may also survive from colonial or post-Revolutionary years.

Federal Direct Taxes

Although ordered by Congress, federal direct taxes were collected and recorded at the county or local level, as part of larger districts and divisions. The 1798 direct taxes on real estate and slaves are especially interesting because some of the records contain details about houses over one hundred dollars in value and about outbuildings, including dimensions and construction materials. Of course, these tax lists pertain only to the states admitted by 1798:

the original thirteen plus Vermont, Kentucky, and Tennessee. Check state archives and historical societies, including the New England Historic Genealogical Society in Boston, for surviving schedules on microfilm, as well as for any surviving schedules from the 1814–1816 direct tax lists. The National Archives has only the Pennsylvania 1798 lists, which are microfilmed on M372. Apparently, no surviving 1798 lists have been found for the Carolinas, Kentucky, New Jersey, and Virginia (including West Virginia).

Congress levied a number of taxes during the Civil War: a direct tax, with each state given a quota based on their population; an income tax; and internal revenue duties. The Tennessee **direct tax assessment lists,** based on a law of June 1862, are the only ones on microfilm (T227). These lists name landowners, including some women and estates or heirs, alphabetically by surname within their county and show the number of acres owned (or ownership of town lots), the valuation, the amount of tax charged, the amount paid within sixty days, and the amount of interest and penalty charged for late payments. A large landowner in Madison County, Tennessee, was Robert A. Connerly, whose 1,150 acres were valued at $16,000 and whose mill was valued at $500. The tax charged to him was $57.75, of which he paid $56.00 within sixty days. Nearly everyone listed on the same page as Connerly was charged $1.75 interest regardless of the amount of tax due and varying amounts of penalty. Even Confederate soldiers were listed, though they were not identified as soldiers. Because the forms were filled out with a varying degree of thoroughness, it is impossible to tell whether some landowners ever paid a penny or what the federal officials did about those who paid nothing. Probably the most useful aspect of the lists is the identity of landowners and their holdings in the 1862–1865 time period.

The Civil War **internal revenue assessments** taxed many people and products. Monthly, quarterly, and/or special levies were placed on raw materials; products of manufacture, including all kinds of spirits; wholesalers and retailers; numerous kinds of businesses; horses and jacks; interest paid on bonds; receipts from sales of slaughtered livestock; and even gross receipts from newspaper advertisements. People in nearly all crafts, professions, and trades, from lawyers and doctors to cattle brokers and fish peddlers had to pay annual license fees. **Annual taxes were charged on luxury items such as carriages, pianos, billiard tables, silver plate, and gold watches.** Figure 3-7, on page 102, is an 1866 "special annual" list for the North Carolina district that included Cabarrus, Davie, Rowan, and Stokes counties. Notice the variety of occupations listed, including distillers, physicians, a peddler, and a bowling alley.

Notes

Monthly, yearly, and special schedules make for a number of lists to read. However, the descriptive pamphlets and some of the introductory material on the microfilm help identify the counties in each district and division; if the county is not named on the schedule heading, the residences of the named individuals help you scan for your ancestral county. The lists name the taxed individuals alphabetically, their residence and occupation, any taxable luxury items they owned, and the taxes they were assessed. The surviving records are numerous; the microfilm publications are mentioned in chapter five, in the state list on pages 170–175. These are available through a Family History Center. Check with the National Archives regional branches for the their holdings beyond what is available on microfilm.

DEED RECORDS

Deed records as a class are among the most valuable sources for genealogists. In addition to land transactions, some clerks recorded a number of other records in their deed books, including wills, inventories, and estate settlements; sheriffs' sales of property; bills of sale for

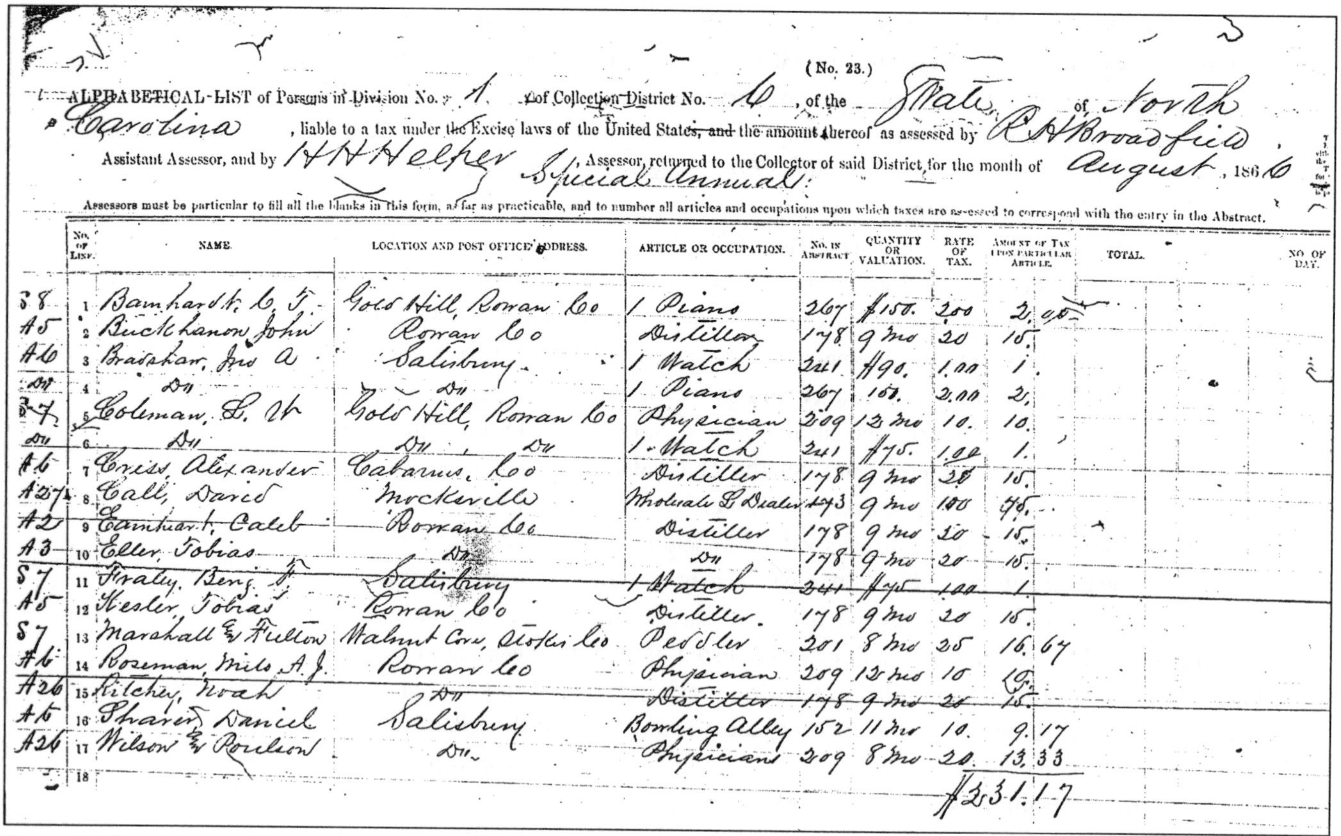
(No. 23.)

ALPHABETICAL-LIST of Persons in Division No. 1 of Collection District No. 6, of the State of North Carolina, liable to a tax under the Excise laws of the United States, and the amount thereof as assessed by R H Broadfield Assistant Assessor, and by H H Helper, Assessor, returned to the Collector of said District for the month of August, 1866

Special Annual:

Assessors must be particular to fill all the blanks in this form, as far as practicable, and to number all articles and occupations upon which taxes are assessed to correspond with the entry in the Abstract.

	No. of Line.	Name.	Location and Post Office Address.	Article or Occupation.	No. in Abstract	Quantity or Valuation.	Rate of Tax.	Amount of Tax upon Particular Article.	Total.	No. of Day.
S8	1	Bamhardt, C. F.	Gold Hill, Rowan Co	1 Piano	267	$150.	2.00	2.00		
A5	2	Buckhanon, John	Rowan Co	Distiller	178	9 mo	20	15.		
A6	3	Bradshaw, Jno A	Salisbury	1 Watch	241	$90.	1.00	1.		
Do	4	Do	Do	1 Piano	267	150.	2.00	2.		
S7	5	Coleman, L. W	Gold Hill, Rowan Co	Physician	209	12 mo	10.	10.		
Do	6	Do	Do Do	1 Watch	241	$75.	1.00	1.		
A6	7	Criss, Alexander	Cabarrus, Co	Distiller	178	9 mo	20	15.		
A27	8	Call, David	Mocksville	Wholesale L Dealer	243	9 mo	100	75.		
A2	9	Earnheart, Caleb	Rowan Co	Distiller	178	9 mo	20	15.		
A3	10	Eller, Tobias	Do	Do	178	9 mo	20	15.		
S7	11	Fraley, Benj. F.	Salisbury	1 Watch	241	$75	1.00	1.		
A5	12	Kesler, Tobias	Rowan Co	Distiller	178	9 mo	20	15.		
S7	13	Marshall & Fulton	Walnut Cove, Stokes Co	Peddler	201	8 mo	25	16.67		
A6	14	Roseman, Miles A. J.	Rowan Co	Physician	209	12 mo	10	10.		
A26	15	Ritchey, Noah	Do	Distiller	178	9 mo	20	15.		
A6	16	Sharer, Daniel	Salisbury	Bowling Alley	152	11 mo	10.	9.17		
A26	17	Wilson & Poulson	Do	Physicians	209	8 mo	20.	13.33		
	18							$231.17		

Figure 3-7 Special Annual list, August 1866, Division No. 1, District 6, Rowan county et al., Internal Revenue Assessment Lists for North Carolina, 1864–1866, NARA microfilm M784, roll 2.

slaves, land, livestock, and other goods; powers of attorney; business contracts; prenuptial agreements; affidavits; apprenticeships and partnerships; and miscellaneous items such as voter lists, slave manumissions, and livestock brands. Regardless of the kind of instrument you find, you can learn about relationships, dates, marriages, deaths, current and former residences, removals and new residences, and other pertinent details of family history.

Power of attorney gives a relative, friend, or attorney authority to handle business on someone's behalf. These documents may appear in deed books. On 6 February 1786, William Harrison, clerk of the town of Petersburg, Virginia, named Edward Pegram, Esquire, his attorney to sue for and recover all money due him (Petersburg Deed Book 1:292).

Business, school, or church connections may be found in deed records. Business partners bought or sold businesses; school trustees received or purchased land for a new schoolhouse. The records may suggest a religious affiliation when church trustees received land as a gift or purchased land for the church.

For example, the Hancock County, Georgia, deed records contain a deed dated 26 March 1828 by which Ann Barbary Robertson conveyed a half acre of land, at the price of one dollar, to Barnaby Shivers, John M. Shivers, Cullen Battle, John S. Lane, and A.E. Reeves, all of Hancock County, "commissioners for erecting a Baptist meeting house or church" (Deed Book N:586). The record identifies the six individuals as residents of the county and suggests that at least the five men were local Baptists given the task of obtaining land for their church. Although some nonmembers occasionally gave, or almost gave, as Ann Robertson did, land to churches, the record should prompt Robertson's researchers to look for a Baptist connection as well.

Contracts sometimes appear in deed books. E.G. Coleman and D.L. Kokernot signed an agreement on 1 April 1876 in Gonzales County, Texas. By the instrument, Coleman bound himself to complete within thirty days the following job:

> [Coleman will] in a good and workmanlike manner well and substantially build a two-story house 20 × 30 feet on a tract of 1 acre of land on the water of Peach Creek it being a portion of the Hill League and donated by William E. Jones for the purpose of erecting said building thereon to be used as a school house and such other purposes as the school trustees may agree, with such lumber and other materials as the said Kokernot may furnish (Deed Book W:225).

Upon completion, Coleman was to receive $200. If either party defaulted on their part of the agreement, the penalty would be $250. On May 15, Coleman received $210 in payment for the job and extra work required.

Prenuptial agreements may also be recorded in deed books. Between February 1786 and March 1789, William Harrison's wife, Lucy, apparently died, and Harrison made plans to remarry. On 26 March 1789, he executed a document according to the agreements made with his bride-to-be prior to the marriage (Petersburg Deed Book 1:492). Whereas they promised to marry each other, William, for love of Nancy, gave her his mansion house called Porter Hill where he then resided, four lots, the house and lot called Lark Hall, one hundred acres in Dinwiddie County, £500 (five hundred pounds), and two slaves. "I further oblige myself to enable Nancy to give her brother Spencer £50 (fifty pounds) when he goes to Great Britain to finish his studies." Both William and Nancy signed the document, witnessed by her father, David Vaughan, and two others. This particular agreement was made between a young woman and a much older man who seems to have had no living children at the time. This may have been an agreement to guarantee her certain property and rights in the event of his death. Such a prenuptial agreement was often made when each party had separate property coming into the marriage and/or had children by a former marriage whose interests they wanted to protect.

Affidavits are instruments of great genealogical value sometimes recorded in deed books. The affidavit described here is one of several made within the same family because of intestate (without a will) deaths. John F. Oldham of Robertson County, Texas, in 1909 created an affidavit that he was the son of B.F. Oldham and grandson of J.N. Oldham, who died in June 1879 or 1880. (Because J.N. was enumerated in the 1880 census, the death must have occurred in 1880.) J.N.'s wife, Mary, died in 1886. The only heirs at law of the said J.N. and Mary were J.C.L. and B.F. Oldham, sons of J.N. and Mary; M.A. McDaniel, wife of J.H. McDaniel; A.S. Jelks, wife of R.L. Jelks; and V.A. Hightower, wife of J.Q. Hightower, the last three being daughters of J.N. and Mary. Both grandparents died intestate, and land inherited by their heirs and described in the document was sold to J.M. Oldham in 1887 (Deed Book 67:334). Other deeds and marriage records supplied most of the given names for the initials in the affidavit.

A number of other documents dealing with the transfer and division of property may be recorded in deed books. Many of the records are self-explanatory when you read the contents. In addition to deed books, documents concerning property may be found in various other record books, depending on the county. Examples include Small Estates Record, Wills Filed for Safekeeping, and Probate Court records, dockets, and minutes.

Although clerks recorded a number of other legal documents in deed books, the bulk of the instruments are deeds of various kinds. Deeds of gift, deeds of trust and mortgages, quitclaim deeds, and warranty deeds are all transfers of title to property and all may provide good information for genealogists. To find the records you need to read, go first to the indexes.

Step By Step

Indexes

To gain the most from the deed records in a county for your time period:

1. Look in both direct and reverse (indirect) indexes where both exist. Direct indexes are arranged by grantor or seller; reverse indexes, by grantee or buyer. Sometimes these are in separate volumes; sometimes they are on facing pages of the same volume. Indexes vary in style and rarely are strictly alphabetical. Most are alphabetical by initial letter of the surname; sometimes, by given name within each surname section. Take time to familiarize yourself with each index style you encounter. Most indexes are also chronological, in the order the documents were brought in for filing or recording. Be aware that recording, and therefore indexing, sometimes took place years, even fifty to eighty years, after the date of the original instrument.

2. Some indexes include both the date of the original instrument and the date of filing, as well as the document type (mortgage, deed, deed of trust, power of attorney, etc.) and the volume and page number where the copy appears. The volume and page number, of course, are your key to finding the text of the document. Other indexes give only the parties' names, the year of the instrument, and the volume and page number for finding the record.

3. Note all entries under your surname(s), whether you recognize the given names or not. If you are reading the index on microfilm, making microprint copies of (photocopying) the pages saves time and gives you the original as a thorough reference for planning and studying.

4. Look for generations of the surname before and after your focus ancestor; be alert for spelling variations of the surname.

5. Pay attention to index entries saying *et al* (*et alii*, "and others") or *et ux* (*et uxor*, "and wife"). The "others" sometimes are heirs selling property they inherited.

6. Write down the source of your information so that you or someone else could find it again. Photocopy or abstract all information given in each deed, including dates, witnesses, residences, conditions and considerations, property descriptions, and whether parties signed their names or signed by mark. (Signatures and marks in deed books are normally in the clerk's handwriting; rarely are they the signatures of the parties.)

7. Be alert for relationships mentioned or implied. Witnesses sometimes were relatives of one party or the other. States vary in their practices of involving relatives as witnesses. If you study the deed books, you can tell whether the same people witnessed documents again and again or whether they appear to be specific to certain deeds.

8. Look at deeds recorded at the same time, within a few pages before or after your ancestor's deeds, to see if family members appear as witnesses to other instruments.

9. Sheriffs' sales of property, usually to satisfy a court judgment against a defendant and usually for payment of debts, are often indexed under *S* for *Sheriff*. The text of the document usually names the debtor, but the index may or may not do so.

10. Sometimes, deeds and mortgages are recorded in separate books and may be indexed separately.

11. Allow yourself time to do a thorough job the first time. If you are researching at the courthouse, study in the evening what you have found so that you can make a return visit the next day to catch what you might have overlooked the first day.

Parts of a Deed Record

The document sometimes begins by naming the county where the transaction took place and the date. Sometimes this information is at the end of the document.

Names of the parties to the transaction normally appear at the beginning of the text. A simple sale of property usually involved two parties: the buyer and the seller, sometimes including their wives. Usually deeds named the county where each party resided at the time.

If the document was a deed of trust, three parties were usually named. John "sold" or deeded a tract of land to Samuel to hold as security because John owed Edward money. If John could not pay what he owed by a stated date, then Samuel had the authority to sell the land at public auction to the highest bidder to get the money to pay Edward.

The nature, conditions, and considerations of the transaction were presented in the body of the document. This section included the price the buyer was to pay, whether he or she had already paid or made a down payment, information about buying on credit at interest, and how and when payment was to be made. The legalese does not always say things in a simple and direct manner, as in "this is a deed of trust." But noticing key elements of what the text says will help you determine what kind of document you are reading. The words "quit claim" or "quitclaim" in the text identify it as a quitclaim deed. Usually, the words "for the love and affection," or something similar, identify a deed of gift, or donation in Louisiana. The term "warrant" or "warrant and defend" usually signifies a warranty deed. See the examples on pages 107–109.

The legal description of the land being bought and sold is an important part of the deed. This part of the record sometimes includes a history of the tract's ownership and sometimes names neighbors, watercourses, or landmarks on or near the property. This information can help genealogists reconstruct the ancestral neighborhood for study and/or locate the property on a map.

Signatures and marks indicated in land records may tell you whether an ancestor could sign his or her name. The actual signatures and marks are not in the deed books, which are the official court copies of the originals, but the clerk indicated whether the individual signed or made a mark. He was supposed to copy the mark as the person made it, whether an *X*, an initial, or a symbol.

Witnesses usually signed the document to say they had watched the parties sign their names. In the deed book copy of the document, the clerk added the witnesses' names along with the indication of whether they signed their names or made their marks. Both men and women, who may or may not have known the parties in advance, served as witnesses; there is no guarantee that witnesses were related to the buyer or the seller.

Recording took place when the buyer filed the document at the courthouse. At this phase, the clerk may also have copied one of two kinds of records dealing with the wife of the seller—her consent to the sale of her relinquishment of dower rights (see below).

Evidence of Wives

A valuable aspect of deed research is the possibility of learning about the seller's wife. In some areas, the wife signed the deed as a joint seller with her husband. At the time of the sale or later, an official of the court took the wife aside and apart from her husband, explained the transaction to her, and asked whether she willingly assented to the sale. Her declaration of assent then became part of the official record. For the genealogist, it provides evidence that she was alive on the date she agreed to the sale.

Important

At other times or places, the seller's wife was asked to relinquish her dower rights in the property. **In states where this was done, the wife acquired by marriage a legal right to part of her husband's estate—her dower or "widow's third"—for her use during her lifetime if she survived him.** Therefore, when a husband sold property while his wife was living, the buyer usually insisted that the wife relinquish her rights to the property so that she could not claim a share of the property after her husband's death. The relinquishment often follows the recording of the deed in the deed book.

For genealogists, the primary value of these two records is the identification of the wife's name and the knowledge that she was living at the time she signed the paper. Sometimes, it is the only record of the wife's name. The dates of multiple acknowledgments or relinquishments may also help determine which wife bore which children.

Legal Descriptions

Part of the purpose of creating deeds is to identify and register the specific property an individual has bought. In the thirty public land states, property—especially rural property—is usually identified by the section or fraction of section, township, and range where it is located. (See chapter six.) Towns and cities nationwide often use block and lot numbers, the neighborhood or addition name or number, or other designations to identify specific properties.

The twenty states that are "state land states" are areas that the federal government never owned. These states include

- the thirteen original states
- the five states that came out of their claimed territory: Vermont, settled early but partially claimed by New York and New Hampshire; Maine, out of Massachusetts; Kentucky, out of Virginia; Tennessee, out of North Carolina; West Virginia out of Virginia
- Hawaii and Texas, which entered the Union after being independent republics

Deeds in these twenty states use(d) a variety of descriptive measures, including lot numbers within a township or survey, lot and block numbers within a town, number of acres within a larger tract originally granted to an individual (e.g., "200 acres in the Powell survey"), or boundary descriptions using metes and bounds.

A metes and bounds system of surveying property designates property lines with natural features, such as watercourses and trees; artificial markers, such as rock piles and a stake in the prairie; and distances and directions between these markers. Figure 3-8, on page 107, illustrates a metes and bounds property description from an 1811 Kentucky deed, along with a rendering of the tract's shape based on that description.

Whoever wrote the deed or copied it into the record did not add some of the specific language that would have made the document easier to understand, but apparently such things were commonly understood then and there seemed no need to elaborate. When he spoke of "south 65 [degrees] west 112 poles," he was giving the length of that part of the property line and the compass direction it followed. In other words, the line ran for 112 poles (1,848 feet), not due south or due west, but southwest. How much south and how much west? "South 65 degrees west." On paper, when you draw a cross for the four compass directions over the spot where that line begins (at a post oak tree), there are ninety degrees (a quarter of a circle) between the south line and the west line. A protractor measures sixty-five of those ninety degrees, as shown in Figure 3-8, on page 107. Thus, the line runs sixty-five degrees west of south (or twenty-five degrees south of west). Plotting such legal descriptions on paper may or may not reflect exactly the reality in the field. The quality of the instruments used, the skill of the surveyor, the difficulty of the terrain, and even weather conditions could have affected the accuracy of the survey. Metes and bounds legal descriptions do not all use the same terms of measurement or descriptive language.

"... land containing 125 acres...more or less...on the waters of the east fork of little river...and bounded as follows...beginning at a post oak in Cravens line thence with it south 65[°] west 112 poles to two post oaks, thence south 30 west 125 poles to a black oak sappling thence south 50 east 150 poles to a black oak on a...[?]...thence north 9 east 250 poles to the beginning..."

1 pole = 16½ feet

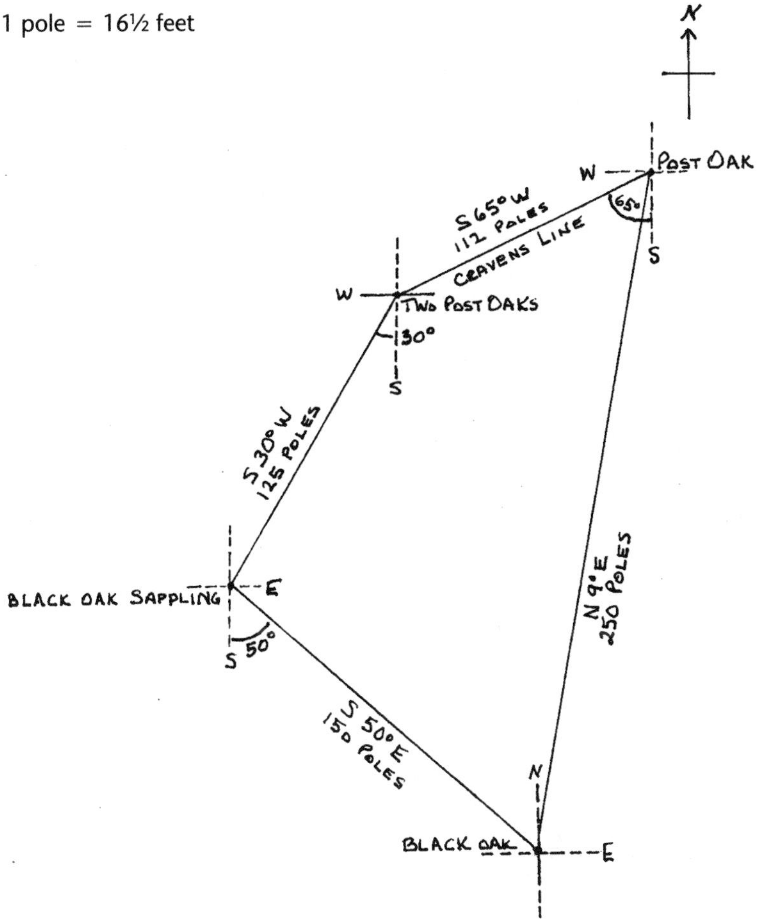

Figure 3-8 Mapping a tract of land with metes and bounds.

Deeds of Gift

Deeds of gift were often used to distribute property among one's children. In this way, Jesse Croom Sr. of Wayne County, North Carolina, gave his son Charles 150 acres on 17 January 1787. The key wording is "for and in consideration of the Natural Love and Affection he hath and bears unto the said Charles Croom his son, . . . [Jesse] hath given, granted, and confirmed . . . unto the said Charles Croom a certain Plantation . . . " containing 150 acres, originally granted to Jesse Croom on 27 April 1767 (Deed Book 3:424). Such a record is music to a genealogist's ears.

When daughters were involved in such deeds, you may discover maiden names. In Hancock County, Georgia, in 1803, Rosey Swinney for love of her daughter Ann Barbara Robertson gave her a Negro boy Sealy (Deed Book N:96). This deed of gift was recorded in August 1824, twenty-one years after its creation. Not only does the record indicate that Rosey Swinney was Ann's mother and that Swinney could well have been Ann's maiden name (if her mother had not remarried), the document also indicates that Ann was already married by 1803. (Other records indicate that her husband was Nathaniel Robertson.) Furthermore, the document would help descendants of Sealy discover how he went from one household to another.

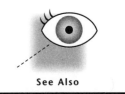

See Also

See chapter nine for more about researching slave ancestors.

Deeds of Trust

The deed of trust is an instrument made to secure payment of debt by transferring property title to one or more trustees. Especially after the Civil War in the South, such deeds were common. Everyone was in debt, and few had money with which to pay those debts. When E.G. Coleman of Hardeman County, Tennessee, had to execute a deed of trust in June 1867, he listed among his property a number of notes due him for several thousand dollars. He also owed money that he was having trouble paying. This deed of trust gave him one year to pay the debts he owed or face the sale of his property at public auction. Thus, as security for payment of the debts, he turned over to George Wood and brother A.A. Coleman his livestock, his home, wagons and buggy, all his farming utensils, the pianoforte, his growing crops of cotton, corn, and fodder, and "all interest I have in real and personal estate of my late father Ferdinand G. Coleman dec'd late of Cumberland County, Virginia." (Deed Book U:56). Since Coleman is a common name and thus sometimes tedious to research, this one statement was the key that unlocked the door to previous generations for his descendants.

Quitclaim Deeds

A quitclaim deed transfers a person's interest in property to another without a guarantee of clear title. In January 1870, in their home county of Appanoose in Iowa, Mary Ellen Ryals and her husband, Solomon Ryals, executed a quitclaim deed to Abel Brown. The preprinted original document, with its handwritten, fill-in-the-blank additions in italics, reads

> This Indenture, Made and Executed, This *Eighth* day of *January* A.D., 18*70*, by and between *Mary Ellen Ryals and Solomon Ryals her husband* of the first part, and *Abel Brown party* of the second part, witnesseth: That the said partys of the first part, for the consideration of the sum of *One hundred and sixty six and 66/100* dollars, to *be* paid, do by these presents sell and forever Quit Claim unto the second party, *his* heirs and all *our* interest, claim and demand, in and to the following described Real Estate, situated in the County of *Monroe* and State of *Ohio*, to-wit: *Lands heretofore subject to sale at Marietta, Ohio the* [*W half of the NW quarter of Section 12 Township 4 Range 4 containing 78.90 acres; the E half of the NE quarter of Section 18 Township 4 Range 4 containing 77.25 acres; and East part of West half of NE quarter of Section 18, Township 4 Range 4 containing 50 acres*] *Situated in Monroe County Ohio* To have and to hold the same, with the appurtenances thereto belonging, unto the said party of the second part *his* heirs and assigns forever, signed this *Eighth* day of *January* 18*70*.

Mary Ellen signed with her mark; Solomon, with his signature. Apparently, the instrument was recorded in Monroe County, Ohio, in January 1874 (Vol. 30:374–375). Notice that the wife's name appears first in the document; this suggests they were selling her interest in the property. Perhaps it was an inheritance to which she and siblings were entitled. A married woman in the nineteenth century was usually not allowed by law to own property on her own or conduct legal business on her own, and thus her husband accompanied her in transactions. On the original of this deed, someone wrote in pencil, "no transfer," which gives the genealogist something else to study.

Warranty Deeds

Warranty deeds, also known by the shorter term *deed*, transferred property with the guarantee or warrant of a good title. **The grantors (sellers) and grantees (buyers) are the parties to the document.** Instead of using every possible synonym for *sells*, as older deeds often did, the one transcribed here is an authorized short form that includes the basic and necessary information in easy-to-understand language, at the same time providing the women's maiden name. Because South Dakota is one of the thirty federal land states, the legal description of the tract is in the language of the rectangular survey system, giving the location in section, township, and range designations. (See chapter six for more on federal land records.)

The deed was executed in Minnesota and recorded in South Dakota. The italics show what the clerk in South Dakota copied and typed onto the preprinted form to file in the Brookings County deed book.

> Deed Record No. 64 [Book 64:608]
>
> Warranty Deed—Short Statutory Form
>
> *Helen R. Steele, nee Helen Revell, and George Steele, her husband, and Lucy R. Palmer, nee Lucy Revell, and Herald K. Palmer, her husband,* grantor of *Hennepin,* County, State of *Minnesota*, for and in consideration of *Twelve Thousand and 00/100* Dollars, GRANTS, CONVEYS AND WARRANTS TO *Frank A. Revell,* grantee, of *Brookings, South Dakota,* P.O. the following described real estate in the County of Brookings, in the State of South Dakota: *The East Half (E$\frac{1}{2}$) of Section Two (2) in Township One Hundred Nine (109) North, of Range Fifty (50) West of the 5th P.M.* [Principal Meridian],
> Dated this *30th* day of *August*, 1943
>
> Revenue Stamps: $13.20 Helen R. Steele George H. Steele
> Lucy R. Palmer Herald K. Palmer
>
> State of *MINNESOTA, Hennepin* County, ss.
>
> On this *the 29th* day of *September* 1943 before me *a Notary Public, the undersigned officer,* personally appeared *Helen R. Steele, nee Helen Revell and George Steele, her husband, and Lucy R. Palmer, nee Lucy Revell and Harold* [*sic*] *K. Palmer, her husband* known to me *or satisfactorily proven* to be the person[s] whose *names are subscribed to* the within instrument, and acknowledge that *they* executed the same *for the purposes therein contained. In witness whereof I hereunto set my hand and official seal. Effie E. Lundquist*
>
> [notary seal] Notary Public, *Hennepin County Minn.*
>
> My commission expires *Dec. 18th,* 1946.

Deeds were often made between relatives, as in the South Dakota example, but relationships were not always expressed. Being alert to the possibilities may help you identify relationships.

For further reference on matters of property and inheritance, see such books as these:

- *Inheritance in America: From Colonial Times to the Present*, by Carole Shammas, Marylynn Salmon, and Michel Dahlin. New Brunswick, N.J.: Rutgers University Press, 1987.

Notes

The document was asking for the post office address of the grantee (Brookings, South Dakota). At that time, residents of small towns and rural areas could receive mail that was addressed to them using only the town and state names. They needed no street address or box number, and zip codes were not yet in use.

- *Land & Property Research in the United States*, by E. Wade Hone. Salt Lake City: Ancestry, 1997.
- *Locating Your Roots: Discover Your Ancestors Using Your Land Records*, by Patricia Law Hatcher. Cincinnati: Betterway Books, 2003.
- *Women and the Law of Property in Early America*, by Marylynn Salmon. Chapel Hill, N.C.: The University of North Carolina Press, 1986.

COURT RECORDS

Because each state sets up its own court system, researchers need to ask or read about the particular names and jurisdictions of courts in their research area at the time the ancestors lived there. Some of this information can be found in (1) the many books and articles on research in each state, (2) some of the Martindale-Hubbell legal directories, (3) some encyclopedias, especially ones in the legal field, and (4) state almanacs. However, most states have a multilevel court system. At the lower level are courts of limited jurisdiction, such as justice of the peace, municipal, family, traffic, small claims, juvenile, and some county courts. These records are usually found in or near the county courthouse in the offices of the court. For various reasons, the early records of some of these courts no longer exist.

The second level of courts are those of general and original jurisdiction, such as district, circuit, and superior courts; courts of common pleas; and some county courts. These courts handle both criminal and civil cases, often including divorce and probate. (Probate is sometimes a jurisdiction of the county court.) Offices and records of these courts are often in county courthouses or courthouse complexes.

Most states have intermediate appeals courts, called district or circuit courts of appeals or superior courts. The highest level court in most states is a supreme court with appellate jurisdiction. Appeals cases at both state and federal levels are illustrated in chapter eight.

County courts, by whatever name the state gives them, usually have jurisdiction over small civil claims and lesser crimes. In some areas, these courts can also sit as probate courts, dealing with wills, estate settlements, guardianship, adoption, and insanity cases. In the early years in Tennessee and North Carolina, the court of pleas and quarter sessions was a kind of county court, made up of justices of the peace. Two representative cases illustrate the kinds of issues brought before this court. In July 1784, James Shaw of Davidson County sued John Montgomery for settlement of a debt of £15.9 (fifteen pounds, nine shillings). When the defendant did not appear in court and Shaw presented his evidence, the court instructed the sheriff to sell the attached property, including one dwelling house and one loom house and loom, to satisfy the debt. In October 1787, Shaw sued William Hopkins who had borrowed a horse and failed to return it. Shaw asked for damages of £30 (thirty pounds). The jury found in favor of the plaintiff, awarded Shaw £22.13.4 (twenty-two pounds, thirteen shillings, four pence) in damages, and charged Hopkins with the court costs.

County court minutes, especially older ones, reflect many activities of the court and community. These examples are representative of the business before the court in Davidson County, Tennessee, 1783–1792:

1. James Shaw was a witness in a trial in April 1783 and testified that he heard William Joiner agree to "pitch and corky" a boat (make it watertight) and give Jonathan Boyd fifteen dollars for the hire thereof.
2. James Shaw served on the grand jury for the July 1784 term and the trial jury in April 1786, October 1787, and numerous other terms.
3. In July 1784, James Shaw was authorized to "keep a Ferry at the place afforesaid

[Nashville] with good and sufficient boats and well attended for the purpose of passage of such as are desirous of crossing the said river [Cumberland]" at the following fees: one shilling for a man and horse, one shilling for every pack horse and pack, eight pence for a lead horse without a pack, six pence for every footman, six pence for every head of horned cattle, and four pence for every head of sheep and hogs.
4. The case of the *State v. John Boyd*, charging the defendant with butchering a beef on the Sabbath Day, came to trial on 8 April 1788. Upon hearing the circumstances, the court acquitted Boyd.
5. On 8 April 1788, James Shaw served on the jury that found Samuel Martin not guilty of stealing a bull from James Bosley.
6. On 8 July 1788, the court appointed one man in each militia company to take a list of taxables (people and their taxable property).
7. On 9 July 1788, James Shaw and others were appointed to lay a road from the Isaac Thomas Ferry (at his residence) to Nashville, with Captain Bosley as overseer.
8. Andrew Jackson, Esquire, produced his license to practice law in Tennessee and took the oath of an attorney on 5 January 1789.
9. On 9 January 1789, the court ordered Colonel Thomas Green to have a tavern license to keep an ordinary in Nashville where "he now is." The next day, the court resolved that the selling price of a quart of whiskey would be one dollar, and in proportion for amounts more or less than a quart.
10. On 10 October 1789, 12 July 1790, and 13 January 1791, Sampson Williams, sheriff, entered his protest against the sufficiency of the county jail.
11. On 13 July 1790, the court exempted Thomas Brown from jury duty because of his being "upon the scout after the Indians."
12. On 13 January 1791, the court established the following rates for tavern keepers: one shilling for breakfast; two shillings for dinner (main midday meal); one shilling for supper; six pence for a half pint of whiskey; one shilling for a half pint of rum or good brandy; one shilling for stabling a horse for twenty-four hours with hay or fodder; and two pence per man for a good bed for one night.
13. On 15 July 1791, William Black took the oath to serve as a deputy sheriff.
14. On 11 January 1792, James Shaw acknowledged the validity of a deed of Robert Wilson to Samuel Shannon, prior to its being recorded in the deed book.

An ordinary was a tavern or eating house or public house where meals were served.

The Rutherford County, North Carolina, Court of Pleas and Quarter Sessions handled the same types of cases and business, with the addition of this example that descendants may find amusing. On Friday, 16 October 1801, William Metcalf was "brought before the court and charged by some of the members of Bills Creek Congregation for disorderly behavior at the place of worship and prays that said Metcalf be bound for his good behavior. [It is] ordered therefore that the said Metcalf be bound for 12 months and [a] day in the sum of £100 with 2 securities in [the amount of] £50 each. Accordingly came the said Metcalf and was bound [for] £100. Thomas Dalton and Benjamin Williams security in £50 each."

State district courts or circuit courts may have both civil and criminal jurisdiction, with civil jurisdiction over suits involving divorce, large amounts of money, and other matters of law. Of course, many of these cases contain genealogical material, as illustrated in chapter eight.

In the district court minutes also are recorded such items as grand jury and trial jury lists, bills of indictment in criminal matters, and civil cases pending before the court. In October 1846, the grand jury of Leon County, Texas, returned bills against Simeon Loyd, William Hightower, William Evans, Daniel McIver, George Floyd, and John McKay for playing at cards and against John McKay for offering a challenge to fight a duel. These details may not be strictly genealogical, but they add interest to the family history.

An early case that contains genealogical information is the *Heirs of Felix A. Richardson, deceased, v. the State of Texas*, filed 30 June 1847. The petition names (1) the minor heirs, Ann, Marian, Elizabeth, and Felix A. Richardson Jr.; (2) their "next friend," Spruce M. Baird; (3) wife and relict of the deceased, Ann Reynolds; and (4) her new husband, Meredith S. Reynolds. In August 1861, the minor heirs were back in court as adults, then living in Kentucky. Named as plaintiffs were Felix A. Richardson Jr.; B.K. McQuann and his wife, Marian; J.L. Smith and his wife, E.A.; and E. Porter and his wife, Elizabeth. Their concern was two large tracts of land in Leon County, Texas, of which William Kinginn (?—name unclear in document) had taken possession with force and arms, from which he had cut and carried off timber valued at ten thousand dollars, and which he refused to vacate.

Other records found in court clerks' offices can include such things as case dockets, witness and jury pay lists, civil court fee books, and other records dealing with the day-to-day operation of the courts. An example is the Jeff Davis County, Texas, jury certificates book showing the 5 July 1907 payment of fifty cents each to the named petit jurors.

Older court records may be stored in basements, attics, and other hard-to-access areas. In one Tennessee county, when I wanted to find a court case pertinent to the settlement of an estate, I was told that the court records from the period I needed were stored in the old jail. The only person who had a key was in the hospital for surgery and would be out of the office at least two weeks. Alas, I couldn't extend my vacation two more weeks and had to return home with that question unanswered. While some court docket and minute books have been microfilmed or abstracted for publication, the case files, which contain the details of the case, are rarely found outside of the courthouse itself.

Divorce

In the early nineteenth century and before, divorce was often the jurisdiction of the state legislature. As the legislatures gave jurisdiction to the state and county courts, they also broadened the laws on grounds for divorce. Depending on the laws of each state, either spouse could file for divorce.

UNCOVERING A MURDER TRIAL

A cousin sparked my interest in my ancestor Mary (Hohn/Hahn) Myers when he told me that Mary and an associate had been convicted of murder for killing Mary's husband (and my ancestor), John Myers. Surprised and curious, I began the adventure of researching Mary. Fortunately, she left a comprehensive Civil War pension application, filed in 1882 and based on the death of one of her unmarried sons. The file listed her twelve children and their birth dates; gave January 1847 as the death date of her first husband, John Myers; and told of her second and third husbands. With some of this information, a cousin, Helen Ray, in the ancestral county, located one of the old trial booklets in the papers of a local estate and had copies made for several of us.

Since the original court records no longer exist at the county courthouse, the booklet, published on rag pages not long after the trial, is the most contemporary evidence of the extraordinary event. The booklet's cover was missing, but the opening page identified its contents: "In The Court of Oyer and Terminer of Venango County of May Term, 1847. Commonwealth vs. Mary Myers & John Parker: Indictment for the murder of John Myers."

With two teams of lawyers, the trial began on 25 May 1847 before a panel of three judges, twelve jurymen, and probably local spectators. In fifty-five pages, the booklet described the testimony in detail, including the alleged conspiracy of Mary Myers and John Parker and the slow and painful death of John Myers over several days from arsenic poisoning. Witnesses for the defense told of John Myers's alcoholism and ill treatment of his wife. Mrs. John Parker wanted to be a witness on behalf of Mary Myers but was not allowed to testify.

After only a week in court, the jury found the defendants guilty and sentenced them to be hanged. The defense asked for an appeal. One of the reasons was "The Prisoners, through the neglect or mistake of the officer, were unable to procure the attendance of one material witness, nor could they lay grounds for an attachment for the witness or the continuance of the cause."

According to an article in the 15 August 1923 issue of the *Venango Citizen Press*, this was the first murder trial held in the county. One of the judges, John Pearson, prepared the "paper book" of the case for the state supreme court. Another of the judges, John McCalmont, rode horseback over the mountains to take the booklet and the case to Harrisburg. This may have been another copy of the same booklet that now tells us about the trial.

According to the newspaper article, the high court reversed the decision and authorized a new trial. However, the second trial never took place, nor was the original sentence carried out. (After all, Mary lived to apply for a pension in 1882.) John Parker escaped from jail, reportedly with the help of "interested parties," and was never apprehended. Mary was eventually released on a "nolle pros," a formal entry in the court record by the prosecution that they would not prosecute the case further. The reason seems to have been that Mary was pregnant with her twelfth child and no one wanted to kill the unborn child. That child, George Myers, was born on 17 August 1847, according to his mother's pension application—almost three months after the trial began and about eight months after John Myers died.

Mary and her children remained in the county for some time before moving to nearby Armstrong County where she lived many more years. She married John Reece on 10 May 1850, just in time to be Mary Reece in the 1850 census. After his death in 1869, she married Alexander McElrarey in 1874 and lived until about 1890 in the midst of her children and their families. *Lona Dee Boudreaux*

Prior to the nineteenth century, divorces occurred, but less frequently than in the following centuries. Before and during the nineteenth century, several kinds of divorce were granted. One was divorce from bed and board (or from table and bed), "divorce *a mensa et thoro*" or a legal separation. In such cases, the parties were still legally married but were prevented from living together and prevented from marrying someone else. Another was divorce with separate maintenance, in which case the wife could live apart from her husband, but he was required to provide support for her and the children. A total divorce, "divorce *a vinculo matrimonii*," dissolved the marriage and allowed the parties to remarry. Although judges could decide some divorce cases, others required a jury. For example, in the superior court of Putnam County, Georgia, in September 1831, a twelve-man jury awarded Betsy Anderson a divorce *a vinculo matrimonii* from Abram Anderson. The court record for this case did not mention the grounds for divorce. Laws varied by state but usually allowed divorce because of adultery or desertion.

Reminder

Divorce cases are often indexed and recorded separately from other cases. The minute book or index usually gives only the fact that a divorce was granted to the two people named. The case file contains the petition from the plaintiff stating the grounds for the divorce as well as other pertinent documents, sometimes including proof of the marriage and information on the children and family property.

The case of *Dave Perkins v. Hulda Perkins* in Leon County, Texas, is an example of the husband asking for divorce. The petition in the case file states that the two were married on 14 December 1882 in Leon County and lived happily together for the first six or eight years. Then the wife began using abusive language and cursing her husband, saying she cared nothing for him and had never loved him. After about 1890, she had refused to care for the household in such matters as cooking and washing for her husband and children. He said he could not afford to hire a servant to do those things for the family. Finally, on 10 January 1896, Hulda abandoned his bed and board, and Dave filed for the divorce, which was granted on 16 November 1896.

In the superior court of Putnam County, Georgia, in March 1831, Sarah Heath sued for divorce against Guilford Heath. The reason apparently was desertion, as the court record indicated that Guilford was "not to be found." One year later, Guilford was indicted for bigamy. John Lee, a justice of the peace, testified that he had married Guilford Heath and Sarah Favers on 6 June 1830. Then William Marchman swore in court that during August 1831, when he was in Houston County, he saw, alive, Margaret Evers, the woman whom Guilford Heath had first married.

Check research guides for your ancestral state or call the courthouse in your ancestral area to determine which court had jurisdiction over divorce cases at the time period of your interest. Consult PERSI for articles on laws and history of divorce in various states.

PROBATE RECORDS

Documents dealing with property and originating in the court with probate jurisdiction include wills, inventories, and estate settlements. This court also handles guardianship of minors and, in some jurisdictions, bastardy, adoption, and insanity cases. For genealogists, probate records can be especially valuable for the relationships, residences, and marriage documentation they contain.

Estates are either testate (with a will) or intestate (without a will). Intestate estates that go through probate generally, but not always, have the opportunity to create more records than estates governed by a will because the court has more oversight in handling intestate estate business.

In charge of settling a testate estate's business is the executor or executrix (female) named in the will; two or more people may serve in this capacity, depending on how the will was written. If a record such as a tax roll names "Moses Eakins, executor of James Eakins, deceased," you know to look for a will and associated documents. If the record says "Moses Eakins, administrator of James Eakins," you know James did not write a will and the court appointed Moses to administer the estate. A widow could act as executrix or administratrix.

The responsibilities of the executor/-trix or administrator/-trix are to pay debts the deceased owed, collect money owed to the estate, provide for the survivors, complete unfinished business, and eventually divide the remaining property among the legal heirs. These heirs in a testate estate are the people named in the will, usually a spouse and children but sometimes grandchildren, siblings, parents, friends, and institutions (church, school, library, etc.). Heirs in an intestate estate are usually the spouse only or the spouse and legitimate children. If a person dies unmarried, the heirs usually are the parents (if living) or siblings (if the parents are deceased). State law determines the rules of heirship in many different circumstances.

Wills can be great genealogical sources. **They and other documents pertaining to an estate can provide such information as**

1. names and relationships of family members, even in three or four generations, who were alive at the writing of the will and/or at the time of the final settlement
2. names of friends and neighbors
3. land descriptions, the disposition of that land, crops growing on the land
4. specific bequests to individuals or organizations
5. clues to the religious affiliation of the deceased or the family, whether in bequests, funeral information, or cemetery preference
6. conditions to be followed in the estate distribution
7. instructions of the testator about continuing the family business; raising and educating the children; or, to a wife, retaining the property unless she remarried, at which time the property would revert to the children
8. burial arrangements and cemetery identity
9. opinions, pronouncements, attitudes of the testator
10. occupation of the testator or family members
11. residence of testator at the time the will was written
12. residences of family members at the time of the will or the final distribution
13. evidence of heirs, executors, or witnesses who married or died between the writing of the will and the final distribution
14. married surnames of daughters
15. names of daughters' husbands, because married daughters could not inherit in their own names and their husbands therefore were often named with them in final distributions
16. names of daughters' husbands, who were sometimes named as executors or specifically singled out not to receive the daughters' inheritances
17. identities of heirs who were minors at the writing of the will or at the time of distribution, especially with language such as "when he arrives at the age of twenty-one"
18. indications of the ages of the testator or heirs, especially with language such as "the child my wife is carrying"
19. indications of whether daughters or sisters were single, especially with language such as "upon her marriage she is to receive . . ." or naming them with a different surname

Notes

A nuncupative will is an oral declaration, usually by an ill testator to several witnesses. Their notes and oral testimony to the court form the only confirmation of the testator's wishes.

Some wills left everything to "my beloved wife and children," all unnamed. At the other end of the spectrum are wills like that of William Coleman Sr. of Cumberland County, Virginia, dated 23 May 1810. It named the heirs in the way we wish all wills would: his son William and William's wife, Parmelia; grandson Spilsby, son of his son William; his son Henry; grandsons Henry and William D., sons of his son Henry; his son Elliott; grandson Ferdinand G., son of his son Elliott; and his daughter Sarah, wife of Wyatt Coleman (Will Book 4:43).

Inventories and appraisals were part of many estate settlement documents. After a person died, the probate court appointed someone to inventory and appraise the deceased person's estate before a settlement and division of property could be made. If the estate had to sell property to pay debts, the inventory and appraisal were sometimes combined with the estate sale in the records. Some estate records reproduce the entire estate sale, listing who bought what and for how much; the widow and other relatives often bought items at the sale. Inventories provide fascinating reading because they give a picture of the home and farm or business. They may also help determine how a family heirloom such as the family Bible or a piece of furniture moved through the family.

The following are a few of the items listed in William Coleman's estate, inventoried on 20 June 1811 in Cumberland County, Virginia (Will Book 4:69):

ITEM	VALUE IN POUNDS.SHILLINGS.PENCE
1 yoke spotted steers	13.10.00
1 cow with the bell on	4.10.00
1 sorrel mare and colt	30.00.00
8 tobacco hogsheads	2.08.00
1 cask w/vinegar, 40 gallons	.12.00
4 spinning wheels	1.16.00
1 lot of coopers and carpenters tools	2.14.00
1 pare [*sic*] flat irons	.06.00
5 grubbing hoes	1.04.00
1 skillet and dutch oven	.06.00
1 loom	1.04.00
1 saddle, bridle	5.02.00
1 dozen pewter plates, 2 dishes, 5 spoons	1.10.00
half dozen knives and forks	.06.00
9 bee hives	4.01.00
1 set of books	1.10.00
1 corner cupboard	3.12.00
1 desk	3.12.00
13 chairs and 1 slate	1.04.09
2 beds and furniture	20.00.00
1 case of razors	.07.06
1 looking glass	.07.06
1 chest	.18.00
15 sheep and a house lamb	9.12.00
3 sows and 13 pigs	4.10.00

Annual or periodic accountings of income and expenses of the estate became part of the estate record. Apart from an estate sale, cash receipts in this Coleman estate included sales of butter, lard, bacon, vinegar, corn, (goose) feathers, brandy, honey, fodder, wheat, tobacco, a skillet, and a cow. Expenses included such items as repairing the small chimney, weaving and cutting out cloth for Negro clothing, paying the executor's wife for "her attendance two days about cleaning up the house & attending to the cooking of the dinner at the funeral sermon of William Coleman," paying the minister for preaching the funeral sermon, and paying John Hudgins for "crying" the auction at the estate sale less items he purchased at the sale.

Final distribution or settlement of the estate occurred when the various reports were accepted by the court. In March 1814, the four heirs of William Coleman each received in slaves and cash an amount equal to £470.5.10½ (470 pounds, 5 shillings, 10½ pence). The final accounting two years later gave each heir another £10.8.3 (10 pounds, 8 shillings, 3 pence) (Will Book 4:307–313, Book 5:199).

Many people, for whatever reasons, did not (and do not) write wills. The court and family or friends still had to settle these intestate estates, especially when property division or settlement was involved. When Elliott Coleman died intestate in 1892 in Hays County, Texas, the court appointed Ed. A. Vaughan administrator. The twenty-one documents in the case file indicate that Coleman had a very small estate, was owed money, and had some outstanding bills left unpaid. According to one letter in the file, by June 1892, his wife and two minor sons, Zeke and Turner, had moved to Mills County, Texas. Another document named some of the other children who were grown and living elsewhere. Thus, the administrator and a family friend, H.C. Wallace, took on the job of paying the creditors and settling the estate. After Wallace collected money due the estate and paid expenses, he had $18.38 left to apportion out to the six creditors who had been only partially paid. Neither the death date nor the cemetery is named in the documents. However, a note dated 17 February 1892 listed funeral expenses. The doctor's bill included treatments prescribed until February 3. These papers thus suggest that Coleman died between about February 3 and 16. (Coincidentally, Coleman's doctor was Dr. Clemons McGarity, a key figure in the case study in chapter nine.)

See Also

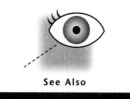

See pages 342–344 for a detailed list of documents from an estate file that were helpful in tracing slave ancestors.

ADMINISTRATIVE AND MISCELLANEOUS RECORDS

County commissioners' minutes and employee records may or may not provide any ancestral information, unless your ancestor was a commissioner or employee. Employee records, like jail records, voter registrations, and automobile registrations, may not be kept more than a few years.

Election returns and polling lists are interesting additions to any family history. They are rather rare but are found in various places. In Caldwell County, Kentucky, they were bundled neatly on a basement shelf. (It is not the kind of basement that requires hard hat, work gloves, and flashlight.) The records revealed that in Princeton on Monday morning, 7 November 1836, Ira Brelsford and Samuel Black had both cast their votes for Martin Van Buren for president. (Van Buren won that election.) Samuel Black remained a Democrat, supporting Van Buren in 1840, Polk in 1844, and Cass in 1848. Ira Brelsford, on the other hand, became a Whig, then supported Fillmore and the American Party in 1856, and Bell's Constitutional Union Party in 1860.

Some early polling lists for Cumberland County, Virginia, can be found in the county deed books. In Book 10, for example, is the evidence that in April 1805 Peter T. Phillips voted for John Randolph for Congress and John Hatcher and German Baker for the assembly. Such records help genealogists understand a little of the political views their ancestors may have held and how they viewed political events. When combined with newspaper reports of election campaigns, such lists add much to the social history of the family.

Business and professional licenses, such as those for physicians, dentists, nurses, tavern keepers, and ferrymen, may show age, address, birthplace, or education information. Other records vary from county to county and in their usefulness for genealogists. Most of them can place an ancestor in a given county on a given date and show that he or she was living.

THE WILL OF C.D. DOUGLAS

This will is typical of many wills written between the colonial era and the present. It contains many standard features and one unique provision in the second item.

IN THE NAME OF GOD, AMEN.

I, C.D. Douglas, of Brookings, S[outh] D[akota] being of sound mind and memory and fully realizing the uncertainties of this frail and transitory life do hereby make, publish and declare this to be my Last Will and testament.

First, I direct that my executrices hereinafter named pay all my just debts and funeral expenses as soon after my decease as conveniently may be.

Second, After the payment of such debts and expenses I give, devise and bequeath unto my grandson, Deloss Revell, the interest and income from the sum of $2,000.00 which amount I hereby set apart therefor, and hereby appoint the First National Bank of Brookings, S.D. as trustee to have and receive said principal sum of $2,000.00, with directions that they keep the same bearing interest at the best rates commensurate with safety and that they pay the interest derived from said sum of $2,000.00 unto the said Deloss Revell annually until he shall arrive of the age of fifty years, and that when he shall arrive at the age of fifty years, then I give and devise the principal of said sum of $2,000.00 to the said Deloss Revell and direct the said First National Bank or their successors as trustees to then pay said principal sum unto the said Deloss Revell.

Third, All the rest, residue and remainder of my estate whether the same be real, personal or mixed and wheresoever situated I give, devise and bequeath to my beloved daughter, Lucy I. Revell and my grandchildren, Mary F. Ely, Alma Mitchell, Grace Bailey, Frank Revell, Lucy Revell and Helen Revell, in equal portions, share and share alike.

Lastly, I do hereby make, constitute and appoint my said daughter, Lucy I. Revell and my granddaughter, Grace Bailey, executrices of this my Last Will and Testament, hereby revoking any and all former wills by me made. said [*sic*] executrices need not give bond or other security.

IN WITNESS WHEREOF I have hereunto subscribed my name and affixed my seal this *14th* day of May, A.D., 1919. [signed] C.D. Douglas.

This instrument was on the day of the date thereof, signed, published and declared by said testator, C.D. Douglas to be his last Will and Testament, in the presence of us who at his request have subscribed our names thereto as witnesses in his presence and in the presence of each other. [Three signatures follow: J.P. Cheever and two that are difficult to read.]

Many of these records are not indexed and take time to research. Ask about specific records or browse among the records; nice surprises sometimes await us.

Warning

COUNTY HISTORIES

Published county histories, like published family histories, can run the gamut of quality and reliability. Many of them include biographical sketches of individuals or families, and these too vary greatly in accuracy. However, these works are worth reading, for they often give good historical background on the local area, as well as capsuled histories of towns, churches, schools, and organizations in the county.

In the 1880s, several companies published county and local histories that included not only information on the first settlers, first officers, and first institutions, but also on the current residents and activities. The Goodspeed Publishing Company of Chicago published such histories of various states, county by county, including autobiographical sketches of citizens who chose to participate. The town sketches identified the trustees of the local academy, elders of the local churches, and officers of the lodges. Some of the Goodspeed's histories have been reprinted to include only the biographical sketches; others have been reissued in their entirety.

Throughout the twentieth century, county genealogical and historical societies published history-and-genealogy compilations in the tradition of the nineteenth-century predecessors. Although space limitations almost always prevent the documentation of family or local data, these volumes provide good clues, and sometimes contacts for continuing research.

In addition to county histories, the following books are useful in county research:

The American Counties, by Joseph Nathan Kane. 4th ed. Metuchen, N.J.: The Scarecrow Press, 1983. Includes independent cities and boroughs.

Ancestry's Red Book: American State, County, and Town Sources, Alice Eichholz, ed. Salt Lake City: Ancestry, 3d ed. to be released 2004.

County Courthouse Book, by Elizabeth Petty Bentley. 2d ed. Baltimore: Genealogical Publishing Co., 1995.

The Handy Book for Genealogists. 10th ed. Draper, Utah: Everton Publishers, 2002.

United States Local Histories in the Library of Congress: A Bibliography, Marion J. Kaminkow, ed. 5 vols. Reprint. Baltimore: Magna Carta Books, 1975.

Works Progress Administration, Historical Records Survey, Inventories of County Archives, variously published. See also *Bibliography of Research Projects Reports: A Checklist of Historical Records Survey Publications*. Washington, D.C.: WPA, 1943.

Local Sources

Local sources can be extremely valuable for genealogists. Whether rural or urban, local resources include cemeteries, churches, and schools. In towns and cities genealogists may find a variety of records related to residents, businesses and professions, organizations, and local government. Local areas vary in the kinds of records available, but most have something of value.

CEMETERIES

In the eastern part of the United States, some cemeteries and legible tombstones date from the seventeenth century. Of course, thousands of ancestors have unmarked graves, and despite laws to the contrary, many cemeteries have been bulldozed in the name of progress and profit. Nonetheless, when you are lucky enough to locate family tombstones, you can often glean valuable information. Using published transcriptions and reading the original inscriptions require caution on the part of the researcher.

Why Research Cemeteries?

Genealogical information on tombstones runs the gamut. How many times have you seen small stones marked "Our Baby" or "Little Bennie, age 5"? Due to expense, rules, or tombstone orders placed by a nongenealogist, some markers show only the years of a person's life instead of complete dates. Sometimes, stones show only a person's initials, perhaps because of space, expense, or the name by which the person was known. Figure 4-1, on page 122, illustrates both limitations on the stone for Nancy Mason, wife of S.D. Williamson. In the same cemetery, the other tombstone in Figure 4-1 does not identify the woman's middle name but does provide her complete dates, her maiden name, and her husband's name. The style of the stone is contemporary with her death date; thus, the people who ordered it were closer to the events it reports than succeeding generations would have been. That proximity does not guarantee correct information, but the greater number of years that intervene between the person's life and the stone's manufacture, the greater the room for error.

The two stones transcribed here also provide maiden names and husbands' names. In addition, the Blackwell stone also indicates a subsequent marriage; the Mood stone gives a specific birthplace.

MARY A. BLACKWELL
formerly widow of Edward Philpot
nee Miss Mary A. Taylor
b 6 May 1809
d 21 July 1886
(Crowder Cemetery, Hardeman County, Tennessee)

SUSAN RICHARDSON LOGAN
wife of Rev. F. A. Mood
b Bloomhill, South Carolina
5 Aug. 1843
d 13 Nov. 1916
(IOOF Cemetery, Georgetown, Texas)

IOOF is the Independent Order of Odd Fellows, a benevolent fraternal organization.

Important

Genealogists must be alert for family members buried in groups. These groups may represent several generations and different surnames. Having some background in the extended family—the ancestral cluster—is helpful before visiting cemeteries, but copying tombstones around an ancestor's grave may provide clues to help identify those other generations. Tombstones of children often contain their parents' names and help the genealogist understand holes in the family census records or the absence of a young person from one census to the next. Even artwork on the tombstone may contain clues to religious or lodge membership or military service and provide clues to other sources for research. Inscriptions may also include a marriage date, children's names, or cause of death. A mother buried with her infant usually suggests that the mother and child died in or shortly after childbirth.

Case Study: Clues From the Cemetery

Case Study

Cemetery visits can provide new avenues for research. Thomas and Emilia King's names and dates are on two sides of a small obelisk in Houston's Washington Cemetery. On a third side is engraved "William A. Rock, 13 May 187L [*sic*]–2 April 1910." Who was this? In the course of gathering basic vital statistics, descendants had found a local marriage record of a Thomas King to Miss Amelia Rock in December 1880, but the death record of Emilia King's son Alfred gave her maiden name as Preuss. Thus, the family had thought the marriage record was for a different couple. Now, with the tombstone information, the obvious next step was another look at the 1880 federal census, using the surname Rock instead of King or Preuss, which had revealed nothing of this family.

The result was positive, showing Amelia Rock, "widowed or divorced," and her son, William Rock (age seven), and daughters, Emily and Mary (ages four and three). A search of the 1870 census showed Amelia Preuss and William Rock in Travis County, Texas, where their marriage was recorded in August 1872. The shared tombstone was the key to solving several mysteries, but the mystery of the "187L" date remains. The *L* is not an upside-down 7 but may be an incomplete 4. The 1880 census suggests an 1873 birthdate for William, but his 1900 census entry, questionable in several other aspects, gives November 1876. Unfortunately for genealogists, William died before the 1910 census. (And of course, the King-Rock marriage record contained an error; the bride was *Mrs.* Amelia Rock.)

Case Study: Transcriptions Raise Questions

Case Study

As helpful as cemetery transcriptions are, especially when you are researching from a distance, they can contain errors. One such error was a mistake in reading the original stones. A published transcription of Samuel and Keturah Black's tombstones in Caldwell County, Kentucky, actually contained six errors. It gave Samuel's dates as 11 October 1779 to 9 October 1859 "in 81rst year of his life" and Keturah's as 13 November 1779 to 19 August 1859 "in 79th year of age."

Figure 4-1 Tombstones from Pine Island Cemetery, Simpson, Vernon Parish, Louisiana, from author's collection.

The first problem appeared to be mathematical. According to the transcription, Samuel would have turned eighty years of age had he lived two more days; thus, he would have been in his eightieth year when he died, not eighty-first. In addition, since Keturah had turned seventy-nine on her last birthday, she was in her eightieth year when she died, if the transcribed *dates* were correct. If the transcribed *ages* were correct, then birth or death dates could be wrong.

Two further discrepancies appeared from public records. One was the 1850 census, reporting their ages as seventy-seven and seventy, which matched the tombstone birthdate for Keturah but suggested a 1772 birth year for Samuel. County records showed Samuel signing a deed of gift on 30 August 1852, and the inventory of his estate, following his death, was made on 25 November 1852. His estate inventory would not have taken place before his death; thus, the 1859 death date was questionable.

The problem was solved by obtaining good photographs of the actual tombstones. The errors had occurred in the 9s. Every 9 except the one in Keturah's birth date was actually a 2 in the photograph. These were strange 2s with a large loop at the top. Perhaps the engraver had used a 9 and extended a line at the bottom to create a 2. Nevertheless, the photographs were clear. The correct dates for Samuel were 11 October 1772–26 October

1852 and for Keturah, 13 November 1779–12 August 1852. Samuel had just turned eighty when he died and was indeed in his eighty-first year. Keturah was already seventy-two when she died, and the inscription on her tombstone was correct: "in 72nd year of age."

Locating Cemeteries

If you know the name and location of a cemetery where your ancestors were buried, half the task is done, and you can plan a visit or arrange for someone to photograph tombstones for you. If you do not know of a particular cemetery in which to look, you have several options:

1. A number of sources may supply the name of a cemetery where an ancestor was buried: newspaper obituaries, death certificates, probate records, family Bibles and papers, older family members, county and local histories, church registers, some organization or lodge records, city or cemetery interment records, and funeral home files may supply the name of the cemetery and sometimes its location. Churches often had burial grounds adjacent to or in the churchyard, and members of the congregation may have used that space for family grave sites.

2. Many transcribed cemetery interment records or tombstone inscriptions have been published. Often arranged by county or by surname, they are relatively easy to investigate. Some repositories, such as the New Orleans Public Library, have card indexes to interments. The Family History Library has some transcriptions available through the Family History Centers. Remember, ancestors were not buried in alphabetical order but often in family groups; thus, the most helpful transcriptions are those that list names as they appear in the cemetery rather than in alphabetical order.

3. The Graves Registration Project of the WPA (Works Progress Administration) during the 1930s and 1940s recorded cemeteries and/or individual tombstones in many states; some of these projects focused on veterans' burials. A number of state archives hold these files and indexes; they are often not complete but can be helpful in locating cemeteries or gravesites.

4. National Archives microfilm M1845 contains card records of headstones provided for deceased Union Civil War veterans (more than 160,000) from about 1879 to about 1903. The twenty-two rolls are arranged alphabetically by surname. For a roll list, do a film/fiche search on the Family History Library Web site <www.familysearch.org/Eng/Library/FHLC/frameset_fhlc.asp> using the first film number in the series: 2155576; click on "search results," then on "view film notes."

5. If you know the county in which the person lived at the time of death, you can begin by focusing on the cemeteries in that county. If no transcriptions exist for that county, get a map that shows the known cemeteries and begin investigating or visiting them. Some cemeteries have associations or commercial offices that keep the records and take care of the grounds. They often have maps that identify the burials in each plot. These plot maps may indicate where and when a person was buried even if no stone marks the spot. Check with a local funeral director or library to use one of the national directories of cemeteries to get contact information for cemeteries in other cities. Funeral directors in small towns and near rural areas may be able to help you locate a specific cemetery if a county map does not show its location. Some local genealogy libraries have cemetery files of various kinds, including directions for finding each one. Local genealogists often know the location of cemeteries in the county.

6. Especially in the twentieth century, some ancestors were buried in cemeteries near their previous residences.

You will not find cemeteries or tombstones for all your ancestors. In rural areas and in cities, cemeteries have been lost or forgotten over the years, and the sites have been covered with roads, buildings, parks, and national forests. In the way of "progress," some stones have been moved to new locations.

See Also

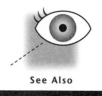

See page 246 for more on using maps; see page 74 for more on the 1886 Social Statistics Reports.

County and city maps show the location of numerous cemeteries, and older maps may show cemeteries no longer in use or whose locations are unknown today. In addition, the Census Office's 1886 *Report on the Social Statistics of Cities*, compiled after the 1880 census, describes the location of cemeteries for many of the 222 cities included in the report. For example, after describing the six cemeteries in Jersey City, New Jersey, the compiler commented that Saint Peter's cemetery "is in a rather poor location, facing the western ends of the tunnels of [two] railroads, and for some time there has been trouble between the railroads and the owners of the cemetery. The lots are all bought up; none are now buried here except lot-owners, and the cemetery will probably have to be removed."[1] If you read such comments about an ancestral cemetery, try to determine what happened.

In the same 1886 report for Burlington, Vermont, the compiler listed five city cemeteries. For all cemeteries, the city health officer issued burial permits based on a certificate of the attending physician; genealogists should ask about the existence of these records. In addition, a family had to obtain a permit from the priest before a burial in Mount Saint Joseph Cemetery (Catholic) or Calvary Cemetery (French Catholic). However, the compiler answered the next question genealogists would ask by adding: "For a long series of years no record was kept of the interments in the several cemeteries . . . [Burial records are] from 1860 for Mount Saint Joseph; 1868 for Lake View; 1878 for Calvary; and 1879 for the other two."[2]

Technique

This process would be the same for many of the sources listed in this book.

Thus, the genealogist's next question is "Do *these* records still exist, and where?" You could begin by (1) looking in WorldCat or other library catalogs to determine whether the interment records have been published or (2) consulting the Family History Library catalog to learn whether such records are available on microfilm through a Family History Center. You could also contact the public library in Burlington (or any other ancestral location) to see (1) whether they hold the records or copies of them and (2) whether they have a researcher list from which you could contact someone who could search the records for you, send you copies of pertinent years' entries, or visit a cemetery and photograph stones for you.

Visiting Cemeteries

Upon determining a burial location, some families pool their resources to honor ancestors with new markers. Although this is a generous gesture, some such stones do not contain correct information. Especially if the stones were not erected soon after the death (and you can often tell by the appearance of the stone or other data gathered during research), genealogists must be cautious in accepting the information they show.

Once you identify an ancestral resting place, copy the inscriptions carefully. If possible, photograph the stones and record their location within the cemetery. If daylight does not highlight the inscription well enough, use mirrors to reflect light onto the stone; use cardboard to shade a glare. When photographing tombstones, also walk away and photograph the stone from enough distance that you see the stone in the context of its surroundings. Label your photographs with the cemetery name and location, the date of your visit, and the name of the person buried there, especially if the inscription is dim.

If the cemetery does not provide a map of the plots, sketch your own. Note landmarks, such as large monuments, roads, fenced plots, gates, row numbers, and even trees, that could help you find the grave site in the future. Measure your pace before leaving home or carry a measuring tape in order to locate grave sites on your map in relation to other features. You can also use a Global Positioning System (GPS) handheld device to find the longitude and latitude coordinates of the plot to show on your map. Some automobiles are now equipped with these devices that could be used at the cemetery gate or on its roads.

ADVICE FOR ENHANCING INSCRIPTIONS

(The following applies only where cleaning and rubbing are not prohibited by law or cemetery rules.) If a tombstone appears unstable (flaking, crumbling, or chipping), do nothing to the stone. Because some stones, for many reasons (age, plant growth, mold, etc.), are not entirely legible, you may consider cleaning a stone only with *distilled* water and a very soft nylon or plastic brush, followed by a gentle rub with a clean cloth. To highlight the inscription, you may rub *only* white blackboard chalk on the stone, not "sidewalk" chalk, crayons, or other compounds. Before leaving, again use only distilled water to remove the chalk. *Sharon DeBartolo Carmack,* Your Guide to Cemetery Research. (See this book for more on cemetery research and on photographing and rubbing tombstones.)

RELIGIOUS RECORDS

Religious records of the greatest genealogical value are usually those of events such as baptism, confirmation, bar mitzvah and bas mitzvah, marriage, and burial. Sometimes family papers contain certificates from these events. In addition, congregational minutes, officer lists, and membership rolls may contain interesting and pertinent historical information on ancestors.

Genealogy in Church Records

Church records of religious events can provide valuable information on births, marriages, deaths, and parentage of ancestors. For example, churches have kept baptism records for centuries. This example contains good genealogical information

> Alfred Thomas King, residence 6004 Sherman, Houston, born 14 May 1925, son of Alfred Thomas King and Annie E. King, baptized 14 June 1925, by Rev. Thomas J. Windham, Clemens Memorial Chapel (later the Episcopal Church of the Good Shepherd), Houston, Texas. Sponsors: Louis Edward DelHomme and Emma Louise DelHomme.

In the case of these sponsors, who were aunt and uncle of the baby, the church record provided their full names, which had not been found in other sources.

In the same family and church, the parents were confirmed as adults: Annie E. King, in 1921; her husband, in 1930. His confirmation record gave the additional information that he had been born in 1886 in Houston and was baptized in the Lutheran church. This information provided new clues for research into his childhood. Sometimes, such records created for adults provide wives' maiden names.

The same church record books reflect the burial of Annie King's father, Joseph T. Wells, age sixty-seven, who died on 9 December 1912 and was buried in Houston's Glenwood Cemetery on December 10, with Rev. Thomas J. Windham officiating. Finding the death date in the church record was especially helpful since Mr. Wells had no civil death certificate and no dates on the obelisk that bears his name and identifies the family cemetery plot.

This church's early marriage records do not offer much information besides the most basic facts: Jewell Black married Oscar T. Hansard at the rectory on 6 June 1928. Later marriage certificates contain full names, ages, parentage, and family addresses of the bride and groom as well as full names of two witnesses. In this set of record books, Rev. Windham recorded weddings that he performed at the church, at the rectory, at the bride's home, and one at the James Furniture Store. Although this church closed in the mid-1980s, its records are housed at another Episcopal church in the area.[3]

Figure 4-2, below, shows the beginning of the 1835 baptism register for the United German Lutheran Churches of New York City. These records occasionally identify a relationship between the baby and the sponsors, as in the case of Henry William Garbe, for whom one sponsor was his grandmother, Jane Baptist. Often the sponsors were relatives or close friends of the parents. These church records, created with great precision and detail, also include a lengthy biography of the pastor, Rev. Frederick William Geissenhainer, D.D., 1771–1838, written within a day or two of his death.

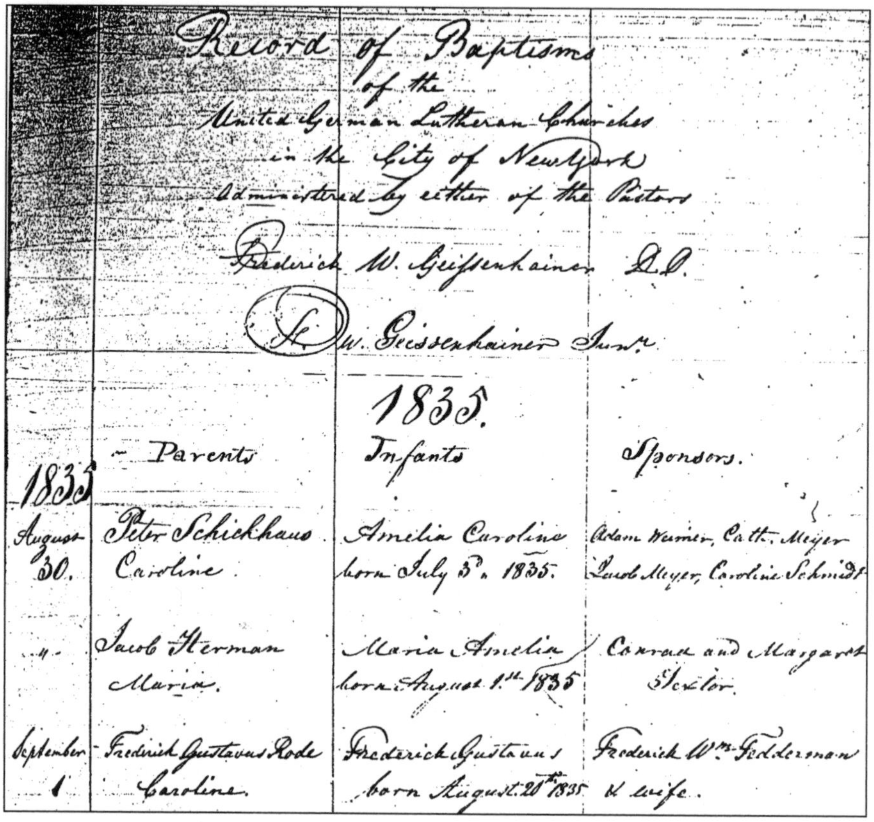
Record of Baptisms of the United German Lutheran Churches in the City of NewYork Administered by either of the Pastors Frederick W. Geissenhainer D.D. F. W. Geissenhainer Junr.

1835.

1835	Parents	Infants	Sponsors
August 30.	Peter Schickhaus Caroline.	Amelia Caroline born July 5th 1835.	Adam Werner, Cath. Meyer Jacob Meyer, Caroline Schmidt
" 4	Jacob Herman Maria.	Maria Amelia born August 1st 1835	Conrad and Margaret Sexlor.
September 1	Frederick Gustavus Rode Caroline.	Frederick Gustavus born August 20th 1835	Frederick Wm. Feddermann & wife.

Figure 4-2 Record of Baptisms, 1835, United German Lutheran Churches, New York City, p. 69, FHL microfilm 1901796.

The same church's marriage records, illustrated in Figure 4-3, on page 127, provide not only the names and ages of the bride and groom but also their residences and occupations and the names and residences of witnesses. Notice that John Hendricks, a "taylor," was marrying Jane Sloan, "widow of Bernard Sloan dec^{d} 3 Years." For genealogists, such evidence of the bride's previous marriage is important information and sometimes a surprise.

The burial records, shown in Figure 4-4, on page 127, provide the date of burial, name of the deceased, birthplace of some immigrants, age at death, cause of death, and other notes. One interesting entry from the same register page as Figure 4-4 noted the 22 September 1835 burial of Leonard Fischer, "an old worthy member of our Congregation aged nearly 82 years, died of old age, and was burried [*sic*] in a Vault on his own land."

Each congregation keeps its records in its own way, often depending on the wishes and

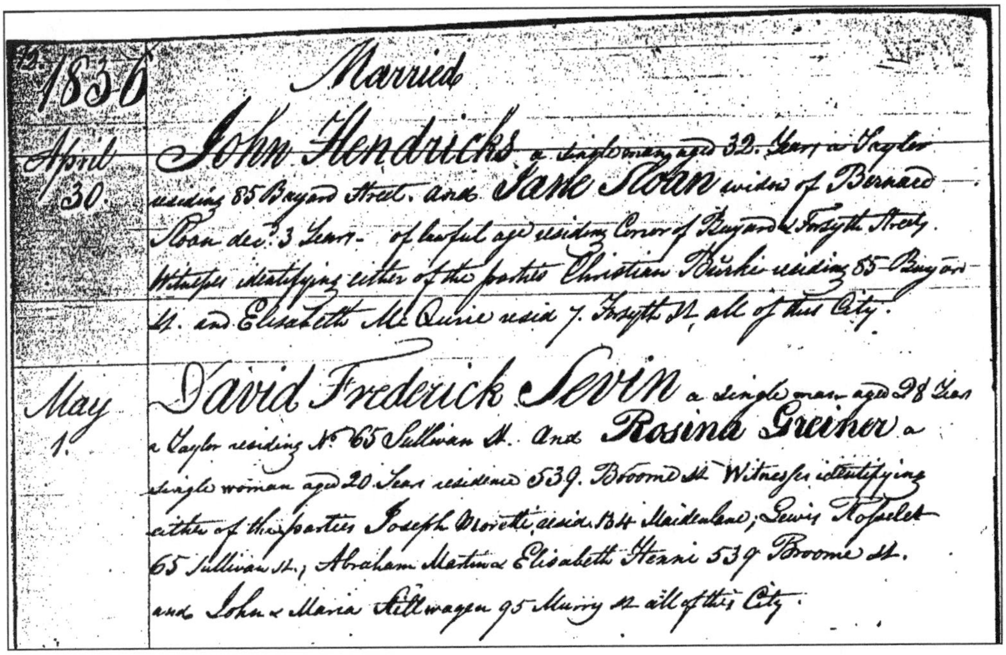

1836 Married

April 30. John Hendricks a single man aged 32 Years a Taylor residing 85 Bayard Street. and Sarah Sloan widow of Bernard Sloan dec'd 3 Years of lawful age residing Corner of Bayard & Forsyth Streets. Witnesses identifying either of the parties Christian Bürki residing 85 Bayard St. and Elisabeth McQuire residing 7 Forsyth St. all of this City.

May 1. David Frederick Sevin a single man aged 28 Years a Taylor residing No 65 Sullivan St. and Rosina Greiner a single woman aged 20 Years residing 539 Broome St. Witnesses identifying either of the parties Joseph Morotti residing 134 Maidenlane; Lewis Hofselet 65 Sullivan St., Abraham Martin & Elisabeth Henni 539 Broome St. and John & Maria Hillwagen 95 Murray St. all of this City.

Figure 4-3 Marriages, 1836, United German Lutheran Churches, New York City, p. 12, FHL microfilm 1901796.

choices of the clergy at the time. In small or rural congregations, especially before the twentieth century, the clergyman was often the record keeper, if records were kept at all. If he or his family did not pass the records to the person who followed him in the role of spiritual leader, the records could well have been lost over the succeeding years.

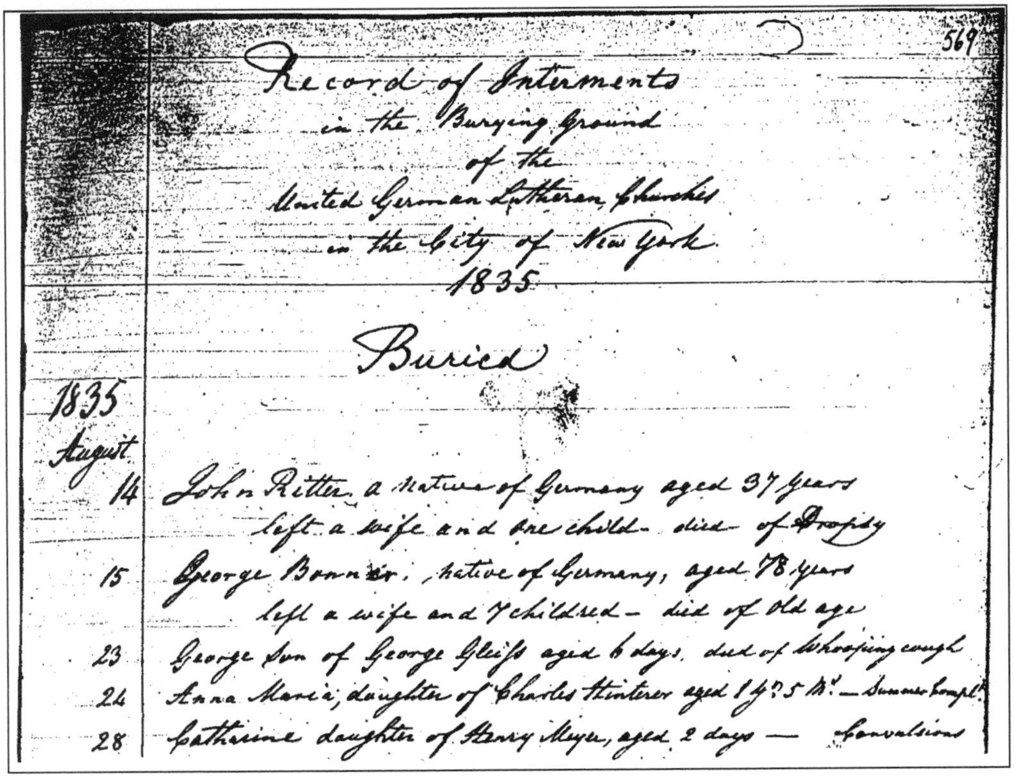

569

Record of Interments in the Burying Ground of the United German Lutheran Churches in the City of New York 1835

Buried

1835 August

14 John Ritter a native of Germany aged 37 years left a wife and one child — died of Dropsy

15 George Bonner, native of Germany, aged 78 years left a wife and 7 children — died of Old age

23 George Son of George Gleiss aged 6 days, died of Whooping cough

24 Anna Maria; daughter of Charles Hinterer aged 1 y. 5 Mo. — Summer Compl.

28 Catharine daughter of Henry Meyer, aged 2 days — Convulsions

Figure 4-4 Record of Interments, 1835, United German Lutheran Churches, New York City, marked p. 569 (but is not), FHL microfilm 1901796.

Clues and History in Church Records

Records of the Presbyterian Church in Bolivar, Tennessee, reflect the same events in the lives of the members: baptism, membership, marriage, death. In addition, they give information on the leadership of the congregation and clues for further genealogical research. For example, E.G. Coleman was admitted to membership by examination on 4 September 1854, two years after his wife and brothers joined. He was ordained a deacon on 19 June 1858 and dismissed on 9 January 1872, with his wife, Catherine, when they moved to Texas. James Fentress, installed an elder on 26 April 1868, was dismissed 7 March 1881, going to First Church, New Orleans.[4]

The colonial Anglican (now Episcopal) churches kept, besides church registers, record books on the business operations of the individual parishes by the committee called the vestry. For each meeting of the vestry, the report listed the names of members present and items of business handled, including the rector's salary, tithes assessed within the parish, and monies spent on indigents, repairs, and supplies. The Bristol Parish vestry, at Petersburg, Virginia, voted to receive Rev. William Harrison as rector on 22 November 1762. On 13 February 1763, they recorded the spending of nine shillings on two bottles of "clarrot" for communion; on 27 September 1763, a little more than £4 (4 pounds) on 11¼ yards of Irish linen and one ounce of thread for "suples" (surplices). In June 1752, when they expanded the south side of the church, they set down in the vestry book the specifications for the addition, including dimensions, thickness of the brick walls, kind of windows, size of floor planks, style of pews, and kind of roof, to be covered with "good cypress heart shingles." In 1765, it was reported that due to "an uncommon winter and the long and continued severity of it," nine bottles of "clarrett" stored for Communion had turned "sow^r [sour] and useless."[5] These details in themselves are not genealogical, but if your ancestors were part of the vestry or the congregation, you would want to study this most interesting kind of historical source. An amazing number of vestry books and similar records survive. Many, such as those of Bristol Parish, have been published or microfilmed.

Nearly one hundred years later, in June 1849, the Session of the Fishing Creek Presbyterian Church of Chester County, South Carolina, became so deeply concerned about some members of the church allowing their children to indulge in a particular worldly sin that they issued a lengthy and stern "Testimony against Dancing." They had marked with "painful anxiety the prevalence of worldly amusements" among the youth of the church. After proclaiming the amusement as "sinful, offensive in the sight of God," and "exerting a most pernicious influence on the minds and morals of the young," and quoting several scripture passages to support their position, the Session issued a warning to parents in the congregation to forbid their children from engaging in dancing or "bring swift destruction on their own souls" and be subject to disciplinary action by the Church.[6] From the genealogical point of view, the Session's greatest sin of omission was not listing the names of the guilty families.

The county museum in Monroe County, Alabama, holds the manuscript minutes of the Salem Baptist Church's monthly conferences, beginning in November 1817. Members were both black and white, and the minutes reflect ordinary, uneventful church business—"conversed about many things and concluded by prayer." They also noted over the winter of 1819–1820 that the church did not assemble because the creeks were too full. However, these minutes reflect some of the same concerns about behavior of members as did the Presbyterian Session records. In 1828, the Baptists chose Brother Ellis to call on Brother (William) Cato to know whether he had joined another church and, if not, to admonish him of his duty and report at the next conference. That report "proved satisfactory," but the brothers who were appointed to converse with Brother Elbert Chism had an unfavorable report, upon which the church agreed to exclude him for immoral conduct such as drinking spiritous [*sic*] liquors to excess and not attending conference when cited. In 1829, they excluded Marian Wiggins for joining the Methodist Society.[7]

Such social history enlivens family history and helps genealogists understand the world in which ancestors lived. Occasionally, these records also give us information about a specific ancestor.

Finding Religious Records

The first task is to try to identify the faith or denomination of each ancestral family or individual and the name of a specific congregation. This effort is sometimes more difficult the farther back in time you reach. However, when the population of an area was more homogeneous than it is now or when fewer choices of religious affiliation existed, history may help narrow your choices.

Remember, not all ancestors affiliated with a religious group. Family members did not always join the same denomination or church, and some family members changed denominations. In addition, some denominations have merged and changed their names over the years, especially the United Methodist Church, the Evangelical Lutheran Church in America, and the United Church of Christ. Baptist, Episcopal, and Presbyterian denominations and others have also experienced mergers and name changes. Check denominational Web sites, where they sometimes explain their history. Do the background research, and let it guide you.

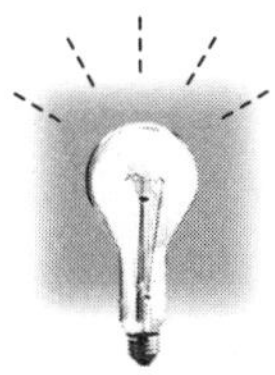

Idea Generator

Clues to ancestral affiliation may be in

- family tradition and interviews with family members
- family papers, including family Bibles, baptism and confirmation certificates of parents or children, funeral programs or cards, evidence of membership in a religious organization related to a particular faith or denomination, diaries, baby books, wedding pictures, wedding guest books, scrapbooks, letters
- newspaper obituaries or local newspaper mentions during the lifetime of the ancestor
- death notices in an organization's publication or files
- death certificates, indicating place of burial; funeral home records, especially if the funeral home dealt primarily with one religious or ethnic group; the cemetery where ancestors were buried; artwork on tombstones within the family
- marriage records, particularly the name and denomination or faith of a clergyman who married the couple
- probate records and estate settlements, naming a place of burial, revealing a bequest to a house of worship, or listing a clergyman who conducted the burial service
- ancestral neighborhoods—a church close to their home, their friends' religious affiliation
- an ancestor's family—siblings, cousins, other relatives who may have been part of the same congregation; wedding announcements of siblings; relatives who were married or buried by the same clergyman
- interviews with older members of the community in which the family lived who know of the predominant organized religious bodies in the area at the time the ancestor lived there
- census records, if a family member was a member of the clergy and reported such as an occupation
- published county, local, and church histories, including biographical sketches of the family

Once you determine or have evidence of a religious affiliation and/or a specific congregation, try to locate and inspect the records. You may need to survey several congregations

Tip

near the family home. **Most congregations keep their own records; begin there.** The clergy, staff, or current lay leadership can often tell you where the records are available for research. Keep in mind that each faith or denomination has its own procedures for keeping or storing congregational records; ask within each religious group where you are likely to find the records you seek.

Although many congregations have historical records, not all fellowships of which our ancestors were members have records beyond more recent years. Like courthouses, churches sometimes suffer fires as the offices of my church did on Palm Sunday night, 1979. We lost the baptism, marriage, and death records but were able to reconstruct the membership list. When my mother was gathering documents for a delayed birth certificate, she requested a copy of her baptism record from the church where that event took place. She was told that those records had been stored in the parsonage for years, but a minister's wife, tired of the old books taking up closet space, had burned them!

If original records no longer exist, transcriptions may be available. Extant records may be stored at

- the church or other house of worship
- a member's house
- a parsonage, vicarage, or clergy's home
- a local or county historical or genealogical society library, or a public or academic library
- a state historical society, archives, museum, or library's special collections

Some church records have been transcribed and published in books or historical and genealogical periodicals. Check the indexes and contents of the state's periodicals, as well as compiled periodical indexes (see chapter eight). Some of these records have been microfilmed and placed in special collections in the state; some are available for rent from the Family History Library.

For congregations that are no longer active, records are often held at (1) a neighboring congregation of the same denomination or faith or (2) a denominational or faith-based archive, especially at the regional or district jurisdictional office: Catholic, Episcopalian, and Greek Orthodox dioceses; Methodist annual conferences; Lutheran synods; etc. Some of these administrative offices maintain archives of inactive congregations; some do not. To contact such offices, check their Web sites. For example, a Catholic diocese directory is online at <www.catholic-usa.com/dioceses.html>. The Catholic Internet Directory (CID) is online at <www.catholic-church.org/cid/>. Some of these Web sites post information about archives. The General Commission on Archives and History of the United Methodist Church and its predecessor churches provides information for genealogists at <www.gcah.org/Searching.htm>.

The Archives of the Evangelical Lutheran Church in America divides the United States into nine regions. Records include those of various predecessor churches, synods, and some individual churches as well as some congregational histories. A list of the regional archives is online at <www.elca.org/os/archives/regsyn.html>. Important information for genealogists is on the Web site at <www.elca.org/os/archives/geneal.html>.

If the jurisdictional offices do not hold the records you need, contact the libraries of denominational and faith-based universities, seminaries, and historical societies. The collections at these institutions vary in their focus. Some hold historical church records, especially for inactive congregations; some focus more on general church history and theology. Either way, their collections may contain records of historical congregations or biographical information on clergy. The reference staff may be able to suggest additional repositories or historical centers for you to contact.

To locate religious archives, libraries, and historical societies and their addresses, or to identify other repositories with church record collections, use library catalogs, Internet search engines, WorldCat, the various online sources of manuscript collections (see chapter seven), Cyndi's List <www.cyndislist.com>, the state-by-state list below, links from the Web sites of institutions in the state-by-state list, and the following reference books:

American Library Directory. New York: R.R. Bowker, latest edition. In the organization index, look for individual church, university, or religious organization names; generic words such as *congregation* and *diocese*; names of denominations. Survey libraries in each state.

Directory of Archives and Manuscript Repositories in the United States. 2d ed. Phoenix, Ariz.: Oryx Press, 1988.

Directory of Historical Organizations in the United States and Canada. Nashville, Tenn.: American Association for State and Local History, latest edition.

Directory of Religious Archival and Historical Depositories in America. St. Louis: Society of American Archivists, Church Records Committee, 1963–1968.

Encyclopedia of Associations: A Guide to National and International Organizations and *Encyclopedia of Associations: Regional, State, and Local Organizations*. Detroit: Gale Research, latest editions.

A Guide to Archives and Manuscripts in the United States, Philip M. Hamer, ed. New Haven, Conn.: Yale University Press, 1961, for National Historical Publications Commission.

Handbook of Denominations in the United States, by Frank Mead. Nashville: Abingdon Press, 1970.

National Union Catalog of Manuscript Collections. Washington, D.C.: Library of Congress, 1990. See p. *xl* under Religion, lists reporting repositories 1975–1990. See also online versions (chapter eight).

Preliminary Guide to Church Records Repositories, by August R. Suelflow. St. Louis [now Chicago]: Society of American Archivists, 1969.

Source Book and Bibliographical Guide for American Church History, by Peter G. Mode. Boston: J.S. Canner and Co., 1964 reprint of 1921 original.

A Survey of American Church Records, by E. Kay Kirkham. 4th ed. Logan, Utah: Everton Publishers, 1978.

Yearbook of American and Canadian Churches. Nashville: Abingdon Press, latest edition.

Church Record Repositories and Historical Collections

No complete list of church records has been made or can be made. The Works Progress Administration (WPA) during the 1930s inventoried church records in many areas, under the Historical Records Survey project (see state listings below). Although these inventories are outdated, they may still provide good references and clues. The National Archives holds the WPA inventories of church archives for at least New Jersey, New York, Oklahoma, and Utah.

The following repositories report collections of church history, which may include archives, congregational records, and denominational or faith-based newspapers:

Alabama—Department of Archives and History (many denominations); Samford University, Birmingham (Baptist).

CHURCH RECORDS SOLVE A MYSTERY

I had always wondered why my maternal great-great-grandparents John Haywood East and Mary Ann (Storm) East named their first child Wiley H. East. At first I thought that John's father might have been William since I knew Mary Ann's father was John Storm. Thus, I knew Wiley was not named for his maternal grandfather. Could he have been named for his paternal grandfather?

John East and Mary Ann Storm married in 1835 in Hendricks County, Indiana, and moved to Iowa. Census records reported he was born in North Carolina in 1807; perhaps the 1810 census of North Carolina would suggest a father and family for him. The only East in that census with a son of the age to be John was Thomas East Jr. in Surry County. Checking marriage records in surrounding counties, I discovered that Thomas East Jr. had married Anna Maria Hauser in 1799 in Bethania, now Forsyth County, then Stokes County, which had been formed out of Surry.

The book *Forsyth County, N.C., Cemetery Records*, compiled by Donald W. Stanley, Ann Ellis Sheek, and Hazell R. Hartman (Kernersville, N.C.: Stanley, 1976–1978), indicates that the cemetery at Bethania was a Moravian cemetery. Were the Easts or Hausers Moravians? I had no idea. Wondering whether I could find Moravian church records, I used an online search engine to try to find out.

A chain of Web sites led me eventually to the archives of the Moravian Church in America <http://moravianarchives.org>, located in Forsyth County, North Carolina, at Winston-Salem. I wrote to them for information on the East and Hauser families and, for a small fee, received transcriptions of all the christening records for the families and everything else they found on various family members. One entry from church minutes indicated that Thomas East Jr. was the son of Thomas East Sr., a prominent official in the Baptist Church in the area, and that Thomas East Jr. was an "outsider," not a Moravian. According to the christening records, my great-great-grandfather John H. East was indeed a son of Thomas and Anna Maria East, and was born on 20 April 1807. The church records also showed that Thomas and Anna Maria had had a son named Ville (Wiley in another record) Hamilton East, born 29 July 1815, who died 1 January 1820 and was buried in Bethania. This meant that John H. East named a son for his younger brother who died at age four-and-a-half. The sad ending is that the second Wiley Hamilton East also died young: He died on 3 July 1862 in Arkansas from an illness while serving as a Union Army private in the Civil War. *Marilyn Finer-Collins*

Alaska—See *Alaskan Russian Church Archives Records, 1733–1938*, by Russian Orthodox Greek Catholic Church of America, Diocese of Alaska. Washington, D.C.: Library of Congress, 1984 (in Russian).

Arizona—See Archives of the Evangelical Synod at Eden-Webster Library, St. Louis, Missouri (United Church of Christ and predecessor churches).

Arkansas—Arkansas History Commission Archives, Little Rock (mostly Baptist records); Southwest Arkansas Regional Archives, Washington (Baptist and Presbyterian mostly); University of Arkansas, Little Rock (several denominations); Hendrix College (Methodist) and Central Baptist College in Conway.

California—Western Jewish History Center, Judah L. Magnes Museum, Berkeley; Hebrew Union College Library, Los Angeles; Jewish Federation Council of Greater Los Angeles; Archdiocese of San Francisco in Menlo Park (Catholic); Santa Barbara Mission, Archive-Library (Catholic); School of Theology at Claremont (Methodist and Protestant Episcopal); United Methodist Church Research Library, University of the Pacific, Stockton; Fresno Pacific University, Center for Mennonite Brethren Studies; Whittier College Library in Whittier (Quaker); Registrar of the Greek Orthodox Diocese of San Francisco (records after 1979 for Alaska, Arizona, California, Hawaii, Nevada, Oregon, Washington); Pacific Lutheran Theological Seminary, Berkeley (Evangelical Lutheran Church in America, archives for Arizona, California, Colorado, Hawaii, New Mexico, Nevada, Utah, Wyoming).

Colorado—Colorado Historical Society (some records, denominations not specified); Iliff School of Theology, Denver (Methodist); Registrar of Greek Orthodox Diocese of Denver (records after 1979 for Colorado, Idaho, Kansas, Louisiana, Missouri, Montana, Nebraska, New Mexico, North Dakota, Oklahoma, South Dakota, Texas, Utah, Wyoming).

Connecticut—Connecticut State Library, Hartford (hundreds of Connecticut churches, partial name index, most on microfilm); Divinity Library at Yale University, New Haven (Congregational); Hartford Theological Seminary (Congregational); Episcopal Diocese of Connecticut, Hartford.

Delaware—Historical Society of Delaware, Wilmington (many copies, some originals); Delaware State Archives, Dover (not comprehensive, but some).

District of Columbia—Archives Department of Catholic University of America, Washington; Archdiocese for the Military Services U.S.A., the Military Ordinariate, Washington (Catholic, sacramental records for service personnel and families dating back to 1917; records available to the individuals or their family members); *Inventory of Church Archives in the District of Columbia*, by Charles Hancock Wentz and the District of Columbia Historical Records Survey (Washington, D.C.: Historical Records Survey, 1940).

Florida—Florida State Archives (some Catholic records from Pensacola, St. Augustine, and Tallahassee; Methodist and Baptist records from various counties).

Georgia—Georgia Department of Archives and History (church and synagogue records); Emory University, Atlanta (Methodist and Episcopalian); Columbia Theological Seminary, Decatur (Presbyterian); Shorter College, Rome (Baptist); Thomas College, Thomasville (church histories); Registrar of the Greek Orthodox Diocese of Atlanta (records after 1979 for Alabama, Florida, Georgia, Mississippi, North Carolina, South Carolina, Tennessee); Georgia Baptist Historical Collection at Mercer University, Macon; Georgia Historical Society, Savannah (Savannah churches).

Hawaii—Hawaii State Archives, Honolulu (Episcopal church in Hawaii records); Hawaii Mission Children's Society, Honolulu (Archives of Congregational Church in the Pacific); Roman Catholic Diocese of Hawaii, Honolulu (some parish records); see Directory of Historical Records Repositories in Hawaii online at <www.hawaiianhistory.org/recrep.html>.

Idaho—Boise State University, Albertsons Library, Boise (records of the Episcopal Diocese of Idaho, including some parish registers and confirmation records; records of the Catholic Women's League); Archives of the Evangelical Synod, Eden-Webster Library, St. Louis, Missouri (United Church of Christ and predecessor churches); *Catholic Church Records of the Pacific Northwest* (St. Paul, Ore.: French Prairie Press,

1972–; Portland, Ore.: Binford & Mort, 1987), various compilers. See also *Finnish Church and Cemetery*, by Darlene Hill Bosworth and Carl A. Bosworth. (Boise: the authors, 1987), focusing on Lake Fork, Idaho.

Illinois—Central Illinois Conference, Bloomington (Methodist); Jesuit-Krauss-McCormick Library, Chicago (Catholic, Lutheran, Presbyterian); Spertus Institute of Jewish Studies, Chicago (Jewish); Church of the Brethren General Board, Elgin; Eureka College, Eureka (Disciples of Christ); Archives of the Evangelical Lutheran Church in America Library, Elk Grove Village (congregational histories; microfilm of some congregational records, especially Norwegian-American); Garrett-Evangelical and Seabury-Western Theological Seminaries, The United Libraries, Evanston (United Methodist, Evangelical United Brethren, Episcopal); American Theological Library Association, Evanston (published church history and records); Registrar of the Greek Orthodox Diocese of Chicago (records after 1979 for Illinois, Indiana [part], Iowa, Minnesota, Missouri, Wisconsin). See also at Illinois State Archives, Springfield, *Inventory of Church Archives, 1941–1942* (Illinois Historical Records Survey, 1941–1942).

Indiana—Indiana State Library, Indianapolis (many Roman Catholic diocesan records, church histories from many denominations); Franklin College, Franklin (Baptist); DePauw University, Greencastle (Methodist); Hanover College, Hanover (Presbyterian); Christian Theological Seminary, Indianapolis (Disciples of Christ); Earlham College, Richmond (Quaker); Archives of the University of Notre Dame, South Bend (Catholic, including early New Orleans); Indiana Historical Society, Indianapolis (various denominations; various locations; many Quaker records); Allen County Public Library, Fort Wayne (some church records and histories).

Iowa—State Historical Society of Iowa, Des Moines and Iowa City (a few church records); Iowa Genealogical Society, Des Moines (some local Lutheran records); William Penn College, Oskaloosa (Quaker); Evangelical Lutheran Church in America, Archives for Region 5, Dubuque (synod and historical records for Illinois, Iowa, Wisconsin, upper Michigan; see ELCA Web site).

Kansas—Kansas State Historical Society, Topeka (church histories; original and microfilmed church records; Topeka funeral home records, some associated with specific religious or ethnic groups); Bethel College, North Newton (Mennonite and Anabaptist); Friends University, Wichita (Quaker); Church of the Brethren Archives at McPherson College, McPherson; Evangelical Lutheran Church in America Archives, Bethany College, Lindsborg (synod archives for Kansas, Missouri).

Kentucky—Filson Historical Society, Louisville (Catholic, Evangelical, and United Church of Christ records from Louisville area); Kentucky Department for Libraries and Archives, Frankfort (some church records, arranged by county); Lexington Theological Seminary (Disciples of Christ); Louisville Presbyterian Theological Seminary; Kentucky Wesleyan College, Owensboro (Methodist); Southern Baptist Theological Seminary, Louisville.

Louisiana—Louisiana State Library, Baton Rouge (some Catholic and Baptist records, also available on microfilm via interlibrary loan); Centenary College of Louisiana, Shreveport (Methodist). See also under Indiana.

Maine—Maine Historical Society, Portland (Congregational, Quaker, Unitarian, and others); Shaker Library, New Gloucester (Quaker collection).

Maryland—Maryland Historical Society, Baltimore (good collection of church records, including Maryland Episcopal Diocese Archives); Maryland State Archives, Annapolis (good collection); Mount Saint Mary's College and Seminary, Emmitsburg (Catholic);

University of Maryland, College Park. In Baltimore: Johns Hopkins University; Ner Israel Rabbinical College; Saint Mary's Seminary and University (Catholic); Baltimore-Washington Conference Archives of the United Methodist Church at Lovely Lane United Methodist Church. See also (1) *Inventory of the Church Archives of Maryland: Presbyterian Churches*, by Ellis Archer Wasson, Candace Watson Belfield, and Maryland Historical Records Survey (Philadelphia: Presbyterian Historical Society, 1969); (2) *Inventory of the Church Archives of Maryland, Protestant Episcopal: Diocese of Maryland*, by Historical Records Survey (U.S.), Maryland (Baltimore: Historical Records Survey of Maryland, 1940); (3) *Directory of Maryland Church Records*, Edna A. Kanely, comp. (Silver Springs, Md.: Family Line Publications, 1987), organized by county and including some Washington, D.C., churches.

Massachusetts—New England Historic Genealogical Society, Boston (Boston area churches); Andover Newton Theological School, Newton Centre (Baptist); American Jewish Historical Society Library, Waltham; Harvard University Divinity School, Cambridge (Unitarian, Congregational). In Boston: American Congregational Association, Congregational Library and Archives <www.14beacon.org> (extensive collection, primarily Congregational, from various states); Episcopal Diocese of Massachusetts Archives; New England Conference Commission on Archives and History and New England United Methodist Historical Society, at Boston University School of Theology Library (Methodist for all of New England); Diocese of Boston (Catholic); Archives of the Unitarian-Universalist Association; Registrar of Greek Orthodox Diocese of Boston (records after 1979 for all of New England). See also the *Genealogist's Handbook for New England Research*, Marcia D. Melnyk, ed. (Boston: The Society, 1999) for locations of others.

Michigan—Library of Michigan, Lansing (WPA inventories of church records); Burton Historical Collection, Detroit Public Library (especially Catholic records); Albion College, Albion (Methodist); Hope College and Western Theological Seminary, Holland (Reformed Church in America); Finnish-American Historical Archives, Hancock (ethnic Lutheran affiliations); Kalamazoo College, Kalamazoo (Baptist); Calvin College and Seminary, Grand Rapids (Christian Reformed Church-Dutch); Registrar of the Greek Orthodox Diocese of Detroit (records after 1979 for Arkansas, Kentucky, Michigan, New York, Tennessee, part of Indiana, and part of Ohio).

Minnesota—Minnesota Historical Society, St. Paul (originals and copies); Bethel Theological Seminary, Arden Hills (Baptist); Baptist General Conference History Center (and Archives), Bethel College, St. Paul (Swedish Baptist and Baptist General Conference); Minnesota Annual Conference Archives and Historical Library, United Methodist Church, Minneapolis; College of St. Thomas, St. Paul (Catholic); Luther Seminary, St. Paul Evangelical Lutheran Church in America, Region 3 Archives (records for Minnesota, North Dakota, South Dakota).

Mississippi—Mississippi State Department of Archives and History, Jackson (originals and copies; see Donna Pannell's *Church Records in the Mississippi Department of Archives and History*); Mississippi College, Clinton (Baptist); Mississippi Baptist Convention Board, Clinton; Reformed Theological Seminary in Jackson (Presbyterian); Millsaps College, J.B. Cain Archives of Mississippi Methodism, Jackson; Mississippi State University Library, State College (Baptist records). See also *Guide to Vital Statistics Records in Mississippi: Volume II, Church Archives* (Jackson: Mississippi Historical Records Survey, 1942).

Missouri—Missouri State Archives, Jefferson City, and Missouri Historical Society, St.

Louis (various denominations and locations); Culver-Stockton College, Canton (Disciples of Christ); Conception Abbey and Seminary, Conception (Catholic); Central Methodist College, Fayette; Missouri Baptist Historical Society at William Jewell College, Liberty; Missouri Valley College, Marshall (Cumberland Presbyterian); Concordia Historical Institute, Department of Archives and History of the Lutheran Church—Missouri Synod, St. Louis (Lutheran history and synod records; family papers; some congregation records); Episcopal Diocese of Missouri, St. Louis; Archives of the Evangelical Synod, Eden-Webster Library, St. Louis (Evangelical and Reformed Church, Evangelical Synod of America, German Protestant, United Church of Christ; records from these congregations in many states). See also *Guide to Vital Statistics, Church Records in Missouri* (St. Louis: Missouri Historical Records Survey, 1942).

Montana—See Archives of the Evangelical Synod, Eden-Webster Library, St. Louis, Missouri (United Church of Christ and predecessor churches). See also at Montana Historical Society, Helena, *Inventory of the Vital Statistics Records of Churches and Religious Organizations in Montana, 1942* (Bozeman, Mont.: Inventory of Public Archives, Montana Historical Records Survey, 1942).

Nebraska—Nebraska State Historical Society, Lincoln (reference guide *Nebraska Church Records at the Nebraska State Historical Society* online at <www.nebraskahistory.org/lib-arch/research/manuscrt/church.htm>); Historical Center of the United Methodist Church, Nebraska Wesleyan University, Lincoln; Evangelical Lutheran Church in America Archives, Nebraska Synod, Omaha.

Nevada—Nevada Historical Society, Reno (archives of Episcopal Church in Nevada from 1862, including records of Indian reservation missions).

New Hampshire—New Hampshire Historical Society, Concord (mainly Congregational and Baptist); New Hampshire State Library, Concord (some records); Dartmouth College, Hanover (Congregational).

New Jersey—New Jersey State Library, Trenton (inquire for specifics); Rutgers, The State University of New Jersey, Alexander Library, Special Collections, New Brunswick; New Brunswick Theological Seminary (Reformed Church in America); United Methodist Archives Center and the General Commission on Archives and History of the United Methodist Church, at Drew University Library, Madison (conference journals; agency records; family/personal papers; denominational history); Princeton Theological Seminary, Princeton (Presbyterian); Registrar of the Greek Orthodox Diocese of New Jersey, New Providence (records after 1979 for Delaware, Maryland, New Jersey, Virginia, and part of Pennsylvania; the archdiocese office at the same location for nationwide records before 1979). See *A Guide to Original and Copied Records of Religious Organizations—Largely New Jersey Churches—in the Special Collections and University Archives of Rutgers University*, by Donald A. Sinclair (New Brunswick, N.J.: Genealogical Society of New Jersey, 1999).

New Mexico—Commission of Public Records, New Mexico State Archives, Santa Fe (Catholic Church records); Albuquerque Public Library (some Catholic records); Archdiocese of Santa Fe, Albuquerque. See also *Locating Catholic Church Records in New Mexico*, an online project by volunteers of the New Mexico Genealogical Society, New Mexico GenWeb, and the Hispanic Genealogical Research Center of New Mexico, <www.nmgs.org/chrchs-intro.htm>. The New Mexico Genealogical Society has published a number of baptism records for the state; see their Web site <www.nmgs.org/>.

New York—New York Public Library, Genealogy Section (statewide church records);

New York Genealogical and Biographical Society, New York City (a major collection, mostly Protestant denominations, especially for Manhattan); New York State Library, Albany (good collection, includes Shaker collection); World Jewish Genealogy Organization, Brooklyn; American Federation of Jews from Central Europe, New York City; Huguenot Historical Society, New Paltz; American Baptist Historical Society, at the American Baptist-Samuel Colgate Library, Colgate Rochester Divinity School, Rochester (denominational history, minutes, agency records; some personal papers); Holland Society, New York City (Reformed Church); Greek Orthodox Archdiocese of America (nationwide records prior to 1979; records after 1979 for District of Columbia and parts of Connecticut and New York). Many county historical societies have local collections.

North Carolina—North Carolina State Archives, Raleigh (many denominations, statewide; permission from the church is needed in order to duplicate); Duke University, Durham (Methodist); Elon College Library, Elon (United Church of Christ); Catawba College Library, Salisbury (German Reformed); Guilford College Library, Greensboro (Quaker); Carolina Discipliana Collection, Harper Hall, Barton College, Wilson (Disciples of Christ); High Point University, Smith Library (Methodist Archives); Presbyterian Historical Society, Montreat (Presbyterian Church USA); Southeastern Baptist Theological Seminary and Wake Forest University, Wake Forest (Baptist); North Carolina Baptist Historical Collection, Winston-Salem; Free Will Baptist Historical Collection, Mount Olive; the Moravian Church in America, Southern Province, Archives and Research Library, Winston-Salem (see Web site <http://moravianarchives.org>, a comprehensive archive of personal and church records; will not photocopy records but will search and send transcriptions for fee; open for researchers); Evangelical Lutheran Church in America, North Carolina Synod, Salisbury (archives for North Carolina Synod). There are no known surviving Church of England parish registers for colonial North Carolina.

North Dakota—State Historical Society of North Dakota, Bismarck (various churches; see <www.state.nd.us/hist/sal/infreligion.htm>).

Ohio—Western Reserve Historical Society, Cleveland (holdings include Jewish History Archives and Shaker manuscripts); Ohio Historical Society, Columbus (some church records, often compilations by chapters of the Daughters of the American Revolution); State Library of Ohio, Columbus (scattered church records, varies from county to county); Mennonite Historical Library, Bluffton College, Bluffton (Mennonite and Amish); Malone College, Canton (Quaker); United Theological Seminary Library, Dayton (Evangelical United Brethren, Methodist, and related groups); Ohio Wesleyan University and Methodist Theological Seminary, Delaware (Methodist); Jacob Rader Marcus Center of the American Jewish Archives, Cincinnati Campus of Hebrew Union College-Jewish Institute of Religion, Cincinnati (synagogue records from various states, family/personal papers, Jewish organization records; see <www.huc.edu/aja/collect.htm>); Wilmington College, Wilmington (Quaker); Catholic Diocese of Cleveland (records from 1840s; archives closed, but archivist search available for a fee; for details, see <www.dioceseofcleveland.org/archivist/archiveform.htm>); Evangelical Lutheran Church in America, Region 6 Archives, Trinity Lutheran Seminary, Columbus (records for Indiana, Kentucky, Ohio, and lower Michigan).

Oklahoma—Oklahoma Baptist University, Shawnee; Evangelical Lutheran Church in America, Arkansas-Oklahoma Synod, Tulsa; check with Oklahoma Historical Society, Oklahoma City.

Oregon—Oregon State Library (Catholic Church records, Pacific Northwest); Northwest Christian College, Eugene (Disciples of Christ); George Fox College, Newburg (Quaker); Western Seminary, Portland (Baptist); Willamette University, Salem (Methodist).

Pennsylvania—The Historical Society of Pennsylvania, Philadelphia (many denominations, concentrating in Delaware Valley: Pennsylvania and New Jersey); Friends Historical Association at Haverford College, Haverford (Quaker); Archives of the Evangelical and Reformed Historical Society, Lancaster Theological Seminary, Lancaster (German Reformed, United Church of Christ; see also Archives of the Evangelical Synod, Eden-Webster Library, St. Louis, Missouri); Lancaster Mennonite Historical Society (Mennonite, Amish); Mennonite Historians of Eastern Pennsylvania, Lansdale; Moravian Historical Society, Nazareth; Reformed Presbyterian Theological Seminary, Pittsburgh; Friends Historical Library of Swarthmore College, Swarthmore (Quaker); Lutheran Theological Seminary, Gettysburg (records of the General Synod of the Evangelical Lutheran Church in America and central Pennsylvania, Delaware, Maryland, and metropolitan District of Columbia); Tri-Synod Archives, Evangelical Lutheran Church in America, Thiel College, Greenville (synod records for western Pennsylvania, West Virginia, western Maryland); Archives of the Moravian Church, Bethlehem; Registrar of the Greek Orthodox Diocese of Pittsburgh (records after 1979 for most of Pennsylvania, West Virginia, part of Ohio); Archives of the Roman Catholic Diocese of Harrisburg; American Catholic Historical Society, Philadelphia Archdiocesan Historical Research Center, campus of the Seminary of St. Charles Borromeo, Overbrook; Balch Institute for Ethnic Studies (Jewish archives), Philadelphia; Evangelical Lutheran Church in America Archives, Lutheran Theological Seminary, Philadelphia (Northeastern region except for metropolitan New York); Presbyterian Historical Society (Presbyterian Church USA), Philadelphia; State Library of Pennsylvania, Harrisburg (some records); Historical Society of Western Pennsylvania, Pittsburgh (Christian denominations and Jewish archives; ethnic archives); Genealogical Society of Pennsylvania, Philadelphia (various denominations).

Rhode Island—Rhode Island Historical Society, Providence (mostly Baptist, Congregational, Unitarian, Quaker; some others); University of Rhode Island, Kingston (records of Rhode Island Episcopal Diocese); Rhode Island Jewish Historical Association, Providence.

South Carolina—South Carolina Department of Archives and History, Columbia (some published denominational and church histories; small collection of individual church records); Furman University, Greenville (Baptist); Charleston Diocese (Catholic); Charleston Library Society (South Carolina Jewish collection); Huguenot Society of South Carolina, Charleston; Evangelical Lutheran Church in America Archives, Lutheran Theological Southern Seminary, Columbia (synod archives for Alabama, Florida, Georgia, Mississippi, South Carolina, Tennessee, Bahamas, Caribbean); College of Charleston; Wofford College, Spartanburg (Methodist); South Caroliniana Library, University of South Carolina, Columbia. See *A Guide to the Manuscript Collection of the South Caroliniana Library*, by Allen H. Stokes (Columbia: South Caroliniana Library, University of South Carolina, 1982).

South Dakota—South Dakota State Historical Society, Pierre (scattered small collections); Center for Western Studies, Augustana College, Sioux Falls (church records collection, especially Episcopal, Lutheran, United Church of Christ); North American

Baptist Seminary, Sioux Falls; Catholic Diocese of Rapid City; Oglala Lakota College, Kyle (Catholic).

Tennessee—Tennessee State Library and Archives, Nashville (originals and microfilm copies); Emmanuel School of Religion, Johnson City (Church of Christ and Disciples of Christ); Memphis Theological Seminary, Memphis (Cumberland Presbyterian); Southern Baptist Historical Library and Archives, Nashville; Disciples of Christ Historical Society, Nashville; Archives of the Jewish Federation of Nashville and Middle Tennessee; University of the South, Sewanee (Protestant Episcopal, Southern Diocese).

Texas—Baylor University, Waco (Baptist); Bridwell Library, Southern Methodist University, Dallas; Texas Catholic Historical Society, Austin; Catholic Archives of Texas, Diocese of Austin, Austin; Southwestern Baptist Theological Seminary, Fort Worth; Texas Christian University, Fort Worth (Disciples of Christ); Episcopal Diocese of West Texas, San Antonio; Roman Catholic Archives, San Antonio; University of Texas, Austin (copies of early Protestant Episcopal records); Texas Baptist Historical Collection, Baptist General Convention of Texas, Dallas; Evangelical Lutheran Church in America Archives, Texas Lutheran University, Seguin (synod records for Texas, Louisiana).

Utah—Family History Library, Salt Lake City (print and microfilm church records and histories from various denominations; check library catalog for holdings; Catholic Diocese, Salt Lake City.

Vermont—Vermont Historical Society, Montpelier (scattered church records); Special Collections at the Library of the University of Vermont, Burlington.

Virginia—Library of Virginia, Richmond (see *A Guide to Church Records in the Archives Branch, Virginia State Library*, by Jewell T. Clark and Elizabeth Terry Long [Richmond, Va.: Virginia State Library, 1981]); Virginia Historical Society, Richmond; University of Virginia, Charlottesville; Randolph Macon College, Ashland (Methodist); Eastern Mennonite College and Seminary, Harrisonburg (Anabaptist and Mennonite); University of Richmond (Baptist); Union Theological Seminary and Presbyterian School of Christian Education, Richmond (Presbyterian); Saint Paul's College, Lawrenceville (Episcopal). The Virginia Historical Society has published most vestry books for colonial Virginia Episcopal parishes. See also *A Guide to Episcopal Records in Virginia*, by Edith F. Axelson (Athens, Ga.: Iberian Publishing Co., 1988). At the Virginia Beach Public Library, see *Guide to the Manuscript Collections of the Virginia Baptist Historical Society: Supplement* (Richmond: Historical Records Survey of Virginia, 1940–1941).

Washington—University of Washington, Seattle: See *Records, 1932–1940* (Washington Historical Records Survey, 1932–1940) for churches in Kittitas and Whatcom counties and Swedish American church archives, primarily Lutheran; Catholic Diocesan Archives, Spokane; Episcopal Diocese of Olympia, Seattle; Faith Evangelical Lutheran Seminary, Tacoma; Evangelical Lutheran Church in America Archives, Pacific Lutheran University, Tacoma (synod records for Alaska, Idaho, Montana, Oregon, Washington).

West Virginia—West Virginia Division of Culture and History, Archives and History Library (a few church records); Bethany College, Bethany (Disciples of Christ); West Virginia Wesleyan College, Buckhannon (Methodist); West Virginia University, West Virginia and Regional History Collection, Morgantown.

Wisconsin—University of Wisconsin, Milwaukee (Milwaukee Urban Archives, churches from Milwaukee, Ozaukee, Sheboygan, Washington, and Waukesha counties, on microfilm; detailed finding aid available at this archives); Seventh Day Baptist Historical Society, Janesville; State Historical Society of Wisconsin, Madison; Marquette University Library, Milwaukee (Catholic special collections).

Wyoming—Contact individual churches; see diocese, synod, conference, and other jurisdictional bodies whose territory includes Wyoming.

SCHOOLS AND UNIVERSITIES

Records of and about schools and universities sometimes provide interesting information about ancestors. Records of individual schools or public school districts usually fall into two categories: those that answer the demands of the county or state government and those that deal with students and faculty. In the first group, school census records taken at the local or county level may provide names and ages of schoolchildren in the district at a given time. If such records are not in the school district office or county courthouse, they may exist in local or state archives and historical societies. Some school district tax offices have records that show taxes paid by heads of household within their jurisdiction, but these records are often kept only about twenty years.

In the second group, all kinds of schools and academies generate enrollment records and transcripts that document a student's attendance, classes, and grades. These records can be vital in an effort to prove age or perhaps parentage, residence, or citizenship, depending on the information provided on the record. Otherwise, they are merely interesting for the historical information they provide. Figure 4-5, on page 141, is a partial page of a college transcript from the 1882–1883 class at Sam Houston Normal Institute (now University) in Huntsville, Texas, where a number of students prepared to be teachers. The two-page record shows class rankings, classes, and the grades of the students. Their curriculum included not only standard geography, math, science, grammar, literature, history, and government courses, but also various teacher training classes, penmanship, drawing, music, calisthenics, elocution, rhetoric, and a graduating essay. The second page of this class record indicates that J.B. Haston ranked fourth in the class; Mattie Harrison ranked eighth of at least ninety-five students.

Because each college kept records in its own way, you will find different information from one record to another. A 1909 individual student transcript from a different university shows not only classes and grades for each year but gives the student's year of birth, patron or parent's name, the family's address, the high school from which the student graduated, the date of entrance to the university, the degree earned, and the graduation date.

Warning

Because of privacy laws, some schools and universities no longer release transcripts, or they make the process tedious. The laws and their interpretation vary considerably from state to state and institution to institution. You usually have to have permission from the person whose record you are requesting, or from the legal executor or guardian, especially if the record is less than fifty years old. If you request a record older than seventy-five years, explain that you want it for family history and identify your relationship to the person whose transcript you seek; you may have no problem getting the record.

Lists or directories of former students and alumni may be more readily available than transcripts. For older colleges and universities, a number of these lists have been published, either in book form or in historical and genealogical periodicals. Alumni associations and university archives may also maintain some of these lists. Other records such as yearbooks, graduation programs, literary publications, alumni publications, newspapers, catalogs, and

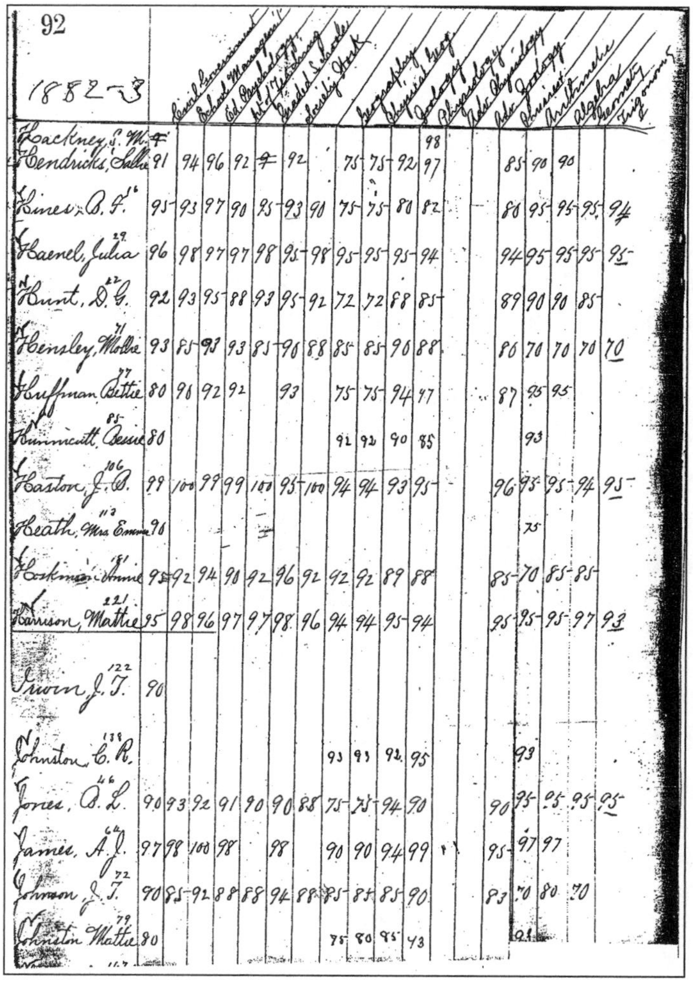

Figure 4-5 Record of class of 1882–1883, p. 92, Registrar's Office, Sam Houston State University, Huntsville, Texas, photocopy sent to author, 1975.

scrapbooks may be available at a school archives or within a special collection in the school library.

Nationally affiliated organizations, such as Greek-letter sororities and fraternities, honor societies, and service organizations, may maintain chapter history on the campus or at the national office. From the headquarters you may learn membership dates, and perhaps a birth or death date, for your ancestor. Chapter histories may reflect offices the ancestor held, but school yearbooks may also provide this information. Besides the organizations' Web sites, one source of information on some of these organizations is *Baird's Manual of American College Fraternities* (Menasha, Wis.: Baird's Manual Foundation, Inc., latest edition).

Many of these national organizations have published periodicals since the late nineteenth and early twentieth centuries. These publications often report initiations, marriages, and deaths of members and the births of their children. However, they also contain member-contributed poetry, articles, and collegiate chapter reports. If these items mention your ancestor or the ancestor's chapter, you learn interesting tidbits of social history from your ancestor's life. For example, the December 1911 issue of *The Adelphean* of Alpha Delta Pi contains a report from Ethel G. Clark, chapter reporter of the Theta Chapter at Lawrence College, Appleton, Wisconsin. The highlight of the quarter on which she reported was the day President Taft visited the campus and addressed the students and local citizens from the Main Hall steps. The senior class—dressed in white and with streamers of red, white, and blue—lined either side of the hallway through which the president passed. "As the President entered the south door, our own Florence Plantz had the honor of presenting to him a bunch of roses in behalf of the college."[8] Descendants of Ethel Clark, Florence Plantz, and any one of the other eighteen young ladies in the chapter at that time can't help but be interested in this report.

For colleges and universities, yearbooks, annual catalogs of classes and rules, handbooks, literary society publications, graduation programs, other memorabilia, and published histories are often housed in the school's library or archives. Such collections may also contain the personal papers of prominent faculty or alumni. Faculty lists and photographs may also be available in the archives, publications, and yearbooks, but life history on faculty and employees may not be available. Personnel records would be subject to the same legal restrictions as students' records, or they may not be kept beyond a certain time period. Each school district or university has its own policy.

STUDENTS' HAND-BOOK OF THE UNIVERSITY OF TEXAS, 1909–1910

Prepared by the Christian Associations (YMCA and YWCA), the handbook presented all kinds of useful information for incoming students, their descendants, and descendants of faculty, advertisers, and local citizens:

- Ads for dentists, doctors, tailors, barbers, shoe shops, banks, laundries, cafes, and other necessary business establishments, including livery stables and several shops that advertised "We loan Kodaks."
- Calendar of admission exams and term exams for the fall and spring semesters; list of the faculty and their office numbers; information on campus organizations and athletics (with the football schedule); words to varsity yells; and traditions of the university, including "All-Fool's Day" (April 1), when students cut class and spent the day picnicking and trolley riding.
- Information on the city of Austin, churches, street cars, mail pick-up and delivery, and the location of the campus telephone booth.
- Names and addresses of eight women who operated rooming and boarding houses for students. Only one woman mentioned her rates: Mrs. W.R. Storey charged eighteen dollars for room and board, and thirteen dollars for meals only.

Especially for small town and rural public schools, early records simply may no longer exist. Yearbooks and school publications may be found in the local public library or museum or in the possession of families who have lived in the area for years. Other materials may be in the possession of descendants of teachers and principals. Some research libraries and archives have school records collections; one such facility is the Milwaukee Urban Archives at the University of Wisconsin in Milwaukee.

Aids for finding school records include the *National Union Catalog of Manuscript Collections* (NUCMC, see page 279), both printed and online versions; online databases, such as OCLC and RLIN (see pages 273 and 281); *A Guide to Archives and Manuscripts in the United States*, Philip M. Hamer, ed. (New Haven, Conn.: Yale University Press, 1961); *The Directory of Archives and Manuscript Repositories in the United States* (Phoenix: Oryx

Press, latest edition); and online guides to specific manuscript collections. Consult the Family History Library catalog for any school records in that library's collection.

In the absence of school records, try local newspapers. The *Bolivar (Tennessee) Bulletin* of 5 January 1867 printed the list of tuition and fees for the excellent Bolivar Select School and announced that the spring term would begin on January 21. On 15 June 1867, the *Bulletin* covered the closing exercises. The faculty were Mrs. M.J. Thompson, principal and math teacher; Miss Anna C. Safford, teacher of English, Latin, and French; Rev. W.H. Thompson (the Presbyterian minister), mental and moral science; and Miss Maggie Q. Wilkerson, vocal and instrumental music. For the ceremony, the Presbyterian church was decorated with "rare flowers and foliage green," and the forty to fifty young ladies of the student body were dressed in white with wreaths of flowers. The vocal class sang a "joyous gushing Welcome Song," and, after a prayer, "the celebrated Echo Song." Among the festivities were the giving of prizes and certificates for "unexceptional scholarship and honorable exertion." The next fall, the *Bulletin* announced a new faculty for the school, as the Thompsons were moving to Columbus, Kentucky, and Miss Safford, to Georgia. The new principal would be Mrs. William E. Glover, a native of North Carolina, educated in Virginia.

Although school records do not usually contain genealogical data other than birth dates or age information and, sometimes, a parent's name, they place ancestors in a given place at a given time, identify their role in the community, and add to our understanding of the community and society in which they lived.

CITY DIRECTORIES

City directories as we know them date back to the 1780s for the cities of Philadelphia, Charleston, and New York, with other cities following throughout the nineteenth century. These began basically as business directories but have long included many residents, with or without occupation being specified.

These directories contribute to genealogical research in a number of ways. Along with telephone directories, they furnish addresses of ancestral families in or near a census year to help you find them in the census. An illustration of this process is on page 60. Some directories include maps of the city, as did the 1857 directory for Richmond, Indiana, as shown in Figure 4-6, on page 144. This map shows not only most street names but ward numbers and the railroad. It gives genealogists another perspective on the community in which ancestors lived.

Idea Generator

Directories also provide interesting details about the cities and counties—their history and government, economy and prices of goods, progress and transportation, churches and schools, climate and watercourses. Even the advertisements can be entertaining and enlightening, especially if your ancestor advertised his or her business in the directory. The Richmond, Indiana, 1857 directory listed fifty-six Quaker families who lived there in 1807–1808, along with the number of individuals in each family, according to "a manuscript" provided by one Charles F. Coffin. Jeremiah Cox's family had ten members; Joseph Comer and his mother lived together; David Baily lived with his mother and sister; Sarah Burgess lived alone.

City directories also give information on ancestors in the years between censuses, especially their presence in a place and indications of deaths and removals. Figure 4-7, on page 145, shows a fairly typical city directory page from the nineteenth century. This page of the Richmond, Indiana, 1857 directory shows name, occupation, and street of residence but not a street address. In order to locate an ancestral property specifically, you would need

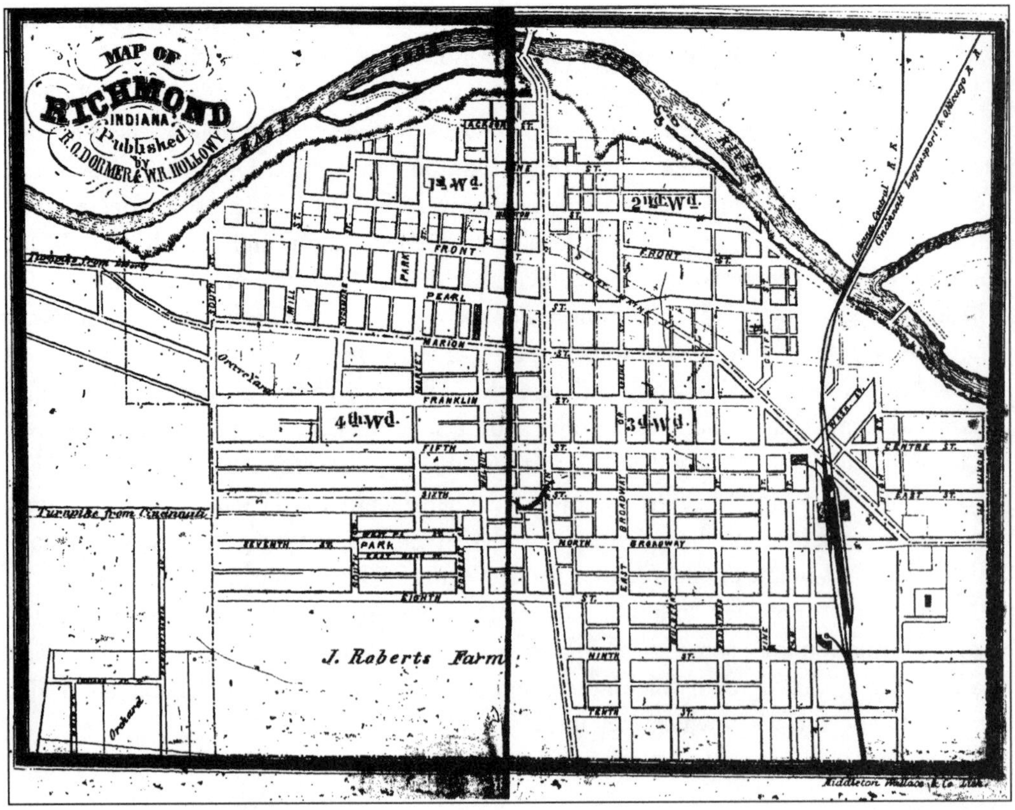

Figure 4-6 Map of Richmond, Indiana, *A Directory to the City of Richmond . . .* (Richmond, Indiana: R.O. Dormer and W.R. Holloway, 1857).

to find the person in another directory or record that gives a house number. The residents listed on this page include several retired people, several women, and at least three who perhaps were willing to pay a little more to get their names in capital letters.

The Stockton, California, directory for 1856 provides helpful information about occupation, residence, and former residence. For example, Thomas Blair, cook at the Eagle Hotel, came from Scotland, and Charles R. Bowen, grocer on Hunter Street near Levee, was from Massachusetts. The Baltimore broadside considered one of the first directory-like compilations was a "list of families and other persons residing in the town of Baltimore, was taken in the year 1752, by a lady of respectability, and who was well acquainted with the place at the time, and is believed to be correct." It too gave information about the persons listed. Mrs. Hughes was the "only midwife among the English families," and Bill Adams was the "barber, the only one."

City directories can give clues to the death or removal of family members. The 1897–1898 Houston city directory listed John A. Iiams as a truck operator with the Texas and New Orleans Railroad. Although he was not reported in the next directory, the 1900–1901 edition listed him as a "moulder" with the Houston and Texas Central Railroad and provided clues to help find the family in the 1900 census. However, the 1902–1903 city directory reported Mary Iiams as widow of John A. The directory was probably compiled during 1901 or early 1902, and the census indicated that John was still living on 1 June 1900. Thus, the directories narrow the date of his death to mid-1900 to mid-1902; this helps the genealogist look for cemetery, interment, or probate records. No civil death record exists for John because Texas did not begin death registration until 1903.

An interesting phenomenon, perhaps a result of the early deaths of parents in the extended Iiams family and the need for the young people to take jobs, was that several of the children were named in the city directory at a young age. Mary Iiams, then as Miss Mary

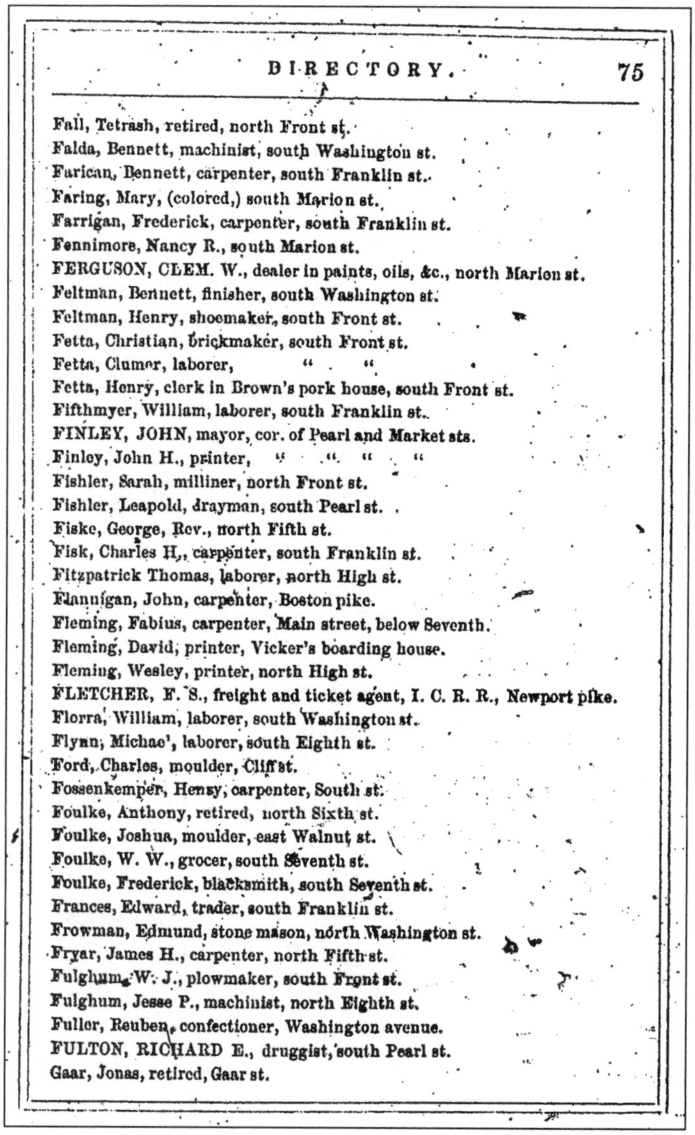

DIRECTORY. 75

Fall, Tetrash, retired, north Front st.
Falda, Bennett, machinist, south Washington st.
Farican, Bennett, carpenter, south Franklin st.
Faring, Mary, (colored,) south Marion st.
Farrigan, Frederick, carpenter, south Franklin st.
Fennimore, Nancy R., south Marion st.
FERGUSON, CLEM. W., dealer in paints, oils, &c., north Marion st.
Feltman, Bennett, finisher, south Washington st.
Feltman, Henry, shoemaker, south Front st.
Fetta, Christian, brickmaker, south Front st.
Fetta, Clumer, laborer, " "
Fetta, Henry, clerk in Brown's pork house, south Front st.
Fifthmyer, William, laborer, south Franklin st.
FINLEY, JOHN, mayor, cor. of Pearl and Market sts.
Finley, John H., printer, " " " "
Fishler, Sarah, milliner, north Front st.
Fishler, Leapold, drayman, south Pearl st.
Fiske, George, Rev., north Fifth st.
Fisk, Charles H., carpenter, south Franklin st.
Fitzpatrick Thomas, laborer, north High st.
Flannigan, John, carpenter, Boston pike.
Fleming, Fabius, carpenter, Main street, below Seventh.
Fleming, David, printer, Vicker's boarding house.
Fleming, Wesley, printer, north High st.
FLETCHER, F. S., freight and ticket agent, I. C. R. R., Newport pike.
Florra, William, laborer, south Washington st.
Flynn, Michae', laborer, south Eighth st.
Ford, Charles, moulder, Cliff st.
Fossenkemper, Hensy, carpenter, South st.
Foulke, Anthony, retired, north Sixth st.
Foulke, Joshua, moulder, east Walnut st.
Foulke, W. W., grocer, south Seventh st.
Foulke, Frederick, blacksmith, south Seventh st.
Frances, Edward, trader, south Franklin st.
Frowman, Edmund, stone mason, north Washington st.
Fryar, James H., carpenter, north Fifth st.
Fulghum, W. J., plowmaker, south Front st.
Fulghum, Jesse P., machinist, north Eighth st.
Fuller, Reuben, confectioner, Washington avenue.
FULTON, RICHARD E., druggist, south Pearl st.
Gaar, Jonas, retired, Gaar st.

Figure 4-7 Richmond, Indiana, City Directory, 1857, p. 75.

Rock, candymaker, and her brother, William Rock (no occupation given), had entries in the 1892–1893 directory under their own names; they were teenagers—about fifteen and seventeen—at the time, living at the home of their mother, Amelia King. (Their stepfather, Thomas King, had died in 1891.) Mary Iiams' half brother, Alfred King, was first listed in the 1902–1903 directory at about age sixteen, giving Mary's address as his residence. Then Mary's son Claxton Iiams (orphaned by 1910) appeared in the 1913 city directory at about age eleven; his residence was his uncle Alfred King's home. Some directories also indicate the number of people living in each household. This information helps genealogists establish the makeup of the family.

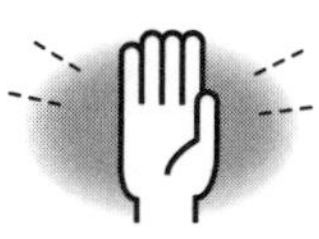

Warning

City directories can help you determine when a family moved in or out of town, **but a single omission from a directory does not necessarily mean they were gone.** They may have chosen not to pay for a listing, in cases where payment was necessary, or may have been away when the directory representative came to their home. Although telephone directories may help identify changes of address or families not in the city directories, not everyone had a telephone, especially from the late 1870s to the 1940s.

ANSWERS FROM THE CITY DIRECTORY

I was puzzled for years on the family of Isabella Morrison Hartley, who was born in October 1811 and married John Packer Jr. in 1836 in Gloucester County, New Jersey.[9] Various records contained clues that Philadelphia was her birthplace. Her mother was documented as Isabella Morrison, married first to William Henry Smiley (by whom she had at least one daughter) and second to a Mr. Hartley, by whom she had Isabella (Hartley) Packer.

Finding Mr. Hartley's given name was the problem. After several years of trying a number of sources without success, I decided to try city directories to check on Morrison and Hartley families, especially between censuses, both before and after Isabella (Hartley) Packer's birth. The breakthrough to identifying Mr. Hartley came in the Philadelphia city directories in the following entries, which contained another surprise—the identification of Isabella Packer's grandparents:

1794—Alexander Morrison, cordwainer [shoemaker], 487 S. Front St.
1797—Alexander Morrison, cordwainer, S. Front St.
1799—Alexander Morrison, shoemaker, opposite the Swedish Church in Front St.
1800—Alexander Morrison in Philadelphia for the federal census.
1801—Alexander Morrison, shoemaker, Front St.
1802—Alexander Morrison, shoemaker, *499 S. Front St.* (I later learned his estate administration was in 1809.)
1810—Morrison (no given name listed), widow of Alexander, *499 S. Front St.*
1810—Federal census of Philadelphia (p. 93) identified Isabella Smiley and household on E. Southwark. (This is mother Isabella before she married Mr. Hartley.)
1811—Isabella Smilie, tayloress, *499 S. Front St.* (This is mother Isabella before she married Mr. Hartley. Information for directories is compiled sometimes before the publication year. Isabella Smiley may have married Mr. Hartley in late 1810 or early 1811, but after the city directory was compiled. However, listed at the same address as the widow Morrison, she was apparently living with her widowed mother at this time.)
1813—Isabella Morrison, widow, *499 S. Front St.* (This is grandmother Isabella, widow of Alexander! I later learned her estate administration was in 1814.)
1814—"Mrs. Hartley, of Matthias," *499 S. Front St.* (This is mother Isabella after she married Mr. *Matthias* Hartley and after he died, although the city directory entry omitted the word *widow* (of Matthias). I later learned that his estate administration was in 1813. Thus, it appears mother Isabella was married to Matthias only from late 1810 or early 1811 to 1813. With the widowed mother and grandmother living at the same address, it was possible to connect the three Isabellas.)
1830—Federal census, Deptford Township, Gloucester County, New Jersey (p. 81), showed Isabella Hartley with two other females in the household; they were of the right ages to be her two daughters, Deborah Smiley (born 1804) and Isabella Morrison Hartley (born 1811).

The city directories tied together clues from previous research and provided clues for the next steps. The information taken as a whole makes the case. *Aryl-Jeanne Reed*

Finding City Directories

City directories (original or in microform) are available for use in many local public and academic libraries, state libraries and archives, and historical societies. Significant collections are housed at the Library of Congress; the National Archives; the American Antiquarian Society of Worcester, Massachusetts; the New England Historic Genealogical Society in Boston; Cornell University; the library of the National Society, Daughters of the American Revolution in Washington, DC; Newberry Library in Chicago; the Family History Library; the New York Historical Society; the New York Public Library; Allen County Public Library in Fort Wayne, Indiana; and Clayton Library Center for Genealogical Research in Houston. The Family History Library's microform copies of various directories are available through Family History Centers; these include some mid-nineteenth-century directories.

Directories on microfilm and microfiche may be purchased from the Gale Group <www.galegroup.com>, but they are expensive. The early collection, available on microfiche from the publisher, is based on *Bibliography of American Directories Through 1860*, by Dorothea N. Spear (Worcester, Mass.: American Antiquarian Society, 1961), which can help you identify which cities had directories before the Civil War. The publisher also has guides to the collection: *City Directories of the United States 1860–1901: Guide to the Microfilm Collection* and temporary reel guides to the 1902–1960 segment. (New directories in this segment are continually being added.) You may have access to these guides at your local library or from home using your library card if your local library subscribes to the database.

If your public library does not have copies of its own city directories, acquiring them would make a worthwhile project for local genealogists and historians. The following chart lists the cities available in early 2003. Available directory dates vary considerably from only one or two years to more than a century; consult the reel guide or contact the publisher for available dates. Much of this list shows directories available for the major cities in each area; some of their directories contain an entire metropolitan area or other towns in the area. If you don't find your ancestral town listed, consult the publisher's roll list and library catalogs under the name of the nearest large town.

Alabama—Andalusia, Anniston, Bessemer, Birmingham, Decatur, Dothan, Gadsden, Greene County, Mobile, Montgomery, Selma, Tuscaloosa. See also "Southern Region."

Alaska—Statewide.

Arizona—Bisbee, Douglas, Phoenix, Tucson.

Arkansas—Blytheville, El Dorado, Fayetteville, Fort Smith, Helena, Hot Springs, Little Rock, Texarkana. See also "Southern Region."

California—Alhambra, Bakersfield, Baldwin Park and Covina, Bellflower, Burbank, Burlingame, Chico, Compton, Eureka, Fresno, Imperial Valley, Inglewood, La Jolla, Long Beach, Los Angeles, Marysville and Yuba City, Merced-Madera, Modesto, Monrovia, Napa, Nevada City, North Hollywood and Studio City, Oakland (with Alameda and Berkeley), Orange County, Palo Alto, Pasadena, Pomona, Redlands, Richmond (and Martinez), Riverside, Sacramento, San Bernardino, San Diego, San Fernando Valley, San Francisco, San Jose (and Santa Clara County), San Pedro, Santa Anna, Santa Barbara, Santa Cruz, Santa Monica, Santa Rosa, South Pasadena, Stockton, Tuolumne County, Ventura, Watts, Westwood Hills, Whittier.

Colorado—Boulder, Boulder County, Colorado Springs, Denver, Grand Junction, Leadville, Pueblo, Salida, Trinidad.

Connecticut—State of Connecticut, Ansonia, Berlin, Branford, Bridgeport, Bristol, Connecticut River Valley, Danbury, Danielson, Darien, Derby, Enfield, Greenwich, Hartford, Hartford Suburban area, Manchester, Meriden, Middletown, Milford, Mystic, New Britain, New Canaan, New Haven, New London, New Milford, Norwalk, Norwich, Putnam, Rockville, Southington, Stamford, Torrington, Wallingford, Waterbury, Willimantic, Winstead. See also "New England Region."

Delaware—Delaware State, New Castle County, Wilmington.

District of Columbia—Washington.

Florida—Arcadia, Bartow, Boca Raton, Bradenton, Clearwater, Daytona Beach, Deland, Delray Beach, Eustis, Fort Myers, Fort Pierce, Gainesville, Jacksonville, Key West, Lakeland, Leon County, Miami, Ocala, Orlando, Palatka, Palmetto, Pensacola, St. Augustine, St. Petersburg, Tallahassee, Tampa, West Palm Beach. See also "Southern Region."

Georgia—Albany, Americus, Atlanta, Atlanta Suburban, Augusta, Brunswick, Columbus, Dalton, Gainesville, Georgia Regional, Griffin, Macon, Rome, Savannah. See also "Southern Region."

Hawaii—Honolulu.

Idaho—Boise, Caldwell; Canyon, Gem, Payette, Washington, Adams counties; Clearwater, Nez Perce, Latah counties; Coeur D'alene; Idaho County and Grangeville; Idaho Falls; Bonneville, Bingham, Fremont, Jefferson, Madison counties; Kootenai, Bonner counties; Shoshone, Benewah, and Boundary counties; Twin Falls.

Illinois—State of Illinois, Alton, Aurora, Beardstown, Belleville, Bloomington, Bureau County, Cairo, Canton, Champaign-Urbana, Chicago, Cicero, Danville, Decatur, De Kalb, Dixon, East St. Louis, Edwardsville, Elgin, Evanston, Freeport, Galena, Galesburg, Harvey, Hyde Park, Jacksonville, Joliet, Illinois Regional, Kane County, Kankakee, Kewanee, Lake, Lake View, LaSalle, Moline, Oak Park, Ottawa, Pana, Pekin, Peoria, Peru, Quincy, Randolph County, Rock Falls, Rockford, Rock Island, Springfield, Sterling, Streator, Waukegan, Will County.

Indiana—State of Indiana, Anderson, Bedford, Bloomington, Bluffton, Clinton, Columbus, Connersville, Crawfordsville, Decatur, Elkhart, Elwood, Evansville, Fort Wayne, Frankfort, Gary, Hammond, Huntington, Indianapolis, Jefferson County, Kokomo, Lafayette, Laporte, Lawrenceburg, Logansport, Madison, Marion, Michigan City, Mishawaka, Muncie, New Albany, New Castle, Pocatello, Princeton, Richmond, Shelbyville, South Bend, Terre Haute, Vincennes. See also "Pennsylvania Region."

Iowa—State of Iowa, Ames, Boone, Burlington, Cedar Falls, Cedar Rapids, Charles City, Clinton, Council Bluffs, Creston, Davenport, Des Moines, Dubuque, Fort Dodge, Fort Madison, Henry County, Iowa City, Keokuk, Marshalltown, Mason City, Muscatine, Ottumwa, Sioux City, Waterloo, Woodbury County.

Kansas—Arkansas City, Atchison, Chanute, Coffeyville, Dodge City, El Dorado, Emporia, Fort Scott, Hutchinson, Independence, Kansas City, Lawrence, Leavenworth, Ottawa, Parsons, Pittsburgh, Salina, Topeka, Wichita.

Kentucky—State of Kentucky, Ashland, Bowling Green, Covington, Danville, Frankfort, Hopkinsville, Lexington, Louisville, Maysville, Middlesboro, Owensboro, Paducah. See also "Pennsylvania Region," "Southern Region."

Louisiana—Alexandria and Pineville, Baton Rouge, Lake Charles, Monroe, New Orleans, Shreveport and Bossier City. See also "Southern Region."

Maine—State of Maine, Androscoggin and Androscoggin County, Augusta, Bangor, Bar Harbor, Bath, Biddeford, Brunswick, Casco Bay, Eliot and York, Falmouth, Houlton, Kennebec County, Lewiston and Auburn, Oxford County, Portland, Rockland, Saco,

Sanford and Springvale, Waterville, Westbrook. See also "New England Region."

Maryland—Annapolis, Baltimore, Cumberland, Easton, Frederick, Hagerstown.

Massachusetts—State of Massachusetts; Acton and Maynard; Adams; Amherst; Andover; Arlington; Ashland, Hopkinton, and Upton; Athol and Orange; Attleboro; Ayer, Groton, Harvard, and Littleton; Barnstable, Falmouth, and Bourne; Belmont; Beverly; Boston; Brighton; Brockton; Brookline; Cambridge; Central Berkshire; Charlestown; Chelsea; Chicopee; Clinton; Concord; Acushnet, Dartmouth, and Westport; Dedham and Westwood; Dighton, Rehoboth, Seekonk, Somerset, and Swansea; Dorchester; East Boston; Essex County; Everett; Fall River; Fitchburg; Fitchburg Suburban; Framingham; Franklin; Franklin County; Gardner; Gloucester; Greenfield; Hamilton; Haverhill; Holyoke; Hyde Park; Lakeville; Lawrence; Lee and Lenox; Leominster; Lexington; Lowell; Lowell Suburban; Lunenberg; Lynn; Lynn Suburban; Malden; Marlboro; Medford; Melrose; Methuen; Middleboro; Middlesex County; Milford; Milton; Nantucket; Natick; Needham, Wellesley, and Dover; New Bedford; Newburyport; Newton; North Adams; North Andover; North Essex; Northampton and Easthampton; Norwood; Orange; Palmer; Pepperell and Townsend; Pittsfield; Plymouth; Quincy; Revere; Rockland; Roxbury; Salem; Somerville; South Berkshire; Southbridge; Southern Berkshire County; Springfield; Taunton; Wakefield; Waltham; Ware; Westfield; Weymouth; Whitman; Woburn; Worcester. See also "New England Region."

Michigan—Adrian, Alpena, Ann Arbor, Battle Creek, Bay City, Benton Harbor, Birmingham, Cadillac, Cheboygan, Coldwater, Dearborn, Down-River, Detroit, East Detroit area, Escanaba, Flint, Grand Rapids, Hillsdale, Holland, Houghton County, Ionia, Ironwood, Jackson, Kalamazoo, Lansing, Lincoln Park, Ludington, Manistee, Marquette, Marshall, Menominee, Muskegon, Owosso, Petoskey, Port Huron, Royal Oak, Saginaw, Sault Ste. Marie, St. Joseph, Three Rivers, Traverse City, West Bay City. See also "Wisconsin/Michigan."

Minnesota—Albert Lea and Freeborn County, Austin, Bemidji, Brainerd, Duluth, Faribault and Northfield, Fergus Falls, Hibbing, Mankato, Minneapolis, Owatonna and Steele County, Rochester, St. Anthony, St. Cloud, St. Paul, Stillwater, Winona.

Mississippi—Biloxi, Clarksdale, Columbus, Greenville, Gulfport, Hattiesburg, Jackson, Meridian, Vicksburg. See also "Southern Region."

Missouri—State of Missouri, Cape Girardeau, Carthage, Columbia, Hannibal, Independence, Jefferson City, Joplin, Kansas City, Sedalia, Springfield, St. Charles, St. Joseph, St. Louis. See also "Pennsylvania Region."

Montana—Anaconda, Billings, Bozeman, Butte, Chouteau County, Dillon, Great Falls, Helena, Kalispell, Lewistown, Livingston, Miles City, Missoula, Montana Territory.

Nebraska—Beatrice, Fremont, Hastings, Kearney, Lincoln, Norfolk, Omaha.

Nevada—Nevada Territory/State of Nevada, Reno area.

New England Region—1849, 1856, 1860 for Connecticut, Massachusetts, Maine, New Hampshire, Vermont.

New Hampshire—State of New Hampshire, Berlin, Claremont, Concord, Derry and Chester, Dover, Exeter and Newmarket, Franklin, Great Falls, Keene, Laconia, Lebanon, Manchester, Nashua, New Ipswitch, Peterborough, Portsmouth. See also "New England Region."

New Jersey—State of New Jersey, Asbury Park, Atlantic City, Belleville and Nutley, Bloomfield, Bridgeton, Burlington, Camden, Clifton, Cumberland, Cumberland County, Elizabeth, Essex County, Hackensack, Harrison and Kearny, Jersey City, Millville, Montclair and Bloomfield, Morris County, Morristown, Newark, New

Brunswick, Newton, North Hudson County, Ocean City, Orange, Passaic, Paterson, Perth Amboy, Plainfield, Princeton, Rahway, Rutherford, Salem, Summit, Trenton. See also "Pennsylvania/New Jersey."

New Mexico—Albuquerque, Artesia, Carlsbad, Roswell, Santa Fe.

New York—Albany, Albion, Amsterdam, Auburn, Batavia, Beacon, Binghamton, Brooklyn, Buffalo, Canandaigua, Carthage, Corning, Cortland, Dunkirk and Fredonia, Elmira, Endicott, Erie County, Freeport, Fulton, Geneva, Glens Falls, Gloversville, Granville, Greenpoint, Herkimer, Hoosick Falls, Hornell, Hornellsville, Hudson, Ithaca, Jamestown, Kingston, Little Falls, Lockport, Long Island, Masena and Potsdam, Mechanicville, Middletown, Mohawk Valley, Morrisania, Mt. Vernon, Newburgh, New Rochelle, New York City (with Manhattan and Bronx), Niagara County, Niagara Falls, Ogdensburg, Olean, Oneida, Oneonta and Cooperstown, Orleans County, Ossining, Oswego, Peekskill, Penn Yan, Plattsburgh, Port Chester and Rye, Poughkeepsie, Queens, Rochester, Rome, Saratoga Springs, Schenectady, Seneca Falls, Staten Island, Syracuse, Tonawanda and North Tonawanda, Troy, Utica, Watertown, Waverly, Westchester, Westchester County, White Plains, Williamsburgh, Yonkers.

North Carolina—Asheville, Belmont, Burlington, Chapel Hill, Charlotte, Concord, Durham, Fayetteville, Gastonia, Goldsboro, Greensboro, High Point, Kinston, Raleigh, Wilmington, Wilson, Winston-Salem. See also "Southern Region."

North Dakota—Bismarck, Dickinson, Fargo, Grand Forks, Jamestown, Mandan.

Ohio—State of Ohio, Akron, Ashland, Ashtabula, Bedford and Maple Heights, Bellaire, Bellefontaine, Bowling Green, Bryan, Bucyrus, Canton, Celina, Chillicothe, Cincinnati, Circleville, Cleveland, Columbus, Columbus Suburban, Coshocton, Dayton, Dayton Suburban, Defiance, Delaware, Delphos, East Liverpool, Elyria, Findlay, Fostoria, Galion, Hamilton, Ironton, Lancaster, Lima, Mansfield, Marietta, Marion, Massillon, Middletown, Montgomery County, Mt. Vernon, Newark, Norwood, Piqua, Portsmouth, Sandusky, Springfield, Steubenville, Tiffin, Toledo, Urbana, Warren and Niles, Youngstown, Zanesville. See also "Pennsylvania Region."

Oklahoma—State of Oklahoma, Ardmore, Bartlesville, Blackwell, Chickasha, El Reno, Enid, Lawton, McAlester, Miami, Muskogee, Oklahoma City, Shawnee, Tulsa.

Oregon—Astoria, Baker, Baker City, Bend, Coos Bay and North Bend, Coos County, Corvallis, Dalles, Eugene, Jackson County, Pendleton, Portland, Salem.

Pennsylvania—State of Pennsylvania, Albion, Allentown, Altoona, Beaver Valley, Berks and Lehigh counties, Bethlehem, Braddock, Bradford, Brookville, Butler, Carbondale, Carlisle, Carnegie, Chambersburg, Chester, Chester County, Clearfield, Coatesville, Connellsville, Corry and Union City, Du Bois, Easton, Erie, Erie County, Franklin, Greensburg, Greenville, Grove City, Hanover and McSherrystown, Harrisburg, Hazleton, Homestead, Johnstown, Kane, Kittanning and Ford City, Lancaster, Lancaster County, Lebanon, McKeesport, Meadville, Monongahela, Monongahela Valley, Nanticoke, New Castle, New Kensington, Norristown, Oil City, Philadelphia, Pittsburgh, Pittston and West Pittston, Plymouth, Pottsville, Reading, Scranton, Shamokin, Sharon, Sunbury, Titusville, Warren, Washington, West Chester, Wilkes-Barre, Williamsport, York.

Pennsylvania/New Jersey—Easton and Phillipsburg area, including Alpha, New Jersey.

Pennsylvania Region—1837 business directory that includes Pittsburgh, Pennsylvania; Wheeling, Virginia (now West Virginia); Cincinnati, Dayton, Portsmouth, and Zanesville, Ohio; Madison, Indiana; Louisville, Kentucky; and St. Louis, Missouri.

Rhode Island—State of Rhode Island, Bristol, Warren, and Barrington; Cranston, Cumberland, East Providence, Hopkinton and Charlestown, Jamestown and New Shoreham, Newport, North Providence and Johnston, Pawtucket, Pawtuxet Valley, Providence, Westerly, Woonsocket.

South Carolina—Anderson, Camden, Charleston, Columbia, Greenville, Greenwood, Spartanburg. See also "Southern Region."

South Dakota—Aberdeen, Huron, Mitchell, Sioux Falls.

Southern Region—1854, selected areas of Kentucky, Tennessee, North Carolina, South Carolina, Georgia, Florida, Alabama, Mississippi, Louisiana, Texas, Arkansas.

Tennessee—State of Tennessee, Athens, Chattanooga, Clarksville, Cleveland, Columbia, Jackson, Johnson City, Knoxville, Memphis, Nashville. See also "Southern Region," "Virginia/Tennessee."

Texas—Abilene, Amarillo, Austin, Beaumont area, Beeville, Big Spring, Brownsville, Brownwood, Cleburne, Corpus Christi, Corsicana, Dallas, Denison, Edinburg, El Paso, Fort Worth, Galveston, Greenville, Houston, Lubbock, Marshall, Mineral Wells, Palestine, Pampa, Paris, Port Arthur, San Angelo, San Antonio, Sherman, Tyler, Waco, Wichita Falls. See also "Southern Region."

Utah—Logan, Ogden, Provo, Salt Lake City.

Vermont—State of Vermont, Barre, Bellows Falls and Springfield, Bennington, Brattleboro, Burlington, Montpelier, Rutland, St. Albans, St. Johnsbury. See also "New England Region."

Virginia—State of Virginia, Alexandria, Arlington, Arlington County, Charlottesville, Danville, Lynchburg, Newport News, Norfolk and Portsmouth, Petersburg, Richmond, Roanoke, Staunton, Wythe County.

Virginia/Tennessee—Bristol.

Washington—Adams, Franklin, Lincoln counties; Bellingham; Benton, Franklin, Klickitat counties; Bremerton, Centralia and Chehalis; Chelan, Douglas, Grant, Okanogan counties; Cowlitz County and Kelso; Ellensburg; Everett; Grays Harbor; Grays Harbor County; Lewis County; Lewis and Pacific counties; Lincoln County; Olympia; Port Angeles and Port Townsend; Seattle; Spokane; Tacoma; Vancouver; Walla Walla; Whitman County; Yakima.

West Virginia—Beckley, Bluefield, Charleston, Clarksburg, Elkins, Fairmont, Huntington, Martinsburg, Morgantown, Parkersburg, Wheeling.

Wisconsin—State of Wisconsin, Appleton, Ashland, Baraboo, Beloit, Chippewa Falls, Eau Claire, Fond du Lac, Green Bay, Janesville, Kenosha, La Crosse, Madison, Manitowoc, Milwaukee, Mineral Point, Oshkosh, Racine, Rock County, Sheboygan, Superior, Watertown, Waukesha, Wausau, West Allis, Whitewater.

Wisconsin/Michigan—Marinette and Menominee.

Wyoming—Casper, Cheyenne, Laramie, Sheridan.

Regional Directory of 1844—Includes Memphis, St. Louis, New Orleans, Pittsburgh, Beaver, Steubenville, Wheeling, Portsmouth, Maysville, Cincinnati, Lawrenceburgh, Madison, Louisville, Vicksburg, Natchez.

Business Directories

Business directories included the names, addresses, and business identification for merchants, manufacturers, professional men, government officeholders, and notaries public. Varying with the publisher, some also included information on the principal towns, their populations, and their economies, as well as advertisements, maps, calendars, and other convenience reference material. The R.L. Polk Company produced statewide gazetteers and business directories biennially for a number of states, and some of these have been microfilmed or reprinted as facsimile editions. Titles and dates vary, but many began in the 1880s and continued into the 1930s. These are some of the states or regions covered: Alaska-Yukon, Arizona-New Mexico, Idaho, Illinois, Indiana, Iowa, Kansas, Maryland, Maryland-District of Columbia, Michigan, Oklahoma, Oregon-Washington (early 1900s), Oregon-Washington-Alaska (1901–1902), Pennsylvania, Texas, Utah, Utah-Idaho, Utah-Wyoming, Wisconsin, Wyoming (1908–1909).

A number of nineteenth-century companies published these directories. The following are only a sampling of the numerous such guides published:

Brown's Gazeteer of the Chicago and Northwestern Railway, and Branches, and of the Union Pacific Rail Road: A Guide and Business Directory . . . South of It to Salt Lake City. Also to Denver, Golden City, Central City, Nevada, Idaho, Georgetown. C. Exera Brown, comp. Chicago: Bassett Brother's Steam Printing House, 1869. Western Americana, Frontier History of the Trans-Mississippi West, 1550–1900, reel 76, no. 769.

Elliott & Nye's Virginia Directory and Business Register. Richmond: Elliott & Nye, 1852.

The Illustrated Commercial, Mechanical, Professional, and Statistical Gazetteer and Business-Book of Connecticut, for 1857–8. A.D. Jones, comp. New Haven, Conn.: T.J. Stafford, 1857.

The Massachusetts Register and Business Directory. Boston: George Adams, 1852–1873.

McKenney's Pacific Coast Directory for 1883–4 . . . of California, Oregon, Washington, British Columbia, Alaska, Nevada, Utah, Idaho, Montana, Arizona, and New Mexico. . . . San Francisco: L.M. McKenney, 1882.

The Medical Register for New England. Francis H. Brown, comp. Boston: Houghton, Osgood, 1880. Directory and business guide, including medical associations, schools, hospitals, benevolent associations and asylums, and others.

Minnesota Gazetteer and Business Directory for 1865: Containing a List of Cities, Villages, and Post Offices in the State, a List of Business Firms, State and County Organizations. . . . Originally published, Saint Paul: Groff & Bailey, 1865. Western Americana, Frontier History of the Trans-Mississippi West, 1550–1900, reel 372, no. 3655.

The New England Business Directory. Boston: George Adams, 1856–1881.

The New-England Mercantile Union Business Directory, Six Parts in One. New York: Pratt & Co., 1849.

The Pacific Coast Business Directory . . . Containing . . . the States of California, Oregon, and Nevada; the Territories of Washington, Idaho, Montana, and Utah; and the Colony of British Columbia . . . . San Francisco: H.G. Langley, 1867–?

The Western Reserve Register for 1852: Containing Lists of the Officers of the General Governments and of the Officers and Institutions on the Reserve. Hudson, Ohio: Sawyer, Ingersoll, and Co., 1852.

LOCAL BUSINESSES

Newspapers, city and business directories, and telephone directories all carried advertisements and notices about local businesses, their merchandise and services, and their proprietors or agents. For descendants of these owners, these publications are interesting, add spice to a family history, and are further evidence of an ancestor's presence in a particular place at a given time. Occasionally, such advertisements went a step further and listed the entire board of directors or trustees, especially of banks, insurance companies, and private schools. For companies with a state government charter, the state law providing for the incorporation of the business sometimes named the individual directors or stockholders. In addition, the various censuses of manufacturers and products of industry (see pages 70–74) name hundreds of individuals and provide some degree of detail about their businesses. The agriculture schedules provide similar details for farmers and ranchers.

For many businesses and professional offices, the only records we have are their advertisements. For others, journals, ledgers, and other records still exist, some even from the colonial period, in library and archives manuscript collections and in museums. The Texas State Archives, for example, holds papers of at least two early Texas physicians, Alexander Ewing and James R. Kerr. Such papers and books often tell about customer or client accounts; who spent how much for what and sometimes whether they paid their bills on time. Like advertisements, these records at least place ancestors in a given place on a given date.

One account book of an unnamed business in Jasper County, Mississippi, survived a destructive courthouse fire and is held in the county courthouse and labeled *Claim Docket and Chancery Court Minutes, Second District, Paulding*. Apparently, Henry M. Round became justice of the peace and after 14 April 1840 used the book for county records. Was he also the merchant who kept the ledger? Nevertheless, the business record identifies its customers. For example, listed under "Sundries D" is an entry that on 23 February 1838, Alfred Shelby "paid $128 on account—cotton." Then on 11 August 1838, A. Shelby bought a shirt for $3.50 and a pair of pants for $5.00. Last, in August 1839, is the note "A. Shelby, amount to grocery ticket, $1.25." Although two land grant records exist for this Shelby in 1836 and 1837 in that county, the business records tell us that he was actually living and farming there and add a human quality to the facts available on him. Some such records contain more substantial genealogical information, such as death dates.

Although mercantile records are interesting and revealing, funeral home records are more genealogical. More and more of these records are being given to libraries and archives, but some companies allow researchers to look at the files in their offices. If genealogists do not abuse this privilege, we all may reap the benefit for years to come. However, companies are not in business to search for our ancestors; they cannot use their work time for researchers who do not know what they are looking for or do not have some specific search in mind and specific facts with which to work.

A good illustration of the value of funeral home records comes in the file of Mrs. Maggie (Kane) Wells of Houston, Texas, who died in 1934. Her death certificate on file at the state bureau of vital statistics gave her birth and death dates and places, cause of death, and the names of the funeral home and cemetery. With a specific funeral home to visit, I made an appointment with the secretary, and she pulled the file ahead of time. The contents were enlightening. They showed that the lady was five feet, one inch tall and weighed about 130 pounds. She had blue eyes, gray hair, and false teeth. She died on 27 December 1934, when the weather was cloudy and warm, not unusual for Houston. The obituaries from all three city newspapers were in the file. They named the thirty-one pallbearers and honorary pallbearers as well as her children, but not her twelve grandchildren or nine great-grandchildren. The published notices also mention "four nieces and nephews all of Cincinnati, Ohio." However, the funeral home folder had the original copy for the obituaries, and it said "four nieces and two nephews of Cincinnati." The slight error in publication could make a difference in trying to identify those Ohio relatives. Furthermore, the death certificate named the cemetery where she was buried, but the funeral home file contained a map that showed exactly where in the family plot she was buried and who was already buried in the same plot. Although she has no tombstone, her descendants still can know the location of her grave.

When Mrs. Wells's son-in-law died in 1941, the same funeral home was called in. That folder contained completely new information for the family record: an order of service for the funeral, the exact location in the cemetery where he was buried, the name of his surviving stepsister and her residence, and the name of his church and Masonic lodge.

Insurance company records also can contain pertinent genealogical information, such as birth date and place, spouse and children or other beneficiaries, residence, occupation, death date, and cause of death. If you know a specific insurance company that handled an ancestor's insurance needs, contact them for the particular information you need and have not found elsewhere. Usually family records and interviews with older relatives are the best sources for determining an insurance company to contact. Some beneficial societies existed, and still exist, primarily as insurance societies. Many are listed in the *Encyclopedia of Associations.* Also consult the catalog of the Family History Library for microfilmed records. One example in the Family History Library catalog is *Record of Benefits, 1883–1924* of the Bavarian Beneficial Society of Cincinnati; the original records are at Wright State University in Dayton, Ohio.

Reminder

Funeral home, insurance, medical, and legal records and, to some extent, other business records can aid in genealogical searches. Ask in the local area about such records, especially in public and academic libraries and museums. Consult the Family History Library catalog under the name of your research state and town. If a business that is still in operation seems likely to have information pertinent to a search, then make the contact and try to find the information. Again, discretion and consideration are key. Taking up employee time, especially talking about family history, is not good public relations for genealogy in general, however polite and interested the employee might act. The few who abuse the privilege of access may well cause the records to be closed to others.

Getting information about or from records of defunct businesses can be a challenge. Many such records do not exist, but some do. Try to determine locally whether the business was sold, who purchased it, and whether the new owners retained the records. (Sometimes, the seller kept the records.) In this effort, you can contact other businesses of a similar nature, the chamber of commerce, or a trade association. Local newspapers or city directories may give you clues to when a business ceased operation or who took it over.

In addition, local public libraries, museums, universities, or state historical societies, libraries, and archives often hold some business records. Survey the repositories in your research area to determine which libraries and archives hold such materials on local companies. For example, the special collections department at the University of Idaho at Moscow, Idaho, houses records of the First National Bank of Wallace, Idaho, which opened in 1887. When the bank failed in 1890 and was reorganized, some families never claimed personal papers they had deposited in the vault for safekeeping. These items are now part of the bank papers. An online inventory of this collection is at the University of Idaho library's Web site <www.lib.uidaho.edu/special-collections/manuscripts/index.html#Business> under "Special Collections-Primary Sources-Business." This library also holds mining, lumbering, and insurance company papers.

Business and Professional Ancestors

Another side of the question is getting information about the businesspeople themselves. Many professional and trade associations publish directories of members from time to time.

Legal, medical, and dental organizations are well known, but such organizations also exist for engineers, dairymen, morticians, architects, teachers, bankers, lawyers, and many others. Their directories vary in genealogical usefulness. Most contain at least members' names and business addresses. Others give birth year, school, and graduation year. Their journals, annual reports, and published transactions often contain obituaries and the more extensive biographical information that genealogists want. (See page 303 for a discussion of legal directories.)

An early trade association, the Carpenters' Company of Philadelphia, published its rules of work in 1786 and included names of over 130 members, some by then deceased. This little volume was reprinted in 1971 as a facsimile edition: *The Rules of Work of the Carpenters' Company of the City and County of Philadelphia*, Charles E. Peterson, annotator, (New York: Bell Publishing, for the Carpenters' Company, 1971).

Directories and records pertaining to clergy are usually in denominational or religious archives. Law, medical, and dental schools usually have collections of their professional directories. Although legal directories have been published since 1868, the American Medical Association directory began in 1906. If you had an ancestor in such a profession or trade, inquire also about biographical dictionaries and compiled obituaries.

Medical Obituaries: American Physicians' Biographical Notices in Selected Medical Journals Before 1907, by Lisabeth M. Holloway (New York: Garland Publishing, 1981) is an extensive work compiled from society journals and other sources, with each entry documented. The volume lists physicians alphabetically with birth and death dates and educational and professional information as found in the listed sources. For example, George Logan (1778–1861) graduated from the University of Pennsylvania medical school in 1802; served in the United States Navy, 1810–1829; practiced medicine in Charleston, South Carolina; and died in New Orleans. George's son, Thomas Muldrup Logan, was incorrectly listed as Charles in his own biographical sketch. This source and others give Thomas's birth date as 31 July 1808, but a family Bible gives January 31. However, the published sketches and this family Bible are secondary sources. The Bible was kept by Thomas's daughter and son-in-law, probably with input from his wife or another family record. Nevertheless, these discrepancies illustrate the warning that even though the compiler of *Medical Obituaries* was thorough and careful, previously published information or family sources may contain mistakes. The genealogist, therefore, must seek to verify the information with other records.

In related fields, several biographical dictionaries are available. At least two in the dental profession were compiled from questionnaires sent to American Dental Association members: *America's Dental Leaders: A National Biographic Volume of the Dental Profession* (Chicago: Distinction Press, Inc., 1953) and *Who's Who in American Dentistry*, by Alvin J. DeBre (Los Angeles: Dale Dental Publishing Co., 1963). These two volumes overlap somewhat, but together they represent a significant portion of the profession between 1900 and 1963. Generations were well represented, with participating dentists giving birth dates at least back to 1874. The information included address, birth date and place, parents' names, spouse and children, education and professional involvement, publications, military service, hobbies, and extra-professional activities.

A more recent addition to the field of biographical dictionaries is *Who's Who in Health Care*, 2d ed. (Rockville, Md.: Aspen Systems Corporation, 1981). The entries give birth date, spouse and children, education, professional positions, memberships, publications, and address. Another late-twentieth-century publication is *Who's Who in American Nursing* (Washington, D.C.: Society of Nursing Professionals, 1984–1989).

Histories, both books and articles, written on professions and occupations can help pro-

For More Info

Another source, if you have doctors in your ancestry, is the American Medical Associations Deceased Physician File, 1864–1970. In this file you may find an obituary and other information, such as medical schools attended and biographical data. This file is available on microfilm at the Family History Library and through its rental program. The names are arranged in alphabetical order. The National Genealogical Society (4527 Seventeenth Street North, Arlington, Virginia 22207-2399) also has the AMA files and will search them for you for a fee.

vide information on ancestors. One example is *The History of Dentistry in the Republic of Texas, 1836–1945*, by Ernest Beerstecher Jr. (Houston: Dental Branch, The University of Texas Health Science Center at Houston, 1975). This book includes a documented biographical directory of dental practitioners in the republic, compiled from many of the same sources that genealogists would use: city directories, newspapers, professional journals, and manuscript sources. A more general history is *The New England Merchants in the Seventeenth Century*, by Bernard Bailyn (New York: Harper and Row, 1964, reprint from original by Harvard University, 1955). See pages 282–287 for discussion of periodical indexes that could help you find articles about ancestors or their occupations.

Employee Records

Employee records are another category of business records. Larger companies and labor unions may be the best sources of information on employees. Family records, obituaries, city directories, and census records are standard sources of identifying an occupation and the employer's name or company. When they still exist (and many do not), the historical employee records or publications of the employee union or association are usually in company, state, or historical society archives. In addition, histories of occupations or products abound, especially for craftsmen such as watchmakers, jewelers, silversmiths, gunsmiths, cabinetmakers, and others. One example is *Arms Makers of Philadelphia 1660–1890*, by James B. Whisker (Lewiston, N.Y.: E. Mellen Press, 1990). Check WorldCat and individual library catalogs for such works that might give you insight on ancestral occupations or the ancestors who worked in them.

Railroad employees. For example, records of Great Northern and Northern Pacific railroad employees are held at the Minnesota Historical Society <www.mnhs.org>. The Virginia Historical Society holds manuscripts relating to the Richmond, Fredericksburg and Potomac Railroad. Employee lists for another railroad have been compiled and published: *Baltimore and Ohio Railroad Employees, 1842 and 1852, 1855 and 1857*, by Edna A. Kanely ([n.p.]: the author, 1982). The book is in major genealogical libraries and is available on microfiche from the Family History Library. On the other hand, railroad magnate James J. Hill and family donated their family and business papers to create the James J. Hill Library in St. Paul, Minnesota <www.jjhill.org>. These records contain family information and some records on their domestic employees, not railroad employees. Other repositories with railroad records include the Chicago Historical Society, Newberry Library in Chicago, San Diego Historical Society, and Northern Illinois University. For others, see the manuscript collection finding aids discussed in chapter seven and *The Directory of North American Railroads, Associations, Societies, Archives, Libraries, Museums and Their Collections*, Holly T. Hansen, comp. (Croydon, Utah: the compiler, 1999).

Nineteenth-century railroads were numerous, and many were short-lived. Likewise, with mergers and business failures came the loss or destruction of records not considered pertinent to reorganization or current operations. Existing company archives may or may not house employment records on specific individuals. However, you never know until you look into the possibilities. The Railroad Retirement Board <www.rrb.gov>, created in the mid-1930s, maintains pension files only on railroad employees who worked from 1936 forward. The Web site gives advice and procedures for genealogists seeking information on ancestral railroad retirees. (See also page 224.)

Colonial and early federal-era employees included indentured servants and apprentices. Thousands of immigrants came in the seventeenth, eighteenth, and early nineteenth centuries as indentured servants (some called redemptioners) bound to an employer for a specified number of years (usually two to seven) to pay for their passage, to work off other debts, or to serve out a criminal sentence. They worked on farms, especially in Maryland, Virginia, and the Carolinas, and in towns, especially in Pennsylvania. An example of a 1738 indenture document is in Figure 7-7, on page 269. Apprentices were usually minors, often orphans, who were bound to an employer, usually until the age of twenty-one, to learn the skills of a craft or trade.

Some records of indentures and apprenticeships survive. A few have been abstracted or transcribed and published, primarily in periodicals. Archives and manuscript collections sometimes hold such records within family or business papers. To identify such collections, consult the sources discussed earlier in this chapter. In addition, the Family History Library has available on microfilm the 1796–1797 indenture book of Philadelphia County, Pennsylvania.

ORGANIZATIONS

Ancestors joined civic and fraternal organizations just as they joined churches and professional groups. Local newspapers, family papers, tombstones, obituaries, and local histories can help you determine which organizations your ancestors belonged to. Notices of meetings, special functions, and election of officers were regular parts of some community newspapers.

For example, the *Bolivar (Tennessee) Bulletin* noted on 24 February 1866 that the IOOF (Independent Order of Odd Fellows) Lodge 27 met each Tuesday night and that A.S. Coleman was an officer. By 13 June 1868, this same Coleman was an officer in the Sons of Temperance, Magnolia Division No. 96, which met each Saturday night at the Odd Fellows Hall. In October 1874, he was Senior Warden of the Worth Encampment No. 16 of the IOOF, which met two Wednesday nights a month. Where can you look for more information?

Tip

If a local chapter of an ancestor's organization still exists, contact the chapter for any information they might share. If the local chapter no longer functions but the national or state headquarters exists, ask there about records from defunct chapters. Also ask where you might find old copies of the organization's periodical, for many organizations publish one. The *Encyclopedia of Associations*, either the national organization volumes or the regional, state, and local organization volumes (cited earlier in this chapter, page 131), can give you addresses for many organizations. The *Greenwood Encyclopedia of American Institutions* (Westport, Conn.: Greenwood Press) is a series of books that helps identify organizations and gives background on them: *Fraternal Organizations*, by Alvin J. Schmidt (1980); *Social Service Organizations*, Peter Romanofsky, ed. (1978); *Farmers' Organizations*, by Lowell K. Dyson (1986); and *Labor Unions*, Gary M. Fink, ed. (1977). Other sources for fraternal organizations include these:

- *The Cyclopædia of Fraternities*, 2d ed., by Albert C. Stevens. New York: E.B. Treat, 1907, reprint by Gale Research, 1966.
- *A Dictionary of Secret and Other Societies*, compiled by Arthur Preuss. St. Louis: B. Herder Book Company, 1924, reprint by Gale Research, 1966.
- *Handbook of Secret Organizations*, by William J. Whalen. Milwaukee: Bruce Publishing Company, 1966.

Whether or not the organization still exists, records may be in libraries, archives, or museums on the local or state level. The *National Union Catalog of Manuscript Collections*,

A Guide to Archives and Manuscripts in the United States, and the *Directory of Archives and Manuscript Repositories in the United States* cited on page 131 can help locate organizational records housed in these institutions.

One organization that often has information on its members is the Masons. Because the organization is more than two hundred years old in this country, some records reach back into the eighteenth century. Much depends on the individual lodge or state grand lodge. The information varies considerably in its completeness, especially for early records. In addition, most Masonic records deal with membership, not biographical data. Sometimes they include a death date.

The emblem on the tombstone of Rev. William Harrison indicated he was a Mason. The Grand Lodge of Virginia graciously provided the following information. Their earliest record of him was on the 1755 bylaws of the Blandford Lodge No. 3 at Petersburg. The other records showed that he did not appear on the lodge roster for 1792, but served as mayor of the city in 1799–1800, served as lodge chaplain from 1800 to 1804, and was listed under "deaths" from the lodge in 1813. No exact death date was sent in, but his tombstone gives the month and day. This information comes from lodge rosters, a lodge history, and grand lodge proceedings. Other records of that lodge were lost in a fire before 1850. The librarian also mentioned that petitions for membership from the nineteenth century and before had little personal information, and few of these have survived in Virginia.[10]

LOCAL GOVERNMENT RECORDS

Town and city governments sometimes have records useful to genealogists. These may be minutes of the governing body, tax rolls, municipal court records, vital records, and perhaps personnel records, but each town or city has its own priorities and state regulations on what to keep and for how long. Contact your particular city of interest for specific holdings, and ask whether they have a city archives. In addition, consult the Family History Library catalog for microfilmed records. For example, the Family History Library catalog contains a number of records from the Philadelphia Alms House and the Guardians of the Poor.

The town of Calvert, Texas, suffered a city hall fire in the early twentieth century but still has some of the city tax rolls back to 1905. One resident on the tax rolls was John P. Shelby, living in town at least from 1905 to 1908. His city tax of $2.20 in 1906 was based on the value of his lot, valued at $160, one vehicle, and a horse. By 1908, he had acquired three cows. It is interesting that this lot, designated with block and lot number in the tax books and deed records, does not appear on the city map for that period, nor has the abstract company yet determined its exact location.

Some towns and cities maintain vital records for births and deaths that occurred within the city limits; some cities required burial permits before someone could be buried in the city. These regulations vary with the city, county, or state. The 1886 *Report on the Social Statistics of Cities* often included these regulations for specific cities (see pages 74–75).

Contact the town clerk or city secretary in the ancestral town to learn what records exist and for what time period. Once you know the extent of existing records, you will be able to determine whether you need to visit city hall or hire someone to look there. In addition, some early town records, mostly from New England, have been published or microfilmed. Check the Family History Library catalog and the New England Historic Genealogical Society for rental availability.

State Records

Using federal census records along with county and local records often gives genealogists a good body of material on specific ancestors. One jurisdiction where ancestors lived and therefore created other records was the state. The records described in this chapter are those found in records of the current states, even if those records were created during colonial or territorial years. The term *state* here applies to the geographic area, not solely to the governmental period after official statehood. Many of these records are housed at the state archives or historical society. Among the most important state-level records, when available, are state censuses.

STATE CENSUSES

A census is a counting of people. Federal censuses began primarily for the purpose of determining representation in the federal House of Representatives, and states too have used census totals for state legislative representation. Because federal enumerations need to be as complete as possible, they include citizens and noncitizens, adults and children, males and females, and, before 1865, the free and the slave. Many state censuses have followed the federal practice.

According to the process set out in the Northwest Ordinance of 1787, a territory could form a legislature when it had five thousand free white males age twenty-one or older and could become a state when it had a population of sixty thousand free persons. This process is a primary reason for the frequent territorial censuses, even statistical ones.

The decennial federal census records are valuable and necessary records for genealogists, but they are not complete. To fill the gaps between federal enumerations and to help make up for the missing schedules, genealogists must rely on other sources. Censuses taken under the authority of the state, territorial, or colonial governments can provide such assistance.

Not all states have made state censuses, and many enumerations were statistical only, without names. Although some named only heads of household, others named each individual within the household. The purely statistical censuses do not provide genealogical information and, therefore, are not considered here.

Important

How Can State Censuses Help?

State censuses help genealogists in exactly the same ways that federal censuses do. They present a picture of each family between decennial censuses, can indicate children born since the last census, and can suggest whether family members had died or moved away. If for some reason the enumerator missed the family in a federal census, the state census may help fill the gap in information.

Especially useful state censuses, even the ones that name only heads of households, are those in states that have suffered the loss of courthouse records in fires. The 1866 Mississippi census for Jasper County is a good example. The 1860 federal census had shown John Moffitt (age eighty-six, born in South Carolina) and his wife, Elisabeth (eighty-two, born in Virginia). In the state census, dated 4 December 1865, both were enumerated. John was listed in the 90-100 age column; his wife, in the 80-90 bracket. This information helps narrow the range of possible death dates for this long-lived couple.

Case Study: Following Clues From the State Census

Case Study

The 1866 state census for Smith County, Mississippi, enumerated the John P. Shelby family. From information in previous census records and family records, both parents can be identified as the male and female in the 40–50 age bracket. From the same sources, names could be put with the two boys under ten and the two boys between ten and twenty. The interesting statistics fall in the remaining two categories. John and his wife had two sons who should have been in the 20–30 age group: George, about twenty to twenty-one, and William, about twenty-two to twenty-three. However, only one was marked in that column. Later census records and his Confederate service record and pension application revealed that George lived and moved with the family to Texas by 1870. On the other hand, the last known record of William was the 1860 census. His name did not appear in Civil War records or later censuses, and apparently he was not with the family in this state census. Although this census did not solve the problem of his whereabouts, it did aid in identifying another family member.

In the same family, in the column for females under ten, the census indicated two young girls. The only one shown in the 1860 census was Mary, born between 1854 and 1858 according to various other records. Who was the second girl? The answer seems to be in the deed records of the Texas county to which the family moved. When the older brother, Irvin Shelby, died intestate in 1912, his heirs sold his land. Because Irvin never married, had no descendants, and died after both of his parents, his heirs were his brothers and sisters, or their heirs. In the deed record, all the brothers except William were listed, as was sister Mary, now a widow. However, besides the Shelby siblings, the deed named five additional people as heirs. Census and marriage records showed that these five were Oldham children born to Lafayette and Anna/Annie M. (Shelby) Oldham. According to the marriage record in the Robertson County courthouse, this couple married in 1878 "at Mr. Shelby's." The marriage record did not indicate whether Mr. Shelby was her father. Nevertheless, Annie was one of Irvin's heirs. In order for Annie's children to be heirs in 1912, she must have already died.

For whatever reason, this Shelby family was not enumerated in the 1870 census in this county although deed records and a legislative petition show they were there. Therefore, it is not possible to know whether Annie was living with the John P. Shelby family in 1870. We do know she was a Shelby and she was a legal heir of Irvin. That gives two possible scenarios. Either she was a daughter of John P. and Matilda and therefore a sister to Irvin and the others, or she was the only heir of deceased brother, William. If she was a daughter of William, she would have been born when William was about seventeen or eighteen years old, quite young for a man to marry in those years. If Annie was a daughter of John P. and his wife, she would have been born in the five-year gap between two known siblings, when the mother was thirty-nine. This seems the most likely possibility. Nevertheless, the state census in 1866 seems to show her, at age five, with the family as the other girl under ten years of age. This state census was the first indication that there might have been another child in the family.

State Censuses That Name Family Members

Some states did not enumerate their population by name other than in the federal decennial censuses. The geographic areas that were territories before becoming states sometimes took territorial censuses, often to determine whether the territory had a large enough population to qualify for statehood. Also, before the American Revolution, when future states were colonies, a few conducted enumerations of the population. If your ancestors lived in a state that took state censuses, you need to use these for additional clues and to help corroborate what you find in federal censuses and other records.

Tip

Since 1840, a number of states have taken censuses in at least some of the "5" years—1855, 1865, etc.—between decennial federal censuses: Florida, Illinois, Iowa, Kansas, Massachusetts, Minnesota, New Jersey, New York, North Dakota, Oregon (limited counties), Rhode Island, South Dakota, Washington (various years), and Wisconsin. Michigan took these censuses in the "4" years. The joint state-federal census of 1885 included Colorado, Florida, Nebraska, New Mexico Territory, and Dakota Territory. Most of these censuses contain information similar to that in the federal censuses: name, age, race, relationship, occupation, citizenship, etc.

South Dakota recorded its 1905–1945 state censuses on individual cards, as shown in Figure 5-1, below. Notice that the 1915 census card for Frank Haskins also gave his church affiliation as Lutheran, his wife's maiden name as Julia Gunderson, and their marriage date as 1895, although by 1915 Frank's wife had died. These pieces of information all become

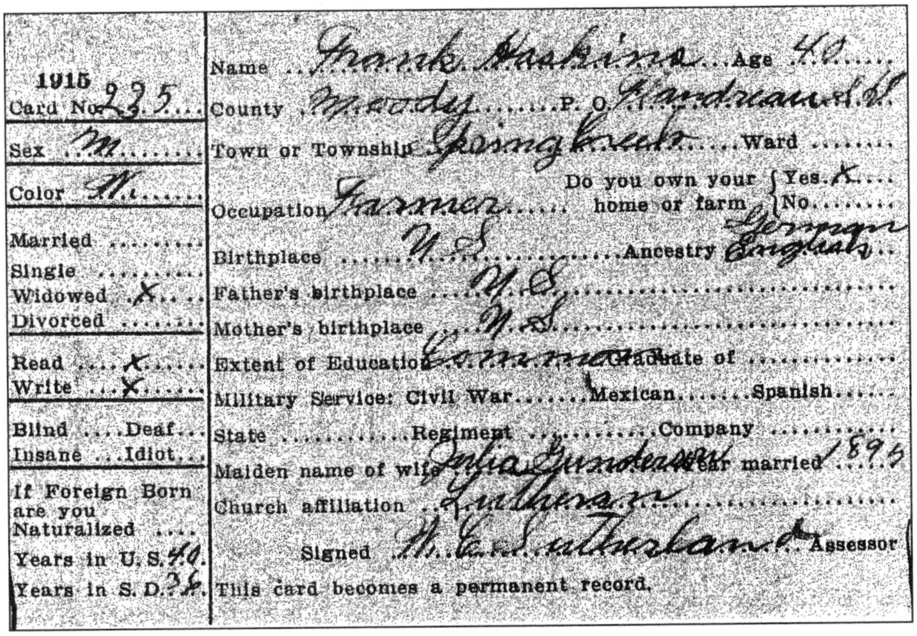
1915
Card No. 235
Sex M
Color W
Married
Single
Widowed X
Divorced
Read X
Write X
Blind ... Deaf ...
Insane ... Idiot ...
If Foreign Born are you Naturalized ....
Years in U. S. 40
Years in S. D. 36

Name Frank Haskins Age 40
County Moody P. O. Flandreau S.D.
Town or Township Spring Creek Ward ....
Occupation Farmer Do you own your home or farm { Yes X No ....
Birthplace U.S. Ancestry German English
Father's birthplace U.S.
Mother's birthplace U.S.
Extent of Education Common Graduate of ....
Military Service: Civil War ...... Mexican ...... Spanish ......
State .... Regiment .... Company ....
Maiden name of wife Julia Gunderson Year married 1895
Church affiliation Lutheran
Signed W. C. Sutherland Assessor
This card becomes a permanent record.

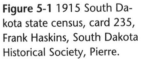

Figure 5-1 1915 South Dakota state census, card 235, Frank Haskins, South Dakota Historical Society, Pierre.

clues for further research. As happens in so many records, however, this card gives the birthplaces of Frank and his parents simply as "U.S."

Oklahoma took its first territorial census in 1890, at the same time as the 1890 federal decennial census but using a different form. Similar to, but not the same as, previous federal censuses, the territorial census asked for street name, dwelling/visitation number, name, relationship to head, color, sex, age; birthplace, number of years in the United States, length of residence in the territory, naturalization status, ability to read and write, and whether a person was a soldier. Figure 5-2, below, is an example from this territorial census.

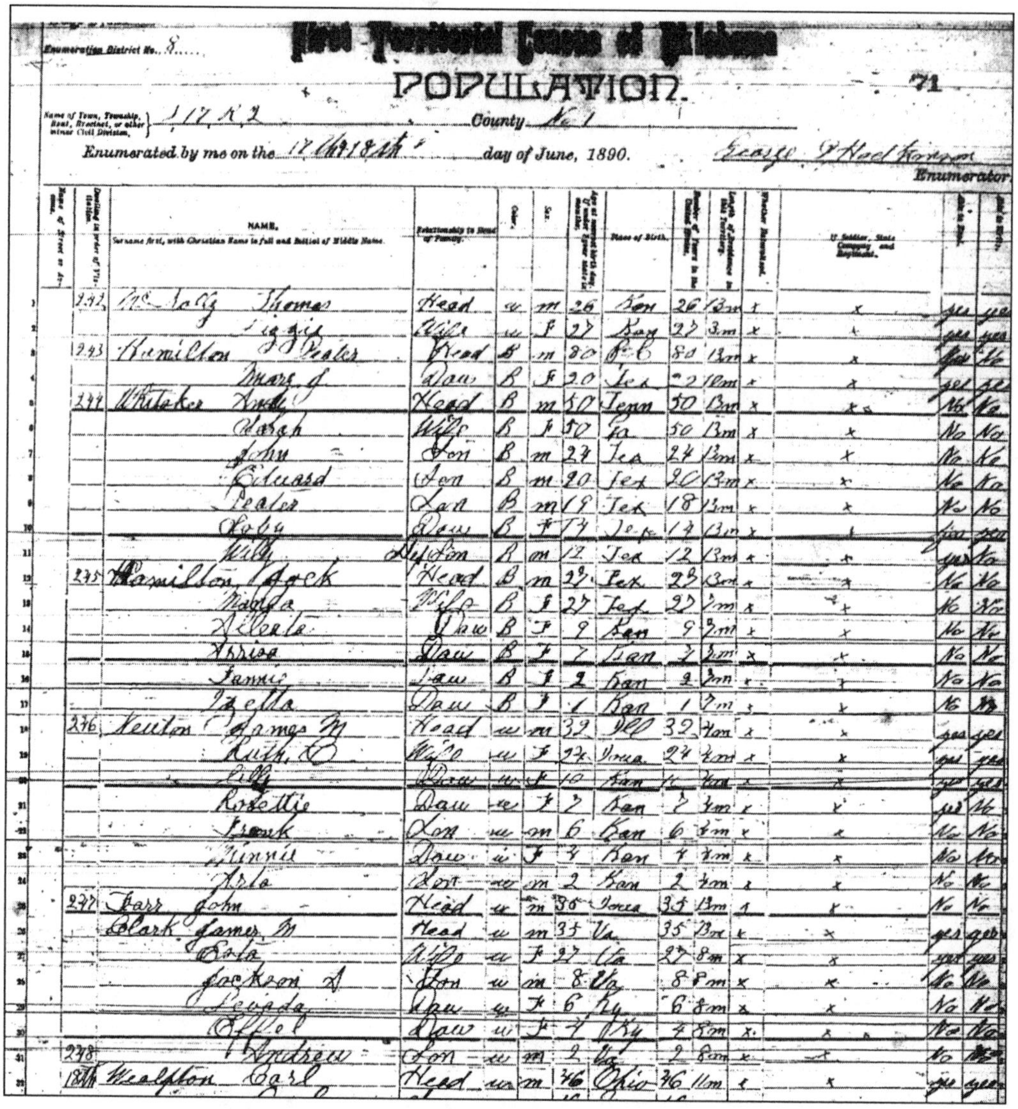

Figure 5-2 First Territorial Census of Oklahoma, 1890, p. 71 for T17 R2, NARA microfilm M1811, 1 roll.

A partial finding aid is *Smith's First Directory of the Oklahoma Territory for the Year Commencing Aug 1st 1890* (Guthrie, Okla. Terr.: James W. Smith, 1890; reprint by Histree, 1989). The directory covers seven counties: Beaver, Canadian, Cleveland, Kingfisher, Logan, Oklahoma, and Payne; it does not include Indian Territory or Greer County, Texas, that became part of Oklahoma in 1896. After listing town residents, Smith listed homesteaders by the location of their land, with quarter section, township, and range, using *e* if the land was east of the Indian meridian or nothing if it was west of the meridian. The census page in Figure 5-2 is for township 17, range 2. Thus, the directory lists Jack Hamilton as a homesteader on the northwest quarter of section 20, township 17, range 2, and the census enumerates him and his family as household number 245 on one of the census pages for "T17, R2." Finding residents without homesteads or not living in the towns in Smith's directory usually requires a page-by-page search of the census.

New York provides researchers with a variety of state censuses. For example, the 1865 census was ahead of the federal censuses by asking for each person's county of birth (if within New York) or state or country of birth (if outside New York); the number of children the women had borne; the number of times an adult had been married; whether one was, at the time, married or widowed; whether one was native-born, naturalized, or alien; and whether one was then in or had been in the army or navy. On the other hand, the 1892 census, organized with two columns of names per page, asked only for basics: name, sex, age, color, native country (not state), citizen or alien status, and occupation.

The 1925 New York census asked only for the country of birth but asked for specifics on immigration and naturalization. For example, on Merrick Road, in Hempstead, Nassau County, Michael McHugh, age seventy-six, reported being a native of Ireland who had been in the United States forty-six years; he was naturalized at New York City Hall in 1879. His wife, Mary, age sixty-nine and an Irish native, had been in the United States forty-four years. Their neighbor Minnie Wanser, a thirty-year-old native of Norway, had been in the United States for fifteen years and had become a citizen "through husband," in this case, by marrying a native-born U.S. citizen.

State-Specific Census Reference List

For the ease of presentation and because we usually think in terms of finding records based on the geographic boundaries of the state, regardless of whether it was legally a state, a territory, or a colony at the time, the list given here combines various enumerations pertaining to the geographic area we now know as the state. Check also in the area that was the parent state, territory, or colony.

The list below concentrates only on censuses that named heads of household or family members, not on substitutes or statistical censuses. It assumes heads of household only, unless otherwise noted. Check archives Web sites and library catalogs for county and year availability. Many of these censuses are available on microfilm on interlibrary loan from the state library, archives, or historical society. Consult their Web sites or ask your local interlibrary loan librarian to contact the institutions for availability. Many are available from the Family History Library through Family History Centers. A number of state and territorial censuses have been published and may be available from state historical societies, libraries, or archives as well as from commercial publishers. See PERSI (page 284) and library catalogs for published schedules or indexes. The *M* or *T* numbers refer to National Archives microfilm publications that can be purchased from NARA or Scholarly Resources.

Alabama—1855, for sixteen counties, has printed index. 1866, most counties, not indexed. See also 1816 Mississippi territorial census for Alabama counties. Partial 1820 census (Baldwin, Conecuh, Dallas, Franklin, Limestone, St. Clair, Shelby, Wilcox counties) as published in *Alabama Historical Quarterly* 6 (1944): 339–515. *The Alabama Genealogical Register* published early Washington County enumerations (1801, 1808, 1810) in vol. 9 (Sept. 1967): 123–126, and Madison County (1809) in vol. 10 (Dec. 1968): 175–182. Madison County, 1809, is also in *Territorial Papers* (see page 176).

Enumerations in and near Mobile in 1706, 1721, 1725 are published in the *Deep South Genealogical Quarterly*, 1 (August 1963): 30; 1 (March 1964): 136–139; and 1 (December 1963): 86, respectively. Enumeration of 1785 is published in *Everton's*

For More Info

For further details, see *State Census Records*, by Ann S. Lainhart (Baltimore: Genealogical Publishing Co., 1992). For more on colonial enumerations, see *American Population Before the Federal Census of 1790*, by Evarts B. Greene and Virginia D. Harrington (Reprint of 1932 original, Baltimore, Md.: Genealogical Publishing Co., 1993).

Genealogical Helper 36 (Sept.-Oct. 1982): 5–6. Enumerations of 1786, 1787, 1789, 1805 are published in *Spanish Census Reports at Mobile*, by Johnnie Andrews Jr. and William David Higgins (Prichard, Ala.: Bienville Historical Society, 1973), FHL film 908670, item 10. Enumerations between 1781 and 1795 are published in *Anglo-Americans in Spanish Archives: Lists of Anglo-American Settlers in the Spanish Colonies of America: A Finding Aid*, by Lawrence H. Feldman (Baltimore: Genealogical Publishing Co., 1991).

Alaska—Early Alaska censuses were lists of native inhabitants of individual towns or islands and can be found in the US Serial Set. (See page 292 for explanation of the Serial Set.)

1870	Sitka census, House Executive Document 5 (42d Congress, 2d session, vol. 1) serial 1470, pp. 13–26. Family members with name, age, birthplace, occupation, relation to head, and remarks on conditions.
1880	Sitka census in *Report of Commander of Navy Ship Stationed at Sitka, 1879–1880, on Affairs in Alaska* (Captain L.A. Beardslee), Senate Executive Document 71 (47th Congress, 1st session, vol. 4) serial 1989, p. 34. April 1880, U.S. citizens by birth, names heads of household only. Naturalized citizens listed with birthplace.
1881	Sitka census, February 1881, in *Report of Naval Officers Cruising in Alaska Waters*, House Executive Document 81 (47th Congress, 1st session, vol. 19) serial 2027, pp. 14–22. Family members with name, age, nationality, occupation. Page 23, Indian village at Sitka, heads of household only.
1885	Cape Smyth, Pt. Barrow, House Executive Document 44 (48th Congress, 2d session), serial 2298. Page 49, Eskimo families. Page 50, individuals and their age, height, weight.
1890–1895	St. George Island, House Executive Document 92, part 1 (55th Congress, 1st session) serial 3576. Family members with age, relationship to head. 1890–p. 256. 1891–p. 315. 1892–p. 357. 1893–p. 441. 1894–p. 464, includes birth, marriage, death records. 1895–p. 485.
1890–1895	St. Paul Island, same document as above. Family members with age, relationship to head. 1890–p. 253, includes birthplace, occupation. 1892–p. 354. 1894–p. 462. 1895–p. 481, includes birthplace.
1904	St. George (p. 58) and St. Paul (p. 43) islands, native population, Senate Document 98 (59th Congress, 1st session) serial 4911. Family members with age, relationship to head. St. George gives birth dates, and lists government employees by name only. Page 50, St. Paul births and deaths from doctor during 1903–1904 year.
1905	St. George (p. 113) and St. Paul (p. 105) islands, serial 4911 (same as above). Family members with age, relationship to head. St. George gives birth dates.
1907	St. George (p. 118) and St. Paul (p. 101) islands, Senate Document 376 (60th Congress, 1st session) serial 5242. Family members with age, relationship to head. St. George includes birth dates.

Arizona—1864, 1866, 1867–1882 (usually on the even years), county availability varies. Names only, by town and county. Arizona excerpts from the Territory of New Mexico census 1860, Arizona territorial census 1864, and Arizona territorial census 1870 are in Senate Document 13 (89th Congress, 1st session) serial 12668–1. Contact state archives for specifics. Several Mexican enumerations published in *Mexican Census—Pre-Territorial [Arizona]*, Eugene I. Sierras, trans. (Tucson: Arizona State Genealogical Society, 1986): vol. 1, Pimeria Alta, 1801; vol. 2, Pimeria Alta, 1852; vol. 3, Tucson, Tubac, and Santa Cruz, 1831.

Arkansas—1823 (Arkansas County only). 1829 (about half the counties) sheriff censuses.

California—1852. See also Historical Society of Southern California's *Southern California Quarterly* for Spanish-period censuses of Los Angeles area, 1790, 1816, 1836, 1844. See state archives for early mission censuses, 1790s, and for town/city censuses, scattered years from 1897 forward; a few transcripts of the city censuses are available through the Family History Library.

Colorado—1885; family members included; with agriculture, industry, and mortality schedules; see also on M158; Garfield County has been lost.

Connecticut—1669–1670, heads of household with numbers of family members and grain inventory; part of the Wyllys papers in the Historical Society, vol. 21; see also *Connecticut 1670 Census*, by Jay Mack Holbrook (Oxford, Mass.: Holbrook Research Institute, 1977). Other censuses are statistical only.

Delaware—No state censuses.

District of Columbia—Though not a state, the district has population and censuses. 1867, 1878 at the Maryland State Archives.

Florida—Fragments exist for several early censuses: 1825 (Leon County); 1855 (Marion County); 1867 (Hernando, Madison, Orange, Santa Rosa counties); 1875 (Alachua County); 1885 (except Alachua, Clay, Nassau, and Columbia counties), see also M845 and FHL. 1935, 1945, both are missing a few precincts.

Scattered colonial censuses 1783–1814, see PERSI for schedules published in journals; see also *The Spanish Censuses of Pensacola, 1784–1820: A Genealogical Guide to Spanish Pensacola*, by William S. Coker and G. Douglas Inglis (Pensacola, Fla.: Perdido Bay Press, 1980). See also *Last Days of British Saint Augustine, 1784–1785: A Spanish Census of the English Colony of East Florida*, by Lawrence H. Feldman (Baltimore: Clearfield Co., 1998).

Georgia—Georgia took septennial censuses, 1798 to about 1879; existing fragments in the state archives include heads of household with number in household. For 1838 (Laurens, Newton, Tattnall counties) and 1845 (Dooly, Forsyth, Warren counties), see *Indexes to Seven State Census Reports for Counties in Georgia, 1838–1845*, Brigid S. Townsend, comp. (Atlanta, Ga.: R.J. Taylor Jr. Foundation, 1975). For 1859 Columbia, see *Georgia Genealogical Society Quarterly* 13 (Winter 1977): 253 ff. For 1827 Taliaferro, 1838 Lumpkin, and 1845 Chatham, see *Censuses for Georgia Counties* (Atlanta, Ga.: R.J. Taylor Jr. Foundation, 1979). Others in the archives include these counties: 1800 Oglethorpe; 1852 Jasper, Chatham, and city of Augusta; 1859 Terrell. Additional schedules may be found in county courthouses and in the Telamon Cuyler Collection, Rare Books and Manuscripts Library, University of Georgia, Athens; see also PERSI for those published in periodicals.

Hawaii—Fragments of 1866 (mostly Maui), 1878, 1890, 1896 (part of Honolulu only). Scattered districts on various islands. No complete coverage. See FHL films 1010681–1010.

Idaho—No state censuses.

Illinois—1818, see *Illinois Census Returns 1810 and 1818*, Margaret Cross Norton, ed. (Baltimore: Clearfield Co., 2002, reprint of 1935 original and 1969 reprint); 1820

(Edwards County missing), see *Illinois Census Returns, 1820*, Margaret Cross Norton, ed. (Baltimore: Genealogical Publishing Co., 1969, reprint of 1935 original); 1825 (Edwards, Fulton, Randolph counties only); 1830 (Morgan); 1835 (Fayette, Fulton, Jasper, Morgan); 1840 (thirty-five of eighty-seven counties extant); 1845 (Cass, Putnam, Tazewell); 1855 (90 percent extant); 1865 (all but Gallatin, Mason, Monroe; only Elm Grove Township in Tazewell County). See Illinois State Archives Web site for additional information: <www.cyberdriveillinois.com/departments/archives/research_series/rseries5.html>.

Indiana—No state censuses record names of households; the censuses are enumerations of eligible voters. Some of these may be in a county auditor's office or the state library. 1807, early territorial census with heads of household for Dearborn, Knox, and Randolph counties; see *Census of Indiana Territory for 1807* (Indianapolis: Indiana Historical Society, 1980).

Iowa—1836 (as part of Wisconsin Territory; Dubuque and Des Moines counties; heads of household and numbers of family members in age categories). Besides 1836, incomplete censuses include 1838 (as part of Wisconsin Territory); 1844 (Keokuk); 1846 (Louisa, Polk, Wapello); 1847, 1849, 1851, 1852 (multiple counties, on FHL films 1022204–05); 1853 (part of Warren County only); 1854 (many counties, beginning on FHL film 1021290); 1856 (many counties); 1859; 1863 and 1869 (both for Henry County only); 1881 and 1882 (both are fragments); 1885 (on FHL films beginning with roll 1021316); 1888, 1889, 1891–1893 (all are fragments); 1895–1897 (fragments); 1905 (incomplete and very difficult to read); 1915; 1925. (Note that 1856–1925 are whole-family censuses.) See *Hawkeye Heritage* and *The American Genealogist* for many that have been published. For interlibrary loan information, see Web site of the State Historical Society of Iowa: <www.iowahistory.org/library/library_offers/microfilm_loan_purchase.html>.

Kansas—1865, 1875, 1885, 1895, 1905, 1915, 1925. Contact State Archives for list of available enumerations made for organization of new counties. (1855 "census" was a voter list.)

Kentucky—No state censuses that name heads of household or family.

Louisiana—No state censuses that name heads of household or family. Louisiana residents were included in some Spanish Texas enumerations now held in the Bexar Archives, University of Texas, Austin, with transcriptions in the R.B. Blake Papers, Vol. 18: 71–284, at East Texas Research Center, Stephen F. Austin University, Nacogdoches, Texas, and Clayton Library Center for Genealogical Research, Houston. For French- and Spanish-period enumerations from various archives, see these publications: (1) *The Census Tables for the French Colony of Louisiana, From 1699 Through 1732*, by Charles R. Maduell Jr. (Baltimore: Genealogical Publishing Co., 1972); (2) *Natchitoches Colonials: Censuses, Military Rolls, and Tax Lists, 1722–1803*, by Elizabeth Shown Mills (Chicago, Ill.: Adams Press, 1981); (3) *Some Late Eighteenth-Century Louisianians, Census Records 1758–1796*, by Jacqueline K. Voorhies (Lafayette, La.: University of Southwestern Louisiana, 1973); (4) *Ancestry's Red Book*, Alice Eichholz, ed., (Salt Lake City: Ancestry, 3d ed. to be released 2004), for information on French- and Spanish-period enumerations; (5) *Louisiana Census and Militia Lists, 1770–1789*, by Albert J. Robichaux Jr. (New Orleans: Polyanthos, 1977).

Maine—1837 fragments for Bangor, Portland, and unincorporated towns (at Maine State Archives); 1837, town of Eliot (at Maine Historical Society). No statewide censuses.

Maryland—No statewide censuses taken. Also see *1776 Census of Maryland*, Rev. ed., by Bettie Stirling Carothers (Westminster, Md.: Family Line Publications, 1989). See also *Maryland Records, Colonial, Revolutionary, County, and Church, From Original Sources*, 2 vols., by Gaius Marcus Brumbaugh (Baltimore: Genealogical Publishing Co., 1993, reprint of 1915 original); this includes the 1776 census.

Massachusetts—1855 and 1865 list family members, the only extant state censuses with names.

Michigan—Only a few state census records survive. The archives has partial enumerations for 1845 (males over twenty-one are named); 1854, 1864, 1874 (in these three, males over twenty-one are named; the rest of the population are in age categories); 1884 and 1894 (family members named, with other information). See PERSI for eighteenth- and nineteenth-century enumerations that have been published.

Minnesota—1836, as part of Crawford and Dubuque counties, Wisconsin Territory; 1838, as part of Crawford and Clayton counties, Wisconsin Territory. 1849, 1853 (fragments), 1857 territorial censuses; see also T1175 for 1857. 1865, 1875, 1885, 1895, 1905 state censuses.

Mississippi—Colonial enumeration of Natchez, 1723, published in "Natchez 1723 Census," by Winston DeVille, *National Genealogical Society Quarterly* 59 (June 1971): 94–95. Colonial enumeration, 1792, transcribed in *History of Mississippi, The Heart of the South*, by Dunbar Rowland (Spartanburg, S.C.: The Reprint Company, 1978). Other eighteenth-century enumerations are in the Cuban papers in the General Archives of the Indies in Seville, Spain; see *Descriptive Catalogue of the Documents Relating to the History of the United States in the Papeles Procedentes de Cuba Deposited in the Archivo General de Indias at Seville*, by Roscoe R. Hill (New York: Kraus Reprint Corp., 1965, from 1916 original).

Territorial enumerations in 1805, 1808, 1810, 1813, 1816. 1805 Wilkinson County in the *Journal of Mississippi History* (Vol. 11: 104–111). 1809 Madison County in *The Territorial Papers of the United States* (Vol. 5: 684–692). 1809 Washington County in *The Territorial Papers of the United States* (Vol. 5: 693–696). 1810 censuses in the *Journal of Mississippi History*: Amite (Vol. 10: 150–171); Baldwin (Vol. 11: 207–213); Claiborne and Warren (Vol. 13: 50–63); Franklin (Vol. 13: 249–255); Jefferson (Vol. 15: 34–46); Washington (Vol. 14: 67–79); Wilkinson (Vol. 11: 104–111). Originals of these 1805 and 1810 schedules are in the State Archives: Territorial Archives, Series A, Vols. 10, 23, and 24.

State enumerations in 1822–1825, 1837, 1841, 1845, 1853, 1866; none are complete for the state. Various county enumerations are published in the *Mississippi Genealogical Exchange*. Scattered town censuses exist. See PERSI for numerous schedules that have been published in periodicals. Various censuses between 1792 and 1866 are on FHL films 899868–70.

Missouri—A few colonial enumerations are in *The Spanish Régime in Missouri*, by Louis Houck (New York: Arno Press, 1971, reprint of 1909 original); this work is reproduced in *Western Americana, Frontier History of the Trans-Mississippi West, 1550–1900*, reel 270, no. 2672.

A few territorial enumerations remain. See *Enumeration of the County of St. Charles, Missouri Territory for the Years 1817 and 1819, With Some Selected Marriage and Cemetery Records . . .*, by Melvin B. Goe (Owensboro, Ky.: Cook-McDowell Publications, 1980). Consult the Missouri State Archives for others.

State censuses for a few counties—1844 (Callaway and Greene counties), 1852 and

1856 (for both, fragments remain), 1876 (the most complete). Check with individual counties. 1787 (St. Louis and Ste. Genevieve). 1791 (St. Louis area). 1803 (New Madrid and Cape Girardeau). 1845 (St. Louis).

Montana—A state census was apparently approved but never taken.

Nebraska—1854–1856, fifteen counties in eastern Nebraska; also published in *Nebraska and Midwest Genealogical Record* (see PERSI); also published as *1854, 1855, 1856 Nebraska Territory Censuses*, by E. Evelyn Cox (Ellensburg, Wash.: 1977). 1865 (Otoe and Cuming counties); 1869 (Stanton and Butler counties). 1885 statewide census, film M352; available for rent from FHL. See also "Nebraska Research," by Sylvia Nimmo, *National Genealogical Society Quarterly* 77 (December 1989): 260–276.

Nevada—1862–1863, one census completed over a period of time, varies from county to county because instructions were not clear; some counties list male heads of household only; some are statistical only; some list all family members. Counties available for 1862 [Douglas, Humboldt (part), Lyon, Ormsby, Storey, Washoe]; 1863 (Lander County). Other censuses called for by statute, but only the 1875 census was taken.

New Hampshire—No state censuses were taken.

New Jersey—1855 (incomplete), 1865 (incomplete), 1875 (Essex and Sussex counties only), 1885, 1895, 1905, 1915. Some do name family members, especially 1895–1915.

New Mexico—Some early Spanish and Mexican censuses. Pre-territorial censuses are incomplete. See *Spanish and Mexican Colonial Censuses of New Mexico, 1790, 1823, 1845*, by Virginia L. Olmsted (Albuquerque: New Mexico Genealogical Society, 1975). A second volume from the society covers the 1750, 1790 (part), and 1830 Spanish and Mexican colonial censuses. 1885 territorial census is the only one since 1845; 1885 is on film M846; available also from FHL. See PERSI for several enumerations that have been published in the *New Mexico Genealogist.*

New York—1825, 1835, 1845, 1855, 1865, 1875, 1892, 1905, 1915, 1925. (From 1855 forward, schedules name each member of household; 1855 is especially helpful because it gives county of birth and length of residence in current location.) Originals of most state censuses are kept at county clerk's office; some are with the county historian. New York State Library has many on microfilm, but not all counties for all years; also check FHL catalog. Consult county clerks and county historians for what they have. For colonial censuses, see PERSI and guides to research in the state. For specific state library holdings, see the Web site <www.nysl.nysed.gov/genealogy/nyscens.htm>.

New York County (Manhattan) 1905, 1915, 1925 available at county clerk's office. That county's 1890 Police Census is available at the Division of Old Records, New York County Clerk. Kings County (Brooklyn) 1855, 1865, 1875, 1892, 1905, 1915, 1925 available at the county clerk's office, New Supreme Court Building, Brooklyn. Bronx County 1915, 1925 at county clerk's office, Bronx. Queens County 1892, 1915, 1925 at county clerk's office, Jamaica. Staten Island 1915, 1925 at county clerk's office, County Courthouse, Staten Island.

North Carolina—1784–1787, for Bertie, Burke, Caswell, Chowan, Duplin, Gates, Granville, Halifax, Hyde, Johnston, Jones, Martin, Montgomery, New Hanover, Northampton, Onslow, Pasquotank, Perquimans, Pitt, Rowan (part), Richmond, Surry, Tyrrell, Warren, and Wilkes counties; not all complete. None after 1790. For published transcriptions of most extant counties, see *State Census of North Carolina, 1784–1787*, 2d ed. rev., by Alvaretta K. Register (Baltimore: Genealogical Publishing Co.,

1973, reprinted 1978, 1993). See PERSI for schedules found or corrected after Register's book.

North Dakota—1857 Pembina County, as part of Minnesota Territory; 1885, northern part of Dakota Territory; 1915, 1925 (both show names and ages of all family members). 1885 also gives occupation and birthplace and includes agricultural, manufacture, mortality schedules, and Civil War veterans.

Ohio—Ohio had no state census as such. 1803 census of Ohio, Northwest Territory, in preparation for statehood; see M1803, Washington County, 1803 schedule.

Oklahoma—1890 First Territorial Census of Oklahoma (of unassigned lands, not Indian Territory), names family members; available from FHL. (See also page 162.)

Oregon—1842–1846, a few counties; 1849, males over age twenty-one, territorial apportionment census (see also "Washington"); 1849, territorial census; 1850–1859, various counties; 1865 (Benton, Columbia, Marion, Umatilla counties). 1870 and 1875 (Umatilla County). 1885 (Linn, Umatilla counties). 1895 (Linn, Morrow, Multnomah, Marion counties). 1905 (Baker, Lane, Linn Marion counties). Oregon 1841–1849, indexes. 1842–1859 provisional and territorial censuses on FHL film 899786. Contact Oregon State Archives for specific holdings of pre-1859 schedules.

Pennsylvania—No real state censuses. (See page 174 below.)

Rhode Island—1865, 1875, 1885, 1905, 1915, 1925, 1935; these name all household members with other information. See also (1) *Census of the Inhabitants of the Colony of Rhode Island and Providence Plantations, 1774*, arranged by John R. Bartlett from the original 1858 publication (Baltimore: Genealogical Publishing Company, 1969); (2) *The Rhode Island 1777 Military Census*, transcribed by Mildred M. Chamberlain (Baltimore: Genealogical Publishing Co., 1985); (3) *Rhode Island 1782 Census*, by Jay Mack Holbrook (Oxford, Mass.: Holbrook Research Institute, 1979).

South Carolina—1829 (Fairfield, Laurens districts). 1839 (Kershaw, Chesterfield districts). 1869 (all counties except Clarendon, Oconee, Spartanburg). 1875 (Clarendon, Newberry, Marlboro, and partial schedules for Abbeville, Beaufort, Fairfield, Lancaster, and Sumter counties). Check PERSI for schedules published in periodicals.

South Dakota—1885, 1895, 1905, 1915, 1925, 1935, 1945. 1895 state census available for Beadle, Brule, Pratt (now Jones), Presho (now Lyman), Campbell, Charles Mix counties only. 1885 census, available for these counties: Beadle, Butte, Charles Mix, Edmunds, Fall River, Faulk, Hand, Hanson, Hutchinson, Hyde, Lake, Lincoln, Marshall, McPherson, Moody, Roberts, Sanborn, Spink, Stanley, and Turner. 1905–1945 are in card file at South Dakota State Historical Society.

Tennessee—No state censuses extant.

Texas—No state censuses. Mexican censuses: (1) 1830, San Antonio and Nacogdoches, transcribed in *1830 Citizens of Texas*, by Gifford E. White (Austin, Tex.: Eakin Press, 1983); (2) 1829, 1834–1836 in *National Genealogical Society Quarterly*, Vol. 40–44; reprinted as *The First Census of Texas, 1829–1836*, by Marion Day Mullins (Washington, D.C. [now Arlington, Va.]: National Genealogical Society, 1976). See also R.B. Blake Papers, transcriptions of these censuses at East Texas Research Center, Stephen F. Austin State University, Nacogdoches; Blake Papers also in transcribed and bound volumes at Clayton Library Center for Genealogical Research, Houston. Some differences in transcription exist between Mullins and Blake. These censuses do not enumerate all residents, only a few towns.

Utah—1856 territorial census with every-name index; returns are on FHL film 505913.

Index is in *1856 Utah Census Index: An Every Name Index*, Bryan Lee Dilts, comp. (Salt Lake City: Index Publishing, 1983).

Vermont—No state censuses. See *Vermont 1771 Census*, by Jay Mack Holbrook (Oxford, Mass.: Holbrook Research Institute, 1982), for head-of-household census of what became Cumberland and Gloucester counties, Vermont.

Virginia—No state censuses.

Washington—Territorial censuses, compiled by county assessors, include family members: 1856–1892, not all years, not all counties; on FHL microfilm beginning with roll 1841781; use this film number in the FHL catalog to see list of counties and years available. Interlibrary loan is available through Washington State Archives and Washington State Library. See PERSI and library catalogs for those that have been published.

West Virginia—No state censuses.

Wisconsin—Not all counties for all years. 1836 (included area that became Iowa Territory). 1838, 1842, 1846, 1847, 1855, 1865 (only Dunn, Green, Jackson, Kewaunee, Ozaukee, Sheboygan counties). 1875, 1885, 1895. 1905 (names family members). 1885, 1895, 1905 available on film from FHL; check FHL catalog for others. Some town enumerations are at county register of deeds or in circuit court files. Check with State Historical Society of Wisconsin for interlibrary loan.

Wyoming—1869, family members included.

CENSUS SUBSTITUTES AND SPECIAL ENUMERATIONS

When a census is lost or none is available for a given time, genealogists and historians sometimes pull together information of a similar nature and time period to help overcome the loss or lack. This substitute census, then, is an effort to identify as many of the people as possible who may have been enumerated in the original record or who lived in the area at a given time. Usually these substitutes include only heads of household because they are most often identified in the records used to compile the substitute. Married women and children were not normally named in tax records and were not eligible to vote, subject to military service, or called for jury duty. Thus they do not usually appear in census substitutes. Nor are most substitutes able to give numbers of family members or age and birthplace information for the people they list, unless the compiler annotated and edited the work to include that kind of data. Nevertheless, substitutes can be useful for identifying a community of people at a given time.

Occasionally, lists of residents are called censuses, in the broadest sense of the term—an effort to identify a large group of people in a given place at a given time. One example is Jay Mack Holbrook's *Connecticut 1670 Census* (Oxford, Mass.: Holbrook Research Institute, 1977), which has amplified an existing head of household census made in Hartford, Wethersfield, and Windsor. Holbrook used tax, land, probate, church, and other records to identify over two thousand people, almost all men, in the colony in the period between 1667 and 1673. No attempt is made to identify relationships or family groups. For other examples, see pages 14–19, in the discussion of the 1790 census.

Various sources that include large numbers of people are used as substitute censuses—taxpayer, voter, and landowner lists as well as city and telephone directories. However, in a narrower sense, any source that identifies an individual and/or family in a given place at a given time becomes a substitute for a census record. In this way, every record of an individual is like a census substitute and is sometimes more helpful than the best census.

Whether the source places the individual among a community or family group, an extended family cluster, or several friends who acted as witnesses to a document, the genealogist can learn something more about the ancestor.

Some states took other enumerations for the purpose of taxation or militia service—as when counting males over age twenty-one—or to identify veterans or school-age children. These enumerations can be valuable sources for locating a household or individual in a place at a given time, and some of them list each household member by name and age. State archives or historical societies, county or town courthouses, or county or local school offices usually hold these additional enumerations. Check PERSI and the Family History Library catalog for availability.

State-by-State List

Sources

The following shows some of the special enumerations and lists, other than city or telephone directories, that are used as census substitutes or enhancers. Many of the records listed are in the state archives or historical society; some are in county courthouses, town halls, or research libraries. For others, consult guides to research in your state(s) of interest and Web sites of and guides to the states' archives. Consult the Family History Library catalog, under the name of the state, then county or city. See also PERSI and library catalogs for published lists and indexes.

Alabama—Enumeration of Confederate soldiers in 1907; veterans and widows in 1921; veterans and widows over age eighty in 1927. M754, federal internal revenue assessment lists, 1865–1866.

Alaska—1903–1904 school list, St. Paul Island, Senate Document 98 (59th Congress, 1st session) serial 4911, p. 50, forty pupils with name, age, attendance, and marks. 1871, Petition of St. George residents, pp. 25–26 of Senate Executive Document 12 (44th Congress, 1st session) serial 1664. 1876, memorial of citizens of California, Oregon, Washington Territory, Alaska Territory, and British Columbia stationed at Ft. Wrangel, Senate Executive Document 14 (44th Congress, 2d session) serial 1718, pp. 4–5. (See page 292 for explanations of the serial set.)

Arizona—Great Registers of Voters, various years, 1866–1938. School superintendent censuses, various years, 1870–1963.

Arkansas—Census of Confederate pensioners, 1911–1912. M755, federal internal revenue assessment lists, 1865–1866.

California—Mission and presidio residents lists, late eighteenth century. Some twentieth-century town and city enumerations. Great Registers of Voters, various years. M756, federal internal revenue assessment lists, 1862–1866.

Colorado—1861 poll lists (voters only), 1866 enumeration of northeastern Colorado. M757, federal internal revenue assessment lists, 1862–1866.

Connecticut—Salisbury, Litchfield County, taxpayers in 1746, 1756, 1760, in an article by Donna Valley Russell, *National Genealogical Society Quarterly* 71 (1983): 94–98. M758, federal internal revenue assessment lists, 1862–1866.

Delaware—"Delaware Settlers, 1693," by Alice Reinders, *National Genealogical Society Quarterly*, 53 (1965): 205–206. Various resident lists for seventeenth century, incomplete. M759, federal internal revenue assessment lists, 1862–1866.

District of Columbia—Police censuses exist for various years between 1885 and 1919 and are contained in the *Annual Reports of the Commissioner of the District of Columbia* at the National Archives. M760, federal internal revenue assessment lists, 1862–1866.

Florida—1855 and 1866 children's census; census of Union-occupied district of Florida, 1864–1865. M761, Internal Revenue Assessment Lists for Florida, 1865–1866.

Georgia—Poor School censuses; see *Research in Georgia*, by Robert Scott Davis Jr. (Greenville, S.C.: Southern Historical Press, 1981), for list of surviving schedules; some available on microfilm. Families supplied with salt, 1862–1864. Men subject to military duty, March 1862. M762, federal internal revenue assessment lists, 1865–1866.

Hawaii—Various compiled materials, including school censuses.

Idaho—1863 poll list, men only. M763, federal internal revenue assessment lists, 1865–1866. M1209, federal internal revenue assessment lists, 1867–1874.

Illinois—Military census, 1861–1863. M764, federal internal revenue assessment lists, 1862–1866.

Indiana—Voter enumerations (men over age twenty-one), every six years beginning 1853; veterans' enrollments, 1886, 1890, 1894. M765, federal internal revenue assessment lists, 1862–1866.

Iowa—Iowa Old Age Assessment Rolls, 1934–1938, half the state. M766, federal internal revenue assessment lists, 1862–1866.

Kansas—Voter censuses 1855, 1856, 1857, 1859. Kansas Board of Agriculture enumerations 1873–1924, 1926–1936, 1950–1979. See also *The Census of the Territory of Kansas, February, 1855*, Willard C. Heiss, comp. (Knightstown, Ind.: Bookmark, 1973, reprint). M767, federal internal revenue assessment lists, 1862–1866.

Kentucky—School censuses, late nineteenth and early twentieth centuries; consult local boards of education, state archives, and Kentucky Historical Society. See *The 1795 Census of Kentucky* (Miami Beach, Fla.: TLC Genealogy Books, 1991), from statewide tax list. M768, federal internal revenue assessment lists, 1862–1866.

Louisiana—Early residents lists, *Louisiana Historical Quarterly* (Vols. 1–6); 1804 Free Persons of Color, in *The Territorial Papers of the United States* (Vol. 9, p. 174–75). Other early lists have been published by Genealogical Publishing Co., Polyanthos Press, and University of Southwestern Louisiana. M769, federal internal revenue assessment lists, 1863–1866.

Maine—1820–1861 militia rolls and rosters. M770, federal internal revenue assessment lists, 1862–1866.

Maryland—1778 oaths of allegiance: St. Mary's County, *National Genealogical Society Quarterly* 41 (1953): 69–74, 119–124; Queen Anne County, *Daughters of the American Revolution Magazine* 101 (1967): 545–546. Lists of eighteenth-century residents in Calendar of Maryland State Papers and Maryland State Archives. M771, federal internal revenue assessment lists, 1862–1866.

Massachusetts—*The Pioneers of Massachusetts [1620–1650]*, compiled by Charles Henry Pope from contemporary documents (Baltimore: Genealogical Publishing Co., 1991, reprint of 1900 original). *List of Freemen of Massachusetts, 1630–1691*, by Lucius R. Paige (Baltimore: Genealogical Publishing Company, 1988, reprint of 1849 original).

Michigan—1888 enumeration of Civil War veterans. *National Genealogical Society Quarterly* and Detroit Society for Genealogical Research have published some early residents lists. One is "Detroit 1796 Census," by Donna Valley Stuart, *National Genealogical Society Quarterly* 69 (1981): 185–194. M773, federal internal revenue assessment lists, 1862–1866.

Minnesota—Alien Registration Records Microfilm Index (February, 1918). M774, federal internal revenue assessment lists, 1862–1866.

Mississippi—1723 Natchez residents, *National Genealogical Society Quarterly* 59 (1971): 94–95. 1798–1799 oaths of allegiance, Natchez district, *National Genealogical Society Quarterly* 52 (1964): 108–116. Spanish censuses of 1792 and 1797 are in state archives. 1907, 1925–1933 enumerations of Confederate soldiers and widows. M775, federal internal revenue assessment lists, 1865–1866.

Missouri—*Anglo-Americans in Spanish Archives*, by Lawrence Feldman (Baltimore: Genealogical Publishing Company, 1991), includes settlers in upper Louisiana; see *The Territorial Papers* for various lists of territorial settlers. M776, federal internal revenue assessment lists, 1862–1866.

Montana—At the Montana Historical Society: (1) 1864 listing of eligible voters, names only; (2) polling lists for various counties in various years, about 1884–1914; (3) school censuses, about 1884–1969, various counties, various years. For details, see Web site at <www.his.state.mt.us/departments/Library-Archives/Pamphlets/genealogy.html>. M777, federal internal revenue assessment lists, 1864–1872.

Nebraska—School censuses exist from the second half of the nineteenth century for some counties and continue well into the twentieth century; contact the Nebraska State Historical Society. See also *Territorial Papers of the U.S. Senate 1789–1873*, M 200 (roll 16) and State Department Territorial Papers, M228.

Nevada—Voter registers from 1865. M779, federal internal revenue assessment lists 1863–1866.

New Hampshire—*Genealogical Dictionary of Maine and New Hampshire*, compiled by Sybil Noyes, Charles T. Libby, and Walter G. Davis, on families established before 1699 (Baltimore: Genealogical Publishing Co., 1991, reprint of 1928–1938 volumes). *New Hampshire 1732 Census*, by Jay Mack Holbrook (Oxford, Mass.: Holbrook Research Institute, 1981), compiled from tax lists, land ownership, church, and town records. *New Hampshire 1742 Estate List*, by Pauline Johnson Oesterlin (Bowie, Md.: Heritage Books, 1994), landowners. *New Hampshire 1776 Census*, by Jay Mack Holbrook (Oxford, Mass.: Holbrook Research Institute, 1976), from New Hampshire Association Test of 1776, adult males only, but the most complete listing of that year. M780, federal internal revenue assessment lists, 1862–1866.

New Jersey—Tax lists from various years, 1773–1786, in *Revolutionary Census of New Jersey: An Index, Based on Ratables . . .*, rev. ed., by Kenn Stryker-Rodda (Lambertville, N.J.: Hunterdon House, 1986). M603, federal internal revenue assessment lists, 1862–1866.

New Mexico—*Territorial Papers*, T17 and M364 (see page 180). M782, federal internal revenue assessment lists, 1862–1870, 1872–1874.

New York—*Lists of Inhabitants of Colonial New York: Excerpted from the Documentary History of the State of New York*, by Edmund B. O'Callaghan (Baltimore: Genealogical Publishing Co., 1979, reprint of excerpts from 1849–1851 original). Various counties and towns, 1675–1799, called both censuses and lists of freeholders, indexed. *Early New York State Census Records, 1663–1772*, 2d ed., Carol M. Meyers, comp. (Gardena, Calif.: RAM Publishers, 1965), indexed. M603, federal internal revenue assessment lists, 1862–1866.

North Carolina—*North Carolina Taxpayers, 1701–1786* and *North Carolina Taxpayers, 1679–1790*, by Clarence E. Ratcliff, comp. (Baltimore: Genealogical Publishing Co., 1989, 1990). M784, federal internal revenue assessment lists, 1864–1866.

North Dakota—Pioneer biography file for more than five thousand North Dakotans born before 1870 and (1) in North Dakota prior to territorial division into North and South Dakota, or (2) considered the first settlers in a township.

Ohio—Quadrennial (voter) enumerations 1803–1911, which included white male inhabitants over twenty-one only until 1863, when they began including black males; various counties for various years. Some schoolchildren censuses; contact Ohio Historical Society. *The 1812 Census of Ohio: A Statewide Index of Taxpayers* (Miami Beach, Fla.: TLC Genealogy Books, 1992). Contact state archives for microfilm of "Special Enumeration of Blacks Immigrating to Ohio, 1861–1863."

Oklahoma—Numerous Indian tribal censuses.

Oregon—1893 school census, Jackson County. 1905 military census, Lane County. M1631, federal internal revenue assessment lists, for Oregon District, 1867–1873.

Pennsylvania—1779–1863, septennial enumerations of taxpayers, available at state archives; some earlier tax rolls exist. M372 contains direct tax lists, 1798. M787, federal internal revenue assessment lists, 1862–1866.

Rhode Island—*The Rhode Island 1777 Military Census*, transcribed by Mildred M. Chamberlain (Baltimore: Genealogical Publishing Co., 1985). *Rhode Island Freemen, 1747–1755: A Census of Registered Voters*, by Bruce C. MacGunnigle (Baltimore: Genealogical Publishing Co., 1982, reprint). *Rhode Island 1782 Census*, by Jay Mack Holbrook (Oxford, Mass.: Holbrook Institute, 1979). M788, federal internal revenue assessment lists, 1862–1866.

South Carolina—Incomplete agricultural censuses in 1868 and 1875. M789, federal internal revenue assessment lists, 1864–1866.

South Dakota—School census records, various counties. Special veterans census, 1885.

Tennessee—1891 incomplete census of males over twenty-one. T227, Civil War direct tax assessment lists.

Texas—See *1840 Citizens of Texas*, 3 vols., by Gifford White (Austin, Tex.: privately published, 1983–1988) compiled from land grants and tax rolls. *The 1840 Census of the Republic of Texas*, Gifford E. White, ed. (Austin, Tex.: Pemberton Press, 1966), compiled from tax lists. *Republic of Texas: Poll Lists for 1846*, by Marion Day Mullins (Baltimore: Genealogical Publishing Co., 1982, reprint of 1974 original). 1854–1855 scholastic census of school-age children, for forty-seven counties (Ellis through Wharton Counties). 1867–1870 voter registrations. School census records, 1920s forward, Robertson County, county judge's office; inquire in other counties. M791, federal internal revenue assessment lists, 1865–1866.

Utah—1851, 1852 Church of Jesus Christ of Latter-day Saints bishops' reports of residents.

Vermont—Town records of many kinds. M792, federal internal revenue assessment lists, 1862–1866.

Virginia—*Early Virginia Immigrants, 1623–1666*, compiled from state records by George Cabell Greer (Baltimore: Genealogical Publishing Co., 1989, reprint of 1912 original). *Virginia in 1740: A Reconstructed Census*, compiled from many sources (Miami Beach: TLC Genealogy Books, 1992). M793, federal internal revenue assessment lists, 1862–1866. For information on the 1790-era tax rolls used to create a substitute census, see page 16.

Washington—*Territorial Papers*, M26, M189 (see pages 180–181).

West Virginia—Land and personal property tax rolls of Virginia, 1782–1863. M795, federal internal revenue assessment lists, 1862–1866.

Wisconsin—Petitions and voter lists in *The Territorial Papers of the United States*, Volumes 11, 12, 17, 27, 28.

Wyoming—*Territorial Papers*, M85, M204 (see pages 180–181).

TERRITORIAL PAPERS

Long lists of inhabitants are good genealogical tools because they identify many people in one place and can be checked rather quickly. These can help you determine the county in which your ancestor lived at a given time and give you a specific location in which to research.

One of the best sources for such lists, though not available for all states, is *The Territorial Papers of the United States*. These are Congressional and executive department documents pertaining to the economy, politics, Indian affairs, geography, citizens' concerns, and other matters relating to governing the territories. They include letters between territorial officials and the government in Washington, postal schedules, militia muster rolls, appointments of civil and militia officers, occasional maps, and numerous petitions to Congress about specific concerns. The records contain lists of voters, jurymen, landowners, merchants, planters, and others. The letters, petitions, memorials, recommendations, and protests address such concerns as the need for closer land offices, requests for roads, requests for clearing navigable streams of obstructions, advice on which men to appoint or not appoint to various offices, and views on the effects of Congressional decisions concerning boundaries and land distribution.

Although they are technically federal documents, they are also state and local history. Because many of the matters handled in these documents would have been the jurisdiction of the state or county governments had the entity been a state, the papers are included in this chapter. The twenty-eight volumes of transcribed records and the microfilmed records represent a small portion of the whole collection at the National Archives.

The indexed books of transcriptions, originally published by the Government Printing Office for the State Department and the National Archives between 1934 and 1975, and the microfilmed original documents cover the early period of each area when population was sparse and local records may not exist. They also record ancestral presence before or between federal census records. For example, Figure 5-3, on page 176, contains the signatures (not a clerk's copy) on an 1866 petition of citizens of Colorado residing in New York City. Contrary to views expressed by other citizens, these men were requesting that (1) Congress admit Colorado as a state according to the constitution then before them and (2) they not strike the word "white" from the document since it applied to ninety percent of the territorial population.

Other documents pertain to individual citizens. Figure 5-4, on page 177, shows letters to two local postmasters from two postmasters general, expressing concern over their performance or lack of appropriate supervision. Documents such as these bring humanness to history, especially if such individuals were your ancestors.

The Territorial Papers are available for use in many large public, university, and research libraries throughout the country. Microfilm copies of volumes one through twenty-six may be purchased from the National Archives (M721) or Scholarly Resources. If you live in one of these former territories and your public library does not own the volume(s) or microfilmed papers pertaining to the state's territorial period, perhaps acquisition of the hard-copy edition or the microfilm would be a worthy project for local genealogists to pursue.

The reference list below is but a sampling of the contents of *The Territorial Papers* and

Figure 5-3 Petition of citizens of Colorado living in New York City, to Congress, 25 January 1866, Territorial Papers of the U.S. Senate, 1789–1873, NARA microfilm M200, roll 17, Colorado, April 1860–February 1868.

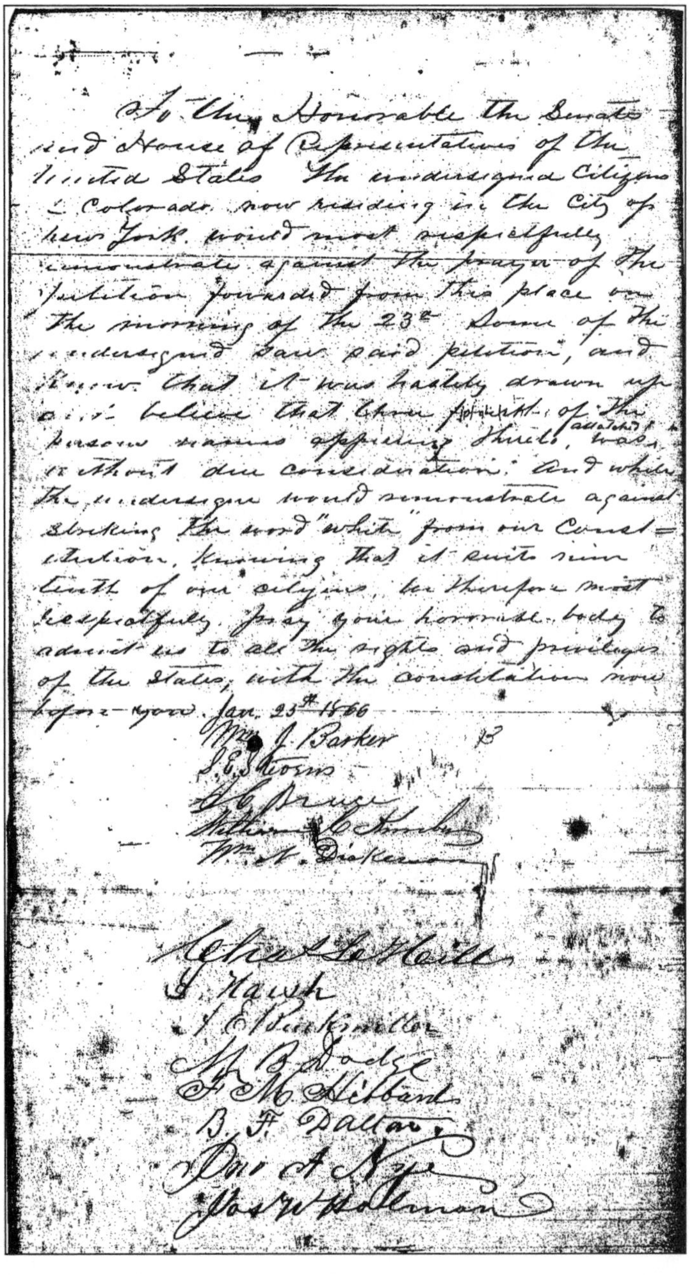

To the Honorable the Senate and House of Representatives of the United States The undersigned Citizens of Colorado now residing in the City of New York would most respectfully remonstrate against the prayer of the petition forwarded from this place on the morning of the 23d. Some of the undersigned saw said petition, and know that it was hastily drawn up and believe that the [illegible] of the persons names appearing thereto, was without due consideration; and while the undersigned would remonstrate against striking the word "white" from our Constitution, knowing that it suits nine tenths of our citizens, we therefore most respectfully pray your honorable body to admit us to all the rights and privileges of the states, with the constitution now before you. Jan. 25th 1866

Wm. J. Barker
[illegible]
B. F. Dalton
[illegible]

is presented to encourage researchers to use these valuable sources. The page numbers given are for the actual lists of names, some of them chosen because of the large numbers of names included. The documents to which these names are attached precede them. In these petitions, as in any petition drive or public issue, not all people who could express their views did. Therefore, the lists do not represent all inhabitants of the area at that date. The specific references included here were chosen to represent the variety of documents in the published volumes as well as their geographic diversity. Some states also had a parent territory, in whose territorial papers earlier material can be found.

ALABAMA, TERRITORY 1817–1819 (VOL. 18)

The first federal census available is 1830.

Volume 5 (Mississippi Territory): pp. 684–692, census of Madison County, Alabama, 1809. Heads of household plus age categories of family members.

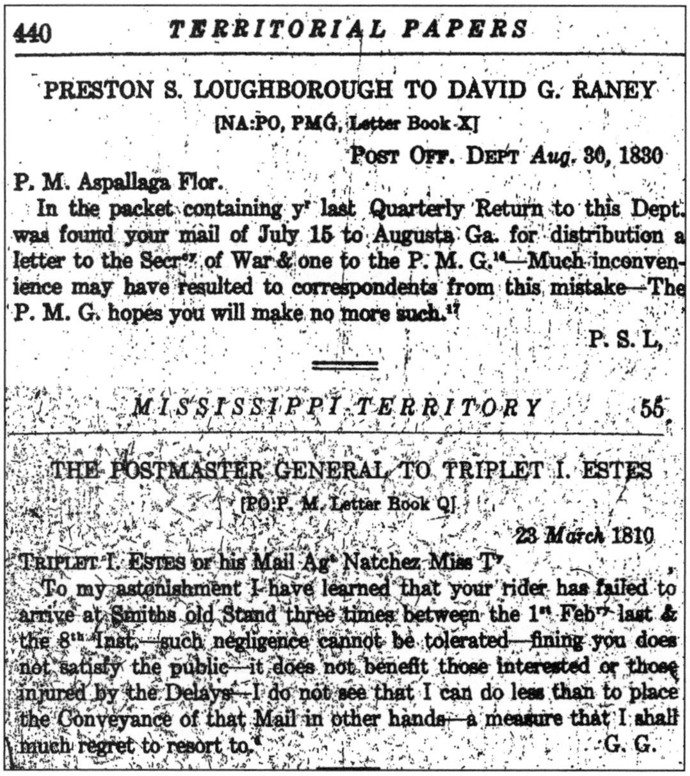
440 *TERRITORIAL PAPERS*

PRESTON S. LOUGHBOROUGH TO DAVID G. RANEY

[NA:PO, PMG, Letter Book X]

POST OFF. DEPT *Aug.* 30, 1830

P. M. Aspallaga Flor.

In the packet containing y^{r} last Quarterly Return to this Dept. was found your mail of July 15 to Augusta Ga. for distribution a letter to the Secr^{ey} of War & one to the P. M. G.[16]—Much inconvenience may have resulted to correspondents from this mistake—The P. M. G. hopes you will make no more such.[17]

P. S. L,

MISSISSIPPI TERRITORY 55

THE POSTMASTER GENERAL TO TRIPLET I. ESTES

[PO:P. M. Letter Book Q]

23 *March* 1810

TRIPLET I. ESTES or his Mail Ag^{t} Natchez Miss T^{y}

To my astonishment I have learned that your rider has failed to arrive at Smiths old Stand three times between the 1st Feb^{ry} last & the 8th Inst.—such negligence cannot be tolerated—fining you does not satisfy the public—it does not benefit those interested or those injured by the Delays—I do not see that I can do less than to place the Conveyance of that Mail in other hands—a measure that I shall much regret to resort to.[4]

G. G.

Figure 5-4 Letters from Postmaster General, *The Territorial Papers of the United States*, Clarence E. Carter, comp. (Washington, D.C.: Government Printing Office, 1934), XXIV (Florida):440; VI (Mississippi):55.

PERSONAL ITEMS IN *THE TERRITORIAL PAPERS*

Occasionally, nongovernmental matters appear in *The Territorial Papers*. In the papers for Louisiana-Missouri Territory is a letter dated 5 July 1806 from James L. Donaldson of St. Louis, to his father-in-law, Dr. William Stewart of Baltimore. The letter reported on business and politics and sent loving greetings to Mrs. Stewart. Donaldson also updated his in-laws on his wife's pregnancy: "About the middle of Sepr I expect Jane will lie in, she begins to grow very large, and I should not be surprized [*sic*] if it happened much earlier." In an era when death frequently came early and health was a concern expressed often in letters to family and friends, it is not surprising that Donaldson ended his letter with a reassuring comment: "Jane never was heartier in her life." (Volume 13: 537)

Volume 6 (Mississippi Territory): p. 743, petition from merchants of St. Stephens, December 1816.

Volume 18: pp. 195–200, petition of about 300 residents of Clarke, Monroe, Washington, Mobile, and Baldwin counties, fall 1817.

ARKANSAS, TERRITORY 1819–1836 (VOLS. 19, 20, 21)

The first federal census available is 1830.

Volume 14 (Louisiana-Missouri Territory): p. 528, 545, petitions of inhabitants of Arkansas District, early 1812.

Volume 15 (Louisiana-Missouri Territory): p. 88, Arkansas Grand Jury, October 1815.

Volume 19: pp. 596–598, jurors for the Superior Court at Little Rock, August and December 1822.

Volume 20: pp. 69–76, Arkansas militia commissions, 1820–1825.
p. 536, list of preemption rights granted at the land office at Batesville, September 1827.

Volume 21: pp. 211–212, bills of review filed with the Superior Court for adjudication of Spanish land claims, April 1830.
pp. 544-551, muster roll of 110 mounted rangers, September 1832.

FLORIDA, TERRITORY 1821–1845 (VOLS. 22, 23, 24, 25, 26)

First available federal census is 1830.

Volume 22: pp. 314–315, petition of Spanish citizens of West Florida, December 1821.

Volume 23: pp. 676–678, petit jurors for the Superior Court at St. Augustine, November 1826.

Volume 24: pp. 685, trustees of the Presbyterian Church, St. Augustine, March 1832.

Volume 25: pp. 77–79, stockholders of Tallahassee Railroad Company, December 1834.

Volume 26: pp. 717–721, permits to applicants for land, with land descriptions in section, township, and range, August 1843.

ILLINOIS, TERRITORY 1809–1818 (VOLS. 16, 17)

First federal census is 1810.

Volume 3 (Northwest Territory): (See page 18 for 1790 list.)
pp. 12–13, petition of inhabitants of the Illinois Country, January 1799.

Volume 7 (Indiana Territory): p. 432, memorial from inhabitants of Peoria, February 1807.

Volume 16: pp. 226–227, 232–237, muster rolls of Illinois militia, June 1812.

Volume 17: pp. 138–139, 106 volunteers for a company of rangers, March 1815.
pp. 321–324, contains a petition from many citizens of Vermont, March 1816.
pp. 568–570, Illinois men who were volunteers with George Rogers Clark against the post of Vincennes, 1779, during the Revolution, list dated February 1818.

INDIANA, TERRITORY 1800–1816 (VOLS. 7, 8)

First federal census is 1820.

Volume 2 (Northwest Territory): p. 621, petition from inhabitants of Knox County, August 1797; list includes seven widows.

Volume 3 (Northwest Territory): pp. 448–449, 454, civil and militia appointments for Wayne County, August–September 1796.

Volume 7: pp. 651–655, poll book of the election in Dearborn County, May 1809.

Volume 8: pp. 333–335, memorial from citizens of the territory, February 1815.

IOWA, TERRITORY 1838–1846

First federal census is 1840.

Volume 12 (Michigan Territory): pp. 1170–1171, petition of inhabitants of Dubuque and Des Moines counties, April 1836.

Volume 27 (Wisconsin Territory): pp. 978–982, petition from inhabitants of Dubuque County, April 1838.

LOUISIANA (TERRITORY OF ORLEANS), 1803–1812

First federal census is 1810.

Volume 9 (Territory of Orleans): pp. 174–175, "free people of color" of Louisiana, January 1804.

MICHIGAN, TERRITORY 1805–1837 (VOLS. 10, 11, 12)

First federal census is 1820.

Volume 7 (Indiana Territory): pp. 230–231, memorial from citizens of Detroit, October 1804.

Volume 10: pp. 393–395, list of land patents received from land office, July 1812.

Volume 11: pp. 465–479, voters of Detroit and counties of Monroe, Oakland, Macomb, St. Clair, and Michilimackinac, September 1823. Over 1200 names.
pp. 735–737, men discharged at Ft. Brady, Sault Ste. Marie, 1824–1825. Gives birthplace, place of enlistment, date of discharge.
pp. 787–806, tax rolls for Wayne and Washtenaw counties, with place of residence, 1825.

Volume 12: pp. 621–624, petition of inhabitants of St. Joseph County, November 1833.

MISSISSIPPI, TERRITORY 1798–1817 (VOLS. 5, 6)

First federal census is 1820.

Volume 5: pp. 66–68, jury report and list from Pickering (now Jefferson) County, 1799.

Volume 6: pp. 108–113, petition by intruders on Chickasaw Lands, September 1810. About 450 names.
pp. 308–315, report on aliens, August 1812.

MISSOURI (ORIGINALLY LOUISIANA TERRITORY), 1803–1821 (VOLS. 13, 14, 15)

First federal census is 1830.

Volume 13: pp. 330–349, petition from inhabitants of Districts of St. Louis, St. Charles, and St. Genevieve, December 1805–January 1806.

Volume 14: pp. 560–562, muster rolls of Nathan Boone's company, June 1812.

Volume 15: pp. 558–561, petition of inhabitants of Howard Land District, December 1819.

OHIO (TERRITORY NORTHWEST OF THE OHIO RIVER), 1787–1803 (VOLS. 2, 3)

See page 18 for 1790 inhabitants. First federal census available is 1820.

Volume 2: pp. 424–425, petition of French inhabitants of Gallipolis, December 1792.

Volume 3: pp. 476–478, civil and militia appointments for Jefferson County, July 1797.

TENNESSEE (TERRITORY SOUTH OF THE OHIO RIVER), 1790–1796 (Vol. 4)

See page 19 for 1790 material. First federal censuses are 1810 (fragments only) and 1820.

Volume 4: pp. 464–470, civil and militia appointments for 1795.

WISCONSIN, TERRITORY 1836–1848 (VOLS. 27, 28)

First federal census is 1820, as part of Michigan Territory.

Volume 17 (Illinois Territory): pp. 518–519, petition of inhabitants of Green Bay, July 1817.

Volume 11 (Michigan Territory): p. 199, voter list from Green Bay and Brown County, September 1821.

Volume 12 (Michigan Territory): pp. 110–112, petition from inhabitants of Prairie du Chien, January 1830.

Volume 27: pp. 1080–1086, Oneida Indians, October 1838.

Volume 28: pp. 1141–1142, petition of 123 female residents at Rosendale, February 1848.

Additional territorial papers have been microfilmed by the National Archives in four sets:

- **Iowa**, 1838–1846 (M325, with descriptive pamphlet).
- **Minnesota**, 1849–1858 (M1050).
- **Oregon**, 1848–1859 (M1049).
- **Wisconsin**, 1836–1848 (M236, a supplement to the volumes listed above, not indexed).

Territorial Papers of the U.S. Senate, 1789–1873 is another microfilm collection of similar materials from the National Archives (M200, 20 rolls). The dates given below are the range of the documents, not necessarily the dates of territorial existence. The documents are not cataloged or indexed but are generally filmed in chronological order. After 1873, territorial affairs were handled by the Department of the Interior. Be sure to consult records of the parent territory for any additional information.

Alabama and Arkansas (1818–1836), roll 8.
Arizona and the Dakotas (1857–1873), roll 18.
Colorado and Nevada (1860–1868), roll 17.
Florida (1806–1845), rolls 9–11.
Idaho, Montana, Wyoming (1863–1871), roll 19.
Indiana (1792–1830), roll 4.
Kansas and Nebraska (1853–1867), roll 16.
Louisiana-Missouri (1804–1822), roll 7.
Louisiana (Territory of Orleans) (1803–1815), roll 5.
Michigan (1803–1847), roll 6.
Minnesota (1847–1868), roll 14.
Mississippi (1799–1818), roll 3.
New Mexico (1840–1854), roll 14.
Ohio (Territory Northwest of the River Ohio) (1791–1813), roll 1.
Oregon (1824–1871), roll 13.
Tennessee (Territory South of the River Ohio) (1789–1808), roll 2.
Utah and Washington (1849–1868), roll 15.
Wisconsin (1834–1849), roll 12.
Miscellaneous Papers (1806–1867), roll 20.

The western states for the most part were the last to be settled and the last to become states. Additional territorial papers created before 1873 are in the records of the State Department; documents created thereafter are with the records of the Department of the Interior. Many of those records have been microfilmed by the National Archives and are available for purchase from the National Archives or Scholarly Resources.

STATE	STATE DEPT. COVERAGE		INTERIOR DEPT. COVERAGE	
Alaska	none (acquired 1868)		1869–1913	M430
Arizona	1864–1872	M342	1868–1913	M429
Colorado	1859–1874	M3	1861–1888	M431
Dakotas	1861–1873	M309	1863–1889	M310
Florida	1777–1824	M116	none (statehood 1845)	
Idaho	1863–1872	M445	1864–1890	M191
Kansas	1854–1861	M218	none (statehood 1861)	
Missouri	1812–1820	M1134	none (statehood 1821)	
Montana	1864–1872	M356	1867–1889	M192
Nebraska	1854–1867	M228	none (statehood 1867)	
Nevada	1861–1864	M13	none (statehood 1864)	
New Mexico	1851–1872	T17	1851–1914	M364
Oklahoma	none (organized as territory 1890)		1889–1912	M828
Oregon	1848–1858	M419	none (statehood 1859)	
Orleans Territory	1764–1823	T260	none (Louisiana statehood 1812)	

Northwest of River Ohio	1787–1801	M470	none (Ohio statehood 1803, Indiana Territory 1800)	
Southwest of River Ohio	1790–1795	M471	none (Tennessee statehood 1796)	
Utah	1853–1873	M12	1850–1902	M428
Washington	1854–1872	M26	1854–1902	M189
Wyoming	1868–1873	M85	1870–1890	M204

INDEX OF ECONOMIC MATERIAL IN DOCUMENTS OF THE STATES OF THE UNITED STATES

Between 1907 and 1922, the Carnegie Institute in Washington, DC, published a series of books (reprinted by Kraus Reprint) that were the project of Adelaide R. Hasse. These books are comprehensive indexes to printed reports of departments and legislatures within thirteen states. The reports all relate in some way to the economy of the state and are indexed chronologically under such topics as agriculture, education, mining, public health, labor, industry, railroads, climate, imports and exports, and the state's defective, dependent, and delinquent populations. These documents contain much state history. While many of them are statistical summaries, others contain information about specific individuals, companies, institutions, and towns. Because of these specifics, they are potentially valuable for genealogists. Although the original plan was to cover all the states, the actual publications covered only thirteen:

California 1849–1904
Delaware 1789–1904
Illinois 1809–1904
Kentucky 1792–1904
Maine 1820–1904
Massachusetts 1789–1904
New Hampshire 1789–1904
New Jersey 1789–1904
New York 1789–1904
Ohio 1787–1904
Pennsylvania 1790–1904
Rhode Island 1789–1904
Vermont 1789–1904

The Maine volume of the index, for example, lists a number of reports on Swedish settlements in the state in the late nineteenth century. If your ancestors were Swedish immigrants in Maine, you should read these. If your family were farmers, you might be particularly interested in several reports about the effects of climate on agriculture. An 1865 report of the Board of Agriculture mentioned the large exodus of New England farmers to Ohio in 1816 due to an unusually long cold season. Another report discussed the 1880 drought as one of the severest on record and the agricultural damage it caused in various parts of Maine. The index cites the agency, publication name, date, and page numbers for each entry.

The California volume includes many items that could be of specific genealogical value. The following is a sampling. (Specific references for locating these are in the California volume.)

1852–1865	Historical list of county superintendents of education.
1856	A petition from the San Rafael Orphanage for Boys praying for state aid, with a list of the orphans.
1873–1900	Annual reports of the state superintendent of public instruction listing holders of state teacher's certificates.
1890	"History of the horse life" of J.C. Simpson, California's most successful breeder.
1891	Directory of grape growers, wine makers, and distillers of California and principal grape growers and wine makers of the eastern states.

Appendixes to the Senate and Assembly Journals in the California Archives contain the lists of county superintendents and certified teachers. In Humboldt County, for example, Rev. W.L. Jones was superintendent from 1861–1868; and in Calaveras County, Robert Thompson served from 1858–1863 (II [1866]:293). Teachers with life diplomas in effect in 1873 included Miss Minnie F. Austin and Theodore Bradley, whose certificates were issued 27 December 1866. (I [1873–1874]:285). The Senate Journal for 1856 (p. 434) listed the thirty-three boys of the San Rafael Orphanage, including Thomas, John, and Daniel McAuliff of Sacramento, ages fourteen, nine, and eight. The youngest was James Nugent of Nevada, age four.

Timesaver

These indexes can save a researcher time because they cover a massive number of state documents in one convenient place. Many public and university libraries have the set; Kraus Reprint Co. reissued the set in 1965. If you find an entry that affects your research, contact the state library or archives or other state document depositories. In addition, the compiler gave credit to the New York Public Library and the Library of Congress for the use of their collections in locating the materials to index. Perhaps their staff could help locate materials cited.

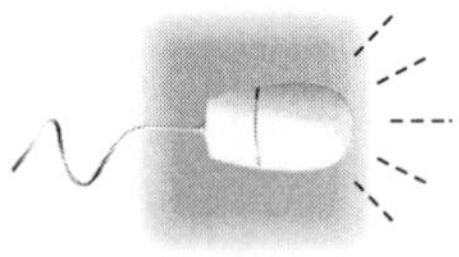

Internet Source

For more on Confederate pension records and for links to the state archives sites mentioned here, see the National Archives Web site at <www.archives.gov/research_room/genealogy/military/confederate_pension_records.html>.

CONFEDERATE PENSION INFORMATION

Union military pensions from the Civil War are federal records. Confederate pensions, for obvious reasons (as in losing the war), had to be state matters. The former Confederate states, plus Kentucky, Missouri, and Oklahoma, eventually authorized pensions. The chart on page 183 outlines each state's decision on Confederate pension authorization; the files may contain both accepted and rejected applications.

Texas passed a Confederate pension law in May 1899, and some fifty-eight thousand veterans and widows filed applications. These included men and women who had spent the Civil War years in many places, for the original law stated they had to have been a resident of Texas since 1 January 1880. The law was amended in later years to relax the requirements. One Mississippi veteran who applied for and received a pension was John P. Shelby. He appeared before the county judge of Robertson County, Texas, on 14 August 1899 to make application and was accompanied by three "credible citizens," who under oath stated that he indeed enlisted in the service of the Confederacy and that he was now "unable to support himself by labor of any sort." These three witnesses were two sons, I.R. and J.A. Shelby, and a daughter, Mrs. M.V. Liels [*sic*]. (The application does not ask for or state the relationships.) The affidavit of Dr. G.M. Abney testified to the applicant's inability to support himself due to age (eighty-one). The application itself gave his name, age, and residence (Petteway, Texas) where he had lived for twenty-nine years. This information coincides with other evidence that he was in the county in early 1870, even though he was not enumerated in the 1870 census. He further said he had served in Company B (Nixon's), Denny's Regiment, Mississippi Cavalry for twelve months, owned no real or personal property, and was in feeble health, suffering from diabetes and old age. The medical information was particularly interesting to his descendants since several of his grandchildren also developed diabetes.

STATE ARCHIVES

Archives are public records. They are kept by many institutions, organizations, and governments. At the state level, archives contain thousands of documents generated by departments

Alabama	1867	Granted pensions for veterans who had lost limbs; 1886, pensions for veterans' widows; 1891, pensions for indigent veterans or their widows; state archives Web site has database of men from Alabama who served in the Confederate army.
Arkansas	1891	Granted pensions for indigent veterans; 1915, pensions for their widows or mothers.
Florida	1885	Granted pensions for veterans; 1889, pensions for their widows; state archives Web site has database of pension application files.
Georgia	1870	Granted pensions to veterans with artificial limbs; 1879, pensions for disabled veterans or their widows living in Georgia; state archives Web site has index to pension applications.
Kentucky	1912	Granted pensions for Confederate veterans or their widows.
Louisiana	1898	Granted pensions for indigent veterans or their widows; state archives Web site has index to pension application files.
Mississippi	1888	granted pensions for indigent veterans or their widows.
Missouri	1911	Granted pensions for indigent veterans only, not their widows; applications for the home for disabled Confederate veterans are mixed in the pension applications.
North Carolina	1867	Granted pensions for veterans who had lost limbs or were blinded; 1885, pensions for all other indigent and disabled veterans or their widows.
Oklahoma	1915	Granted pensions for Confederate veterans or their widows; state archives Web site has index to pension applications.
South Carolina	1887	Authorized pensions for indigent veterans or their widows, but few early applications survive. More are available from the 1919–1925 period, when pensions were authorized regardless of need. Some Confederate Home applications and inmate records from 1909–1957 survive, as do 1925–1955 applications of veterans' wives, widows, daughters, or sisters.
Tennessee	1891	Authorized pensions for indigent Confederate veterans; 1905, pensions for their widows; state archives Web site has index to pension applications, index to the Tennessee Confederate Soldiers Home applications, and Tennessee Confederate physicians.
Texas	1881	Set aside land for disabled veterans; 1899, pensions for indigent veterans or their widows; state archives Web site has index to pension applications, 1899–1975, and lists of Confederate indigent families.
Virginia	1888	Granted pensions to veterans or their widows. Library of Virginia Web site has a card index to pension rolls, a pension roll database, and a list of Confederate disability applications and receipts (for artificial limbs).

and agencies of the government as well as correspondence from citizens to those agencies. Each state is organized in its own way. Some states have separate state library and state archives. In other states, these two are basically one institution. In other states, the state historical society houses the archives. Regardless of the location, each state archives has its own finding aids to help researchers know what is in its collection. Finding aids are sometimes on the institution's Web site or the USGenWeb sites for each state.

Many of the state archives include research materials that are not government documents. Newspapers published in the state, atlases of the state, and private or business papers of citizens often are housed at the archives. These types of special collections are discussed in chapter seven. In addition, local and county histories, genealogical periodicals, cemetery transcriptions, church records, and county and city records may also form part of the archives or related library.

Important

Much of what is kept in state archives has genealogical use. State censuses and census substitutes discussed earlier are good examples. Appellate court records and legislative memorials and petitions are others. (See also pages 295–297.) States in the eastern United States have colonial and Revolutionary War records in their archives. Other archives hold originals or microfilm copies of records generated during their Spanish, French, Mexican, Dutch, Swedish, or territorial periods.

Certain elected officials, as they took office, had to sign bonds that they would faithfully execute their offices or owe a penalty in the amount specified on the bond. A separate file of these bonds and oaths of office are in some state archives. When one J. Orville Shelby (not the Confederate general) was elected presiding justice of the police court of Liberty County, Texas, in December 1869, he and two friends as securities signed a bond that he would safely keep the records and faithfully discharge his duties or be subject to a $500 penalty. In addition, because he was in the South after the Civil War, he also had to swear as part of his oath of office that he had never been an elected official swearing to support the Constitution of the United States and then "engaged in insurrection or rebellion against" the United States or "given aid or comfort to the enemies thereof." These papers are filed in the Texas State Archives, along with those of thousands of other elected officials.

State Records Holdings

Below is a list of other types of records that state archives or historical societies may hold; depending on the state's organization, some of these records may be at the state library. Each archives collection is unique to the state, and its history, laws, and population; yet, many states have similar materials. Some states keep these records longer than others do, especially items such as auto license registrations, voter registrations, and driver's licenses. Some records may not be open to the public, but family members of the persons involved may be able to get copies. Files of some commissions or departments may concern communities and the state in general rather than individual citizens. (The list does not include copies of National Archives microfilm or published genealogical materials, which many state archives also hold.) Use this list to stimulate your interest in finding out about the archives of your research locales and to purchase or read online the guides to their collections.

- Adjutant general department records
- Admittances to state orphans' home, state hospitals
- Agriculture commission records
- Alien registrations
- Apprentice bonds
- Attorney general department records
- Auditor general department records
- Auto license registrations
- Banking commission records
- Biographical files of officeholders, pioneers, prominent citizens
- Business papers and directories
- Card indexes to various record groups
- City directories
- Civil service commission records
- Colonial government records, including courts, legislature, militia, governors
- Colonial records of counties, towns
- Commerce department records
- Comptroller records
- Conservation and natural resources department records
- Constitutional convention(s) records
- County government records
- County record books, especially from early years
- Driver's licenses
- Economic development office records
- Education department records
- Election commission records
- Energy department files
- Ethics commission records
- Family and personal papers
- Fish, wildlife, game commission records
- Forestry department records

French or Spanish land grants
Funeral home records
General services commission records
Government records of territorial or colonial period or of former governments (Confederacy, Republic of Texas, etc.)
Governors' records
Higher education system records
Highway and transportation department records
History commission records
Insurance commission records
Internal affairs department records
Judicial system records
Justice department records
Labor and industry department records
Land office records (state land)
Legislative records, including petitions received
Licenses for professions, vocations, occupations
Lieutenant governors' records
Maps and atlases
Mental hospital/asylum records
Military and veterans affairs department records
Military history of units from the state
Military records of state residents
Militia records, rolls
Mines and minerals department records
Municipal records
Naturalization records from state or county courts
Navigation, waters, rivers, ferries, port authority records
Newspapers published in the state
Notary records
Oaths and bonds of officeholders
Old-age assistance records
Online databases on state archives Web site
Oral history
Organizations' records and publications
Parks, recreation, tourist commission records
Payroll records for state employees
Penitentiary and prisoner records
Pensions granted by the state (officeholder, Confederate, etc.)
Photographs
Public employee records (may or may not be open)
Public employee retirement commission records
Public health department records
Public utility commission records
Public welfare records
Railroad commission records
Reconstruction-era oaths and voter registrations
Residential institution records (state hospitals, soldiers' homes, etc.)
Revenue office records
Revolutionary War–era government and militia records
School district records, records of teaching certificates issued
Secretary of state or department of state records
State censuses and special enumerations
State court records, trial and appellate courts
State government documents and publications
State hospital/asylum records
State inspector general records
State police, highway patrol, law enforcement records
State supreme court opinions and records
Tavern or liquor licenses
Tax records
Teacher retirement system records
Territorial government records
Territorial period records of counties, towns
Township minutes
Treasury department records
Veterans' organizations records
Vital records, especially early ones
Voter registrations
World War I service medal application cards
WPA veterans' graves registration project files

OTHER RECORDS

State institutions such as prisons, residential institutions, and hospitals sometimes maintain their own records. Getting genealogical information from these may require a statement of why the information is needed and the relationship of the researcher to the person who was in the institution. One family discovered in the county probate files that a relative had been sent to the state "insane asylum" early in the twentieth century. The probate record contained an affidavit from the father that said that insanity was hereditary in the family. Somewhat concerned at this development, the researcher then requested information from the state hospital in an effort to find out more and was told that an unnamed uncle was the other person affected by insanity. Now the researcher is trying to identify that uncle.

As the Great Depression deepened, more states authorized old-age assistance benefits, usually for those over sixty-five. (This was an important reason for the increased demand for proof of age, which in turn led to the Soundexing of the 1900 and other census records so that proof could be found more quickly.) These laws provided for new departments or commissions within the state government, although local offices usually accepted, investigated, and granted or denied the applications. Sometimes the same commission handled child welfare cases and relief for the indigent and sometimes coordinated their efforts with the federal relief programs within the state. As these agencies changed focus over the years and as Social Security became the substitute benefit for many retirees, local offices closed and files were stored or destroyed, especially for lack of storage space. Thus, the case files of specific families or individuals may or may not still exist. Some states have kept only the administrative papers; check with your ancestral state archives and county clerks about their holdings.

States and cities began registering vital statistics (births, deaths, marriages) at different times and in different ways. Because these records are usually generated in the county or town, they are discussed in chapter three. Birth and death records may be available in some states only through the state vital statistics or vital records office, but most marriage records are accessible at the county level (town in New England; independent towns and cities in Virginia).

State court systems, other than the appellate courts, usually do the bulk of their business at the county level. Each state has its own court structure. Chapter three discusses court records as genealogical tools. Chapter eight discusses appellate courts.

BIBLIOGRAPHY OF RESEARCH GUIDES TO THE STATES

Sources

The Family History Library has research outlines for all the states. You can order them from the customer service phone number—(800) 537-5971—or read them online or print them from the Web site <www.familysearch.org/Eng/Search/Rg/frameset_rhelps.asp>. The state-specific books and articles listed below are usually more comprehensive than the research outlines, but the research outlines may be more readily available to you. Some of the books listed are out of print but available in libraries; some are updated in revised editions periodically. Even the older publications contain worthwhile information. Sometimes, the USGenWeb state page provides basic information about research in the state.

The *National Genealogical Society Quarterly*, which has published a number of the guides in the list below, is available as a Family Tree Maker CD-ROM publication (Family Archives CD #210) for issues published between 1908 and 1997. More recent issues are in libraries and are available from the society. This two-CD set is a helpful addition to a personal library, as is a current subscription to the quarterly.

HIGHLIGHTING THE SOUTH DAKOTA STATE HISTORICAL SOCIETY: STATE ARCHIVES

To encourage you to visit your ancestral state's archives and Web site, this list focuses on some of the holdings of the South Dakota State Archives.

Web site: <www.sdhistory.org> with links to archives, both within and out of South Dakota.

Online databases: Holdings of South Dakota newspapers; descriptions of new acquisitions, serials collections, other collections.

Collections: State and regional history; about 800 county and town histories; church histories; more than 250 county atlases from 1893 (some with landowners' names, directories of the rural population, photographs of farms; plats of townships, towns, cities); New England genealogy (since many South Dakotans have New England roots); over 1,000 family histories; biographical file on notable South Dakotans and South Dakota authors; organization records; family papers and photographs; women's history, including personal and organization papers; WPA Graves Registration Project for most counties, many cemeteries from their beginning through 1941, including some small family cemeteries and the Union County Poor Farm Cemetery (an abstract of this cemetery is on the South Dakota GenWeb page); numerous county records; special collection related to the Missouri River; microfilm of federal records pertinent to the state, such as homestead land tract books, federal census records, copies of Bureau of Indian Affairs records and Indian reservation censuses.

Serials collection (with growing online listing): Extensive collection of South Dakota newspapers; city and business directories; high school and college yearbooks, such as *The Jack Rabbit* of the South Dakota Agricultural College/South Dakota State University dating back to 1907; publications of South Dakota organizations, such as the *South Dakota Clubwoman* of the South Dakota Women's Christian Temperance Union, dating from 1913, and the *South Dakota Wheat Grower* from the state's Wheat Growers' Association, from 1947 forward; historical society journals from states in the region.

Railroad records: History of railroads in South Dakota and their impact on the settlement and development of the state; maps and photographs of crossings; Milwaukee Road deeds; right-of-way files from railroad closings in the 1970s; Chicago and North Western Railroad, Huron division records, 1931–1981 (no employment records).

State records: State censuses, school censuses, naturalizations, penitentiary prisoner files, veterans' bonus files, and others.

State library, also part of the South Dakota State Historical Society: State government documents depository library; federal government documents depository library.

Multiple States—Stryker-Rodda, Kenn, ed. *Genealogical Research: Methods and Sources*. Vol. 2. Rev. ed. Washington, D.C.: The American Society of Genealogists, 1983. Chapters on Alabama, Arkansas, Florida, Illinois, Indiana, Iowa, Kentucky, Louisiana, Michigan, Mississippi, Missouri, Ohio, Tennessee, Wisconsin.

Multiple States—Rubincam, Milton, ed. *Genealogical Research: Methods and Sources.* Vol. 1. Rev. ed. Washington, D.C.: American Society of Genealogists, 1980. Chapters on Delaware, Georgia, Maryland, New England, New Jersey, New York, North Carolina, Pennsylvania, South Carolina, Virginia.

New England—Melnyk, Marcia D., ed. *Genealogist's Handbook for New England Research*. 4th ed. Boston: New England Historic Genealogical Society, 1999. Also: Crandall, Ralph J., ed. *Genealogical Research in New England*. Baltimore: Genealogical Publishing Co., 1984. Also: Lainhart, Ann S. "Records of the Poor in Pre-Twentieth-Century New England." *National Genealogical Society Quarterly* 81 (December 1993): 257–269.

Alabama—Barefield, Marilyn Davis. *Researching in Alabama: A Genealogical Guide*. Rev. ed. Birmingham: Birmingham Public Library, 1998.

Alaska—Lake, Gretchen L., and David A. Hales. "Alaska's Native Population: Sources for Genealogical and Historical Research." *National Genealogical Society Quarterly* 83 (December 1995): 277–292. Also: FHL Research Outline for Alaska, sales catalog item 31038.

Arizona—FHL Research Outline for Arizona, sales catalog item 31039.

Arkansas—Norris, Rhonda S. *Arkansas Links: A Comprehensive Guide to Genealogical Research in the Natural State*. Kearney, Nebr.: Morris Pub., 1999.

California—Ogle, Sandra K. "Genealogical Research in California." *National Genealogical Society Quarterly* 76 (Sept. 1988): 194–211.

Colorado—Hinckley, Kathleen W. "Genealogical Research in Colorado." *National Genealogical Society Quarterly* 77 (June 1989): 107–127.

Connecticut—Kemp, Thomas Jay. *Connecticut Researcher's Handbook*. Detroit: Gale Research, 1981. Also: Sperry, Kip. *Connecticut Sources for Family Historians and Genealogists*. Logan, Utah: Everton Publishers, 1980.

Delaware—Doherty, Thomas P., ed. *Delaware Genealogical Research Guide*. Wilmington: Delaware Genealogical Society, 1997.

District of Columbia—Cook, Eleanor M.V. *Guide to the Records of Your District of Columbia Ancestors*. Silver Spring, Md.: Family Line Publications, 1987. Also: Angevine, Erma Miller. "Genealogical Research on Families of the District of Columbia." *National Genealogical Society Quarterly* 78 (March 1990): 15–32.

Florida—Michaels, Brian E. "Genealogical Research in Florida." *National Genealogical Society Quarterly* 76 (June 1988): 89–111.

Georgia—Davis, Robert Scott Jr., comp. *Research in Georgia*. Greenville, S.C.: Southern Historical Press, 1981.

Hawaii—Duey, John V., and Rose Marie H. Lindsey Duey. *A Beginner's Guide for Genealogical Research in Hawaii*. Honolulu: Alu Like, Inc., 1989. A short booklet. Also: FHL Research Outline for Hawaii, sales catalog item 31048.

Idaho—FHL Research Outline for Idaho, sales catalog item 31049.

Illinois—Schweitzer, George K. *Illinois Genealogical Research*. Knoxville, Tenn.: the author, 1997. Also: Gooldy, Pat, and Ray Gooldy. *Manual for Illinois Genealogical Research*. Indianapolis: P. Gooldy, 1994.

Indiana—Beatty, John D. "Genealogical Research in Indiana." *National Genealogical Society Quarterly* 79 (June 1991): 100–122.

Iowa—FHL Research Outline for Iowa, sales catalog item 31052.

Kansas—FHL Research Outline for Kansas, sales catalog item 31053.

Kentucky—Hogan, Roseann Reinemuth. *Kentucky Ancestry: A Guide to Genealogical and Historical Research*. Salt Lake City: Ancestry, 1992.

Louisiana—FHL Research Outline for Louisiana, sales catalog item 31055.

Maine—FHL Research Outline for Maine, sales catalog item 31056. See also "New England" above.

Maryland—Peden, Henry C., and Mary K. Meyer. *A Guide to Genealogical Research in Maryland.* 5th ed. Baltimore: Maryland Historical Society, 2001.

Massachusetts—Schweitzer, George K. *Massachusetts Genealogical Research.* Knoxville, Tenn.: the author, 1999. See also "New England" above.

Michigan—McGinnis, Carol. *Michigan Genealogy Sources and Resources.* Baltimore: Genealogical Publishing Co., 1987.

Minnesota—Warren, Paula Stuart. "Genealogical Research in Minnesota." *National Genealogical Society Quarterly* 77 (March 1989): 22–42.

Mississippi—Hatten, Ruth Land. "Genealogical Research in Mississippi." *National Genealogical Society Quarterly* 76 (March 1988): 25–50.

Missouri—Porter, Pamela Boyer, and Ann Carter Fleming. "Genealogical Research in Missouri." *National Genealogical Society Quarterly* 87 (June 1999): 85–116.

Montana—Richards, Dennis L. *Montana's Genealogical and Local History Records, A Selected List of Books, Manuscripts, and Periodicals.* Detroit: Gale Research, 1981.

Nebraska—Sones, Georgene G., comp. for Nebraska State Genealogical Society. *Nebraska: A Guide to Genealogical Research.* Lincoln: The Society, 1984. Also: Nimmo, Sylvia. "Nebraska Research." *National Genealogical Society Quarterly* 77 (December 1989): 260–276.

Nevada—Greene, Diane E. *Nevada Guide to Genealogical Records.* Baltimore: Genealogical Publishing Co., 1998.

New Hampshire—Towle, Laird C., and Ann M. Brown. *New Hampshire Genealogical Research Guide.* Bowie, Md.: Heritage Books, 1983. See also "New England" above.

New Jersey—Stryker-Rodda, Kenn. "That Genealogical Quagmire: New Jersey." *National Genealogical Society Quarterly* 48 (June 1960): 59–71.

New Mexico—FHL Research Outline for New Mexico, sales catalog item 31068.

New York—Schweitzer, George K. *New York Genealogical Research.* Knoxville, Tenn.: the author, 1988. Also: Guzik, Estelle M., ed. *Genealogical Resources in the New York Metropolitan Area.* New York: Jewish Genealogical Society, 1989. Also: Remington, Gordon L. *New York State Towns, Villages, and Cities: A Guide to Genealogical Sources.* Boston: New England Historic Genealogical Society, 2002. Also: Remington, Gordon L. *New York State Probate Records: A Guide to Testate and Interstate Records.* Boston: New England Historic Genealogical Society, 2002.

North Carolina—Leary, Helen F.M., ed. *North Carolina Research: Genealogy and Local History.* 2d ed. Raleigh: North Carolina Genealogical Society, 1996. Also: Leary, Helen F.M. "A Master Plan for North Carolina Research." *National Genealogical Society Quarterly* 75 (March 1987): 15–36.

North Dakota—Winistorfer, Jo Ann B., and Cathy A. Langemo. *Tracing Your Dakota Roots: A Guide to Genealogical Research in the Dakotas.* Bismarck, N.D.: Dakota Roots, 1999.

Ohio—Sperry, Kip. "Genealogical Research in Ohio." *National Genealogical Society Quarterly* 75 (June 1987): 81–104. Also: Bell, Carol Willsey. *Ohio Genealogical Guide.* 6th ed. Youngstown, Ohio: Bell Books, 1995.

Oklahoma—FHL Research Outline for Oklahoma, sales catalog item 31073.

Oregon—Lenzen, Connie. "Genealogical Research in Oregon." *National Genealogical Society Quarterly* 79 (March 1991): 33–55.

Pennsylvania—Freilich, Kay Haviland. "Genealogical Research in Pennsylvania." *National Genealogical Society Quarterly* 90 (March 2002): 7–36.

Rhode Island—Taylor, Maureen A. "Genealogical Research in Rhode Island." *National Genealogical Society Quarterly* 88 (March 2000): 5–31.

South Carolina—Holcomb, Brent Howard. *A Guide to South Carolina Genealogical Research and Records*. Columbia, S.C.: the author, 1998.

South Dakota—Winistorfer, Jo Ann B., and Cathy A. Langemo. *Tracing Your Dakota Roots: A Guide to Genealogical Research in the Dakotas*. Bismarck, N.D.: Dakota Roots, 1999.

Tennessee—Bamman, Gale Williams. "Research in Tennessee." *National Genealogical Society Quarterly* 81 (June 1993): 99–125. Also: Schweitzer, George K. *Tennessee Genealogical Research*. Knoxville: the author, 1986.

Texas—Ericson, Carolyn R., and Joe E. Ericson. *A Guide to Texas Research*. Nacogdoches, Tex.: Ericson Books, 1993. Focuses on the kinds of records created in Texas. Also: Kennedy, Imogene Kinard, and J. Leon Kennedy. *Genealogical Records in Texas*. Baltimore: Genealogical Publishing Co., 1987. Focuses on county-by-county records availability and early Texas reference material.

Utah—FHL Research Outline for Utah, sales catalog item 31081.

Vermont—FHL Research Outline for Vermont, sales catalog item 31082. See also "New England" above.

Virginia—McGinnis, Carol. *Virginia Genealogy: Sources & Resources*. Baltimore: Genealogical Publishing Co., 1993. Also: Grundset, Eric G. "Genealogical Research in Virginia." *National Genealogical Society Quarterly* 82 (Sept. 1994): 179–206. Also: Good, Rebecca H., and Rebecca A. Ebert. *Finding Your People in the Shenandoah Valley of Virginia*. Alexandria, Va.: Hearthside Press, 1988.

Washington—FHL Research Outline for Washington, sales catalog item 31084. Also: *Genealogical Resources in Washington State: A Guide to Genealogical Records Held at Repositories, Government Agencies, and Archives*. Olympia, Wash.: Secretary of State, Division of Archives and Records Management, 1983.

West Virginia—McGinnis, Carol. *West Virginia Genealogy Sources and Resources*. Baltimore: Genealogical Publishing Co., 1988. Also: Good, Rebecca H., and Rebecca A. Ebert. *Finding Your People in the Shenandoah Valley of Virginia*. Alexandria, Va.: Hearthside Press, 1988.

Wisconsin—Herrick, Linda M. *Wisconsin Genealogical Research*. 2d ed. Janesville, Wis.: Origins, 1998.

Wyoming—Spiros, Joyce V. Hawley. *Genealogical Guide to Wyoming*. Gallup, N. Mex.: Verlene Publishing, 1982.

General—Eichholz, Alice, ed. *Ancestry's Red Book: American State, County & Town Sources*. Salt Lake City: Ancestry, 3d ed. to be released 2004. Capsuled but very helpful guide to each state.

General—Prucha, Francis Paul. *Handbook for Research in American History: A Guide to Bibliographies and Other Reference Works*. 2d ed. Rev. ed. Lincoln: University of Nebraska Press, 1994.

Federal Records

Federal records are essential sources for history and genealogy research, and many are accessible to the public in books or microform. **Federal records discussed elsewhere in this book are these:**

See Also

- Federal census records—chapter two.
- Federal direct taxes—chapter three.
- *The Territorial Papers of the United States*—chapter five. (These do not apply to states that were never territories: California, Kentucky, Maine, Texas, Vermont, West Virginia, and the original thirteen states.)
- Maps published by the United States Geological Survey and other agencies—chapter seven.
- Government documents, Serial Set, public statutes, appellate courts—chapter eight.
- Records relating to African Americans—chapter nine.
- Records relating to American Indians—chapter ten.
- Immigration and naturalization records—chapter eleven.
- National Archives microfilm is discussed and referenced throughout the book.

Researchers are fortunate to have available the massive records and resources in two primary federal repositories, the Library of Congress and the National Archives. Because it is beyond the scope of this book to describe in detail the holdings of either institution, you are encouraged to study the published guides to the collections, especially before visiting.

LIBRARY OF CONGRESS

The Library of Congress, often called the largest library in the world, contains extensive collections of published, manuscript, and microform works that would keep a genealogist busy for years. Numerous finding aids and subject bibliographies describe its holdings, and some of these are listed throughout this book. Also, the library catalog is accessible online at <http://lcweb.loc.gov>. Some maps, books, and other sources are available through the Photoduplication Service. Check with the library or its Web site for current fees and instructions. Other guides to the library include these:

- *The Center: A Guide to Genealogical Research in the National Capital Area*, by Christina K. Schaefer. Baltimore: Genealogical Publishing Co., 1996. Covers more facilities than the Library of Congress.
- *A Guide to the Microfilm Collection of Early State Records*, Lillian A. Hamrick, ed. Washington, D.C.: Library of Congress, 1950. Supplement with the same title is by William Sumner Jenkins, 1951.
- *The Library of Congress: A Guide to Historical and Genealogical Research*, by James C. Neagles. Salt Lake City: Ancestry, 1990. Very useful. A must before visiting.
- *Manuscripts on Microfilm: A Checklist of the Holdings in the Manuscript Division.* Washington, D.C.: Library of Congress, 1973.
- *Special Collections in the Library of Congress*, Annette Melville, comp. Washington, D.C.: Library of Congress, 1980.

NATIONAL ARCHIVES

The National Archives and Records Administration (NARA or National Archives) holds primarily federal records, beginning with the American Revolution and Continental Congress. When the Archives II building in College Park, Maryland, opened in the spring of 1994, records were shifted to new locations. Categories of records scheduled to remain in Archives I (Washington, DC) include genealogical materials and records of the following: Congress and the Supreme Court; American Indians; pre–World War II army and navy; and World War I, Great Depression, and New Deal agencies. Archives II and the regional branches hold other civilian and military record groups. If you plan to visit these facilities, ask ahead of time about the location of the records you need to use, and contact regional branches about records added to their collections.

National Archives records are organized by department and function. To guide researchers through over 450 record groups, many publications are available. A useful guide is *The Archives: A Guide to the National Archives Field Branches*, by Loretto Dennis Szucs and Sandra Hargreaves Luebking (Salt Lake City: Ancestry, 1988).

The titles listed below are all National Archives publications. The General Information Leaflets are available free of charge through the NARA Web site; the other titles are available for purchase through NARA or booksellers. See <www.archives.gov/publications/index.html> for other publications about National Archives holdings; see <www.archives.gov/publications/general_information_leaflets.html> for free pamphlets on the regional archives.

- *Black History: A Guide to Civilian Records in the National Archives*, Debra L. Newman, comp. 1984. A helpful guide for any researcher.
- *Guide to Federal Records in the National Archives of the United States.* 3 vols. 1996. Now online at <www.archives.gov/research_room/federal_records_guide/>.
- *Guide to Genealogical Research in the National Archives of the United States.* 3d ed. 2000. Very useful, whether you are planning a visit or not.
- *A Guide to Pre-Federal Records in the National Archives*, Howard H. Wehmann, comp. Revised by Benjamin L. DeWhitt. 1989.
- *Guide to Records in the National Archives Relating to American Indians*, Edward E. Hill, comp. 1984.
- *Guide to Records Relating to U.S. Military Participation in World War II*, by Timothy P. Mulligan. Part I, 1996. Part II, 1998.
- *Microfilm Resources for Research: A Comprehensive Catalog.* 2000. Handy guide to microfilm publications by record group, publication number, subject, and title.

- *Military Service Records in the National Archives.* 1985, revised. General Information Leaflet #7.
- *The National Archives: Washington, DC, and College Park, MD: Information for Visitors.* 1994. General Information Leaflet #61.
- *The National Archives in the Nation's Capital: Information for Researchers.* 2001. General Information Leaflet #71.
- *Our Family, Our Town: Essays on Family and Local History Sources in the National Archives.* Timothy Walch, comp. 1987.
- *Research in the Land Entry Files of the General Land Office.* Rev. ed. 1998. General Information Leaflet #67.
- *The Trans-Mississippi West, 1804–1912: A Guide to Federal Records for the Territorial Period.* 4 vols. Robert M. Kvasnicka, comp. 1993–1996.
- *Using Records in the National Archives for Genealogical Research.* 1990, revised. General Information Leaflet #5.

The following subject catalogs of National Archives microfilm all have the subtitle *A Select Catalog of National Archives Microfilm Publications*. They are online at <www.archives.gov/publications/online_publications.html> and contain detailed descriptions of the records and roll-by-roll listings. For many of the microfilm publications, NARA has prepared descriptive pamphlets (DP) with more information about the contents of the publication.

American Indians (1998)
Black Studies (1996)
Diplomatic Records (1986)
Federal Court Records (online only)
Genealogical and Biographical Research (1991)
Immigrant and Passenger Arrivals (1991)
Military Service Records (1985)

In addition to the guides, microfilm catalogs, and descriptive pamphlets, NARA has published inventories, preliminary inventories, and special lists descriptions to various record groups. These finding aids describe record series or groups in depth; they are not indexes to the records or to individuals named in the records. The NARA Web site lists currently available inventories and special lists at <www.archives.gov/publications/inventories_and_lists.html>.

Copies of National Archives Records

Researchers may request copies of records in four areas of the National Archives: ship passenger arrivals, census, land-entry files, veterans' benefits, and military service. Request the necessary forms online at <www.archives.gov/ global_pages/inquire_form.html>. You will need a separate form for each record requested. The forms come with detailed instructions, including payment options and prices. Be prepared to wait two to four months for your copies.

For ship passenger arrival records, use Form NATF 81 to request copies. The request must contain the following information: (1) full name of the arriving passenger, (2) the port of arrival, (3) exact date of arrival or name of the ship. Additional information, such as passenger's age or names of accompanying passengers, can aid in the search.

Request copies of census records on Form NATF 82. The National Archives staff does not research the census for patrons. If you want a copy of a particular record from a census that has been opened to the public, you must provide the county and state, the census year, the exact page number, and for 1880 and later censuses, the enumeration district number. If you have access to the microfilm for passenger arrival records or censuses and a microprint copier, it is easier, cheaper, and quicker to make such copies yourself. (See page 64 for information on getting copies of closed census records.)

For copies of land-entry files, use Form NATF 84. This form requires the following information: (1) type of land files to be searched; (2) name of "entryman," or person obtaining the land; (3) approximate date of entry; (4) state and legal description of the land, including section, township, and range; (5) patent or final certificate number; and (6) name of the processing land office.

For veterans' benefits records (pension and bounty-land warrant applications), use Form NATF 85. You will need to supply specific information, including (1) full name of veteran and widow or other claimant; (2) the war in which he served or the dates of his service; (3) the state from which he served; (4) branch of service, unit, rank, volunteer or regulars; (5) date and place of birth; and (6) date and place of death. **When requesting pension files, request the complete file—all pages, every document—regardless of the size of the file.** If you don't request it, you will get only the pages the staff person feels are most pertinent. If you furnish your credit card number with your request, the process is usually faster. Otherwise, they have to write you with the price of the file, and you must send your payment before they process your request.

Important

Copies of military service records require Form NATF 86 and the same kind of information about the veteran that you need for NATF 85. For Civil War records, indicate Union or Confederate forces. (Confederate pensions are state records and not held at the National Archives.) Request Standard Form 180 to obtain more recent service records.

MILITARY RECORDS

Most of the military records of genealogical interest fall into two groups: compiled service records and veterans' benefits. Federal military records begin with the American Revolution. The original thirteen states have militia records from the colonial period, and many of these have been published. Eastern state archives and historical societies also have some Revolutionary records because units in the Revolution were organized both by states and by the Continental Congress. Thousands of original records and abstracts for individual veterans are at the National Archives.

After "thrashing around many Civil War Web sites," a person once asked on a genealogy e-mail list where to find an online list of all Civil War soldiers, listed alphabetically with their dates of birth, places of enlistment, and places of residence! Although the Internet now includes various databases to help identify servicemen and their units or their pensions, most of the information about them, including details of birth, enlistment, and residence, comes not from an online database but from research, including the military records at the National Archives. Various microfilm publications are listed in this chapter; consult *Military Service Records: A Select Catalog of National Archives Microfilm Publications* in paperback or online for roll lists. For comprehensive coverage of military records, see *U.S. Military Records: A Guide to Federal & State Sources: Colonial America to the Present*, by James C. Neagles (Salt Lake City: Ancestry, 1994).

For More Info

A fascinating article, "Women Soldiers of the Civil War," by DeAnne Blanton, was in the National Archives *Prologue* 25 (spring 1993): 27–33. Read it online at <www.archives.gov/publications/prologue/spring_1993_women_in_the_civil_war_1.htm>.

Compiled Service Records and Other Evidence of Service

The National Archives has microfilmed numerous compiled service records and other evidence of service for volunteer soldiers, navy personnel, and marines who served between 1775 and the early twentieth century. These records are abstracts compiled from muster rolls, pay lists, hospital and prison records, and other sources. Many records give little more than the serviceman's name, rank, unit, and dates of muster rolls or rosters. The abstracts of service records are arranged by war or time period, then by state and unit, with surnames alphabetical in each unit. Indexes and other records can help determine the regiment in which the soldier served.

A brief example of a service record is that of Confederate Private S.D. Williamson of Company E, 38th Alabama Regiment. His record contains two abstracts: (1) His name appeared on a roll of prisoners of war captured at Blakely, Alabama, on 9 April 1865 and received at Ship Island, Mississippi, 15 April 1865; and (2) he was listed on a roll of prisoners of war transferred from Ship Island to Vicksburg, Mississippi, on 1 May 1865.

On the other hand, some service record abstracts show age, birthplace, physical description, and residence, as well as enlistment, imprisonment, transfer, desertion, absence, leave, medical, or death information. Service records for officers may contain other records about their service and documents they created and signed in the course of their service. When J.A.P. Campbell was lieutenant colonel over the 40th Mississippi Infantry (Confederate Volunteers), one of the documents he approved and signed was a requisition from First Lieutenant E.L. Williford, commanding Company H of the regiment. Williford was requisitioning equipment and cooking utensils for nine men of his company. On 19 July 1862, he received for the group one ax, ax handle, spade, cooking kettle, mess pan, camp hatchet, skillet, and water bucket. His receipt does not show that they received the nine plates, spoons, and cups they had requisitioned.

Such documents are not genealogical but they do give descendants a better picture of the life of the soldiers. Thus, researchers interested in a more thorough study of their ancestors' military service could benefit from looking at the service records of the officers of the company and regiment. On the microfilmed records, the regimental officers' files are filmed in alphabetical order along with the enlisted men, by regiment and company.

Revolutionary service records are in the National Archives Record Group 93. Records from later periods are primarily in Record Groups 94 and 407, and Confederate records are in Record Group 109. To check periodically for new microfilm publications in these and other record groups, visit the National Archives Web site at <www.archives.gov/research_room/genealogy/> and scroll down to "New Microfilm Publications."

The National Archives holds numerous records that have not been microfilmed, including at this writing a large number of Union Civil War service records. However, the following list of microfilm publications represents the records readily accessible to researchers at the National Archives or other research libraries. The film is available for purchase from the National Archives or Scholarly Resources and for rent from the Family History Library (check catalog for availability). Each item refers to compiled service records or their indexes, unless otherwise described. (M and T numbers are National Archives publication numbers.)

Research Tip

1. **Records of Revolutionary War soldiers, 1775–1783.**
   a. General index (M860). Units from the thirteen colonies, Continental troops, some sailors and civilian employees. Compiled service records of this group (M881).
   b. Index, Connecticut soldiers (M920).
   c. Index, soldiers in Georgia units (M1051), soldiers in North Carolina units (M257).
   d. Revolutionary War rolls, 1775–1783 (M246). Muster rolls, payrolls, etc., arranged by state and unit.
   e. Index to compiled service records, American naval personnel (M879 and T516). About a thousand sailors and civilian employees (duplicated in M860).
   f. Compiled service records of American naval personnel and members of the depart-

See Also

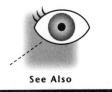

See chapter nine for other military records relating to African-American servicemen and chapter ten for other military records relating to American Indians.

ments of Quartermaster General and Commissary General . . . (M880).

g. Personnel returns (with physical descriptions) of some Massachusetts units (M913).

h. Central treasury records (M1015). Roll 6, certificates of indebtedness issued to Continental soldiers, 1783–1786. Roll 7, pension payments to Pennsylvanians, 1785–1804.

i. Special index to numbered records, War Department collection of Revolutionary War records, 1775–1783 (M847). Miscellaneous numbered records, called "The Manuscript File," are in M859, pertaining to pay, procurement, personnel records, enlistment papers, etc.

j. Numbered record books, War Department records (M853). Roll 1, index. Includes oaths of allegiance, oaths of office, commissions, pay, and settlement of accounts.

k. War Department correspondence, 1791–1797 (M1062). Indian affairs, pensions, etc.

2. **Compiled service records of volunteer soldiers who served from 1784 until 1811** (M905). Index (M694).

3. **Records of volunteer soldiers who served in the War of 1812** (and concurrent Indian Wars).
   a. Index (M602). Indexes to volunteers in Louisiana units (M229), North Carolina units (M250), South Carolina units (M652).
   b. Compiled service records, volunteers in units from the Territory of Mississippi (M678).
   c. Muster rolls, payrolls, militia and regular army, Battle of Tippecanoe, 1811 (T1085).

4. **Records of volunteer soldiers who served during Indian Wars and disturbances, 1815–1858.**
   a. Index (M629).
   b. Cherokee disturbances and removal: indexes to volunteers in Alabama units (M243), Georgia units (M907), North Carolina units (M256), Tennessee units, and the field and staff of the Army of the Cherokee Nation (M908). No microfilmed service records for these groups.
   c. Creek War: index to volunteers in Alabama units (M244); compiled service records, Florida militia (M1086).
   d. Florida War (Second Seminole War 1836–1843); indexes to volunteers in Alabama units (M245), Louisiana units (M239).
   e. Florida Indian Wars, 1835–1858: Compiled service records, Florida volunteers (M1086).
   f. War of 1837–1838: index, volunteers in Louisiana units (M241).

5. **Records of volunteer soldiers who served during the Patriot War, 1838–1839.** Indexes to Michigan units (M630), New York units (M631). No microfilmed service records.

6. **Records of volunteer soldiers who served during the Mexican War, 1846–1848.**
   a. Index (M616).
   b. Compiled service records, units from Mississippi (M863), Pennsylvania (M1028), Tennessee (M638), Texas (M278); Mormon units (M351).

7. **Records of volunteer Union soldiers who served during the Civil War, 1861–1865.**
   a. U.S. Colored Troops, index (M589). (See chapter nine for more records on the U.S. Colored Troops.)
   b. Veterans Reserve Corps, index (M636).
   c. U.S. Volunteers, 1st–6th regiments, compiled service records (M1017). Former Confederate soldiers.

d. Indexes, volunteer Union soldiers in organizations not raised by states or territories (M1290). Includes Veteran Volunteers, Confederate POWs who enlisted in U.S. Army, Indian Home Guards, U.S. Sharp Shooters, etc.
e. Units by state (Film numbers: index and service records). One number indicates index only. At this writing, the service records are still in the process of being filmed.

Alabama: M263, M276
Arizona: M532
Arkansas: M383, M399
California: M533
Colorado Territory: M534
Connecticut: M535
Dakota Territory: M536, M1960
Delaware: M537, M1961
District of Columbia: M538
Florida: M264, M400
Georgia: M385, M403
Idaho: See "Washington Territory"
Illinois: M539
Indiana: M540
Iowa: M541
Kansas: M542
Kentucky: M386, M397
Louisiana: M387, M396
Maine: M543
Maryland: M388, M384
Massachusetts: M544
Michigan: M545
Minnesota: M546
Mississippi: M389, M404
Missouri: M390, M405
Montana: See "Washington Territory"
Nebraska Territory: M547, M1787
Nevada: M548, M1789
New Hampshire: M549
New Jersey: M550
New Mexico Territory: M242, M427
New York: M551
North Carolina: M391, M401
Ohio: M552
Oregon: M553, M1816
Pennsylvania: M554
Rhode Island: M555
South Carolina: None
Tennessee: M392, M395
Texas: M393, M402
Utah Territory: M556, M692
Vermont: M557
Virginia: M394, M398
Washington Territory: M558
West Virginia: M507, M508
Wisconsin: M559
Wyoming: See "Washington Territory"

8. **Records of movements and activities of volunteer Union organizations** (M594, by state). Compiled service histories of units, mergers, disbandment, dates of service, etc.
9. **Records of Confederate soldiers who served during the Civil War, 1861–1865.** Many of the Confederate records were lost in the final days of the war. The service records in the National Archives are compiled from the surviving Confederate and state records, and from Union prison and parole records.
   a. Consolidated index to compiled service records of Confederate soldiers (M253).
   b. Organizations raised by the Confederate government, index (M818), compiled service records (M258).
   c. General and staff officers and nonregimental enlisted men, including military judges, chaplains, agents, drillmasters, and aides-de-camp. Index (M818), compiled service records (M331).
   d. Unfiled papers belonging to Confederate service records (M347). Alphabetical.
   e. Records of Confederate naval and marine personnel (M260).
   f. Selected records of Confederate prisoners of war (M598), general and by prison.
   g. Register of Confederates who died in federal prisons and military hospitals (M918).
   h. Records of Virginia forces, 1861 (M998), primarily correspondence.
   i. Confederate Army casualty lists and reports (M836), by state and unit.

j. Case files, applications of former Confederates for presidential pardons, 1865–1867 (M1003).
k. Reference files relating to Confederate medical officers (T456).
l. Units by state, index and records film numbers.

Alabama: M374, M311	Mississippi: M232, M269
Arizona Territory: M375, M318	Missouri: M380, M322
Arkansas: M376, M317	North Carolina: M230, M270
Florida: M225, M251	South Carolina: M381, M267
Georgia: M226, M266	Tennessee: M231, M268
Kentucky: M377, M319	Texas: M227, M323
Louisiana: M378, M320	Virginia: M382, M324
Maryland: M379, M321	

10. **Records of Confederate movements and activities** (M861). Compiled unit histories, by state.
11. **Records of volunteer soldiers who served during the War with Spain, 1898.**
    a. Index (M871); index to volunteers in Louisiana units (M240), North Carolina units (M413).
    b. Compiled service records, Florida infantry (M1087).
12. **Records of volunteer soldiers who served during the Philippine Insurrection, 1899–1903.** Index (M872). No compiled service records have been microfilmed.
13. **Registers of enlistments, U.S. regular army, 1798–1914** (M233).
14. **Returns from military posts, 1800–1916** (M617).
15. **Returns, regular army:** infantry regiments, 1821–1916 (M665); cavalry regiments, 1833–1916 (M744); artillery regiments, 1821–1901 (M727); field artillery, 1901–1916 (M728); Coast Artillery Corps, 1901–1916 (M691); Corps of Engineers 1832–1916 (M851); engineer battalions, 1846–1916 (M690).
16. **Index to navy rendezvous reports (enlistments):** 1846–1861, 1865–1884 (T1098). Civil War years, 1861–1865 (T1099). Armed Guard personnel 1917–1920 (T1101). Naval Auxiliary Service, 1917–1918 (T1100).
17. **Abstracts of service records, naval officers, 1798–1893** (M330).
18. **Records, navy courts-martial and courts of inquiry, 1799–1867** (M273). Rolls 1–2, index.
19. **Muster rolls, U.S. Marine Corps, 1789–1892** (T1118).
20. **United States Military Academy cadet application papers, 1805–1866** (M688). Roll 1, index.
21. **United States Naval Academy** registers of delinquencies, 1846–1850 and 1853–1882, and academic and conduct records, 1881–1908 (M991).
22. **List of mothers and widows of American World War I soldiers, sailors, and marines entitled to make a pilgrimage to the war cemeteries in Europe, 1930** (M1872). (See Figure 6-1.)
23. **Card records of headstones provided for deceased Union Civil War veterans, ca. 1879–ca. 1903** (M1845).

Figure 6-1, on page 199, is from microfilm M1872, the list of mothers and widows of American World War I soldiers, sailors, and marines entitled to make a pilgrimage to the war cemeteries in Europe where their loved ones were buried. The eligible women were asked whether they wanted to make the trip and whether they wanted to go in 1930. Of over 11,000 who were eligible, about 6,730 were interested and 5,323 of those expressed a desire to go in 1930. If all of the latter group made the trip, the government's cost was estimated to be over $5.5 million. The list reproduced on microfilm is also available as part of the Serial Set—House Document 140 (71st Congress, 2d session) serial 9225. (See page 292 for more on the Serial Set.) An interesting article about the project and the trips is "World War I Gold Star Mothers Pilgrimages," by Constance Potter in *Prologue* 31 (1999): 140–145, 210–215. The article is available on the National Archives Web site under "publications" and "*Prologue*."

The page shown in Figure 6-1 names some of the Wisconsin widows and mothers who were questioned about their interest in making the pilgrimage. Both the mother and the widow of Private Edwin A. Lange were interested in visiting his grave site at Meuse-Argonne in France. On the other hand, Mrs. Mary Arnett of Marshfield, Wood County, apparently had not responded (response listed as unknown); she had lost two sons in France.

WISCONSIN

Name and address	Relationship	Name of deceased	Rank	Organization	Cemetery	Desires pilgrimage 1930	Desires pilgrimage Later
		WINNEBAGO COUNTY—con.					
LANGE, Mrs. BERTHA, 288 High St., Oshkosh	Mother	LANGE, EDWIN A.	Pvt.	Co. I, 312th Inf.	Meuse-Argonne	Yes.	
LANGE, Mrs. EDWIN A., 1203 5th St., Oshkosh	Widow	LANGE, EDWIN A.	Pvt.	Co. I, 312th Inf.	Meuse-Argonne	Yes.	
MACHEN, Mrs. ALICE, 9 Jay St., Oshkosh	Mother	MACHEN, RAYMOND O.	Pvt. 1 cl.	Co. H, 127th Inf.	Oise-Aisne		No.
MERTES, Mrs. KATIE, Box 63, Oshkosh	Mother	ORSCHENS, MICHAEL	Pvt.	Co. L, 168th Inf.	St. Mihiel		No.
REAM, Mrs. MARGARET A., 17 Park St., Oshkosh	Mother	REAM, WARD H.	1st lt.	Co. C, 305th Engrs.	Meuse-Argonne	Yes.	
REGNERY, Mrs. ANDREW, 826 S. Park Ave., Oshkosh	Mother	REGNERY, JAMES J.	Pvt.	2d Co., M. G. Bn., 1st Brig.	St. Mihiel		Yes.
SMITH, Mrs. MARTHA W., 22½ Mount Vernon St., Oshkosh.	Mother	SMITH, HOWARD LOWELL	1st lt.	3d Tn. Hq. and M. P.	Aisne-Marne	Yes.	
TIMMERMAN, Mrs. GEORGE, 424 15th St., Oshkosh	Mother	TIMMERMAN, JOHN A.	Pvt.	Co. B, 146th M. G. Bn.	Oise-Aisne		No.
WILSON, Mrs. CLARA S., 322 9th St., Oshkosh	Mother	WILSON, IRVING F.	Pvt.	Co. M, 353d Inf.	Meuse-Argonne		No.
ZIMMERMAN, Mrs. GRACE, 934 10th St., Oshkosh	Mother	OBERSTEINER, FRANK	Sgt.	Co. C, 150th M. G. Bn.	Meuse-Argonne		No.
		WOOD COUNTY					
ARNETT, Mrs. MARY, 612 E. 3d St., Marshfield	Mother	ARNETT, GEORGE	Pvt.	Hq. Det., 57th F. A. Brig.	Oise-Aisne		(1)
		ARNETT, WM.	Pvt.	Co. A, 127th Inf.	Suresnes		
BRESEMANN, Mrs. MARGARET, 1006 S. Vine St., Marshfield.	Mother	BRESEMANN, FREDERICK W.	Pvt.	Co. B, 18th Inf.	Meuse-Argonne		No.
BUCKLEY, Mrs. G. A., 840 1st St., Wisconsin Rapids	Mother	BUCKLEY, JOHN W.	1st lt.	2d Corps, Aero School	St. Mihiel		Yes.
FISHER, Mrs. GEORGE P., Route 7, Box 61, Wisconsin Rapids.	Mother	FISHER, JOHN P.	Pvt.	Hq. Co., 350th Inf.	Meuse-Argonne		No.

Figure 6-1 List of Mothers and Widows of American Soldiers, Sailors, and Marines Entitled to Make a Pilgrimage to the War Cemeteries of Europe, 1930, NARA microfilm M1872, 1 roll, p. 338, Wisconsin.

Pension and Bounty Land Warrant Applications

The records of veterans' benefits are pension applications and bounty land warrants. Pension records based on Revolutionary War service cover the entire nineteenth century. Applications prior to 1800 burned in a War Department fire in November 1800. Until 1818, a Revolutionary pension applicant had to be a needy and disabled (invalid) veteran or the indigent heir of a deceased veteran. In 1818, Congress authorized the first service pensions, based on service without disability as a requirement, but financial need was still a prerequisite. In 1828 and 1832, Congress liberalized this program so that need was no longer a consideration.

Most of the veterans who qualified for pensions met the requirements set down in laws of Congress. However, other veterans or heirs had special circumstances necessitating individual attention beyond or in exception to the public statutes. Congress dealt with these cases through private relief acts. These private acts appear in the *Congressional Record* and journals as well as the Serial Set. Those that occurred between 1789 and 1845 appear also in volume six of the *Public Statutes of the United States*. Later cases appear in the *Statutes* volume for each session of Congress. The Serial Set is the source for the documents relating to each case. (See chapter eight for further discussion.)

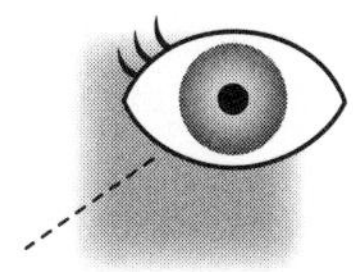

See Also

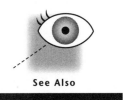

Pension records from Confederate Civil War service are state records. See pages 182 and 183.

Bounty land. Some men enlisted in the military because of the government's promise of free land after the war. This bounty land was offered to those with wartime service between

1775 and 1855—Revolutionary War, War of 1812, Indian wars, and Mexican War (1845–1848). Unlike the early pensions, bounty land warrants did not have a requirement of indigence. One reason that so many veterans sold their warrants was that until 1830 the warrants could be used for land only in the U.S. Military District in Ohio. Gradually that restriction was relaxed, and by 1842 they could be redeemed at any federal land office. During the Revolution, some of the thirteen colonies also offered land to men who served in units organized there. These included Georgia, Massachusetts, New York, North Carolina (land in Tennessee), Pennsylvania, and Virginia (land in Kentucky and what became known as the Virginia Military District of Ohio). Records of state bounty land grants are state records; consult the state archives and published books of abstracts.

Virginia half-pay pensions (M910). In 1779, Virginia authorized to certain officers who served to the end of the Revolutionary War payment for life of half the amount of pay they had received, or half-pay pensions. When a number of candidates filed their applications, the state disallowed them. After nearly fifty years of litigation between Virginia and the veterans' families, Congress directed the Secretary of the Treasury to make the payments. The files reproduced on the microfilm sometimes cover several generations as heirs of the deceased soldiers applied for back payments. Thus, the files are important for genealogists.

For example, the file of Joseph Calvitt showed he had served as a lieutenant in Clarke's Illinois Regiment of Virginia State Troops. He married Sidney, and they moved to the Natchez, Mississippi, area about 1785. Joseph died there in August 1819, and his widow later married a man named Rundell. The file lists Joseph and Sidney's four children with genealogical information about them. Then the file mentions a fifth child, an illegitimate daughter named Mariah Louise, born 28 July 1814, the daughter of Mrs. Sisson, a widow. Joseph made provision for the maintenance and education of this child, whom he called "the innocent offspring of my indiscretion in my old age."

Remarried widows. The indexes to pension application files of remarried widows (M1784 and M1785) provide a convenient research tool. Figure 6-2, below, shows four of the cards from pre-Civil War pensions. They are alphabetical by the widow's remarried name but identify her soldier's name and unit, the war in which he fought, and the pension file number.

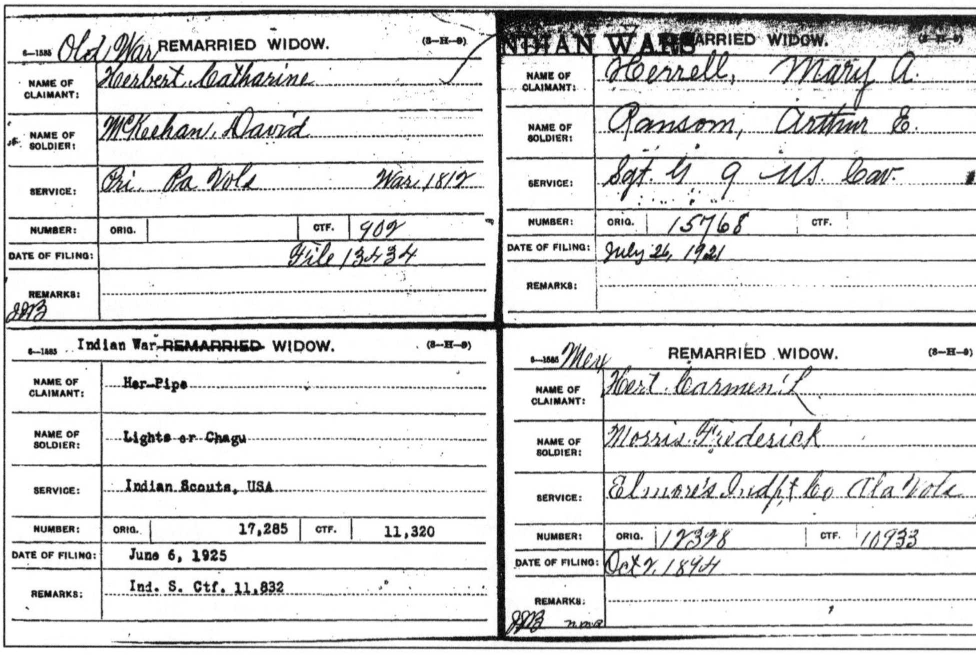
6—1585 Old War REMARRIED WIDOW. (8—H—9)
NAME OF CLAIMANT: Heerbert, Catharine
NAME OF SOLDIER: McKeehan, David
SERVICE: Pri. Pa. Vols. War, 1812
NUMBER: ORIG. | CTF. 902
DATE OF FILING: File 13434
REMARKS:

Indian Wars REMARRIED WIDOW.
NAME OF CLAIMANT: Herrell, Mary A.
NAME OF SOLDIER: Ransom, Arthur E.
SERVICE: Sgt. G 9 U.S. Cav.
NUMBER: ORIG. 15768 | CTF.
DATE OF FILING: July 24, 1921
REMARKS:

6—1585 Indian War REMARRIED WIDOW. (8—H—9)
NAME OF CLAIMANT: Her-Pipe
NAME OF SOLDIER: Lights-or-Chagu
SERVICE: Indian Scouts, USA
NUMBER: ORIG. 17,285 | CTF. 11,320
DATE OF FILING: June 6, 1925
REMARKS: Ind. S. Ctf. 11,832

6—1585 Mex REMARRIED WIDOW. (8—H—9)
NAME OF CLAIMANT: Hert, Carmen L.
NAME OF SOLDIER: Morris, Frederick
SERVICE: Elmore's Indpt. Co. Ala. Vols.
NUMBER: ORIG. 12398 | CTF. 10933
DATE OF FILING: Oct. 7, 1894
REMARKS:

Figure 6-2 Index to Pension Application Files of Remarried Widows Based on Service in the War of 1812, Indian Wars, Mexican War, and Regular Army Before 1861, NARA microfilm M1784, 1 roll, alphabetical order.

Pension Applications

In order to get a pension or bounty land, the veteran, his widow, or other legal heirs had to document his service and their relationship to him. Thus, pension applications are very important genealogical sources. The files often contain information not found elsewhere—parents' and/or siblings' names; maiden names; birth, marriage, and death dates; birthplaces; places of residence at the time of the application; religious affiliation or a specific congregation name; and family problems. These problems may have involved illnesses, the mental debilities of the elderly, economic difficulties within the family, homes and possessions lost in fires, and even accusations of "friends" or relatives against other family members. One supporting affiant to a widow's pension application accused the widow's son of managing her meager income for his own interest and profit. (See pages 376 and 378 for other types of accusations from a pension file.)

Figure 6-3, below, is part of the pension application for Thomas Gulliver, who had served in Company D of the 149th New York Infantry (Civil War). This page provides his residence

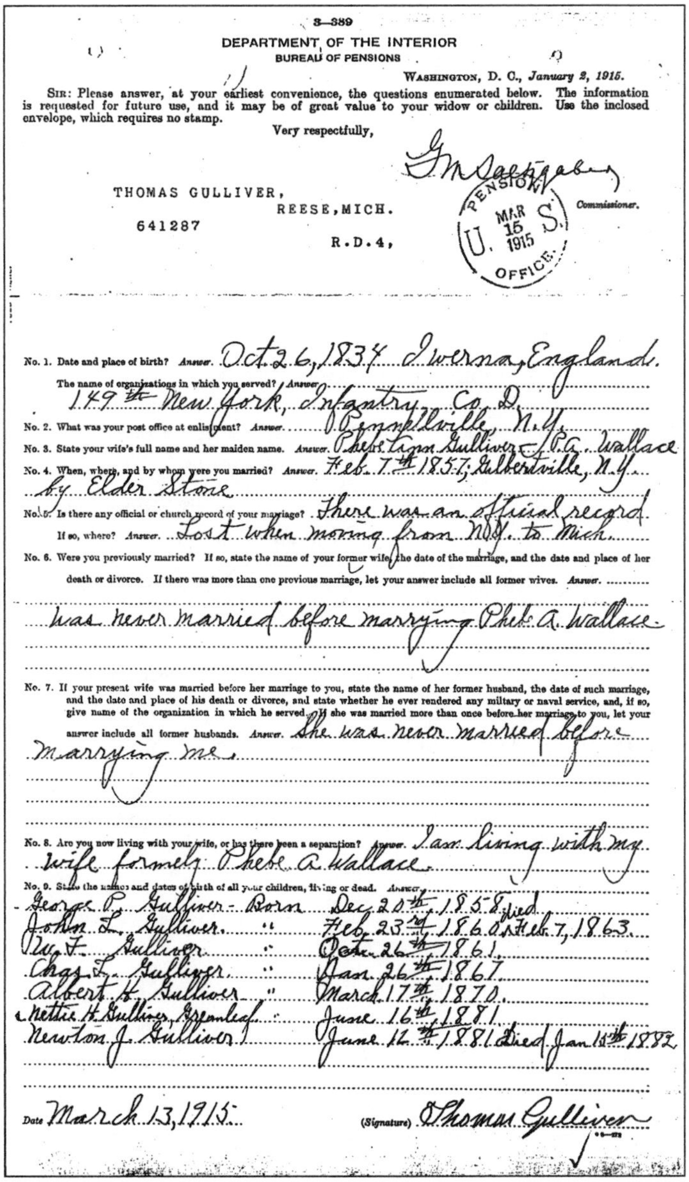
3—389

DEPARTMENT OF THE INTERIOR

BUREAU OF PENSIONS

WASHINGTON, D. C., *January 2, 1915.*

SIR: Please answer, at your earliest convenience, the questions enumerated below. The information is requested for future use, and it may be of great value to your widow or children. Use the inclosed envelope, which requires no stamp.

Very respectfully,

[signature], *Commissioner.*

THOMAS GULLIVER,
REESE, MICH.
641287
R.D.4,

PENSION OFFICE MAR 15 1915 U. S.

No. 1. Date and place of birth? *Answer.* Oct 26, 1834 Iwerna, England.

The name of organizations in which you served? *Answer.* 149th New York, Infantry, Co. D.

No. 2. What was your post office at enlistment? *Answer.* Pennellville, N.Y.

No. 3. State your wife's full name and her maiden name. *Answer.* Phebe Ann Gulliver—P.A. Wallace

No. 4. When, where, and by whom were you married? *Answer.* Feb. 7th 1857; Gilbertville, N.Y. by Elder Stone

No. 5. Is there any official or church record of your marriage? There was an official record

If so, where? *Answer.* Lost when moving from N.Y. to Mich.

No. 6. Were you previously married? If so, state the name of your former wife, the date of the marriage, and the date and place of her death or divorce. If there was more than one previous marriage, let your answer include all former wives. *Answer.* was never married before marrying Phebe A. Wallace

No. 7. If your present wife was married before her marriage to you, state the name of her former husband, the date of such marriage, and the date and place of his death or divorce, and state whether he ever rendered any miltary or naval service, and, if so, give name of the organization in which he served. If she was married more than once before her marriage to you, let your answer include all former husbands. *Answer.* She was never married before marrying me.

No. 8. Are you now living with your wife, or has there been a separation? *Answer.* I am living with my wife formely Phebe A. Wallace

No. 9. State the names and dates of birth of all your children, living or dead. *Answer.*

George P. Gulliver - Born Dec 20th, 1858 died
John L. Gulliver " Feb. 23rd 1860 Feb. 7, 1863.
W. F. Gulliver " Oct. 26th 1861.
Chas. L. Gulliver " Jan. 26th 1867.
Albert H. Gulliver " March 17th 1870.
Nettie H. Gulliver, Greenleaf " June 16th 1881
Newton J. Gulliver June 12th 1881 Died Jan 15th 1882

Date March 13, 1915. (Signature) Thomas Gulliver

Figure 6-3 Pension application questionnaire of Thomas Gulliver, 1915, certificate #641287 (private, Co. D, 149th NY Infantry), Pension Applications Based Upon Service in the Civil War or Later, Records of the Veterans Administration, RG 94, National Archives Building, Washington, DC.

in 1915, specific birthplace in eastern Dorsetshire in England, his wife's maiden name, their marriage date and place, and the birth dates and some death dates of their children. For the genealogist, this is amazing information—and all on one page.

Case Study

The Miller research is a good example of cluster genealogy.

ALL IN THE BROTHER'S PENSION FILE

Philene (Miller) Simms was one of the older children of George and Margaret Miller of Green County, Pennsylvania. She and her brother George Jr. were grown and married before the Civil War began. A search for her mother's maiden name had been unfruitful but ended when the pension file based on her brother Andrew's Civil War service arrived in the mail:

Andrew Miller was twenty-two years old when he enlisted for three years as a private in Company D of the 1st West Virginia Volunteers on 7 September 1861. Still at home with his parents, George and Margaret (Myers) Miller, were Ann, born 4 May 1829; Margaret, born 31 May 1837; William, born 10 December 1841; Lusinda [*sic*], born 31 December 1843; and Drusilla, born 23 September 1848. Lusinda married and left home shortly after Andrew enlisted. The remaining four siblings were "Invaleads," unable to provide a living for themselves.

During the battle of Moorefield (now West Virginia) just after the second anniversary of his enlistment, Andrew was captured. He was held in Richmond until the following March when he was imprisoned at Andersonville in southwestern Georgia. A year later, he was exchanged at Vicksburg and was immediately admitted to the Union army hospital there, suffering from advanced scurvy. He died in the hospital on 14 April 1865, the day Lincoln was assassinated and five days after Lee surrendered at Appomattox.

The soldier's death was a great personal loss to his family but also an economic loss. Before his capture and imprisonment, he wrote letters to his father and sent home money out of his pay. With Andrew no longer at home to help on the farm or in the service sending home five or ten dollars at a time, the Millers were feeling the difference. With four invalid children (a crippled son and three "idiotic" daughters, according to census records), the parents had their hands full.

The mother, Margaret Miller, died on 23 September 1876. By this time George Sr. had become disabled by an injury to his knee, caused by "falling with a log of wood." He had never fully recovered and was therefore unable to work; he estimated that he could earn only a third of the wages a sound man could earn. Since his son's death, he had been compelled to rent out his land and, thus, his income from all sources was not more than $100 a year.

Since Andrew was single when he died and left no wife or child, his father applied for a pension as a dependent parent of a deceased soldier. He filed his application in Marshall County, West Virginia, which was the most convenient location for him. One of his affiants, John Myers of Jefferson County, Ohio, remembered George and Margaret marrying about 1822. Another affiant, Michael Myers, recalled being present at the wedding of George Miller and Margaret Myers on or about 13 August 1823 at the residence of Jacob Miller in Jefferson County, Ohio. (The county marriage book shows the marriage as 18 August

1825.) After fifty-plus years, how many folks can remember exactly? Michael Myers affirmed that George Miller was then seventy-eight years old and they had known each other for sixty years. Thus, in early 1880, at about eighty years of age, George Miller was granted a pension of eight dollars a month, retroactive to the day after his wife had died.

What happened to Andrew was tragic, and George and Margaret had a most unfortunate set of circumstances with which to cope. However, as Philene Simms' great-great-granddaughter who requested the pension file, I got not only copies of the letters Andrew had written to his father but also more family history than I could have imagined. And there it was, waiting for me, in Philene's brother's name. *Virginia Simms Toney*

Pension Payments

Paying the pensioners was the job of the War Department beginning in 1792. In 1849, the Pension Office was transferred from the War Department to the Interior Department and later became the Bureau of Pensions. In 1930, the bureau and other agencies dealing with veterans were merged into the Veterans Administration. In 1907, the pension office stopped using ledger books to record pension payments and began using cards. Several series of microfilm reproduce pension payment records.

The series **Ledgers of Payments, 1818–1872** (T718), from the Treasury Department,

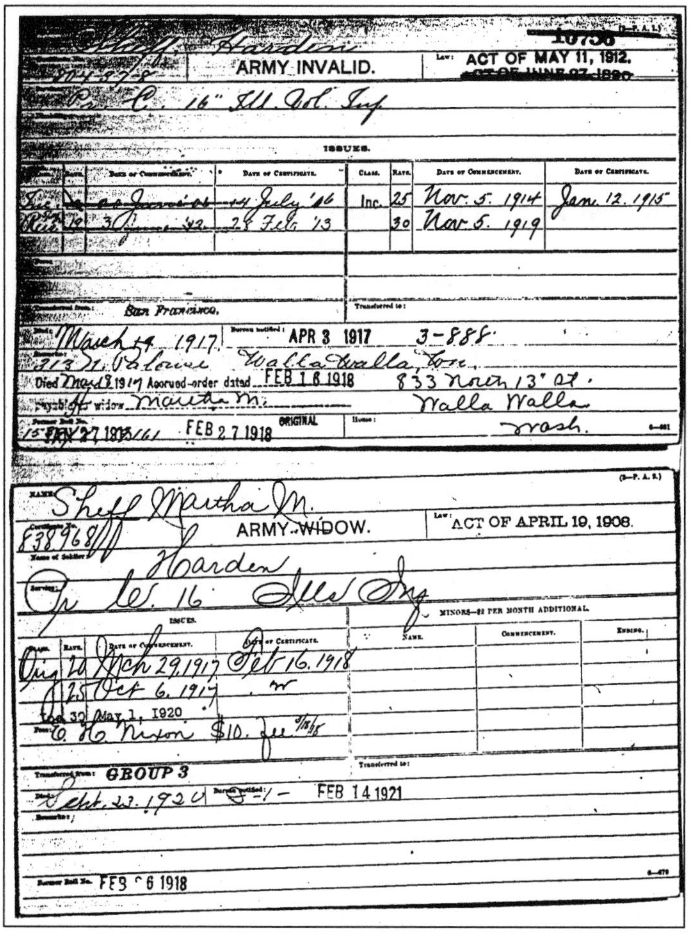
ARMY INVALID.
ACT OF MAY 11, 1912.
ISSUES.
Inc. 25 Nov. 5. 1914 Jan. 12. 1915
30 Nov. 5. 1919
San Francisco.
APR 3 1917
Walla Walla, Wn.
Died March 1917 Accrued-order dated FEB 16 1918
widow Martha M.
Walla Walla Wash.
FEB 27 1918 ORIGINAL

Sheff Martha M.
ARMY WIDOW.
ACT OF APRIL 19, 1908.
Harden
MINORS—$2 PER MONTH ADDITIONAL.
Mch 29 1917 Feb 16. 1918
Oct 6. 1917
May 1, 1920
GROUP 3
Sept. 23. 1920 FEB 14 1921
FEB 6 1918

Figure 6-4 Payment records of Harden Sheff and widow Martha M. Sheff, Veterans Administration Pension Payment Cards, 1907–1933, NARA microfilm M850, roll 2032, alphabetical order.

reproduces the records of the semiannual payments that were sent to pensioners each March and September. The microfilm includes records of Revolutionary War pensioners, invalid pensioners, and widows. The entries are divided according to the act under which the pension was granted and the pension agency. Each volume is divided by state and shows the pensioners' names in rough alphabetical order. These are available at some research libraries and through the Family History Library.

Sometimes, the record shows a death date or a person's move to a new place of residence. The New Jersey record for 1833–1849 (roll 5) shows that John Curry received two payments in 1833 before his death on November 6; Richard Clark received pension payments from 1833 until his death on 6 April 1837. William Stanley of Virginia got his pension from 1820 to 1836, when a note was written on the record saying "transf[erre]d to Ohio." The Ohio record then showed his payments from 1837 to 1842, with no indication of payment in 1843 and no indication of his death. His researcher should try the next volume to determine whether he received further payments.

The **Veterans Administration pension payment cards, 1907–1933** (M850), are a huge series of microfilm, arranged alphabetically by surname of the pensioner. The series includes pensioners on the rolls during the given dates, excluding those from World War I. The cards show the name of the army or navy veteran or veteran's widow, the certificate number, the military unit and basic facts of the service, the nature of disabilities, and the pensioner's residence and death date. Some cards also identify the alias by which the veteran was known. The back of the card details the amounts and dates of payments. Figure 6-4, on page 203, shows the cards for Private Harden Sheff of Company C, 16th Illinois Volunteer Infantry (Civil War), and his widow Martha M. Sheff. Residents of Walla Walla, Washington, they died on 18 March 1917 and 23 September 1920, respectively.

Pension-Related Microfilm

Indexes to the pension records are numerous, as shown in the list below. If you find an ancestor listed as a veteran or a widow in such an index, get the pension file. **National Archives microfilm relating to pension and bounty land warrant applications and files include the following:**

Microfilm Source

1. Selected records from Revolutionary War pension and bounty land warrant application files, 1800–1900 (M805). Not complete files, but selected for genealogical interest.
2. Revolutionary War pension and bounty land warrant application files, 1800–1900 (M804). Complete files of some eighty thousand applications. Published index by National Genealogical Society in bibliography on page 208. Rolls are arranged alphabetically.
3. U.S. Revolutionary War bounty land warrants used in the Military District of Ohio (M829). Roll 1 contains indexes.
4. Register of Revolutionary War land warrants, Act of 1788 Military District of Ohio, 1799–1805 (T1008).
5. Virginia half-pay and other related Revolutionary War pension application files (M910).
6. Index to War of 1812 pension application files (M313).
7. War of 1812 military bounty land warrants, 1815–1858 (M848).
8. Old War index to pension files, 1815–1926 (T316). Pensions based on disability or death from service between 1783 and 1861.
9. Ledgers of payments to pensioners, 1818–1872 (T718).
10. Index to Mexican War pension files, 1887–1926 (T317).

11. Selected pension application files, Mormon Battalion, Mexican War (T1196).
12. Index to Indian Wars pension files, 1892–1926 (T318).
13. General index to pension files, 1861–1934 (T288). 544 rolls, mostly relating to Civil War service but including some pensioners from later conflicts.
14. Organization index to pension files of veterans who served between 1861 and 1900 (T289). Same material as number 13 above, but by unit instead of alphabetical.
15. Veterans Administration pension payment cards, 1907–1933 (M850).
16. Index to general correspondence of Record and Pension Office, 1889–1920 (M686).
17. Index to pension application files of remarried widows based on service in the War of 1812, Indian wars, and Regular Army before 1861 (M1784, 1 roll).
18. Index to pension application files of remarried widows based on service in the Civil War and later wars and in the Regular Army after the Civil War (M1785). 7 rolls.

Military-Related Records

Draft registration cards for World War I are located at the National Archives branch in East Point, Georgia, and are available on microfilm M1509 at research libraries and from the Family History Library. Ancestry.com is gradually putting the World War I draft registrations online as part of its subscription database. As of this writing, only two states had been completed.

The "Selective Service Act" of May 1917 required registration of all men who had reached their twenty-first birthday on or before registration day but had not reached their thirty-first birthday. Congress and President Wilson ultimately chose four registration dates: 5 June 1917, 5 June 1918, 24 August 1918, and 12 September 1918, the last being for men of the age of eighteen and not yet forty-six. Thus, the entire registration process included men born between 13 September 1872 and 12 September 1900. The registration dates were slightly different in Alaska, Hawaii, and Puerto Rico but still fell between mid-1917 and late-1918. Except for those on active duty in the military or naval service on 5 June 1917, all men were supposed to register—citizens, aliens, Indians, felons, prisoners, the ill, the insane, and the disabled. More than twenty-four million did so. Registration did not make every man a candidate for service. Many who registered, including non-citizen Indians, prisoners, aliens, the ill, the disabled, or the incompetent, were not subject to the draft.

For a small fee you can request a search of the records using the form furnished by the East Point regional archives. You must be able to furnish the man's full name and address at the time of registration. The information on the registration varies but may include name, residence, age, birth date, citizenship status, occupation, physical description, signature, and sometimes birthplace and nearest relative (relationship not always specified).

Printed Source

A good reference book for the subject and for microfilm roll numbers is *Uncle, We Are Ready! Registering America's Men 1917–1918*, by John J. Newman (North Salt Lake, Utah: HeritageQuest, 2001).

Figure 6-5, on page 206, shows the registration card of Sukesaburo Doi, born 2 November 1882 and a Japanese citizen working as a fisherman in Wilmington, Los Angeles County, California on 12 September 1918. He named as his nearest relative his mother in Japan. Like Doi's card, the following abstracts contain genealogically pertinent information that may otherwise be difficult to find:

- Horace Duffy, Caucasian, born 31 December 1888 in San Pedro, California, where he lived on 5 June 1917; worked as theatrical stage employee for Auditorium Theatre; single; claimed exemption from draft due to a stiff finger on his right hand; registered 5 June 1917.
- Herbert Lawrence, Caucasian, born 11 July 1889 in Bradford, Yorkshire, England; naturalized citizen living in Wilmington, Delaware; worked as pipe fitter for General Chemical Co. in Claymont, Delaware; married with three children as of 5 June 1917.
- Vincenzo DiMeglio, Caucasian, born 11 January 1887 in Ischia (Naples) Italy; an

alien (not yet a declarant for citizenship); worked as a fisherman in San Pedro, California; married; had served two years in the Italian army artillery; registered 5 June 1917.

- Robert Lee, Negro, born 20 July 1879; lived in Wilmington, Delaware; worked as a roofer helper; nearest relative was George Lee, his father, of Amherst County, Virginia; registered 12 September 1918.
- Andrew Dorotich, Caucasian, born 16 July 1883 in Austria; had filed declaration of intent to become a U.S. citizen; an unemployed fisherman living in San Pedro, Los Angeles County, California; nearest relative was his wife, Martha Dorotich, living then in Comisa, Austria; registered 16 September 1918.

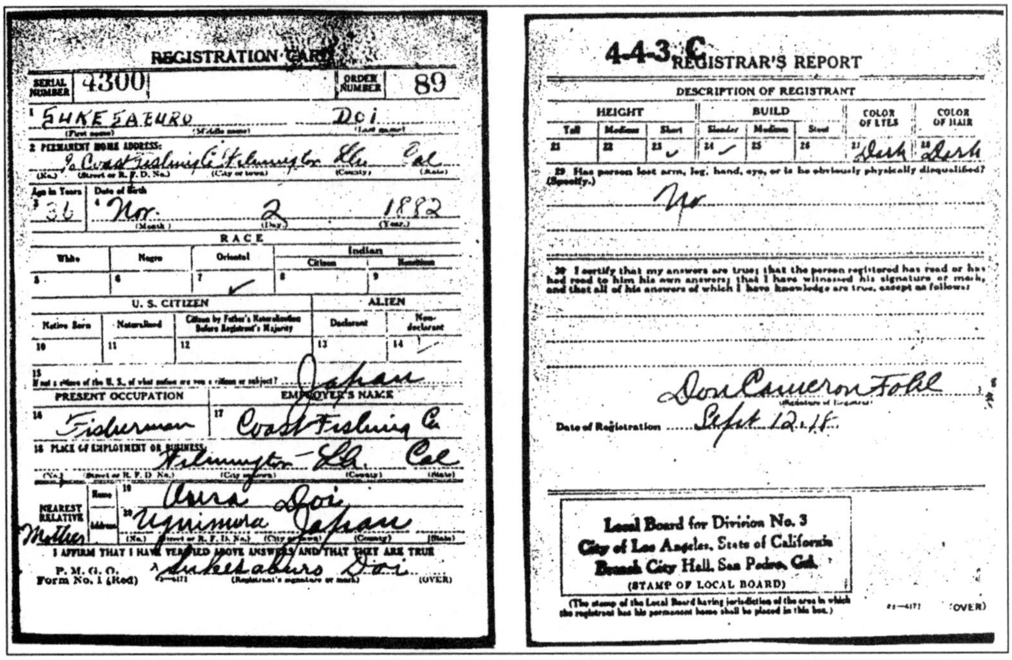
REGISTRATION CARD
SERIAL NUMBER 4300 ORDER NUMBER 89
1 SUKESABURO Doi
(First name) (Middle name) (Last name)
2 PERMANENT HOME ADDRESS:
c/o Coast Fishing Co Wilmington L.A. Cal
(No.) (Street or R. F. D. No.) (City or town) (County) (State)
Age in Years 3 36 Date of Birth 4 Nov. 2 1882
(Month) (Day) (Year)
RACE
White 5 | Negro 6 | Oriental 7 ✓ | Indian: Citizen 8 | Noncitizen 9
U. S. CITIZEN: Native Born 10 | Naturalized 11 | Citizen by Father's Naturalization Before Registrant's Majority 12
ALIEN: Declarant 13 | Non-declarant 14 ✓
15 If not a citizen of the U. S., of what nation are you a citizen or subject? Japan
PRESENT OCCUPATION 16 Fisherman
EMPLOYER'S NAME 17 Coast Fishing Co
18 PLACE OF EMPLOYMENT OR BUSINESS: Wilmington L.A. Cal
(No.) (Street or R. F. D. No.) (City or town) (County) (State)
NEAREST RELATIVE Name 19 Aura Doi
Address 20 Ugnimura Japan
Mother
I AFFIRM THAT I HAVE VERIFIED ABOVE ANSWERS AND THAT THEY ARE TRUE
P. M. G. O. Form No. 1 (Red) Sukesaburo Doi (Registrant's signature or mark) (OVER)

4-4-3 C
REGISTRAR'S REPORT
DESCRIPTION OF REGISTRANT
HEIGHT: Tall 21 | Medium 22 | Short 23 ✓
BUILD: Slender 24 ✓ | Medium 25 | Stout 26
COLOR OF EYES 27 Dark
COLOR OF HAIR 28 Dark
29 Has person lost arm, leg, hand, eye, or is he obviously physically disqualified? (Specify.) No
30 I certify that my answers are true; that the person registered has read or has had read to him his own answers; that I have witnessed his signature or mark, and that all of his answers of which I have knowledge are true, except as follows:
Don Cameron Folle (Signature of Registrar)
Date of Registration Sept 12, 18
Local Board for Division No. 3
City of Los Angeles, State of California
Branch City Hall, San Pedro, Cal.
(STAMP OF LOCAL BOARD)
(The stamp of the Local Board having jurisdiction of the area in which the registrant has his permanent home shall be placed in this box.)
(OVER)

Figure 6-5 World War I draft registration card of Sukesaburo Doi, 1918, World War I Selective Service System Draft Registration Cards, NARA microfilm M1509, roll 30, FHL microfilm 1530800, California board 4-4-3, Los Angeles County, cards Dah-Z.

Military discharge papers from the Spanish-American War forward are often filed in county courthouses and can provide valuable information for the genealogist. (Veterans have often been asked to file a copy for safekeeping for their protection and later use if their original is lost.) The World War I honorable discharge of William Taylor Oldham, filed in Robertson County, Texas, gives the following information about the serviceman:

> Served as Private First Class, Laundry Company 307. Inducted 15 June 1918 at Franklin, Texas. Member of the American Expeditionary Force (AEF), 2 September 1918 to 8 July 1919. Assigned to 351 Butcher Company, 5 September 1918; to 307 Laundry Company, 25 January 1919; to Cas. Det. Demot. Group, 14–19 July 1919. Discharged 21 July 1919 at Camp Pike, Arkansas. Entitled to travel pay to Bremond, Texas. Paid in full $128.21, including $60 bonus pay. This was his first service. Born at Bremond, Texas. Farmer, age 27, single. Fair complexion. 5 feet 7½ inches tall. Not qualified as marksman or gunner. Not mounted. Received immunizations 21 June 1918. Not wounded. Good physical condition at time of discharge. Excellent character, no AWOL, no absence.

Although the National Archives has the early records of most of the services, existing records of more recent veterans are at the National Personnel Records Center, 9700 Page Avenue, St. Louis, Missouri 63132-5100. Their release of information form states,

"Although the Privacy Act (1974) does not apply to the records of deceased individuals, Department of Defense instructions indicate that we must have the written consent of the next of kin if the individual is deceased. For the purposes of the release authorization, the next of kin is defined as any of the following: unremarried widow or widower, son, daughter, father, mother, brother, or sister."

A fire at this facility on 12 July 1973 destroyed many of the records of twentieth-century military personnel, including these: (1) army personnel separated from the service between 1912 and 1959 (about 80 percent loss); (2) air force and army air corps personnel separated between 1947 and 1963, especially servicemen whose surnames begin with *I* through *Z*. Records remaining at the records center include (1) army officers separated after 30 June 1917; (2) army enlisted personnel separated after 31 October 1912; (3) air force personnel separated after 1947; (4) navy enlisted men separated after 1885; (5) navy officers separated after 1902; (6) Marine Corps officers separated after 1895; (7) Marine Corps enlisted personnel separated after 1904; (8) Coast Guard officers separated after 1928 (possibly some earlier ones); (9) Coast Guard enlisted men separated after 1914; and (10) civilian employees of the Coast Guard predecessor agencies (Revenue Cutter, Life-Saving, and Lighthouse Services), 1864–1919. You can request a search on their Standard Form 180 available from the NPRC office, the National Archives, and other federal centers.

A CD-ROM available at the Family History Library and Family History Centers is the index to *U.S. Military Personnel Who Died in Korea or Vietnam, 1950–1975*. These government-generated databases are also online at Ancestry.com. The Korean Conflict Death Index, 1950–1957 (prepared by the Department of Defense), contains 33,642 files; information includes name, age, race, citizenship, hometown and state, rank and branch of service, type of casualty, and death record number. The Vietnam Casualty Index (Orem, Utah: Ancestry, 1997) from a Department of Defense data file, contains 58,181 files; information includes name, birth and death dates, hometown and state, date the tour of duty began, length of service, service number, branch of service, type of casualty, marital status, and religious preference. On Ancestry.com, the databases are listed in the alphabetical list of "all databases" under Korea and Vietnam. Search engines may help you find non-subscription sites with these databases.

Records of the merchant marine from 1937 forward are housed at the office of the Commandant of the Coast Guard. These records give birth date, service information, and sometimes death date, if the family notified the office of the death. Information can be obtained with a signed release by a living mariner, a court order in case of litigation, or a copy of the death certificate for records of a deceased mariner. The office is required to keep the records for sixty years. Thus, records more than sixty years old may have been destroyed. The National Archives has a few records prior to 1937 but does not receive records as they pass the sixty-year requirement. The address for merchant marine records since 1937 is Commandant (G-MVP-1), U.S. Coast Guard, 2100 Second Street SW, Washington, DC 20593-0001. This same office keeps Coast Guard military records only a short time before sending them on to the National Personnel Records Center in St. Louis, Missouri.

For More Info

For more information on merchant marine history and service records, visit <www.usmm.org>.

Tennessee Civil War Questionnaires. An interesting and valuable source that came about because of Civil War service is *Tennessee Civil War Veterans Questionnaires*, 5 volumes, compiled by Gustavus W. Dyer and John Trotwood Moore (Easley [now Greenville], S.C.: Southern Historical Press, 1985). Questionnaires were sent to all known living Civil War veterans (Union and Confederate) in Tennessee in 1914, 1915, and 1920. Some 1,650 were completed and returned and are housed at the Tennessee State Library and Archives. The responses concern family history as well as military service.

New York Town Clerks' Records of Soldiers and Officers in the Military Service are important resources resulting from the Civil War. Many of the registers show for each serviceman information such as enlistment, rank, promotions, unit, engagements, disabilities, and discharge or death while in the service. A bonus for genealogists is additional details on race, birth date, birthplace, marital status, previous occupation, and parents' names, sometimes including the mother's maiden name. Microfilmed from originals at the New York State Archives, the records are organized alphabetically by county and thereunder by town. The microfilm is available from the Family History Library on film numbers 1993401–1993437.

For Further Reference: Military Topics Other Than Civil War

The bibliographies given here are a sampling of some basic reference materials and resources other than general histories. In addition, check library catalogs for books and PERSI for articles and abstracts with military history, maps, Loyalists, veterans' tombstone inscriptions, and other military-related subjects. Through interlibrary loan and university and research libraries, you have access to hundreds of published and manuscript materials, from both the government and the private sector. (See chapter eight for use of government documents. See also bibliographies in chapters seven and eight.)

American Loyalist Claims, 1730–1835, microfilmed records from Public Record Office, London. Available from the Family History Library.

American Military Cemeteries: A Comprehensive Illustrated Guide to the Hallowed Grounds of the United States, Including Cemeteries Overseas, by Dean W. Holt. Jefferson, N.C.: McFarland and Co., 1992.

A Bibliography of Loyalist Source Material in the United States, Canada, and Great Britain, Gregory Palmer, ed. Westport, Conn.: Meckler Publishing Co., 1982.

Blacks in the American Armed Forces, 1776–1983: A Bibliography, by Lenwood G. Davis and George Hill. Westport, Conn.: Greenwood Press, 1985.

Genealogical Abstracts of Revolutionary War Pension Files, Virgil D. White, abstracter. Waynesboro, Tenn.: National Historical Publishing Co., 1990. An important work.

German Allied Troops in the American Revolution: J.R. Rosengarten's Survey of German Archives and Sources, Don Heinrich Tolzmann, ed. Bowie, Md.: Heritage Books, 1993.

Historical Register of Officers of the Continental Army During the War of the Revolution, April, 1775–1783, by Francis B. Heitman. Washington, D.C.: 1914. Reprint, Baltimore: Genealogical Publishing Co., 1982.

Index of Revolutionary War Pension Applications, Max E. Hoyt, Frank Johnson Metcalf, et al., eds. Washington, D.C. [now Arlington, Va.]: National Genealogical Society, 1966, revised and enlarged, 1976.

Index to Mexican War Pension Files, Virgil D. White, transcriber. Waynesboro, Tenn.: National Historical Publishing Co., 1989.

Index to the War of 1812 Pension Files, Virgil D. White, transcriber. Waynesboro, Tenn.: National Historical Publishing Co., 1989.

Index to U.S. Invalid Pension Records, 1801–1815, by Murtie June Clark. Baltimore: Genealogical Publishing Co., 1991.

Index to Volunteer Soldiers, 1784–1811, Virgil D. White, transcriber. Waynesboro, Tenn.: National Historical Publishing Co., 1987.

Known Military Dead During the Spanish-American War and the Philippines Insurrection, 1898–1901, Clarence Stewart Peterson, comp. Baltimore: the compiler, 1958.

Others by same compiler: (1) *Known Military Dead During the Mexican War, 1846–1848* (1957); (2) *Known Military and Civilian Dead in the Minnesota Sioux Indian Massacre in 1862* (1958); (3) *Known Military Dead During the War of 1812* (1955).

List of Log Books of U.S. Navy Ships, Stations, and Miscellaneous Units, 1801–1947, Claudia Bradley, et al, comp. Washington, D.C.: National Archives and Records Service, 1978.

List of Pensioners on the Roll January 1, 1883. 5 vols. Washington, D.C.: U.S. Pension Bureau, as part of the Serial Set, Senate Executive Document 84 (47th Congress, 2d session) serial 2078–2082. Reprint. Baltimore: Genealogical Publishing Co., 1970.

Major Index to the Pension List of the War of 1812, 6 vols., by Annie Walker Burns. Washington, D.C.: the author, n.d. Alphabetical abstracts.

Naval Historical Foundation Manuscript Collection: A Catalog. Washington, D.C.: Library of Congress, 1974.

Naval Records of the American Revolution, 1775–1788, by Charles Henry Lincoln. Washington, D.C.: Government Printing Office, 1906. Reprint, Bowie, Md.: Heritage Books, 1992. A calendar of records from originals in the Library of Congress.

Official Army Register. Washington, D.C.: Office of the Secretary of War, annual, 1875–1978.

The Pension List of 1792–1795: With Other Revolutionary War Pension Records, Murtie June Clark, comp. Baltimore: Genealogical Publishing Co., 1991. Indexed. Includes the claims reports from the *American State Papers: Claims* and abstracts of acts of Congress, 1789–1815, invalid pension claims.

Pension List of 1820. War Department document originally published 1820 by Gales and Seaton, Washington, D.C. Reprint, Baltimore: Genealogical Publishing Co., 1991.

Pension Roll of 1835. Originally published in 1835 as part of the Serial Set, Senate Document 514 (23d Congress, 1st session) serial 249–251. Reprint, Baltimore: Genealogical Publishing Co., 1992. 4 vols., with index. Names and records of 60,700 soldiers.

Pensioners of the Revolutionary War Struck off the Roll. War Department report to the House of Representatives. Originally published in 1836 as part of the Serial Set, House Document 127 (24th Congress, 1st session) serial 289. Reprint, Baltimore: Genealogical Publishing Co., 1969.

Pierce's Register: Register of the Certificates Issued by John Pierce, Esquire, Paymaster General and Commissioner of Army Accounts for the United States, to Officers and Soldiers of the Continental Army Under Act of July 4, 1783. War Department document, originally published 1915. Reprint, Baltimore: Genealogical Publishing Co., 1987.

Preliminary Guide to the Manuscript Collection of the U.S. Military Academy Library, by J. Thomas Russell. West Point, N.Y.: Military Academy, 1968.

Records of the Revolutionary War, by W.T.R. Saffell. Baltimore: 1894. Reprint by J.T. McAllister, 1913, with index to Saffell's list of Virginia soldiers in the Revolution. Reprint, Baltimore: Genealogical Publishing Co., 1969. Reprint, Baltimore: Genealogical Publishing Co., for Clearfield Company Reprints, 1991. Lots of lists, including officers with bounty land warrants issued before the end of 1784.

Register of the Army and Navy of the United States. Washington, D.C.: Peter Force, 1830.

Register of the Army of the United States. Washington, D.C.: Adjutant and Inspector General's Office, 1813.

Research Guide to Loyalist Ancestors: A Directory to Archives, Manuscripts, and Published Sources, by Paul J. Bunnell. Bowie, Md.: Heritage Books, 1990.

Revolutionary Pensioners: A Transcript of the Pension List of the United States for 1813. Reprint of 1813 original. Baltimore: Southern Book Co., 1953.

U. S. Naval History Sources in the United States, Dean C. Allard, et al, comp. Washington, D.C.: Government Printing Office, 1979. Department of the Navy, History Division.

The West Point Atlas of American Wars, Volume I: 1689–1900, Vincent J. Esposito, ed. New York: Henry Holt and Co., 1995.

For Further Reference: Civil War

Academic and large public libraries have many of these works.

The Appomattox Roster: A List of Paroles of the Army of Northern Virginia Issued at Appomattox Court House on April 9, 1865. Reprint of 1887 original. New York: Antiquarian Press, 1962. Indexed.

Civil War Claims in the South: An Index of Civil War Damage Claims Filed Before the Southern Claims Commission, 1871–1880, by Gary B. Mills. Laguna Hills, Calif.: Aegean Park Press, 1980. See these records on National Archives microfilm publication M87.

Compendium of the Confederate Armies, 11 vols., by Stewart Sifakis. New York: Facts on File, 1992. Regimental histories arranged by state. Companion to Frederick H. Dyer's *Compendium of the War of the Rebellion* (Union), 3 vols., 1909.

Compendium of the War of the Rebellion [Union], 2 vols., Frederick H. Dyer, comp. Reprint of 1908 original. Dayton, Ohio: Morningside Press, 1994.

The Confederacy: A Guide to the Archives of the Government of the Confederate States of America, by Henry Putney Beers. Washington, D.C.: National Archives and Records Administration, 1998.

Confederate P.O.W.'s: Soldiers & Sailors Who Died in Federal Prisons & Military Hospitals in the North. Reprint of 1912 War Department original. Nacogdoches, Tex.: Carolyn Ericson and Frances Ingmire, 1984. Gives name, prison, cemetery, rank and unit, death date.

Confederate Research Sources: A Guide to Archives Collections, by James C. Neagles. Salt Lake City: Ancestry, 1986.

The Confederate States Marine Corps: The Rebel Leathernecks, by Ralph W. Donnelly. Rev. ed. Shippensburg, Pa.: White Mane Publishing Co., 1989.

The Era of the Civil War—1820–1876, by Louise Arnold and Richard Sommers. Army Military History Institute. Washington, D.C.: Government Printing Office, 1982. Bibliography of the institute's collection on the Civil War.

A Guide to Civil War Maps in the National Archives. Rev. ed. Washington, D.C.: National Archives, 1986.

The Medical and Surgical History of the Civil War, 12 vols. plus 3 vols. index, by Joseph K. Barnes, Joseph J. Woodward, et al. Reprint of 1870s original. Wilmington, N.C.: Broadfoot Publishing Co., 1990. Includes information on hundreds of individual servicemen, largely Union.

Military Bibliography of the Civil War, C.E. Dornbusch, comp. New York: New York Public Library, 1961–1987. Revision and supplement to *Bibliography of State Participation in the Civil War, 1861–1866*, 3d ed., by War Department Library, 1913. Volume I—Regimental Publications and Personal Narratives, Northern States (1961, reprint 1971). Volume II—Regimental Publications and Personal Narratives, Southern, Border, and Western States and Territories; Federal Troops, Union and Confederate Biographies (1967). Volume III—General References; Armed Forces; Campaigns and Battles (1972). Volume IV—Regimental Publications and Personal narratives; Union and Confederate Biographies, General References, Armed Forces, Campaigns and Battles (1987).

Military Operations of the Civil War: A Guide-Index to the Official Records of the Union and Confederate Armies, 1861–1865, 5 vols., Dallas Irvine, comp. Washington, D.C.: National Archives, 1966–1980.

Official Army Register of the Volunteer Forces of the United States Army for 1861, '62, '63, '64, '65. Washington, D.C.: Adjutant General's Office, 1865. Reprint, Gaithersburg, Md.: Ron R. Van Sickle Military Books, 1987. Each volume indexed. Part I—New England States. Part II—New York, New Jersey. Part III—Pennsylvania, Delaware, Maryland, District of Columbia. Part IV—Confederate States plus West Virginia, Kentucky. Part V—Ohio, Michigan. Part VI—Indiana, Illinois. Part VII—Missouri, Wisconsin, Iowa, Minnesota, California, Kansas, Oregon, Nevada. Part VIII—Territorial Troops (Washington, Utah, New Mexico, Nebraska, Colorado, Indian Territory, Dakotas, Arizona, Idaho, Montana), U.S. Troops (Veteran Reserve Corps, First Army Corps [Veterans], Colored Troops, and miscellaneous). Lists by unit within each state or territory.

Personnel of the Civil War, William Frayne Amann, ed. New York: Thomas Yoseloff, 1961. Volume I—Confederate Volume II—Union. Popular names and official names of units. Volume II includes troops from the Indian nations and U.S. Colored Troops.

Register of Officers of the Confederate States Navy, 1861–1865. Washington, D.C.: Department of the Navy, 1898. Reprint, Mattituck, N.Y.: J.M. Carroll and Co., 1983. Reprints by the same company: (1) *List of Staff Officers of the Confederate States Army, 1861–1865*, Marcus J. Wright, comp. Washington, D.C.: Government Printing Office, 1891. Reprint, 1983. (2) *General Officers of the Confederate Army*, General Marcus J. Wright, comp., 1911. Reprint, 1983. (3) *List of Field Officers, Regiments, and Battalions in the Confederate States Army, 1861–1865*. Reprint, 1983.

Service Records of Confederate Enlisted Marines, by Ralph W. Donnelly. Washington, N.C.: the author, 1979. Alphabetical abstracts.

Southern Historical Society Papers. 52 vols. Millwood, N.Y.: Kraus Reprint, 1977. Reprint of the 1876–1943 edition, vols. 1–49, published by the Southern Historical Society. Reprint of the 1953–1959 edition, vols. 50–52, published by the Virginia Historical Society, Richmond. Impressive collection of records from the Confederate period. Easier to search with *Index-Guide to the Southern Historical Society Papers, 1876–1959*, 3 vols. James I. Robertson Jr., ed. Wilmington, N.C.: Broadfoot Publishing Co., 1992.

The Union: A Guide to Federal Archives Relating to the Civil War, by Kenneth W. Munden and Henry Putney Beers. Washington, D.C.: National Archives, 1998.

United States Navy: Official Records of the Union and Confederate Navies in the War of the Rebellion. 30 vols., plus index volume. Washington, D.C.: Government Printing Office, 1927. Reprint, New York: Antiquarian Press, Ltd., 1961.

The War of the Rebellion: A Compilation of the Official Records of the Union and Confederate Armies. Washington, D.C.: Government Printing Office, 1893. Series I (53 vols.)—Reports and Operations. Series II (8 vols.)—Prisoners of War, etc. Series III (5 vols.)—Union Correspondence, etc. Series IV (3 vols.)—Confederate Correspondence, etc. In addition to an index in each volume, there is a general index. Letters, reports, other documents.

AMERICAN STATE PAPERS

The *American State Papers* is a compilation of legislative and executive department documents, organized, transcribed, and published in topical units. Gales and Seaton in Washington, DC, originally published them between 1832 and 1861. Many academic and research libraries own sets of the originals. Since these volumes are part of the Serial Set, microform or print copies are usually available in libraries holding the Serial Set. (See page 292.)

Class I	Foreign Relations, 1789–1828	6 volumes
Class II	Indian Affairs, 1789–1827	2 volumes
Class III	Finance, 1789–1828	5 volumes
Class IV	Commerce and Navigation, 1789–1823	2 volumes
Class V	Military Affairs, 1789–1838	7 volumes
Class VI	Naval Affairs, 1794–1836	4 volumes
Class VII	Post Office Department, 1790–1833	1 volume
Class VIII	Public Lands, 1789–1837	8 volumes
Class IX	Claims, 1789–1823	1 volume
Class X	Miscellaneous, 1789–1823	2 volumes

In the Class IX volume are claims against the government for work done, compensation for losses during the Revolution, and pensions for Revolutionary War military service. Several reports between 1792 and 1795 list disabled Revolutionary pensioners. These reports are especially important now because all pension applications submitted before November 1800 were destroyed in a War Department fire that month. The reports do not duplicate the lost applications but identify a sizable number of veterans approved for pensions. Typical of the invalid pensioners in a 1792 report was Joshua Gilman of New Hampshire, who had been a private in Colonel Hubbard's Regiment and was wounded in the left arm on 16 August 1777 at the Battle of Bennington. He was supposed to receive a monthly pension of $1.11, but the government was $20 in arrears on his payments (1:58).

Class VIII contains reports, with occasional maps, of hundreds of public land grants and claims. A chart of land claims in Mississippi Territory, abstract for December 1806, shows Alexander Armstrong with a certificate dated 17 December 1806 for one hundred acres on the Bayou Pierre (1:902). Volume three contains a "supplementary list of actual settlers" in Louisiana east of the Mississippi River and west of the Pearl River. Volume seven contains a statement of the amount of military land scrip issued to officers and soldiers of the Virginia Continental Line under an act of relief, 15 November 1834. The same volume contains long lists of "Indians owning farms in the Choctaw Nation 1831."

Each book has an index, but a more complete index for the Gales and Seaton Class VIII and IX volumes is *Grassroots of America: A Computerized Index to the American State Papers Land Grants and Claims (1789–1837)*, with other aids to research, edited by Philip W. McMullin (Salt Lake City: Gendex Corp., 1972). One helpful reference in *Grassroots* is a map of the seventy-seven federal land offices opened before 1840, although not all of them were open *in* 1840. The book identifies land offices in the central states and gives researchers a better understanding of why so many public-land settlers complained of the distance and difficulty of travel to the nearest land office.

The New American State Papers, 1789–1860, edited by Thomas C. Cochran (Wilmington, Del.: Scholarly Resources, 1972–1981) is another series from manuscript collections at the National Archives and Library of Congress, with some of the documents from the Gales and Seaton volumes and the Serial Set. These volumes are facsimile reproductions of the original manuscript and published documents. They follow a topical arrangement similar to that of the older *American State Papers*, but they are subdivided into subject headings within each set. These books are not indexed.

Agriculture, 1789–1860	19 volumes
Commerce and Navigation, 1789–1860	47 volumes
Indian Affairs, 1789–1860	13 volumes
Military Affairs, 1789–1860	19 volumes
Naval Affairs, 1789–1860	10 volumes
Public Finance, 1789–1860	32 volumes
Public Lands, 1789–1860	8 volumes

PUBLIC LANDS

Colonial land grants are not federal records. They are state records usually found in the archives of the original states, and many of the records have been published. Sales and other distribution of state lands, such as the Georgia land lotteries or the Texas headright (to Republic settlers) and pre-emption (homestead) grants, are also state records found at state land offices, surveyor general offices, and archives. Abstracts of many such records are published. Over the years, the federal government acquired land in the state land states for government offices, military use, and post offices. Subsequent sale of such land back to private hands may also be shown in federal records.

As the original states ceded their western land claims to the Confederation government in the 1780s, Congress had to decide not only on a government for the new lands and a policy for the native peoples still living on much of that land, but also on a system of surveying and selling the land. This public domain was a vast area, still east of the Mississippi River, but soon to expand into the Louisiana Purchase and on to the Pacific Ocean. Debating the New England system of presurveyed townships and the Southern system of indiscriminate and irregular tracts, Congress adopted the Ordinance of 1785, which established the basis for public land organization and policy in areas now called the public land states. They include all states west of the Mississippi River, except Texas and Hawaii, and these states east of the river: Alabama, Florida, Illinois, Indiana, Michigan, Mississippi, Ohio, and Wisconsin. Louisiana and Minnesota, split by the river, are public land states considered part of the first tier west of the river.

Under the Ordinance of 1785, all federal lands were to be surveyed into six-mile-wide vertical strips called ranges and six-mile-wide horizontal strips of townships. Like the longitude lines on which they are based, ranges are numbered east or west of a principal meridian, e.g., Range 14 West (R14W). Like latitude lines, township strips are numbered north or south of base lines, e.g., Township 10 North (T10N). Range and township strips intersect to form blocks of land (townships), each six miles square. Within each block, six miles by six miles, are thirty-six one-mile-square-sections, and they are numbered, e.g., S1, S2, etc., to S36, as shown in the chart "One Standard Township in the Rectangular Survey System," on page 214. Each section typically contains 640 acres, although some may be surveyed at a little less than that amount. Some townships have fewer than thirty-six sections, and some sections may have irregular shapes due to natural features of the land, such as lakes, swamps, canyons, and rivers.

Sections can be subdivided into quarter-sections—Northeast ¼, Northwest ¼, Southeast ¼, and Southwest ¼—each containing 160 acres. Smaller tracts may exist within the quarter sections, as shown in the chart "One Section of Land," on page 215. Sections with irregular shapes may have lot numbers.

One Standard Township in the Rectangular Survey System

36 T3N R3W	31 T3N R2W	32	33	34	35	36 T3N R2W	31 T3N R1W
1 T2N R3W	6	5	4	3	2	1 T2N R2W	6 T2N R1W
12	7	8	9	10	11	12	7
13	18	17	16	15	14	13	18
24	19	20	21	22	23	24	19
25	30	29	28	27	26	25	30
36 T2N R3W	31	32	33	34	35	36 T2N R2W	31 T2N R1W
1 T1N R3W	6 T1N R2W	5	4	3	2	1 T1N R2W	6 T1N R1W

Showing neighboring sections in adjoining townships (N & S) and ranges (E & W)

Tract Books

The tract book contains the record of each patent—the first transfer of each piece of public domain from the federal government to an individual citizen or company. County deed records reflect subsequent sales.

The tract book is one place to look for a legal description of ancestral land. Since the tract books and the related township plats (maps) are arranged by range, township, and section, they can also help researchers identify ancestral neighbors, especially in an area where many tracts were purchased within the same time frame. In this way, tract books also act as an index to original purchasers (patentees) in an area. These federal records are especially useful in counties that have lost deed records in courthouse fires.

Two sets of tract books were kept. The federal government set of tract books also continued to record the ownership history of land that reverted back to the government. Tract books and plats for eastern public land states (east of the Mississippi River and the first tier of states on the west bank of the river) are located at the Bureau of Land Management (BLM) Eastern States Office, 7450 Boston Boulevard, Springfield, Virginia 22153. (This BLM office was formerly in Alexandria, Virginia.)

Federal tract books, local land office tract books, or copies for the western states are housed in various places—a Bureau of Land Management state office, state land offices, state historical societies or archives, county courthouses, or the National Archives or its regional branch that serves the state. The Fort Worth regional archives, for example, has Oklahoma tract books. The NARA regional branches in Los Angeles (Laguna Niguel), San Francisco (San Bruno), and Denver have some tract books and plats for their regions.

One Section of Land

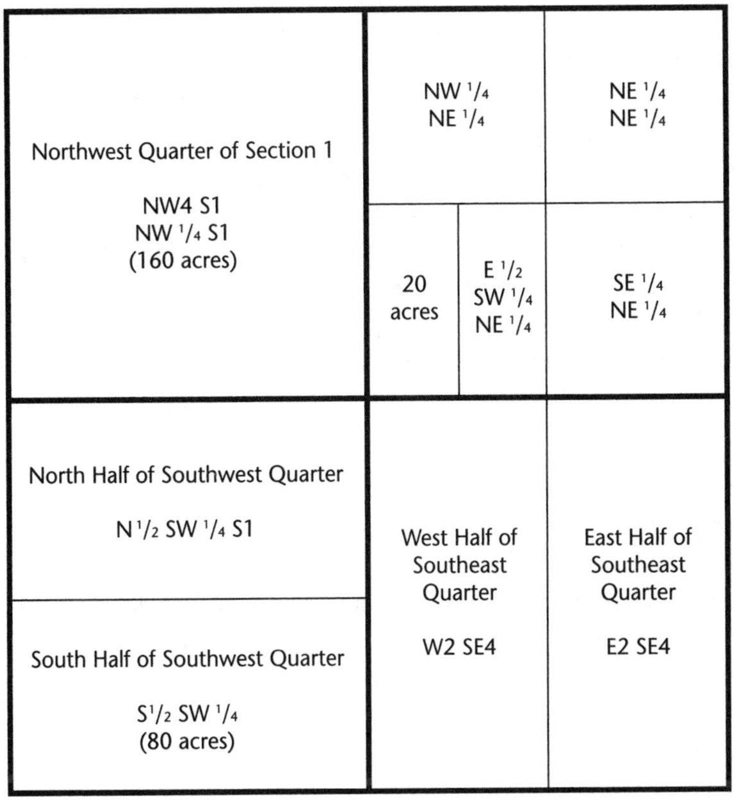

Contact other regional archives for their holdings. Some tract books are available on microfilm at research libraries and from the Family History Library. The Cartographic Branch of the National Archives has some township plats.

Electronic Searches

Information from the BLM Eastern States tract books is available in two electronic formats: CD-ROM and Internet database. **Of the two, the Internet option is newer, quicker, and easier to use.** The CD-ROMs are available from some booksellers and through the Government Printing Office, Superintendent of Documents, P.O. Box 371954, Pittsburgh, Pennsylvania 15250-7954; phone (202) 512-1800. The states available on CD-ROM are Alabama, Arkansas, Florida, Louisiana, Michigan, Minnesota, Mississippi, Ohio, and Wisconsin. The CDs allow a search by name, including spelling variations, or legal description. The results show you the patentee's name, the legal description of land, the land office, the acreage, the document (certificate) number, and the signature date, which is the recording/filing date and not necessarily the purchase/patent date.

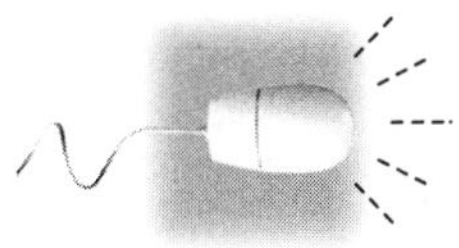

Internet Source

You can also search an entire section or township to identify the original patentees for the ancestral neighborhood. They may or may not have lived on the land when your ancestor lived there, but the process is one way of beginning to re-create the ancestral cluster of neighbors.

Patent information for the Eastern States through the 1950s, some pre-1908 patents (for Kansas, Oklahoma, and Nebraska), and post-1908 patents for western states are also available on an easy-to-use database on the BLM Web site <www.glorecords.blm.gov/> under "Search Land Patents." Using a "basic search," you can determine whether a specific ancestor received a land patent in a specific state and learn the location, acreage, land office, signature date, and document number. Using the "standard search," you can identify other patentees in the township by (1) using the township and range numbers and the state and land office names as search criteria and (2) choosing a display of results by patentee names. If you also limit the search with a section number, you can identify other patentees in a specific section. (At this writing, Iowa is the only Eastern State with records not online; the plan is to have them in the database in 2004.)

Use the chart "One Standard Township" to identify the sections that adjoin each other within each township. Sometimes, ancestors lived in one section but had relatives or close friends whose land was in an adjoining section or township. Thus, either the CD-ROM or online search can facilitate study of the ancestral neighborhood as a tool of cluster genealogy. From the Web site, you can view and print out a copy of the final patent document. Figure 6-6 shows the patent of Israel Walkup of Pettis County, Missouri, who purchased his eighty acres through a cash entry sale.

Patents and Land Entry Files

Using the document or certificate number given in the CD-ROM or online search, you can request the complete land entry file.

The patent was the transfer of land from the government to private ownership. The tract book and the patentee's final certificate document that transfer. However, other documents were created in the process, depending on the act of Congress under which the land was sold—cash entry, credit, homestead, military bounty land warrants, timber culture, mining, and others. Some of these laws provided for the transfer without the need for other documents; the file may contain only the receipt for payment. Other laws, especially for homesteads and timber culture land, set up a list of prerequisites that the patentee had to meet in order to get the final certificate. These requirements generated records for the individual's case file as the applicant documented his or her compliance with the law: marriage, citizenship, military service, length of residence on the land, improvements to the land, and/or affidavits of supporting witnesses (often relatives or neighbors).

Thus, the individual case file for each land entry is the source of potentially valuable information for genealogists, especially in the case of settlers under the Homestead Act of 1862 or the Timber Culture Acts of 1873, 1874, and 1878. According to the Homestead Act, 160 acres of unclaimed land was available to any citizen (or alien who had legally declared his intention to become a citizen) for a small filing fee, as well as five years residence on and improvement of the land. In the case of immigrants, the case file often includes naturalization papers. In order to obtain the final patent, the applicant had to provide proof of residency and land improvement. Proof involved affidavits of the claimant and witnesses answering a number of questions, including descriptions of the dwelling, outbuildings, and cultivation. When Minerva P. Shores, an unmarried native-born citizen, filed her final papers for her Nebraska homestead in 1889, she and witnesses confirmed that she had lived on the land since April 1883, had built a sod house ten feet by twelve feet with one window and one door, had planted trees and cultivated fifteen acres in crops for three years, and had made continuous residence on the land except for about three months when she left to earn money for her support.

According to the Timber Culture Acts, created "to encourage the growth of timber on the western prairies," an applicant had to be a citizen over age twenty-one or the head of a family, choose land that was naturally void of timber, plant and maintain trees on a certain number of acres (which changed over the years), provide proof of fulfilling the requirements, and pay a filing fee. Because it was difficult on the Great Plains to keep a

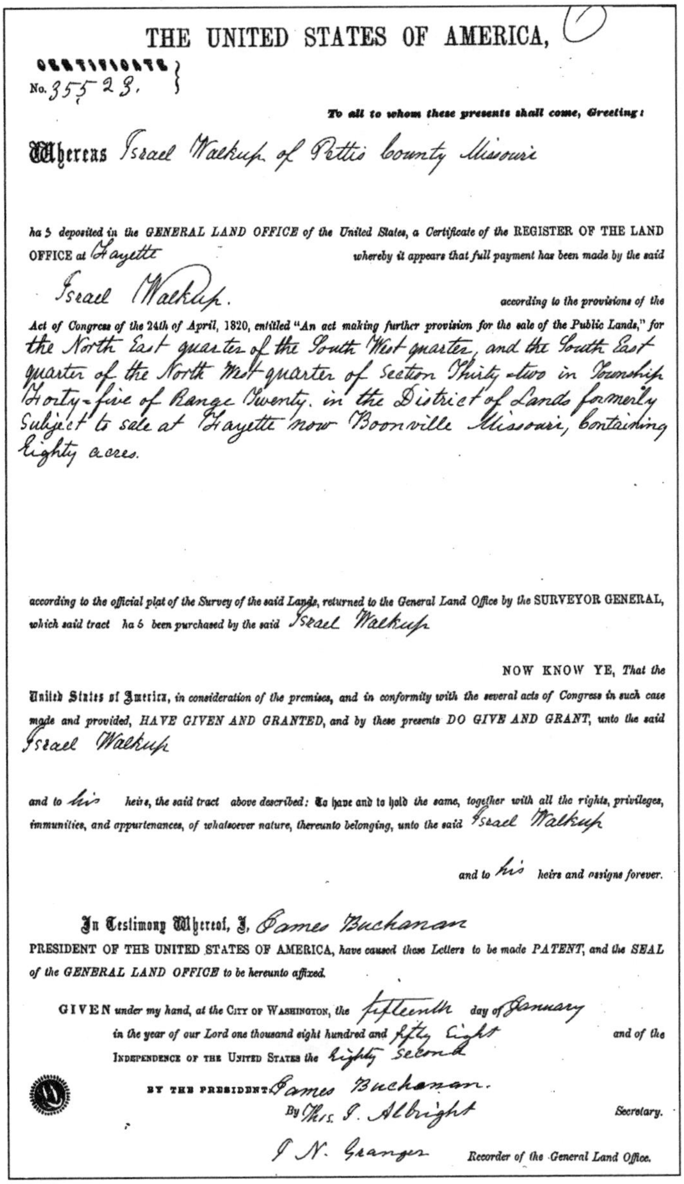

THE UNITED STATES OF AMERICA,

CERTIFICATE No. 35523.

To all to whom these presents shall come, Greeting:

Whereas Israel Walkup of Pettis County Missouri

has deposited in the GENERAL LAND OFFICE of the United States, a Certificate of the REGISTER OF THE LAND OFFICE at Fayette whereby it appears that full payment has been made by the said Israel Walkup. according to the provisions of the Act of Congress of the 24th of April, 1820, entitled "An act making further provision for the sale of the Public Lands," for the North East quarter of the South West quarter, and the South East quarter of the North West quarter of Section Thirty-two in Township Forty-five of Range Twenty. in the District of Lands formerly Subject to sale at Fayette now Boonville Missouri, containing Eighty acres.

according to the official plat of the Survey of the said Lands, returned to the General Land Office by the SURVEYOR GENERAL, which said tract has been purchased by the said Israel Walkup

NOW KNOW YE, That the United States of America, in consideration of the premises, and in conformity with the several acts of Congress in such case made and provided, HAVE GIVEN AND GRANTED, and by these presents DO GIVE AND GRANT, unto the said Israel Walkup

and to his heirs, the said tract above described: To have and to hold the same, together with all the rights, privileges, immunities, and appurtenances, of whatsoever nature, thereunto belonging, unto the said Israel Walkup

and to his heirs and assigns forever.

In Testimony Whereof, I, James Buchanan PRESIDENT OF THE UNITED STATES OF AMERICA, have caused these Letters to be made PATENT, and the SEAL of the GENERAL LAND OFFICE to be hereunto affixed.

GIVEN under my hand, at the CITY OF WASHINGTON, the fifteenth day of January in the year of our Lord one thousand eight hundred and fifty Eight and of the INDEPENDENCE OF THE UNITED STATES the Eighty Second

BY THE PRESIDENT: James Buchanan.

By Jas. S. Albright Secretary.

J. N. Granger Recorder of the General Land Office.

Figure 6-6 Federal land patent of Israel Walkup, Pettis County, Missouri, 1858, certificate 35523, from <www.glorecords.blm.gov/Patent/Search/Image.asp>, accessed 13 January 2003.

large number of trees alive and in good condition for eight to ten years, as required, many applicants never completed their patents.

Additional information in the land entry files may include a former residence and the date of the receipt for actual payment for the land. The final patents were issued later. The "signature date" in the database is usually the date of the patent and is often several months to a year after the patentee actually acquired and settled the land. Some applicants died between the two events, and genealogists have been confused by the appearance of someone acquiring land after death. However, land offices often did a large volume of business ("land-office business") and record keeping stacked up.

The National Archives has land-entry case files of the General Land Office dating from 1788 (Bureau of Land Management, RG49). When requesting copies of case files, you need to provide the state and land office names, legal description, name of patentee, and type of entry. (See pages 193–194 in this chapter for information on getting copies.)

In Florida, Oregon, and Washington, the federal government gave land to settlers to strengthen the U.S. claims to the land. Because the land was a gift or "donation," the records

TESTIMONY OF NICKOLAS BIEVER

When Nickolas Biever moved to Dakota Territory, he applied for a homestead on 19 August 1882. At the Yankton land office, he recorded his 160 acres of land in the northwest quarter of section 17, Township 100, and Range 56 in Hutchinson County. When he turned in his final paperwork in October 1887, at age twenty-six, his testimony and documents contained these statements pertinent to family history:

- "I am a farmer." Post office address: "Bridgewater, McCook County, Dakota."
- "I lived a part of the time here in Bridgewater & a part of the time at my brothers 1½ miles from this land."
- "I am a naturalized citizen of the U.S."
- "I have not voted since filing on this land."
- "Aug. 28th 1882. Built a frame house 10×12 value $30"
- "I built house myself. Present house was built in fall of 1883 and is habitable at all times of the year. . . . Frame house 16×22. Val. $200.00, Granary val. $10.00, Sod Barn 16×30, val. $25.00, 2 wells val. $25.00, 70 acres broken val. $210.00"
- Implements: "Wagon, 2 plows, seeder and drag, have owned same 3 years"
- Livestock: "2 horses, 2 cows, 8 hogs"
- "I was married in June 1887."
- "Once [absent from land], I went to West Bend Wis. in October 1884 to bring my father and mother out and returned in Nov. 1884."
- Furniture: "6 chairs, 1 table, 1 coupboard, 1 bedstead & bedding therefor, 1 stove and cucking utensils"
- Crops: "4 seasons, wheat, oats, corn & flax"
- United States District Court, Second Judicial District of Dakota Territory, 11 June 1884. "Nickolas Biever, having resided in the United States for more than three years preceding his twenty-first birthday and at least five years in the United States and at least one year in the Territory of Dakota, and having declared his intention to become a United States citizen, renounces allegiance to the King of Prussia and is permitted to take the oath of citizenship in the United States." *Alice Ellis*

of the patents are called donation land entries. Files at the National Archives include Florida records of 1842–1850 and Oregon-Washington records for 1851–1903.

When surveying and selling public lands, the federal government had to consider private claims on land granted by foreign governments (Britain, France, and Spain) when they owned the land. Evidence of these claims and the determinations made on their validity can be found in the *American State Papers*; the Serial Set; court records; possibly state archives; and, for Texas (state land, not federal), the General Land Office in Austin. One such report in the Serial Set is *Reports of the Committees on Private Land Claims of the Senate and*

House of Representatives, from the 19th Congress, 2d Session to the 44th Congress, 1st Session, Senate Miscellaneous Document 81 (45th Congress, 3d session) serial 1836. Many of the case files for such private claims are in the National Archives. Consult the *Guide to Genealogical Research in the National Archives* for more specific information; consult library catalogs for abstracts that have been published.

For Further Reference: Public Land

Academic and large public libraries often hold the books listed below. Consult library catalogs and WorldCat for books of land grant abstracts for specific counties or states.

Federal Land Grants in the Territory of Orleans, the Delta Parishes, adapted from the *American State Papers,* Class VIII *Public Lands*, Volume II and arranged by counties as they existed in 1812, by Charles R. Madwell Jr. New Orleans: Polyanthos Press, 1975.

Federal Land Series: A Calendar of Archival Materials on the Land Patents Issued by the United States Government, With Subject, Tract, and Name Indexes, 4 vols., by Clifford Neal Smith. Chicago, Ill.: American Library Association, 1972–1986. Volume I—1788–1810. Volume II—Federal Bounty Land Warrants of the American Revolution, 1799–1835. Volume III—1810–1814 (continuation of Volume I). Volume IV—Grants in the Virginia Military District of Ohio.

History of the Rectangular Survey System, Bureau of Land Management. Washington, D.C.: Government Printing Office, 1991.

Land & Property Research in the United States, by E. Wade Hone. Salt Lake City: Ancestry, 1997.

"Land and Tax Records," by William Thorndale. In *The Source: A Guidebook of American Genealogy*, Arlene Eakle and Johni Cerny, eds., 216–253. Salt Lake City: Ancestry, 1984.

Land Claims, Vincennes District: A Report and Documents From the Commissioner of the General Land Office in Relation to Land Claims in the Vincennes Land District in the State of Indiana, 1835, House Document 198 (23rd Congress, 2d session) serial 275, vol. 5. Reprint, Indianapolis: Indiana Historical Society, 1983.

The Land Office Business: The Settlement and Administration of American Public Lands, 1789–1837, by Malcolm J. Rohrbough. New York: Oxford University Press, 1968.

Land Title Origins: A Tale of Force and Fraud, by Alfred N. Chandler. New York: Robert Schalkenbach Foundation, 1945. Chapters on regions. Bibliography.

Opportunity and Challenge: The Story of BLM, by James Muhn, Hanson R. Stuart, and Peter D. Doran. Washington, D.C.: U.S. Department of the Interior, Bureau of Land Management, 1988.

Preliminary Inventory of the Land-Entry Papers of the General Land Office, by Harry P. Yoshpe and Philip P. Brower. Washington, D.C.: National Archives, 1949, 1981. Preliminary Inventory number 22. Inventory of National Archives holdings. Inquire about any changes due to redistribution of records and completion of Archives II.

BUREAU OF REFUGEES, FREEDMEN, AND ABANDONED LANDS

The federal government organized the bureau that was popularly called the Freedmen's Bureau under the War Department at the close of the Civil War, primarily to assist freed slaves in dealing with the many changes they faced after emancipation. However, the refugees in the name of the bureau were often white southerners displaced from their homes by the war. In many of the bureau records, researchers find white ancestors. See page 313 for an 1866 page from the North Carolina district of the bureau showing destitute families and individuals, both white and black, receiving food rations of corn meal and pork or bacon. Figure 6-7, below, is a letter from the acting assistant commissioner for South Carolina requesting government transportation for an old white man, reportedly a "soldier of the war of 1812," to travel from Columbia to Richmond, Virginia. As in this case, most of the transportation requests gave as a standard reason, " . . . and will relieve the government of his support."

Abandoned Lands

The bureau was involved in many varied activities, including surveying, seizing, leasing, and restoring to their owners "abandoned" lands in the former Confederate states. The microfilmed records describing these abandoned lands contain information on both black and white ancestors. The microfilmed records of the assistant commissioner for Tennessee, in *Descriptions of Abandoned Property and Its Former Owner*, contain information from Nashville that Mrs. Luzinca C. Brown owned and "abandoned" at least five pieces of property, of which the first was this house:

> One large 2 Story Brick Dwelling house on Cedar Street Nashville fronting the Capitol with Lot Extending from High Street to Vine & from Cedar to the Alley, & also has stable & outbuildings attached. This building was occupied by Gov Johnson as a residence upon his arrival here & up to Dec 17 1864 is still so occupied & no rent has been paid on the same. This Mrs. Brown left here at or about the time of the Stampede of the Confederates & went South, but where she is at this Date Dec 17 1864 is not known, having been reported to be in Europe &c, &c, &c. [Undated note added in margin: "restored."]

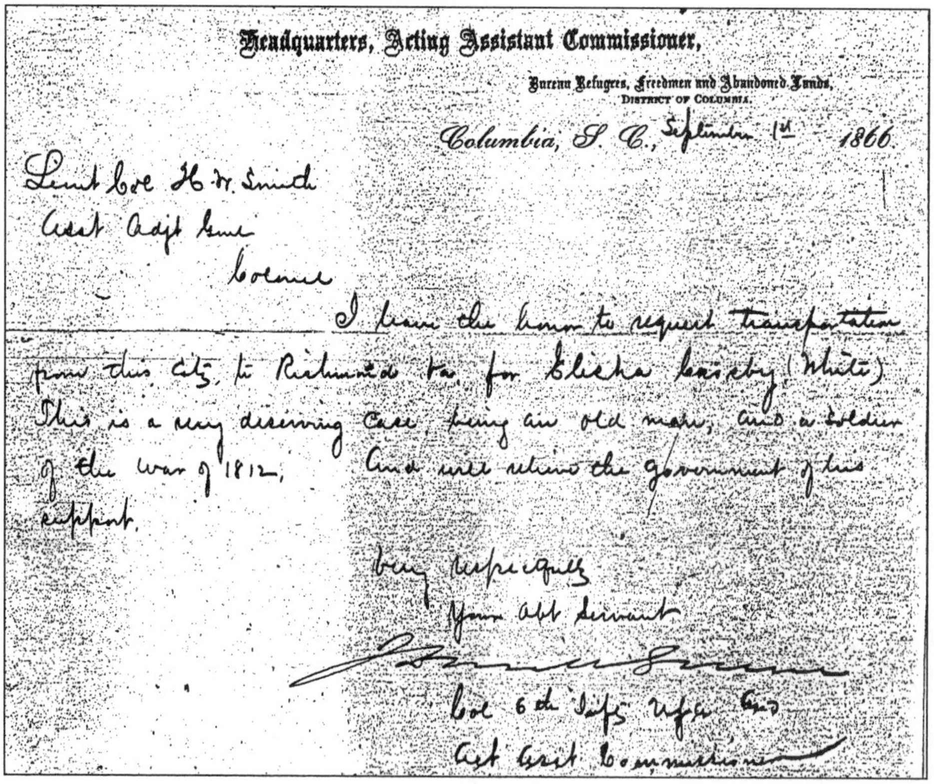

Headquarters, Acting Assistant Commissioner,
Bureau Refugees, Freedmen and Abandoned Lands,
Columbia, S. C., September 1st 1866.

Lieut Col H. W. Smith
Asst Adjt Genl
Colonel
I have the honor to request transportation from this City to Richmond Va. for Elisha [illegible] (White). This is a very deserving case being an old man, and a soldier of the war of 1812, and will relieve the government of his support.
Very respectfully
Your obt Servant
[illegible]
Col 6th Infy [illegible]
Act Asst Commissioner

Figure 6-7 Request for transportation, September 1866, to Lt. Col. H.W. Smith, in records of Assistant Commissioner for the state of South Carolina, Bureau of Refugees, Freedmen, and Abandoned Lands, 1865–1870, NARA microfilm M869, roll 44, target 5.

Also in Nashville were three brick dwellings owned by George Leascher, who "left here in Feb 1862 as a Capt in the Confederate Army & is at date *viz* Dec 17 1864 a prisoner of war at some point north of the Ohio River." One of his dwellings, on Jefferson Street, lot 49 on the map, was occupied by "Mrs. L." without rent. The government was using the other two to house laborers. (Although the owner's wife may well have been the Mrs. L. who lived in the house, the authorities considered it abandoned.)

On the same roll of microfilm, in *Lists, Reports, and Correspondence Pertaining to Land and Property, 1864–1868*, is information about George W. Holden of Bedford County, Tennessee. His farm, in the Ninth Civil District, was 112 acres, of which twenty were tillable. The property was seized on 22 March 1865, with the owner in the "Confederacy & reported in rebel service." A year later, in April 1866, a note was added to the entry: "Is in possession & has taken the Amnesty Oath."

Certainly not all Southern lands were considered abandoned, but the records are worth reading if you had families in these states. (See chapter nine for more on the bureau.)

The Freedmen's Bureau records also contain correspondence between the populace and the bureau offices as well as indentures and contracts made with former slaves. These are potential sources for identifying activities of ancestors, male and female, between censuses and in a very tumultuous period of Southern history. For more details about the records of the bureau, see also

- *Preliminary Inventory of the Field Offices of the Bureau of Refugees, Freedmen, and Abandoned Lands*, Elaine Everly and Willna Pacheli, comp. NM-95. Washington, D.C.: National Archives and Records Service, 1974.
- *Records of the Bureau of Refugees, Freedmen, and Abandoned Lands, Washington Headquarters*, Elaine Everly, comp. Preliminary Inventory No. 174. Washington, D.C.: National Archives and Records Service, 1973.

FEDERAL COURTS

The majority of court cases in the United States originate in state court systems. Therefore, their records are likely to have pertinent information for more genealogists than do federal courts. However, many federal cases do contain genealogical material.

The federal court system that Congress created in 1789 remained virtually the same until 1891. The lower level is still the district courts, of which ninety-four now exist, with at least one in each state or territory and the District of Columbia. These are the federal trial courts with original jurisdiction. Until 1891, the circuit courts were "circuit-riding" judges who had both original and appellate jurisdiction and heard cases in various locations within the circuit. In 1891, Congress created the federal courts of appeals, one for each judicial circuit, as an intermediate appellate level and took away the appellate jurisdiction of the circuit courts. Then in 1911, Congress discontinued the circuit courts. The high court remains the Supreme Court.

The list of states assigned to most of the federal circuits has changed significantly over the years since 1789, especially as new states were admitted to the Union. Before 1980, for example, states now in the Eleventh Circuit were in the Fifth. Before 1929, states in the Tenth Circuit were in the Eighth. *The Archives: A Guide to the National Archives Field Branches* and each regional *Guide to Records in the National Archives* (both cited earlier in this chapter) can help you identify the location of specific records. (After these publications were issued, many of the Alaska records were transferred to the Anchorage regional archives.) In addition, the Federal Judicial Center Web site <www.fjc.gov/history/home.nsf> under "U.S. Circuit Courts, 1789–1912," presents a detailed description of the changes in the U.S. circuits as states were moved from one to another and a description of the makeup of the territory served by the federal courts of appeals. Records from the federal courts of appeals are spread among the regional National Archives branches, the records from each circuit housed in the branch serving the city where the court usually sits.

Certain special courts exist outside this ladder, notably the Court of Claims, which began in 1855 to hear cases against the United States based on any federal law, regulation, or government contract. Later called the U.S. Claims Court, since 1992 this body has been called the U.S. Court of Federal Claims. Claims Court records are at the National Archives (RG123), as are Supreme Court records (RG267). Appeals of claims cases used to go to the Supreme Court but since 1982 have gone to the Court of Appeals for the Federal Circuit, which also replaced the U.S. Court of Customs and Patent Appeals. U.S. Court of Claims docket cards for Congressional case files for 1884–1943 have been microfilmed as M2007.

Tip

If you know of a federal case involving an ancestor or another family member, try to determine the court and the approximate date before making a search. (See page 297.) Most of the federal district and circuit court records, including case files, are arranged chronologically by court. Such records are kept at the court for only twenty-five to thirty years before being sent to the National Archives regional branch that serves the state where the court is located. (See Appendix A for National Archives branches and states they serve.) Contact the regional archives for their specific holdings.

The kinds of judicial records available vary from court to court but may include minute and docket books, record and final record books, case files, and some indexes. Cases involve such issues as bankruptcy, naturalization, patent and copyright infringement, land disputes, water and fishing rights, civil rights, Indian rights, draft evasion, income tax evasion, admiralty cases, mail theft, counterfeiting, and prohibition violations (1920s). Several examples of genealogical material in federal cases are presented in chapter eight under "Appellate Courts." The National Archives regional branches whose states were once territories also have some territorial court records. The Fort Worth and Atlanta (East Point) regional branches also have some Confederate court records for their states. Some of the branches have a few colonial and state court records.

OTHER FEDERAL RECORDS

Millions of federal records illustrate the government's interaction with individuals. See books such as *Guide to Genealogical Research in the National Archives of the United States* for more information on the hundreds of record groups that contain information on ancestors. Most remain unfilmed, but microfilming continues.

Passports

Passports were not required for U.S. citizens traveling abroad until the early twentieth century, and the issuing process was not standardized. However, in the records of the State Department (RG59 and RG84), the National Archives has applications for passports issued from about 1789 forward. In order to make a search, you need the name of the individual receiving the passport and the approximate date of departure or issue. Indexes are arranged by date and then loosely by alphabet. The applications themselves have been filmed. Information on applications varies but can include age, birthplace, citizenship and naturalization, residence, physical description, occupation, affidavits of character, and family data. Passport applications of naturalized citizens often show the court and date of their naturalization. (See pages 397 and 407.)

Figure 6-8, below, shows the passport application filed on 20 May 1867 for the not-yet-well-known Samuel L. Clemens (whom we know best as Mark Twain) as he prepared for a trip abroad. He sailed from New York on 8 June 1867 on the *Quaker City* for a transatlantic pleasure and "reporting" trip. One result of the trip was his introduction to Charles Langdon, whose sister Clemens later married. The other result was the entertaining 1869 book *The Innocents Abroad.*

Microfilmed indexes and passport applications are available at research libraries and through the Family History Library. National Archives microfilm publications include the following:

- M1371—*Registers and Indexes for Passport Applications, 1810–1906* (13 rolls)
- M1372—*Passport Applications, 1795–1905* (694 rolls)
- M1490—*Passport Applications, January 2, 1906–March 31, 1923* (2,740 rolls)
- 1834—*Emergency Passport Applications (Passports Issued Abroad), 1877–1907* (56 rolls)
- M1848—*Index to Passport Applications, 1850–52, 1869–80, 1881, 1906–23* (61 rolls)

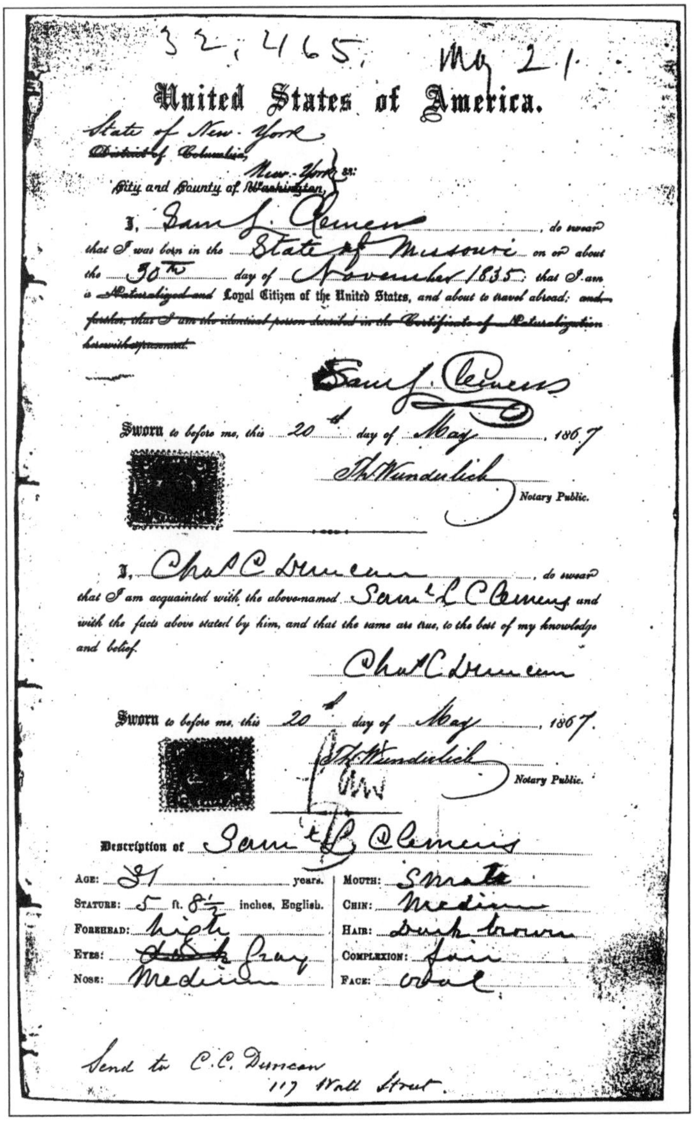

32465, May 21.

United States of America.

State of New York
~~District of Columbia~~
City and County of ~~Washington~~ New York ss:

I, Sam L. Clemens, do swear that I was born in the State of Missouri on or about the 30th day of November 1835; that I am a ~~Naturalized and~~ Loyal Citizen of the United States, and about to travel abroad; ~~and further, that I am the identical person described in the Certificate of Naturalization herewith presented.~~

Sam L. Clemens

Sworn to before me, this 20th day of May, 1867

Th. Wunderlich, Notary Public.

I, Chas C Duncan, do swear that I am acquainted with the abovenamed Sam L Clemens and with the facts above stated by him, and that the same are true, to the best of my knowledge and belief.

Chas C Duncan

Sworn to before me, this 20th day of May, 1867.

Th. Wunderlich, Notary Public.

Description of Sam L Clemens

Age: 31 years.	Mouth: Small
Stature: 5 ft. 8½ inches, English.	Chin: Medium
Forehead: high	Hair: Dark brown
Eyes: Dark Gray	Complexion: fair
Nose: Medium	Face: oval

Send to C.C. Duncan 117 Wall Street.

Figure 6-8 Passport application of Samuel L. Clemens, vol. 318, #32465, 20 May 1867, New York, in Passport Applications, 1795–1905, NARA M1372, FHL microfilm 1429880.

Social Security

Congress passed the Social Security law in August 1935, including state- and locally-administered programs for the aged needy and the blind. Post offices distributed the first Social Security applications in November 1936, and the Social Security administration (SSA) issued more than thirty-five million cards in the first two years. As of 1 January 1937, when the first payroll taxes were collected, qualified workers began accumulating credits to apply toward old-age insurance benefits. From 1937 to 1940, retirees received a lump-sum payment, not monthly benefits, with about fifty-three thousand receiving small payments in 1937. In 1939 Congress added survivor benefits for spouses and minor children. At first, mostly industrial workers paid payroll taxes in order to be covered under the "old-age pension," and numerous categories of workers were "exempt" from coverage, including domestic and farm workers, itinerant and hospital workers, small-store proprietors, and the "casually employed." At the time Social Security began, a number of states were also instituting old-age assistance programs for the needy. (For more Social Security history, visit the Web site <www.ssa.gov>.)

For More Info

See "Railroad Records for Genealogical Research," by Wendy L. Elliott in the *National Genealogical Society Quarterly* 75 (December 1987): 271–277.

Government employees, railroad workers, and church employees participated in other programs. The Civil Service Retirement System began in 1920, and Congress created the Railroad Retirement Board in 1934. Visit the Railroad Retirement Board Web site at <www.rrb.gov/geneal.html> for information concerning genealogical use of the records. (See also page 156.) At this writing, the research fee is twenty-seven dollars—the same as for Social Security records—and records searches pertain only to deceased retirees. Living retirees may request their own records. You can write to the board at Office of Public Affairs, United States Railroad Retirement Board, 884 North Rush Street, Chicago, Illinois 60611-2092. Also see Cyndi's List for more Web sites dealing with railroad employment and research.

The U.S. Social Security Death Index (SSDI, mostly 1962 forward), which includes railroad retirees, is available on CD-ROM at Family History Centers and research libraries. The database is also available free-of-charge on the FamilySearch and Ancestry.com Web sites. By entering the name of the deceased person, you can learn birth and death dates, the place where the Social Security card was issued, the Social Security number, and usually the residence of the person at the time of death. The index, though extensive, does not reflect all deaths since 1962. It includes deaths reported to the SSA for those with Social Security numbers or railroad retirees.

If the ancestor's name appears on the SSDI on the Ancestry.com Web site <www.ancestry.com>, **you can print out a letter of request to send to the Social Security Administration with the search fee for a copy of the person's original Social Security application (form SS-5).** This letter acknowledges that the person's name appears on the Social Security Death Index and saves you from having to provide further proof of death.

Timesaver

If you don't use the letter from the Web site, you can request an SS-5 by writing to the Social Security Administration, Freedom of Information Workgroup, 300 North Greene Street, P.O. Box 33022, Baltimore, Maryland 21290. Provide the ancestor's name, death date and proof of death (such as a death certificate), the Social Security number (often on the death certificate), and the search fee. At this writing, the fee is twenty-seven dollars.

The application for a Social Security number contains such information as full name, birth date and birthplace (especially helpful if the applicant was an immigrant), residence, employment information, and often either parents' names or spouse's name. The death date may be included if the number was issued in order to process survivor benefits. (This situation occurred especially in the early years of the system.) Because the form was usually completed by the applicant, a parent, or the spouse, it can be a reliable source for research. It may be the only available source of birth information, especially for persons born before their states or cities required birth registration. If the person whose record you seek is living, he or she must sign a release authorizing you to obtain the information. An example of an SS-5 is shown in Figure 6-9, below.

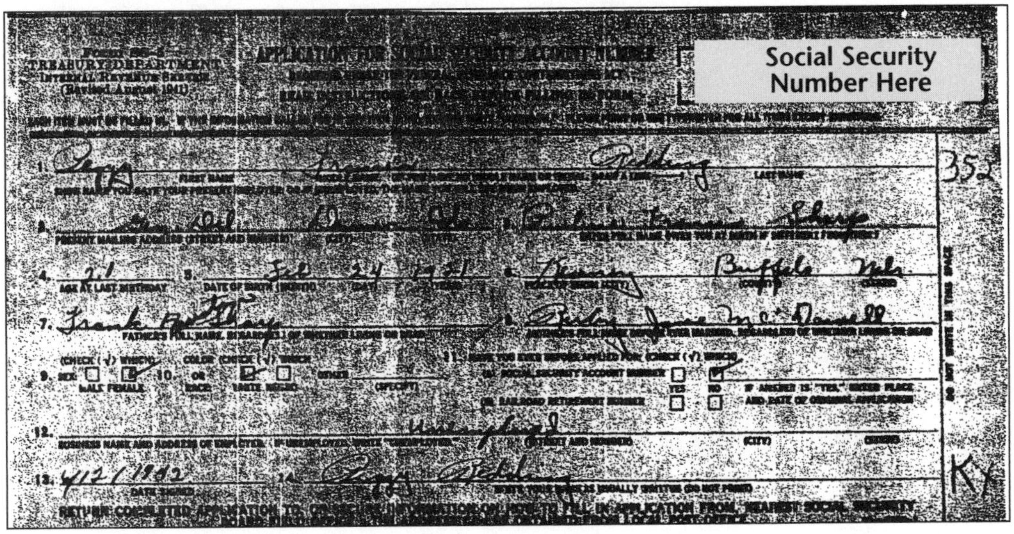

Figure 6-9 Social Security application of Peggy Frances Redding, 1942, 524-xx-xxxx, copy from Social Security Administration, Baltimore, Maryland.

Civilian Employees of the Government

Records of retired or former civil service (civilian) employees of the government are kept at the National Personnel Records Center, 111 Winnebago Street, St. Louis, Missouri 63118. Information on file usually includes birth date, employment data, and death date (if the person died while still employed). Records do extend back into the nineteenth century. To obtain copies, you need to provide the ancestor's name; birth date; place and years of employment; Social Security number, if applicable; and proof of death, such as death certificate or newspaper obituary.

Southern Claims Commission

Many claims grew out of the Civil War, especially from property seizures by the Union Army. In 1871, Congress authorized a board of three commissioners to consider claims of Southern citizens who had been loyal to the Union during the war. Popularly called the Southern Claims Commission, this body received claims of many kinds. The commission had to decide on the true loyalty of the claimants and the nature and monetary value of the claims and then report its findings to Congress. Of more than 22,000 claims submitted, the commission approved about 7,100. The records generated are voluminous; some have been published in microform.

- M1407—*Barred and Disallowed Case Files of the Southern Claims Commission, 1871–1880*, on 4,829 microfiche cards.
- M1658—*Southern Claims Commission Approved Claims: Georgia, 1871–1880*, on 1,100 microfiche cards.
- M2062—*Southern Claims Commission Approved Claims, 1871–1880: Alabama*, on 36 rolls of microfilm.
- M87—*Records of the Commissioners of Claims (Southern Claims Commission), 1871–1880*, on 14 rolls of microfilm. Roll 13 contains a geographical index to the submitted claims, arranged by state, then by county, and thereunder by the names of individual

ANSWERS ON LOCATION

Family records showed that James Thomas Mitchum died in an accident on the docks at Charleston, South Carolina, on 20 February 1919. An article in the *Charleston News & Courier* the following day reported the accident. About 4:15 P.M., Mitchum, a switchman, was switching some boxcars at the Navy Yard when he fell between them while attempting to make a coupling and was "so crushed that he died about an hour later" at the Navy Yard dispensary.

Since he died on navy, thus federal, property, would records at the National Archives add further information? Given the date and location of the accident, National Archives staff pulled records of the Judge Advocate General's office at Charleston. These papers are organized by date, each file being the investigation of a separate case. The inquiry began the day after Mitchum's death.

The medical officer reported that Mitchum was a civilian employee who received multiple fractures and crushed bones; his body had been turned over to Stuhr Undertaking Establishment (funeral home) at the request of the family and the Brotherhood of Railway Trainmen, of which he was a member. A naval officer of the Yard corroborated the medical officer's report. The yardmaster testified that Mitchum had gone to work at the Yard on February 6, only two weeks prior to his death. He had a work history as a switchman and brakeman with several railroads between 1911 and 1918, some in Charleston and the most recent in Bridgeport, Connecticut. Co-workers explained the accident in detail and affirmed that at the time of the accident the cars were on a curve, a position that required special precautions. Mitchum had assured them that, with his prior experience, he was aware of the safety precautions they were instructed to follow. The board concluded that the victim "was performing duties proper for his rating and for which he was qualified by his experience" and that his death was "due primarily and solely to his own carelessness in going between cars which were being coupled." They blamed no one else and concluded their report, which they forwarded to the Secretary of the Navy, Office of the Solicitor. Yes, some answers and further clues for genealogical research were in this file. This is one of thousands of examples of research possibilities at the National Archives. *Karen F. Stanley*

claimants. Roll 14 contains a consolidated alphabetical index to the claimants. The consolidated index is also published in *Southern Loyalists in the Civil War: The Southern Claims Commission*, by Gary B. Mills (Baltimore: Genealogical Publishing Co., 1994). A typical claim is that of William Sherwood of Virginia, commission number 22111. In 1875, he submitted a claim for the loss of a horse, oats, and fodder, which he valued at $410. Of that amount, the commission allowed $180. Claims for livestock, crops, foodstuffs, provisions, and quartermaster stores make up the majority of the claims.

Special Collections

Genealogists often benefit from using special collections, especially newspapers, maps, and manuscripts. These collections are found at many state, academic, and other research libraries and may contain genealogical, historical, or reference information.

NEWSPAPERS

Newspapers can be remarkable sources of information for local history and genealogy. Although some newspapers exist from the eighteenth century, for the most part, they are tools for nineteenth- and twentieth-century research. The most significant genealogical information researchers might find in local newspapers includes notices about marriages and deaths and facts that link individuals into specific families. However, from these pages also come advertisements, business announcements, legal notices, real estate notices, social news, personal news, and much local history and flavor. Merely finding an ancestor in a given place at a given time can be important to research. In rural areas, the newspaper in the county seat often served the entire county and generally carried more local news and personal items than did newspapers of large cities, which focused more on state, national, and international politics.

Marriage, Birth, and Death Notices

Simple marriage notices may contain little more than the names of the bride and groom and the wedding date, but sometimes they provide clues to other information. A typical brief announcement was one of 4 December 1869 in which the *Bolivar* (*Tennessee*) *Bulletin* reported: married on November 30 at the residence of the bride's father [unnamed] by Rev. F.P. Mullally, Pitser Blalock and Mary C. Coleman.

The *New York Tribune* on 29 April 1868 gave more information (italics added for illustration): married "on *Monday*, April 27, *at Hartford*, by the Rev. Mr. Fisher, Wm. F. Geisse to Ella D., *only daughter of D. B. Coe, esq., of Brooklyn*." More elaborate notices included names of other relatives and attendants and descriptions of the celebration. Of course, the clergymen's names may be clues to religious affiliation.

USING NEWSPAPERS TO SOLVE A GENEALOGICAL PROBLEM

A book of Juneau County, Wisconsin, tombstone inscription transcriptions showed that Martha H. Grote, wife of C.H. Grote, died on 5 March 1889, age thirty-one years. However, an Iowa newspaper contained a notice that Martha's brother had attended the funeral of his last remaining sister, Marcella, in 1883. If Marcella was the last living sister, then Martha's death date must not have been 1889. The censuses of 1870 and 1880 enumerated Charles H. Grote, Martha's husband, with a wife named Elizabeth. The 1860 census showed his wife as Martha H. Since Elizabeth and Martha H. are not names likely to have been confused with each other, these were more likely two different wives. Since previous research had shown death notices in issues of the *Mauston Star* of Juneau County, Wisconsin, where the family lived, perhaps the newspaper would help determine when Martha H. Grote died. Because 8s and 6s can be confused in reading old handwriting or tombstone inscriptions, perhaps Martha died in 1869 instead of 1889. Thus, I decided to get on interlibrary loan the issues of this newspaper for March and April 1869. The 11 March 1869 issue contained Martha's death notice, actually showing her death date as 5 March 1868. The year is likely a typographical error; it is not likely her death notice in her local newspaper would have appeared exactly a year after her death. Nevertheless, it was newspapers that demonstrated first the problem with the published tombstone transcription and then the solution. *Pat (Palmer) Metcalfe*

Births seemed to get the least attention in nineteenth-century newspapers, perhaps due to the fact that families were often large and the infant mortality rate was high. On 2 November 1900, an advertisement in *The (Franklin, Texas) Central Texan* reported that one-fourth of babies died before their first birthday; one-third, before they were five; and half before reaching fifteen. Because it is an advertisement, we may question the source and accuracy; however, the statistics make us aware of the risks to health and life before the days of "modern medicine." On 4 June 1914, the *Williamson County (Texas) Sun* published a fairly typical early-twentieth-century birth announcement: "Born last Thursday to Mr. and Mrs. C.R. Starnes of Granger, a boy." What was his name?

Warning

Often deaths were reported as simple notices, giving vital information but leaving the reader with unanswered questions. In New York, the *Daily Albany Argus* on Tuesday morning, 9 February 1830, reported that "WILLIS, the famous bugleman and leader of the West Point band died at that post on Monday and was buried with the honors of war." Did he have only one name? On which Monday did he die? Yesterday? Was he buried at West Point? Did he leave family?

The 2 November 1900 issue of the *Calvert (Texas) Chronicle* reported, as paraphrased here:

> Died four miles east of Calvert last Saturday, of malarial fever, Mrs. J.M. Oldham, who leaves a husband and a large number of children; burial was at Mt. Vernon with twenty to thirty members of the W.O.W. [Woodmen of the World fraternal organization], of which her husband is a member, attending.

From what was given, the researcher can calculate Mrs. Oldham's death date: the paper was printed on Friday; the previous Saturday was October 27. The researcher receives helpful clues about the cemetery, the family's residence, and the husband's W.O.W. membership. Unanswered, unfortunately, are the questions of her given and maiden names, the number and names of her surviving children; her age; and, in an area with many Oldhams, her husband's given name.

Even elaborate obituaries do not answer all questions, but they may furnish many details. A lengthy obituary for Rev. Henry Metcalf, printed 6 September 1887, gave the date of his birth in Georgia; the name of the Alabama town where he grew up; his wedding date and wife's maiden name; his conversion date; the date he was licensed as a Methodist preacher; the dates of his ordination as deacon and elder; information about his preaching and his last sermon; the dates of his death and burial; and the cemetery near Corsicana, Texas, where he was laid to rest. Not included in the obituary were names of the "many relatives" who mourned his death. His family kept the clipping (although no one recorded the name of the newspaper from which it came) because it contains much information not available elsewhere. For example, the couple married in 1845, probably in Dale County, Alabama, where marriage records were lost in a courthouse fire in 1884.

The genealogical information in this announcement from the *New York Tribune*, Wednesday, 29 April 1868, is the kind researchers hope to find: died "at Chatham Four Corners, on Sunday evening last, Mrs. Mary C. Woodbridge, wife of W.A. Woodbridge and daughter of the late Joshua Wingate of Hallowell, Maine."

Figure 7-1, on page 230, shows typical examples of nineteenth-century newspaper items, taken from issues of the *Painesville (Ohio) Telegraph* between January 5 and March 15 of 1848. The first column shows two death notices and two marriage announcements. Refer to the chart on date references when reading Figure 7-1.

Internet Source

Current obituaries may be online if the newspapers in which they appear are online. Depending on the newspaper, issues may be online only a few days, several months, or longer. Two Web sites that link to many daily newspapers are <www.gebbieinc.com/dailyint.htm> and <www.newspaperlinks.com/>.

DATE REFERENCES OFTEN FOUND IN NEWSPAPERS AND OTHER SOURCES

the 9th instant	means	the 9th of this month
the 30th ultimo	means	the 30th of last month
Tuesday last	means	the most recent Tuesday
Thursday next	means	the nearest Thursday to follow
February last	means	the most recent February
December last	means	the most recent December, even though it fell in a previous year

Although newspaper accounts of births, marriages, and deaths are sometimes the only accounts of the events that genealogists find and were usually published soon after the event with information furnished by family or friends, they may contain typographical or factual errors. Editors got a fair amount of their news by word of mouth and may not have checked out all the details or proofread their typesetting before printing. For example, what appears to be a retraction notice, although not an apology, in the *New Orleans Advocate* of 20 January 1866 said, "The reported death of M. Thiers has been contradicted." The box on page 228 illustrates one probable typographical error.

Figure 7-1 Composite of articles from *Painesville (Ohio) Telegraph*, January-March 1848, microfilm.

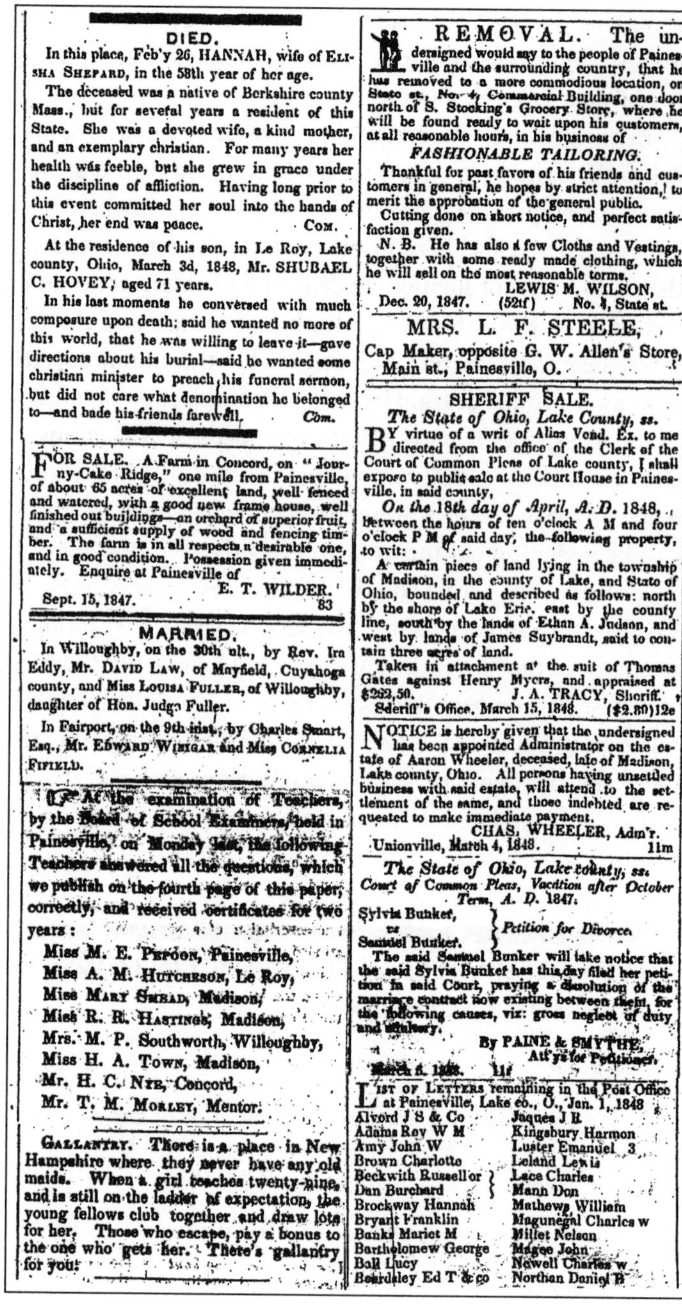

DIED.

In this place, Feb'y 26, HANNAH, wife of ELISHA SHEPARD, in the 58th year of her age.

The deceased was a native of Berkshire county Mass., but for several years a resident of this State. She was a devoted wife, a kind mother, and an exemplary christian. For many years her health was feeble, but she grew in grace under the discipline of affliction. Having long prior to this event committed her soul into the hands of Christ, her end was peace. COM.

At the residence of his son, in Le Roy, Lake county, Ohio, March 3d, 1848, Mr. SHUBAEL C. HOVEY, aged 71 years.

In his last moments he conversed with much composure upon death; said he wanted no more of this world, that he was willing to leave it—gave directions about his burial—said he wanted some christian minister to preach his funeral sermon, but did not care what denomination he belonged to—and bade his friends farewell. *Com.*

FOR SALE. A Farm in Concord, on "Journy-Cake Ridge," one mile from Painesville, of about 65 acres of excellent land, well fenced and watered, with a good new frame house, well finished out buildings—an orchard of superior fruit, and a sufficient supply of wood and fencing timber. The farm is in all respects a desirable one, and in good condition. Possession given immediately. Enquire at Painesville of

E. T. WILDER.

Sept. 15, 1847. 83

MARRIED.

In Willoughby, on the 30th ult., by Rev. Ira Eddy, Mr. DAVID LAW, of Mayfield, Cuyahoga county, and Miss LOUISA FULLER, of Willoughby, daughter of Hon. Judge Fuller.

In Fairport, on the 9th inst., by Charles Smart, Esq., Mr. EDWARD WINIGAR and Miss CORNELIA FIFIELD.

☞ At the examination of Teachers, by the Board of School Examiners, held in Painesville, on Monday last, the following Teachers answered all the questions, which we publish on the fourth page of this paper, correctly, and received certificates for two years:

Miss M. E. PERDON, Painesville,
Miss A. M. HUTCHESON, Le Roy,
Miss MARY SMEAD, Madison,
Miss R. R. HASTINGS, Madison,
Mrs. M. P. Southworth, Willoughby,
Miss H. A. TOWN, Madison,
Mr. H. C. NYE, Concord,
Mr. T. M. MORLEY, Mentor.

GALLANTRY. There is a place in New Hampshire where they never have any old maids. When a girl reaches twenty-nine, and is still on the ladder of expectation, the young fellows club together and draw lots for her. Those who escape, pay a bonus to the one who gets her. There's gallantry for you!

REMOVAL. The undersigned would say to the people of Painesville and the surrounding country, that he has removed to a more commodious location, on State st., No. 4, Commercial Building, one door north of S. Stocking's Grocery Store, where he will be found ready to wait upon his customers, at all reasonable hours, in his business of

FASHIONABLE TAILORING.

Thankful for past favors of his friends and customers in general, he hopes by strict attention, to merit the approbation of the general public.

Cutting done on short notice, and perfect satisfaction given.

N. B. He has also a few Cloths and Vestings, together with some ready made clothing, which he will sell on the most reasonable terms.

LEWIS M. WILSON,

Dec. 20, 1847. (52tf) No. 4, State st.

MRS. L. F. STEELE,

Cap Maker, opposite G. W. Allen's Store, Main st., Painesville, O.

SHERIFF SALE.

The State of Ohio, Lake County, ss.

BY virtue of a writ of Alias Vend. Ex. to me directed from the office of the Clerk of the Court of Common Pleas of Lake county, I shall expose to public sale at the Court House in Painesville, in said county,

On the 18th day of April, A. D. 1848, between the hours of ten o'clock A M and four o'clock P M of said day, the following property, to wit:

A certain piece of land lying in the township of Madison, in the county of Lake, and State of Ohio, bounded and described as follows: north by the shore of Lake Erie, east by the county line, south by the lands of Ethan A. Judson, and west by lands of James Suybrandt, said to contain three acres of land.

Taken in attachment at the suit of Thomas Gates against Henry Myers, and appraised at $262,50. J. A. TRACY, Sheriff.

Sheriff's Office, March 15, 1848. ($2.80)12e

NOTICE is hereby given that the undersigned has been appointed Administrator on the estate of Aaron Wheeler, deceased, late of Madison, Lake county, Ohio. All persons having unsettled business with said estate, will attend to the settlement of the same, and those indebted are requested to make immediate payment.

CHAS. WHEELER, Adm'r.

Unionville, March 4, 1848. 11m

The State of Ohio, Lake county, ss.

Court of Common Pleas, Vacation after October Term, A. D. 1847.

Sylvia Bunker, vs Samuel Bunker. } *Petition for Divorce.*

The said Samuel Bunker will take notice that the said Sylvia Bunker has this day filed her petition in said Court, praying a dissolution of the marriage contract now existing between them, for the following causes, viz: gross neglect of duty and adultery.

By PAINE & SMYTHE, Att'ys for Petitioner.

March 6, 1848. 11f

LIST OF LETTERS remaining in the Post Office at Painesville, Lake co., O., Jan. 1, 1848

Alvord J S & Co	Jaques J R
Adams Rev W M	Kingsbury Harmon
Amy John W	Luster Emanuel 3
Brown Charlotte	Leland Lewis
Beckwith Russell or Dan Burchard	Lace Charles
	Mann Don
Brockway Hannah	Mathews William
Bryant Franklin	Magunegal Charles w
Banks Mariet M	Millet Nelson
Bartholomew George	Magee John
Ball Lucy	Newell Charles w
Beardsley Ed T & co	Northan Daniel B

Other Notices

Besides state and national political and/or economic news and some serial literature, newspapers filled much of their space with advertisements, legal and personal notices, editorials, and local news.

Advertisements make up a considerable portion of early newspapers. In the twenty-four columns (four pages) of the 9 February 1830 issue of the *Daily Albany (New York) Argus*, advertisements filled 12½ columns, just over half the issue; 4½ columns concerned debtors; another 1½ columns were other legal notices; 4½ columns reported news of the New York legislature; and the remaining column reported general news.

Although books of newspaper abstracts often do not include advertisements and notices, these items can provide information for the genealogist. One example from the 9 February

1830 *Daily Albany Argus* reads: "TO LET, from the first of May next, that elegant three story brick dwelling house and lot No. 28 Montgomery st. [*sic*] occupied by G.W. Stanton. Also that commodious three story brick dwelling house and lot No. 33 Columbia st. occupied by B.G. Staats. Apply to C.W. Groesbeck & Co." Descendants of these families could find here the location and description of family residences, indication of a move, and the possibility that these families rented rather than owned their homes.

Figure 7-1 shows several advertisements. In column two, Lewis W. Wilson, a tailor, announced his removal to "a more commodious location," and Mrs. L.F. Steele advertised her cap-making business.

Legal notices in the *Daily Albany Argus* give good genealogical information. Besides notices about the many debtors in and out of jail, the 9 February 1830 issue printed an announcement that Charlotte Selby, of New York City, the widow and devisee of Skeffington Selby, deceased, was applying to the legislature for an act releasing to her the title to lot number 620 on the easterly side of Broadway in the city's Ninth Ward, extending from Broadway to Crosby Street. Was this the family residence? Do deed records give further information about this property?

Figure 7-1, column two, displays (1) a notice of a sheriff's sale (auction) of property to satisfy a debt resulting from a court case against Henry Myers; (2) an estate administrator's notice for persons having unsettled business with Aaron Wheeler, deceased, to "attend to the settlement of the same"; and (3) the announcement of a petition of divorce that Sylvia Bunker filed against Samuel Bunker for "gross neglect of duty and adultery."

Individual or personal notices and local gossip appear in newspapers as well. This one appears in the *Houston (Texas) Daily Post*, 20 October 1897. Why did he leave? Where did he go? Was he returned to the home?

> Corsicana, Texas, October 18.—John Holyby, a boy about 12 years of age, light hair and grey eyes, has left the State Orphans' Home. Any information that will lead to his discovery will be very much appreciated. Parties will please corre-

NEWSPAPER ADVERTISEMENT LEADS TO BREAKTHROUGH

All that was known about Eugenia C. Frierson, born about 1844 in Lafayette County, Mississippi, was that she married a Mr. Clardy and had two daughters. In the 1880 census, two Clardy children—Perl [*sic*], age eight, and Myra Lynn, age six—were enumerated with Frierson relatives in Lafayette County, Mississippi. Both girls were shown as "orphans" and born in "Miss." This information seemed to indicate that the parents were dead by 1880. While reading microfilm of the *Oxford (Mississippi) Falcon*, I was excited to notice an ad in the 14 June 1866 issue for "James G. Frierson & Martin L. Clardy, Attorneys At Law and Solicitors in Chancery," in Oxford, Mississippi. Recognizing James G. Frierson as Eugenia's brother, I thought it probable that Martin L. Clardy was her unidentified husband. Armed with a full name, I soon discovered that not only was Martin L. Clardy alive and well in 1880, he was a member of Congress from St. Francois County, Missouri! I was then able to locate Martin with wife Eugenia in St. Francois County in 1870 and learn that the couple's first child was a son, Charles. One lead from a newspaper advertisement gave me the full name of Eugenia's husband, a correct list of their children, and an appreciation for the admonition, "Never assume!" *Gay E. Carter*

> spond with the undersigned. All papers in the state are requested to copy this notice. Jink Evans, president of board of trustees, Corsicana, Texas.

Personal mentions may include local citizens who had returned from travels, former residents coming back for a visit, out-of-town visitors in town on business, and even local farmers who had brought fresh vegetables to the editor. Personal names also appear in lists of letters remaining in post offices—letters that had been sent to persons believed to be in the area and that were still unclaimed at a given date. Figure 7-1, second column, shows part of the 1 January 1848 list of letters at the Painesville, Ohio, post office.

NEWSPAPER HELPS DATE A FAMILY PHOTO

Someone labeled a three-generation photo of the F.A. Mood family with some, but not all, of the names. The ladies' dresses placed the picture in the mid-1890s; the family Bible register of births, marriages, and deaths suggested a date between November 1896 and April 1897. Then, a story in the *Williamson County (Texas) Sun* at Christmas 1896 named all the members of this family who had gathered for the holiday, the first time in ten years they had been together. The newspaper article confirmed the presence of the fifteen family members in the photo, secured the identity of the unlabeled faces in the photo, and indicated the photo was probably made during this holiday reunion.

Figure 7-1 contains a for sale notice through which E.T. Wilder was trying to sell a quite desirable farm and orchard on "Journey-Cake Ridge," originally advertised in September 1847 and still for sale in mid-February 1848. It is not clear whether Wilder was the owner or his agent; many resources present genealogists with good information but leave such pertinent questions unanswered. Although the local residents probably understood, we should not make assumptions without further study.

The *Bolivar* (*Tennessee*) *Palladium*, on 24 June 1831, advertised that William G. Steele was selling his tan-yard at Bolivar along with the forty acres adjoining it and twenty-three acres with a dwelling and an apple and peach orchard. Why was he selling out? He said, "I am entirely unacquainted with the business."

The *Mauston* (*Wisconsin*) *Star* repeated on 20 May 1869 Nicholas McCormick's "information wanted" notice, originally dated a month earlier:

> My son, Michael McCormick, left home in the town of Plymouth, Juneau county [Wisconsin] on the 12th of April. He is thirteen years old, five feet in height, light complexion, slightly freckled, hair light inclined to red, and shingled close; had a brown spot on his neck; had on at the time of leaving dark tweed pants, dark Garibaldi jacket with new sleeves and black wool hat. The undersigned will reward any one who will give information of his whereabouts, but will not be responsible for any debts of his contracting.

Editorial comments give readers an insight into local politics and circumstances. After the Civil War, the *Bremond* (*Texas*) *Central Texan* editor commented in his paper's second issue (4 June 1870) that the military still patrolled the streets of Calvert, and they could have better served the country by patrolling the frontier. (Post–Civil War military rule in Texas had officially ended on April 16, but this editor complained that not all the "enemy" troops had left the state.)

Editors also used fillers that included poetry, jokes, and interesting items from other cities or states. The *Painesville (Ohio) Telegraph* editor on 19 January 1848 informed his readers of six eclipses that would occur during the coming year, four of the sun and two of the moon, with their dates and visibility. In the same issue, as Figure 7-1 shows, the *Telegraph* editor, under the heading "Gallantry," told his readers why, in an unnamed (and fictitious?) place in New Hampshire, "they never have any old maids."

Local news, especially in rural areas and small cities, included epidemics, merchants with new buildings or new merchandise, ships arriving or departing, updates on railroad building in the area, fires, escapes from jail, fund-raising efforts, lists of hotel guests, voter lists, school and social events, church and lodge functions, political meetings, reports on the local economy, and area farm and crop news. The *Houston (Texas) Daily Post* announced proudly on 20 October 1897:

> The last of the patients pronounced by Dr. Guiteras as having yellow fever, made his appearance upon the street yesterday, Officer Henry Lee. He is still feeble from the effects of his long illness, but expects to be able to resume work today or tomorrow. This clears up all Dr. Guiteras' yellow fever patients in Houston, each having recovered with not a single death and no contagion with the period of incubation long since passed. These facts speak for themselves even more potently than health bulletins.

The community fund-raising project reported in the *Bolivar (Tennessee) Bulletin* during the summer and fall of 1866 was a Grand Tournament held at the local fairgrounds. The proceeds from the contests and food sales were to be used for a monument to the Confederate dead. Long lists of names appeared in the newspaper as committees, entrants, and judges were announced. The "Grand Gala Day" was actually two days of tilting contests, a "grand concert" by the ladies, and a "grand Masquerade." Miss Irene McNeal was crowned Queen of Love and Beauty by the winning Knight of the White Plume, N.B. Cross. The masquerade prize went to "the man on the mule."

As shown in column one of Figure 7-1, the Painesville, Ohio, Board of School Examiners had awarded two-year teaching certificates to eight teachers, based on a thirty-five-question exam. The questions dealt with teaching, language, arithmetic, and geography. Questions the successful candidates answered correctly included these:

1. Mention some of the *motives* that may properly be placed before pupils to incite them to exertion, and dispose them to obedience.
2. Write the second person plural of the verb *try*, in each tense of the Potential mode.
3. When may a noun be used without a governing word?
4. How many ways can you change the *form* of a fraction, without changing the value?
5. What mountains on the Globe rise above the limits of perpetual snow?
6. What advantages are gained by requiring all pupils in Geography to draw the outlines of countries?

Not only were the Grand Gala Day and the teacher's examinations local news, they are also social history. **Newspapers are full of such local "flavor,"** including detailed descriptions of graduation ceremonies, concerts and theatrical productions, church revivals, ice cream socials, funerals, political rallies with barbecues, parades, "entertainments," weddings, fiftieth wedding anniversary celebrations, bridal showers, and even bridge parties. This kind of news along with illustrations of fashions, automobiles, houses, furniture, farm-

Hidden Treasures

ing implements, and other merchandise help us understand more fully the world in which our ancestors lived.

When you find ancestors mentioned in such coverage, you have documentation of the ancestor in that place at that time. When you know your ancestors lived in the locale at the time, you can learn of the ancestor's friends, neighbors, associates, activities, and community. You begin to "know" your ancestor as a person and a community member, not just a name on a family group sheet or in a database. You may also begin to develop a sense of connection between generations. Read about Mother's Day celebrations on 10 May 1914, the first nationwide observance of the day; read about the grocer's supply of cranberries, pumpkins, turkeys, and other Thanksgiving fare in late-nineteenth- and early-twentieth-century advertisements. Some events have maintained continuity with which we can identify.

Ancestors were real people, with the same life events that we observe and experience. In addition to family letters and diaries, newspapers provide an insight into life in the past that few other sources can.

Religious/Denominational Newspapers

Besides local newspapers, many ancestors had access to religious papers, such as the *Connecticut Catholic* and *The Catholic Herald* (Nashville) in the late-nineteenth century. A number of interesting titles with apparent religious leanings were published in Providence, Rhode Island: the *Religious Intelligencer* of the 1820s, the *Gospel Messenger* of the 1840s, the *Christian Soldier* of the 1840s, the *Israelite* of the 1890s, the *Pentecostal Christian* about 1913, and the *Rhode Island Jewish Review* of the 1920s.

Long-running examples from the Methodist Episcopal Church were the *Northern Christian Advocate* (Auburn, New York; at least 1845–1878), the *Southern Christian Advocate* (1837–1948, published in various cities), the *New Orleans Christian Advocate* 1850–1946), and the *Pacific Christian Advocate* (1855–1929). These and the papers of other denominations and faiths carried marriage and death notices, advertisements, sermons, reports on conferences and schools, church history and biography, news from clergy or congregations in other cities or states, general information about the denomination or faith, reports from the "Young Men's Department," freedmen's issues after the Civil War, essays, poetry, and other literature considered appropriate for their readers. Figure 7-2, on page 235, is a section from the 20 January 1866 *New Orleans Advocate*, showing advertisements, marriage notices, and the last section of a long article on the state of the Methodist Episcopal church in Canada and the United States.

As items of interest to 1866 readers of the *New Orleans Advocate*, the editor included riddles, conundrums, and anecdotes such as the following from the January 6 and January 20 issues:

> What fishes have their eyes nearest together? (The smallest.)
> What must you keep, after giving it to another? (Your word.)
> Why is an old man's house more easily entered than a young one's? (His gait is broken and his locks are few.)
> A bright little girl, in playful anger, caught hold of an older sister, saying, "Now I'll shake the saw-dust out of you," thinking the human species was got up on the same plan as her dolls.

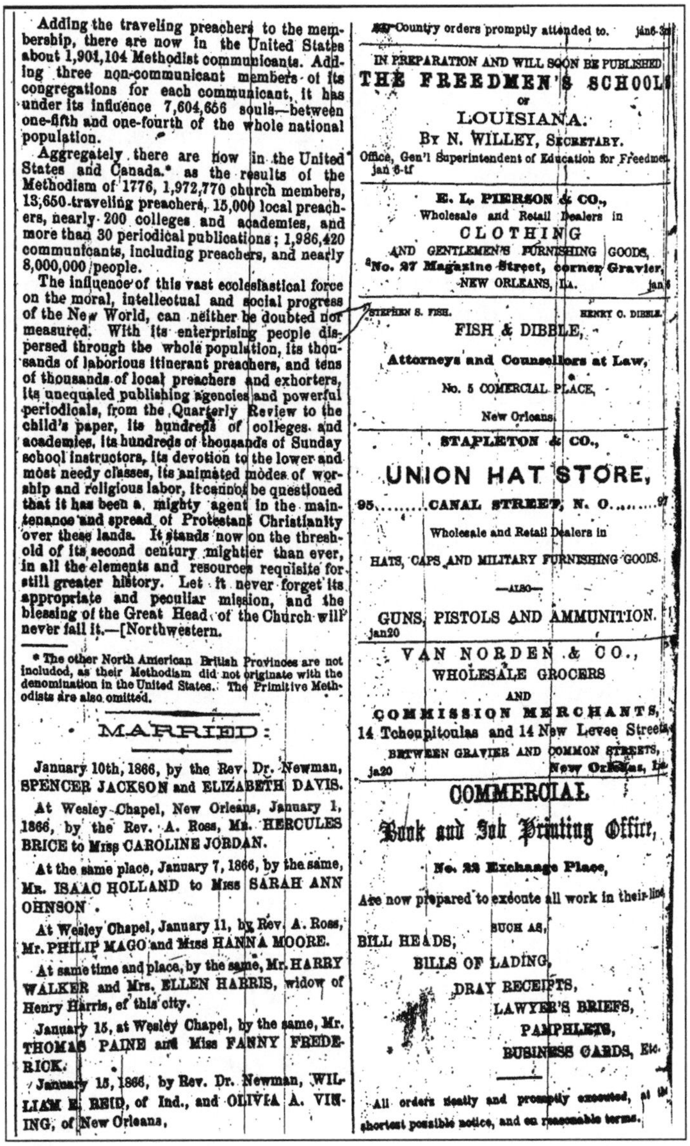

Adding the traveling preachers to the membership, there are now in the United States about 1,901,104 Methodist communicants. Adding three non-communicant members of its congregations for each communicant, it has under its influence 7,604,656 souls—between one-fifth and one-fourth of the whole national population.

Aggregately there are now in the United States and Canada,* as the results of the Methodism of 1776, 1,972,770 church members, 13,650 traveling preachers, 15,000 local preachers, nearly 200 colleges and academies, and more than 30 periodical publications; 1,986,420 communicants, including preachers, and nearly 8,000,000 people.

The influence of this vast ecclesiastical force on the moral, intellectual and social progress of the New World, can neither be doubted nor measured. With its enterprising people dispersed through the whole population, its thousands of laborious itinerant preachers, and tens of thousands of local preachers and exhorters, its unequaled publishing agencies and powerful periodicals, from the Quarterly Review to the child's paper, its hundreds of colleges and academies, its hundreds of thousands of Sunday school instructors, its devotion to the lower and most needy classes, its animated modes of worship and religious labor, it cannot be questioned that it has been a mighty agent in the maintenance and spread of Protestant Christianity over these lands. It stands now on the threshold of its second century mightier than ever, in all the elements and resources requisite for still greater history. Let it never forget its appropriate and peculiar mission, and the blessing of the Great Head of the Church will never fail it.—[Northwestern.

* The other North American British Provinces are not included, as their Methodism did not originate with the denomination in the United States. The Primitive Methodists are also omitted.

MARRIED:

January 10th, 1866, by the Rev. Dr. Newman, SPENCER JACKSON and ELIZABETH DAVIS.

At Wesley Chapel, New Orleans, January 1, 1866, by the Rev. A. Ross, Mr. HERCULES BRICE to Miss CAROLINE JORDAN.

At the same place, January 7, 1866, by the same, Mr. ISAAC HOLLAND to Miss SARAH ANN OHNSON.

At Wesley Chapel, January 11, by Rev. A. Ross, Mr. PHILIP MAGO and Miss HANNA MOORE.

At same time and place, by the same, Mr. HARRY WALKER and Mrs. ELLEN HARRIS, widow of Henry Harris, of this city.

January 15, at Wesley Chapel, by the same, Mr. THOMAS PAINE and Miss FANNY FREDERICK.

January 15, 1866, by Rev. Dr. Newman, WILLIAM E. REID, of Ind., and OLIVIA A. VINING, of New Orleans.

Country orders promptly attended to. jan6-3m

IN PREPARATION AND WILL SOON BE PUBLISHED
THE FREEDMEN'S SCHOOLS
OF
LOUISIANA.
BY N. WILLEY, SECRETARY.
Office, Gen'l Superintendent of Education for Freedmen.
jan 6-tf

E. L. PIERSON & CO.,
Wholesale and Retail Dealers in
CLOTHING
AND GENTLEMEN'S FURNISHING GOODS,
No. 27 Magazine Street, corner Gravier,
NEW ORLEANS, LA. jan6

STEPHEN S. FISH. HENRY C. DIBBLE.
FISH & DIBBLE,
Attorneys and Counsellors at Law,
No. 5 COMERCIAL PLACE,
New Orleans.

STAPLETON & CO.,
UNION HAT STORE,
95.........CANAL STREET, N. O..........97
Wholesale and Retail Dealers in
HATS, CAPS AND MILITARY FURNISHING GOODS.
—ALSO—
GUNS, PISTOLS AND AMMUNITION.
jan20

VAN NORDEN & CO.,
WHOLESALE GROCERS
AND
COMMISSION MERCHANTS,
14 Tchoupitoulas and 14 New Levee Streets,
BETWEEN GRAVIER AND COMMON STREETS,
ja20 New Orleans, La.

COMMERCIAL
Book and Job Printing Office,
No. 23 Exchange Place,
Are now prepared to execute all work in their line
SUCH AS,
BILL HEADS,
BILLS OF LADING,
DRAY RECEIPTS,
LAWYER'S BRIEFS,
PAMPHLETS,
BUSINESS CARDS, Etc.

All orders neatly and promptly executed, at the shortest possible notice, and on reasonable terms.

Figure 7-2 *New Orleans Advocate*, 20 January 1866, p. 8, col. 7–8, microfilm.

Finding Religious Newspapers

Faith-based and denominational newspapers are often held in the special collections of the principal colleges and universities of the faith or denomination, archives of the denominational administrative bodies, various divinity colleges and theological seminaries, large academic libraries, and state historical societies and archives. For example, Notre Dame University at South Bend, Indiana, maintains an extensive collection of Catholic newspapers (see <www.nd.edu/~archives/cathnews/>), as does the American Catholic Historical Society in Philadelphia <www.amchs.org>. The Presbyterian Historical Society in Philadelphia (for northern and western states) and in Montreat, North Carolina (for southern states), holds numerous Presbyterian newspapers.

Search engines and library catalogs are helpful in identifying special collections and books of abstracted genealogical information. One of the largest search mechanisms is WorldCat, often accessible through a local public or academic library. A subject search for Presbyterian newspapers identified numerous titles, including the long-running *Africo-American Presbyterian* (1879–1938) and the *Christian Observer* published in Kentucky (1870–1968), along with libraries that hold original or microfilm copies.

Other Newspapers

Ancestors also subscribed to ethnic, foreign language, labor, political, and special interest newspapers, such as those that supported the temperance movement. Titles from Providence, Rhode Island, illustrate the variety that at least the publishers thought worthy of the venture: the *Anti-Universalist* (1820s), *Masonic Mirror and Intelligencer* (1825), the *Freemasons Repository* (1870s), the *Temperance Herald* (1830s and 1840s), the *Voice of the Truth* (1867–1872), the *National Wine Merchants and Brewers Gazette* (1890s), the *Labor Advocate* (1910s), and the *Italian Review* (mid-1920s). Rochester, New York, for a few years around 1830, had the *Anti-Masonic Enquirer*, whose name apparently reflected its editorial leanings.

Ethnic and foreign language newspapers have existed in what is now the United States since the early eighteenth century, with German-language papers being among the earliest, most numerous, and most widely circulated. A number of these were published in Pennsylvania and New York. According to one source, by 1856, fifty-six German-language newspapers existed in the United States.[1] Ethnic papers, including African-American and Jewish papers, were published throughout the nineteenth and twentieth centuries; many are available on interlibrary loan.

Tip

Use subject or title searches in WorldCat to identify specific titles, available dates, holding institutions, and union lists. A subject search for Swedish-language newspapers, for example, revealed numerous titles published from the mid-nineteenth century to more recent decades in New York, Massachusetts, Illinois, Washington, Texas, California, Minnesota, and Michigan. WorldCat and library catalogs also can help you identify finding aids and histories such as these:

- *The Black Press in the Middle West, 1865–1985*, Henry Lewis Suggs, ed. Westport, Conn.: Greenwood Press, 1996.
- *Ethnic Newspapers and Periodicals in Michigan: A Checklist*, Richard Hathaway, ed. Ann Arbor: Michigan Archival Association, 1978. Part of the J. William Gorski Polish Genealogy and Historical Collection.
- *The Ethnic Press in the United States: A Historical Analysis and Handbook*, Sally M. Miller, ed. New York: Greenwood Press, 1987.
- *The German-Language Press in Indiana: A Bibliography*, by James P. Ziegler. Indianapolis: Max Kade German-American Center, Indiana University-Purdue University at Indianapolis and Indiana German Heritage Society, 1994.
- *The German Language Press of the Americas, 1732–1968: History and Bibliography*, by Karl John Richard Arndt and May E. Olson. Pullach/München: Verlag Dokumentation, 1973.
- *Norwegian-Americana Papers, 1847–1946*, by Olaf Morgan Norlie. Northfield, Minn.: Eilron Mimeopress, 1946.
- *Outsiders in 19th-Century Press History: Multicultural Perspectives*, by Frankie Hutton and Barbara Straus Reed. Bowling Green, Ohio: Bowling Green State University Popular Press, 1995. Ethnic, foreign-language, and dissenters' newspapers.

The *Cherokee Phoenix*, the first American Indian paper, began publication in 1828 in Georgia in the Cherokee language, using Sequoyah's table of syllables, or alphabet. Publication lasted about six years. The Oklahoma Historical Society holds this and other microfilmed Native American newspapers in its collection.

Political newspapers or newspapers that focused on political issues were among the earliest. One history reported thirty-seven newspapers in the colonies in 1775. Of those, twenty-three were said to have "patriotic" leanings, seven were of "loyalist" persuasions, and seven rode the fence.[2] As the political situation deteriorated toward war, circulation increased substantially. In the nineteenth century, papers often used political party names in their titles: *Democrat*, *Whig*, and *Republican*.

Reportedly, the first labor paper in the United States was the *Mechanics Free Press* of Philadelphia, published from 1828 to 1835. In other large cities, a variety of papers circulated among the general working population or specific groups of workers, such as stenographers or ironworkers. The Robert F. Wagner Labor Archives at the Tamiment Institute Library in New York holds numerous historical records of New York City labor and socialist organizations, including newsletters, monthly journals, and newspapers. Other collections of labor publications are at Johns Hopkins University in Baltimore. Bibliographies and finding aids for labor publications include these:

- *American Labor Union Periodicals: A Guide to Their Location*, by Bernard G. Naas and Carmelita J. Sakr. Ithaca: Cornell University, 1956.
- *The Immigrant Labor Press in North America, 1840s–1970s: An Annotated Bibliography*, by Dirk Hoerder. New York: Greenwood Press, 1987–.
- *Labor History Archives in the United States: A Guide for Researching and Teaching*, Daniel J. Leab and Philip P. Mason, eds. Detroit: Wayne State University Press, 1992. Contains information on forty libraries, archives, and historical societies in the United States.
- *Labor Papers on Microfilm: A Combined List*, by the State Historical Society of Wisconsin. Madison: State Historical Society of Wisconsin, 1965. The society maintains a large archive on the labor movement and social action movements.

Collections of Newspapers

Many of the institutions in the list on pages 241–246 hold ethnic and special interest newspapers. These are examples of collections with ethnic newspapers:

Arkansas—University of Arkansas, Little Rock (American Indian newspaper collection)

Illinois—Center for Research Libraries, Chicago (U.S. Ethnic Newspaper Collection, foreign-language newspapers printed in the United States; see a list of titles at <www.crl.edu/DBsearch/Ethnic.asp>)

Illinois—University of Illinois, Urbana-Champaign, Slavic and Eastern European Library (includes newspaper collection)

Minnesota—University of Minnesota, Minneapolis, Immigration History Research Center (extensive collection of ethnic newspapers)

New York—New York University, Tamiment Library (includes microfilm of the long-running Yiddish *Jewish Daily Forward*)

Pennsylvania—Historical Society of Pennsylvania, Philadelphia (includes the Balch Institute's extensive collection of ethnic newspapers)

Texas—University of Texas, Austin, Center for American History (includes some ethnic and religious newspapers; see <www.lib.utexas.edu/tnp>)

Indexes

One time-consuming aspect of some newspaper research is that most papers are not indexed. If only a few issues of a newspaper exist for the time period you need, you can read the issues easily without using an index. Even if you have a death date and want to search for an obituary in a small community newspaper, you will not spend much time checking issues of the paper that appeared from a day to a month or more after the death occurred. However, working without specific dates or with larger newspapers requires more research time.

Fortunately, individuals and societies are providing more indexes, some as separate publications, some in society periodicals. The Works Progress Administration (WPA) during the 1930s indexed some newspapers. Public and historical society libraries often maintain indexes to local obituaries. Some library and archive Web sites that explain newspaper holdings also mention available indexes; some indexes are now online.

One source for locating indexes is *Newspaper Indexes: A Location and Subject Guide for Researchers*, 3 vols., by Anita Cheek Milner (Metuchen, N.J.: Scarecrow Press, 1977–1982). In addition, several companies have published indexes for recent city newspapers. Some of these indexes began in the 1970s. Most of the online newspaper indexes are for issues published from the late 1980s forward.

One of the most comprehensive indexes for a U.S. newspaper is *The New York Times Index: A Book of Record.* The index began in 1851. From 1913 to 1929, it was issued quarterly. In the January–March 1914 volume appears the entry *Novak, Rev. Alexis–death, Mar 6, 1:7.* This is the reference for the Rev. Novak's death notice, which was printed in the March 6 issue, the first page, column seven.

Another helpful resource for this newspaper is the *Personal Names Index to 'The New York Times Index' 1851–1974*, 22 vols., compiled by Byron A. and Valerie R. Falk (Succasunna, N.J.: Roxbury Data Interface, 1976). These books are an index to an index. With each name is a citation to help find the item in the larger index. It certainly beats looking through 123 years of books! For the years 1913–1929, the citations give the year the name appeared and the quarterly index (I, II, III, or IV) in which you will find it. For example, the entry *George Craig Severance–d 1922, I, 472* means that his death notice reference appears in the January–March 1922 (first quarter) index, page 472.

For items that appeared in the other years, the citation gives the year and the page number of that year's index. The researcher then looks in that index to find the issue date and page reference. With such a specific reference, it is sometimes possible to obtain a photocopy of the item directly from an institution that has a collection of the newspapers, especially if they are on microfilm. Other sources for searching the *Times* are *The New York Times Obituaries Index, 1858–1968* and *The New York Times Obituaries Index, 1969–1978*, (New York: New York Times, 1970, 1980). Check a library reference section for these books.

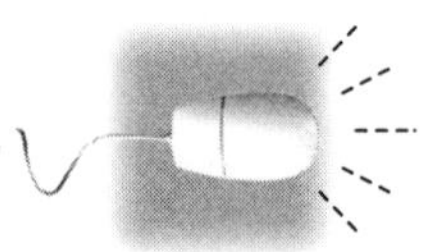

Internet Source

Another exciting finding aid for *The New York Times* is the ProQuest database Historical Newspapers that contains the 1851–1999 *Times* issues and a friendly search engine. For example, a search for the name of Proctor Knott and the date range of 1867–1911 (the bulk of Governor Knott's professional life) yielded about 200 notices and articles mentioning the Kentucky governor or a winning race horse of the same name. The online index and digitized text are available through many libraries that subscribe to ProQuest online databases and to members of the New York Genealogical and Biographical Society on their Web site <www.nygbs.org/members/proquest.html>. Set-up instructions for society members is currently available at <www.nygbs.org/info/articles/ProQuest1.html>.

The ProQuest (formerly Bell and Howell) and University Microfilms (UMI) group publishes indexes, many dating from the 1970s, for the newspapers listed below. These books contain a personal name index at the back and do include obituaries, listed under "deaths," with abstracts and references for the issue date, section, page number, and column number. Many indexes are available in electronic (CD-ROM or online) databases, and current newspapers are often searchable online.

Atlanta Constitution and *Atlanta Journal* (1983+)

Barron's (1975–1980)
Chicago Sun-Times (1979–1982)
Chicago Tribune (1972+)
The Christian Science Monitor (1949+)
The Denver Post (1999+)
The Detroit News (1976+)
The Houston Chronicle (1993+)
The Houston Post (1976–1994)
The Los Angeles Times (1972+)
Minneapolis *Star and Tribune* (1984–1985)
National Observer (1962–1968)
New Orleans Times-Picayune (1972+)
New York Times Tribune (1875–1906)
St. Louis Post-Dispatch (1975+)
The Wall Street Journal (1955+)
The Washington Post (1971+)
Washington Star-News (1894–1973)
The Washington Times (1986–1993)

Finding Newspapers

Sometimes researchers find original issues of newspapers to read at county courthouses, public and academic libraries, historical societies, and state archives. However, many newspapers on microfilm are available on interlibrary loan through your local library. Because of time and staff constraints, most of the holding institutions cannot research for you but may send a photocopy of a particular item from a specific issue.

Newspaper abstracts often appear in genealogical periodicals, and many have been published in books. For example, Brent H. Holcomb has published numerous abstracted marriages and death notices from South Carolina Lutheran, Methodist, Baptist, and city newspapers. Consult library catalogs for titles of these and similar books. Consult Cyndi's List <www.cyndislist.com> for links to online newspapers and abstracts. Remember that published abstracts do not mention all names in newspaper issues; try to view the original or microfilmed copy whenever possible.

Tip

One way to determine which newspapers exist for your research area and how to find them is to consult union catalogs, bibliographies, and histories of journalism, such as the works listed below. Such references often identify which libraries or other institutions hold which editions of which newspapers. (See pages 280–281 for further discussion.)

- *American Journalism: A History, 1690–1960*, 3d ed., by Frank Luther Mott. New York: Macmillan, 1962.
- *American Newspapers, 1821–1936: A Union List of Files Available in the United States and Canada*, Winifred Gregory, ed. New York: H.W. Wilson, 1937. Reprint, New York: Kraus Reprint Corporation, 1967. If not held in the main library stacks, this work may be in the reference section. Volume is arranged by state, city, and title. Entries give dates of publication, other titles the paper had, and the repositories holding the paper at the time the book was compiled. The repositories are listed as abbreviations which are translated at the front of volume.
- *A Checklist of American Eighteenth Century Newspapers in the Library of Congress*, John Van Ness Ingram, comp. Washington, D.C.: Government Printing Office, 1912. Organized by state, city, and title; indexed.

- *Gale Directory of Publications and Broadcast Media.,* 5 vols. Detroit: Gale Research, latest edition. Directory of current newspapers, other periodicals, and broadcasting stations in the United States and Canada. Reference work found in many medium to large libraries.
- *History and Bibliography of American Newspapers, 1690–1820,* 2 vols., by Clarence S. Brigham. Worcester, Mass.: American Antiquarian Society, 1947. Rev. ed., Hamden, Conn.: Archon Books, 1962.
- *Newspapers in Microform, United States, 1948–1983,* 2 vols. Washington, D.C.: Library of Congress, 1984. Organized by state, city, and title. Listings are only for holdings on microform, not originals or reprinted copies.
- *The Popular Press, 1833–1865,* James D. Startt and William David Sloan, eds. Westport, Conn.: Greenwood Press, 1999.
- UMI Division of ProQuest Information and Learning, catalog of Newspapers in Microform at <www.umi.com/nim/search> using the "advanced search" query. You can supply the date range, country, and state for which you want to search even if you don't have a specific title. You can search by city as well, but not all city newspapers are now available in microform. The results of the search give titles of papers that are available for purchase, mostly on microfilm, from this company at (800) 521-0600. However, the catalog functions as a finding aid to let you know which papers existed for your ancestral community and date range. You may be able to borrow the same paper via interlibrary loan or help your library purchase pertinent rolls of microfilm. A sample search for U.S. newspapers published between 1730 and 1930 resulted in 2,530 titles, with something from nearly every state.

The United States Newspaper Program is an attempt to update and consolidate newspaper finding information in every state and U.S. trust territory. This project is a major effort by hundreds of repositories to locate and inventory all extant newspapers in the country. A master bibliographic database is maintained by OCLC (Online Computer Library Center), based in Ohio. If you have access to the OCLC database at or through your local public or academic library, you can access information about newspaper holdings in your research state. Ask your librarian about access to and use of the catalog WorldCat to help identify titles published in your ancestor's area during the ancestral lifetime.

The U.S. Newspaper Program Web site <www.neh.gov/projects/usnp.html> offers links to at least one participating institution in the newspaper project in each state. Use the link to your research state to learn more about the state's efforts to catalog and preserve its newspapers. Some of the sites can help you determine whether your ancestral community had a newspaper and whether copies still exist. The Web sites vary considerably in content and ease of accessibility.

Most states have printed bibliographies, inventories, or union catalogs on newspapers within that state; some are available from the institution with the most extensive collection. An example is the *Guide to Wyoming Newspapers, 1867–1967,* by Lola Homsher (Cheyenne, Wyo.: Wyoming State Library, 1971). Under the city of Cheyenne is listed, among others, the *Daily Hornet* published between 10 March and 11 April 1878, with the information that the Wyoming Archives has all issues, and the University of Wyoming at Laramie has one edition. In libraries using the Library of Congress call number system, these guides for various states may be found under Z6952-6953. Libraries using the Dewey Decimal system would catalog these under 011.35, bibliographies on newspapers.

Family History Library

A few newspapers, union lists, and published abstracts are available on microfilm or microfiche from the Family History Library. In the online catalog at <www.familysearch.org>, use a "Place Search" for the state name and look on the resulting list for newspapers. A few titles, such as the *Savannah (Georgia) Morning News*, the District of Columbia's *Daily National Intelligencer*, and the German-language *New Yorker Staats-Zeitung* are available through the Family History Centers.

On film or fiche, researchers can also rent, for example, the *Union List of Arkansas Newspapers, 1819–1942: A Partial Inventory of Arkansas Newspaper Files Available in Offices of Publishers, Libraries and Private Collections in Arkansas* (Little Rock: Historical Records Survey, Division of Community Service Programs, Work Projects Administration, 1942). Although the work is old and probably outdated, as some newspapers files have likely changed hands since 1942, the list is a valuable reference for titles and dates of publication.

For other states, materials available for rent include published newspaper abstracts or collected clippings. These, too, are good finding aids if they include newspaper titles and dates. Most abstracts furnish this information; scrapbooks of clippings often do not. If you find an ancestor mentioned in such works, try to borrow the microfilm of the original issue of the paper to (1) check the details and (2) gather additional information that the abstracter may have omitted.

Major Newspaper Collections

Among the nation's largest newspaper repositories, often with newspapers from many parts of the country, are the American Antiquarian Society in Worcester, Massachusetts; the Kansas State Historical Society in Topeka; the Center for Research Libraries in Chicago; New York Public Library; the New York Historical Society in New York City; the Library of Congress, Washington, DC; Rutgers University, New Brunswick, New Jersey; the Wisconsin Historical Society in Madison; and the Western Reserve Historical Society, Cleveland, Ohio.

The list on pages 241–246 is to help researchers find, in each state, the most comprehensive newspaper collections of that state's papers. **Numerous city, historical society, and academic libraries hold microfilm of their local or county newspapers;** not all can be listed here. Consult staff members or individual library catalogs for details. Bear in mind that newspapers may or may not be listed in online library catalogs. Also try a subject search by town or title in WorldCat to identify titles published during an ancestor's life and learn of libraries that hold issues you may need to read.

Library/Archive Source

The information in this list was supplied by the institutions and the U.S. Newspaper Project in each state. Many of these collections contain city, ethnic, labor, special interest, and religious newspapers. In many of these institutions, newspapers are part of their special collections; consult the collections in your ancestral state for specific holdings. Library and archive holdings and interlibrary loan policies are not static, and collections may grow or change focus over the years.

Alabama—Alabama Department of Archives and History, Montgomery (see also <www.archives.state.al.us/newsp/newsp.html>); Auburn University, Auburn; Birmingham Public Library; University of Alabama, Tuscaloosa.

Alaska—Alaska State Library (ASL), Juneau; Consortium Library at the University of Alaska Anchorage (UAA); Rasmuson Library at the University of Alaska Fairbanks (UAF); Anchorage Municipal Libraries, Loussac Library (AML). See also <www.library.state.ak.us/hist/newspaper/news.html>.

Arizona—Arizona State Library, Archives and Public Records, History and Archives Division, Phoenix (largest collection in the state); Arizona Historical Society, Tucson (extensive collection); University of Arizona, Tucson (extensive collection); also consult Phoenix Public Library and Arizona State University, Tempe.

Arkansas—Arkansas History Commission Archives, Little Rock (largest collection in state; searchable list of holdings at <www.ark-ives.com> under "resource types," "newspapers"); University of Arkansas Libraries, Fayetteville (significant collection, especially for northwest Arkansas).

California—California State Library, Sacramento (extensive collection plus indexes to San Francisco papers); Los Angeles Public Library (extensive Los Angeles collection); Sutro Library of the California State Library, San Francisco (San Francisco and other papers); University of California at Berkeley in the Periodicals, Newspapers, Microforms Library (extensive collection). In San Diego, the three large universities, historical society, and public library all hold San Diego newspapers.

Colorado—Colorado Historical Society, Denver (most extensive collection in the state). See also *Guide to Colorado Newspapers, 1859–1963*, by Donald E. Oehlerts (Denver: Bibliographical Center for Research, Rocky Mountain Region, 1964).

Connecticut—Connecticut Historical Society and Connecticut State Library, both in Hartford, are the two largest collections. For more information, visit <www.cslib.org/newspapers.htm> and click on "Find newspapers in the State Library's catalog" for State Library holdings, or "Locating Connecticut Newspapers in Other Institutions." The staff requests that you read the directions before linking to "reQuest" and use "Conn." instead of "CT" for the state abbreviation. You can search the database by title, subject, or town name. Interlibrary loan is available from the Connecticut State Library. For a comprehensive guide to newspaper holdings in the state, contact the Connecticut Newspaper Project, Connecticut State Library, 231 Capitol Avenue, Hartford, Connecticut 06106; phone (860) 757-6527.

Delaware—Delaware Public Archives, Dover; Delaware Technical and Community College, Owens Campus, Betze Library, Georgetown; Historical Society of Delaware, Wilmington; University of Delaware Library, Newark.

District of Columbia—Washingtoniana Division of the Martin Luther King Jr. Memorial Library; microfilm listed on <www.dclibrary.org/washingtoniana/gd-microfilm.html>.

Florida—Florida State University, Strozier Library, Tallahassee; University of Florida Library, P.K. Yonge Library of Florida History, Gainesville (extensive collection, largest in the state); State Library of Florida, Florida Collection, Tallahassee (extensive collection, second largest in the state); University of Miami, Richter Library, in Coral Gables; University of West Florida, Pace Library, Pensacola.

Georgia—University of Georgia, Athens (largest collection of newspapers in the state; some indexes; growing online database at <http://dlg.galileo.usg.edu/>); Emory University, Atlanta; Georgia Historical Society, Savannah (primarily Savannah papers); State Archives of Georgia, Atlanta.

Hawaii—Bishop Museum Library, Honolulu; Hawaiian Historical Society, Honolulu (early newspapers date from 1834; some indexes to marriages, birth notices, obituaries); Hawaii State Archives, Honolulu; Hawaii State Library, Honolulu (comprehensive collection); University of Hawaii at Manoa, Hamilton Library, Honolulu (comprehensive collection). See also *Guide to Newspapers of Hawaii 1834–2000*, by Helen G. Chapin (Honolulu: Hawaiian Historical Society, 2000).

Idaho—Idaho State Historical Society, Historical Library and State Archives, Boise (the most complete collection in the state); Idaho State University, Pocatello, and University of Idaho, Moscow (substantial collections); Boise State University, Boise (good collection).

Illinois—Chicago Historical Society (mostly Chicago newspapers); Illinois State Historical Library, Springfield (extensive collection); Newberry Library, Chicago (extensive Chicago collection, with some other Illinois papers; includes foreign-language papers; see description at <www.newberry.org/nl/genealogy/L3gabout.html>); University of Illinois at Urbana-Champaign (extensive collection).

Indiana—Indiana State Library, Indianapolis (largest collection in the state); Indiana University, Bloomington; Indiana Historical Society, Indianapolis, has master negatives of the microfilm from which they sell copies. See *Indiana Newspaper Bibliography: Historical Accounts of All Indiana Newspapers Published from 1804 to 1980 and Locational Information for All Available Copies, Both Original Microfilm*, by John W. Miller (Indianapolis: Indiana Historical Society, 1982).

Iowa—Iowa State Historical Society, locations in Des Moines and Iowa City (also a clippings file of Iowa biographies) are the two major newspaper repositories in the state.

Kansas—Kansas State Historical Society, Topeka (excellent, extensive collection). See <www.kshs.org/library/news.htm>.

Kentucky—Filson Historical Society, Louisville (second largest collection of periodicals in state, especially good collection of pre–Civil War newspapers); University of Kentucky, Lexington (largest collection in the state).

Louisiana—Largest collections: Louisiana State Archives, Baton Rouge; Louisiana State University, Hill Memorial Library, Baton Rouge; New Orleans Public Library; Tulane University, Howard-Tilton Library, Special Collections, Manuscripts and Rare Books Department, New Orleans. Other significant collections are held at Historic New Orleans Collection, Williams Research Center, 410 Chartres Street <www.hnoc.org>; Louisiana State Museum Historical Center, New Orleans; and State Library of Louisiana, Baton Rouge.

Maine—Maine Historical Society, Portland; Maine State Library, Augusta (see <www.state.me.us/sos/arc/> for ongoing list of holdings); University of Maine, Orono (largest collection in the state). Other substantial collections: Bangor Public Library; Bowdoin College, Brunswick; Dyer Library and Saco Museum (formerly York Institute Museum), Saco; and Portland Public Library.

Maryland—Enoch Pratt Free Library, Baltimore (extensive collection); Maryland Historical Society, Baltimore (includes some indexes); Maryland State Archives, Annapolis (largest collection in the state).

Massachusetts—American Antiquarian Society, Worcester; Boston Public Library; smaller collections at Massachusetts Historical Society and New England Historic Genealogical Society, both in Boston.

Michigan—Central Michigan University, Clarke Historical Library, Park Library Building, Mount Pleasant; Detroit Public Library, Burton Historical Collection; Library of Michigan, Lansing (most extensive collection); Michigan Technological University, Copper Country Historical Collection, Houghton; Western Michigan University, Archives and Regional History Collection, Kalamazoo. See also *Michigan Newspapers: Preliminary Bibliography: A Partial Listing of Michigan Newspapers Based Upon a Survey of Public Libraries and Newspaper Offices in the State of Michigan* (Lansing: State Department of Education, Michigan State Library, Michigan Unit, 1966).

Minnesota—Minnesota Historical Society, St. Paul (largest collection in the state); University of Minnesota, Wilson Library, Minneapolis campus (second largest collection).

Mississippi—Mississippi Department of Archives and History, Jackson (extensive collection); Mississippi State University, in Mississippi State (extensive collection); University of Mississippi, in Oxford (substantial collection); University of Southern Mississippi, Hattiesburg (substantial collection).

Missouri—Missouri Historical Society, St. Louis (*Missouri Republican*; *Missouri Gazette*; St. Louis German-language and African-American papers); State Historical Society of Missouri, Columbia (largest, most comprehensive collection in the state); St. Louis Public Library (large collection of St. Louis papers; ongoing development of online index to obituaries, death notices, and burial permits published in the *St. Louis Post-Dispatch* and of WWI and WWII casualty lists; see <www.slpl.lib.mo.us>).

Montana—Montana Historical Society Library and Archives, Helena (strongest collection in the state; has most of the newspapers ever published in Montana).

Nebraska—Nebraska State Historical Society, Lincoln (largest collection in the state).

Nevada—Nevada Historical Society, Reno (with index to *Territorial Enterprise* from 1859); Nevada State Archives, Carson City; University of Nevada, Las Vegas; University of Nevada, Reno. See *The Newspapers of Nevada: A History and Bibliography, 1854–1979*, by Richard E. Lingenfelter and Karen Rix Gash (Reno: University of Nevada Press, 1984).

New Hampshire—Largest collections at New Hampshire Historical Society and New Hampshire State Library, both in Concord; good collection at Dartmouth College, Baker/Berry Library, Hanover.

New Jersey—Rutgers, The State University of New Jersey, Alexander Library, New Brunswick (major collection); New Jersey Historical Society, Newark; New Jersey State Archives, Trenton (major collection; location 225 West State Street); New Jersey State Library, Trenton (substantial collection; location 185 West State Street). See also the *Directory of New Jersey Newspapers, 1765–1970*, William C. Wright and Paul A. Stellhorn, eds. (Trenton, N.J.: New Jersey Historical Commission, 1977).

New Mexico—Fray Angélico Chávez History Library at the Museum of New Mexico, Santa Fe; New Mexico State Archives, Santa Fe; New Mexico State Library, Santa Fe; University of New Mexico, Albuquerque; and New Mexico State University, Las Cruces.

New York—Center for Migration Studies Library and Archives in Staten Island <http://cmsny.library.net/#About>; New York City Public Library; New York Genealogical and Biographical Society, New York City (with pre-1900 abstracts of deaths, marriages); New York Historical Society, New York City (one of the largest collections of eighteenth-century newspapers in the country); New York State Library, Albany (extensive collection; listing of microfilm by city and county at <www.nysl.nysed.gov/nysnp>).

North Carolina—North Carolina State Archives, Raleigh (extensive collection); State Library of North Carolina, Raleigh (extensive collection); smaller collection at the University of North Carolina, Wilson Library in Chapel Hill.

North Dakota—State Historical Society of North Dakota, Bismarck (the newspaper depository for the state; statewide inventory available for sale; full in-state listing of newspapers at <www.state.nd.us/hist/newshome.htm>).

Ohio—Ohio Historical Society, Columbus (largest Ohio collection); Western Reserve Historical Society, Cleveland (extensive collection). See also *Ohio Newspapers: A Liv-*

ing Record, Robert C. Wheeler, comp. (Columbus: Ohio Historical Press, 1950).

Oklahoma—Oklahoma Historical Society, Newspaper Archives, Oklahoma City (has nearly all Oklahoma newspapers ever published, including Indian papers); University of Oklahoma, Bizzell Library, Norman (selected titles).

Oregon—Oregon Historical Society Research Library, Portland (comprehensive collection of major Oregon newspapers; vertical file of clippings); Oregon State Library, Salem (selected titles); University of Oregon, Knight Library, Eugene (most complete collection of Oregon newspapers, 1841 to the present).

Pennsylvania—Four most extensive collections: Carnegie Library of Pittsburgh (focus on Pittsburgh area); Free Library of Philadelphia (focus on Philadelphia area); Pennsylvania State University, State College; State Library of Pennsylvania, Harrisburg (the most comprehensive collection, with interlibrary loan available within the contiguous U.S.). See Web sites for descriptions and information on indexes. Two other strong collections: Historical Society of Pennsylvania, Philadelphia (includes the newspaper collection of the Balch Institute, an extensive collection of ethnic newspapers); Historical Society of Western Pennsylvania, Pittsburgh.

Puerto Rico—University of Puerto Rico, San Juan.

Rhode Island—Rhode Island Historical Society Library (official repository of state newspapers; holds almost every known state newspaper from 1732 to the present).

South Carolina—Charleston Library Society (especially Charleston papers); Furman University, Greenville (upstate newspapers); South Carolina Department of Archives and History (*The South Carolina Gazette*, 1732–1782 only); University of South Carolina, South Caroliniana Library, Columbia (largest collection in the state). See John Hammond Moore's *South Carolina Newspapers* (Columbia: University of South Carolina Press, 1988).

South Dakota—South Dakota State Historical Society–State Archives, Pierre (most extensive collection of the state's newspapers; union list online at <www.sdhistory.org>).

Tennessee—Knox County Library, McGhee Library, McClung Historical Collection, Knoxville; Tennessee State Library and Archives, Nashville; University of Memphis (formerly Memphis State University), McWherter Library, Memphis; University of Tennessee, Knoxville.

Texas—Texas State Library and Archives, Austin; Texas Tech University; University of Texas at Austin, Center for American History (CAH), Austin (the largest collection of Texas newspapers, including ethnic and military-post papers; online catalog of the CAH collection at <www.cah.utexas.edu/newspapers/newspapers_fa.pdf>).

Utah—Extensive collections at Utah Valley Regional Family History Center, Harold B. Lee Library, Brigham Young University Library, Provo; Family History Library, Salt Lake City; Utah State Historical Society Library, Salt Lake City; University of Utah, Marriott Library, Salt Lake City. See also *Guide to Newspapers Located in the Utah State Historical Society Library*, Linda Thatcher, comp. (Salt Lake City: Utah State Historical Society, 1985).

Vermont—State of Vermont State Department of Libraries, Montpelier (largest collection, mostly on microfilm); University of Vermont, Bailey-Howe Library, Burlington; Vermont Historical Society Library, Montpelier (second largest collection, mainly pre-1900 in hard copy). See also *A Union List of Vermont Newspapers*, by staff of Vermont Newspaper Project (2000), available on the VNP Web site <http://danalib.uvm.edu/vtnp/vnphome.htm>.

Virgin Islands of the U.S.—Virgin Islands Public Library System, Enid M. Baa Library, Von Scholten Collection, on St. Thomas, Virgin Islands.

Virginia—College of William and Mary, Swem Library, Williamsburg; Library of Virginia, Richmond, <www.lva.lib.va.us/whatwedo/vnp/index.htm> and <www.lva.lib.va.us/whatwehave/news/index.htm>); University of Virginia, Alderman Library, Charlottesville; Virginia Historical Society, Richmond.

Washington—University of Washington, Suzzallo Library, Seattle (extensive Washington collection, some other Pacific Northwest newspapers); Washington State Library, Olympia (largest Washington collection).

West Virginia—Marshall University, Huntington; West Virginia University Library, West Virginia and Regional History Collection, Morgantown (largest collection of this state's newspapers); West Virginia State Archives and History Library, Charleston, <www.wvculture.org/history/newspapers/newsmic>.

Wisconsin—Milwaukee Public Library; Wisconsin Historical Society, Madison (the major Wisconsin newspaper collection; extensive collection of early trans-Appalachian newspapers, labor, black, Native American, ethnic, women's, U.S. Army Camp newspapers, and nineteenth-century religious newspapers). See also *Guide to Wisconsin Newspapers, 1833–1957*, by Donald E. Oehlerts (Madison: State Historical Society of Wisconsin, 1958).

Wyoming—Wyoming Archives and Records Management, Historical Research Division, Cheyenne; University of Wyoming, Laramie.

MAPS

Important

Maps are essential tools for the study of history and genealogy. Every genealogist needs at least a road map or atlas of the state(s) and counties of research interest. In addition, historical atlases provide much interesting information about each region and its social, economic, religious, political, and military history. Most research libraries have map collections, including atlases, and those with federal depository library collections often include topographic, navigation, and other types of maps. Maps can also be purchased. Thus, various kinds of maps are available to aid genealogical research.

Maps, of course, help locate places and get us where we are going. In genealogy, their functions are varied:

1. To help locate cemeteries and ancestral residences. This process works in both directions. (a) Finding a known family residence on a county or city map can help narrow the search for cemeteries in which family members are buried or churches and schools they may have attended. (b) If you know the name of an ancestral school, church, or cemetery, a city or county map may help you locate it and perhaps narrow the search for an ancestral residence. (Remember, many churches have adjacent cemeteries.)
2. To pinpoint, using information from other records, where ancestors lived, worked, or worshipped. Locating such ancestral places may be the key to discovering or gathering more family history—learning where to look for additional records, meeting old-timers who may know something about the family, discovering a house where ancestors lived, photographing the school an ancestor attended. Even if the house no longer exists, locating the property where it stood gives you a sense of connection with the family who lived there.
3. To locate ancestral property or addresses in order to study the neighbors. Ancestors

often lived near other relatives and in-laws. Studying the neighborhood can help identify such connections.

4. To identify neighboring counties, especially if your ancestor lived near a county boundary line. Sometimes ancestors filed records at a neighboring courthouse because it was closer to home and easier to reach. Some ancestors married in a neighboring county, especially if it was the bride's home.
5. To show you the terrain and vegetation of the ancestral neighborhood and help you understand more about how ancestors might have traveled, crops they may have raised, or the difficulties they may have had in constructing shelter and outbuildings.
6. To study historical events that happened in the ancestral neighborhood and study the genealogy of the county—its parent county or counties and how its boundaries changed. If ancestors were early residents, the parent county may hold records about them.
7. To help determine name changes of towns and villages. Historical atlases, historical travelers' maps and guidebooks, county maps, and others can indicate, for example, that Martinsville, Missouri, became Platte City, and Arkapolis, Arkansas, became Little Rock.

County Maps

Some of the most useful maps are the general highway maps of each county, published by state highway or transportation departments in cooperation with the U.S. Department of Transportation, Federal Highway Administration. Although their comprehensiveness varies from state to state, county maps often show main and rural roads, waterways, communities, rural churches, and cemeteries. They are extremely useful for cemetery hunting. Rural maps sometimes identify the location of buildings and residences but not landowners' names. To buy these maps for the states you search, you can locate the proper agency in each state through a guide such as *The National Directory of State Agencies* (Gaithersburg, Md.: Cambridge Information Group Directories, Inc., latest edition), available in library reference sections. Also look on the state government's Web site for the highway or transportation department. (Search engines can find such sites quickly.)

The Web site <www.firstgov.gov> links to both federal and state government Web sites. As the site is arranged at this writing, under "Agencies," click on "state, local & tribal" for a page for state, local, tribal, and U.S. territory resources. Each jurisdiction's home page is unique; maps may be under travel, tourism, department of transportation, economic development, or other parts of the site. Some, such as the Idaho Transportation Department's Geographic Information System page <www3.state.id.us/itd_gis/> and the Wisconsin Department of Transportation page <www.dot.wisconsin.gov/travel/maps/docs/county.htm>, lead to printable county maps showing township and range numbers, essential in studying ancestors in federal land states. Such sites also provide department contact information for ordering maps.

Perhaps a quicker option from the FirstGov.gov Web page is a search for a single state and topic, such as "county maps" for Connecticut. That search led to the Department of Economic and Community Development site <vvv.ecd.state.ct.us/research/maps/index.html> which contains state, county, and road maps in PDF and JPG formats.

If you had ancestors in several counties in a state, you may benefit from buying an atlas for the entire state rather than separate county maps. At least four publishers provide detailed atlases; commercial booksellers also may stock them:

1. County Maps (County Map Books), Puetz Place, Lyndon Station, Wisconsin 53944. Phone: (608) 666-3331. States: Arkansas, Florida, Indiana, Kentucky, Michigan,

North Carolina, Ohio, Pennsylvania, South Carolina, Tennessee, West Virginia, Wisconsin. Detailed county road maps based on those of the state departments of transportation, including location of cemeteries and rural churches.

2. DeLorme "Atlas & Gazetteer" Series, DeLorme, P.O. Box 298, Yarmouth, Maine 04096. Phone: (207) 846-7000. Web site: <www.delorme.com>. Topographical maps for all fifty states.
3. Shearer Publishing, 406 Post Oak Road, Fredericksburg, Texas 78624. Phone: (800) 458-3808. Web site: <www.shearerpub.com/travel.htm>. Detailed atlases that also show townships and ranges for the applicable states. States in series at this time: Arkansas, Colorado, Louisiana, New Mexico, North Carolina, Oklahoma, Texas.
4. University Press of Mississippi, Jackson, Mississippi. Web site: <www.upress.state.ms.us/books/m/ms_road_atlas.html>. *Mississippi Road Atlas*, with detailed county maps and fifty city maps, published in 1997. Shows townships and ranges. Cartography by the Mississippi Department of Transportation. Excellent source for Mississippi research.

County or state atlases from the nineteenth century were sometimes quite detailed, naming not only roads, creeks and rivers, lakes and ponds, and rises in elevation but also post offices, ferries, communities, and some specific residences. Such maps may help determine whether ancestors lived near other relatives or who their nearest neighbors were. A valuable research tool of this kind for early South Carolina is the 1825 *Mills' Atlas* (Reprint, Easley, S.C.: Southern Historical Press, 1980). The surveys for the atlas were made largely in 1819 and 1820 with some additions before publication in 1825. Each county map shows waterways, roads, churches, mills, stores, fords, ferries, and family residences in the rural areas at the time the map was made. The Chesterfield County map aided in a Shelby family search for a wife's maiden name by identifying nearest neighboring families. (See page 69.) The atlas has been printed several times, including the 1965 edition by Robert Pearce Wilkins and John D. Keels Jr. in Columbia, South Carolina. It is available at many research libraries, as are such atlases for other states.

Atlases of Historical County Boundaries

Standard road maps and atlases show current county boundaries, but these lines have not always been the same. Combining knowledge of a family's residence with the history of county boundary changes can help determine whether the family moved from one county to another or whether the family stayed in one place and became part of a newly created county. **Knowing which counties surrounded an ancestor's residence gives you additional courthouses in which to look for ancestral records and records of other relatives.** A family who lived near a county line or state line sometimes lived near relatives in the neighboring county or state. Title abstract companies in the locale, historical atlases, and census maps often show general boundary changes and parent counties.

Research Tip

However, the Gale Group <www.galegroup.com> has a series of atlases (listed in their catalog of print materials) that focus on the details of county boundary changes. Since genealogists look for ancestral records in the context of specific times and places, researchers need to know which county had jurisdiction over an ancestral location at any given time; these atlases provide this kind of information. Many of the maps identify modern towns and watercourses, which assist researchers in visualizing the changes that took place in the area. The atlases resulted from research in primary sources, especially the laws that created the counties, in an effort to be as accurate as possible.

Each volume contains an alphabetical list of county creations, including "paper" counties that never officially organized; a chronology of state and county boundaries from the initial settlement of the area, including name changes and actions of any foreign governments with jurisdiction over the area; an impressive collection of individual county maps showing each boundary change, often with the historical boundary superimposed over a modern map; lists of colonial, state, and federal censuses pertinent to the state; maps of the state showing counties as they existed at census time; and a bibliography for further reference on state laws, maps, geography, and history.

At this time, the series includes eighteen volumes, although the Illinois and Pennsylvania volumes are apparently out of stock and must be obtained through used-book dealers. The books have different individual editors, but John H. Long has been general editor of the series; Charles Scribner's Sons and Simon & Schuster published the books between 1992 and 2000. The volumes in the series include the following, all titles beginning with *Atlas of Historical County Boundaries*:

1. Alabama
2. Connecticut-Maine-Massachusetts-Rhode Island
3. Delaware-Maryland-Washington, DC
4. Florida
5. Illinois
6. Indiana
7. Iowa
8. Kentucky
9. Michigan
10. Minnesota
11. Mississippi
12. New Hampshire-Vermont
13. New York
14. North Carolina
15. Pennsylvania
16. South Carolina
17. Tennessee
18. Wisconsin

Other published references to help you with historical county boundaries, boundary and name changes, and parent counties include these:

Ancestry's Red Book: American State, County & Town Sources, Alice Eichholz, ed. Salt Lake City: Ancestry, 3d ed. to be released 2004.

Atlas of County Boundary Changes in Virginia, 1634–1895, by Michael F. Doran. Athens, Ga.: Iberian Publishing Co., 1987.

The Handy Book for Genealogists, 10th ed., George B. Everton Sr., ed. Logan, Utah: The Everton Publishers, Inc., 2002.

Historical Atlas and Chronology of County Boundaries, 1788–1980, John H. Long, ed. Boston: G.K. Hall, 1984. Five volumes covering the states of Delaware, Illinois, Indiana, Iowa, Maryland, Michigan, Minnesota, Missouri, New Jersey, North Dakota, Ohio, Pennsylvania, South Dakota, Wisconsin. This editor is the general editor of the series of Atlases of Historical County Boundaries.

Historical U.S. County Outline Map Collection, 1840–1980, Thomas D. Rabenhorst and Carville V. Earle, eds. Baltimore: University of Maryland Department of Geography, 1984.

Map Guide to the United States Federal Censuses, 1790–1920, by William Thorndale and William Dollarhide. Baltimore: Genealogical Publishing Co., 1987. An excellent guide to boundary changes and how they affected each census.

A Series of County Outline Maps of the Southeastern United States for the Period 1790–1980. Chapel Hill, N.C.: University of North Carolina Department of Geography, 1973.

Fire Insurance Maps

Maps produced for various fire insurance companies, primarily by the Sanborn Company, helped insurance companies assess the risk involved with insuring specific properties. One of the earliest known maps of this kind is Edmund Petrie's 1790 map of Charleston, South Carolina, made for the Phoenix Fire Insurance Company of London. Only a few such maps exist for years between 1790 and 1867. From 1867 to 1970, the Sanborn Company produced thousands of maps, covering more than twelve thousand large and small towns.

Research Tip

These maps can help genealogists pinpoint homes or businesses of ancestors. Besides street names, street width, block numbers, some house numbers, and lot boundary lines, the Sanborn maps often show the shape and height of buildings, information on size and construction material, building use (residence, church, etc.), locations of doors or chimneys, and water lines or fire hydrants. For genealogists, such information on ancestral homes or businesses is fascinating and may help answer other questions in research, such as the location of the school or church nearest the ancestral home, whether a house was standing at the time of the map, or whether a house was rebuilt after a fire.

Figure 7-3, on page 251, is the 1927 Sanborn map for Marfa, Texas, showing the "original town" with both frame and adobe homes. On the corner of West Washington and North Davis, at the opposite end of the block from the Methodist Church, still stands a home that has gone through two major remodelings. The 1927 map shows the shape of the house after its first remodeling, as it existed from about 1926 to about 1939. The map, when compared with family photos, actually helped date that remodeling. Superimposed on the map is a photo of the house as it looked in 1927, showing that the original frame siding had been covered with decorative stucco and one side porch had been taken in as a room. Even without photos, such maps give genealogists information about ancestral towns and neighborhoods.

The largest public collection of Sanborn maps is in the Library of Congress, from which you can request photocopies or microfilm copies. For a comprehensive listing of the Library of Congress collection, available cities and dates, and map numbers necessary for requesting duplication, see *Fire Insurance Maps in the Library of Congress: Plans of North American Cities and Towns Produced by the Sanborn Map Company* . . . (Washington, D.C.: Library of Congress, 1981. Gov Doc LC5.2:F51). The book is indexed but is also arranged alphabetically by state and city. It can be found in many federal depository libraries. When contacting the photoduplication department, specify the city and state, the date, and the street location for the map you want.

In 1983, Chadwyck-Healey <www.chadwyck.com>, now part of ProQuest Information and Learning, produced the maps listed in the Library of Congress book on a series of 1,099 rolls of microfilm. University Publications of America, part of Lexis-Nexis Academic and Library Solutions, and the Library of Congress also sell microfilm of the map collection. The Sanborn Company's Map Library is now part of Environmental Data Resources, which can be reached at (800) 352-0050.

In addition to the Library of Congress, a number of other repositories have Sanborn map collections. See *Union List of Sanborn Fire Insurance Maps Held by Institutions in the United States and Canada*, by R. Philip Hoehn and others (Santa Cruz, Calif.: Western Association of Map Libraries, 1976–77). Many public and academic libraries have paper copies or microfilm of the Sanborn maps for their city or region or access through an online subscription database. In many locations, you can view the maps online at

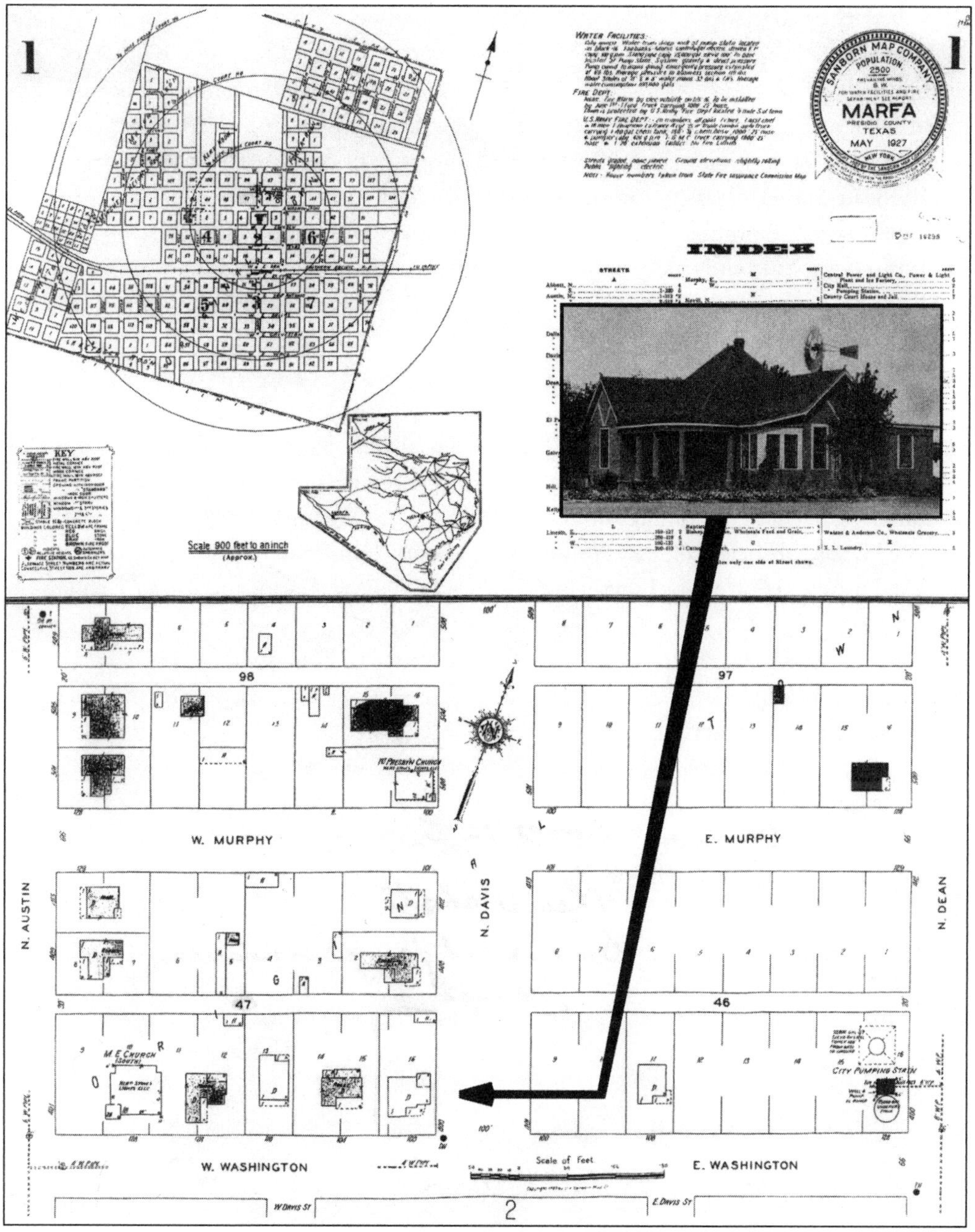

Figure 7-3 Marfa, Texas, Sanborn Co. map, with photo of house added, May 1927. Used with permission of Sanborn Map Co., The Sanborn Library, LLC; all rights reserved; further reproductions prohibited without written permission from The Sanborn Library, LLC.

home, through the library's databases, using your library card. On the Web site of the University of Utah <www.lib.utah.edu/digital/sanborn/index.html>, at this writing, researchers can view the Utah Sanborn maps in color without a subscription or password, under the J.W. Marriott Library's digital collections. If you've never seen Sanborn maps, visit this site.

You can also rent a few of these maps on microfilm through the Family History Library. In the online catalog <www.familysearch.org>, do a "place search" for the state; under "related places," click on the county or independent city of interest and look for "maps." Four such cities identified in the catalog are St. Louis, Missouri; Helena and Fort Smith, Arkansas; and Lyons, New York. Others may be available as well.

This chart lists some of the major research facilities whose collections include Sanborn maps:

University of Alabama
Alaska State Library
University of Arizona
University of Arkansas, Fayetteville
Arkansas History Commission Archives
California State University, Northridge
University of Colorado, Boulder
Connecticut, Yale University
Historical Society of Delaware
University of Florida
University of Georgia
University of Hawaii
University of Idaho
University of Illinois, Urbana
Indiana University, Bloomington
State Historical Society of Iowa, Iowa City
State Historical Society of Iowa, Des Moines
University of Kansas
University of Kentucky
Louisiana State Library
Louisiana State University
University of Maine
University of Maryland
Massachusetts, Harvard University
Library of Michigan
Michigan, Detroit Public Library
Minnesota Historical Society
Mississippi State Archives
Mississippi State University
University of Missouri
Montana Historical Society
University of Nebraska
University of Nevada, Reno
New Hampshire, Dartmouth College
New Jersey, Princeton University
University of New Mexico
New York Public Library
University of North Carolina
University of North Dakota
Ohio, Kent State University
University of Oklahoma
Oregon State University
Pennsylvania State Library
Pennsylvania State University
Rhode Island, Brown University
South Caroliniana Library University of South Carolina
South Dakota, History Resource Center, Pierre
University of Tennessee
University of Texas, Center for American History
University of Utah
Utah State Historical Society
University of Vermont
Library of Virginia
University of Virginia (microfilm)
University of Washington
Washington, Tacoma Public Library
West Virginia University
State Historical Society of Wisconsin
University of Wyoming, Laramie

Other Maps, Atlases, and Gazetteers

Sometimes maps identify individual family residences or property. Especially in the North and Midwest, the late nineteenth and early twentieth centuries saw the publication of comprehensive county atlases. These often showed private land ownership, sometimes with boundary lines.

Railroad maps. *Railroad Maps of North America: The First Hundred Years*, by Andrew M. Modelski (Washington, D.C.: Library of Congress, 1984), is another interesting source. As in county atlases, towns and villages dot some of these maps. Some maps identify boundaries of individual tracts of land, and some name individual family residences. An excellent example in the book is the Winchester-Potomac area of Virginia in 1832. The map shows many family homes as well as taverns, stores, churches, and other landmarks. These maps can also help you study migration routes if your ancestral families moved at a time when railroads were a travel option.

The University of Alabama online map library (see page 258) includes some railroad maps. Also, the Library of Congress American Memory Web site has a number of railroad maps online at <http://memory.loc.gov/ammem/gmdhtml/rrhtml/rrhome.html>.

Military maps can be sources for finding family residences in limited locations and time frames as well as studying ancestral participation in military engagements. A good example is *The Official Atlas of the Civil War*, which has been published at least four times:

- Originally *Atlas to Accompany the Official Records of the Union and Confederate Armies*. Washington, D.C.: Government Printing Office, 1891.
- *The Official Atlas of the Civil War*. New York: T. Yoseloff, 1958.
- *The Official Military Atlas of the Civil War*. New York: Arno Press, 1978.
- *The Official Military Atlas of the Civil War*. New York: Fairfax Press, 1983.

The very helpful index to the atlas is *Civil War Maps: A Graphic Index to the Atlas to Accompany the Official Records of the Union and Confederate Armies*, Noel S. O'Reilly et al., comp. (Chicago: Newberry Library, 1987). This book is arranged alphabetically by state but with maps showing each area of the state that is covered by the plates in the atlas. Many of the maps cover small areas in which individual family residences are labeled, as well as ferries, fords, and other landmarks that often carry the owner's name.

A similar work is *The West Point Atlas of American Wars*, Volume I, *1689–1900*, with Vincent J. Esposito as chief editor (New York: Henry Holt and Co., 1995). Many of the maps pinpoint and name taverns, bridges, farmhouses, plantations, communities, churches, railroads, trails and roads, ferries, swamps, and even vegetation and bluffs in their relation to troop placement and battle positions. These can aid genealogists in their study of ancestors and their geographic settings.

Land ownership maps can help with research for ancestral residences and neighbors. Consult abstract companies in your research area for availability of such maps in their files. General land offices in the various states may be another source of these maps, and most research libraries and archives have map collections. Another finding aid is *Land Ownership Maps: A Checklist of Nineteenth Century United States County Maps in the Library of Congress*, Richard W. Stephenson, comp. (Washington, D.C.: Library of Congress, 1967). The book lists about 1,450 county land ownership maps, mostly in the Northeast and Midwest, along with good coverage of Virginia, California, and Texas. Copies of these maps may be ordered from the Photoduplication Service at the Library of Congress, specifying the county name, date, and map entry number from Stephenson's book. A large collection of these maps is at the Newberry Library in Chicago.

Most maps, of course, do not show family residences, but you can use many sources for clues and identify the locations on current maps. In studying ancestors who lived in public land states where land was surveyed and sold in sections, townships, and ranges, get maps with these divisions already on them. Using deeds, patents, and other records, you can plot accurately where the family property was. If you can find such a map that also shows roads, you can more easily visit the site. You may need to pool information from several maps to pinpoint a location.

When deed records show rural property descriptions by metes and bounds, locating the site may be more difficult. With county atlases, abstract company maps, topographic and other maps, it is possible to pinpoint many ancestral home sites. Texas researcher Gay Carter used family tradition, deed records, and a National Oceanic and Atmospheric Administration (NOAA) nautical map to locate and visit the actual house, built in 1699, where her colonial Glascock ancestors had lived on Virginia's Northern Neck.

For ancestors who lived in a town or city, you can also plot on a city map information gained from other sources, such as deeds, family papers, and city directories. With an address

Reminder

SPELLING CHANGES

The surname Glasscock is a good example of spelling changes that genealogists find. The colonial family was consistently "Glascock" or "Glascocke." By the mid-nineteenth century, the spelling was consistently "Glasscock," as it is today. The question is not "Which spelling is correct?" but "Have I identified the correct ancestors?"

or a description of city property using block and lot number, you can often find historical and current maps in the courthouse, city hall, library, tax appraisal district, or abstract company files to show you the exact location so you can visit the site. The use of both old and current maps can be important since city streets sometimes undergo name changes. Perhaps you can see the very house in which the family lived or the buildings where they worked. Even if the residence or workplace no longer stands, a Sanborn map may show you characteristics of the original building or changes made over the years. These may also give you an understanding of the immediate neighborhood that you cannot get any other way.

Migration routes, such as trails, roads, or railroads, often appear on maps in addition to waterways and mountain ranges. All of these features can help you determine ancestors' possible migration routes or nearest market towns. In addition, **maps dealing with migrations, frontiers, and territorial development can be found in many history books and historical atlases.** Check library catalogs for specific titles. The numerous sources that can aid in one's understanding of migration routes and frontiers include these examples:

Printed Source

An Atlas of Appalachian Trails to the Ohio River (1998), *An Atlas of Northern Trails Westward From New England* (2000), *An Atlas of Southern Trails to the Mississippi* (1999), and *An Atlas of Trails West of the Mississippi River* (2001), by Carrie Eldridge. Chesapeake, Ohio: the author.

Atlas of Early American History: The Revolutionary Era, 1760–1790, Lester J. Cappon, Barbara Bartz Petchenik, and John Hamilton Long, eds. Princeton, N.J.: Princeton University Press, for Newberry Library, 1976. Maps show Indian villages, counties in 1790, churches, Masonic lodges, taverns, ferries, schools, and other aspects of economic and cultural life, ratification of the Constitution by county, and towns, with some city maps. A fascinating resource.

The Development of Early Emigrant Trails in the United States East of the Mississippi River, by Marcus W. Lewis. Washington, D.C. (now Arlington, Va.): National Genealogical Society, 1933.

Maps Showing Explorers Routes, Trails, & Early Roads in the United States: An Annotated List, Richard S. Ladd, comp. Washington, D.C.: Library of Congress, 1962. Indexed.

Panoramic maps of the late nineteenth and early twentieth centuries give a different perspective of ancestral towns and cities. As if looking down on the city from a height just outside town, the artists showed prominent buildings, waterways, wharves, railroads, parks, churches, factories, and a general view of residential areas. These "bird's eye" views usually didn't detail individual residences unless a homeowner paid the artist to include a little inset picturing the home. Commissioned often to promote growth and economic development by demonstrating the city's attractive qualities, the maps give you a sense of the city's size and density at the time of the drawing and the hustle and bustle of everyday life. Such details could help you describe the setting or environment in which your ancestors lived.

Such drawings are in map collections around the country. Some panoramic maps appear in state and county atlases and in U.S. historical atlases, such as the American Heritage publication listed below. Existing panoramic drawings include those of large cities but also of numerous aspiring communities from Blue Hill, Maine, to Tumwater, Washington, and from Placerville, California, to Cedar Key, Florida.

More than seventeen hundred renderings are identified in *Panoramic Maps of Cities in the United States and Canada: A Checklist of Maps in the Collections of the Library of Congress, Geography and Map Division*, 2d ed. (Washington, D.C.: Library of Congress, 1984. Gov Doc LC5.2:P19). If you identify a panoramic map of an ancestral community in the Geography and Map Division of the Library of Congress, you can order a photocopy from the Library of Congress at (202) 707-5640. More information, an index of town and city panoramic maps, and views of many maps are on the American Memory Web site, at this writing available at <http://lcweb2.loc.gov/ammem/gmdhtml/gmdhome.html> and <http://memory.loc.gov/ammem/pmhtml/panhome.html>. (Several paths on the Library of Congress Web site will take you to the panoramic maps.)

Historical atlases vary in content, often focusing on acquisition of territory and military campaigns. Many also provide information on population density, the location of specific ethnic populations, terrain, rainfall and climate, electoral college votes in presidential elections, roads and railroads, economic development, the "shape" of the United States at specific times, and other data that helps genealogists understand the world in which ancestors lived. One comprehensive reference is *The American Heritage Pictorial Atlas of United States History* (New York: American Heritage, 1966). This book includes reprints of historical maps, several panoramic city maps, and demographic maps, along with text about major periods of U.S. history.

Other such atlases include the following; check library catalogs for more titles:

- *Atlas of American History*, rev. ed., Kenneth T. Jackson, ed. New York: C. Scribner's Sons, 1978.
- *Historical Atlas of the United States*, centennial ed., by the National Geographic Society. Washington, D.C.: The Society, 1988.

Gazetteers are good references and finding aids. These books are geographical indexes published for individual states, regions, or the nation as a whole. They usually list and describe towns, counties, and other named places, often including waterways. One typical gazetteer is *Fanning's Illustrated Gazetteer of the United States* (New York: Ensign, Bridgman, and Fanning, 1855; reprint, Bowie, Md.: Heritage Books, 1990). It contains maps of the thirty-one states and fourteen cities, history and statistics about the United States in the 1850s, locations of hundreds of towns and other named places, and descriptions of major cities. For example, Fanning's 1855 gazetteer identifies Blue Hill, Maine (population: 1,939), as a post town in Hancock County, about seventy-five miles east of Augusta.[3] The U.S. Gazetteer at the Web sites <www.census.gov/cgi-bin/gazetteer/> and <http://tiger.census.gov/> shows Blue Hill's 1990 population with a slight growth to 1,941.

Fanning's Gazetteer described larger towns and cities in more detail, giving the following information for Dover, Delaware: In the Dover Hundred, capital of the state, county seat of Kent County, a borough on Jones' Creek, ten miles from its entrance into Delaware Bay; fifty miles south of Wilmington; 120 miles from Washington; built on four principal streets, which form a square in the center of town; has an elegant statehouse and several churches, banks, and other public buildings, neat and mostly of brick; population in 1810 was about 900; population in 1820, about 600 [*sic*]; population in 1830, about 1,300; population in 1840, about 3,790; population in 1850, about 4,207.[4] If your ancestors lived in Dover, you would want to know these details to help you understand the environment in which your ancestors lived.

Various gazetteers are online. At this writing, one for Kentucky is on the University of Kentucky Web site <www.uky.edu/KentuckyPlaceNames/>. One for Washington state is at the Tacoma Public Library Web site <www.tpl.lib.wa.us/v2/NWRoom/WaNames.htm>. Use search engines, USGenWeb <www.usgenweb.org>, Cyndi's List <www.cyndislist.com>, and library catalogs to find other maps and gazetteers online or in libraries.

A number of facsimile reprints are available in libraries and from booksellers and publishers; for some states, these have been reprinted for a number of different years. The reprints include such titles as these:

- *Dictionary of Alaska Place Names*, by Donald J. Orth. Washington, DC: U.S. Government Printing Office, 1967. Geological Survey Professional Paper 567.
- *Eastin Morris' Tennessee Gazetteer, 1834, and Matthew Rhea's Map of the State of Tennessee, 1832*, Robert M. McBride and Owen Meredith, eds. Nashville: Gazetteer Press, 1971. From 1834 original.
- *A Gazetteer of Illinois, in Three Parts*, by J.M. Peck. Bowie, Md.: Heritage Books, 1993. Reprint of 2d ed., originally published in Philadelphia by Grigg and Elliot, 1837.
- *A Gazetteer of Texas*, 2d ed., by Henry Gannett. Washington, D.C.: Government Printing Office, 1904. U.S. Geological Survey. Bulletin no. 224. Series F. Geography, 36.
- *A Gazetteer of the State of Georgia*, by Adiel Sherwood. Bowie, Md.: Heritage Books, 2001. Facsimile reprint of the 1837 gazetteer published by P. Force in Washington, DC.
- *A Gazetteer of the State of Maine: With Numerous Illustrations,* by Geo. J. Varney. Bowie, Md.: Heritage Books, 1991. Reprint of 1881 original, published in Boston by B.B. Russell.
- *Gazetteer of the State of Missouri: With a Map of the State . . . ,* Alphonso Wetmore, comp. St. Louis: C. Keemle, 1837. Microfilm. Woodbridge, Conn.: Research Publications, 1975. Western Americana, Frontier History of the Trans-Mississippi West, 1550–1900; reel 595, no. 6149.
- *A Gazetteer of the State of New-Hampshire*, by John Farmer and Jacob B. Moore. Bowie, Md.: Heritage Books, Inc., 1997. Facsimile reprint of 1823 original, including map. Index.
- *Gazetteer of the State of New York . . .*, by J.H. French. Baltimore, Md.: Genealogical Publishing Co., 1994. Reprint of J.H. French's 1860 gazetteer, published in Syracuse by R.P. Smith. Indexes.
- *A Gazetteer of the State of Pennsylvania*, by Thomas F. Gordon. New Orleans: Polyanthos Press, 1975. Reprint of 1832 original published in Philadelphia.
- *A Gazetteer of the States of Connecticut and Rhode-Island . . . ,* by John C. Pease and John M. Niles. Bowie, Md.: Heritage Books, 1991. Facsimile reprint of the 1819 original published by W.S. Marsh, Hartford, Connecticut. Index.
- *A Gazetteer of Vermont: Containing Descriptions of All the Counties, Towns, and Districts in the State*, by John Hayward. Bowie Md.: Heritage Books, 1990. Reprint of the 1849 original published by Tappan, Whittemore, and Mason in Boston. Index.
- *A Geographic Dictionary of Massachusetts*, by Henry Gannett. Baltimore: Genealogical Publishing Co., 1978. Reprint of 1894 bulletin no. 116, U.S. Geological Survey, published by the U.S. Government Printing Office, Washington, D.C.

- *A Geographic Dictionary of New Jersey*, by Henry Gannett. Baltimore: Genealogical Publishing Co., 1978. Reprint of 1894 bulletin no. 118, U.S. Geological Survey, published by the U.S. Government Printing Office, Washington, D.C.
- *A New and Comprehensive Gazetteer of Virginia, and the District of Columbia . . .*, by Joseph Martin. Westminster, Md.: Willow Bend Books, 2000. Bibliography and index. From *A Comprehensive Description of Virginia*, undated but circa 1830s, originally published in Richmond.

Topographic Maps

Other helpful maps for locating cemeteries and sites of ancestral residences, as well as for understanding how geography may have affected ancestors' lives, are topographic maps, made from aerial photographs by the U.S. Geological Survey (USGS). These maps show longitude and latitude designations, township and range numbers for applicable states, elevations, waterways, roads and trails, communities, some cemeteries, some vegetation, and often the locations of buildings at the time the map was made. Like general highway maps, these do not name individual residences or landowners.

Internet Source

Read more about the USGS and "topo" maps at <http://mcmcweb.er.usgs.gov/topomaps/>. Another online database of "topo" maps is TopoZone <www.topozone.com>.

Topographic maps may be used at the federal depository libraries that receive the published maps of the USGS. The maps may be purchased from the USGS Information Services [P.O. Box 25286, Denver, Colorado 80225; phone (888) 275-8747] or from the many "commercial dealers" in each state who are listed on the Web site <http://mapping.usgs.gov/esic/to_order.html>. Map depository libraries, other libraries, and map retailers in each state may also have the *Catalog of Topographic and Other Published Maps* for various states. Each state catalog, available on request from the USGS, not only lists commercial dealers and ordering information but also includes the *Index to Topographic and Other Map Coverage* for the state. This essential booklet helps you identify which map you need to order.

Another way to identify the standard 7.5-minute topographic map you need is to use Map Finder on the USGS Web site <http://edcwww.cr.usgs.gov/mapfinder>. Map Finder allows you to search for a map by entering a zip code or the name of a populated place or by clicking on a map. Once you have found the name of the map, you can place an order online with USGS or take the information to a local map dealer.

Geographic Names Information System (GNIS)

The GNIS of the USGS provides a service to help the public locate place names and geographic features. A twenty-five-year project began in 1976 to find such names on maps of all kinds, old and new, for a huge database. The information in this database includes the name, former names, and the location of every kind of feature except roads and commercial establishments. One exception to the noncommercial rule is the inclusion of ferries, fords, stores, mills, boat landings, and the like on old maps. Current military installations are not shown; historical ones are.

You can use GNIS to identify the topographic map that shows the town, Indian reservation, cemetery, creek, or other named feature you want to locate. Currently, this query system is at <http://geonames.usgs.gov/pls/gnis/web_query.gnis_web_query_form>. (Some search engines will take you close to the query page if you search using "GNIS query form.")

When your query result shows on the screen, scroll down the page to various options that allow you to view the feature on a topographic map or aerial photo. One option is to view the feature via the Census Bureau's Tiger Map Server. Especially for cemeteries, this feature helps pinpoint the location in relation to towns and roads in the vicinity and makes it easier to compare with road maps if you want to visit.

Many of the features shown in the GNIS are also published in the multivolume *Omni Gazetteer of the United States of America*, Frank R. Abate, ed. (Detroit: Omnigraphics, Inc., 1991). Numerous academic and research libraries have map collections with this set and other cartographic references. Large map collections include, but are not limited to, the following:

- Brown University, John Carter Brown Library, Providence, Rhode Island.
- Illinois State Library, Springfield.
- Newberry Library, Chicago.
- Massachusetts Historical Society, Boston; <www.masshis.org>.
- Michigan State University, Main Library, Map Library, East Lansing.
- University of Alabama, Map Library, Tuscaloosa; heavily involved in developing the GNIS database. See numerous historical and contemporary maps of the southeastern United States and other locations online at <http://alabamamaps.ua.edu>.
- University of Chicago, Regenstein Library, Chicago.
- University of Michigan, Clements Library, Ann Arbor.
- University of Texas, Austin, the Perry-Castañeda Library.
- University of Virginia, Alderman Library, Charlottesville; maintains an online Virginia gazetteer based on the GNIS database that helps identify the quadrangle (topographic) map showing the searched feature, <http://fisher.lib.virginia.edu/vagaz/frontpage.phtml>.
- University of Washington, Suzzallo Library, Seattle.
- Utah Valley Regional Family History Center, Harold B. Lee Library, Brigham Young University, Provo.

If you have difficulty finding a particular cemetery, church, or landmark in an ancestral area, or if you are trying to locate a community or other feature that no longer exists, try the GNIS. You can reach the GNIS by mail at U.S. Geological Survey, Branch of Geographic Names, 523 National Center, Reston, Virginia 20192 and by telephone at (703) 648-4544.

Defunct Communities

One challenge for genealogists is locating ancestral communities that no longer appear on road maps or county maps. If this is your problem after querying family members and searching family papers, **try these ideas**:

Idea Generator

1. Search maps and gazetteers contemporary with the ancestors, especially in libraries, archives, or museums in the target state or county.
2. Talk to old-timers in the county or parish.
3. Compare census and other information on families in the community with deed and plat book records, and plot this data on a grid map of the county.
4. Read local and county histories and newspapers.
5. Search postal directories, mail routes, and postal route maps. (Some communities, of course, did not have post offices.) At this writing, the Tennessee State Library provides an online database of Tennessee place names and post offices, based on the National Archives microfilm M1131 and M841, *Record of Appointment of Postmasters*, 1789–1871 at <www.state.tn.us/sos/statelib/pubsvs/postoff.htm>. A book based on these microfilm records and other records is *Tennessee Postoffices and Postmaster Appointments, 1789–1984*, D.R. Frazier, comp. (Dover, Tenn.: the compiler, 1984). The book and the online list give the name of the post office, its county, and the date the post office opened and closed. For example, the post office of Frierson, in Maury County, operated from 1884 to 1901. This information could give Frierson family researchers ideas for further investigations.

GNIS MAPS IN RESEARCH

Three locations in the teaching career of Stephen J. Ford of Louisiana were Sunflower, New Hope, and Hard Times, which are not identified on current road maps. A search using the online GNIS Web Query Form showed several Louisiana features that included the name Sunflower, but only one in the area where Ford lived—Franklin Parish. Located on the Bee Bayou quadrangle topographic map, that feature is Sunflower Cemetery, which could well have been the site of a church or community in the 1870s when Ford was there. Cemeteries and churches on a map are often remnants of a community that once was in the same location, and school classes were sometimes held at church buildings. At least, research can focus on a specific site. Figure 7-4, on page 260, shows Sunflower Cemetery on the map resulting from the GNIS query.

A GNIS search for New Hope revealed fifty-eight features in Louisiana, mostly churches of that name, four of which were in the rural area where Ford lived—Franklin, Tensas, and East Carroll parishes. The one in Franklin Parish was less than twenty miles from the Sunflower Cemetery.

GNIS located no place called Hard Times in Franklin Parish. However, on both the Newellton quadrangle "topo" map and several antique maps, a Hard Times Bend appears on the Mississippi River in neighboring Tensas Parish. The GNIS reported a historical site, Hard Times Landing Post Office, in that area but of unknown longitude and latitude coordinates. *Bullinger's Postal and Shippers Guide* (see below) listed Hard Times Landing as a post office in Tensas Parish but gave no further information.

Plotting on an area map the GNIS information and other known locations from Ford's life creates a broad "neighborhood" for further study in an attempt to learn more about his sibling(s) and identify his wife's family. This focus, especially for these three locations where Ford taught, involves research on the families of his students, whose names he recorded in an attendance record book still held by one of his descendants.

Case Study

This type of search is a good application of cluster genealogy.

6. Consult such references as *Bullinger's Postal and Shippers Guide for the United States and Canada*, published since 1871. In 1976, this Westwood, New Jersey, company issued a centennial reprint of *The Monitor Guide to Post Offices and Railroad Stations in the United States and Canada–1876*. The guide lists hundreds of towns that were post offices and/or railroad stations, with their county and state locations. Thus, it does not include communities that had neither a post office nor a railroad station. The guide also distinguishes between post offices and railroad stations in the same place if their names were different. Thus, it is a guide to double names and name changes. For example, Youngsville in Franklin County, North Carolina, is listed with a double name. Youngsville, as it is called today, was the railroad station name in 1876. At that time, its post office was called Pacific. In Prince George's County, Maryland, today's Oak Grove was then the post office name, with Brick Church as its railroad station. Spelling variations are not a new problem. This guide cautions, "If you do not find the place for which you are looking, try some other way of spelling the name, and look again."
7. Consult the Geographic Names Information System database (see page 257).

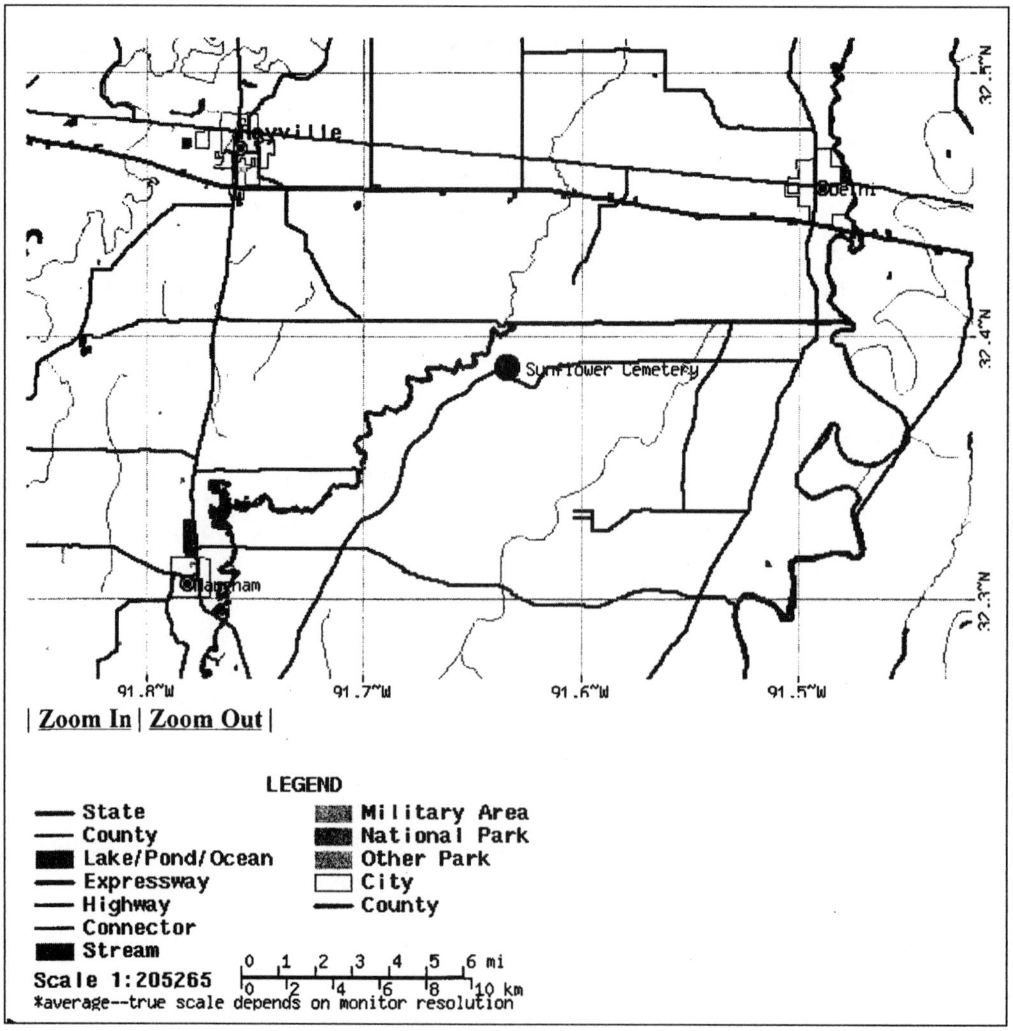

Figure 7-4 Map showing location of Sunflower Cemetery, Franklin Parish, Louisiana, USGS GNIS Map Server, online, <http://geonames.usgs.gov/pls/gnis/web_query.gnis_web_query_form>, accessed 8 January 2003.

Other Government Maps

Topographic maps are only one kind of map that can be located through the *Monthly Catalog of Government Publications*. (See page 291.) By looking for a place name such as a river or county in this index, you can sometimes find maps issued by various government agencies, such as the U.S. Geological Survey, the Corps of Engineers, the Forest Service, the Soil Conservation Service, or the National Oceanic and Atmospheric Administration. Maps published by these agencies often show landmarks, cemeteries, schools, and the location (not names) of individual residences.

The Post Office Department Reports of Site Locations, 1837–1950 (National Archives microfilm M1126) are forms, diagrams, and homemade maps sent to the department when a post office was established or moved. They were meant to identify the location of that post office, whether by section, township, and range or in relation to other landmarks, such as stores or houses. Most of the reports are post–Civil War, and some are for communities that no longer exist.

The *U.S. Serial Set*, including the *American State Papers*, is a major source of all kinds of maps. Especially during westward expansion and other exploration projects, reports to Congress often contained maps, from town plats to maps of trails and surveys for roads or ferries. The sixteen-volume *CIS U.S. Serial Set Index, Part XIV: Index and Carto-Bibliography of Maps, 1789–1969*, Donna P. Koepp, ed. (Bethesda, Md.: Congressional Information Service,

1995–) provides access to an estimated fifty thousand maps. The maps are indexed by geographic area, subject, title, and personal name. *The Territorial Papers* also contains scattered maps. An early Missouri map, about 1816, appears in *The Territorial Papers: Louisiana–Missouri Territory* (XV:118). Although it does not specify individual residences, it shows some ferries, villages, and courthouses, whose names may be the same as the families who established them.

GENEALOGICAL USE OF NAVIGATION MAPS

Family lore said that the Glasscocks of Bridgeport, Alabama, lived on nearby Long Island in the Tennessee River. Some maps showed the northern tip of the island above the state line in Tennessee; others showed the entire island below the state line in Alabama. Since at the time I did not have access to Alabama topographic maps, this question was a point of frustration and possibly a problem when it came to jurisdiction and finding appropriate records. Luckily, I discovered in the government documents collection of the Neumann Library, University of Houston-Clear Lake, a U.S. Army Corps of Engineers navigation chart of the Tennessee River. (Such navigation charts have been published for other rivers including the Cumberland, Allegheny, Ohio, and Mississippi.) It confirmed that Long Island (now Bridgeport Island) is mostly below the Alabama state line with its northern tip in the state of Tennessee. One piece of the puzzle was solved!
Gay E. Carter

For Further Reference

The publications listed below may help you find ancestral locations and maps in the Library of Congress and other collections. Some of the Library of Congress maps are available from the Photoduplication Service.

Internet Source

To learn more about maps of a state, consult WorldCat and see <www.cyndislist.com> under the state's name.

Published References

Alaska and the Northwest Part of North America, 1588–1898, P. Lee Phillips, comp. Washington, D.C.: Government Printing Office, 1898.

Atlas of the American Revolution. Chicago: Rand McNally, 1974. Has some city maps and a few that show family residences.

Atlases in Libraries of Chicago: A Bibliography and Union Check List. Chicago: University of Chicago Libraries, Document Section, 1936.

Checklist of Printed Maps of the Middle West to 1900, 14 vols., Robert W. Karrow Jr., ed. Chicago: Newberry Library, 1981–1983.

Civil War Maps: An Annotated List of Maps and Atlases in the Library of Congress, 2d ed. Richard W. Stephenson, ed. Washington, D.C.: Library of Congress, 1989. Indexed.

Detroit and Vicinity Before 1900: An Annotated List of Maps, Alberta G.A. Koerner, comp. Washington, D.C.: Library of Congress, 1968. Arranged chronologically.

A Genealogical and Historical Atlas of the United States of America, by E. Kay Kirkham. Salt Lake City: E.K. Kirkham, 1976.

The Geography and Map Division: A Guide to its Collections and Services. Rev. ed. Washington, D.C.: Library of Congress, 1975. Includes fire insurance, railroad, county maps, etc.

A Guide to Civil War Maps in the National Archives, rev. ed., Charlotte M. Ashby et al., comps. Washington, D.C.: National Archives, 1986.

Guide to U.S. Map Resources, 2d ed., David A. Cobb, comp. Chicago: American Library Association, 1990. Directory of facilities with map collections, by state.

A Handy Guide to Record-Searching in the Larger Cities of the United States, by E.K. Kirkham. Logan, Utah: Everton Publishers, 1974. Includes city maps with ward boundaries.

The Historical Atlas of United States Congressional Districts, 1789–1983, Kenneth C. Martis, ed. New York: The Free Press, division of Macmillan, 1982.

A List of Geographical Atlases in the Library of Congress, 9 vols., Philip Lee Phillips et al., comps. Washington, D.C.: Government Printing Office, 1909–1992. Annotated, indexed.

List of Manuscript Maps in the Edward E. Ayer Collection, Clara A. Smith, comp. Chicago: The Newberry Library, 1927.

A List of Maps of America in the Library of Congress, P. Lee Phillips, comp. Washington, D.C.: Government Printing Office, 1901. Includes states, counties, and cities. Alphabetical by place name.

A List of Nineteenth Century Maps of the State of Alabama, by Sara Elizabeth Mason. Birmingham, Ala.: Birmingham Public Library, 1973.

The Map Catalog. New York: Vantage Press, division of Random House, 1990.

Map Collections in the United States and Canada: A Directory. 4th ed. New York: Special Libraries Association, 1984.

Maps and Charts Published in America Before 1800: A Bibliography, 2d ed., rev., by James Clements Wheat and Christian F. Brun. London: Holland Press, 1985.

Maps Relating to Virginia in the Virginia State Library and Other Departments of the Commonwealth, Earl G. Swem, ed. Richmond, Va.: Virginia State Library, 1914.

The National Gazetteer: A Geographical Dictionary of the United States, by L. de Colange. London: Hamilton, Adams and Co., 1884.

Panoramic Maps of Anglo-American Cities: A Checklist of Maps in the Collections of the Library of Congress, Geography and Map Division, John R. Hébert, comp. Washington, D.C.: Library of Congress, 1974.

Township Atlas of the United States, John L. Androit, comp. McLean, Va.: Androit Associates, 1977. Shows villages in townships.

Ward Maps of United States Cities: A Selective Checklist of Pre–1900 Maps in the Library of Congress, Michael H. Shelley, comp. Washington, D.C.: Library of Congress, 1975. Covers thirty-five cities.

A useful reference guide is *Using Maps in Genealogy*, published by the USGS as Fact Sheet 099-02, September 2002. This revision is available on the USGS Web site in HTML and PDF versions at <http://mac.usgs.gov/mac/isb/pubs/factsheets/fs09902.html>. Paper copies can be found in many federal depository libraries or may be obtained by calling (888) ASK-USGS.

Library/Archive Source

MANUSCRIPT COLLECTIONS

Manuscript means handwritten, and handwritten documents are often found in libraries' special collections. Manuscript collections contain a great variety of items in small and large groupings, especially family, business, and organization papers. Most large collections have printed catalogs, guides, or calendars to help researchers identify and access their contents.

Libraries and archives in every state have manuscript collections important to the history, government, business—and therefore genealogy—of the state and its neighbors. Genealogists learn of these collections in books on research in the state or on Web sites of its libraries and archives.

What's in These Collections?

Probably the most useful type of collection for genealogists is family papers, the same types of records that many families keep: diaries, letters, family Bibles, scrapbooks, photographs, newspaper clippings, household accounts, deeds, family business papers, pre–Civil War plantation records, and personal memorabilia. Manuscript collections may include business papers with ledgers, journals, receipts, and employee or customer records. Families of lawyers, doctors, undertakers, merchants, and other businessmen have donated records to some special collections; these often contain information on citizens of the town or county, including employees of the company. School and organization papers may include enrollment and membership lists, publications, catalogs, yearbooks, memorabilia, and newspaper clippings.

Figure 7-5, on page 264, is an example of a school record from family papers in an academic library's special collections: the monthly "Record of the Daily Recitations, &c, of Master F.A. Mood" from the High School of Charleston, South Carolina, dated 1 April 1846. The principal had sent this report to the student's father. It shows that school teaching and class structure were different from what we know today and prompts the genealogist to learn more about high school education in the 1840s.

Diaries are important resources in manuscript collections, and many have been published. Even if your ancestors did not keep diaries or journals, or if none survive, the diaries of others may mention your family members. Diarists wrote about their friends and relatives, commented on meals and daily activities, divulged private emotions and thoughts, memorialized deceased children or spouses, editorialized on current events and local courtships, and reported on celebrations and funerals among their cluster of associates. They relate humorous, tragic, and humdrum events.

Many diaries and compiled letters from the Civil War years reflect the hardships of the time and often mention other people. Even in later years, when Civil War veterans wrote regimental and company histories, much in the form of journals or memoirs, they mentioned relatives, tentmates, officers, and others with whom they came in contact. Perhaps as important as anything else, these personal accounts help us "moderns" remember that human nature is human nature. Technology, attitudes, and cultural influences change the details of daily life, but human nature remains fairly constant.

Consult library catalogs and WorldCat for published diaries from your ancestral locations. Even those from the general area where your ancestors lived may give you insight into customs and people in the area. We cannot know with certainty that our ancestors thought or behaved in the same ways as diarists in their community, but the more we know of these patterns and of our ancestors' circumstances, the more we may be able to suggest common experiences. An interesting book about women's diaries and the social context in which they were written is *Read This Only to Yourself: The Private Writings of Midwestern Women, 1880–1910*, by Elizabeth Hampsten (Bloomington: Indiana University Press, 1982).

A delightful series of children's books, "Diaries, Letters, and Memoirs," from Blue Earth Books (an imprint of Capstone Press of Mankato, Minnesota), combines history with excerpts from the childhood diaries of boys and girls. The diaries are from ultimately famous people—Louisa May Alcott, Charles Lindbergh, and Theodore Roosevelt—and others not

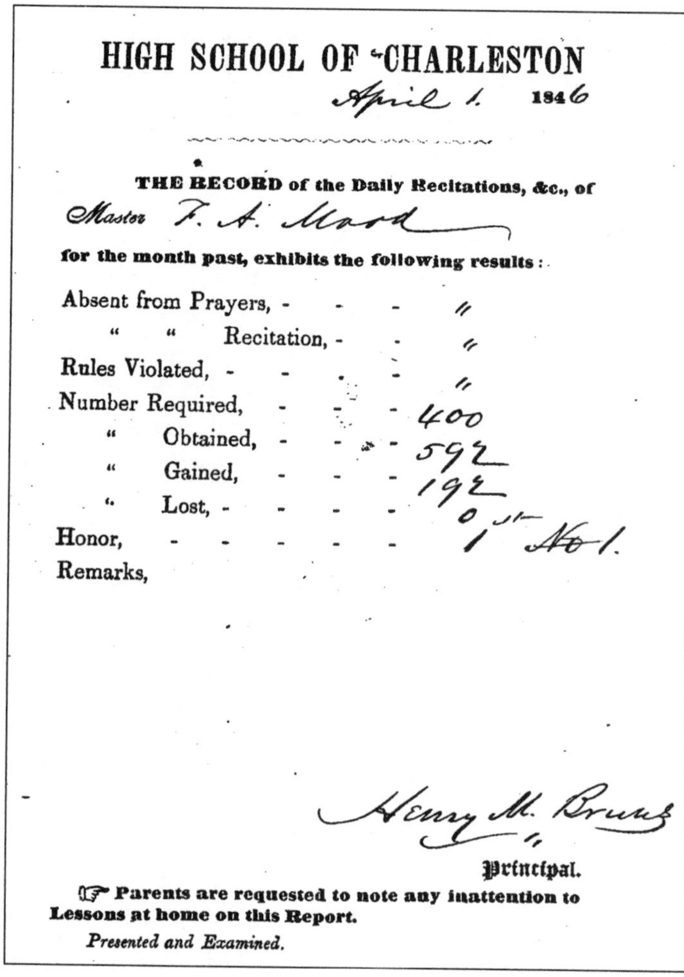

HIGH SCHOOL OF CHARLESTON

April 1. 1846

THE RECORD of the Daily Recitations, &c., of

Master F. A. Mood

for the month past, exhibits the following results:

Absent from Prayers,	"
" " Recitation,	"
Rules Violated,	"
Number Required,	400
" Obtained,	592
" Gained,	192
" Lost,	0
Honor,	1st No 1.
Remarks,	

Henry M. Bruns

Principal.

☞ Parents are requested to note any inattention to Lessons at home on this Report.

Presented and Examined.

Figure 7-5 Record of F.A. Mood, High School of Charleston, April 1846, from the Special Collections, A. Frank Smith Jr. Library Center, Southwestern University, Georgetown, Texas.

well known: a colonial Quaker girl, a Civil War drummer boy, a pioneer farm girl, a free black girl in the 1850s, a whaling captain's daughter, and others.

Bibliographies of diaries, both manuscript and published, include the following:

American Diaries, Laura Arksey et al., comp. Detroit: Gale Research Co., 1983–1986. Volume 1—diaries written 1492–1844. Volume 2—diaries written 1845–1980. The books include subject, name, and geographic indexes.

American Diaries: An Annotated Bibliography of American Diaries Written Prior to the Year 1861, William Matthews, comp. Berkeley, Calif.: University of California Press, 1945.

And So to Bed: A Bibliography of Diaries Published in English, by Patricia Pate Havlice. Metuchen, N.J.: Scarecrow Press, 1987. Indexed by name, subject, and place. Includes an index to Matthews' *American Diaries*.

The Published Diaries and Letters of American Women: An Annotated Bibliography, by Joyce D. Goodfriend. Boston: G.K. Hall, 1987.

Travels in the Confederate States: A Bibliography, E. Merton Coulter, comp. Baton Rouge: Louisiana State University Press, 1994, reprint of the 1948 original by the University of Oklahoma Press. Bibliography of memoirs, diaries, and recollections, written during or after the Civil War.

Women's Diaries, Journals, and Letters: An Annotated Bibliography, by Cheryl Cline. New York: Garland Publishing Co., 1989.

Women's Diaries of the Westward Journey, by Lillian Schlissel. New York: Schocken Books, 1982. History, photos, and bibliography; chart showing the ninety-six diaries consulted.

Diversity in Collections

Hundreds of manuscript collections exist throughout the United States. Descriptions of two must suffice. Genealogists with ancestors from Minnesota westward to Oregon often consult the Great Northern Railroad Records and Northern Pacific Railroad Records at the Minnesota Historical Society in St. Paul as they look for evidence of ancestors in the railroad employee records. This important facility also houses records from numerous businesses, organizations, and families. Descriptions of many collections are available on the society's Web site at <www.mnhs.org/library/collections/manuscripts/manuscripts.html>.

The University of Texas Center for American History <www.cah.utexas.edu> also provides a number of important collections and online descriptions. The Southern Historical Archival Collection contains antebellum family and plantation records as well as archives from the Natchez Children's Home, 1816–1945. The Natchez Trace Papers include documents of the Lower Mississippi Valley—primarily Louisiana, Mississippi, and Arkansas—from about 1759 to about 1813. Two guides to this collection are *Inside the Natchez Trace Collection: New Sources for Southern History*, Katherine J. Adams and Lewis L. Gould, eds. (Baton Rouge: Louisiana State University Press, 1999), and *Calendar of the Natchez Trace Collection: Provincial and Territorial Documents, 1759–1813*, by Judy Riffel (Baton Rouge: La Comité des Archives de la Louisiane, 1999).

Most such collections contain family papers and correspondence; these manuscripts are often the most useful for genealogists. Many collections include papers of businesses, churches, schools, and organizations, although these documents are often more historical than genealogical. In other words, if your ancestor was a member of the leadership of one of the businesses or other institutions, he or she could be mentioned in connection with its official business but probably not in relation to family. Nevertheless, hundreds of families are represented in the manuscript collections around the country.

The Draper Manuscripts

Important

One of the most extensive manuscript collections for early American history and genealogy is the Draper Manuscripts housed at the State Historical Society of Wisconsin. They deserve discussion here due to the large region to which they pertain. The manuscripts are largely letters, documents, and notes about the South and trans-Allegheny West that Lyman Copeland Draper collected during the second half of the nineteenth century. The collection contains fifty series representing such topics as frontier life and wars, the American Revolution, interviews with pioneers and their descendants, genealogical information, and papers of prominent men, including Daniel Boone, George Rogers Clark, and Thomas Sumter. The documents include payroll and muster roll lists, court documents, newspaper articles, memos, bills of sale and receipts, obituaries, information from family Bibles, sketches and maps, and numerous letters to and from Draper about regional genealogy and history. For example, series SS includes a payroll of Captain Joseph Ogle's company of Ohio County militia in 1781; series VV includes an 1874 letter to Draper about the marriage of Colonel Moses Shelby and an 1874 letter from Draper asking for genealogical information about the Sumter family.

The descriptive *Guide to the Draper Manuscripts*, by Josephine L. Harper (Madison, Wis.: State Historical Society of Wisconsin, 1983), is available at libraries and from the society. The documents are organized into these series:

A	George Bedinger Papers
B	Draper's Life of Boone
C	Boone Papers
D	Border Forays
E	Brady and Wetzel Papers
F	Joseph Brant Papers
G	Brant Papers and Brant Miscellanies
H	Daniel Brodhead Papers
J	George Rogers Clark Papers
K	George Rogers Clark Miscellanies
L	Jonathon Clark Papers
M	William Clark Papers
N	William Groghan Papers
O	Daniel Drake papers
P	Draper's Biographical Sketches
Q	Draper's Historical Miscellanies
R	Draper's Memoranda Books
S	Draper's Notes
T	Thomas Forsyth Papers
U	Frontier War Papers
V	Georgia, Alabama, and South Carolina Papers
W	Josiah Harmer Papers
X	William Henry Harrison
Z	Illinois Papers
AA	William Irvine Papers
BB	Simon Kenton Papers
CC	Kentucky papers
DD	King's Mountain Papers
EE	London Documents at Albany
FF	Mecklenburg Declaration, by Draper
GG	Mecklenburg Declaration Papers
HH	Mecklenburg Declaration Miscellanies
JJ	Newspaper Extracts
KK	North Carolina Papers
LL	Paris Documents at Albany
MM	Robert Patterson Papers
NN	Pittsburgh & Northwest Virginia Papers
OO	Pension Statements
PP	Potter Papers
QQ	William Preston Papers
RR	Rudolph Ney Papers
SS	David Shepard Papers
TT	South Carolina Papers
UU	South Carolina in the Revolution Miscellanies
VV	Thomas Sumter Papers
WW	John Cleves Symmes Papers
XX	Tennessee Papers
YY	Tecumseh Papers
ZZ	Virginia Papers

For More Info

For more information, see "The Draper Manuscripts: An Important Tool in Historical Research," by Ora Kasten in *Heritage Quest* Magazine no. 79 (January/February 1999): 12–16.

Although the collection is not indexed, six volumes of "calendars" describe eleven of the series in detail, with indexes to names and places mentioned in the descriptions. These are not every-name indexes to the collection but are very helpful in identifying potentially helpful documents. In the calendars, each document is identified by a finding code such as 8VV321, which means "volume 8 of series VV, page 321." The calendar series is available in most of the libraries that have the microfilm collection, and it includes these volumes:

1. *The Preston and Virginia Papers of the Draper Collection of Manuscripts*, by Mabel Clare Weaks. Madison, Wis.: The State Historical Society of Wisconsin, 1915. Publications of the State Historical Society of Wisconsin, Calendar Series, vol. 1. Describes Series QQ and ZZ.
2. *Calendar of the Kentucky Papers of the Draper Collection of Manuscripts*, by Mabel Clare Weaks. Madison: The State Historical Society of Wisconsin, 1925. Publications of the State Historical Society of Wisconsin, Calendar Series, vol. 2. Describes Series CC.
3. *Calendar of the Tennessee and King's Mountain Papers of the Draper Collection of Manuscripts*, by the State Historical Society of Wisconsin. Madison: The Society, 1929. Publications of the State Historical Society of Wisconsin, Calendar Series, vol. 3. Describes Series XX and DD.
4. *Calendar of the George Rogers Clark Papers of the Draper Collection of Manuscripts*,

SUCCESS IN MANUSCRIPT COLLECTIONS

The 1910 census of Castleton, Richmond County, New York, listed my great-uncle, Alexander Perry, as a widower living with his parents; this suggested a first marriage of which I had been unaware. Then, a 1993 history of Christ Episcopal Church, New Brighton, Staten Island referred to a plaque in the 1906 sanctuary that memorialized an Alice Martin DeWolf Perry; the plaque was dedicated on All Saint's Day, 1908. The name DeWolf struck me because the Perry family had strong ties with DeWolfs of Bristol, Rhode Island. A granddaughter of Alexander Perry and his second wife confirmed that Alexander had been married previously and thought the wife's name was Tucker, not DeWolf. Was she divorced? A widow?

An online guide to the special collections at the University of Rhode Island Library showed papers of the Colt-DeWolf families of Bristol, Rhode Island, containing not only a 1793 will for a DeWolf ancestor but a wedding invitation of an Alice Martin DeWolf Tucker, the daughter of Mr. and Mrs. John Hryne Tucker, at the Collegiate Church in New York City. The library staff sent me copies of both documents.

The archivist of the Dutch Reformed Collegiate Church of New York City confirmed that Alice Tucker of Bristol, Rhode Island, and Alexander Perry married at that church on 9 August 1907. Indeed, the 1900 census of Bristol enumerated the John Hryne Tucker household that included twin daughters Ethel D. and Alice Martin D.W. Tucker, born in July 1876, and in-laws Jacob and Ann Martin. Since Alexander Perry and his siblings had spent their childhood summers with their Perry grandparents, both DeWolf descendants, in Bristol, he and Alice probably had known each other for many years before they married. The tragedy of their situation was her death a little more than a year after their marriage; perhaps she died in childbirth.

The couple apparently became members of Christ Church on Staten Island. Yet, why did they marry in New York City and not in the bride's hometown or Staten Island? Why did they marry in the Dutch Reformed church when the bride's family was likely Episcopalian? The research continues, but the manuscript collections were important in getting the search this far. *Alexander Perry Scott*

by the State Historical Society of Wisconsin, indexed by Samuel McDowell. Utica, Ky.: McDowell Publications, 1985. Publications of the State Historical Society of Wisconsin, Calendar Series, vol. 4. Describes Series J.

5. *Calendar of the Thomas Sumter Papers of the Draper Collection of Manuscripts*, by the State Historical Society of Wisconsin, indexed by Sandra Howell. Utica, Ky.: McDowell publications, 1986. Publications of the State Historical Society of Wisconsin, Calendar Series, vol. 5. Describes Series VV.
6. *Calendar of the Frontier Wars Papers of the Draper Collection of Manuscripts*, by the State Historical Society of Wisconsin, indexed by Samuel McDowell. Utica, Ky.: McDowell Publications, 1991. Publications of the State Historical Society of Wisconsin, Calendar Series, vol. 6. Describes Series U, SS, TT, and UU.

In addition, at least four histories, compiled from documents in the collection and other sources, contain transcriptions of documents from several series.

1. *Documentary History of Dunmore's War, 1774*, Reuben Gold Thwaites and Louise Phelps Kellogg, eds. Madison: Wisconsin Historical Society, 1905. Reprint, Harrisonburg, Va.: C.J. Carrier Co., 1974.
2. *The Revolution on the Upper Ohio, 1775–1777*, Reuben Gold Thwaites and Louise Phelps Kellogg, eds. Madison: Wisconsin Historical Society, 1912. Reprint, Port Washington, N.Y.: Kennikat Press, 1970.
3. *Frontier Defense on the Upper Ohio, 1777–1778*, Reuben Gold Thwaites and Louise Phelps Kellogg, eds. Madison: Wisconsin Historical Society, 1912.
4. *Frontier Advance on the Upper Ohio, 1778–1779*, Louise Phelps Kellogg, ed. Madison: The Wisconsin Historical Society, 1916. Wisconsin Historical Publications; Collections, vol. 23, Draper Series, vol. 4.

Two very different documents illustrate the diversity of the Draper collection. Figure 7-6, below, is from a "register of persons killed, wounded, or taken prisoner by the enemy in Augusta County, Virginia, or who have made their escape" over a period of months during the French and Indian War, beginning in October 1754. This page reported for 30 July 1755 into September 1755. Surnames on the list included Draper, Cull, Leonard, Griffith, and White. The last on the page was "an old man his Wife & a Schoolmaster." The first name on this page of the list was that of Colonel James Patton, of North River, who was killed.

Figure 7-6 Register of persons killed, wounded, or taken prisoner by the enemy . . . , Augusta County, Virginia, July–September 1755, Draper Manuscripts, 1QQ83, microfilm.

A number of the documents in this series pertained to James Patton, including the one in Figure 7-7, on page 269. Dated 28 April 1738, this document was an indenture by which Peter Burn (or Burke in the calendar) "of his own freewill and consent" bound himself for five years to James Paton [*sic*], Merchant, in return for his passage to America. Although there appears to be an error in the twelfth line, where Peter's name was written instead of

Paton's, the intent was clear. During the term of service and employment, Paton was to supply meat, drink, apparel, lodging, and other "Necessaries" and pay the "usual Allowance" at the end of the five years. The parties then "interchangeably set their Hands and Seals" to the document. Thus, Peter Burn made his mark on the copy that James Paton kept; Burn kept the half that Paton had signed. The curved line at the top no doubt separated the two halves of the document, so that they would have fit together into a whole.

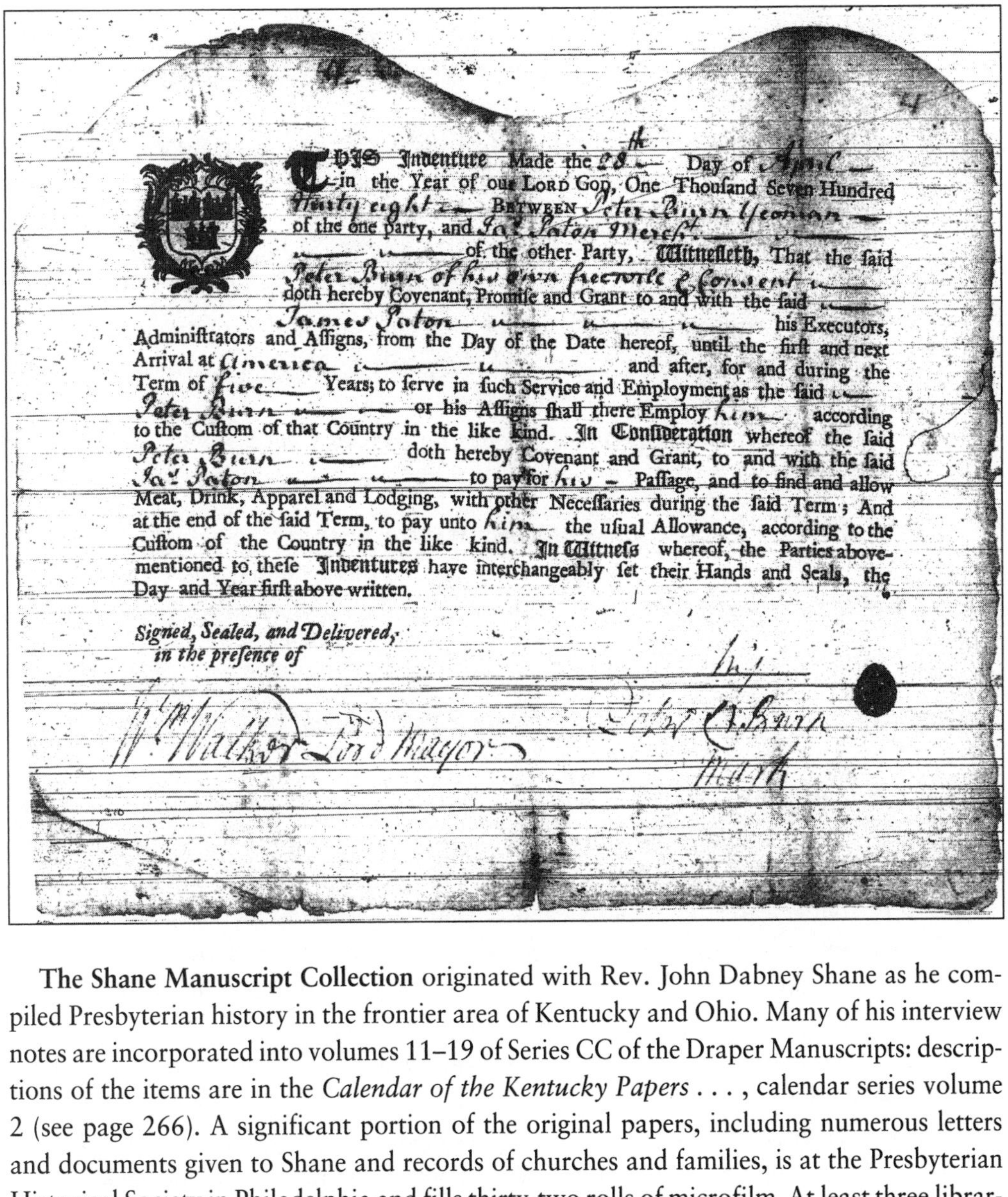

THIS Indenture Made the 28th Day of April in the Year of our LORD GOD, One Thousand Seven Hundred thirty eight BETWEEN Peter Burn Yeoman of the one party, and Jas. Paton Merch.t of the other Party, Witnesseth, That the said Peter Burn of his own freewill & Consent doth hereby Covenant, Promise and Grant to and with the said James Paton his Executors, Administrators and Assigns, from the Day of the Date hereof, until the first and next Arrival at America and after, for and during the Term of five Years; to serve in such Service and Employment as the said Peter Burn or his Assigns shall there Employ him according to the Custom of that Country in the like kind. In Consideration whereof the said Peter Burn doth hereby Covenant and Grant, to and with the said Jas. Paton to pay for his Passage, and to find and allow Meat, Drink, Apparel and Lodging, with other Necessaries during the said Term; And at the end of the said Term, to pay unto him the usual Allowance, according to the Custom of the Country in the like kind. In Witness whereof, the Parties above-mentioned to these Indentures have interchangeably set their Hands and Seals, the Day and Year first above written.

Signed, Sealed, and Delivered, in the presence of

W.m Walker Lord Mayor

Peter Burn his mark

Figure 7-7 Indenture of Peter Burn with James Paton, 28 April 1738, Draper Manuscripts, 1QQ4, microfilm.

The Shane Manuscript Collection originated with Rev. John Dabney Shane as he compiled Presbyterian history in the frontier area of Kentucky and Ohio. Many of his interview notes are incorporated into volumes 11–19 of Series CC of the Draper Manuscripts: descriptions of the items are in the *Calendar of the Kentucky Papers . . .*, calendar series volume 2 (see page 266). A significant portion of the original papers, including numerous letters and documents given to Shane and records of churches and families, is at the Presbyterian Historical Society in Philadelphia and fills thirty-two rolls of microfilm. At least three libraries with this microfilm collection are the Family History Library, Allen County Public Library in Fort Wayne, and Clayton Library in Houston. A finding aid to this part of the Shane collection is *The Shane Manuscript Collection: A Genealogical Guide to the Kentucky and Ohio Papers*, by William K. Hall (Galveston, Tex.: Frontier Press, 1990).

Finding Manuscript Collections

You can identify a manuscript collection in several ways. Two major resources are the *National Union Catalog of Manuscript Collections* (NUCMC), discussed in chapter eight, and the *National Inventory of Documents Sources* (NIDS). NIDS, published by Chadwyck-Healey, is a microfiche collection of finding aids, catalogs, and indexes to help researchers locate and learn more about manuscript collections held in libraries and archives in the United States, the United Kingdom, and Ireland. Both NUCMC and NIDS are searchable electronically in Chadwyck-Healey's subscription database *ArchivesUSA*.

As a follow-up to these sources, you can contact the individual holding institution for a catalog or guide to a particular collection; some institutions have these guides on their Web sites. Often you can order copies of manuscripts for a fee, even if you cannot visit the collection.

Three handy sources for identifying or surveying manuscript collections in your state of interest are the following:

- *Directory of Archives and Manuscript Repositories in the United States*. 2d ed. Phoenix: Oryx Press, 1988. Revised and updated version of the Yale guide; covers more than forty-five hundred depositories.
- *A Guide to Archives and Manuscripts in the United States*, Philip M. Hamer, ed. New Haven, Conn.: Yale University Press, 1961, for the National Historical Publications Commission. Arranged alphabetically by state and city; indexed; describes holdings for over one thousand institutions, including state archives and historical societies, research and public libraries, and museums.
- *Guides to Archives and Manuscript Collections in the United States: An Annotated Bibliography*, by Donald L. DeWitt. Westport, Conn.: Greenwood Press, 1994.

Library/Archive Source

Look for manuscript collections especially at state, historical society, and academic libraries in your research area. With access to the Internet, you may be able to identify a collection that contains material pertinent to your search. Search engines can help you find Web sites for these libraries; many of their Web sites post guides to their special collections. If your local public or academic library provides access to WorldCat, you can search for your subjects of interest, such as diaries, family papers, account books, and ledgers.

Guides to Manuscript Collections

The following is a sampling of bibliographies on manuscript collections. Many special collections have such guides. If a guide is not online, ask how you can acquire one that is pertinent to your research. Use library catalogs and WorldCat to identify others.

African American Genealogy: A Bibliography and Guide to Sources, by Curt Bryan Witcher. Fort Wayne, Ind.: Round Tower Books, 2000. Includes holdings of white and black family papers in major repositories nationwide.

Catalogued Manuscripts and Diaries of the California Section, Thomas H. Fante, comp. Sacramento, Calif.: California State Library, 1981.

Civil War Manuscripts: A Guide to Collections in the Manuscript Division of the Library of Congress, John R. Sellers, comp. Washington, D.C.: Library of Congress, 1986.

A Guide to Major Manuscript Collections Accessioned and Processed by the Library of the Western Reserve Historical Society Since 1970, by Kermit J. Pike. Cleveland: Western Reserve Historical Society, 1987.

Guide to Private Manuscript Collections in the North Carolina State Archives, by Barbara T. Cain. Raleigh: North Carolina Department of Cultural Resources, Division of Archives and History, 1981. Indexed.

A Guide to the Manuscripts and Archives of the Western Reserve Historical Society, by Kermit J. Pike. Cleveland, Ohio: Western Reserve Historical Society, 1972.

Manuscript Sources in the Library of Congress for Research on the American Revolution,

John R. Sellers et al., comps. Washington, D.C.: Library of Congress, 1975.

Manuscripts on Microfilm: A Checklist of the Holdings in the Manuscript Division. Washington, D.C.: Library of Congress, 1973.

Members of Congress: A Checklist of Their Papers in the Manuscript Division, Library of Congress. Washington, D.C.: Library of Congress, 1980.

Overland Passages: A Guide to Overland Documents in the Oregon Historical Society, Kris White and Mary-Catherine Cuthill, eds. Portland: Oregon Historical Society Press, 1993.

Preliminary Listing of the San Francisco Manuscript Collections in the Library of the California Historical Society, by Diana Lachatnere. San Francisco: California Historical Society, 1980.

The Shaker Collection of the Western Reserve Historical Society: A Reel List to the Manuscripts and a Short Title List of the Printed Materials Contained in the Microform Collection, by Mary L. Hart Richmond. Glen Rock, N.J.: Microfilming Corp. of America, 1977.

Genealogically Important Collections

The nature of manuscript collections means they vary both in content and in usefulness to a given research project. However, they are well worth investigating, both for the fascinating social history they contain and for the potential discovery of genealogical information. Besides the collections whose guides are listed above, the following list is a sampling from the hundreds of manuscript collections in the United States that hold materials of potential value for genealogists—diaries, family papers and Bibles, letters, early U.S. printed materials, photographs, organization and business documents, and historical documents.

- American Antiquarian Society, Boston <www.americanantiquarian.org>
- Bancroft Library, University of California at Berkeley <http://bancroft.berkeley.edu>
- The Filson Historical Society, Louisville, Kentucky <www.filsonhistorical.org>
- Historic New Orleans Collection, Williams Research Center, New Orleans <www.hnoc.org>
- Library of Virginia, Richmond <www.lva.lib.va.us>
- Maryland Historical Society, Baltimore <www.mdhs.org> under "library collections"
- Massachusetts Historical Society, Boston <www.masshist.org>
- New England Historic Genealogical Society, Boston <www.newenglandancestors.org>
- The Newberry Library, Chicago <www.newberry.org>; also a large collection on Native American history
- Society for the Preservation of New England Antiquities, Archives Library, Boston <www.spnea.org>; architectural history, photographs, drawings, papers
- State Historical Society of Wisconsin, Madison <www.wisconsinhistory.org>
- University of Arkansas, Fayetteville, Libraries, Special Collections <http://libinfo.uark.edu/specialcollections/about/overview.asp>
- University of North Carolina at Chapel Hill <www.unc.edu>
- Western Kentucky University, Bowling Green <www.wku.edu> and <http://digilib.kyvl.org/dynaweb/oak> for digital guides to many collections in the state

Libraries

PART I—PUBLIC, PRIVATE, AND ACADEMIC LIBRARIES

Public, private, and academic libraries often own research materials that are valuable for genealogists. These collections may include books and periodicals on historical or genealogical subjects, local history collections, vertical files of genealogical information, and reference materials that aid you in finding information. Many of these libraries also have local or regional manuscript, map, and newspaper collections and documents from federal or state governments. Regardless of the sizes of their collections, libraries are valuable for research. Large libraries have enough material to keep researchers busy for weeks or months. They make wonderful excuses for extended vacations.

In addition to local public and university libraries, genealogists are fortunate to have available the huge Library of Congress and a number of private (not government-funded) libraries that have large historical and genealogical collections. Some of the private institutions that are major research facilities are the Library of the National Society, Daughters of the American Revolution (Washington, DC), the Newberry Library (Chicago), The Filson Historical Society Library (Louisville, Kentucky), the New England Historic Genealogical Society (Boston), the American Antiquarian Society (Worcester, Massachusetts), the Harold B. Simpson History Complex Research Center (Hillsboro, Texas), and the Family History Library of the Church of Jesus Christ of Latter-day Saints (Salt Lake City).

To identify libraries with genealogy and/or local history collections, consult the *Directory of American Libraries With Genealogy or Local History Collections* by P. William Filby (Wilmington, Del.: Scholarly Resources, 1988) and the *American Library Directory* (New Providence, N.J.: R.R. Bowker, division of Reed Publishing, latest edition). The library directory is organized by state and city; each library's entry may mention collections such as genealogy or local history. This directory does not always include archives.

Identifying libraries or searching their catalogs is now possible through the Internet. Sites such as LIBWEB: Library Servers via WWW <http://sunsite.berkeley.edu/Libweb/>, LibrarySpot <www.libraryspot.com/>, or Librarians Serving Genealogists: Genealogy Libraries on the WWW <www.genealogy.org/~holdiman/LSG/libraries.html> have links to different types of libraries. USGenWeb <www.usgenweb.org/> is another good place to look for local libraries in your research area.

When visiting libraries, genealogists want to find books and periodicals with abstracts of marriage records, deeds, wills, and newspaper articles; family and county histories; and census and cemetery records. These sources are most often found in genealogy libraries and departments, but many libraries have such materials. In fact, these are not the only sources that contain genealogical information and the historical studies that place ancestors in the perspective of their times and places.

History is a large category in many libraries, and each state, region, and territorial possession of the United States has its section of shelves with books and scholarly journals pertaining to its history. For instance, one rather typical university library, far from Pennsylvania, contains several sections of shelving dedicated to books on historical topics in Pennsylvania, including books of letters, personal papers, diaries, biographies, town and state histories, and passenger lists. The ethnic and social histories include a wide range of subjects of interest to genealogists working on Pennsylvania ancestors. These subjects include the Irish, Jews, and African Americans in Philadelphia; Slovak Catholics and Lutherans in Pittsburgh; the Moravian town of Bethlehem; and the Scotch-Irish of colonial Pennsylvania.

Reminder

Many libraries have local or regional history collections that contain genealogical materials. Such a collection may also include a vertical file that contains folders on families of the area. These folders may hold letters, documents, scrapbooks, photographs, Bible records, family group charts, newspaper articles, obituaries, and other information on family members. Such a file may help you take your family back several generations, may help you find living family members who can share information, and is certainly a way for you to share with other searchers what you have collected and documented. Even if you cannot leave materials for the vertical file while you are visiting a library, you can send information at any time and ask that it be placed in the vertical file under the family name.

If your local public library does not have such a vertical file, perhaps you can help form one. After all, family records make a valuable complement to public records, and the public library is a central, accessible location for such information to be kept. In fact, two especially successful research days stand out in my mind because of vertical files on local families; one was in the city of Wilmington, Delaware, and one was in the very small town of Alto, Texas.

Interlibrary Loan

Interlibrary loan is an important part of research. It can provide access to books, microfilm, periodicals, master's theses, and doctoral dissertations. The subject matter is wide-ranging, but genealogists are usually interested in history—biographies, county and local histories, military unit histories, and some family histories.

Loans through other libraries are usually handled by the library reference departments, which also have many of the directories and other materials that researchers use time and time again. Thus, for researchers, reference librarians are important. However, they are not there to do research for you but to point you toward references, to offer suggestions, to answer questions, and to handle interlibrary loan requests. One habit that gives genealogists a bad reputation in libraries and public records repositories is being unprepared before asking questions, thus expecting too much assistance from the staff, who have many patrons to help and their own work to do. In the case of interlibrary loan, the sending and receiving librarians can work more effectively for you if you provide accurate title, author, and publication information, and page numbers where applicable. It is your job to get that information *before* requesting interlibrary loan.

OCLC is one subscription service that libraries may join for the purpose of uniform cataloging and for interlibrary loan. The system contains a large database of holdings from libraries throughout the country. If your library participates in OCLC or a similar cataloging service, you have access to millions of books. Many libraries offer access to WorldCat, the OCLC online union catalog and part of the OCLC FirstSearch group of searchable databases.

In the area of genealogy, however, few libraries lend materials. Those that do sometimes have limitations and restrictions. Some public or state libraries will lend to other libraries within their state. It is not important that the borrower know the lending policy of each library, for you probably would not be contacting the library that holds the material you would like to borrow. The reference or interlibrary loan librarians take care of the communication. These resource people usually are very helpful and conscientious in their efforts to acquire the materials we patrons need. The fee you pay for such interlibrary loan is minimal and well worth the cost.

Interlibrary loan is also possible through various genealogical and historical institutions, some of which are listed elsewhere in this book. Several independent lending (rental) libraries, in addition to those listed on pages 2–3, include the following:

- Duke University, Perkins Library, Durham, NC 27706-2597. For interlibrary loan of microfilm of supplemental census schedules, contact their Newspapers and Microforms Department. See <www.lib.duke.edu/access/news/census.htm>. For purchase of these films, contact Photographic Services Section, CB #3934, Wilson Library, University of North Carolina, Chapel Hill, NC 27514-8890. A reel index is available online at <www.lib.unc.edu/ncc/phs/census.html>.
- Genealogical Center Library, P.O. Box 71343, Marietta, GA 30007-1343; e-mail: gencenlib@aol.com; Website <http://homepages.rootsweb.com/~gencenlb/index.htm l>. Rents books only. Has a sizable collection including some materials from almost every state; largest concentration is from states east of the Mississippi River. Reasonable annual membership fee.
- Mid-Continent Public Library, 15616 East 24 Highway, Independence, MO 64050-2057. Interlibrary loan catalog, *Genealogy From the Heartland*, available online at <www.mcpl.lib.mo.us/branch/ge/heartland>.
- National Genealogical Society (NGS) in Arlington, Virginia. Circulating collection located at Special Collections, St. Louis County Library, 1640 South Lindbergh, St. Louis, MO 63131-3598. NGS members may borrow books through interlibrary loan. Online catalog accessible from <www.ngsgenealogy.org/libprecat.htm>; books available for loan are indicated by the code "SLCL—NGS Collection."
- New England Historic Genealogical Society, 101 Newbury, Boston, MA 02116. Large research library of books and manuscripts is open to visitors; circulating collection is housed in separate facility in Framingham, Massachusetts, and available for loan to members only. Collection especially strong for New England, but includes Canadian, European, and U.S. materials. Search online catalog at <www.newenglandancestors .org/libraries/sydneyplus.asp>.

Tip

Some institutions have published descriptions of their loan materials, and some lists are published on their Web sites. One such booklet is *Searching for Your Ancestors—And All That Jazz!* compiled by Virginia Rogers Smith (Baton Rouge: State Library of Louisiana, 1997), a description of the genealogy collection in the Louisiana Section of the State Library. The text of this booklet is also on the State Library of Louisiana's Web site at <www.state.lib.la.us/Dept/LaSect/searchin.htm>. Microfilm and duplicate titles of books are available for interlibrary loan.

Family History Library and Family History Centers

Although it is beyond the scope of this book to discuss libraries individually (and there are many), the Family History Library merits attention. The Church of Jesus Christ of Latter-day Saints, sometimes abbreviated LDS, maintains in Salt Lake City, Utah, the largest genealogical library in the world. Through more than thirty-seven hundred branches—Family History Centers—worldwide, researchers have access to numerous microprint materials from the library's holdings. To get a more complete idea of the size and scope of this library, consult these books:

- *The Library: A Guide to the LDS Family History Library*, Johni Cerny and Wendy Elliott, eds. Salt Lake City: Ancestry, 1988.
- *Your Guide to the Family History Library: How to Access the World's Largest Genealogy Resource*, by Paula Stuart Warren and James W. Warren. Cincinnati: Betterway Books, 2001.

As with many libraries, some Family History Library materials are available on loan and some are not. Materials for loan are available through the Family History Centers and can be borrowed for a period of about four weeks, with a similar renewal period. You can also receive materials on indefinite loan. Fees vary for each loan period. The Family History Library catalog is available on microfiche and CD-ROM at Family History Centers and online at <www.familysearch.org>. The catalog shows you most of what the library holds in Salt Lake City and which materials are available for rent. Materials include county and state records, military records, passenger lists, censuses, church and cemetery records, family histories, county and family histories, and numerous other materials for the United States and many countries around the world. These materials come to the Family History Centers on microfilm or microfiche. Unless microfilmed, books are not available via the rental program.

In addition, Family History Center patrons have available for use several CD-ROM collections. One is Ancestral File, a compilation of descendancy reports, family group sheets, and pedigree charts submitted by church members, nonmembers, and genealogical organizations specifically to this collection, which is updated periodically. Although living persons may be named in the file's alphabetical surname list, vital information is provided for deceased persons only. This information includes birth, marriage, and death dates and places; spouses' and children's names; and the names and addresses of those who submitted the information. Ancestral File is also available without charge at <www.familyseach.org> under "Search."

Warning

The Family History Department of the LDS Church does not attempt to verify the accuracy of the information submitted for Ancestral File; therefore, be cautious when using this or any other databases. Some databases contain very valuable information, but conflicting details appear frequently. One ancestor may be listed several times, but with different vital dates, different birthplaces, or other differing details. Thus, finding an ancestor or someone with the same name in the file is itself not proof of anything.

Perhaps the file's greatest value is helping descendants find others who are working on the same family. It may also supply new clues about ancestors who are in the file.

Persons interested in submitting reliable data to this collection may write to FamilySearch Support Unit, 4 WW, 50 East North Temple Street, Salt Lake City, Utah 84150. For further details on submitting information, call the FamilySearch Support Unit at (801) 240-2584.

International Genealogical Index (IGI) is an alphabetical list by surnames and region taken largely from (1) abstracted vital records and (2) group sheets processed through the

Temple of the LDS Church. In this file, one may find birth, marriage, and death information; parents' names; and other family data on deceased persons from more than ninety countries. This periodically updated collection is published on microfiche, on CD-ROM, and at <www.familysearch.org> under "Search." Each entry has a reference number that allows you to find the "input source" and get a copy of the individual record. Assistance is available from the library staff or center volunteers.

Each Family History Center (FHC) usually maintains a collection of microfilm or microfiche on indefinite or permanent loan. These are placed in the center by patrons and by local societies. The materials may include census records and other items pertaining to the local or regional area. For example, the Houston, Texas, Stake (Bering) FHC has an extensive microfiche collection of old Scottish parochial registers as well as indefinite loan microfilm of U.S., French, Irish, and German records.

Other collections at the FHCs may include atlases, reference books, the Family History Library research outlines for countries and states, and CD-ROM sources such as the *Periodical Source Index* (PERSI), the *U.S. Social Security Death Index*, *U.S. Military Personnel Who Died in Korea or Vietnam*, the *Freedman's Bank Records*, and the *1880 United States Census and National Index*.

Besides meeting and consulting with other avid genealogists at Family History Centers, researchers find that the real strength of these facilities is the access to the vast collection of microfilm and microfiche from Salt Lake City. Even those doing European research are often amazed at the depth of materials they can rent for very reasonable fees—for example, Polish, French, and Irish parish records and British, Canadian, and Norwegian censuses.

U.S. research is a primary focus of the Family History Library. Going to the library or renting microfilm is a way of using courthouse records when it isn't possible to travel to the county or state of interest. As mentioned throughout this book and shown in its endnotes, Family History Library microfilm is accessible and comprehensive. If you live near Salt Lake City, can visit there, or have a Family History Center near you, take advantage of the opportunity provided to church members and non-members. You just might knock down your brick wall.

SPECIAL REFERENCE MATERIALS IN LIBRARIES

Public, academic, and special libraries contain many kinds of reference materials. Some, such as encyclopedias and dictionaries, are particularly useful for finding specific information on a given subject. Bibliographies, on the other hand, help locate books and materials that aid in your research. Two groups of these bibliographic sources are especially helpful to genealogists and historians. The first group is references that help you find materials in individual libraries: library catalogs and union catalogs. The second group assists you in finding materials on a given subject: subject bibliographies, indexes, and abstracts.

Library Catalogs

One of the most helpful bibliographic sources in any library is, of course, the library catalog, either on computer or on cards. This catalog is a type of bibliography that lists, ideally, all the materials in a given library, or division of a library, by subject, author, and title. As more libraries convert to computerized catalogs, patrons are often faced with an out-of-date card catalog, sometimes still in use, and an incomplete computerized catalog. In addition, the computerized systems often require patrons to think very creatively to find materials on a given subject. If you cannot find what you need using a subject search, ask whether the system can do a keyword search. Patrons should consult both card and computer catalogs when both exist and should ask for help from a librarian when necessary.

Internet Source

With more libraries providing access to their catalogs via the Internet, it is getting easier to learn before you travel to a library what resources are available there, whether you are planning a local research trip or that dream vacation to the ancestral home county. Arriving at your research destination already armed with titles and/or call numbers allows you to make the most of your time. Web sites to help you find library online catalogs were discussed on page 272.

Some library catalogs have been published as reference guides for not only in-house patrons but also those who live elsewhere and may wish to visit, request a copy of something, or borrow materials on interlibrary loan. Catalogs may cover an entire library or a particular collection within the library. Check the Web sites of individual libraries for online guides and catalogs. Published catalogs include the following examples:

- *Daughters of the American Revolution, Library Catalog*. 3 vols. Washington, D.C.: National Society, DAR, 1982–1992. Vol. 1—family histories and genealogies; Vol. 2—state and local histories; Vol. 3—acquisitions, 1985–1991. Note that the DAR Library does not participate in interlibrary loan.
- *Denver Public Library, Catalog of the Western History Department*. 7 vols. plus supplements. Boston: G.K. Hall & Co., 1970.
- *Descriptive Inventory of the Archives of the State of Illinois*, 2d ed., by Robert E. Bailey and Elaine Shemoney Evans. Springfield, Ill.: Illinois State Archives, 1997.
- *Dictionary Catalog of the Local History and Genealogy Division [of the New York Public Library]*. 18 vols. Boston: G.K. Hall & Co., 1974.

Some subject bibliographies for large collections may be considered catalogs in the broad sense because they list books available in a particular place even though these books deal with only one collection of the overall holdings. Check online catalogs for these bibliographies. Examples of printed bibliographies include the following, which may be available in libraries around the country:

- *Bibliographic Guide to Black Studies*. Boston: G.K. Hall & Co., annual, 1975–1997. Supplements *Dictionary Catalog of the Schomburg Collection of Negro Literature and History [in the New York Public Library]* (below). Continued by *Interdisciplinary Bibliographic Guide to Black Studies* (1998) and *G.K. Hall Interdisciplinary Bibliographic Guide to Black Studies* (annual, 1999–).
- *The Black Experience: A Guide to Afro-American Resources in the Florida State Archives*. Tallahassee, Fla.: Florida Department of State, Division of Library and Information Services, Bureau of Archives and Records Management, 1988, reprinted 1991.
- *Dictionary Catalog of the Schomburg Collection of Negro Literature and History [in the New York Public Library]*. 9 vols. Boston: G.K. Hall & Co., 1962. Supplements 1967, 1972, 1974. Now the Schomburg Center for Research in Black Culture, with many resources available online at <www.nypl.org/research/sc/sc.html>.
- *A Genealogist's Guide to the Allen County Public Library, Ft. Wayne, Indiana*, 3d ed., by Karen B. Cavanaugh. Watermill, Ind.: the author, 1983.
- *Genealogy: A Guide to the UC Berkeley Library*, by Barbara Lee Hill, Patricia A. Davison, and Bette G. Root. Berkeley, Calif.: The Library Associates, The General Library, University of California, Berkeley, 1984.
- *Guide to Civil War Records in the North Carolina State Archives*. Raleigh, N.C.: North Carolina Archives, 1966.

- *A Guide to Genealogical Notes and Charts in the Archives Branch, Virginia State Library*, Lyndon H. Hart III, comp. Richmond, Va.: Virginia State Library, 1983.
- *Guide to Local and Family History at The Newberry Library*, by Peggy Tuck Sinko. Salt Lake City: Ancestry Publishing, 1987. (The Newberry Library is in Chicago.)
- *Local History and Genealogy Resources of the California State Library*, rev. ed., Gary E. Strong and Gary F. Kurutz, eds. Sacramento, Calif.: California State Library Foundation, 1991.
- *Preliminary Guide to Pre-1904 County Records in the Archives Branch, Virginia State Library and Archives*, Suzanne S. Ray et al., comps. Richmond, Va.: Virginia State Library, 1987.
- *Preliminary Guide to Pre-1904 Municipal Records in the Archives Branch, Virginia State Library and Archives*, Lyndon H. Hart and J. Christian Kolbe, comps. Richmond, Va.: Virginia State Library, 1994.
- *Virginia Genealogy: A Guide to Resources in the University of Virginia Library*. Rev. ed. Charlottesville, Va.: University Press of Virginia, 1983.

Many libraries have finding aids that are mini-catalogs showing the library's holdings on a particular subject, such as military records, immigration and passenger lists, census records, county records, or periodicals. In libraries with open stacks and microform files, many finding aids provide the call numbers and locations within the library. Finding aids are most often found at reference areas in the library. They may be in published form, in notebook binders, or on microfiche. Ask for information about finding aids at the reference desk.

Browsing, fortunately, is permitted in many libraries. It may not be efficient, but it can help make up for gaps in the cataloging system or holes in the researcher's work list for the day. Besides, browsing is fun and often rewarding. This wandering in the stacks does not take the place of using the library catalog, but it can help you find things you may not know to look for and might not find otherwise. I still remember the delight I felt while browsing in one university library. While hurrying down an aisle of history books with a call number in hand, looking for something else, I spotted a book of eighteenth-century passenger lists (oaths of allegiance) that I had not seen before. Thank goodness for titles on the spines of books. On a lark, I decided to pause long enough to inspect its index and found, much to my surprise, the only one of my ancestors I have ever found on such a list.

Union Catalogs

Union catalogs are combined lists of holdings from two or more libraries. This kind of reference can help you find out which libraries own which materials. One such series, the *National Union Catalog* (Washington, D.C.: Library of Congress), lists thousands of books on many subjects in hundreds of libraries. The catalog is most useful for identifying the locations of specific books or works of specific authors; books are listed alphabetically by author. A separate series lists the same books by subject. This catalog was issued in microfiche from 1983 to 2002.

More than seven hundred volumes comprise *The National Union Catalog Pre-1956 Imprints*. These books are arranged alphabetically by author, and the process of using them is the same as for the *National Union Catalog* (NUC). When I wanted to find a family history written by a Blakeney in 1928, I pulled the volume covering the *Bl* part of the alphabet. I found the author's full name, correct title, publication information, the Library of Congress card number, and the coded names of other reporting libraries that own the book. The volumes on Locations are supplements for both the NUC and *Pre-1956 Imprints*, are arranged by Library of Congress card numbers, and list additional libraries that own the books having Library of Congress numbers. (In other words, books without Library of Congress numbers will not be listed in the Locations supplements.)

National Union Catalog of Manuscript Collections

Probably of greater use to genealogists than NUC or the *Pre-1956 Imprints* is the *National Union Catalog of Manuscript Collections*, or NUCMC (pronounced nuck-muck). It began as a series of books describing the contents and location of various manuscript collections around the country. These manuscript collections are often family and business papers that have been given to libraries or archives. The contents may include letters, diaries, business ledgers, genealogical notes, Bibles, deeds, memorabilia, and other documents pertaining to a family, business, town, county, school, church, or organization. Because families and businesses do not exist in a vacuum, their papers are likely to mention or include information on their relatives, friends, neighbors, and business associates. Cluster genealogy becomes important again when you are looking for manuscript collections that may include an elusive ancestor. The ancestor may not have saved letters and documents, but one of his neighbors or cousins might have.

Publication of NUCMC began in 1962, covering cataloging done 1959–1961. New volumes were published annually, when possible, to include newly contributed or newly reported collections. Because of the massive nature of the project, there is a time lapse between reporting and publication. The 1991 volume, for example, was issued in the spring of 1993.

Cumulative indexes cover these years: 1959–1962, 1963–1966, 1967–1969, 1970–1974, 1975–1979, 1980–1984, 1985, 1986–1990, 1991–1993. In these indexes, researchers can look for these topics:

1. Surnames, to find references to individuals or families.
2. State, city, and county names, to find manuscript records pertaining to a locality. Under state names are subheadings for newspapers, churches, family and personal papers, maps, slavery, vital records, genealogy, organizations and societies, and legal affairs, with further subheadings for lawyers' and judges' papers.
3. General subject headings, such as religious denominations or names of ethnic groups.
4. Specific companies, organizations and institutions, universities and schools, churches, ships, or occupations.
5. Types of records (wills, deeds, etc.), genealogy, and other subject headings. For example, under the topic "Blacksmithing" are references to that occupation in various states, as reflected in the manuscript collections being reported.

Each topic, name, or subheading listed in the index has a coded number beside it, as in "Emily Ann Steenberg Mitchell (1826–1847) 84–1720." In parentheses are the life dates of the person named. The "84" refers to the catalog of 1984, and "1720" refers to item number 1720 in that year's list. The 1984 volume shows MS 84-1720 at the head of the entry and the title of the collection: "Mitchell and Barnes family papers, 1791–1911." This collection, the gift of a family member in 1977, is housed in the Cornell University Library, Department of Manuscripts and Archives, Ithaca, New York. The description of the collection tells that it is chiefly correspondence, legal documents, daybooks, photos, and clippings. The letters include some to Emily (Minnie) Ann Mitchell, daughter of William L. (1825–1904) and Emily Ann Steenberg Mitchell (1826–1847). The entry also shows (1) names and life dates of other family members who were correspondents and (2) the New York counties represented in the collection. Some entries also tell you whether the repository has a catalog of the collection to help locate specific items quickly.

The ***Index to Personal Names in the National Union Catalog of Manuscript Collections, 1959–1984*** (Alexandria, Va.: Chadwyck-Healey, 1987) is an important two-volume resource to supplement the use of NUCMC. Volume one covers alphabetical entries A–K; volume two, L–Z. The entries in this index are the same as those in the main indexes, but isolate the personal names from place and institutional names and topical references.

The **"Geographical Guide to Repositories"** at the front of the most recent volume tells you about manuscript collections reported in the catalogs in a particular city. This guide could be helpful when you are planning to research in the city. This reference is alphabetical by state and lists each reporting repository and the year(s) of its reports. You can then refer to the catalog of the year(s) listed, in the alphabetical list of repositories, and find the number of each collection that repository has reported. If a listing in the "Geographical Guide" sent you to the volume for 1974, and that volume showed 74-1200–1237 with the name of the repository you want to visit, then you would know that items 1200–1237 in the 1974 catalog are descriptions of collections housed in that repository. You can read these descriptions to determine whether you need to plan time during your visit to study them.

A **"General Guide to Repositories"** is another reference at the front of the NUCMC volumes and is arranged by subject area and by type of repository. Genealogists would probably be most interested in the repositories listed under the subjects "Religion," "Ethnic Groups," and "Regional History." The types of repositories include, for example, college and university libraries, historical societies, museums, public libraries, special libraries, and religious institutions. Under "city archives" in the 1975–1990 list are only three repositories: Baltimore, Maryland; Camden, South Carolina; and Charleston, South Carolina. The only two listed under "county archives" in the same volume are Bexar County, Texas, and Saratoga County, New York. This does not mean that these are the only three cities and two counties with archives collections. It means that these are the only ones reporting descriptions of special collections between 1975 and 1990. Furthermore, NUCMC usually does not report official records housed in archives or courthouses if those records were created there or would ordinarily be found there. The collections reported are those found in more-or-less unexpected places.

Warning

Most manuscript collections are limited to use within the repository. You should contact the staff to find out if any items of the collection or its catalog are available on interlibrary loan. If they are not, you have a perfect excuse for a vacation.

In 1986 NUCMC began using the Research Libraries Group (RLG) database to produce the published catalog. Production of the print catalog ceased at the end of 1993, and the records are now available only in the RLG database, searchable at <www.loc.gov/coll/nucmc/>. This NUCMC Web site also allows searching for manuscript records in the OCLC catalog. For a comprehensive search, one should use both catalogs.

Another way to search for manuscript records is to use the subscription database ArchivesUSA by Chadwyck-Healey. All of the records contained in the print version of NUCMC are available in ArchivesUSA with additional indexing provided by the National Inventory of Documentary Sources (NIDS). Information about the repositories is also searchable, with links to Web sites for more information.

Other Union Lists

Another union list of particular interest to genealogists is *American Newspapers, 1821–1936*, Winifred Gregory, ed. (New York: Wilson, 1937; reprint Millwood, N.Y.: Kraus

Reprint Corp., 1967). This huge volume reports in detail the newspapers held by nearly six thousand repositories in the United States and Canada. As in most books of this kind, the repositories are listed by abbreviations, which are explained at the beginning of the book. The entries themselves are arranged alphabetically by state, within the state by city, and under each city, by newspaper title. Under each newspaper title is its frequency (weekly or daily), its dates of publication, any changes in its name, and which repositories hold which dates. For example, who has copies of the *New York Evening Post* for the year 1821? The entry in Gregory's book shows that existing 1821 copies of this newspaper are scattered among such places as the New York Public Library, the New York Historical Society, the American Antiquarian Society, Lehigh University, and others.

You also may wish to consult the union catalog *Newspapers in Microform: United States, 1948–1983* (Washington, D.C.: Library of Congress, 1984). In addition, many states now have union lists of newspapers published in their state. See chapter seven for further discussion of newspapers and these finding aids.

The *Union List of Serials in the Libraries of the United States and Canada*, Edna Brown Titus, ed. (New York: H.W. Wilson Co., 1965), lists thousands of periodical publications by state and city. For example, to learn about the *New Orleans Advocate*, consult the *Union List of Serials*. It identifies the *Advocate* as "a weekly journal devoted to Christianity, our country, and literature," published from 1866 to at least 1869, and that Ohio Wesleyan University owns copies.

Union lists on computerized databases are also very useful tools for finding materials. The first was OCLC, which began in 1967. Others include Research Libraries Information Network (RLIN) and Western Library Network (WLN). The original purpose of such computerized systems was to provide uniform cataloging. A valuable by-product is advanced, efficient assistance with interlibrary loan. The OCLC catalog is now available electronically as WorldCat, discussed earlier.

Subject Bibliographies

Library catalogs and union catalogs focus on sources in particular libraries. Subject bibliographies as well as indexes and abstracts help you identify sources on specific subjects. These reference materials do not always specify where to find a particular book or article, but they indicate that it exists. When limited to the description of all or part of a particular collection, these guides act as a special kind of library catalog or finding aid. Examples of subject bibliographies useful to genealogists are the following:

- *The American Colonies in the Seventeenth Century*, Alden T. Vaughan, comp. New York: Appleton-Century-Crofts, Meredith Corporation, 1971.
- *A Bibliography of American Autobiographies*, Louis Kaplan, comp. Madison, Wis.: University of Wisconsin Press, 1961. Includes subject index.
- *A Bibliography of American County Histories*, P. William Filby, comp. Baltimore: Genealogical Publishing Company, 1985.
- *Confederate Imprints: A Bibliography of Southern Publications From Secession to Surrender*, by T. Michael Parrish and Robert M. Willingham Jr. Austin, Tex.: Jenkins Publishing Co., [ca. 1984]. This is an expansion and revision of earlier works by Marjorie Crandall and Richard Harwell.
- *Documents of the American Revolution, 1770–1783 (Colonial Office Series)*, 21 vols., K.G. Davies, ed. Shannon, Ireland: Irish University Press, 1972–1981. Records in the Colonial Office of the Public Records Office, London. Indexed. Calendar and abstracts of documents, 1770–1776. Transcripts of documents, 1775–1783.

- *Genealogies in the Library of Congress: A Bibliography*, 5 vols., Marion J. Kaminkow, ed. Baltimore, Md.: Genealogical Publishing Co., 1972–1987. Reprinted, 2001.
- *Goldentree Bibliographies in American History*. Arlington Heights, Ill.: Harlan Davidson/Forum Press, various dates. John Hope Franklin compiled the volume on African-American history. John Shy prepared the one on the American Revolution.
- *Guide to American Indian Documents in the Congressional Serial Set: 1817–1899*, by Stephen L. Johnson. New York: Clearwater Publishing Co., 1977. Reprinted by Congressional Information Service, 2000.
- *A Guide to Manuscripts Relating to American History in British Depositories Reproduced for the Division of Manuscripts of the Library of Congress*, by Grace Gardner Griffin. Washington, D.C.: Library of Congress, 1946.
- *Revolutionary America, 1763–1789: A Bibliography*, 2 vols., Ronald M. Gephart, comp. Washington, D.C.: Library of Congress, 1984. A guide to sources in the Library of Congress.
- *Travels in the Old South: A Bibliography [1527–1860]* and *Travels in the New South: A Bibliography [1865–1955]*, by Thomas D. Clark. *Travels in the Confederate States: A Bibliography [1861–1865]*, by E. Merton Coulter. Norman, Okla.: University of Oklahoma Press, 1956–1959, 1962, and 1948, respectively.
- *United States Local Histories in the Library of Congress: A Bibliography*, 5 vols., Marion J. Kaminkow, ed. Washington, D.C.: Library of Congress, 1975. Reprint. Baltimore: Magna Carta Book Co., with supplement, 1986.

See Also

See chapter nine for bibliographies concerning African-American history and genealogy.

Bibliographies on various aspects of U.S. history have Library of Congress call numbers in the range of Z1236 forward. The American Revolution bibliographies are cataloged under Z1238; Civil War bibliographies, under Z1242. From Z1251 to about Z1360 are the works on each state, in alphabetical order. For example, Colorado is Z1263; Minnesota is Z1299; and Vermont is Z1343. Bibliographies pertaining to specific ethnic groups are under Z1361. Sometimes you can find useful materials by browsing in this area of a library.

Books in Print

The kinds of bibliographies mentioned above help researchers find sources in a particular library or subject area. *Books in Print* (New Providence, N.J.: R.R. Bowker, annually) is another kind of resource; it lists by author, title, or subject books currently available as well as books taken out of print ("OP") and those that are out of stock indefinitely ("OSI"). To find books of genealogical value and interest, look in the subject volumes under state, county, and city names as well as topics such as census, history, genealogy, records, registers, pension, Afro-American, slavery, free Negroes, American Indians, tribal names, and ethnic group names. Publishers' names, addresses, and phone numbers are in the publishers volume.

Books in Print is also available electronically through subscription. Many libraries have this valuable resource. The printed volumes are usually found in special reference sections or at the reference desk.

Indexes and Abstracts

Indexes and abstracts are another kind of bibliographic source. One of the best-known examples of such an index, though one of limited genealogical use, is *Readers' Guide to Periodical Literature* (New York: H.W. Wilson, 1900–). You can look up periodical articles by author, title, or subject and learn the name and issue of the periodical in which the article may be found. This index covers mostly popular magazines and few of the ones genealogists find most useful. However, the subject heading "Genealogy" can lead readers to interesting articles in such magazines as *Life*, *Hobbies*, *Ms.*, *House and Garden*, and *Essence*. *Readers' Guide Full Text* is the electronic version available by subscription as part of H.W. Wilson's *WilsonWeb*. The online database begins coverage with 1983.

For older articles, consult *Nineteenth Century Reader's Guide to Periodical Literature, 1890–1899, with Supplementary Indexing 1900–1922* (New York [now Bronx]: H.W. Wilson, 1944) and *Poole's Index to Periodical Literature, 1802–1906* (Gloucester, Mass.: Peter Smith, 1963 reprint).

America: History and Life (Santa Barbara, Calif.: ABC-Clio Information Services, 1964–) is a helpful reference that includes both index and abstracts. From 1955 through 1963, the same kind of information appeared in *Historical Abstracts*—by the same publisher—which is now an index for subjects other than American history. However, *America: History and Life* now has a volume zero which contains an index and more than six thousand abstracts from the years 1954–1963.

Until 1989, each annual edition was divided into four separate publications: (A) abstracts of articles, (B) book reviews, (C) abstracts of dissertations, and (D) index by author, subject, or title. Beginning with volume 26 (1989), five issues appear each year. Issues 1–3 contain abstracts, reviews, and dissertation citations plus an index to these. Issue 4 contains only abstracts, reviews, and citations, with no index because it is followed shortly by issue 5, the annual cumulative subject and author index, with other reference tables. Five-year indexes began in 1964.

Articles mentioned in the index volumes 1–25 have code numbers such as 22A2591. The "22A" means volume 22, part A (abstracts of articles), and "2591" is the abstract number. The abstract gives the name, volume, and page numbers of the periodical in which to find the article.

In this *America: History and Life* index, look first for the names of ancestors or places pertinent to their lives. This is not an every-name index but an index to people, places, and topics that are the subjects of books, articles, or dissertations. Each of these publications is listed under at least four subject headings. For example, in volume 29 (1992), an article about M. LaRue Harrison was listed under his name and under the headings "Arkansas Cavalry"; "First Arkansas, Northwestern"; "Civil War"; and "Unionists." Under each heading, the reference was "1219a." You would look for entry 1219 in volume 29 for the abstract and journal information needed to find the article. The article is "An Experiment in Collective Security: The Union Army's Use of Armed Colonies in Arkansas," by Diane Neal and Thomas W. Kremm, in *Military History of the Southwest* 2 (1990): 169–181.

America: History and Life is also available from ABC-CLIO as an online subscription database; check your public or academic library for availability. An advantage of this format is the ability to search all years at once.

The *Combined Retrospective Index Set to Journals in History, 1838–1974* (CRIS/History), Annadel N. Wile, ed. (Washington, D.C.: Carrollton Press, Inc., 1977), is a nine-volume set of indexes covering some 342 subject categories found in articles in over 240 journals, with two additional volumes of author indexes. The first four volumes deal with world history. Volumes five through nine index first the chronological periods of U.S. history and then topics in U.S. history, in alphabetical order, from Agriculture, AnteBellum South, and Black History to individual states and the West. Most articles appear several times and under different keywords or subject categories. Each reference gives a journal number with volume and page number where the article can be found. The end pages of each index volume list all these journal numbers and identify the journal names. In our library, the staff has been nice enough to add call numbers beside each journal owned by the library. Many of these journals are publications of state historical societies, universities, and professional associations. Titles include *Quaker History*, *Ohio History*, *Filson Club History Quarterly* (Kentucky), *South Atlantic Quarterly*, *William and Mary Quarterly*, *Virginia Magazine of History and Biography*, *New Jersey History*, *Church History*, and the *Register of the Kentucky Historical Society*.

Of special interest to genealogists is volume 6, the Biography and Genealogy index. This massive index lists surnames alphabetically, many with given names. This also is not an every-name index but an index to people who are the subjects of articles. References give the same finding information as in the other volumes: journal, volume, and page number where you can find the article. Remember that the index covers periodicals through 1974.

Writings on American History is a bibliography that has been published almost annually since 1902. Until 1962, it included books and articles, including many family histories. Since 1962 it has focused only on articles. It groups entries by historical time period, state, and topic, including "genealogy" in some volumes. Volumes are indexed by author and subject. (Its publication history is complicated, including at various times the Government Printing Office, the American Historical Association, KTO Press, the Library of Congress, and Kraus, but the volumes are shelved together in the American History reference section or stacks.)

The *Virginia Historical Index*, often called the Swem Index (after the editor Earl Gregg Swem of the College of William and Mary), was originally published in 1934, and reprinted by Peter Smith, Magnolia, Massachusetts, in 1965. The two volumes offer extensive and comprehensive coverage of a small but important group of Virginia periodicals:

- *William and Mary Quarterly Historical Magazine*, Series 1 and 2 (1892–1930).
- *Calendar of Virginia State Papers* and other manuscript papers in the Library of Virginia (1652–1869).
- *Tyler's Quarterly Historical and Genealogical Magazine* (1919–1929).
- *William Walter Hening's Statutes at Large* (1619–1792 laws of Virginia).
- *The Virginia Magazine of History and Biography* (1893–1930).
- *The Virginia Historical Register and Literary Advertiser* (1848–1853).
- *The Lower Norfolk County Virginia Antiquary* (1895–1906).

Many public and academic libraries, especially larger or older ones, have these publications, which are important for genealogists working in Virginia, Kentucky, West Virginia, and even Maryland and other states. The Swem Index is quite comprehensive, including family, individual, business, and place names; events; headings for topics such as journals, churches, courts, Indians, academies, marriages, divorce, and free Negroes; and a myriad of historical and cultural topics such as clothing, furniture, and even ink powder. Because index entries are spelled as they appear in the text, be sure to look under variant spellings. In libraries, the Swen Index is often cataloged and shelved with Virginia materials (call number 975.5 or F221).

The *Virginia Historical Index* is available as CD-ROM #202 of Family Tree Maker's Family Archives (Genealogy.com, a division of A&E Television Networks).

The *Periodical Source Index* (PERSI), a project of Allen County Public Library, Fort Wayne, Indiana, indexes about ten thousand genealogy and local history periodicals that were published from the early-nineteenth century to the present in the United States, Canada, and other countries. Released in book form from 1986 to 1997, PERSI is now available on CD-ROM and by subscription at Ancestry.com.

In the original eight-volume set, the subsequent annual indexes, and the electronic versions of PERSI, you can search by locality, surname, or research methodology. PERSI is not an every-name index but indexes article titles and numerous subjects from the articles, including history; directories; cemeteries; passenger lists; naturalizations; maps; obituaries; and census, church, court, land, military, tax, voter, and probate records. Entries give the article description, journal title, volume number, and year of publication but no page numbers. If you need an article from a periodical that your library does not have, you can obtain a copy of the article from Allen County Public Library. Order forms and procedures are available on their Web site <www.acpl.lib.in.us/genealogy/persi.html>. You may also try to get article copies via interlibrary loan at your local library.

Genealogical Periodical Annual Index: Key to the Genealogical Literature (Bowie, Md.: Heritage Books, annual since 1962) indexes over 270 periodicals whose publishers subscribe to the service. It includes surname, locality, and topical categories. References give the volume, issue number, and beginning page number where a particular article or item may be found, and the periodical list includes the address of each publisher. If you do not have access to the periodical you need, you can try interlibrary loan for a copy of the article or contact the publisher to try to purchase that issue. Many back volumes of the *Genealogical Periodical Annual Index* (GPAI) are still in print and available for purchase from Heritage Books <www.heritagebooks.com>. Electronic (Adobe Acrobat PDF file) versions are available for years 1992 through 1999. At this writing, the Heritage Books Web site offered year 2000 of GPAI as a free download for researchers to try.

Other Indexes

Several other indexes exist for multiple genealogical periodicals. One is Donald Lines Jacobus's *Index to Genealogical Periodicals* (New Haven, Conn.: D.L. Jacobus), a three-volume index to over fifty journals and quarterlies that did not have their own comprehensive indexes:

- volume 1 (1932): issues through 1931
- volume 2 (1947): 1932–1946, including Revolutionary War and Family Records sections
- volume 3 (1953): 1947–1952

The three volumes were combined into one easier-to-use book by Carl Boyer and reissued in 1983. This revised edition is divided into name and place indexes, which give the name of the periodical, volume, and page number where the article may be found.

Maud Quigley of Grand Rapids, Michigan, indexed some ninety periodicals received by the Grand Rapids Public Library into three books (Grand Rapids, Mich.: Western Michigan Genealogical Society, 1981):

1. *Index to Family Names in Genealogical Periodicals Plus Addenda*
2. *Index to Hard-to-Find Information in Genealogical Periodicals*
3. *Index to Michigan Research Found in Genealogical Periodicals*

The hard-to-find information in the second volume includes military subjects, migrations, ship passengers, maps and trails, ethnic and religious groups, and headings for individual states. The list of periodicals in each volume tells which years are covered by the index for each journal. The index gives the name of the periodical with volume and issue number, not the page, for each reference.

The *Index to Genealogical Periodical Literature, 1960–1977*, by Kip Sperry (Detroit, Mich.: Gale Research, 1979, now out of print), is in many libraries. It indexes articles about general and ethnic sources, research procedures, bibliographies, maps, and the like, but not persons and places.

Some major genealogical and historical periodicals have published their own comprehensive indexes, including the following examples:

- *Topical Index to National Genealogical Society Quarterly, Volume 1–50 (1912–1962)*, Carleton E. Fisher, comp. Arlington, Va.: National Genealogical Society, 1964. Volumes 1 through 85 of this quarterly are now available and searchable on CD-ROM #210 of Family Tree Maker's Family Archives (Genealogy.com, a division of A&E Television Networks).
- *The New England Historical and Genealogical Register, Index of Subjects, Index of Places, Index of Person, Volumes 1–50*, 4 vols., Josephine Elizabeth Rayne, comp. Baltimore: Genealogical Publishing Co., 1972. Reprint of originals published by the New England Historic Genealogical Society, 1906–1911; reprinted in two volumes by Picton Press, 1989. *The New England Historical and Genealogical Register: Index of Persons, Volumes 51–148*, 4 vols., Jane Fletcher Fiske, ed. Boston: New England Historic Genealogical Society, 1995. In 1989, Jean D. Worden of San Dimas, California, privately published a subject index for volumes 51–142 (1897–1988) of the *New England Historical and Genealogical Register*. The society published the *Register* 1847–1994, including a condensed index, on nine CD-ROMs in 1996. These years are now searchable on the society's Web site <www.newenglandancestors.org/rs3/articles/theregister/>, with plans to add later years in the near future. Anyone may search the database, but only members may view detailed results (non-members are given the number of records found).
- *Fifty Year Index to the Mississippi Valley Historical Review, 1914–1964*. Bloomington, Ind.: Organization of American Historians, 1973. In 1964, the journal title changed to *The Journal of American History*. Both titles are searchable with full-text availability 1914–1999 in libraries participating in JSTOR (Journal Storage), <www.jstor.org>; check with the reference librarian. Additionally, contents of more recent volumes, 1999 to the present, are available to libraries subscribing to *The History Cooperative* <www.historycooperative.org>.
- *Genealogical Guide: Master Index of Genealogy in the Daughters of the American Revolution Magazine, Volumes 1–84, 1892–1950*. Washington, D.C.: DAR Magazine, 1951. An index to volumes 85–89 (1950–1955) was issued in 1956.

See Also

Newspaper indexes and other reference materials are discussed in chapter seven.

Computerized periodical and newspaper indexes are now in use in many academic libraries and businesses and in some public libraries. Check for them in your local library.

Online databases that index or abstract periodicals and newspapers usually include issues dating back only to the late 1980s when the services began. The publishers indicate that they have limited plans or no plans to go into back issues. However, subscriptions sites such as Ancestry.com now offer access to some digitized historical newspapers. For example, I read an obituary for one man I was researching in a 1911 edition of the *Washington Post* on Ancestry.com.

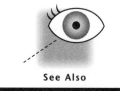

Experiment with different databases and subjects—you never know what you might find. Computerized indexes do include items that could benefit a genealogical search. One company that provides several databases is UMI, part of the ProQuest group. Their *Newspaper Abstracts* covers newspapers (including obituaries from 1986 forward for larger cities such as New York, San Francisco, Boston, Atlanta, Detroit, Houston, Denver, Los Angeles, St. Louis, and Washington. Their *Periodical Abstracts* index covers more than two thousand periodicals in many subject areas. Included are journals of some interest to genealogists, such as *American Heritage, The American Historical Review, American History Illustrated, American Indian Quarterly, Canadian Journal of History, Church History, Civil War History, The Journal of American History, The Journal of Military History, Pacific Historical Review, Southwestern Historical Quarterly, The Western Historical Quarterly*, and *The William and Mary Quarterly*. The company has several products available, with index only or with text; some products are also produced on CD-ROM.

For those who need a particular article from a periodical and cannot find it locally or through interlibrary loan, Ingenta <www.ingenta.com> offers a fee-based service for article copies. Their searchable database contains references to articles from a wide variety of sources including many genealogical titles, 1988 to the present. Fees and availability vary with the journal title, but in many cases copies can be purchased and sent to you either online or by fax.

PUBLISHED FAMILY HISTORIES

Many people who have compiled clusters of family members publish their results. To the extent that the compiler has been careful and accurate and has documented the information, these books can be very useful. **However, even if you find a book that includes your family, use the information as clues for your own research; do not accept without reservation what is given.**

Warning

The example below comes from a family history published in the early twentieth century, but similar problems appear even in recent books. This particular book contains many family groups in a cluster of related families spread over six or seven generations. It gives numerous vital statistics but no documentation. The author appears to have been in contact with a number of his cousins and received information from them. However, this family group illustrates a discrepancy that occurs in many family histories:

John Aaron, b 1825, m 1849, d 1851.
Wife Sarah, b 1829.
Son Aaron Hugh, b 1827, d 1904.
Daughter Elizabeth Miranda, b 1850.

Obviously, John would not have fathered a child at age two, and Sarah would not have had a child two years before she was born! According to the grandfather's estate settlement in the county records, John (no middle name) and Aaron Hugh were brothers, not father and son. John died young, leaving one daughter, Elizabeth Miranda. Now the dates make sense.

Most libraries with genealogy collections have a section of family histories. Large libraries such as the Library of Congress, the Family History Library, Newberry Library in Chicago, and Clayton Library in Houston have hundreds of them. Some are well written and well documented, and many are not. The fact that they are in a library does not automatically make them reliable research sources. Of course, they may be very accurate on one part of the family and not on another. The genealogist, therefore, must be cautious in accepting what is published and should work to verify the data with other sources.

One helpful reference for finding published family histories is *Genealogies Cataloged by the Library of Congress Since 1986: With a List of Established Forms of Family Names and a List of Genealogies Converted to Microfilm Since 1983* (Washington, D.C.: Library of Congress, 1992). Most family histories published before 1900 and now on microfilm at the Library of Congress are available for purchase and for interlibrary loan. Check the catalog above for availability, and make your request at your local library through the interlibrary loan librarian.

BIOGRAPHICAL DICTIONARIES

Many biographical dictionaries have been published since the late nineteenth century. They cover the famous and the not-so-famous throughout the country. Like published family histories, they can be great sources, or not so great. Much depends on the care with which each entry was produced. However, they often contain good clues. Finding entries on a member of your cluster of relatives can give you solid leads to pursue.

You can find the ones available in your library reference section by looking in the library catalog under "Biography–Dictionaries" or "United States–Biography–Dictionaries." Many of them are multivolume sets. Some, such as *Appleton's Cyclopædia of American Biography* (New York: D. Appleton & Co., 1887) and the *Dictionary of American Biography* (New York: Charles Scribner's Sons, 1928–), cover a broad base of people. Others are more specialized, with sketches of governors and persons in Congress, the federal executive branch, the frontier, the Confederacy, various regions, and numerous professions. *Biography and Genealogy Master Index* (Detroit, Mich.: Gale Research, 1975–) is available as a CD-ROM or Web-based subscription; it is also part of an Ancestry.com subscription. It indexes over 450,000 biographical sketches in over ninety-five biographical dictionaries.

Case Study: J. Proctor Knott

Case Study

This case study shows the information gathered on J. Proctor Knott's professional life from fourteen biographical and periodical sources. (Not included here are another eight or more articles on Knott from other biographical directories and encyclopedias.) It is interesting to compare the information from these sources to identify differences and discrepancies and to see the information that is unique to some of the sources. The sources are listed here in the order of their publication; the notes given from each indicate in italics the new or differing details about Knott's career. All the sources mentioned his governorship, his reputation as an orator, and one particularly popular and famous speech he made in Congress in 1871. Some sources mentioned his childhood and family, but that information is not included here. The case study demonstrates (1) the importance of using more than one source to learn more about an individual; (2) the differences that can occur in printed materials; and (3) the need to investigate further what you find, especially the discrepancies.

Knott's death certificate in Marion County, Kentucky, apparently with his widow as informant, stated the following: born 29 August 1830, died 18 June 1911—age eighty years, nine months, nineteen days.[1] Thus, he died two months and eleven days before his eighty-first birthday. This information differs in some of the sources below. The following sources provided information on his career.

1. Z.F. Smith, *The History of Kentucky* (Louisville: Courier-Journal Job Printing Co., 1886), 816. (Published while Knott was governor.)

Born 29 August 1830 near Lebanon, Kentucky; moved to Missouri, May 1850*; admitted to the bar, 1851; elected to Missouri legislature, 1857; resigned from legislature and appointed attorney general, August 1859; elected attorney general, 1862 [all other sources give 1860]; returned to Kentucky, 1863, and practiced law; Democrat member of 40th, 41st, 44th, 45th, 46th, 47th Congresses; elected governor of Kentucky, 1883, for four-year term. *The 1850 census shows him working as a clerk and living with the Jacob Clapper family in Memphis, Missouri.[2]

2. H. Levin, ed., *The Lawyers and Lawmakers of Kentucky* (Chicago: Lewis Publishing Co., 1897; reprint, Easley, S.C.: Southern Historical Press, 1982).

Born in Marion County; after common school education, became professor of natural sciences in Lebanon Seminary; *studied law, admitted to bar, and practiced law in Lebanon* [before moving to Missouri]; practiced law in Missouri; 1860, was delegate to the Democratic national convention; attorney general of Missouri *until 1863*; served in Congress, 1867–1871, 1875–1883; governor of Kentucky, 1883–1887; 1890, delegate from Marion County to Kentucky state constitutional convention; 1897, when this book was published, Knott was dean of law department, Center [*sic*] College, Danville, Kentucky.

3. Rossiter Johnson, ed., *The Twentieth Century Biographical Dictionary of Notable Americans*, vol. 6 (n.p.: The Biographical Society, 1904), 27 May 2002, Ancestry.com.

Born in *Washington County*, Kentucky, later Marion County [established 1834]; *began study of law in 1846* [at age 16]; moved to Missouri in May 1850; worked in circuit and county clerks' offices until he was admitted to the bar, 1851 [1850 census supports this]; served in Missouri legislature, 1858; appointed attorney general, 1859, *to fill a vacancy*; elected attorney general, *1860*, serving in that office 1859–*1861*; when he declined to take the test oath of allegiance [to the Union] and his office as attorney general was declared vacant, he was imprisoned [no date given] in the *arsenal* in St. Louis and released by order of *General Lyon*; returned to Kentucky, *April 1862*; Congressman, 1867–1871 (40th-41st Congresses), 1875–1883 (44th–47th Congresses); received honorary LLD degree from Centre College, 1885; 1892–1894, professor of civics and economics at Centre College, Danville, Kentucky; 1894, professor of law and dean of law department at Centre College.

4. "Death Comes at Eventide to the Hon. James Proctor Knott in Lebanon," *The (Louisville, Kentucky) Courier-Journal*, Monday, 19 June 1911, obituary.

Died Sunday evening, 18 June 1911, age 80; studied law in Memphis, Missouri, and *admitted to the bar at age 16* [implying he was in Memphis at age 16 or in 1846]; practiced law in Memphis, Missouri, and sent from there as *member of the constitutional convention*; elected to Missouri legislature, *1858*; appointed attorney general of Missouri, *1858*; elected attorney general, 1860; arrested for refusing to take the test oath [of allegiance to the Union] and his office was declared vacant, *1863*; disbarred from practicing law in the state; returned to Kentucky, *1863*; member of 40th, 41st (1867–1871) Congresses, 45th, 46th, 47th Congresses (*1877*–1883) [omitted 44th Congress]; offered governorship of Hawaii by President Cleveland and later a place on the Interstate Commerce Commission but declined both positions; elected governor of Kentucky, 1883; 1887–1888, employed by state to assist attorney general in certain cases; practiced law in Frankfort, 1890; elected to represent Marion County in state constitutional convention; instrumental in retaining Frankfort as the state capital; 1894, retired from law practice to become dean of law department, Centre College; held that post six years; suffered stroke of paralysis in 1900; moved back to Lebanon, 1902; remained in feeble health.

5. *Washington Post*, 19 June 1911, p. 6. "J. Proctor Knott is Dead," 27 May 2002, Ancestry.com.

Knott died 18 June 1911, age *82* years; practiced law in Memphis, Missouri, where he lived until *1862*; attorney general of Missouri *until 1862*; elected to Congress, 1867, serving one term; elected again in *1877*, serving *another term*.

6. *Dictionary of American Biography* (New York: Charles Scribner's Sons, 1933), 10: 470.

Knott began study of law, 1846; served in circuit and county clerks' offices, Scotland County, Missouri; elected to Missouri legislature, *1857*, to represent Scotland County; elected Missouri attorney general, *1860*; resigned post as attorney general, *1862*; briefly imprisoned for refusing to take the test oath of allegiance; returned to Kentucky; practiced law; served in Congress 1867–1871, *1875*–1883; after governorship, practiced law in Frankfort, five more years; 1892, professor of civics and economics, Centre College, Danville, Kentucky; 1894, helped organize law department, served as dean and professor of law, Centre College; retired, *1901*, due to ill health.

7. Edwin W. Mills, "The Career of James Proctor Knott in Missouri," *Missouri Historical Review* 31(April 1937): 288–294. (Author lived with Mr. and Mrs. Knott, 1900–1901, and thus had many interviews with them.)

Knott died 18 June *1912*, age *82*; gave family stories and more detail on his early life and career; elected Missouri attorney general, *1860*; after resignation in *1862*, imprisoned *in Jefferson Barracks* [different federal facility from the arsenal, although both were in or near St. Louis] and soon paroled by *General U.S. Grant*; returned to Kentucky; dean of law school, Centre College, 1894–*1902*.

8. Howard W. Robey, "J. Proctor Knott, Congressman, 1867–1871" (master's thesis, University of Kentucky, 1939).

As a teenager, Knott taught school with his father and brother; *began study of law in Lebanon*, Kentucky; served as deputy county clerk, Scotland County, Missouri, before he was admitted to the bar; was an ardent Southern sympathizer but opposed secession; imprisoned briefly in St. Louis although no record exists, but mention of it made in a House debate, 1867, after his election to Congress; he and the Kentucky delegation were subjects of much debate on whether to seat them; no evidence of military service on either side during Civil War; his taking the oath of office in Congress was delayed six months due to the Radicals contesting the election; ill health forced him to request indefinite leave; returned to Kentucky, 4 April 1868; missed the rest of that session of Congress; back in Congress by 23 January 1869; in Congress, respected as a constitutional lawyer and capable speaker; at close of 41st Congress, returned home; did not seek reelection. After his second term in Congress, he practiced law, appearing many times before the U.S. Supreme Court.

This author says Knott returned to Lebanon, Kentucky, at the end of the 41st Congress, which recessed for the summer break on 15 July 1870. The details of his participation in the 41st Congress help place him in Washington at the time of the 1870 census; he was not enumerated in Kentucky with his wife and has not yet been found in the Washington area in that census.[3]

9. G. Glenn Clift, ed., *Governors of Kentucky* 1792–1942 (Cynthiana, Ky.: The Hobson Press, 1942), 93–94.

Knott studied law in Memphis, Missouri, 1846–1851; admitted to the bar *in 1846 at age 16* [implying in Memphis, Missouri]; elected attorney general of Missouri, *1860*; arrested, disbarred, *1861*; moved back to Kentucky, *1862*; employed as special assistant to Kentucky attorney general, 1887–1888.

10. Lowell H. Harrison, ed., *Kentucky's Governors, 1792–1985* (Lexington: University Press of Kentucky, 1985), 96–100 (Article on Knott written by Robert M. Ireland).

Focused on Knott's governorship. Early career: appointed attorney general, 1858; elected to that office, 1860; resigned 1862; imprisoned briefly; returned to Kentucky, 1863; served six terms in Congress; retired 1902; provides nothing new or different about other aspects of his career.

11. Hambleton Tapp, comp., "James Proctor Knott and the Duluth Speech," *The Register of the Kentucky Historical Society* 70 (April 1972): 77–93.

Compiled largely from Edwin Mills (source 7 above) and Lebanon, Kentucky, historian John F. Dahringer; Tapp quoted Dahringer saying that Knott suffered a crippling paralytic stroke in 1900 and was obliged to relinquish his post at the college.

12. Robert A. Powell, *Kentucky Governors* (Frankfort: Kentucky Images, 1976), 66.

Knott served in 40th and 41st Congresses from 4 March 1867 until 3 March 1871. (Robey, source 8 above, discussed at length the Kentucky congressional elections that were held in *May* 1867; the delegation reported to Congress in July, not March.)

13. "James Proctor Knott," *Biographical Directory of the United States Congress, 1774–Present*, 29 June 2002, <http://bioguide.congress.gov/scripts/biodisplay.pl?index=K000290>.

Nothing new or different; compiled from the other sources.

14. "A Kentucky Governor—James P. Knott (1883–1887)," *The Kentucky Explorer* 6 (April 1992): 29.

Studied law in Missouri; after governorship served as *president* of Centre College. [Knott was not college president, according to the college Web site, <www.centre.edu/web/library/sc/presidents.html> accessed 24 April 2003.]

U.S. GOVERNMENT PUBLICATIONS

The U.S. government generates thousands of records each year, and an amazing number of these deal with history or with individuals and events that will become history. Many government publications are useful references for genealogists and historians.

Monthly Catalog and Government Publications

The *Monthly Catalog of United States Government Publications* (Washington, D.C.: Government Printing Office, since 1895) is the index for finding reports, pamphlets, maps, books, manuals, and other publications of the federal government.

The *Monthly Catalog* allows you to look for material by author, title, subject, title keyword, series, and various document numbers. Each index reference gives you a number by which you can look up more complete information in the books of entries. For example, "91-22354" means entry number 22354 in the 1991 volumes. That entry will tell you such information as which department or agency issued the document, whether it is for sale at a government bookstore, whether it is a depository item, and the document's classification number. Similar in concept to Library of Congress or Dewey decimal call numbers, this is the number under which the document is usually cataloged in the stacks of federal depository libraries. The classification begins with a letter indicating the issuing department or agency: *A* for the Department of Agriculture, *I* for the Department of the Interior, *LC* for Library of Congress, C for Department of Commerce, and so forth.

Because the *Monthly Catalog* has been published since 1895, it is helpful that cumulative indexes have been prepared, both by the Government Printing Office (GPO) and by several commercial publishers. Indexes from 1976 to the present are available online or on CD-ROM in many libraries. The electronic version, entitled Catalog of U.S. Government Publications, is available on the GPO Access Web site <www.access.gpo.gov/su_docs/locators/cgp/index.html>. Online coverage is from January 1994 to the present.

For genealogists, the most useful items found through the use of the *Monthly Catalog* are maps, histories, National Archives and Library of Congress reference books, and bibliographies of many kinds. Try looking up place names connected with your ancestor.

The following publications are a selected few of hundreds that could be helpful to genealogists and historians. Check the U.S. Government Online Bookstore <http://bookstore.gpo.gov> for current availability.

- *The Black Experience in Natchez, 1720–1880*, by Ronald L.F. Davis. Special History Study. Denver: U.S. Department of the Interior, National Park Service, 1993.
- *Commanding Generals and Chiefs of Staff, 1775–1991: Portraits and Biographical Sketches . . .*, by William Gardner Bell. Washington, D.C.: Center of Military History, United States Army, 1992.
- *The Continental Army*, by Robert K. Wright Jr. Army Lineage Series. Washington, D.C.: Center of Military History, United States Army, 1983.
- *Generations Past: A Selected List of Sources For Afro-American Genealogical Research*, Sandra M. Lawson, comp. Washington, D.C.: Library of Congress, 1988.
- *Location of the Wilderness Road at Cumberland Gap National Historical Park*, by Jere L. Krakow. Washington, D.C.: U.S. Department of the Interior, National Park Service, 1987.
- *Measuring America: The Decennial Censuses from 1790 to 2000*. Washington, D.C.: U.S. Census Bureau, 2002. An invaluable reference.
- *My History Is America's History: 15 Things You Can Do to Save America's Stories*. Washington, D.C.: National Endowment for the Humanities, 1999.
- *The United States Army in the World War, 1917–1919*. 17 vols. Washington, D.C.: Government Printing Office, 1948.

United States Serial Set and Indexes

The *U.S. Serial Set Indexes* (Bethesda: Congressional Information Service, Inc.—not a government agency) are tools to help researchers access many of the Congressional documents generated between 1789 and 1969 from both the House of Representatives and the Senate. These materials often contain information on ancestors. The indexes fall into twelve parts:

Part I: 1789–1857	Part V: 1897–1903	Part IX: 1925–1934
Part II: 1857–1879	Part VI: 1903–1909	Part X: 1935–1946
Part III: 1879–1889	Part VII: 1909–1915	Part XI: 1947–1958
Part IV: 1889–1897	Part VIII: 1915–1925	Part XII: 1959–1969

Each of these parts contains three volumes: Part 1, Subject Index A–K; Part 2, Subject Index L–Z; and Part 3, Finding Lists. Use the Finding Lists to look for ancestors' names. The Finding Lists include an index of names of individuals and organizations receiving private relief, but it is not an index to every name mentioned in the documents.

Use the Subject Indexes especially to find documents pertaining to your research area. Look under the state, territory, or other locality name. The index gives the titles of documents, but the titles are not always descriptive of all the material that may be found there. Good examples are the various census records of the islands of St. George and St. Paul in Alaska, which are included in various other reports and indexed without any suggestion of a census. Be alert to titles that mention petitions, name lists, depositions, or other indications that groups of names may be in the text. Some longer documents have their own indexes. Be sure to check the end of the document for such an index.

The coded numbers that accompany each entry in the index refer to the related document. H.rp.539 (31-1) serial 585 tells that the information is found in House Report number 539 (from the thirty-first Congress, first session) and may be found in serial number 585. *S.doc.* means "Senate document." *H.misdoc.* means "House miscellaneous document", and *S.ex-doc.* or *H.exdoc.* means "[Senate or House] executive document." Refer also to the user guide at the beginning of each book. The serial number is the key to finding the document quickly, but all the information is necessary once you find the correct serial volume. Some libraries have these volumes in book form; some, in microform.

Another useful index to this set is the sixteen-volume *CIS U.S. Serial Set Index, Part XIV: Index and Carto-Bibliography of Maps, 1789–1969* edited by Donna P. Koepp (Bethesda, Md.: Congressional Information Service, 1995–). The personal name index includes any name appearing on a map, whether it is that of the mapmaker or a name identifying a building or other feature. Be sure to check for your family names in this index.

Case Study: Orgain and Moore

Case Study

Senate Document 37 (17th Congress, 1st session) serial 59 concerned Sterling Orgain, a Tennessee merchant and partner in the firm of Moore and Orgain. From previous research I knew that Orgain and Alfred Moore were brothers-in-law, married to sisters. The document concerning them was indexed in the Finding Lists under both names and yielded an interesting set of events. On 17 September 1818, the two men purchased from one Morris Lindsay an account against the federal government for $120 for blacksmith work. Lindsay had made 120 pairs of horseshoes for the Tennessee volunteer mounted gunmen involved in the Seminole War. Peter Hagner of the Third Auditor's Office, Treasury Department, had refused the claim on the grounds that these soldiers, under an act of 2 January 1795, were given an allowance of forty cents a day to cover their costs, including the use of their horses, arms, and other needs. The government therefore was not responsible for their horseshoes.

Orgain and Moore bought the account and resubmitted it as a petition to the Senate for payment. The Senate Claims Committee twice rejected it as well. Finally in February 1824, the petition was presented a third time and was referred to the Military Affairs Committee. This group differed with the auditor's "most rigid construction" of the 1795 law, saying they could not conceive that the soldiers were intended by the law to shoe their own horses during their service. "[Nor] can the committee believe that the soldier who defends his country, and fights its battles, should be deprived of his well earned reward, by deductions of this kind, without an express provision to that effect, for it is well known, that shoeing horses and providing those shoes, has uniformly constituted an expenditure of the quartermaster's department." Presenting the supporting evidence and precedence for authorizing such payments, the committee begged leave to present to the Congress a bill for paying the account. That bill passed in May 1824, nearly six years after the original work was done.

Other Congressional Sources

Two additional aids for finding information on ancestors are these:

1. *Digested Summary and Alphabetical List of Private Claims Which Have Been Presented to the House of Representatives From the First to the Thirty-First Congress, Exhibiting the Action of Congress on Each Claim With References to the Journals, Reports, Bills, &c, Elucidating Its Progress.* Originally compiled by order of the House of Representatives. Baltimore: Genealogical Publishing Co., reprint, 1970. Although

the bulk of this book deals with claims arising from the Revolutionary War, the volume includes private claims from post-Revolutionary years.

2. *List of Private Claims Brought Before the Senate, From the Commencement of the Fourteenth to the Close of the Thirtieth Congress.* 30th Cong., 2d sess., in vol. 2, 1849. Senate Misc. Doc. 67. Serial 534.

Congressional Information Service, now part of LexisNexis, publishes the Serial Set and also publishes historical indexes to other government materials:

1. *United States Congressional Committee Hearings Index*, early 1800s to 1969.
2. *Unpublished United States Senate Committee Hearings Index*, 1823–1964. Index to personal names. Mostly twentieth-century material.
3. *Unpublished United States House of Representatives Committee Hearings Index*, 1837–1946.
4. *United States Congressional Committee Prints Index*, 1789–1969.
5. *Presidential Executive Orders and Proclamations*, 1789–1983.
6. *United States Supreme Court Records and Briefs*, 1897 to present.
7. *United States Statutes at Large*, 1789 to present.
8. *Congressional Record and Predecessors*, 1789 to present.
9. *United States Congressional Journals*, 1789–1978.

These indexes in book form and the documents themselves are usually housed in library documents or reference sections. User guides in each volume explain the coded references. The indexes are also available electronically as the LexisNexis Congressional subscription service. Check for access at a library near you.

The *Congressional Record*, the *House Journal*, and the *Senate Journal* are reports of the proceedings of each session of Congress. The journals are the official documents published at the end of the session to provide a history of bills, resolutions, and procedural matters. They do not include debates. The *Congressional Record* is a daily report published during each session. It includes texts of bills, debates, votes, and anything else that happens on the floor of either house, as well as material added by members for publication that may or may not be related to the business at hand. Apart from an ancestor who was a member of either house and his participation in its proceedings, the genealogist would probably be most interested in the private acts for relief of individuals. The serial set usually is a more comprehensive coverage of these matters than the *Congressional Record* or the journals because the facts and documents of a case are reproduced in the serial volumes. (See "Public Statutes at Large" below.)

PART II—LAW LIBRARIES

Sources

Law libraries specialize in information pertaining to the legal profession: laws, court decisions, and other reference materials such as professional directories. **These collections contain much genealogical information that has not been abstracted for genealogists but is there for the searching.** Universities with law schools have law libraries that are usually open to the public. In addition, many counties have a law library in or near the courthouse, and other academic libraries have legal references and databases available for research.

STATE LAWS

Books of state statutes make up a sizable section of law libraries. Many volumes of these laws have indexes of varying degrees of usefulness, from mere calendars of titles to actual surname, place name, and subject listings. Cumulative indexes are quick ways to look for ancestors, extended family, or specific businesses. When working on city or county history, you could find such indexes valuable since legislative action sometimes involved city and county boundaries, courts, professional and license fees, officers, businesses, roads and bridges, schools, and other concerns. Three examples of cumulative indexes for state laws are these:

1. Swem's *Virginia Historical Index* (see page 284) includes Hening's Statutes of Virginia (1619–1792) in its listings, although this index is more likely to be found with history reference materials in a public or university library than in a law library.
2. A very good cumulative index to H.P.N. Gammel's editions of the laws of Texas is the *Analytical Index to the Laws of Texas, 1823–1905*, by Cadwell Walton Raines (Austin, Tex.: Von Boeckmann-Jones Co., Printers, 1906, reprint by Fred B. Rothman and Co., 1987). This index contains individual names as well as topics, such as relief acts, memorials and petitions, free Africans, adoption, legalization of certain marriages, legitimation of children, and name changes.
3. *A Complete Index to the Names of Persons, Places, and Subjects Mentioned in Littell's Laws of Kentucky*, by W.T. Smith (Lexington, Ky.: Bradford Club Press, 1931).

Private Acts

Of great interest to genealogists is the fact that our state legislatures, like their national counterpart, in almost every session have enacted laws and resolutions that addressed the needs or wishes of individual citizens in such matters as payment for services rendered to the state, name changes, land titles, financial aid, property and inheritance questions, adoption, marriage, and divorce. These *private acts* or *relief acts* are sometimes indexed separately by subject and name; sometimes they are indexed along with the *public acts*.

In early years, state laws approved name changes. The Mississippi legislature, in January and February 1840, allowed two men to change their names. William Mitchell of Lawrence County became William Mitchell Rayman, and George Washington Grant of Leake County became George Washington Grant Thompson, since he was the son of James J. Thompson. The reader is naturally curious about the circumstances leading to these changes, and often the reason was inheritance, although the records do not always explain. Nor do the published statutes always identify the resident counties of the persons named. That information may be in the petition that initiated the proceeding.

The same Mississippi legislative session declared Mariah E. Marley, natural child of Samuel Marley of Yazoo County, to be his legitimate child, entitled to the rights of any other children of whole blood, including the *right to inherit* from her father's estate should he die intestate. The Alabama General Assembly on 9 January 1835 authorized Louisa Blankenship to change her surname to McAllister, under which she could inherit property bequeathed to her in the will of Edmund McAllister, deceased, of Lawrence County, on the condition that she would take the name McAllister. Some name changes were also granted in divorce decrees.

State legislatures also addressed the issues of marriage and legitimate children. The first legislature of the state of Texas on 4 April 1846 legalized the marriage of Samuel M. Parry and Elizabeth Neese "as though at the time of the celebration of said marriage no legal disability existed thereto" and legitimated their children—Samuel, Mary, Catharine, Rosand, John,

William, David, and Martha. Such information provides a good list of children's and parents' names and the knowledge that these children were all living in 1846. This act does not specify the county of residence or whether Neese was Elizabeth's maiden name or name by a previous marriage.

Adoption was another concern handled by state legislatures. A good example from Texas is the March 1848 act that authorized the name of Zachary Taylor Long, infant (which can mean "infant" or simply "young, a minor") son of Andrew Long, to be changed to Zachary Taylor Winfree and the child to be adopted by Jacob F. Winfree and made "capable of inheriting in the same manner as if the said infant were the lawful child" of J.F. Winfree.

Another special kind of law was for aid and relief of persons in need. The Texas legislature, for example, on 10 April 1901, voted that Mary E. Batchelor, widow of James W. Batchelor, continuing unmarried and in indigent circumstances, was entitled to a pension of $150 a year during her lifetime, to take effect ninety days after adjournment of the session.

In some states, mostly in the years prior to the Civil War, the state legislature had some jurisdiction over divorce. Often the chancery or equity court in each county or district could review the case and issue a decree recommending the dissolution of the marriage, and the legislature had the right of final approval. In some cases, the parties could appeal directly to the legislature. The Alabama Assembly in January and February 1854 granted sixty divorces, and all but two of the cases originated in the Chancery Courts throughout the state. Apart from complete divorce, one option was divorce from bed and board, a legal separation. In January 1834, Laura Bell and Susan Pool, both of Mobile County, Alabama, each received this kind of divorce by act of the state legislature. The divorce records found in the laws of the state can be especially useful when you face a burned courthouse in the county.

In many states, women's rights were severely limited, especially in the matter of property rights. The Alabama act for the relief of Elizabeth Jewell, 20 December 1837, approved for her the right to acquire, hold, and dispose of separate property as if she were a *feme sole* (single female) and declared that her separate property was not liable for payment of any debts of her husband, Thomas Jewell.

Other Legislative Acts

Although many researchers find the laws enacted by state legislatures of limited genealogical usefulness in searching for their ancestors, those who want to know more about the life and times of a given ancestral family may want to read laws of the state on crime and punishment, marriage and divorce, taxation, inheritance, women's rights (or the lack of rights), slavery and freedmen, professional and business licensing, and so forth.

Of course, appropriation bills still come before legislatures to determine the budget of the state government. An ancestor who worked for the state would have had his or her salary determined ultimately by the legislature. For example, the list published in the laws of Texas for the Special Session of August 1901 gives the semi-annual salary of each employee, not by name but by job title. The nurses at the Confederate Home were allowed $144 each. Apart from salaries, the governor's office received a six-month appropriation of $18 for ice. Comparing the final enactment with the state senate's version published in the *Senate Journal* shows that one item denied was a request from the Department of Agriculture, Insurance, Statistics, and History for $100 to purchase a "typewriter machine." However, the Senate allowed $5 per month rent for typewriters for the Senate clerks.

Is this genealogy? If your ancestors were employees affected by these decisions, the information adds detail and spice to your family history. If your ancestors lived in the state and paid the taxes that supported these appropriations, you may find this part of state history enlightening and fascinating. If you live in the state currently, you may find that things have not changed very much!

A series of laws useful when studying the colonial period of U.S. history is the Colony Laws of North America Series, John D. Cushing, ed. (Wilmington, Del.: Michael Glazier, Inc., 1978). Sixteen volumes represent the earliest printed laws for Delaware, Georgia, Maryland, Massachusetts, the Pilgrims of New Plimouth [*sic*], New York, New Hampshire, New Haven and Connecticut, New Jersey, North Carolina, Pennsylvania, Rhode Island and Providence Plantations, South Carolina, and Virginia. The volumes are facsimile reproductions of original printed sources.

A number of law libraries and academic libraries have the entire collection of state and territorial laws, called session laws, on microfiche or in book form. If your local library does not have the session laws for your state, perhaps this could be a project for special donations.

THE PUBLIC STATUTES AT LARGE OF THE UNITED STATES

Laws and resolutions passed by the U.S. Congress as well as ratified treaties to which the United States is a party are collected in the series called *Public Statutes at Large of the United States*, from 1789 to the present. For genealogists, again the most valuable part of these publications is the private acts passed during each session. Just as citizens of the states appealed to their state legislatures for relief, so citizens of the country called on Congress for help with personal claims and concerns.

The great majority of these private acts of Congress concern pensions for military service, but some address other concerns. A bill passed on 28 May 1830 for the relief of John Moffitt directed the Treasury Department to ascertain the value of Continental Loan Office Certificate number 104 issued to John Moffitt by the Loan Commissioners of South Carolina and to pay him the sum due on the certificate, excluding interest.

An outgrowth of any war is the need for support of families of servicemen killed in the war. An 11 August 1790 act approved an annuity in the amount of seven years' half-pay of a lieutenant colonel to be paid to Frances Eleanor Laurens, the orphan daughter of the late Lieutenant Colonel John Laurens, who was killed while in the service of the United States.

Fortunately, the private acts of Congress are included in the indexes of the *Public Statutes*. The first eight volumes of the *Public Statutes* cover the period from 1789 to 1845. Volume 6 is devoted entirely to the private acts approved during those years, with an index. The private acts from 1845 to 1900 are published after the public statutes in each volume and are included in the general index to that volume. Each volume covers one Congress, both sessions. Since 1875, the U.S. Government Printing Office has published the *Public Statutes*, beginning with the forty-third Congress (1873–1875). In 1901 and succeeding years, the public and private acts were separated into two volumes, and part two of each pair covers the private acts. The Serial Set is the place to find documents supporting the action; therefore, individuals who are the recipients of these acts are indexed also in the Serial Set Finding Lists.

APPELLATE COURTS AND COURT REPORTS

In the United States, state and federal governments have a pyramid of courts. The federal and state district courts and county, city, and special courts (family, probate, etc.) are the trial courts where the majority of cases originate. Each jurisdiction provides a smaller number of intermediate appellate courts where decisions of the lower courts can be reconsidered at the request of defendants or plaintiffs. The U.S. Supreme Court and its counterparts in the states are the high courts, often the final stop in the litigation process.

For centuries, written reports of court cases have been part of legal history in courts of original or appellate jurisdiction. Even the county court minute books in our most rural counties from the early years of the nation contain brief summaries of the numerous cases heard and decided there. (See chapter three.) Such cases represent the activities of somebody's ancestors. Furthermore, written records of state and federal appellate courts and their predecessors may give genealogists information on ancestral lives and activities. Some of those details include birth, marriage, and death dates as well as names and relationships of heirs.

Federal Digest Series

For federal appellate cases, a number of published reports exist. The official reports prepared by the courts are one source of information about cases and the individuals involved in them. However, the unofficial reporters—publications of private companies—are additional sources, indexed and readily available for genealogists to consult.

Various digests index reported cases but not all cases that have taken place. The Federal Digest series is a handy set of reference books that indexes reported federal cases, usually appellate cases, from federal and predecessor courts dating back to 1754. (Some of the cases may have begun in state courts but ended up in federal appellate courts.) Usually, these digests are housed in law libraries but are sometimes included with federal documents (although they are not government documents) or special collections in university and research libraries. Larger law firms also maintain law libraries, but access may be restricted to their employees.

The federal digests include the following, all publications of West Publishing Company of St. Paul, Minnesota:

- *Federal Digest* reported cases from 1754 to 1939; 72 volumes published between 1941 and 1956
- *Modern Federal Practice Digest* reported cases from 1939 to 1961, 62 volumes published between 1960 and 1972
- *Federal Practice Digest 2d [series]* reported cases from 1962 to November 1975, 92 volumes published between 1976 and 1979
- *Federal Practice Digest 3d [series]* reported cases after November 1975, 120 volumes published between 1984 and 1987
- *Federal Practice Digest 4th [series]* reported cases after about 1983, more than 114 volumes, published from 1997 to the present and continuing (at this writing)

Most of these volumes are topical indexes covering thousands of subjects, such as occupational safety, bankruptcy, drugs, adoption, land ownership, and civil rights. The index entries refer researchers to cases dealing with nearly any subject. However, the volumes of the most genealogical interest are the tables of cases (alphabetical by the name of the plaintiff) and the defendant-plaintiff tables (alphabetical by the name of the defendant). Because the plaintiffs and defendants were often individuals, families, or family businesses, you can search these tables for your ancestral surnames and perhaps find a case in which ancestors were involved or named. The following guide refers you to the volumes that contain the tables of cases and thus the indexes to surnames:

- *Federal Digest* Table of cases (plaintiff's name listed first), volumes 66–68; defendant-plaintiff table (defendant's name listed first), volumes 69–70

- *Modern Federal Practice Digest* Table of cases, volumes 53–54; defendant-plaintiff table, volumes 55–56
- *Federal Practice Digest 2d* Table of cases, volumes 82–84; defendant-plaintiff table, volumes 85–86
- *Federal Practice Digest 3d* Table of cases, volumes 113–116; defendant-plaintiff table, volumes 117–119
- *Federal Practice Digest 4th* Table of cases, volumes 100–104C (eighteen volumes at this writing); no defendant-plaintiff table yet

The digest (topical and index) entries give citations that allow you to find the reports of cases in which you are interested. For each case, the citation includes the volume and page number in a published report. In listing each case, the digests give an abbreviation for the name of the lower courts (for example, C.C. for circuit court; D.C. for district court) as well as the appellate courts that heard the cases (see list below).

Over the years, the digests have included citations for the published reports of a number of courts. The inclusion of these published reports has changed over the years as the court system and the publication of case reports have changed. The following published reports (Reporters and Reports) are cited in one or more series of the Federal Digests; you will need this information to find the case reports you want to read. The abbreviations in parentheses are the abbreviations to the published reports from each court:

Appeals Cases in the District of Columbia (App.D.C.)
Bankruptcy Reporter (B.R.)
Circuit Courts of Appeals Reports (C.C.A.)
Claims Court Reporter (Cl.Ct.)
Court of Claims Reports (Ct.Cl.)
Court of Customs Appeals Reports (Ct.Cust.App.)
Custom and Patent Appeals Reports (C.C.P.A.)
District of Columbia Supreme Court Reports (D.C.)
Federal Cases (Fed.Cas.)
Federal Claims Reporter (Fed.Cl.)
Federal Reporter (F.)
Federal Reporter 2d [series] (F.2d)
Federal Reporter 3d [series] (F.3d)
Federal Rules Decisions (F.R.D.)
Federal Supplement (F.Supp.)
Lawyers Edition of the *Supreme Court Reports* (L.Ed.)
Military Justice Reporter (M.J.)
Supreme Court Reporter (S.Ct.)
U.S. Reports [U.S. Supreme Court] (U.S.)
Veterans Appeals Reporter (Vet.App.)

Each case cited in a digest has one or more citations that look something like this: 48 U.S. 234. This refers you to volume 48, page 234, of the series called *U.S. Reports* and thus informs you that the case eventually went to the U.S. Supreme Court. Ask the reference librarians for help in finding the reports and reporters that you need. These are multi-volume series that could be spread over a wide range of shelves in a law library.

Many appellate cases contain genealogical information about relationships, dates, and events in people's lives. Some of that data may be available in family and local sources. However, especially in counties with burned courthouses, the information may be found only in such legal sources. For example, the testimony in the following example mentions that the recorder's office where a land record in question was deposited burned before 1806. This case was *Lewis et al. v. Baird et al.* originally from the Circuit Court for the District of Ohio, July 1842. (The several citations for the case included 48 U.S. 234 and 12 L.Ed. 681.) One citation was for the federal case number 8316, found in 15 Fed.Cas. 457. Thus, the lengthy published report is in volume 15 of *Federal Cases*, that includes cases 8125-8734. Page 457 begins the summary of the case. Most of the plaintiffs had a common surname, Lewis; thus, this case is an example of the benefits to common-surname research that could result from the use of such legal reports. The case report contains the following genealogical material:

1. The complainants in the case were Peter K. Wagner and Sidonia Pierce Wagner, his wife; John Lawson Lewis, Louisa Maria Lewis, Theodore Lewis, Eliza Cornelia Lewis, Alfred J. Lewis, John Hampden Lewis, Algernon Sidney Lewis, George Washington Lewis, and Benjamin Franklin Lewis, all of New Orleans, Louisiana; John Bowman and his wife, Mary Pierce (Lawson) Bowman, of Tennessee; and George C. Thompson of Kentucky. Notes from the case indicate that the plaintiffs claimed ownership to a tract of land that was in the hands of the defendants, John Baird et al. Thompson was not a Lawson heir, but the other eleven defendants were heirs of a common ancestor, Robert Lawson.

2. The complainants' ancestor, General Robert Lawson, served in the Virginia Continental Line in the Revolutionary War and received a warrant for ten thousand acres of land. He lived in Fayette County, Kentucky. He died in Richmond, Virginia, between 1802 and 1805, when Columbus, the youngest of three children, was sixteen years old.

3. Robert Lawson's wife, Sarah, of Fayette County, Kentucky, died in Virginia in 1809. Her three children survived her: sons John P. Lawson and Columbus Lawson and a daughter (unnamed) who had married Joshua Lewis. Columbus Lawson died unmarried about 8 January 1815. His brother, John P. Lawson, died about 1 June 1809, leaving only one child, Mary (Lawson) Bowman, wife of John Bowman, as shown on the list of complainants. The last Lawson sibling, Mrs. Lewis (still no given name mentioned), died about 1 October 1830; and her husband died about 20 June 1833. The ten Lewis children and their cousin Mary (Lawson) Bowman were the complainants in the case.

4. Though not mentioned in the index because he was not a party to the lawsuit, James McKinley, a witness, in 1796 lived on the farm of Daniel Feagins, who had two sons, Fielding and Edward Feagins, and who lived near Germantown, Mason County, Kentucky, in 1796. Thus, the case includes genealogical information on others as well as the complainants.

As shown in the Lewis case, researchers may benefit from using cluster genealogy in this legal research because some of the genealogical information provided is for people other than those named in the title of the case. Another example is the case in 10 F. 717 of *Young et al. v. Dunn et al.* from the Circuit Court for the Eastern District of Texas, 1882. A letter that was probated as the will of James A. *Caldwell*, dated 21 March 1842 and addressed to S.C. *Colville*, named Jane *McFarland*, wife of Jacob McFarland, as Caldwell's only blood relation, now in Texas. Caldwell, Colville, and McFarland were not parties to the lawsuit and therefore were not listed in the index.

Some case reports reprint the entire will of an ancestor, as occurred with the will of Samuel DeVaughn of the District of Columbia, who died 5 July 1867, and the will of Mary Vermilya, who died in 1824 in Hudson County, New Jersey (17 S.Ct. 461; 10 F. 857 and 33 F. 201, respectively).

One case, *Aaron Bradshaw v. Nehemiah B. Ashley* (180 U.S. 59; 21 S.Ct. 297), contains genealogical data from another case, *Mitchell v. Mitchell* (1851) from Maryland, involving land of one Francis J. Mitchell (who died in 1825), his son James D. Mitchell, and James's widow, Elizabeth. The Mitchell case was simply cited as part of the argument in the Bradshaw case; thus, the Mitchell dispute does not appear in the *Federal Digest* table of cases.

American Digest System

West Publishing Company also produces a comprehensive series of digests (topical references and indexes) of both state and federal appellate cases that are reported in all of the West reporters. The volumes are arranged alphabetically by legal topics but cover all reported American case law during the stated years. This huge series is called the American Digest System and contains the following sub-series:

American Digest, Century Edition, or *Century Digest* (cases 1658-1896).
First Decennial Digest (1897–1906); volumes 21–25 index this set and the *Century Digest.*
Second Decennial Digest (1907–1916).
Third Decennial Digest (1916–1926).
Fourth Decennial Digest (1926–1936).
Fifth Decennial Digest (1936–1946).
Sixth Decennial Digest (1946–1956).
Seventh Decennial Digest (1956–1966).
Eighth Decennial Digest (1966–1976).
Ninth Decennial Digest, Part 1 (1976–1981), *Part 2* (1981–1986).
Tenth Decennial Digest, Part 1 (1986–1991), *Part 2* (1991–1996).
Eleventh Decennial Digest, Part 1 (1996–2001).
General Digest, 8th Series (1991–1996), *General Digest, 9th Series* (from 1996, continuing the *Tenth Decennial Digest, Part 2*), *General Digest, 10th Series* (2001 forward, continuing the *Eleventh Decennial Digest, Part 2*).

As with the Federal Reporter system, the genealogist using the American Digest system should consult the volumes labeled Table of Cases to identify cases possibly involving family members. These tables are usually in the last books in each series and are arranged alphabetically by the name of the plaintiff. Cases after 1976 are also indexed by defendant. Read the explanations and abbreviations at the beginning of the tables to understand how to access the cases. The principle is basically this: volume number, abbreviation of the reporter or reports series in which the case report appears, topic number under which to find the case mentioned if it appears in one of the Decennial Digests, or the page number in a book of case reports. The slightly different numbering in the *Century Digest* is cross-referenced in the *First* and *Second Decennial Digests.*

References such as 51 Miss. 128 and Cooke 179 (Tenn) refer to case reports from the states—volume 51, page 128 of the Mississippi Reports and page 179 of Cooke's Tennessee Reports. A citation such as 48 C. War 27 refers to volume 48 of the *Century Digest*, the topical heading war and its subheading number 27. A table of abbreviations at the front of the volume helps clarify the terms used in the reference.

National Reporter System

Regional digests refer researchers to a variety of regional or state reporters, which report cases and decisions from state appellate courts. Also published by West, these digests cover each region of the country and each state individually except Delaware, Nevada, and Utah. The Dakotas are combined in one digest, as are Virginia and West Virginia. These series contain references to cases decided in the state courts and reported in the National Reporter System (below).

These volumes are the unofficial reports for decisions issued by appellate courts in the states; in some instances, the official reports prepared by the courts may cover earlier cases than does the National Reporter System. However, the cases are also included in the American Digest System (Decennial Digests) discussed above. (Many states have other digests and reporters as well. Law libraries vary in their holdings. Few can afford to own all published digests and reporters; many focus on the publications pertinent to their state or region.)

Many state cases are searchable electronically in the *LexisNexis* subscription database. The dates of electronic coverage vary from state to state, so be sure to check which cases and time periods are present.

The National Reporter System—the regional reporters (volumes of case reports) with the states they cover—is listed below. The regional digests cover the same groups of states. Check with reference librarians at the law library for help as needed, as these publications and coverage are subject to change:

Atlantic Reporter (began in 1886): Connecticut, Delaware, District of Columbia (Court of Appeals), Maine, Maryland, New Hampshire, New Jersey, Pennsylvania, Rhode Island, Vermont. See Federal Digest for Circuit Court for District of Columbia.

North Eastern Reporter (began in 1885): Illinois, Indiana, Massachusetts, New York, Ohio.

North Western Reporter (began in 1879): Iowa, Michigan, Minnesota, Nebraska, North Dakota, South Dakota, Wisconsin.

Pacific Reporter (began in 1884): Alaska, Arizona, California, Colorado, Hawaii, Idaho, Kansas, Montana, Nevada, New Mexico, Oklahoma, Oregon, Utah, Washington, Wyoming.

South Eastern Reporter (began in 1887): Georgia, North Carolina, South Carolina, Virginia, West Virginia.

Southern Reporter (began in 1887): Alabama, Florida, Louisiana, Mississippi.

Southwestern Reporter (began in 1887): Arkansas, Kentucky, Missouri, Tennessee, Texas. Each state has its own digest now.

New York Supplement (from 1888), *California Reporter* (from 1960), and *Illinois Decisions* (from 1976) are separate reporters for the most litigious states and include some lower court decisions.

Military Law Reporter, covering military appellate decisions, began in the mid-1970s.

LEGAL DATABASES

Massive electronic databases of legal, business, scientific, and news information are now available from various subscription services. These databases cover many subjects with the latest news and information from newspapers, periodicals, business and professional journals, and legal reports, generally from the 1980s forward. Two of the most well known that include the legal field are Westlaw from West Group, a division of Thomson Corporation, and LexisNexis from LexisNexis, a division of Reed Elsevier. For the most part, these services are available to businesses that subscribe to them; in law libraries for students, faculty, and lawyers; and in many academic libraries for patrons whether or not they are connected with the university. Remember that cases contained in these databases are mostly appellate cases that have been reported in the *Reporter* and *Digest* systems. No database includes all cases ever tried.

Legal Directories

Several directories of persons in the legal profession began publication in the late nineteenth century. *The Lawyers Directory* by the Sharp and Alleman Company of Philadelphia has been published under various titles since 1883. *Martindale's American Law Directory* (New York: G.B. Martindale) began in 1868 with annual editions. *Hubbell's Legal Directory* (New York: Hubbell Legal Directory Co.), also an annual publication, began in 1870. The Martindale and Hubbell volumes listed lawyers in the United States, Canada, and some European countries; U.S. bankers (one or more per city); real estate agents (Martindale, 1874); U.S. consuls living abroad (Hubbell, 1929); other groups pertinent to the legal business; a description of the court system in each state; and a synopsis of its laws. These two companies merged in 1931 and continue as a New Providence, New Jersey company, Martindale-Hubbell Law Directory, Inc. The 1993 edition was the first to list lawyers alphabetically throughout the country. Earlier volumes were alphabetical by state and towns within it.

The current Martindale-Hubbell directory is searchable online at <www.martindale.com/xp/Martindale/home.xml>. Another searchable directory for lawyers and law firms is on the FindLaw Web site <http://directory.findlaw.com/>. Both print and electronic directories of law professors and other legal professionals often contain biographical information.

The Martindale directory of 1920 showed that H.O. Metcalfe had been admitted to the Texas bar in 1913, made between two thousand and five thousand dollars annually, and had high recommendations for ability and promptness. Mr. C.E. Mead, with whom he worked, was a very capable lawyer who had been in the profession since 1890. The 1924 and subsequent directories correctly reported Metcalfe's birth year as 1887. Space in the biographical section or business card section could be purchased by those lawyers who wanted their schooling, professional memberships, or specializations advertised.

OTHER REFERENCE MATERIAL

Law libraries also contain sections on foreign law; maritime law; specialized topics such as social security, family law, and commercial law; general books on legal history; biographies; reference tools such as the *Encyclopedia of Associations*, Denise S. Akey, ed. (Detroit: Gale Research Co.) and Congressional directories and biographical lists; and legal research guides to various states.

Legal reference works covering many topics include these:

- *American Jurisprudence 2d.* Rochester, N.Y.: Lawyers Co-Operative Publishing Co., 1962.
- *Black's Law Dictionary*, by Henry Campbell Black. St. Paul, Minn.: West Group, published since 1891, any edition.
- *Corpus Juris*, William Mack and Donald J. Kiser, eds. New York: American Law Book Co., 1932.
- *Corpus Juris Secundum*, Francis J. Ludes and Harold J. Gilbert, eds. Brooklyn: American Law Book Company, 1953.

Focus on African-American Genealogy

United States genealogists searching any ethnic or nationality group will have in common certain sources that are basic to genealogical research, such as census records; land, estate, tax, marriage, and vital records; cemetery and church records; newspapers; and so forth. Besides sources that everyone uses, some African-American-specific sources do exist and may be helpful. In addition to basic family, local, county, state, and federal sources, other possibilities exist in libraries, archives, and electronic sources.

For most African-American researchers, genealogy divides into post–Civil War and pre-1865 periods. The first focus is to work backward in time through basic genealogical records to identify ancestral families in 1870, the year of the first census after the end of the Civil War and the emancipation of slaves. Only then should you undertake research of pre-1865 sources. (The Civil War began in 1861 and ended in 1865. Slaves became free at different times, but the Thirteenth Amendment to the Constitution finalized nationwide emancipation in December 1865.)

For More Info

To connect with other African-American researchers, see the list of member societies of the Federation of Genealogical Societies at <www.familyhistory.com/societyhall/main.asp>.

African-American genealogy before 1865 acquires a particular challenge because of the existence of slavery and the relative scarcity of records concerning individual slaves. Information can be found on many of them and on freedmen, even if it seems buried in obscure places. Patience and perseverance are the keys to this kind of research. The case study at the end of the chapter demonstrates a search for slave ancestors.

POST–CIVIL WAR RECORDS

After the Civil War, the names of recently freed slaves began appearing in censuses, local and county records, newspapers, city directories, and other records that genealogists use. These records, with African-American genealogy in mind, are the focus of this section.

See Also

Review chapter two for more on federal censuses and chapter five for more on state censuses.

Federal Census Records

Federal censuses from 1870 forward present the same excitement and dilemmas to researchers of any ethnic group. Some families were not enumerated, for many reasons. Some individuals were omitted, probably unintentionally. Mistakes occurred in names, ages, gender, birthplaces, and other information. Since census takers and clerks often spelled phonetically,

expect spelling variations in your family's names in census and other records. In spite of these problems, federal census records are valuable and necessary sources readily available to researchers.

Warning

Enumerator Gifts. In the post–Civil War censuses, census takers sometimes interpreted their instructions uniquely and recorded information for which genealogists are grateful and from which they often obtain valuable clues. These gifts to the genealogist may include middle names, marriage dates, designations of twins or triplets, or specific birthplaces, such as city or county. The following are two examples dealing with family relationships.

Remember, the 1870 census forms did not ask for family relationships. Yet, the enumerator in Jasper County, Mississippi, left two examples of such information. An alert researcher can benefit from the clues that such "gifts" contain.

In the African-American household of Crawford (age fifty-eight) and Adeline (age fifty-two) Kelly lived eleven younger family members between the ages of twenty-four and one, listed in order from oldest to youngest, as children in a family usually were. The researcher should ask whether the youngest ones were truly children of a fifty-two-year-old woman. However, after the baby, four more Kellys were listed, ranging in age from four years to one month. The enumerator bracketed these four and marked them "Grandchildren." Perhaps Adeline, therefore, really was the mother of the one-year-old, or perhaps Adeline was not really fifty-two years old. Remember, she probably was born a slave, reportedly about 1818; thus, **she and her family probably had no knowledge of her actual birth date and had to approximate her age.** Such estimates may be off by a few or even ten to fifteen years.

Important

The second example was from the same neighborhood, in the black family of Manuel (age twenty-eight) and Jane (twenty-five) Heidelberg. Besides their four young children, sixteen-year-old Sarah McDonald was living with them. Under the column for Sarah's occupation, the enumerator wrote "living with brother-in-law." Normally Manuel would be Sarah's brother-in-law in one of two ways. The most likely was that Sarah was the sister of Manuel's wife. The other was that Sarah was the wife of Manuel's brother. It is possible that brothers had different surnames, especially in black families after the Civil War, but the record gave no hint whether Sarah was then or had been married. Nevertheless, the genealogist benefits from the information that a relationship existed; studying a cluster of relatives is often a road to progress in research.

Color/Race Designations. Instructions to census takers changed over the years. Among the frequent changes was the census bureau's definition of racial groups. Researchers need to be aware of the changing definitions and choices in order to interpret ancestral censuses accurately. Remember, we do not know who furnished the information or whether the census taker asked the family or guessed.

CD Source

An aid to 1870 census research is *African Americans in the 1870 U.S. Federal Census* (Heritage Quest, 2001, CD-ROM), a national index to African-American heads of household.

- **1870–1880.** "Color" choices were White, Black, Mulatto, Chinese, and Indian. *Mulatto* included persons of mixed race, especially quadroons (one-quarter black ancestry), octoroons (one-eighth black ancestry), and "all other persons having any perceptible trace of African blood." (See Figure 9-4, on page 335.)
- **1890.** Census takers were instructed to record "white, black, mulatto, quadroon, octoroon, Chinese, Japanese, or Indian, according to the color or race of the person enumerated."

  According to the instructions, "black" referred to anyone at least three-fourths Negro; "mulatto" applied to persons who were three-eighths to five-eighths black; "quadroon" described persons one-fourth black; and "octoroon" meant those with one-eighth or any trace of Negro ancestry.

- **1900.** The choices on the census form were White, Black, Chinese, Japanese, or Indian. (Mulatto was not an option on this census.)
- **1910–1920.** Census takers had to choose from White, Black, Mulatto, Chinese, Japanese, Indian, and Other. "Mulatto" was used to describe persons of mixed race "having some proportion or perceptible trace of negro blood."
- **1930.** Individuals of mixed white and black parentage were to be listed as Negro, and Mulatto was withdrawn. Persons of mixed Indian and Negro blood were to be listed as Negro, unless the Indian blood predominated and the person was considered an Indian in the community. People of mixed white and Indian blood were to be considered Indian, unless the individual was accepted as white in the community. "Mexican" was added to the choices.
- **1940.** The "color" choices were White, Negro, Indian, Chinese, Japanese, Filipino, Hindu, and Korean; the census taker could write in any other "race."

Marriage Records

Marriage records, especially in the South immediately after the Civil War, reflect the marriages of freed men and women. Some of these had been couples before the war and registered to legalize their union since slave marriages had not been recognized in the eyes of the law. In some areas, these "cohabitation" records gave additional information about the couple, such as how long they had been a couple or the woman's former name or maiden name.

For example, Craven County, North Carolina, marriage records contain the names of numerous couples who registered their marriages in August 1866, to beat a deadline set by state law. Figure 9-1, below, shows the makeshift record book, formerly a military register. The columns name the groom and the bride, the bride's former name, and the time

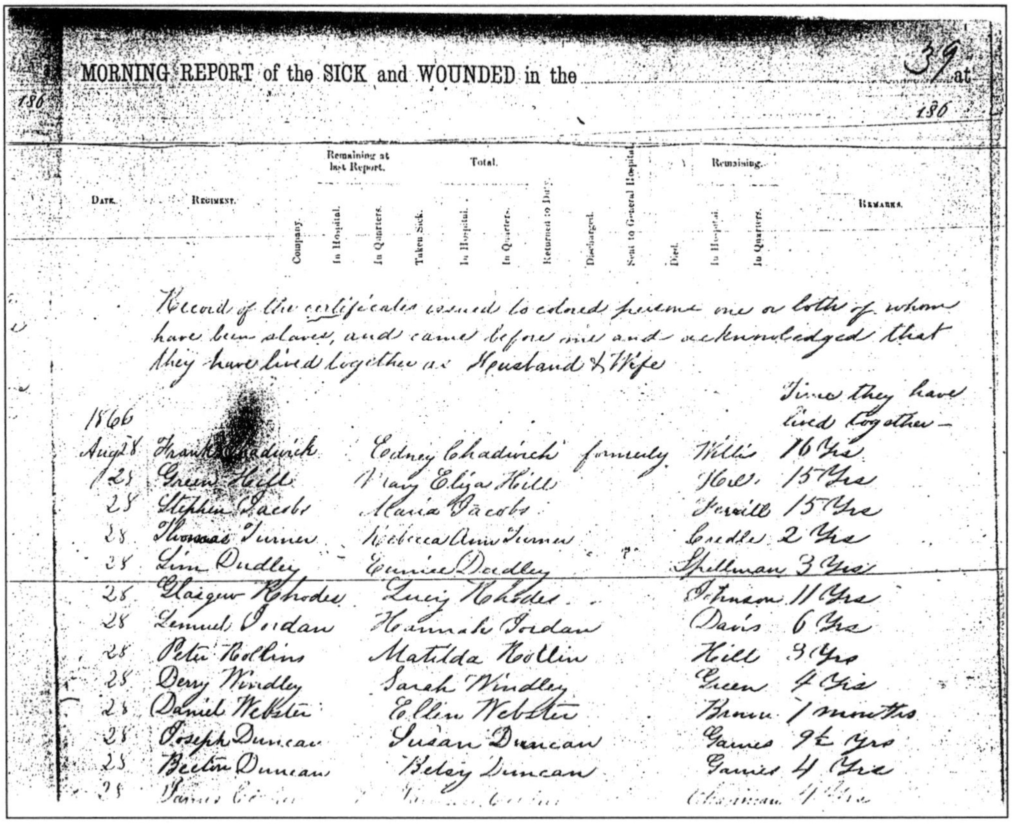

MORNING REPORT of the SICK and WOUNDED in the ... 39 at ... 186

Record of the certificates issued to colored persons one or both of whom have been slaves, and came before me and acknowledged that they have lived together as Husband & Wife

1866				Time they have lived together
Aug 28	Frank Chadwick	Edney Chadwick	formerly Willis	16 Yrs
28	Green Hill	Mary Eliza Hill	Hill	15 Yrs
28	Stephen Jacobs	Maria Jacobs	Farrill	15 Yrs
28	Thomas Turner	Rebecca Ann Turner	Credle	2 Yrs
28	Sim Dudley	Eunice Dudley	Spellman	3 Yrs
28	Glasgow Rhodes	Lucy Rhodes	Johnson	11 Yrs
28	Lemuel Jordan	Hannah Jordan	Davis	6 Yrs
28	Peter Rollins	Matilda Rollins	Hill	3 Yrs
28	Derry Windley	Sarah Windley	Green	4 Yrs
28	Daniel Webster	Ellen Webster	Brown	7 months
28	Joseph Duncan	Susan Duncan	Gaines	9½ Yrs
28	Becton Duncan	Betsy Duncan	Gaines	4 Yrs

Figure 9-1 Cohabitation Records, Craven County, North Carolina, Marriages 1865-1905, Book 2 (1865–1866):39, FHL microfilm 0288298.

they had lived together as husband and wife. This page shows couples recently married as well as those married fifteen or sixteen years.

For some years after the war and in various ways, African-American brides and grooms were often identified as black. Some counties used separate record books for blacks and whites. Some used the abbreviation *col'd* or *col* or *c* (colored) or *fmc* (free man of color) and *fwc* (free woman of color) beside the names. At least from a genealogical point of view, this practice can help researchers identify the correct ancestors and the correct marriage date since many counties had black and white residents of the same names.

In some states, such as Iowa, Virginia, and North Carolina, a number of post-war marriage records named the couple's parents. This practice helps researchers

- identify or confirm another generation of ancestors, often one born in slavery
- determine groups of siblings and re-create family groups
- estimate a parent's death date if marriage records of siblings begin listing a father or mother as deceased
- track several generations or get clues to multiple marriages for a given individual, even an ancestor's parent

Separate marriage books for black and white couples were common practice for a time in many Southern counties. An example is the Hardeman County, Tennessee, Freedmen's Marriage Records, 1865–1870. In this case, racial designation is found only with the names of the men who joined the grooms in signing the marriage bonds. When George W. Morgan got his marriage bond in December 1868, prior to marrying Martha J. Coleman, his surety was Ike Napier, *col'd.*

However, when Thornton Alexander married Lizzie Blaylock in April 1868, the surety on his bond was Jessee [*sic*] Blalock, a white farmer of the county. Further research suggests that Blalock was Lizzie's slaveholder before the war and her employer for several years afterward.

Vital Records

Birth and death records are twentieth-century sources in most states and cities. They are often found in county courthouses, or in city or state health or vital statistics bureaus. These are discussed in chapter three. In the early years of mandated registration, compliance was not universal. Thus, you may identify family births or deaths that were not reported or that were registered years after the event—delayed birth or death certificates. One of the greatest benefits of collecting these records on siblings is the potential of learning more about the parents.

Tax Records

Post–Civil War county tax rolls may be among the earliest records showing the presence of freed men and women. When personal property was taxed, owners of horses and other livestock and farming implements were to report their holdings and pay tax accordingly. Even without taxable personal property, freedmen were among the county residents paying poll taxes (head taxes); not until later were poll taxes sometimes required for voting.

The records are usually annual and may be organized alphabetically or geographically within each county. Many tax records have been microfilmed, at least to 1900. Check the state archives or the Family History Library catalog at a Family History Center or at <www.familysearch.org> for available records.

Research Tip

The case study later in this chapter illustrates the importance of tax rolls in studying one African-American family.

Voter Registrations

In some southern states after the Civil War, voter registration lists may be the first public records of former slaves. Many of the surviving registers are housed in state archives. Check library catalogs and the state archives of your ancestral state to learn whether these have been microfilmed or published. Check the Family History Library catalog at <www.familysearch.org> for microfilm availability.

Some of these records distinguish black and white voters. The amount of information given on each man varies from state to state. The Texas registers often furnish good information. In Austin County, Texas, in August 1867 Thomas Hawkins registered to vote. He stated that he had lived forty-five years in the state and twenty years in Austin County. He gave his birthplace as Guinea, Africa. In November 1869, Harry Bartin and Bob Kerkindoll registered to vote in Robertson County, Texas. Both said they had been in Texas forty years. Bartin, born in South Carolina, had also been in the county forty years (meaning, in the area that became that county in 1837). Kerkindoll, who came to the county only two years before, gave Kentucky as his birthplace.

Indexes to Deposit Ledgers of Branches of Freedman's Savings and Trust Company

The National Archives houses the indexes to deposit ledgers of some branches of the Freedman's Savings and Trust Company, 1865–1874. They are indexes only, incomplete and undated, and the deposit ledgers themselves remain unlocated, either missing or destroyed. The microfilmed indexes, grouped by state and city, are alphabetical by the first letter of the depositor's surname, but not in strict alphabetical order. Thus, all of the New Bern, North Carolina, indexes are together. If there are several volumes for a city, there are, therefore, several sets of *A*s to look through in searching for a surname beginning with *A*.

The lack of dates is not so great a problem when the researcher knows that the Freedman's Savings and Trust Company did business from 1865 to 1874. The company was established for deposits by or on behalf of freed slaves or their descendants. Although thirty-three branches were established, the indexes exist for twenty-six of them. The set of microfilm (M817) contains five rolls:

1. Huntsville, Alabama; Little Rock, Arkansas; Washington, DC
2. Jacksonville and Tallahassee, Florida; Augusta and Savannah, Georgia; Lexington and Louisville, Kentucky
3. New Orleans and Shreveport, Louisiana; Baltimore; Natchez and Vicksburg, Mississippi; St. Louis, Missouri; New York City.
4. New Bern, Raleigh, and Wilmington, North Carolina; Philadelphia; Beaufort and Charleston, South Carolina.
5. Memphis and Nashville, Tennessee; Norfolk and Richmond, Virginia; and unidentified.

Most of the depositors lived in or near the city where the branch bank was located. If your ancestors lived a goodly distance from a branch bank, it is less likely they would have had accounts. Nevertheless, if you find ancestors mentioned, you may learn valuable information. How can these indexes help researchers?

1. They help locate an ancestor in a specific place, sometime between 1865 and 1874. For example, since William Cowper's name appears in several New Orleans ledgers, you know that he was in the city over a period of months, perhaps several years.

2. Some of the records, by supplying the full names of the depositors, help genealogists learn the ancestor's middle name. This record may be the only source of the complete name. Examples from the New Orleans ledgers are Eli Mansfield Goodwin, Ann Gracie Hamilton, and Peter Israel Jones; from Shreveport, Alonzo Gustavus Longuire and Silas Flenoy Priestly.

3. Occasionally the ledger names both husband and wife. Some of these are implied husband-wife relationships, such as Eliza A. and Nelson Mack of Baltimore. Sometimes the relationship is stated, as in these New Orleans entries: Butler Alexander and his wife, Harriet, and John C. McKennon and wife, Delilah. This information can help identify couples whose marriages may not have been recorded or spouses who may have no other records.

4. Other identifying evidence may add to the information about an ancestor:

- Thomas Trusty *Sr.*, of New York City.
- *Major* E.F. Townsend and *Private* James Lewis of Vicksburg.
- J. Walpool's *grocery* in Shreveport.
- In New Orleans, *Rev.* Henry Green, *Widow* Elizabeth Gabriel, and Elizabeth James *alias* Wilson. The term *alias* did not always mean what it implies today but can indicate a married name and a maiden name, or sometimes two married names.

Notes

In the years after the Civil War, a number of organizations formed by or for the benefit of freed slaves. A number of these organizations had accounts in the Freedman's Savings and Trust Company. You will not find an ancestor's name connected with the organizations in these account ledger indexes, but you will get a flavor of the times and ideas for further searching if records or newspaper accounts of these organizations still exist. For example, such accounts in New Orleans included the Union Band No. 1, the Lutheran Benevolent Society, the Louisiana Association for the Benefit of Destitute Colored Orphans, Jeremiah Good Samaritans, the Colored Laboring Men, the First African Baptist Association, and St. James Chapel of the A[frican] M[ethodist] E[piscopal] Church. New York City's branch had accounts from a number of trade associations and lodges as well as the Enharmonic Singing Association.

These account ledger indexes tell us that in these towns and cities,

- black churches were being established
- people in certain occupations were banding together for mutual aid (coachmen, laborers, woolmen, lady draymen, longshoremen, etc.)
- there was a growing concern for education among blacks
- people were seeking social and fraternal outlets
- poverty was a widespread problem that private organizations were trying to address

Registers of Signatures of Depositors in the Freedman's Savings and Trust Company

The National Archives microfilm series M816 is records of account holders from twenty-nine branches of the Freedman's Savings and Trust Company. Most of the branches represented in this set are the same as those in the Indexes to Deposit Ledgers discussed above. However, the Jacksonville, Florida, branch is not included in the signature registers. Genealogists are grateful that four cities not included in the Indexes to Deposit Ledgers do have some surviving signature registers: Mobile, Alabama; Atlanta, Georgia: Columbus, Mississippi; and Lynchburg, Virginia.

These signature registers provide much more genealogical information than the deposit ledgers and, in some cases, have death certificates of the account holders attached. For some organizations' accounts in Philadelphia, names and signatures of officers appear in the registers.

CD Source

Abstracts of these registers are available as a CD-ROM, Freedman's Bank Records, from FamilySearch.org and at many libraries and Family History Centers.

Most of the registers contain personal and family information, just as we provide beneficiary information today. Additional information was sometimes included, such as the wife's maiden name, depositor's age, names of people who could draw on the account, or names of military units in which the depositor had participated during the Civil War. Some widows who had no children of their own named brothers or sisters, along with nieces and nephews. Such a "beneficiary" designation of course may suggest the maiden name of the depositor. Some account holders named their former masters and plantations. Others indicated that they had been free before the war.

Almost every entry contains some genealogical information, but some depositors gave more information than others. The following record is one of the more complete entries. Notice the information on Bell's cluster of relatives.

Branch: New Orleans Account number 66
Depositor: Graham Bell
Date: 2 October 1866, some notes added 31 March 1869
Occupation: 1866, carriage driver; 1869, dining room servant
Born in 1845, Mississippi; in 1866, age 21 years, 4 months, 3 weeks
Came to Louisiana in 1852; no master's name given
Father's name—Sam, died in Mississippi. Mother's name—Nancy Turner. Stepfather's name—William Turner. Wife's name—Mary E. Bell. Wife's mother—Nancy Bright.
Children: "Lewis 5 Bell" [age 5?, added in 1869?] and Ida Victoria [added with "8 mos."]
"Children dead Spencer Jackson and John." Brother Sam in New Orleans. [Brother] Allen dead. [Brother] Ben [?] dead. Sister, Maria, wife of Henry Stewart in Natchez. Mother had 8 children.

Although the following depositor had no children and therefore no descendants to research her life, her signature card could help researchers of family members.

Branch: New Orleans Account number 60
Depositor: Harriet Cobb
Date: 24 September 1866
Occupation: works as a servant
Born in Westmoreland County, Virginia
Master: Philip Chandler, plantation Whitehall, Pointe Coupee, Louisiana
Husband: Robert Cobb
No children
In case of death, her money was to go to Cyrus Ellis for the benefit of two younger sisters, Emily Anna and Charlotte Watson.

Other records of the company housed in the National Archives include letters to and from the commissioners, dividend payment records, loan and real estate ledgers, financial and accounting records, a record of bonds filed for lost passbooks, and records of the liquidation of the company between 1881 and about 1920. One additional set of microfilm is M874, Journal of the Board of Trustees and Minutes of Committees and Inspectors of the company.

Bureau of Refugees, Freedmen, and Abandoned Lands

Congress created the Bureau of Refugees, Freedmen, and Abandoned Lands in 1865 as a part of the War Department, especially to aid former slaves in coping with the realities and hardships of life after the Civil War. Until its termination in 1872, the bureau dealt with many aspects of work, education, health care, family life, adjustment to freedom, political and community participation, race relations, and day-to-day necessities.

Records of the bureau headquarters (Record Group 105) contain letters and records to and from the Commissioner, Superintendent of Education, Quartermaster, and other officials. Some of the microfilmed records (not all the records) are in series M752 (Commissioner's letters and registers), M742 (Selected Commissioner's records), and M803 (Education Division). A description of records, both microfilmed and originals at the National Archives, is the *Preliminary Inventory of the Records of the Bureau of Refugees, Freedmen, and Abandoned Lands Washington Headquarters*, Preliminary Inventory 174, Record Group 105, compiled by Elaine Everly (Washington, D.C.: National Archives and Records Service, 1973). This is available from the National Archives.

Notes

Refugees generally were destitute and/or dislocated whites; *freedmen* were recently freed slaves, often destitute as well.

On the state and local levels were the district or field offices, with an assistant commissioner over the activities in the state, his quartermaster and other officers, superintendents of education, and local agents around the state. Field offices were located in the District of Columbia, Kentucky, Maryland, and the former Confederate states—Alabama, Arkansas, Florida, Georgia, Louisiana, Mississippi, North and South Carolina, Tennessee, Texas, and Virginia. Bordering states of Missouri and Kansas fell under the Arkansas office. Delaware and West Virginia were served by both the District of Columbia and Maryland offices.

Although a number of field office records have been filmed and new microfilm publications will be added, many more records are available for study only at the National Archives. To learn more about the manuscript records from your ancestral state, try to obtain from the National Archives the portion of this manual that pertains to that state: *Preliminary Inventory of the Records of the Field Offices of the Bureau of Refugees, Freedmen, and Abandoned Lands (Record Group 105)*, inventory NM095, compiled by Elaine Everly and Willna Pacheli in 1973.

- Part 1 contains an inventory of records pertaining to Alabama, Arkansas, District of Columbia, Florida, Georgia, Kentucky, and Louisiana.
- Part 2 pertains to records from the field offices in Maryland, Delaware, Mississippi, Missouri, North Carolina, and South Carolina.
- Part 3 surveys records from field offices in Tennessee, Texas, and Virginia.

The field office records may contain such items as labor contracts, records of relief for indigent persons, descriptions and leases of abandoned lands, some marriage records (especially in Mississippi), requests for transportation to return home or join family, complaints registered by freedmen, reports on crimes, records of hospitals, and occasional censuses of local areas. National Archives microfilm M1875—*Marriage Records of the Office of the Commissioner, Washington Headquarters of the Bureau of Refugees, Freedmen, and Abandoned Lands, 1861–1869*—was published in 2002. Most of the Freedmen's Bureau microfilm reproduces the original handwritten records and is not indexed. Reading them can be time-consuming, but they often contain information not found elsewhere.

Figure 9-2, on page 312, shows a page from the Freedmen's Bureau records in South Carolina granting destitute freedmen transportation to go to the places named on the page. Figure 9-3, on page 313, shows both black and white recipients of rations—corn meal and pork or bacon—at New Bern, North Carolina, in December 1866. The small columns on the chart are for (1) the number of days the rations cover, (2) number of adults, (3) number of children, (4) total in the family, (5) number of whites, (6) number of blacks, (7) pounds and ounces of pork or bacon received, (8) pounds and ounces of corn meal received. All

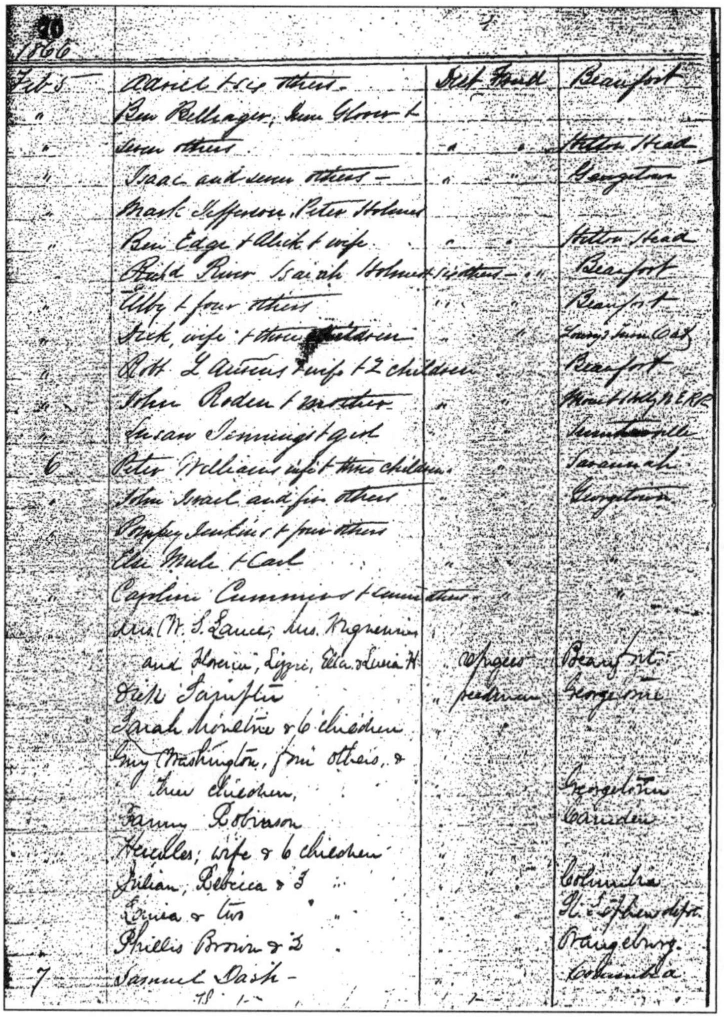

Figure 9-2 Transportation register, February 1866, South Carolina transportation issued, Records of the Assistant Commissioner for the state of South Carolina, Bureau of Refugees, Freedmen, and Abandoned Lands, 1865–1870, NARA microfilm M869, roll 44, target 2.

the recipients signed the receipt with their marks, and, according to the last column of remarks, all were destitute and/or sickly.

Microfilmed bureau records include the following series. (The first number is Records of the Assistant Commissioner for that state. The second number refers to Records of the state Superintendent of Education.)

- Alabama—M809, M180
- Arkansas—M979, M980
- District of Columbia—M1055, M1056
- Florida—M1869
- Georgia—M798, M799
- Louisiana—M1027, M1026
- Mississippi—M826
- North Carolina—M843, M844
- South Carolina—M869 only
- Tennessee—M999, M1000, Selected Records of Field Office, T142
- Texas—M821, M822
- Virginia—M1048, M1053

One kind of record that may contain genealogical information is the indentures of apprenticeship. These records may provide the name of a parent or former slaveholder, the age of the child, and the terms of the indenture. A good illustration comes from M999, roll 20—Hardeman County, Tennessee, where E.G. Coleman, a white farmer, signed the documents to bind seven young orphans into his care. The indentures furnish the following information about the children, as of 6 January 1866:

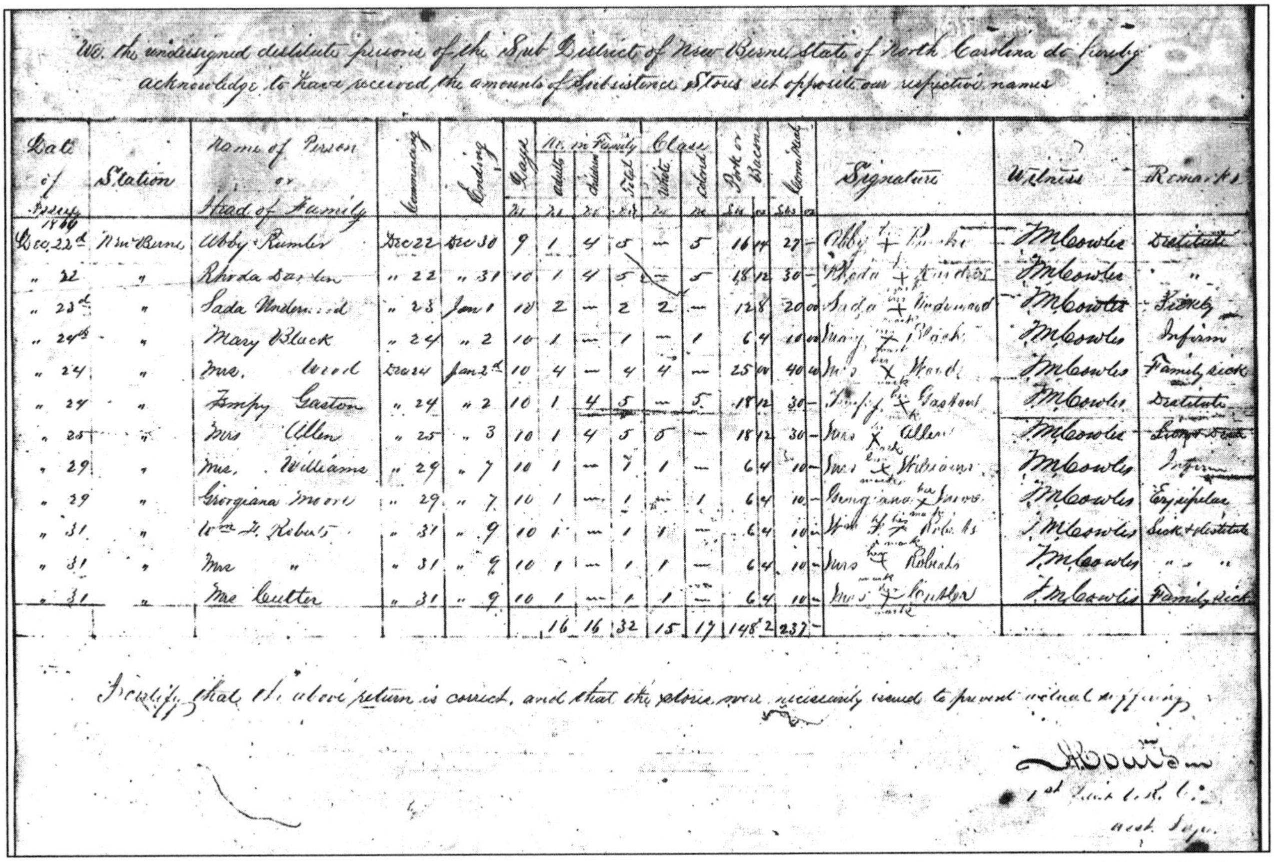

We the undersigned destitute persons of the Sub District of New Berne State of North Carolina do hereby acknowledge to have received the amounts of Subsistence Stores set opposite our respective names

Date of Issue	Station	Name of Person or Head of Family	Commencing	Ending	Days	No. in Family: Adults	Children	Total	Class: White	Colored	Pork or Bacon lbs	oz	Corn Meal lbs	oz	Signature	Witness	Remarks
1866 Dec. 22d	New Berne	Abby Rumler	Dec 22	Dec 30	9	1	4	5	—	5	16	14	27	—	Abby + Rumler	T.M. Cowles	Destitute
" 22	"	Rhoda Darden	" 22	" 31	10	1	4	5	—	5	18	12	30	—	Rhoda + [illegible]	T.M. Cowles	"
" 23d	"	Sada Underwood	" 23	Jan 1	10	2	—	2	2	—	12	8	20	00	Sada + Underwood	T.M. Cowles	Sickly
" 24th	"	Mary Black	" 24	" 2	10	1	—	1	—	1	6	4	10	00	Mary + Black	T.M. Cowles	Infirm
" 24	"	Mrs. Wood	Dec 24	Jan 2d	10	4	—	4	4	—	25	00	40	00	Mrs X Wood	T.M. Cowles	Family sick
" 24	"	Jimpy Gaston	" 24	" 2	10	1	4	5	—	5	18	12	30	—	Jimpy X Gaston	T.M. Cowles	Destitute
" 25	"	Mrs Allen	" 25	" 3	10	1	4	5	5	—	18	12	30	—	Mrs X Allen	T.M. Cowles	[illegible]
" 29	"	Mrs. Williams	" 29	" 7	10	1	—	1	1	—	6	4	10	—	Mrs X Williams	T.M. Cowles	Infirm
" 29	"	Georgiana Moore	" 29	" 7	10	1	—	1	—	1	6	4	10	—	Georgiana X Moore	T.M. Cowles	Erysipelas
" 31	"	Wm. F. Roberts	" 31	" 9	10	1	—	1	1	—	6	4	10	—	Wm F. + Roberts	T.M. Cowles	Sick & destitute
" 31	"	Mrs "	" 31	" 9	10	1	—	1	1	—	6	4	10	—	Mrs + Roberts	T.M. Cowles	" "
" 31	"	Mrs Cutler	" 31	" 9	10	1	—	1	1	—	6	4	10	—	Mrs + Cutler	T.M. Cowles	Family sick
						16	16	32	15	17	148	2	237	—			

I certify that the above return is correct, and that the stores were necessarily issued to prevent actual suffering

[illegible]
1st Lieut. [illegible]
Asst. Supt.

Figure 9-3 Rations issued at New Berne [*sic*], North Carolina, 22 December 1866, Records of the Assistant Commissioner for the state of North Carolina, Bureau of Refugees, Freedmen, and Abandoned Lands, 1865–1870, NARA microfilm M843, roll 27.

1. Louis Cross, turned 10 on 5 Mar. last	(his birth date—5 Mar. 1855)
2. Fillis Cross, turned 8 on 26 Apr. last	(her birth date—26 Apr. 1857)
3. Aaron Cross, turned 6 on 20 Aug. last	(his birth date—20 Aug. 1859)
4. Isham Cross, turned 4 on 24 Sept. last	(his birth date—24 Sept. 1861)
5. Margaret Cross*, turned 5 on 28 Oct. last	(her birth date—28 Oct. 1860)
6. Jane Cross*, turned 8 on 6 Apr. last	(her birth date—6 Apr. 1857)
7. Alice Cross*, will turn 10 next Feb. 15	(her birth date—15 Feb. 1856)

**orphan* scratched out and note added: *abandoned by her mother 1862.*

These were children of at least two different mothers, but the documents do not say anything more about the mothers or name the former slave owner. In some indentures, a child was bound out with the consent of the mother, as when six-year-old Abe Lincoln was bound to G.W. Swinebroad of Hardeman County, Tennessee, in February 1866.

In these and most other cases, boys were indentured until the age of twenty-one, and girls, until age eighteen. The employer agreed to teach them, in these cases, farming and housekeeping, and provide clothes and money ($100 to males, $75 to females) at the end of the term. The employer also had to sign a bond with two other men as sureties that he would honestly and fairly abide by the terms of the indenture. Each indenture was cosigned by a Bureau agent.

PRE–CIVIL WAR RECORDS

Once you have discovered as much as you can about a given ancestral family after the Civil War, you are better prepared to search for them in pre-war records. If they were free before

1865, your search will concentrate in censuses, city directories, county records, and other sources discussed throughout this book. If you believe that certain ancestral families were slaves before 1865, your search will involve trying to identify the slaveholder because the records of that family will be the key to finding your family.

For More Info

For more on tracing African-American ancestry and identifying slaveholders, see *A Genealogist's Guide to Discovering Your African-American Ancestors* by Franklin Carter Smith and Emily Anne Croom (Cincinnati: Betterway Books, 2002).

Research Tip

Identifying a Slaveholder

Usually two avenues of research help identify a slaveholding family: surname and/or location. Remember that slaves generally created no records in their own name. Their public identity came through the slaveholder, by whose surname they were usually known in any records in which they were named. Privately, they may have used a surname of a former slaveholder, even one dating back several generations, as a way of preserving their own family history.

Sometimes a freed slave family or individual, whether before or after 1865, assumed the surname of a former slaveholder. Thus, the surname they used in post-emancipation records may be a clue to identifying the slaveholding family in whose records the slave family was named or counted. **Studying people of that surname in the county of residence or neighboring counties is one way to begin searching for slave ancestors.** Especially after 1865, many freed slaves remained in their pre-war county for some years before moving away. (See the case study beginning on page 333.)

On the other hand, freed men and women and their children sometimes preferred to create their own identity, apart from any slaveholder, by choosing their own surname. The new surname sometimes was that of a prominent citizen (Washington, Lincoln), a symbolic name (Freeman, Justice, Canaan), the name of a parent or grandparent, or another name that had personal significance or appeal. Tracing these ancestors may depend on studying the community in which they lived after emancipation, looking for white families who had held slaves of corresponding genders and ages to your family members.

Either approach will involve looking for slaveholder candidates in federal census records and state tax records, especially the sections that reported slaves. Look in the slaveholding household for slaves who match the genders and ages of your ancestor's family, especially the mother and children. Slave fathers may or may not have lived on the same farm or plantation as the mother and children.

The slave information in such records can help narrow a list of possible slaveholder candidates. The next step is to study the family of and public records created by the leading candidate(s), especially probate records, to determine whether your ancestor or family was named. If one candidate's records do not provide a match, perhaps the slaves came from the spouse's family, another related family, or a neighboring family. It is usually not possible to confirm every former slaveholder, but it is often possible to move several ancestral lines into the early nineteenth century or beyond.

Federal Censuses Before 1870

Federal census records before 1870 vary greatly in their usefulness for tracing slave and free ancestors. For tracing free ancestors, statewide indexes to heads of household are available in libraries, often on CD-ROM, or on online subscription sites such as Ancestry.com and HeritageQuestOnline.com. For tracing slave ancestors, you will have to identify the slaveholder first and search his or her census entries for slave families of the appropriate genders and ages.

Enumerator Gifts. As in later censuses, some enumerators gave more information than was asked for, and these additions can be very helpful to genealogists. For example, the

1860 enumerator in Chatham County, Georgia, not only listed the town or county of birth for everyone, instead of just the state or country, but also gave very specific information on some of the children's ages.

For example, Amanda Rose was a thirty-four-year-old free mulatto seamstress, born in Savannah (in Chatham County). Her family included William Hood (fifteen, a bricklayer, born in Savannah), Theodore Rose (eight years and eight months old, born in Savannah), and Leonora Rose (five years and eight months old, born in Savannah). Giving the ages of children in months helps pinpoint birth dates. Theodore, for example, had already passed his eighth birthday and was eight months into his ninth year. Assuming the reported age was correct, one could figure he was probably born in September 1851. He would have turned eight in September 1859. By June 1860, he would have completed eight more months toward his ninth birthday. The same reasoning would suggest that Leonora may have been born in September 1854.

1850 and 1860. The 1850 census was the first to list all persons in free households by name, age, gender, race, occupation, and birthplace. The 1860 census gives the same type of information.

Separate slave schedules for 1850 and 1860 list slaveholders by name in each county and slaves by age and gender, but rarely by name. (See Figure 9-5, on page 336, for an example.) The Bowie County, Texas, enumerator in 1850 named the slaves in his jurisdiction.

The slave schedules are important for African-American researchers as they try to match a slaveholder's slave community with that of pre-1870 ancestral family members. The goal is to try to determine where the black family was in 1860 or 1850. (See the case study later in this chapter.)

1820–1840. The censuses of 1820 to 1840 enumerated whites, free blacks, and slaves by age groups. Only the heads of household were named.

African-American historian Carter G. Woodson made a thorough study of the census of 1830 since he felt it was taken at a high point of free Negro culture, especially in the South.[1] During the five years after that census, laws and prejudices in the South began making life much more difficult for free Negroes, and many migrated north. One phenomenon of the 1830 census was that some 3,815 free blacks in twenty states, two territories, and the District of Columbia were slaveholders. These were most numerous in Louisiana (966), Virginia (951), Maryland (654), and South Carolina (484). Other areas where free Negroes owned slaves in 1830 were Alabama, Arkansas Territory, Connecticut, Delaware, District of Columbia, Florida Territory, Georgia, Illinois, Kentucky, Mississippi, Missouri, New Hampshire, New Jersey, New York, North Carolina, Ohio, Pennsylvania, Rhode Island, and Tennessee. Only in Indiana, Maine, Massachusetts, Michigan Territory, and Vermont did free blacks not own slaves.

Men who set out to purchase their own freedom and that of their family members often bought their wives first and freed them so that additional children born into the family would be born free. By law, the child received the status of its mother.

Another phenomenon that appears in these early censuses is the presence of households where all are listed as slaves. Carter G. Woodson included the 1830 cases in his book *Free Negro Owners of Slaves in the United States in 1830* as a separate title: *Absentee Ownership of Slaves in the United States in 1830*. Some of these may have been slaves who were hired out to earn their livings. In the District of Columbia, for example, Peter McCoy was named in the head of household column with a household totaling one person, who was a slave. The census did not make clear whether Peter McCoy was the slaveholder or the slave, who happened to be living alone. If he were the slave owner, we would expect to find him listed not far away with his own household. However, the name is listed only once in the District of Columbia index and appears only once on that page. It seems likely, therefore, that the slave was the one named as head of household. Other sources may help answer the question.

In Madison County, Alabama, Pleasant Merrill, overseer for Major Gones, was listed as head of a household of seventeen slaves. No free persons were listed in the household. However, Pleasant Merrill was not one of the slaves. He and his young wife were enumerated in the previous household as whites. The owner may have lived elsewhere, but the overseer was nearby.

A more common situation occurred in Conecuh County, Alabama. The head of household column read "Starke H. Boyakin's slaves." Twenty-four slaves made up the entire household. No free persons of any race were listed living with them. This entry clearly suggests that the owner lived elsewhere or had died. In a clearer example in Richmond, Virginia, the household marked "Peyton Randolph's estate" showed two slaves living apart from any owner. Neither of these examples clarifies who might have been in charge at each location, a trusted slave or a person in the next household.

1790–1810. These federal censuses named free heads of household (white, black, Indian, or people of mixed race) but reported for each household only the total number of slaves or free persons other than white—black or Indian.

The 1790 census generally has two columns for white males (over 16 and under 16), one column for white females, one column for "all other free persons," meaning "other than white," and one column for slaves. For example, in South Carolina, when Dick Knight's family consisted of only seven "other free persons," the census meant "Dick Knight and six others who were not white."

Registers of Free Negroes or Slaves

One useful source of black history is registers or certificates of free Negroes; some states required registration at various times before the Civil War. In addition, a few states required slave registration. Surviving records can be found in some county courthouses or state libraries, archives, or historical societies. Some have been microfilmed, and some of these records are found in books with other county court records or minutes.

The Maryland Archives, for example, holds Prince George's County Certificates of Freedom, 1806–1852, and at least one manumission book from Anne Arundel County, which includes certificates of freedom, 1810–1864. The South Carolina Archives has microfilmed the Charleston Free Negro Tax Books, about 1811–1860. The Indiana State Library has some Indiana free Negro registers and a few Pennsylvania slave registers. The National Archives has some District of Columbia manumission records.

Notes

Manumission and *emancipation* refer to freeing slaves.

Other registers may be found at the Library of Virginia, Virginia Historical Society, South Caroliniana Library, University of Missouri at Columbia, North Carolina Archives, Georgia Archives, and Georgia Historical Society. The Illinois State Archives has an online searchable database of servitude and emancipation records (1722–1863) at <www.cyberdriveillinois.com/departments/archives/servant.html>. Copies of the records can be obtained from the archives.

Many of the free black registers have been published; a sampling of titles is given here. Check library catalogs, publishers' catalogs, and *Books in Print* for others.

Alexandria County, Virginia, Free Negro Registers, 1797–1861, Dorothy S. Provine, comp. Bowie, Md.: Heritage Books, 1990.

Entitled! Free Papers in Appalachia Concerning Antebellum Freeborn Negroes and Emancipated Blacks of Montgomery County, Virginia, Richard B. Dickenson and

Varney R. Nell, eds. Arlington, Va.: National Genealogical Society, 1981.

Register of Black, Mulatto and Poor Persons in Four Ohio Counties, 1791–1861, Joan Turpin, comp. Bowie, Md.: Heritage Press, 1985. Clinton, Highland, Logan, Ross counties.

Register of Free Blacks, Rockingham County, Virginia, 1807–1859, Dorothy A. Boyd-Rush, comp. Bowie, Md.: Heritage Books, 1992.

The Register of Free Negroes: Northampton County, Virginia, 1853–1861, Frances Bibbins Latimer, comp. Bowie, Md.: Heritage Books, 1992.

Register of Free Negroes and of Dower Slaves, Brunswick County, Virginia, 1803–1850, by Frances Holloway Wynne. Fairfax, Va.: the author, 1983.

Registers of Blacks in the Miami Valley [Ohio]: A Name Abstract, 1804–1857, Dayton, Ohio: Wright State University, 1977.

The information in these registers varies, but may include manumission records that originated in that county or elsewhere, affidavits that testified to someone's free status, registration of free persons as they moved into a new county, and evidence of free status from wills and deeds. The Alexandria County, Virginia, registers (listed above) contain much valuable information. The following are three examples:

- Entry number 11 (page 2) tells the background of Nicholas Cammel, who in 1805 was about thirty-five years old. He was born in St. Pierre, Martinique, and came to Virginia in 1793.
- Entry number 73 (page 13) contains an affidavit of Susan Peade, wife of James Peade, who swore that she knew the mother of Kitty Harris, a free black woman. Kitty's mother was a white woman of Fairfax County, Virginia, near Occoquan; therefore, Kitty was born free. (A newborn child carried the status of the mother.)
- Entry number 27 (page 5) shows evidence that the free man Elick was freed by the will of Peter Hellen of Calvert County, Maryland, in 1814.

County Courthouse Records

County courthouses hold many kinds of records valuable for pre-1865 genealogy of both free and slave ancestors. Especially important for slave research are probate and deed records. Once you have identified a potential ancestral slaveholder, look for his or her family's probate and deed records and search them for information on your ancestors.

See Also

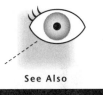

See chapter three for more about records pertaining to free ancestors. See the case study at the end of this chapter for more on using probate and tax records.

Wills may contain slave information. For example, the will of Edmond Jones of Madison County, Tennessee, written in July 1835 and amended in February 1836, distributed his slaves among his children. To the advantage of the researcher, he, like many other slaveholders, named his slaves in the document. Additionally helpful is the naming of some relationships in this will: Sam, *his wife* Dicy, and *their child* Isham went to Thomas M. Jones; Aggy and *her child* Paul, to John Edmund Jones.

Inventories listed and appraised property of value within an estate and sometimes were combined with reports of estate sales. Since slaves were considered property of value, inventories often listed them, either by group or as individuals, sometimes with good genealogical clues. The 1856 estate inventory of Margaret Turley in Caldwell County, Kentucky, named the slave woman Sitha, about *42 years old*, and *her child* Ellen.

Annual reports by the administrator or executor may detail slaves who were hired out or sold, slaves who died or were born, and expenses of the estate in feeding, clothing, or housing the slaves.

Final distribution or partition of an estate may show which heir received which slave(s).

Some reports of distribution provide additional information, such as where the heirs (and thus the slaves) lived and slave relationships or ages.

Deed records and bills of sale also identify slaves and sometimes give information that may be helpful clues for further searching. Hardeman County, Tennessee, deed records show E.G. Coleman's purchase of Jane, about *eighteen years old* in 1850 and of sound mind and body, and Albert, a *carpenter* about *twenty-six years old* in 1851.

The San Augustine County, Texas, deed records contain a bill of sale dated 25 October 1837, for the slave Easther, *age thirty-eight,* sold by B.F. Gates of *Adams County, Mississippi*, to Almanzon Huston of San Augustine. This additional information about Gates' residence might be a clue for further search on Easther.

Fayette County, Tennessee, deeds also give genealogical information on a slave family. In July 1843, a deed of trust of John L. Day and Thomas Patton mentioned the slave woman Mary, age thirty, and *her child* Jane, age two. Eighteen months later, in January 1845, Patton gave to his daughter Sarah Jane Day (wife of John L.) Mary and *her children* Penny, Jane, and Leanna.

Deed and probate records are often found at the county courthouse or, sometimes, at the state archives. Surviving records are often available on microfilm at genealogical libraries and from the Family History Library.

Tax Records

For a number of slaveholding states, pre-war state tax records provide year-by-year listings of property held by free residents, white or black. By tracking a known or potential slaveholder through tax rolls, researchers can sometimes

- learn the number of slaves in a particular household from year to year. This could help pinpoint the births or deaths in the slave community, or sales and acquisitions of slaves. Be aware, however, that some taxpayers may have under-reported their slave holdings to save on their taxes, and rarely were slaves named in these records.
- estimate when a slaveholder died and thus narrow the search for probate records that might name the slaves. Be alert for the words *deceased*, *estate of*, *heirs of*, *administrator of*, or *executor of*.
- track migration of the slaveholding family according to their first or last appearance on the county tax rolls. (See the case study later in this chapter.)

These nineteenth-century records are rarely found at county courthouses. More often they are housed at the state archives and are available for research there or on microfilm through the Family History Library.

Church Records

When they exist, church records can help genealogists of any ethnic group. Pre–Civil War church records sometimes give information on slaves. For example, the Presbyterian Church in Bolivar, Hardeman County, Tennessee, was organized in November 1852, and its records show membership and baptism for some blacks before the Civil War. Rose, a "servant" of E.G. Coleman, was baptized and admitted to membership on 21 November 1858. The next year, on 19 June 1859, her four sons were baptized: Moses Elijah, Lewis Pleasant, Joe Stevens, and Thomas Henry. The church register does not indicate the ages of these sons but is valuable in identifying the children's mother and the slaveholder's name. It was not uncommon for southern churches before the Civil War to show blacks on the membership rolls, even if most members were white.

The 1870 census indicates that this African-American family kept its former master's name after the Civil War. The head of household was Pleasant Coleman, mulatto, age forty, born in Virginia. Rose was age forty, born in North Carolina. Five children were in the family: Thomas (seventeen), Lewis (sixteen), Moses (fourteen), Elvira (twelve), and Adaline (ten), all recorded as black and all born in Tennessee. The other son, Joe Stevens Coleman (?), is not yet accounted for in 1870, nor is it yet known whether he used the Coleman surname. Comparison of the 1870 census with the 1860 slave census schedule shows that the slave population at Coleman's farm in 1860 could accommodate all of this family, including the youngest, for there was a four-month-old female slave in that census. (The slave schedule does not name the slaves.) Post–Civil War deed records in the same county indicate land records in the name of Pleasant Coleman, Moses Coleman, and Thomas Coleman in the 1880s, after the white family had moved away.

City Directories

City directories before and after the Civil War included African-American residents. Those listed before the war were almost always free. Some entries published only names, addresses, and occupations, and many directories gave racial designations: *c*, *col'd*, or *colored* or *fpc* (free person of color). Some had separate sections of the book for black residents. City directories are often available in book form in libraries of the same city. Larger libraries sometimes have microform collections of directories from many cities. Check the Family History Library catalog at <www.familysearch.org> for rental availability and subscription Web sites for online availability.

The Stockton, California, 1856 directory also noted the former residence of each person. Thus, it shows that Virgil Campbell (*colored*) was pastor of the M[ethodist] E[piscopal] Church, lived on Commerce Street, and came from Arkansas. A.L. Newby was a black cook from Connecticut who lived on Sutter Street.

The Boyd's Delaware State Directory of 1859–1860 showed many free black residents, including a number of widows. In the city of Wilmington, Charlotte Bailey, widow of Daniel, was a cook who lived at 604 E. Fifth. Two other entries showed the same address—Twelfth Street at the corner of Tatnall—for Rosana Furron, widow of William, and Harriett Hopkins, widow of James; they may have lived together or as near neighbors. The genealogist would want to investigate whether the two women might have been related and when their husbands died.

STATE GOVERNMENT RECORDS

State government records often contain information on African Americans before and after the Civil War. Such sources may include passports, memorials and petitions to the state legislature, and laws and acts of the legislature.

Passports

One pre–Civil War source in some states (and from the federal War Department) was passports issued to travelers to cross Spanish or Indian lands. Early applicants sometimes had to furnish character references to give assurance that they would not cause trouble with the Spanish or the Indians. Some of the passport recipients were traders, adventurers, Indians, and government officials; many were immigrants moving from eastern states to fertile frontier land farther west. From the time of the Revolution well into the nineteenth century, farmers and planters from Maryland to Georgia poured into what is now the lower South, Arkansas, and Tennessee.

How do these documents aid genealogical research? They help place people in a given place at a given time and thus (1) provide clues to further records they may have generated in that place or (2) identify an event in a timeline of their lives. If your research suggests that a certain planter may have been the slaveholder of your family and he migrated during this period, the passport records may shed light on him and his slaves.

Two published sources of these passports are the following:

- *Passports Issued by Governors of Georgia, 1810 to 1820*, Mary G. Bryan, comp. Washington, D.C.: National Genealogical Society, 1964. Special publication no. 28.
- *Passports of Southeastern Pioneers, 1770–1823*, by Dorothy Williams Potter. Baltimore: Genealogical Publishing Co., 1982. Includes passports issued by Spanish authorities, the U.S. War Department, Mississippi, Pennsylvania, North Carolina, Georgia, Tennessee, and Kentucky.

Two examples illustrate the diversity of information in these records:

1. In May 1813, a justice of the peace in Adams County, Mississippi, issued a passport to Benjamin Orr who was planning to take a free man of color north to Chillicothe, Ohio. The free mulatto man was Samuel Davis, about age twenty-three, a native of Pennsylvania, about five feet nine inches "high."[2] This is one of the more detailed documents.
2. In January 1812, Georgia's executive department ordered passports for these persons from South Carolina "to travel through the Indian Nations to the Western Country": James Hughey, his wife, eight children, and ten negroes [*sic*]; Daniel Colvin, his wife, two children, and two negroes; Charles H. Simms, his wife, five children, and one negro; Mason Hughey, his wife, and five children; James Roden with eleven negroes.[3] This record contains less specific information but potentially useful clues.

Memorials and Petitions

Memorials and petitions are sources usually found in the state archives because they were sent to the state government for special purposes. Finding aids or indexes are often available in the archives to help researchers determine whether an ancestor or relative signed such a petition or request. Sometimes the papers reveal genealogical information; sometimes their value lies simply in identifying an ancestor in a given place at a given time. These petitions may contain signatures of many people subscribing to a special request, or they may concern the needs of one individual or family.

One such petition in Texas in 1870 shows signatures of 445 men of the three-county area of Falls, Robertson, and Limestone. Sixty of the signers were labeled "free men of color." Such designation is helpful to researchers. For example, eleven Wilsons signed the request. Three of the men were named George Wilson. Two were black, Senior and Junior (perhaps but not necessarily father and son), and one was white. Besides the three Georges, six more Wilson men were identified as black and two others were apparently white. Such a set of names becomes a checklist to use in searching other county records and the census for genealogical information and relationships.

Although this kind of petition contains no specific genealogical data, it places these 445 men in that area on or about 28 June 1870. It offers some consolation for the researcher who discovers that an ancestor signed the petition and yet was not enumerated in the census of that same summer. Whether the ancestor remained in the area or moved later that year, he was there at least long enough to be considered a citizen of one of the three counties named.

A more personal kind of petition that asked special help from the legislature often contains genealogical information. Such a plea from Zylpha Husk is in the Texas State Archives. A free black woman living in Harris County, Republic of Texas, in December 1841, Zylpha stated that she was a native of Georgia, about twenty-seven years old, and had come to Texas about five years before and to Houston about 1839. Living with her was her daughter, Emily, about thirteen years old.

The Congress of the Republic of Texas had passed a law on 5 February 1840 requiring free blacks to leave Texas by 1 January 1842. Just before this deadline, Zylpha petitioned the Congress of the Republic for permission to remain, as she "would not know where to go if driven hence." Attached were the signatures of numerous prominent citizens supporting her request and testifying that she had conducted herself well and had earned her living by honest industry as a washerwoman. No specific action on this request appears in the published laws of the Congress. However, in December 1842, President Sam Houston issued a proclamation allowing free Negroes to remain for two years after 5 February 1843 (Gammell's *The Laws of Texas 1822–1897*, II: 879). He stated that the change was made in response to the many "honest and industrious" free persons who had been in the Republic for years and were anxious to remain.

A slightly different petition for special consideration concerned an African-American woman of Houston, Texas, named Liley, or Delilah, "one of the best cooks in the republick of Texas," "honorable," "trustworthy," of "good conduct . . . [and] good moral character." She had "by her industry" earned enough money to purchase her freedom from her mistress, Cynthia Ewing, who was asking the legislature to "pass a Law to Emancipate her." The petition, dated 1 November 1847, was signed by about eighty men and women who supported her request. The acts of the legislature do not reflect how the request was handled. Nevertheless, the document is a valuable source, giving residence information, the slaveholder's name, and insight into Delilah's talent and character.

Private Acts and Resolutions

State legislatures occasionally approve acts for the relief or benefit of individuals, sometimes as a response to a petition or memorial. These *private acts*, found with other laws of the state, contain genealogical information on some slaves and free Negroes, especially since a number of states regulated their activities and their manumission.

One such act from the Alabama legislature, on 19 January 1854, freed John Bell, a slave of William R. King, deceased, with the assent of the heirs. Although the report gave no further information on Bell or the King family, the researcher would want to (1) find William R. King in the 1850 census, the slave schedule of 1850, or county records, especially probate, and (2) look for Bell and any family in the free population schedules of 1860 and public records from 1854 forward. By identifying the slaveholder, the record could help narrow the search for information on Bell prior to 1854.

The 1831 Alabama legislature authorized John Robinson, a "free man of color," to free his wife, Ann, who was a slave, and her two children, Lelia Ann and LaFayette, upon posting a five hundred dollar bond with the Madison County court. The 1830 census of Madison County listed John Robinson (age bracket twenty-four to thirty-six) as a free Negro with a household of seven persons, four of them slaves. These four include three children under age ten and an older woman, more of the age to be Robinson's mother than his wife. The woman closer to his own age is listed as free already, along with another child under ten. Madison County is one Alabama county that has not had a destructive fire.

Therefore, courthouse records may yield more information on Robinson's purchase and emancipation of his wife and children, his dealings with the county court, and the identification of his household.

COURT RECORDS

Court records in county courthouses or federal district courthouses can contain much genealogy. These records can be found in court docket books, court minute books, and case files in the court clerk's office. Each state designates which court handles each type of case. County-level courts often dealt with debt cases, sheriff's sales of property, misdemeanors, small claims, bigamy, and illegitimacy.

Federal court records more than thirty years old are sent to the National Archives branch that services the state in which the court is located. These branches are listed in Appendix A of this book. The kinds of genealogical information found in court cases are illustrated below and in chapters three and eight.

Court records, including appellate records, contain information for some black genealogists. An example is Warren Hall's case against the U.S. and Mary Roach, reported in the U. S. *Court of Claims Reports* (11 Ct.Cl. 197). Although this court is not an appellate court, its published reports are available in law libraries. Hall's case provided this genealogical information:

1. Hall's mother was an Indian and his father, African.
2. His mother was a free woman in Alexandria, Virginia, at the time of his birth; therefore, he was entitled by law to her status.
3. However, he was later sold as a slave in New Orleans and from 1844 to 1864 was a slave on the Bachelor Bend plantation of Benjamin Roach's father in Mississippi.

Appellate courts at the state or federal level can contain similar information in cases appealed from lower courts. One case with considerable genealogical information was argued before the Texas Supreme Court during its December term of 1847 (2 Texas Reports 342). The case of *Robert M. Jones v. Laney et al. by their next friend James Colbert* was an appeal from Lamar County. The case report gives the family's history. Laney was born in 1811, a slave of James Gunn in the Chickasaw Nation, now Mississippi. Gunn was an Indian with an Indian wife living in the Chickasaw Nation. In 1814, when Laney was two years and nine months old, Gunn freed her in writing and recorded the action at the Chickasaw agency. Laney continued living with her mother, still a slave of Gunn, until Gunn's death in 1823. After 1823, but before going to live with Susan Colbert, a Chickasaw woman, Laney had two children, who, with her grandchildren, were the other defendants in the case. In 1842, James Colbert, Laney, and her family as free persons moved to the Choctaw Nation, where they lived together until November 1846.

The slaveholder, Gunn, wrote a will in which he named several slaves and left the balance of his slaves, unnamed in the will, to his daughter Rhoda. Rhoda and her husband, Joseph B. Potts, and the widow, Molly Gunn, sold these slaves to Robert M. Jones, of Indian descent, then living in the Choctaw Nation. The Gunn heirs and Jones considered Laney one of the slaves included in the sale and claimed they did not know of Gunn's manumission of Laney. Jones went to court to get Laney and her children as his slaves by right of purchase. The state Supreme Court affirmed the judgment of the trial court that Laney and her family were indeed free as proven by the written document of manumission, which Gunn had voluntarily executed. The researcher who finds such a case should go to the original trial court for any additional information, such as the names of Laney's children and grandchildren.

Finding Court Records

How does the researcher find these cases? One approach is to look in a library for a copy of *Judicial Cases Concerning American Slavery and the Negro*, 5 vols., Helen Tunnicliff Catterall, ed. (Washington, D.C.: Carnegie Institute, 1926–1937; reprint, Buffalo, N.Y.: W.S. Hein, 1998). These books are abstracts of reported cases from the high courts of states and countries. Each abstract contains the case name, the volume and page number of the digest in which the case report can be found, and the date of the case. The indexes include case names and some individuals mentioned in the cases. The five volumes are organized by the state in which the case originated, according to this table:

- Volume 1: Cases from courts of England, Virginia, West Virginia, Kentucky
- Volume 2: Cases from North Carolina, South Carolina, Tennessee
- Volume 3: Cases from Georgia, Florida, Alabama, Mississippi, Louisiana
- Volume 4: Cases from New England (Connecticut, Rhode Island, Massachusetts, Vermont, New Hampshire, Maine), Middle States (Delaware, Maryland, New Jersey, New York, Pennsylvania), and the District of Columbia
- Volume 5: Cases from courts of states north of the Ohio River, states west of the Mississippi River (Arkansas, California, Illinois, Indiana, Iowa, Kansas, Michigan, Missouri, Nebraska, Ohio, Texas, and Wisconsin), Canada, and Jamaica

If you do not have access to this set, you have at least two other choices. First, if you know that a lawsuit took place within the family you are searching, you can look in the Table of Cases, under the name of the plaintiff, in the *First Decennial Digest* (Volume 25) or subsequent Decennial Digests. These tables are indexes that refer you to the case reports where you can find more about the case. The problem with this approach is that you have to know the plaintiff's name. See chapter eight for more discussion of the Decennial Digests and how to use them.

The more general approach is to conduct a survey in the following books. The references are to the topical, or *key word,* heading of "Slavery." They contain a short statement about each reported case pertaining to slavery during the given time period in federal and state appellate courts. (Cases arising out of slavery were tried long after 1865.)

- *Century Digest*, Vol. 44, beginning column 851, about 165 pages of cases before 1896.
- *First Decennial Digest*, Vol. 18, p. 423–439, about 17 pages of cases 1896–1906.
- *Second Decennial Digest*, Vol. 20, p. 1148–1152, 5 pages of cases 1906–1916.
- *Third Decennial Digest*, Vol. 24, p. 1473–1476, 4 pages of cases 1916–1926.
- *Fourth Decennial Digest*, Vol. 28, p. 483–485, 3 pages of cases 1926–1936.
- *Fifth Decennial Digest*, Vol. 39, p. 1976–1978, 3 pages of cases 1936–1946.
- *Sixth Decennial Digest*, Vol. 27, p. 425, one case between 1946 and 1956.
- *Seventh Decennial Digest*, Vol. 27, p. 1442, reference to a few early cases and laws.

From Finding Aids to Case Information

The very large subject of slavery is divided into subtopics, such as "who is a slave," fugitive slaves, manumission, crimes by or against slaves, property rights of slaves, and hiring of and regulation of slaves. Each subtopic cites cases involving that matter of law. For example, topic 46 concerns the registry of slaves. Cases cited were all Pennsylvania cases arising out of the state laws requiring and detailing the registry of slaves (1780, 1782, 1788). Topics 7 and 8, concerning who were slaves, capsule cases from various states. Cases are listed in outline form under each topic, as in [a], [b], [c], etc. The synopsis of each case gives the state in which it originated, the year of the appeal, an abstract of the case and the decision, the name of the case, and the reference to where the case report may be found. The following is a sample citation and its translation into layman's language:

> *[n] Mo 1827—The children of a negro slave, in Illinois, born after the ordinance of 1787 abolishing slavery, are entitled to their freedom. Merry v. Tiffin. 1Mo725.*
> [*n* in the outline] case heard in Missouri in 1827, using the ordinance of 1787 which prohibited slavery in the Northwest Territory, which included Illinois. Case name: *Merry versus Tiffin.* Report found in Vol. 1 of *Missouri Reports*, original page 725.

To read more about the case, find the *Missouri Reports*, cases heard by the Missouri Supreme Court, volume 1. The case actually had two defendants, Tiffin and Menard, and was appealed from the St. Louis Circuit Court's May term, 1827. The man named John (no surname given), age thirty-six, was born of a slave mother but after 1787. He had been held as a slave from the time of his birth. As the synopsis shows in the citation above, the court agreed that John was indeed entitled to his freedom, as were others in the same circumstances. If this case report shows surnames, slave names, or localities in which you are interested, you should pursue the more detailed information in the records of the St. Louis Circuit Court for the May term, 1827.

The genealogical information in a case may concern people who are not the plaintiff or defendant. This is another reason for searching for cases based on locality rather than case name. An example is a federal case capsuled in the "Slavery" topic of the *First Decennial Digest* (Vol. 44, topic 40–41, fugitive slaves). The case name was *U.S. v. Lewis L. Weld*, from the First Judicial District, at Leavenworth, Kansas Territory, January 1859. The case involved the federal fugitive slave law of 18 September 1850 and Lewis L. Weld, who aided a slave in his escape. The *genealogical* information concerns the slave Peter Fisher, alias Charles Fisher, alias Charley Fisher, a slave in Kentucky and property of John O. and Anna Bell Hutchison, young children of Rain C. Hutchison. Fisher escaped and made his way to Kansas, followed by Hutchison, who had him arrested as a fugitive. Fisher escaped again, with the aid of Lewis L. Weld, whom the grand jury indicted for his part in the escape. In April 1860, Supreme Court of Kansas (in *Pacific States Reports*, Book 24, subtitled *Kansas Supreme Court Reports, Volume I*) voided the indictment.

NEWSPAPERS

After the Civil War, and more so after 1900, newspapers have carried notices of births, marriages, and deaths; local activities in which ancestors may have participated; and advertisements and legal notices that may have concerned ancestors. Obituaries can be important sources of genealogical information.

Runaway Slave Notices

Newspapers prior to 1865 also contained notices of slave sales or runaway slaves. In the attempt to make a sale or find a runaway slave, the owner often publicized such information as the slave's name, age, height, appearance, clothing, occupation, or special talents. These notices usually identified the owner, the residence that the slave left, with whom he or she supposedly traveled, and any reward offered for the slave's return. **Published newspaper abstracts often contain runaway and sale notices.** A useful source for this research is a three-volume work, *Runaway Slave Advertisements: A Documentary History from the 1730s to 1790*, Lathan A. Windley, comp. (Westport, Conn.: Greenwood Press, 1983). The books transcribe notices from Virginia and North Carolina (Volume 1), Maryland (Volume 2), and South Carolina (Volume 3).

Printed Source

Notices that mention pairs or groups of slaves, especially those that identify a parent and child or a husband and wife, could be useful if you already know the names of several family members from that time and place. Other useful notices are those that mention a person whom the researcher already considers a possible slaveholder of family members. Reading these notices as research tools before you have knowledge of specific eighteenth-century ancestors is probably counterproductive for identifying ancestors and their slaveholders. However, these records are full of social history on such topics as slave clothing, travel, and the dangers these individuals faced.

Identifying Newspapers for Research

African-American newspapers existed before the Civil War. In 1969–1970, the Negro Universities Press, later part of the Greenwood Publishing Group, reprinted two series of these along with some early-twentieth-century black periodicals. These are available in many academic or large public libraries. The two series include the following publications, with the dates of the issues that were reprinted.

SERIES I

Alexander's Magazine (1905–1909)
Colored America Magazine (1900–1909)
Competitor (1920–1921)
Crisis: A Record of the Darker Races (1910–1940)
Douglass' Monthly (1858–1863)
Half-Century Magazine (1916–1925)
The Messenger: The World's Greatest Negro Monthly (1917–1928)
National Anti-Slavery Standard (1840–1870)
The National Era (1847–1860)
National Principia (1858–1866)
The Negro Quarterly: A Review of Negro Life and Culture (1942–1943)
Opportunity: Journal of Negro Life (1923–1939)
The Quarterly Review of Higher Education Among Negroes (1933–1960)
Race Relations: A Monthly Summary of Events and Trends (1943–1948)
Radical Abolitionist (1855–1858)
Southern Frontier (1940–1945)
The Voice of the Negro (1904–1907)

SERIES II

The African Observer (1827–1828)
American Anti-Slavery Reporter (1834)
American Jubilee (1854–1855)
The Anti-Slavery Examiner (1836–1845)
The Anti-Slavery Record (1835–1837)
Anti-Slavery Tracts (1855–1861)

The Brown American (1936–1945)
Color Line (1946–1947)
Education (1935–1936)
Fire!! (1926)
Harlem Quarterly (1949–1950)
National Negro Health News (1933–1950)
The National Negro Voice (1941)
The Negro Music Journal (1902–1903)
Negro Story (1944–1946)
New Challenge (1934–1937)
The Non-Slaveholder (1846–1854)
Race (1935–1936)
Slavery in America (1836–1837)

For example, the *National Era*, published in Washington, DC, reported at length on national politics and political personalities. However, it also printed marriage and death notices, presumably from its readers and subscribers, although the paper does not say whether the people in the announcements were black or white. The notices came from New York, Maryland, Pennsylvania, and even as far away as Illinois and Ohio.

Many local newspapers are available on microfilm via interlibrary loan. To identify newspapers in your ancestral county or city, consult such sources as these:

- *African-American Newspapers and Periodicals: A National Bibliography*, James P. Danky, ed. Cambridge, Mass.: Harvard University Press, 1998.
- *American Newspapers, 1821–1936: A Union List of Files Available in the United States and Canada*, Winifred Gregory, ed. New York: H.W. Wilson, 1937. Reprint, New York: Kraus Reprint Corp., 1967.
- "Black American Records and Research," by Charles Blockson. In *Ethnic Genealogy*, Jessie Carney Smith, ed. Westport, Conn.: Greenwood Press, 1983. Contains a list of African-American newspapers and a bibliography of books about them.
- *Newspapers in Microform.* 2 vols. Washington, D.C.: Library of Congress, 1984.
- United States Newspaper Program. <www.neh.gov/>

NATIONAL ARCHIVES RECORDS

The National Archives houses millions of records containing history and genealogy. Numerous civilian and military documents on microfilm show thousands of individuals interacting with the federal government. Earlier, this chapter mentioned records of the Freedmen's Bureau and the Freedman's Savings and Trust Company. Others deal with military service and the District of Columbia.

National Archives microfilm may be purchased from the National Archives or Scholarly Resources, used at and rented from the Family History Library, used at the National Archives in Washington and its regional branches, and used at research libraries nationwide. Many National Archives materials are not on microfilm and require time and patience to study in Washington, DC. The records also vary considerably in their genealogical content but certainly have historical value.

For More Info

For details on National Archives materials relating to African-American history and genealogy, consult

- *Black History: A Guide to Civilian Records in the National Archives*, Debra L. Newman, comp. Washington, D.C.: National Archives Trust Fund Board, 1984.

- *Black Studies: A Select Catalog of National Archives Microfilm Publications.* Washington, D.C.: National Archives Trust Fund Board, 1996. Online at <www.archives.gov/publications/microfilm_catalogs/black_studies/black_studies.html>.
- *Guide to Genealogical Research in the National Archives of the United States*, 3d ed. Anne Bruner Eales and Robert M. Kvasnicka, eds. Washington, D.C.: National Archives and Records Administration, 2000. Chapter twelve.
- National Archives Web site: (1) articles at <www.archives.gov/publications/prologue/genealogy_notes.html/#afram>; (2) <www.archives.gov/research_room/genealogy>, click "Research Topics," then "African-American Research"; and (3) on the same Research Room/Genealogy page, scroll down to "New Microfilm Publications," which includes new film not listed in the Black Studies catalog.

Military Records

Among the many kinds of military records in the National Archives are several groups of special interest to African-American researchers. Research libraries nationwide hold the collections; some are available through the Family History Library. Photocopies of military service files can also be obtained from the National Archives. See <www.archives.gov/global_pages/inquire_form.html> to request the appropriate form.

See Also

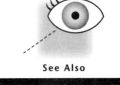

See also chapter six for more on military records.

- M589—*Index to Compiled Service Records of Volunteer Union Soldiers Who Served with U.S. Colored Troops*: Microfilm arranged alphabetically by surname. The index helps identify the soldier's unit and state from which he served; the index does not include those who served in state units.
- M1821—*Compiled Service Records of Volunteer Union Soldiers Who Served With the 8th–13th Infantry Regiments, U.S.C.T.*: Microfilming in progress, over 100 rolls as of this writing.
- M1898—*Compiled Military Service Records of Volunteer Union Soldiers Who Served With the U.S. Colored Troops, 54th Massachusetts Infantry Regiment (Colored).*
- M1801—*Compiled Military Serice Records of Volunteer Union Soldiers Who Served With the United States Colored Troops: 55th Massachusetts Infantry (Colored).*
- M1817—*Compiled Military Service Records of Volunteer Union Soldiers Who Served With the United States Colored Troops: 1st through 5th United States Colored Cavalry, 5th Massachusetts Cavalry (Colored), 6th United States Colored Calvary.*
- M1819—*Compiled Military Service Records of Volunteer Union Soldiers Who Served With the United States Colored Troops: 1st U.S. Colored Infantry, 1st South Carolina Volunteers (Colored), Company A, 1st U.S. Colored Infantry (1 Year).*
- M1820—*Compiled Military Service Records of Volunteer Union Soldiers Who Served With the United States Colored Troops: Infantry Organizations, 2d through 7th, including the 3d Tennessee, the 6th Louisiana, and the 7th Louisiana.*
- M1818—*Compiled Military Service Records of Volunteer Union Soldiers Who Served With the United States Colored Troops: Artillery Organizations.*
- M123—*Schedules Enumerating Union Veterans and Widows of Union Veterans of the Civil War 1890.* These help identify Union Army veterans living in 1890, including African Americans, and their units. (See page 44.)
- M1659—*Records of the Fifty-Fourth Massachusetts Infantry Regiment (Colored), 1863–1865.* Records from this state unit include letters, orders, muster rolls, casualties, morning reports, and other unit records.
- M858—*The Negro in the Military Service of the United States, 1639–1886.* Docu-

ments relating to military participation of blacks as well as reports concerning slaves, fugitives, and prisoners of war.

- M929—*Documents Relating to the Military and Naval Service of Blacks Awarded the Congressional Medal of Honor from the Civil War to the Spanish-American War.*
- M1002—*Selected Documents Relating to Blacks Nominated for Appointment to the U.S. Military Academy, 1870–1887.*

The National Parks Service Web site <www.itd.nps.gov/cwss> includes a database with basic facts about Union and Confederate soldiers and sailors from the Civil War. Books about Confederate or Union military participants from specific states are available in many libraries. Also consult library catalogs for books such as these:

- *Black Soldiers-Black Sailors-Black Ink: Research Guide on African-Americans in U.S. Military History, 1526–1900*, by Thomas Truxtun Moebs. Chesapeake Bay, Va.: Moebs Publishing Co., 1994. A massive work with useful bibliographies, lists of soldiers, sailors, and units; and other reference information.
- *On the Trail of the Buffalo Soldier: Biographies of African Americans in the U.S. Army, 1866–1917*, Frank N. Schubert, comp. Wilmington, Del.: Scholarly Resources, 1995.

District of Columbia

District of Columbia records relating to slaves are found especially in two National Archives record groups.

- M433—*Records of the U.S. District Court for the District of Columbia Relating to Slaves, 1851–1863*: 3 rolls, including manumission papers, 1851–1863; fugitive slave cases, 1851–1863; and emancipation papers, 1857–1863.
- M520—*Records of the Board of Commissioners for the Emancipation of Slaves in the District of Columbia, 1862–1863*: 6 rolls, records created following the 1862 act of Congress abolishing slavery in the District of Columbia.

SLAVE NARRATIVES

Interviews with perhaps as many as six thousand former slaves have been published since the Civil War, and many are available in academic and public libraries. During the Great Depression of the 1930s, the federal Writers Project of the Works Progress Administration (WPA) conducted interviews with more than two thousand former slaves. The typescripts of these stories and reminiscences fill forty-one volumes: Series 1 and 2, originally published in 1941 and reprinted in 1972 by Greenwood Publishing, under the title *The American Slave: A Composite Autobiography*, and Supplemental Series 1 and 2, published in 1978–1979. The set covers the following topics and states, which were the residences of the former slaves when they were interviewed in the 1930s, not always the states where they were born or grew up.

SERIES 1 (VOLS. 1–7) AND SERIES 2 (VOLS. 8–19)

Volume 1—From Sundown to Sunup: The Making of the Black Community
Volumes 2–3—South Carolina Narratives, parts 1 and 2, parts 3 and 4
Volumes 4–5—Texas Narratives, parts 1 and 2, parts 3 and 4
Volume 6—Alabama and Indiana Narratives
Volume 7—Oklahoma and Mississippi Narratives
Volumes 8–10—Arkansas Narratives, parts 1 and 2, parts 3 and 4, 5 and 6
Volume 11—Arkansas Narratives, part 7, and Missouri Narratives

Volumes 12–13—Georgia Narratives, parts 1 and 2, parts 3 and 4
Volumes 14–15—North Carolina Narratives, parts 1 and 2, parts 3 and 4
Volume 16—Kansas, Kentucky, Maryland, Ohio, Virginia, Tennessee Narratives
Volume 17—Florida Narratives
Volume 18—Unwritten History of Slavery (from Fisk University)
Volume 19—*God Struck Me Dead* (from Fisk University)

SUPPLEMENTAL SERIES 1

Volume 1—Alabama Narratives
Volume 2—Arkansas, Colorado, Minnesota, Missouri, Oregon, and Washington Narratives
Volumes 3–4—Georgia Narratives, parts 1 and 2
Volume 5—Indiana and Ohio Narratives
Volumes 6–10—Mississippi Narratives, parts 1, 2, 3, 4, and 5
Volume 11—North Carolina and South Carolina Narratives
Volume 12—Oklahoma Narratives

SUPPLEMENTAL SERIES 2

Volume 1—Alabama, Arizona, Arkansas, District of Columbia, Florida, Georgia, Indiana, Kansas, Maryland, Nebraska, New York, North Carolina, Oklahoma, Rhode Island, South Carolina, and Washington Narratives
Volumes 2–10—Texas Narratives

The *American Slave* interviews are also available on CD-ROM from Ancestry.com and online at <memory.loc.gov/ammem/snhtml/snhome.html> (American Memory). Several indexes are also available from the following:

- The American Memory Web site mentioned above.
- *A Comprehensive Name Index for The American Slave*, by Howard E. Potts. Westport, Conn.: Greenwood Press, 1997.
- *Slaves II: A Deeper Look into the WPA Slave Narratives*, by Brenda Terry. Dallas, Tex.: OneBorn, 1998.

Reminder

These narratives are the reports of the WPA writers' interviews with some men and women who had been "free Negroes" before the Civil War, but mostly with elderly former slaves, some sixty-five to seventy years after emancipation. Naturally, those who remembered life during slavery were older than seventy-five years when they were interviewed, and many reported their ages in the nineties. Many of the interviews used standardized questions about slave life, housing, clothing, food, work, holidays, songs, religious life, weddings, funerals, and superstitions. The genealogist naturally wishes that more attention had been paid to family history in the interviews, but many of them contain good information and provide fascinating reading.

For example, the interview with Mrs. Susan Dale Sanders of Louisville, Kentucky, contained this genealogical information of both black and white families (from Series 2, Volume 16, Kentucky section, pages 43–45):

1. Susan was born near Taylorsville, Spencer County, Kentucky, and lived there until four or five years ago when she moved to Louisville. (This interview is not dated; most were mid-1930s.)
2. Her mother (not named) was raised from infancy by her master, Reuben Dale, a "good ole baptist." He let the slaves go to church. (Church records might give more information.)

3. Susan's father was Will Allen, a slave of Colonel Jack Allen, who permitted him to stay at Dale's farm and work at Allen's.
4. Susan was one of seven children born to this couple. The boys were Harry and Peter. They joined the army and fought in the Civil War.
5. Susan was named for Susan Dale Lovell, Reuben Dale's daughter who lived down the road from his farm.
6. Will Allen died after the war was over and before Susan married.
7. Susan Dale married William Sanders and had six children.
8. William Sanders had fought in the war and was "wounded in the body," but lived a long time after the war. His widow, Susan, was receiving a veteran's pension. (Look for a pension file.)

Will Oats of Mercer County, Kentucky, gave his interviewer information that could be a great help to researchers of his family, especially since he and his brothers used different surnames (Series 2, Volume 16, Kentucky section, pages 18-19).

1. Will Oats was born in 1854 in Wayne County, "up Spring Valley." He said he was eighty-four at the time of the interview. He moved to Mercer County after he was grown.
2. His parents were Betty Oats and Will Garddard of North Carolina. He grew up living with his mother, grandmother, and siblings.
3. His three sisters were living at the time of the interview: Lucy Wilson and Frances Phillips of Ohio and Alice Branton of Mercer County.
4. His two brothers, also still living, were Jim Coffey and Lige Coffey of Harrodsburg, Kentucky. (Lige is a common nickname for Elijah.)
5. His masters were Lewis Oats and his sister.
6. His grandmother (unnamed) walked from Monticello (where they lived?) to Camp Nelson when the war closed to get their "free papers." She bought a little land and house where they all went to live. (Deed records or Freedmen's Bureau records might give more information.)

Both white and black researchers should consult these volumes because they contain valuable clues and information from men and women who knew the people they talked about. These books are sources of cluster genealogy of the black *and* white families who lived on the same land, their neighbors, and relatives.

LIBRARIES

Public, private, and academic libraries hold numerous materials of value in genealogical research. Besides those discussed in chapter eight, several publications deserve attention here: the *Journal of Negro History*, various biographical compilations, and several finding aids.

Journal of Negro History

An important contribution to the study of black history is the *Journal of Negro History*, founded by Carter G. Woodson in 1916 and published by the Association for the Study of Negro (now African-American) Life and History, Inc., in Washington, DC. An index to volumes one through fifty-three (1916–1968) was published in 1970. Even volume one of this quarterly publication contains articles that illustrate the value of this periodical for genealogists and historians. The founder wrote the lead article for the first issue, "The Negro of Cincinnati Prior to the Civil War." A well-documented and fascinating article in a much more recent issue concerned a slave named Free Frank McWhorter of Kentucky and Illinois, his business enterprises, and his amazing efforts to purchase freedom for many family members.[4] Reading such articles gives genealogists further ideas for sources and methods of research.

A companion publication from the same association is the *Negro History Bulletin*, which contains some articles of biographical and genealogical interest. An example is "Willis A. Hodges: Freedom Pioneer [1815–1890]," by Willard B. Gatewood Jr., in volume 43 (1980): 12–13, 16.

Biographical Works

Among the published works that contain information on somebody's ancestors are compiled biographies, usually of prominent people and those with noteworthy achievements. Volumes such as these sometimes contain bibliographies or reference lists showing where the compilers found the information or works the researcher could consult for more information. Such biographical dictionaries can provide good clues, but may contain errors or discrepancies. If you find an ancestor in such a book, try to check the information for accuracy.

The publisher Chadwyck-Healey has produced a microfiche collection entitled *Black Biographical Dictionaries, 1790–1950*, and a three-volume index. On 1,068 microfiche cards, the series contains 297 titles that contain more than thirty thousand biographical references to prominent and ordinary citizens. Academic and large urban libraries are the most likely to have all or parts of this collection.

Other compiled biographical and historical works that mention individuals include titles such as these:

- *Black American Writers Past and Present: A Biographical and Bibliographical Dictionary*, by Theressa Gunnels Rush et al. Metuchen, N.J.: Scarecrow Press, 1975.
- *Black Pioneers of Science and Invention*, by Louis Haber. New York: Harcourt, Brace & World, 1970.
- *Colored Charlotte: Published in Connection with the Fiftieth Anniversary of the Freedom of the Negro in the County of Mecklenburg and the City of Charlotte, North Carolina*, by C.H. Watson. Charlotte, N.C.: A.M.E. Zion Job Print, 1915. Check library catalogs for other city-specific works.
- *Dictionary of American Negro Biography*, Rayford W. Logan and Michael R. Winston, eds. New York: Norton, 1982.
- *Freedom's Lawmakers: A Directory of Black Officeholders During Reconstruction*, rev. ed., by Eric Foner. Baton Rouge: Louisiana State University Press, 1996.
- *The Negro Trail Blazers of California: A Compilation of Records From the California Archives in the Bancroft Library at the University of California in Berkeley*, by Delilah L. Beasley. Originally published Los Angeles: 1919. New York: Negro Universities Press, 1969. Check library catalogs for other state-specific works.
- *Who's Who of the Colored Race: A General Biographical Dictionary of Men and Women of African Descent*, Frank Lincoln Mather, ed. Detroit: Gale Research, 1975, reprint of 1915 original.

Negro Year Book

Between 1912 and 1952, Tuskegee Institute (now University) issued the *Negro Year Book*, which contains biographical and professional information on African Americans in business, agriculture, religion, science, government, education, civil rights, health professions, the military, journalism, the arts, and literature. It also contains a directory of national organizations and news items on current issues. The Depression and World War II years saw some gaps in publication, but these books contain much useful information. They are often found in academic and large public libraries.

Library Finding Aids

The *America: History and Life* social sciences index discussed in chapter eight is found in the reference sections in many academic and public libraries. The index is also available online in many libraries with subscriptions to electronic databases. By looking under specific names, places, and subject headings, researchers can find articles pertaining to many aspects of African-American biography, history, and, ultimately, genealogy.

For example, in volume twenty-nine of the index, number one (1992), listed under the topics "Blacks," "Chaplains," "Civil War," and the names William T. Sherman, Henry M. Turner, and William Waring is an article about two black Union army chaplains (Waring and Turner) and Sherman's march through South Carolina in 1865.[5] The listings in the index refer the reader to abstract 1224 earlier in that volume, where there is a brief description of the article as well as the author, title, and journal information necessary to find the article itself. If your library does not have the journal containing the article, ask a librarian about getting a copy through interlibrary loan or a photo duplication service.

Likewise, the *Combined Retrospective Index Set* (CRIS) for history has sections dealing with black history, slavery, Negroes, the Civil War, the antebellum South, the period of Reconstruction after the Civil War, and other topics useful for finding African-American history and biography. Volume six of the set is an index devoted to biography and genealogy. (See chapter eight for further discussion of this set of reference materials.)

General reading and studying indexes in many different books can reveal interesting and useful information. One such item on a North Carolina man named Lawrence Ward appeared in *Hood's Texas Brigade: A Compendium*, by Harold B. Simpson (Hillsboro, Tex.: Hill Junior College Press, 1977), p. 466. Ward was a slave and a cook with the Rowan County Artillery, officially known as Company D, First Regiment, North Carolina Artillery, and also called Reilly's Battery, which was assigned to Hood's Texas Brigade. He was with others in the unit as a Union prisoner of war at Plymouth, Virginia, on 31 October 1864.

Internet Source

A quick link to state archives and historical societies is at <www.coshrc.org/arc/states.htm>. Check <www.usgenweb.org> and <www.rootsweb.com> for Web sites pertaining to your research counties.

SPECIAL COLLECTIONS AND ARCHIVES

Archives, libraries, and historical societies often house public records and manuscript collections (private, family, organization, church, or business records). These special collections often contain sources helpful to historians and genealogists.

In the United States, the national, state, and some local governments maintain some form of archives of public records pertaining to the administration of the government and its interaction with the people. At the state and national levels, the archival records cover legislative, executive, and judicial branches of government and agencies within those branches. Ask the state archives or state historical society in your ancestral state(s) about published guides to their special collections. Some of the institutions also have such guides on their Web sites.

County archives may also include information from local families and businesses, newspapers, sheriffs' files, poorhouse records, or files of other agencies. Local archives may include such items as city council minutes and ordinances, municipal court records, police and fire department records, civil service employee records, and school district records.

Few of these public records pertain exclusively to black history or genealogy, or to that of any other ethnic group. Black history and genealogy are part of the whole history of the area that the records cover. Some of the repositories that house such public records have indexes, card files, or other finding aids to help researchers know what is there and how to access the material. Staff members of these institutions can assist you in finding materials.

Manuscript Collections

Special collections and manuscript collections from the private sector may contain family diaries, scrapbooks, Bibles, photographs, and letters; business or plantation ledgers, accounts books, and journals; cemetery and funeral home records; and minutes, membership lists, and other records of churches and social and fraternal organizations.

Reminder

Remember that a number of the slave narratives, manumission papers, and indentures of apprenticeship give exact birth dates of people who were born as slaves. These records suggest that someone was keeping slave birth records on some of the farms and plantations. One woman told an interviewer that when she married, she was given a Bible with her family's dates that the mistress had recorded. Sometimes, Bible records or plantation birth records are found in manuscript collections.

Manuscript collections, although seldom indexed comprehensively, may contain good information about the people in that family, business, or organization. Ask about a printed catalog or guide to the collection in which you are interested. Some of these catalogs are online at the institution's Web site.

The *National Union Catalog of Manuscript Collections* (NUCMC) is another resource for finding family, business, plantation, religious, and organizational records. (See chapters seven and eight for more on this resource.) As time passes, more and more people have electronic access to databases that help locate manuscript materials; ask a reference librarian at your public or academic library about access to such databases.

Extensive microfilm collections created from manuscript items include these three titles, usually found in academic or large public libraries:

- *Records of Ante-Bellum Southern Plantations from Emancipation to the Great Migration*, Ira Berlin, ed. Also from University Publications of America, 2000–. See descriptive guide at <www.lexisnexis.com/academic/2upa/Ash/plantMig.htm>.
- *Records of Ante-Bellum Southern Plantations from the Revolution through the Civil War*, Kenneth M. Stampp, ed. Bethesda, Md.: University Publications of America, 1985–. See descriptive guide at <www.lexisnexis.com/academic/2upa/Ash/AnteBellumSouthernPlantations.htm>.
- *Slavery in Ante-Bellum Southern Industries*, Charles B. Dew, ed. Also from University Publications of America, 1991–.

Case Study

Please read the endnotes, beginning on page 440, as you read the case study. The notes not only illustrate how to cite the sources which provided the information but also answer some questions you may have as you read.

CASE STUDY: ONE McGARITY FAMILY

After their emancipation, whenever it occurred, some freed men and women assumed the surname of a former slaveholder—the last, the first, the longest, the favorite—or of a slaveholder farther back in the family's past. Others chose a name of no apparent family or prewar connection. Sometimes, the post–Civil War surname is a clue for the genealogist trying to identify pre–Civil War ancestors.

This case study demonstrates a typical process and set of sources used to take many a family's history into the early nineteenth century. The twentieth-century surname was known. How critical would it be in identifying previous generations of the family? The first step was researching the family backward to 1870.

Results of Research in Post-1870 Records

1. Three McGarity brothers—John, William, and Charley—lived in Guadalupe County, Texas, with their families in the early twentieth century, as shown in the 1900, 1910, and 1920 censuses. Among his children, John had a son named Jason, and living in John's 1920 household was Mary Ellen McGarity (age 70), listed as his mother. Charley had, among other children, a son named Clemons/Clemy.[6]

2. The 1880 census enumerated the three brothers with siblings Tennessee, Mary, George, Eliza, and Alice; stepsister Lizzie Shade; and parents Jason and Mary E. McGarity in neighboring Gonzales County. The father, Jason, was a black farmer, age 36, reportedly born in Mississippi; Mary E., age 33, was born in Missouri. Four households away was Eliza McGarity, age 47, a Tennessee-born mulatto "washerwoman" with two children: son William (15) and daughter Mary E. (9).[7]

3. The 1870 census of Gonzales County listed Jason McGarity (age 27) with wife "Maretta" (23) and three children: Tennessee (4), John (2), and William (1). (See Figure 9-4, on page 335, last family on the page.) They were mistakenly listed as white. Two households from them lived the following McGaritys:[8]

Nancy McGarity, 58, black, born in South Carolina
Eliza, 37, mulatto, born in Tennessee
Florinda, 17, mulatto, born in Mississippi
Merideth, 10, mulatto, born in Mississippi
Willie (male), 5, mulatto, born in Texas

4. The Gonzales County tax rolls listed Jason McGarity, "colored," in 1868 and from 1870 through at least 1880. By 1880, his taxable property included three horses, eleven cattle, ten hogs, and farming implements. About or by 1891, he moved his family to neighboring Guadalupe County, where the tax rolls showed him from 1891 through 1898. Since he was not enumerated on the 1900 census or after, he may have died between 1898 and early 1900.[9] (Texas began keeping death records in 1903.)

The Search for a Slaveholder

In order to study Jason and the other African-American McGaritys in pre-1865 records, it was necessary to determine their slaveholder, for it was fairly certain they had been slaves before 1865. Research would involve the six members of the surname cluster who were born before 1865, as suggested in census records:

- Nancy, born about 1812 in South Carolina, black—about 48 in 1860
- Eliza, born about 1833 in Tennessee, mulatto—about 27 in 1860
- Jason, born about 1843 or 1844 in Mississippi, black[10]—about 17 in 1860
- Florinda, born about 1853 in Mississippi, mulatto (1870)—about 7 in 1860
- Merideth, born about 1860 in Mississippi, mulatto (1870)—possibly an infant at the time of the 1860 census
- William/Willie, born about 1865 in Texas, mulatto (1870) or black (1880)—not expected to be enumerated in the 1860 census

Next door to Nancy and Eliza's household in 1870 and Eliza's household in 1880 was a white physician, Clemons McGarity, reportedly born in South Carolina about 1819.[11]

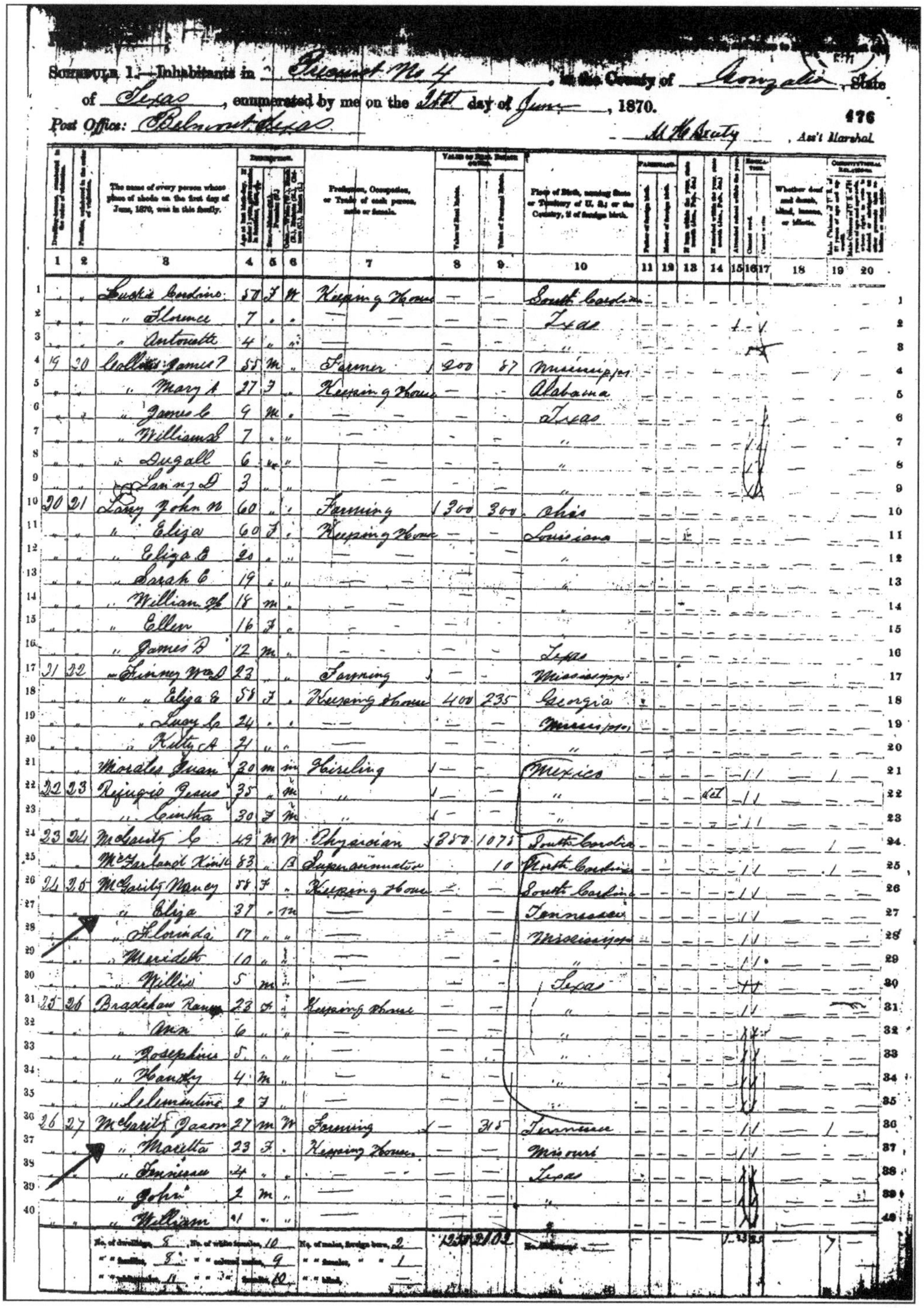

SCHEDULE 1.—Inhabitants in Precinct No 4, in the County of Gonzales, State of Texas, enumerated by me on the 7th day of June, 1870.

Post Office: Belmont Texas — M McBeaty, Ass't Marshal. 476

1	2	3	4	5	6	7	8	9	10
		Lucky Cordina	57	F	W	Keeping House	—	—	South Carolina
		" Florence	7	"	"	—	—	—	Texas
		" Antoinette	4	"	"	—	—	—	"
19	20	Collins James T	55	M	"	Farmer	200	87	Mississippi
		" Mary A	27	F	"	Keeping House	—	—	Alabama
		" James C	9	M	"	—	—	—	Texas
		" William D	7	"	"	—	—	—	"
		" Dugall	6	"	"	—	—	—	"
		Larry D	3	"	"	—	—	—	"
20	21	Lacy John W	60	"	"	Farming	1300	300	Ohio
		" Eliza	60	F	"	Keeping House	—	—	Louisiana
		" Eliza B	20	"	"	—	—	—	"
		" Sarah C	19	"	"	—	—	—	"
		" William H	18	M	"	—	—	—	"
		" Ellen	16	F	"	—	—	—	"
		" James B	12	M	"	—	—	—	Texas
21	22	Finney Wm D	23	"	"	Farming	—	—	Mississippi
		" " Eliza E	58	F	"	Keeping House	400	235	Georgia
		" Lucy C	24	"	"	—	—	—	Mississippi
		" Kitty A	21	"	"	—	—	—	"
		Morales Juan	20	M	M	Hireling	—	—	Mexico
22	23	Refugio Jesus	35	"	M	"	—	—	"
		" Cintha	30	F	M	"	—	—	"
23	24	McGarity C	49	M	W	Physician	1350	1075	South Carolina
		McFarland Kinch	83	"	B	Superannuated		10	North Carolina
24	25	McGarity Nancy	58	F	"	Keeping House	—	—	South Carolina
		" Eliza	37	"	M	—	—	—	Tennessee
		" Florinda	17	"	"	—	—	—	Mississippi
		" Merideth	10	"	"	—	—	—	"
		" Willis	5	M	"	—	—	—	Texas
25	26	Bradshaw Nancy	23	F	"	Keeping House	—	—	"
		" Ann	6	"	"	—	—	—	"
		" Josephine	5	"	"	—	—	—	"
		" Handy	4	M	"	—	—	—	"
		" Celementine	2	F	"	—	—	—	"
26	27	McGarity Jason	27	M	W	Farming	—	315	Tennessee
		" Marietta	23	F	"	Keeping House	—	—	Missouri
		" Tennessee	4	"	"	—	—	—	Texas
		" John	2	M	"	—	—	—	"
		" William	1/12	"	"	—	—	—	"

No. of dwellings, 8; No. of white females, 10; No. of males, foreign born, 2
No. of families, 8; No. of colored males, 9; No. of females, foreign born, 1
No. of white males, 11; No. of colored females, 10; No. of blind, —

Figure 9-4 U.S. Census of 1870, Gonzales County, Texas, p. 476, showing white, mulatto, and black McGarity families.

(See Figure 9-4.) Because the black McGaritys had the same surname as Dr. McGarity, the logical place to begin the pre-1870 search was with the doctor's pre-war records. No other McGaritys, black or white, were in the county's 1870 census or 1870s tax rolls.

The 1860 census enumerated Dr. McGarity living alone in Gonzales County, age thirty-nine. The corresponding slave schedule showed him as holder of six slaves: a seventeen-year-old male, and females age forty-eight, twenty-eight, twenty-three, eight, and six months.[12] (See Figure 9-5, on page 336.) All except the eldest female were listed as mulatto. Compared with the list of known McGaritys, this schedule seemed to place Jason, Nancy, Eliza, Florinda, and possibly Merideth in Dr. McGarity's household, along with an unidentified twenty-three-year-old female. Their ages suggest, but do not confirm, that Nancy may have been the mother of Eliza and Jason, and Eliza may have been the mother of Florinda and Merideth.

Neither the free nor slave schedule of the 1850 census for Gonzales County listed Dr. McGarity. Since three of the African-American McGaritys were reportedly born in Mississippi between about 1843 and 1860, the Mississippi 1850 census seemed the place to look next. In 1850, the black McGarity group would have included only Nancy (about thirty-eight), Eliza (about seventeen), and Jason (about seven).

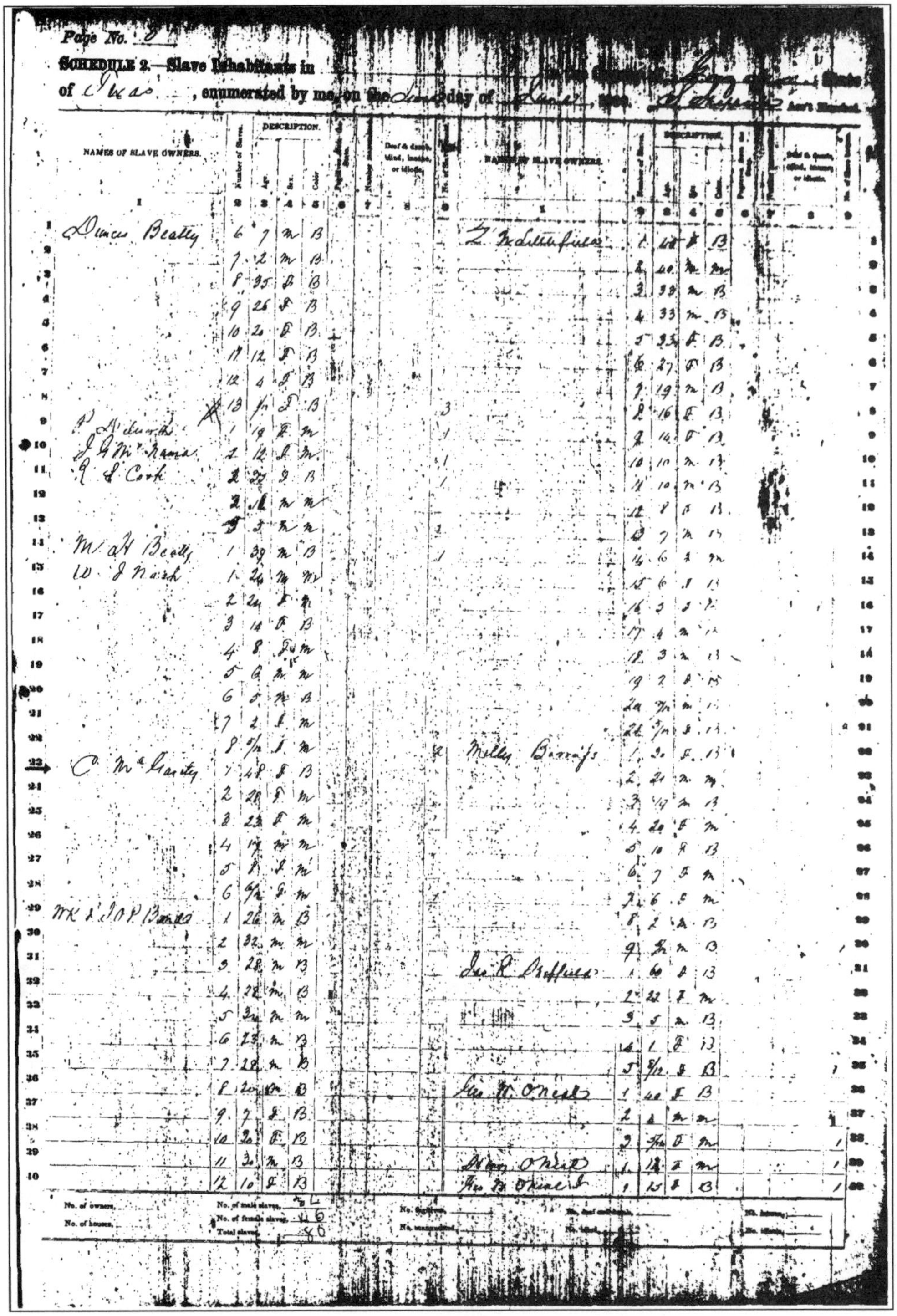
Page No.
SCHEDULE 2.—Slave Inhabitants in
of Texas, enumerated by me, on the day of
NAMES OF SLAVE OWNERS.
DESCRIPTION.
No. of owners,
No. of houses,
No. of male slaves,
No. of female slaves,
Total slaves,

Figure 9-5 U.S. Census of 1860, Slave Schedules, Gonzales County, Texas, p. 3, C. McGarity household.

A white male, C. McGarity, of approximately the appropriate age (twenty-six) was enumerated in Panola County, Mississippi, with no occupation reported, but the slave schedule did not show him as a slaveholder.[13] Nor was a C. McGarity enumerated in 1850 in other southern states. In 1852, presumably the same C. McGarity paid taxes in Panola County but not on slaves.[14] Because some tax rolls no longer exist, it is not possible to determine when C. McGarity arrived in Panola County. Yet, the existing tax rolls suggest he arrived during or after 1845.

Another Panola County taxpayer, at least from 1840 to 1845, was one John H. McGarrity/McGaherty, who claimed three slaves, but only in 1844.[15] One was under age five; two were between five and sixty. The black McGaritys—Nancy, Eliza, and Jason—would have fit into these age brackets in 1844.

However, the 1840 census showed John H. McGarity in Panola County with a probable wife, four children, six adult male slaves, and two other male slaves between ten and twenty-four—no female slaves. The black McGarity family group would have included only Nancy and Eliza in 1840; thus, it appears they were not with John McGarity. Furthermore, no one in John's household in 1840 matched Dr. McGarity's age bracket—fifteen to twenty, or age nineteen.[16] Was John related to Dr. McGarity? Would studying him aid in the search for the African-American McGaritys?

The 1840 Panola County John H. McGarity apparently was the same John H. McGarity who lived within about nine households of Dr. McGarity in Gonzales County, Texas, in 1860. The head of John's 1860 household was another Clemons McGarity, sixteen years younger than the doctor. John H. (sixteen years older than Dr. McGarity), his wife, and seven other children were in the household; another possible son lived next door.[17] These McGaritys did not own slaves, according to the slave schedule. However, four facts suggested a relationship to Dr. McGarity:

- their proximity to Dr. McGarity in 1860
- their former residence in Panola County, Mississippi, where Dr. McGarity had lived
- their naming a son Clemons, Dr. McGarity's given name
- their prior residence and John's and Dr. McGarity's births in South Carolina

The migration pattern of John McGarity's family, implied by the birthplaces reported for the children, indicated they had lived in South Carolina until about 1835, in Tennessee in the late 1830s, in Mississippi from at least 1841 to 1846, and in Arkansas from at least 1848 to 1855. Indeed, the 1850 Arkansas census showed the family in Chicot County, Arkansas, with nine children, but no slaves.[18] Thus, even if John and Dr. McGarity were related, the black McGaritys did not seem to be in either household until after 1852. In addition, the reported birthplaces of the black McGaritys resembled, but did not match exactly, the migration patterns of the white McGaritys.

Because of his birth date of about 1820–1821, Dr. McGarity was not expected to be shown as a head of household in 1840 and was not found as one. Nor was he living with John H. McGarity's family.

So far, the evidence suggested that Dr. McGarity acquired the slaves after 1852, either in Mississippi or Texas. His first appearance on the Gonzales County, Texas, tax rolls was in 1855, at which time his taxable property included no land, no slaves, seven horses, and a watch. Over the next six years, his land ownership increased to 425 acres. In 1861, for the first time, he was taxed for six slaves. He reported 100 acres and six slaves in 1862; the next year, 100 acres and a value of slaves of $5,330. In 1864, he was taxed for 100 acres and eight slaves.[19] By 1865 and with emancipation, slaves were no longer reported on the tax rolls, and in 1868, Jason McGarity entered the poll-tax-only rolls—adult males with no taxable property.

The six slaves Dr. McGarity reported in 1861 were likely the same as those listed in the 1860 slave schedule. These two records suggested he may have acquired the slaves about 1859 or 1860, while he was living in Gonzales County. However, neither a Gonzales County compilation of slave transactions nor the deed index indicated a bill of sale for McGarity's purchase of the slaves.[20] Because Dr. McGarity married in 1873, after emancipation, it was unlikely that the black McGaritys had come into his possession through his wife's family.[21]

Clues From the Web and Probate Records

The Internet offered a breakthrough at this point in the research. A message posted on Genforum <http://genforum.genealogy.com> in the McGarity family forum stated that John H. McGarity was born in 1805 in Union County, South Carolina, and had married Elena Nancy Littlefield, ten years his junior. (The census records supported these facts.) His parents were Clemons McGarity, whose will was recorded in Union County in 1822, and Polly Nance; siblings included Clemons, William, and several sisters.[22] If confirmed, this information meant John H. and Dr. McGarity were probably brothers.

Important

Whenever possible, it is important to go from a derived, transcribed, or abstracted source to the most original version of the record. In this case, the original added information left out of the abstract and corrected several errors in the abstract.

A book of Union County will abstracts provided more information, confirmed or corrected in the microfilm of the original record.[23] In 1822, the only member of the black McGarity family yet born was Nancy, about ten years old. Written on 2 August 1822, Clemons McGarity Sr.'s will named eight slaves: woman/wench Rhoda (left to son Clemons after his mother's death); girls Till/Tilda, Frosty, Betsey, and Phoebe; boys Squire and Charles; and boy Amos (bequeathed to son Clemons). The estate inventory, made in October 1822, named another slave, a man Cesar, and called Tilda a woman instead of a girl. Listed in descending order of monetary value, the young people were perhaps also listed in descending order of their ages: Squire, Frosty, Betty [*sic*], Charles, Amos, and Phoebe. The inventory reported no slave relationships or ages.

The probate file also reported the sale of Charles and Frosty (1826), the purchase of shoes for Squire (1828), and income from hiring out Cesar (1823), Squire (1828), and Tilda (1829). The documents gave no evidence of a slave girl named Nancy. Nor did later records, identified to this point, suggest whether Dr. Clemons McGarity ever had possession of the slaves Rhoda and Amos.

Papers in the file indicate that Clemons Sr. died within ten days of writing his will, perhaps on August 12. They also named several people of the related surnames suggested in the Genforum message: P. Littlefield; appraiser and justice of the peace Zachariah Nance; Z. Nance Sr.; Thomas Nance, paid for shoemaking; James Nance, buying livestock at the estate sale; and witness Jno. [John/Jonathan] Nance. In addition, the will named witnesses John Lawson, Fleming Hall, and William White, who was also the executor. These names formed a cluster of McGarity associates (and possible relatives) for further investigation. Interestingly, no other McGaritys appeared to be involved with Clemons McGarity's estate or its settlement; thus, the path of research turned to the other surnames.

Tip

Remember, "Polly" is a common nickname for Mary. Mary McGarity was called Polly in the will because that was probably the name by which she was called. In the census, she was Mary, the formal name.

The 1820 census showed Clemons McGarity Sr. and wife in Union County, with two white boys or sons, three white girls or daughters, and nine slaves. The 1830 census of the same county listed Mary McGarity as head of household, apparently with all three sons (John H., William, and Clemons, born circa 1820–1821) still at home and four young white females and ten slaves in the household.[24] It is not yet known when or where Mary McGarity died.

Branching Out: The Littlefields

John H. McGarity's wife was reportedly a Littlefield, and P. Littlefield was named in Clemons McGarity Sr.'s probate file. Prior research in Gonzales County, Texas, had shown a number of Littlefield families living there. Thus, they became the next focus of study: Were they the former slaveholders of the black McGaritys?

Before 1825, one Philip Littlefield had married Patsey Nance, daughter of Zachariah Nance of Union County, South Carolina.[25] (Note that Patsey is a common nickname for Martha.) Philip and his family were enumerated in Union County in 1820 with five slaves, none matching the age of Nancy McGarity, who would have been about eight that year. In 1830, Philip and his family were in Gibson County, Tennessee, but without slaves.[26]

Not surprisingly, by 1850 Philip (then age seventy-two) and Martha (sixty-two) were in Panola County, Mississippi, in a cluster of younger Littlefield heads of household: O.H.P., William, Z.M. or Z.N. (enumerated next to C. McGarity), Fleming, and A.J. All these Littlefields reported slaves in the census. At this time, the black McGaritys—Nancy, Eliza, and Jason—would have been about thirty-eight, seventeen, and seven years old. As a family group, they could have fit only into the household of Fleming Littlefield, who reported forty-six slaves ranging in age from fifty-five years to two months, as enumerated in two entries in the slave schedule.[27] County tax rolls and birthplaces reported in the census suggested these Littlefields, like John McGarity, had migrated from South Carolina to Tennessee before moving to Mississippi, and the first wave was in Panola County by 1840. Some of the family remained as late as 1856.[28]

However, by 1851 Fleming Littlefield was in Gonzales County, Texas, where he paid tax on twenty-five slaves. By 1853, he claimed forty slaves and 1,474 acres of land. The following year, the same acreage and thirty-eight slaves were taxed in the name of M.T. Littlefield. The 1855–1860 tax lists identified this taxpayer as Mrs. Mildred T. Littlefield, widow and executrix of F. Littlefield, deceased.[29]

"Executrix" indicated Fleming left a will and, therefore, maybe a probate file. Indeed, that file contained several documents naming twenty-four slaves—eight men, six women, and eight children—in addition to two who had died after the 1853 inventory. Technically and legally, the named slaves were distributed in 1854 among the widow and three minor children, but tax rolls indicate they and others not named in the probate proceedings remained with the widow at least through 1860. In these records, the only slave name that matched one of the black McGaritys was Eliza, a common name in the South for both black and white females. The file contained no indication of any estate sale through which Dr. McGarity could have acquired this Eliza, for she was part of the group assigned to the daughter Martha Mildred Littlefield, still a minor.[30] In 1860, the widow Littlefield, as "guardian of heirs of P. Littlefield dec'd," reported sixteen slaves in the census; no female slave matched the age of Nancy McGarity.[31]

A family sketch in the county history book provided more clues on this part of the Littlefield family. Fleming was reported as the third of eight children of Philip and Martha (Nance) Littlefield, who had moved from Union County, South Carolina, to Carroll County, Tennessee, then to Panola County, Mississippi, and eventually to Gonzales County, Texas. Mildred, a young widow, married Fleming as his second wife in 1841. He died of pneumonia in January 1853, leaving a large estate. His mother, Martha (Nance) Littlefield, died in Gonzales County in 1859; his father, Philip, in 1864. Fleming's mother was again mentioned as daughter of Zachariah Nance, and Fleming's brother Z.N. was Zachariah Nance Littlefield.[32]

Branching Out: The Nance Family

No positive evidence had surfaced to suggest that Dr. McGarity's slaves had come from the Littlefield family. However, Fleming Littlefield's mother was named as a daughter of Zachariah Nance, and Dr. McGarity's mother was reportedly born a Nance. Zachariah Nance had been involved in the estate of Dr. McGarity's father. He would be the next target of investigation.

Reminder

Mary McGarity was listed as a head of household in the 1830 census; thus, we know she died after that.

A Littlefield family history in the Gonzales County Records Center and Archives includes a family group sheet for Zachariah Nance, his wife, and eleven children. The eldest daughter was named as Mary Ann "Polly," wife of Clemons Monroe McGarity; she died after 1830 in an unidentified location. The fifth child and fourth daughter was Martha "Patsy" Nance, wife of Phillip B. Littlefield; she died in Gonzales County in 1859. She and her husband had already been eliminated as the holders of the McGarity slave family.

Five other children of Zachariah Nance died in South Carolina or Tennessee; one son moved to Georgia. Considering their death dates and places, it was unlikely that Dr. McGarity, while he was a minor, would have acquired slaves from aunts' or uncles' bequests or estate sales in those states, or from any distant estate sales after he moved to Texas. Evidence suggested that he got the slaves close to 1860, likely in Texas. The Nance group sheet gave no information on three remaining siblings: son James Nance (living in 1829), son Laurel V. Nance, and daughter Margaret "Peggy" Nance who had married an unidentified man named Hall.[33] (Peggy is a common nickname for Margaret.)

The group sheet also mentioned that Zachariah Nance had died about 1828 in Union County, South Carolina, and left a will. The Union County will abstract book gave preliminary information, later confirmed and corrected from the original on microfilm.[34] Although the 1829 inventory of his estate appraised eleven slaves (Jim, Tom, Joe, Julius, Julia, Haley, Sharlotte, Lucinda, Daniel, Thursey, and Jes), the will mentioned four others, three by name. Nance had given these to three of his children: Solomon to John Nance, Amy to Elizabeth Hall (wife of Martin Hall, according to the group sheet), and the *girl Nancy* to Peggy Hall! Nancy McGarity would have been about 17 in 1829. Were these two Nancys one person? It was time to investigate the Halls. (Figure 9-6, on page 341, shows part of Zachariah Nance's will, naming Nancy in item 9.)

Branching Out: The Hall Family

A message on a FamilyHistory.com message board stated that Zachariah Nance's daughter Margaret/Peggy Nance married Fleming Hall of South Carolina, lived in Tennessee, went to Tippah County, Mississippi, as a widow, and later moved to Texas.[35] This migration pattern resembled that of the Littlefields and McGaritys, and perhaps more importantly, that of Nancy McGarity's family.

The 1850 and 1860 censuses did not show any Nances in Gonzales or neighboring counties. Although six Hall families lived in Gonzales County in 1860, none reported a Margaret or Peggy of the appropriate age, about sixty-two. Only one Hall slaveholder was named in the slave schedule that year, and his five slaves appeared to be a family with three young children. They did not match the McGarity group.[36]

Research Tip

It was time to review:

1. Peggy Hall, daughter of Zachariah Nance in Union County, South Carolina, had reportedly married a Fleming Hall; she was a sister of Dr. McGarity's mother, thus his aunt. (A marriage record probably would not be found as South Carolina, unlike most other southern states, did not require civil marriage registration at that time.)

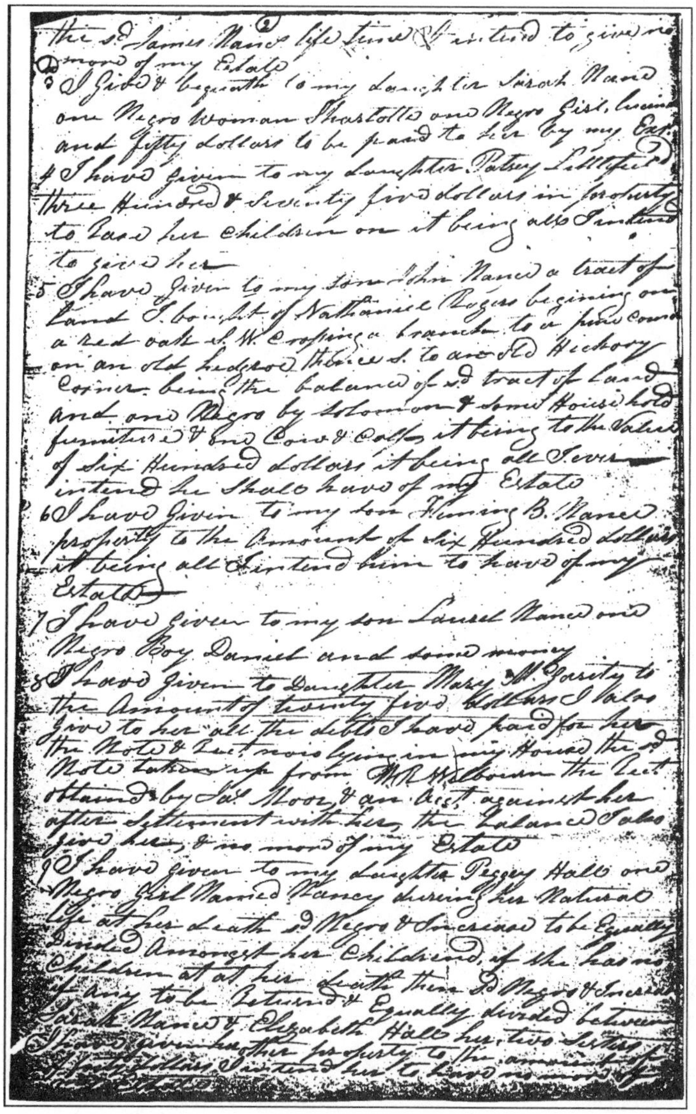
the sd James Nance life time & I intend to give no
more of my Estate
3 I Give & bequeath to my daughter Sarah Nance
one Negro Woman Sharlotte and Negro Girl, [illegible]
and fifty dollars to be paid to her by my Ext
4 I have given to my daughter Patsey Littlefield
three Hundred & Seventy five dollars in property
to Raise her children on it being all I intend
to give her
5 I have given to my son John Nance a tract of
Land I bought of Nathaniel Rogers begining on
a red oak S.W. Crossing a branch to a pine Corner
on an old hedgrow thence S. to an old Hickory
Corner being the balance of sd tract of Land
and one Negro by Solomon & some Household
furniture & one Cow & Calf it being to the value
of Six Hundred dollars it being all I ever
intend he shall have of my Estate
6 I have given to my son Fleming B. Nance
property to the Amount of Six Hundred dollars
it being all I intend him to have of my
Estate
7 I have given to my son Laurel Nance one
Negro Boy Daniel and some money
8 I have given to daughter Mary McGarity to
the Amount of twenty five dollars I also
give to her all the debts I have paid for her
the Note & Acct now lying in my House the sd
Note taken up from M.R. Holbourn the Acct
obtained by Jas Moor, & an Acct against her
after settlement with her, the balance I also
give her, & no more of my Estate
9 I have given to my daughter Peggy Hall one
Negro Girl Named Nancy during her Natural
life at her death sd Negro & increase to be Equally
Divided Amongst her children, if she has no
children at at her death then sd Negro & increase
if any to be Returned & Equally divided between
Sarah Nance & Elizabeth Hall her two sisters
[illegible] property to the amount of
[illegible] I intend her to have no more [illegible]

Figure 9-6 Will of Zachariah Nance, Union County, South Carolina.

2. Thus, the Fleming Hall who had witnessed Clemons McGarity's will in Union County, South Carolina, in 1822 could have been his brother-in-law.
3. Related McGaritys and Littlefields had moved to Gonzales County, Texas, and Halls too were there in 1860, although no Peggy was among them.
4. Of the Gonzales County Halls in the 1860 census, three heads of household—J.M., D.J., and F.B.—were reportedly born in South Carolina between 1819 and 1829. They were near enough in age to be brothers and of the appropriate ages to be sons of a sixty-two-year-old woman, as Peggy would have been that year.[37]
5. These three Hall families exhibited similar migration patterns to Peggy Hall, widow of Fleming Hall—in Mississippi in the late 1840s and early 1850s and moving to Texas by about 1853 or 1854.

Tip

Studying records and families in the known location first is often more productive than striking out for the unknown.

At this point, one strategy could have been to investigate more specifically the Halls' migration pattern—South Carolina, Tennessee, Mississippi, and Texas. A better and quicker option was to study the South Carolina Halls in Gonzales County, where Dr. McGarity lived and thus where he may have acquired the slave family. The birthplaces and ages of the Hall children reported in the 1860 census suggested that all three families were in Gonzales County by about 1853.

That county's tax rolls actually listed them for the first time in 1855.[38] Jesse Hall reported owning no land and no slaves; D.J. Hall, apparently the same as enumerated in the 1860 census, paid tax on 157 acres and no slaves. Neither Jesse or D.J. reported owning slaves between 1855 and the Civil War.

However, a Margaret Hall was on the 1855 tax roll, acknowledging ownership of one horse, eleven slaves, and no land. For the next two years, Margaret Hall paid tax on four slaves and a horse; in 1858, she reported seventy-five acres and four slaves. The 1859 roll helped answer the question of Margaret's absence from the 1860 census. That year and in 1860, J.M. Hall paid tax as administrator of the estate of M. Hall, reporting seventy-five acres and five slaves. *Administrator* meant she had died intestate, without a will, but perhaps a probate file existed.

Could the four slaves Margaret reported from 1855 to 1858 have been the black McGaritys: Nancy, Eliza, Jason, and Florinda? Could Merideth, supposedly born about 1860, have been the fifth slave added to the tax rolls in 1859?

Indeed, the Gonzales County probate records contained a probate file for Margaret Hall.[39] The following documents from the file are pertinent to this study:

1. **Application for letters of administration,** filed 23 August 1858, asking the court to appoint J.M. Hall as administrator of the small estate of *his mother*, Margarett [*sic*] Hall, who died on 21 April 1858, a resident of Gonzales County.
2. **Administrator's bond,** signed on 2 October 1858, with J.M. Hall as principal and G.W. O'Neal and William M. Littlefield as sureties. This shows further interaction between Hall and Littlefield family members.
3. **Inventory and appraisal of the estate,** made 8 October 1858. The list included 75 acres, the homestead of Mrs. M. Hall; one horse, a yoke of oxen, twelve hogs, one wagon, various implements and furniture; growing crops of corn and cotton; and five slaves, named in this order: Eliza (twenty-six), Florida (six, and named as "Florida" in later records), Nancy (age forty-six), Tennessee (twenty-one), and Jason (fifteen). Yes! Notice the addition of Tennessee, who was not previously identified. Why were four slaves on Margaret's tax report from 1855 to 1858 if five were named in the inventory in 1858? Possibly, the youngest (Florida) was too young to be taxed; or Margaret was underreporting; or, less likely for a widow with a small estate, one slave was added through purchase. The ages reported here for Eliza, Florida, Nancy, and Jason were fairly consistent with the ages they later reported to census takers. (Figure 9-7, on page 343, shows this part of the inventory.)
4. **Acknowledgment of payment** and doctor bill for forty dollars from C. *McGarity* to Margaret Hall for visits, prescriptions, medicine, and "attention for self" during June and July 1858 and medical attention to the Negroes of the estate in 1859. This bill begs the question, Was Margaret Hall still alive in June and July 1858? Nevertheless, it is clear that Dr. McGarity was the physician for the Halls; he was paid on 26 December 1859.
5. **Acknowledgment of payment** of thirty dollars to J.G. McNemar for making the coffin for Margaret Hall. Since the bill was dated 22 July 1858, it is likely Margaret had died prior to that.
6. **Voucher** from J.M. Hall claiming a debt of $10.20 against the estate for bacon, beef, and coffee he furnished the Negroes in 1858 while they were "picking out the crop of cotton."

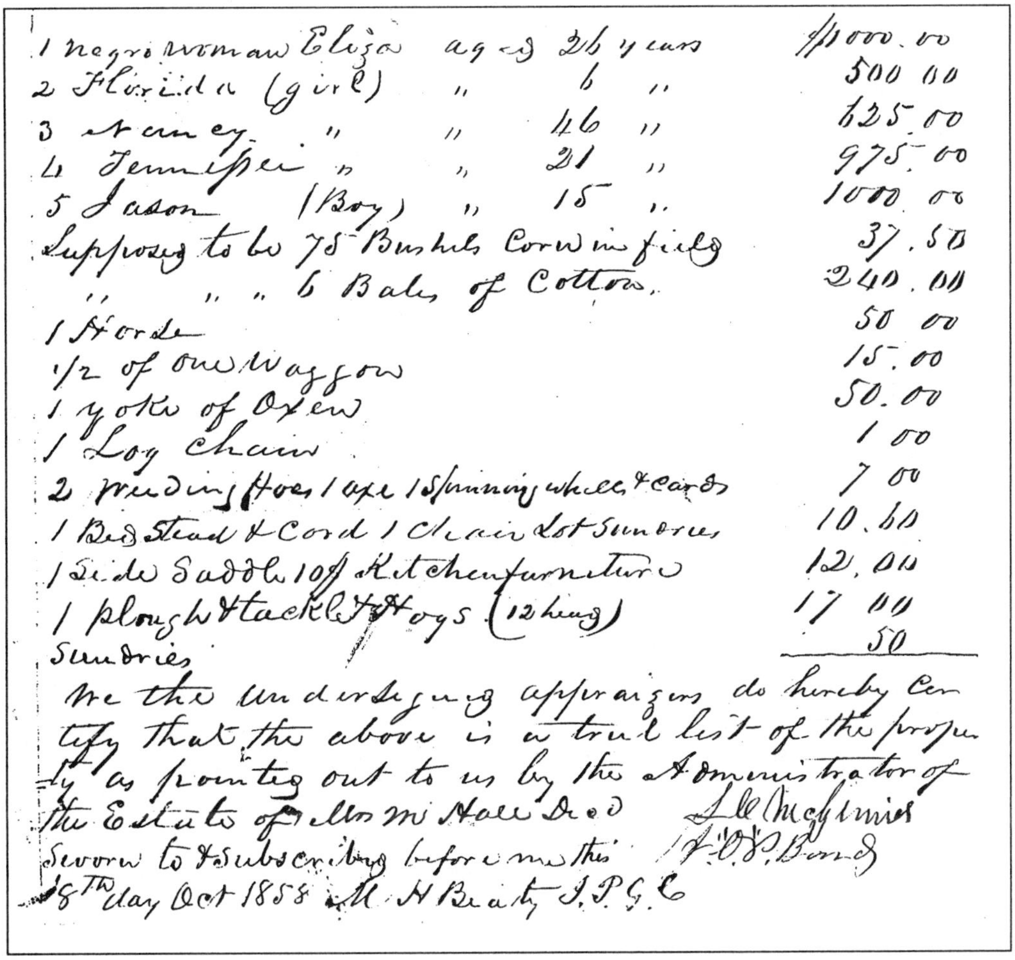
1 Negro woman Eliza aged 26 years $1000.00
2 Florida (girl) " 6 " 500 00
3 Nancy " " 46 " 625.00
4 Tennessee " " 21 " 975.00
5 Jason (Boy) " 15 " 1000.00
Supposing to be 75 Bushels Corn in field 37.50
" " " 6 Bales of Cotton 240.00
1 Horse 50 00
1/2 of one Waggon 15.00
1 yoke of Oxen 50.00
1 Log chain 1 00
2 Weeding Hoes 1 axe 1 spinning wheel & cards 7 00
1 Bed stead & Cord 1 Chair lot sundries 10.60
1 Side Saddle 10 lot Kitchen furniture 12.00
1 plough & tackle & Hogs (12 head) 17 00
Sundries 50
We the undersigned appraisers do hereby certify that the above is a true list of the property as pointed out to us by the Administrator of the Estate of Mrs M Hall Decd
Sworn to & subscribed before me this 8th day Oct 1858 M H Beaty J.P.G.C

Figure 9-7 Inventory of Margaret Hall, 8 October 1858.

7. **Petition of administrator,** J.M. Hall, to the court, 9 November 1858, requesting permission to sell at auction "all the inventoried property except the land & Negroes" and the corn crop and to sell the cotton for cash in order to pay debts and expenses. The petition stated that Hall had kept the Negroes named in the inventory on the place in order to gather the corn and cotton crops. Thus, he had bought their food and clothing on credit, promising to pay as soon as the crops were sold. He estimated that all the unpaid debts of the estate at that time totaled about $350.
8. **Petition of administrator** to the court, 31 January 1859, requesting permission to rent out the farm for the year 1859 and to hire out the Negroes privately rather than at public auction. He requested the private hiring, since the "said Negroes have always been very tenderly treated and worked very moderately and petitioner believes if said Negroes are hired publicly they will probably be maltreated and the interest of said Estate will suffer." This wording suggested the slaves were a family group or at least had been together as a group for some years. In addition, Jesse Hall asserted that "Nancy is decidedly unhealthy being afflicted with Rheumatism—and the girl Eliza is very weakly & unhealthy—and the Girl Florida is now only about 6 years old . . . " The judge agreed to Hall's request "provided the healthy Negroes are hired for the customary price at public auction for the current year." This decree meant Jason and Tennessee were subject to hiring out. A later accounting suggested F.B. Hall had rented the land for twenty-five dollars; there was no further mention of hiring out any slaves.

9. **Petition to the court** from F.B. Hall, filed by his attorney, 15 October 1859, asking that the estate partition be allowed since all debts had been paid and almost all claims due the estate had been collected. The property subject to partition and division included the 75 acres of land and the slaves: Eliza, Florida, Nancy, Tennessee, and "Jackson." The heirs residing in Gonzales County were F.B. Hall, D.J. Hall, Jesse M. Hall, Margaret L.(A?) Reeves (wife of Charles A. Reeves), Martha F. Tronson (wife of J.S. Tronson)—all brothers and sisters of whole blood. Nonresident heirs included Mary A.B. Ward, wife of John W. Ward of DeSoto County, Mississippi; L.V. Hall of Clark County, Arkansas; and the six unknown children of Z.N. Hall, deceased, of Bradley County, Arkansas. Attached was a statement from J.M. Hall, administrator, expressing willingness to have the partition made.
10. **Receipts** from C. McGarity, dated 26 December 1859 and 1 February 1860, acknowledging receipt of $65.75 and $32, partial payment for his claim against the estate.
11. **Court order for distribution of the estate,** 26 December 1859, and appointing Eli Mitchell, C.C. DeWitt, and *C. McGarity* commissioners to make the partition, with one-eighth going to each sibling named in the petition above. The court order named the slaves again in the same order as before: Eliza, Florida, Nancy, Tennessee, Jackson/Jason, and "Nancy Malvina—child of Tennessee about 4 weeks old."
12. **Affidavit** of *C. McGarity* and Eli Mitchell, two of the commissioners charged with making the partition, 26 December 1859, reporting that the estate "is not capable of a fair and equal partition amongst the heirs" and recommending that the land and Negroes be sold in order for the partition to be made in eight equal parts. The valuation placed on the slaves was the same as it had been in the 1858 inventory: Eliza (age 26), $1,000; Florida, $500; Nancy, $625; Tennessee, $975; child of Tennessee, 4 weeks old $100; Jason, $1,000—totaling $4,200.
13. **Bill of sale,** 7 February 1860, by which *C. McGarity* was the highest bidder on twelve months credit for the purchase of Eliza Ann (age 26) for $1,900; Florida (6), $1,410; Nancy (46), $1,100; Tennessee (22) and child, $2,001; and Jason (15), $1,950—a total of $8,361. To provide payment, McGarity, along with Samuel Luckie and William Wade, executed a one-year promissory note to J.M. Hall for $8,361 at 10 percent interest. Then, to secure payment of the promissory note, Jesse Hall paid Clemons McGarity one dollar for all right, title, and interest McGarity had in the Negroes "to have & to hold unto him, the said J.M. Hall, his heirs and assigns forever." This was a mortgage. If McGarity paid the promissory note on time, then the mortgage was void. Otherwise, the mortgage would remain in effect. (Figure 9-8, on page 345, shows this bill of sale.)
14. **Report of administrator,** Jesse Hall, to the court, 27 March 1860, on the sale of the land to J.W. Watson and the slaves to C. McGarity.
15. **Annual accounting** of the administrator, 24 June 1861, including the fact that $8,611 was owed to the estate for the sale of the land and Negroes.

Notes

Interestingly, the probate documents ranging from October 1858 to June 1861 kept the slaves' ages the same; only Tennessee "aged" one year between October 1858 and February 1860.

Since the black McGaritys matched the gender-and-age list under Dr. McGarity's name in the 1860 slave schedule, made after June 1, it appears they were in his possession, but it seems from the annual accounting to the court over a year later that he had not paid the estate. By the time the 1861 accounting was filed with the court, the Civil War had begun, and Texas had seceded from the Union and joined the Confederate States. This in itself did not lessen McGarity's legal obligation, but during the next four years many activities and obligations took a back seat to the war effort and keeping food on the table. More than

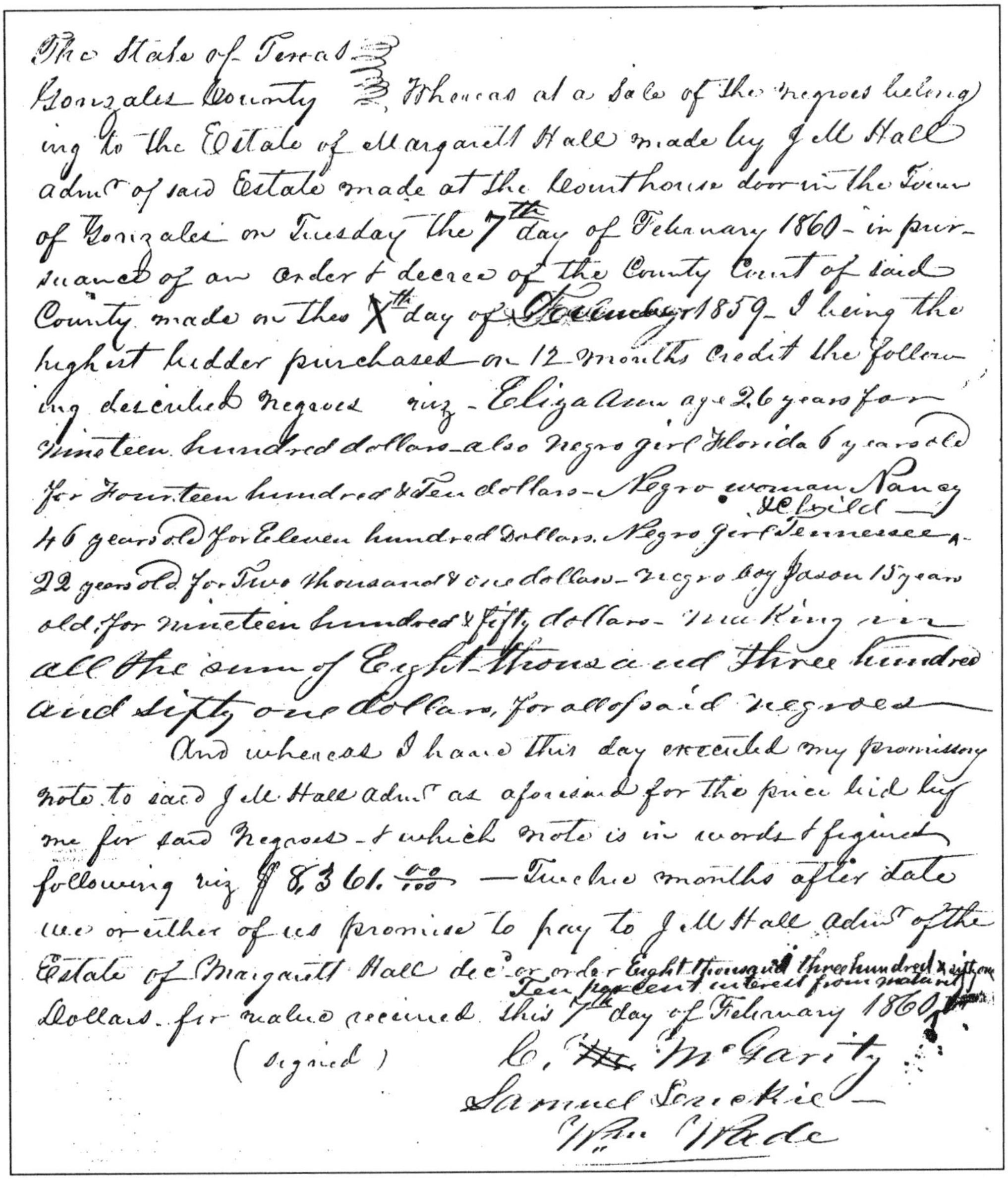

The State of Texas }
Gonzales County } Whereas at a sale of the negroes belonging to the Estate of Margarett Hall made by J. M. Hall
admr of said Estate made at the Courthouse door in the Town
of Gonzales on Tuesday the 7th day of February 1860 - in pur-
suance of an order & decree of the County Court of said
County made on the X th day of December 1859 - I being the
highest bidder purchased on 12 months Credit the following described negroes viz - Eliza Ann age 26 years for
nineteen hundred dollars - also Negro girl Florida 6 years old
for Fourteen hundred & Ten dollars - Negro woman Nancy
46 years old for Eleven hundred Dollars. Negro girl Tennessee & child
22 years old for Two thousand & one dollar - negro boy Jason 15 years
old for nineteen hundred & fifty dollars - making in
all the sum of Eight thousand three hundred
and sixty one dollars, for all of said negroes
And whereas I have this day executed my promissory
note to said J. M. Hall Admr as aforesaid for the price bid by
me for said negroes - & which note is in words & figures
following viz $8361.00/100 - Twelve months after date
we or either of us promise to pay to J. M. Hall admr of the
Estate of Margarett Hall decd or order Eight thousand three hundred & sixty one
Ten per cent interest from maturity
Dollars - for value received this 7th day of February 1860
(signed) C. McGarity
Samuel [illegible]
Wm Wade

Figure 9-8 Bill of sale of C. McGarity, in Margaret Hall probate file.

140 years later, we cannot know exactly what transpired—whether the Hall heirs ever received a distribution, whether they retained or regained use of the slaves, where the black McGaritys lived, how they fared, etc. After emancipation, however, they chose the McGarity surname and remained very near the doctor.

The estate papers had not fully answered the question of relationships among the black McGaritys. Each list began with Eliza and Florida, suggesting that they were mother and daughter—an idea supported by the 1870 census. Next on the list were Nancy, Tennessee and her child, and Jason. The obvious question was whether Nancy was the mother of Eliza and/or Tennessee and/or Jason. The answer may never be known with certainty.

Naming patterns are often useful in tracing African-American ancestors of this period. In this case, Tennessee's daughter seems to have been named for the elder Nancy, probably her grandmother. Tennessee and Nancy Malvina have not been identified in records after 1860, but Jason's eldest daughter, born about 1865–1866, was named Tennessee. Thus, the elder Tennessee and Jason may have been siblings, and Jason may have named his daughter in memory of his sister.

Tennessee ("Tennie") McGarity married John Bond in Gonzales County on 13 January 1881. The 1900 census enumerated this Bond family in Gonzales County and reported Tennie's birth date as March 1864, a bit earlier than what had been reported in the 1870 census for Jason's daughter. However, the age was close enough for her to be Jason's daughter rather than the elder Tennessee.[40] The elder Nancy McGarity has not been identified in census or other records after 1870.

What about the child Merideth, born about 1860, according to the 1870 census? She may well have been born after the February 1860 sale and after the 1860 census enumeration. The six-month-old slave in Dr. McGarity's household in the 1860 census may therefore have been Tennessee's daughter Nancy Malvina, who may have died before the 1870 census. It seems unlikely the two names referred to the same child.

Retracing Margaret Hall's Footsteps

In order to learn more about Nancy McGarity and her proposed family and set the stage for a search for her ancestors, it was necessary to study Margaret Hall between her father's death in 1829 and her own in 1858.

1850s. The 1860 census had suggested that at least three Hall brothers were in Mississippi between 1846 and at least 1852. For the 1850 census, F.B. Hall and L.V. Hall were in DeSoto County, Mississippi, with their wives and children, apparently sharing a house. To the east, Tippah County, Mississippi, was home to Zack Hall and family as well as Jesse M. Hale [*sic*] and his family. None of these sons was listed as a slaveholder.[41] The rest of the family has not been identified in the 1850 census. Nor have the black McGaritys been located in 1850.

However, widow Margaret Hall was in the Panola County, Mississippi, tax roll of 1852, reporting a clock and five slaves under the age of sixty.[42] At this time, the known McGarity group would have included Nancy, Eliza, Tennessee, and Jason. Thus, it is possible they were in Margaret's household. The identity of the fifth slave is unknown.

1840s. Before moving to Panola County, Margaret Hall lived in Tippah County, Mississippi. In 1840, Margaret Hall was enumerated there with apparently four sons and one daughter still at home. Jesse M. Hall lived very near but held no slaves. Margaret's slaves were three females—a female between twenty-four and thirty-six and two females under ten. Indeed, Nancy McGarity was about twenty-eight; Eliza, about seven; and Tennessee, about three.[43] This was one of few pieces of concrete evidence that the McGarity slaves were with Margaret Hall and support the idea that Nancy was the mother of Eliza and Tennessee.

Notes

A poll is a *head* or *person* who was subject to tax. The estate inventory in 1858 listed Tennessee as 21, suggesting she was born about 1837.

The Tippah County tax rolls show Margaret Hall in 1841, 1843 to 1845, and 1847, abstracted and interpreted as follows:[44]

- 1841, 1843—2 black polls [Nancy, Eliza]; Tennessee may have been under 5 and not taxable; Jason was born about 1843.
- 1844, 1845—3 slaves between 5 and 60 [Nancy, Eliza, Tennessee], 1 slave under 5 [Jason].
- 1847—4 black polls [Nancy, Eliza, Tennessee, and possibly Jason].

A Hall researcher provided additional family history and the location of Fleming's probate file, which was available on microfilm through the Family History Library.[45] While living at Ripley, in Tippah County, Margaret and her older children were involved in settling the estate of her husband, Fleming B. Hall, from early 1842 until early 1847. Fleming had died intestate in Carroll County, Tennessee, prior to 13 December 1830, when Zachariah

Bryant was appointed administrator of the estate. Existing Carroll County probate records begin about 1852, with earlier records lost in a courthouse fire.[46] However, the probate file in Abbeville County, South Carolina, indicated that, at his death, Fleming Hall had owned property there. The widow and adult children gave David Hall, "Dear Brother," power of attorney to act in their behalf. One slave man, Lewis, was sold in 1832, but no other slaves were mentioned. This negative evidence suggests that Nancy McGarity did not stay in South Carolina but migrated with the Hall family.

1830s. Fleming Hall was head of household in Carroll County, Tennessee, when the census taker visited in 1830. The family's census entry shows the five sons, all younger than fifteen, and one daughter at home, between ten and fifteen. (The other two daughters were probably living at home but not enumerated.) The only slave in the household was a female between ten and twenty-four. Indeed, Nancy McGarity would have been about eighteen.[47]

Margaret Hall paid tax in Tippah County, Mississippi, 1837 to 1840; in the first two years she reported one black poll, probably Nancy, as Eliza would have been under age five and therefore not taxable. By 1839 and 1840, when Margaret reported two slaves, Eliza would have been five or older, of age to be reported for taxes.[48]

1820s. The Fleming Hall family was enumerated in Pendleton County, South Carolina in 1820, with a son and a daughter under ten. Two slaves were part of the household, a boy and a girl, both under fourteen.[49] Nancy McGarity would have been about eight at that time; perhaps she was in the Hall household that early.

Fleming and Margaret Hall's five sons all reported in the 1850 and/or 1860 censuses that they were born in South Carolina, between about 1819 and 1829. The undocumented Zachariah Nance group sheet found in Gonzales gives Margaret's birth date as 12 January 1798. Figured from census records, Fleming's birth date apparently fell between 1793 and 1800. These birth dates suggest that the couple married probably no earlier than 1815. If Zachariah Nance had given Nancy to Margaret as a wedding gift, Margaret would have had a very young slave child to raise. Nance's will mentions only that he had given Nancy to Margaret, suggesting Nancy may have been with Margaret before 1 August 1828 when the will was written. Besides, Nancy was not listed in Nance's inventory as part of his estate at the time of his death. By 1828, Nancy was about sixteen and Margaret, thirty.

These pieces of evidence suggest that Nancy's 1870 census entry was correct about her South Carolina birth and her age. Any attempt to identify her parents must begin with the estate of Zachariah Nance. The only slave "woman" named in his will was Sharlotte, who was also the female slave with the highest value in the 1829 inventory—three hundred dollars—likely because she was in her prime of age and health. However, the slave Julia, valued at only one hundred dollars and given to Nance's wife, may have been the oldest female in the slave group. This record alone is not enough on which to speculate, but Sharlotte and Julia warrant further study as candidates for Nancy's mother.

Census records, probate files, tax rolls, and clues from various researchers of the McGarity, Littlefield, Nance, and Hall extended families have carried the Jason McGarity family history from the 1920s backward, over a hundred years. The records demonstrate that Jason and his childhood family kept the surname of the most recent slaveholder, Dr. Clemons McGarity, with whom they lived only a few years but undoubtedly knew much longer. However, their longer history lay with the Hall family, eventually identified in the same neighborhood and part of a large, extended family who had migrated more or less together across the South between 1830 and the Civil War. Earlier history of Jason's family will necessarily begin with the Nance household in South Carolina in the 1820s.

FOR FURTHER READING AND REFERENCE

Compiling a bibliography of all books written on black history or for use in African-American genealogy would be a monumental task. However, the genealogist can find a number of helpful books in academic, public, and private research libraries. The following list is but a sampling of books that genealogists use. Look for others pertinent to your ancestors and your research in library and publisher catalogs and in *Books in Print* under subject headings such as Afro-Americans, Blacks, Free Negroes, Free Blacks, or place names. *Books in Print* is available in most libraries in book or electronic format.

Genealogy Guides

African American Genealogy: A Bibliography and Guide to Sources, by Curt Bryan Witcher. Fort Wayne, Ind.: Round Tower books, 2000.

Afro-American Genealogy Sourcebook, by Tommie M. Young. New York: Garland Publishers, 1987 (went out of print in 1992). Contains a lengthy bibliography of black history and genealogy sources.

Black Indian Genealogy Research, by Angela Y. Walton-Raji. Bowie, Md.: Heritage Books, 1993.

Black Roots: A Beginner's Guide to Tracing the African American Family Tree, by Tony Burroughs. New York: Simon & Schuster, 2001. Focuses on research of post-1870 ancestors.

Finding a Place Called Home, by Dee Parmer Woodtor. New York: Random House, 1999.

A Genealogist's Guide to Discovering Your African-American Ancestors, by Franklin Carter Smith and Emily Anne Croom. Cincinnati: Betterway Books, 2002. Step-by-step guide with numerous case studies and research examples to help you work back to 1870 and search for pre-war ancestors.

Slave Genealogy: A Research Guide with Case Studies, by David H. Streets. Bowie, Md., Heritage Books, 1986. Focuses on records in Wayne County, Kentucky.

"Tracing Free People of Color in the Antebellum South: Methods, Sources and Perspectives," by Gary B. Mills. *National Genealogical Society Quarterly* 78 (December 1990): 262–278.

Black History in Specific Places

Black Baltimore, 1820–1870, by Ralph Clayton. Bowie, Md.: Heritage Books, 1987.

Black Yankees: The Development of an Afro-American Subculture in Eighteenth Century New England, by William D. Piersen. Amherst, Mass.: University of Massachusetts Press, 1988.

The Blacks of Pickaway County, Ohio in the Nineteenth Century, by James Buchanan. Bowie, Md.: Heritage Books, 1988.

California's Black Pioneers: A Brief Historical Survey, by Kenneth G. Goode. Santa Barbara, Calif.: McNally & Loftin Publishers, 1974. Mentions many individuals.

The First Hundred Years: A History of Arizona Blacks, by Richard E. Harris. Apache Junction, Ariz.: Relmo Publishers, 1983.

The Freedmen's Bureau in South Carolina, 1865–1872, by Martin Abbott. Chapel Hill, N.C.: University of North Carolina Press, 1967.

A Heritage Discovered: Blacks in Rhode Island, by Rowena Stewart. Providence, R.I.: Black Heritage Society, 1978.

In Search of Canaan: Black Migration to Kansas, 1879–1880, by Robert G. Athearn. Lawrence, Kan.: The Regents Press of Kansas, 1978.

North of Slavery: The Negro in the Free States, 1790–1860, by Leon F. Litwack. Chicago: University of Chicago Press, 1965.

A Peculiar Paradise: A History of Blacks in Oregon, 1788–1940, by Elizabeth McLagan. Portland, Ore.: Georgian Press, 1980.

Pennsylvania's Black History, by Charles L. Blockson. Philadelphia: Portfolio Associates, 1975.

Philadelphia's Black Elite: Activism, Accommodation, and the Struggle for Autonomy, 1787–1848, by Julie Winch. Philadelphia: Temple University Press, 1988.

Books on Pre–Civil War Free Blacks

The Free Black in Urban America, 1800–1850: The Shadow of the Dream, by Leonard P. Curry. Chicago: University of Chicago Press, 1981.

Free Blacks in a Slave Society, Paul Finkelman, ed. New York: Garland Publishing, 1989. A collection of articles from various periodicals on free Negroes in Charleston and South Carolina, North Carolina, Savannah and Georgia, New Orleans and Louisiana, Delaware, Virginia, Alabama, Mississippi, and Florida. Part of a series with other volumes entitled *Fugitive Slaves*; *Slavery in the North and the West*; *Slavery, Revolutionary America, and the New Nation*; *Antislavery*; *Religion and Slavery*; and others.

Free But Not Equal: The Midwest and the Negro During the Civil War, by V. Jacque Voegeli. Chicago: University of Chicago Press, 1967.

The Free Negro Family, by Edward Franklin Frazier. Salem, N.H.: Ayer Co. Publishers, 1968, reprint of 1932 original.

Free Negro Heads of Families in the United States in 1830, Carter G. Woodson, comp. Washington, D.C.: Association for the Study of Negro Life and History, 1925.

The Free Negro in Ante-bellum Louisiana, by H.E. Sterkx. Cranberry, N.J.: Fairleigh Dickinson University Press, 1972.

The Free Negro in North Carolina, 1790–1860, by John Hope Franklin. New York: W.W. Norton and Co., 1971, reprint of 1942 original.

Free Negroes in the District of Columbia, 1790–1846, by Letitia Woods Brown. New York: Oxford University Press, 1972. Includes lists of free Negroes from primary sources and an excellent bibliography.

Slaves Without Masters: The Free Negro in the Antebellum South, by Ira Berlin. New York: Oxford University Press, 1981. Reprint of 1974 edition from Pantheon Books. Includes an extensive bibliography of manuscript sources.

A World in Shadow: The Free Black in Antebellum South Carolina, by Marina Wikramanayake. Columbia, S.C.: University of South Carolina Press, 1973.

History, Biography, and Genealogy

The Black Family in Slavery and Freedom, 1750–1925, by Herbert G. Gutman. New York: Pantheon Books, 1976.

Black Indians: A Hidden Heritage, by William Loren Katz. New York: Aladdin Paperbacks, 1997.

The Black Presence in the Era of the American Revolution, by Sidney Kaplan and Emma Nogrady Kaplan. Amherst, Mass.: University of Massachusetts Press, 1989.

Free Negro Owners of Slaves in the United States in 1830 Together with Absentee Own-

ership of Slaves in the United States in 1830, by Carter G. Woodson. Westport, Conn.: Negro Universities Press, 1968. Reprint of 1924 original.

List of Black Servicemen Compiled from the War Department Collection of Revolutionary War Records, Debra L. Newman, comp. Washington, D.C.: National Archives and Records Service, 1974.

Many Thousands Gone: The Ex-Slaves' Accounts of Their Bondage and Freedom, by Charles H. Nichols. Bloomington, Ind.: Indiana University Press, 1969.

Roll, Jordan, Roll: The World the Slaves Made, by Eugene D. Genovese. New York: Vintage Books, 1976.

Runaway Slaves: Rebels on the Plantation, by John Hope Franklin and Loren Schweninger. New York: Oxford University Press, 1999.

Reference

Antebellum Black Newspapers: Indices to New York Freedom's Journal (1827–1829), The Rights of All (1829), The Weekly Advocate (1837), and The Colored American (1837–1841), Donald M. Jacobs, ed. Westport, Conn.: Greenwood Press, 1976.

Index to The Journal of The Afro-American Historical and Genealogical Society Quarterly Issues of 1980–1990, Barbara D. Walker, comp. Bowie, Md.: Heritage Books, 1992.

Selected Documents Pertaining to Black Workers Among the Records of the Department of Labor and Its Component Bureaus, 1902–1969, by Debra L. Newman. Washington, D.C.: National Archives and Records Service, 1977.

Subject Bibliographies

Subject bibliographies help the genealogist identify books and other materials that might prove helpful. Some libraries now have this kind of information on their Web sites. This is a sampling of bibliographies useful for African-American history and genealogy:

Bibliographic Guide to Black Studies. Boston: G.K. Hall & Co., annual. A supplement to the *Dictionary Catalog of the Schomburg Collection* below. Represents only holdings of the New York Public Library.

A Bibliography of Louisiana Books and Pamphlets in the T.P. Thompson Collection of the University of Alabama Library, Donald E. Thompson, comp. University, Ala.: University of Alabama Press, 1947.

Black Access: A Bibliography of Afro-American Bibliographies, by Richard Newman. Westport, Conn.: Greenwood Press, 1984. Subject index and chronological index. Lists many library catalogs and guides.

The Black Experience: A Guide to Afro-American Resources in the Florida State Archives. Tallahassee: Florida Archives, 1988, reprinted 1991. An excellent and extensive survey of black history in state and local records, manuscript collections, photographic collection, and the state library's Florida Collection.

Black Genealogy: An Annotated Bibliography, by Edith Green Sanders. Atlanta: Atlanta Public Library, Samuel Williams Special Collections, 1978. Catalog of materials in the Williams Collection.

Black Index: Afro-Americana in Selected Periodicals, 1907–1949, by Richard Newman. New York: Garland Publishing Co., 1981. Indexed by subject, place, and author.

Blacks and Their Contribution to the American West: A Bibliography and Union List of Library Holdings Through 1970, by James de T. Abajian. Boston: G.K. Hall, 1977.

Blacks in the American Armed Forces, 1776–1983: A Bibliography, by Lenwood G. Davis and George Hill. Westport, Conn.: Greenwood Press, 1985.

Blacks in the American West: A Working Bibliography, by Lenwood G. Davis. Chicago: CPL Bibliographies, 1976.

Blacks in the Pacific Northwest 1789–1974: A Bibliography of Published Works and Unpublished Source Materials on the Life and Contributions of Black People on the Pacific Northwest, Nos. 767-768. Chicago: CPL Bibliographies, 1975.

Blacks in the State of Ohio, 1800–1976: A Preliminary Survey, by Lenwood G. Davis. Chicago: CPL Bibliographies, 1977.

Catalogue of the Charles L. Blockson Afro-American Collection, Charles L. Blockson, ed. Philadelphia: Temple University Press, 1990. Over thirty-thousand entries. The collection is now housed at Temple University.

Data Relating to Negro Military Personnel in the Nineteenth Century, by Aloha South. Washington, D.C.: National Archives and Records Service, 1973.

Dictionary Catalog of the Negro Collection of Fisk University Library, by Fisk University. Boston: G.K. Hall and Co., 1974.

Dictionary Catalog of the Schomberg Collection of Negro Literature and History in the New York Public Library. Boston: G.K. Hall & Co., 1962, supplements 1967 and 1972.

Guide to Manuscripts and Archives in the Negro Collection of Trevor Arnett Library, Atlanta University. Atlanta: Trevor Arnett Library, 1971.

Focus on American Indian Genealogy

Aboriginal inhabitants (American Indians or Native Americans) have long been in the land that became the United States, but their written history is comparatively short. Prior to the nineteenth century, genealogical information was seldom recorded. Since the first European contact in the sixteenth century, numerous private and government records have named individual American Indian men in connection with trade, treaties, and tribal leadership. Until the mid-nineteenth century, however, relatively few of these records mentioned their wives and families, other than as statistics. In fact, the censuses of southeastern tribes prior to their removal to Oklahoma in the 1830s were among the first records to go beyond the chiefs to name other heads of household and family members.

Genealogists whose Native American ancestors lived with or identified with their tribal group into the twentieth century have a good possibility of finding ancestral records in a number of government-generated documents. However, those who only suspect they have an American Indian ancestor face a more daunting task of confirmation. As with many ancestors of undetermined origin, ethnicity is not always made clear in existing records.

Many Americans have family traditions of Indian ancestors but no clue to who, where, or when; and researchers are left with a process of elimination to try to narrow the candidates. Even as late as World War II, families of mixed blood sometimes preferred to keep the fact quiet, usually for economic or social reasons. After several generations of silence, the facts were forgotten. Often the opposite is true today; many people proudly claim Indian ancestors or wish they had some.

Reminder

Thus, the search for real or tradition-based American Indian ancestors follows the same principles as any other genealogical search, especially the following:

- Begin with yourself and confirm your lineage backward, one generation at a time without skipping a generation.
- Use the methods and sources available to research any member of the general population, regardless of ethnicity.
- Don't limit your success by focusing only on trying to confirm a family tradition, but research with a mind open to whatever the facts show, including erroneous family lore.

- Keep learning. Read guides to genealogy and the history of your ancestral locations, and continually look for "new" sources.
- Practice cluster genealogy, using multiple sources combined with patience and perseverance.

Your research may give you a time frame, a geographic point of reference, and tribal identification for your most recent Native American ancestor, if there is one. Without a tribal name, you must study the ancestor's geographic area—its history and culture—for tribal possibilities that fit the ancestor's life. Once you know an ancestor's tribe, study records created by, for, and about that tribe, including treaties and histories.

If the possibly-Native-American ancestor(s) lived on the fringes of settled areas or miles away from a European-style record-keeping system, you may not find "genealogical" records and the accompanying information genealogists hope for in such records. Since the earliest contact, intermarriage between Indians and other ethnic groups has occurred, especially between Indian women and white men. On the frontier, many of these unions were common law marriages or were established according to Indian custom, and no official written record was made. On the other hand, marriage confirmation may be hidden in "unlikely" places. An example from a tribal enrollment application file is shown in Figure 10-2, on page 360.

FEDERAL DECENNIAL CENSUS RECORDS

As the federal government extended its sovereignty over western lands beyond the original thirteen states, American Indians of course were mentioned in federal records. The research difficulty lies in finding and documenting individuals, especially women. Searching census records is essential in U.S. genealogy, especially for ancestors living in and after 1850.

See Also

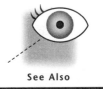

See chapter five for more on the availability of state and territorial censuses.

Besides enumerating the population, the census records reflect naming patterns. As white frontiersmen married Indian brides, their offspring often kept their fathers' surnames. Some Native Americans used their Indian names in dealing with the federal government; others transliterated their Indian name into English and used it as a surname. Much in the manner of Europeans in the Middle Ages or freed slaves after the Civil War, some Indians adopted European surnames related to physical characteristics, accomplishments, occupations, or personal choice.

Native Americans enumerated with only one name are often listed in the census indexes as though "Indian" were their surname. Those with at least two names are indexed by the surname or the Indian name that seemed to the census taker or indexer to be a surname.

Non-Reservation Indians in Federal Censuses

According to the 1880 instructions to federal census takers, Indians not living in a tribal situation were considered part of the general population:

> Indians not in tribal relations, whether full-bloods or half-breeds, who are found mingled with the white population, residing in white families, engaged as servants or laborers, or living in huts or wigwams on the outskirts of towns or settlements are to be regarded as a part of the ordinary population of the country for the constitutional purpose of the apportionment of Representatives among the States, and are to be embraced in the [general population] enumeration.[1]

Such Indians who "mingled with the white population" were identified occasionally in census records. For example, the 1840 census of Attala County, Mississippi, contains a number of Indian families, labeled as such and enumerated in the columns for "free persons of color," meaning persons other than white. Heads of household include those with English names, such as Fisher Durant and Charles Westley; Indian names, such as Comotohana and Chunkchoo; single names, such as George and Washington; and other names, such as Doctor Jack and Choctaw Wallace.

Likewise, in Macon County, North Carolina, in 1860 were families born "in the Cherokee Nation, North Carolina." A few used English names, such as Jim Wood Pecker. Eight families reported the surname Connahuk and Indian given names, including Gay hihigh, Aka, and Chew way laka. They were identified as Indians in the column for color, even though the printed choices were only white, black, or mulatto.

The 1870 census was the first to include Indian as one of the categories of color (race) the enumerators were to use. Jasper County, Mississippi, was home to a number of Indians living among the whites and blacks. Those with English names included John Marsh and wife, Betsy, both born in Mississippi and married in December 1869.

As in some white and black households, genealogical information sometimes creeps into these records. In the 1870 household of Mississippi Indians Tom and Susey Parker was Molly Parker, age sixty, identified as "living with son." In the case of one young Indian family—John, Susy, and infant Nancy—with no recorded surname, the other person in the household was Oliver Deace, identified as "living with brother." The genealogist must ask whether John and Susy ever used the surname Deace and what its significance was—a name of choice, the name of a parent, etc.

The 1880–1930 censuses continued to use "Indian" as a racial category. In 1930, persons of mixed Negro and Indian blood were to be reported as Negro unless the percentage of Indian blood was dominant and the individual was considered Indian in the community. Persons of mixed white and Indian ancestry were to be listed as Indian unless the percentage of Indian blood was very small or the person was accepted as white in the community.

Oklahoma in 1860

Reminder

American Indians in what later became Oklahoma were not enumerated in the general population schedules of the nineteenth century since the area was not an organized territory until 1890. In 1860 whites and free blacks living in that area were enumerated at the end of the Arkansas free schedule under "Indian lands west of Arkansas." The corresponding slave schedule acts as a partial Indian census, at least for the considerable number of Indians who were slaveholders. This enumeration appears at the end of the slave schedule for Arkansas—M653, roll 54. In the Cherokee Nation, the majority of slaveholders were Indians, often marked "Ind." after their names, but all five nations had Native American slaveholders.

Combining the free and slave schedules gives a more complete picture of the region's population than either schedule alone. For example, in the Chickasaw Nation, Georgia Ann Love was listed in the free schedule as the wife of a native, who was not named. In the corresponding slave schedule, Samuel Love was listed as a slaveholder. The researcher should look for other records to answer the question of whether this Samuel was Georgia's husband, as suggested in these census schedules.

Special Federal Indian Schedules

In 1880 the Census Bureau instructed enumerators to take a special census of Indians on or near reservations, using 1 October 1880 as census day. Persons who died after 1 October

1880 were to be included since they were living on census day; children born after 1 October 1880 were to be omitted. Enumerations exist for Indians living near military posts in Washington Territory (Tulalip and Yakama Agencies), California (Round Valley Agency), and Dakota Territory (Standing Rock Agency). These schedules are on five rolls of National Archives microfilm (M1791), available at Archives I, various regional branches, the Family History Library, and other research libraries. This census requested such detailed information as each person's name, translation of the name, relationship to the head of household, marital status, whether the Indian was of full or mixed blood, personal description, occupation, health or disability, education, personal property (horses, cattle, sheep, swine, dogs, firearms), land occupied and cultivated, and sources of subsistence (self or family, government, hunting, fishing, or gathering natural products).

The 1900 and 1910 censuses also included a special Indian schedule for enumerating Indians on and off reservations. Every family composed primarily of Indians was to be reported on the special schedule. Indians living in predominantly white or black households were to be included in the general population schedule. These Indian schedules are found on the microfilm with the general population, usually at the end of the county or the enumeration district in which the families resided. Regardless of the instructions to the census takers, Indians of mixed blood were enumerated in both schedules; if you don't find your family in the general population schedule, check the Indian schedule. Some families and siblings were with the general population in one year and in the Indian schedules the other year. (See Figure 10-9, on page 377, for an example of a 1910 schedule.)

The questions were in two sections on the page. The top section contained questions identical to those asked the general population, such as relationship, age, birth date (1900 census), birthplace, number of children born to women, occupation, and birthplaces of parents. Additional columns asked for information specific to tribal Indians:

- 1900—(column 29) each person's other name, if any; (30) tribe of one's nativity; tribe of father (31) and mother (32); (33) degree of white blood, if any; (34) whether the current marriage was polygamous; (35) whether the Indian was "taxed" (either living among the general population and subject to taxation or living with the tribe but having acquired citizenship through an allotment of land) or "not taxed" (living on a reservation without an allotment); (36) if the Indian was a U.S. citizen, the year of acquiring citizienship; (37) whether the Indian acquired citizenship by receiving an allotment from the government; (38) whether the Indian was living in a "fixed" (permanent) or "movable" (such as a tepee) structure.
- 1910—(column 33) tribe of the individual; tribe of father (34) and mother (35); (36) degree of Indian blood; (37) degree of white blood; (38) degree of Negro blood; (39) number of times married; (40) whether living in polygamy in 1910; (41) if in a polygamous marriage, whether the wives were sisters; to be left blank if marriage was monogamous; (42) educational institution from which the Indian graduated; (43) whether the Indian was "taxed" or "not taxed" (same criteria as 1900); (44) year of land allotment, if any; (45) whether the Indian lived on his or her own land; (46) whether the dwelling was of "civilized" design (log, frame, stone house), marked "Civ." on schedule; or whether the dwelling was of "aboriginal" design (tepee, cliff dwelling, etc.), marked "Abor." on the schedule.

No separate Indian schedule was taken in 1920, and the supplemental schedules taken in 1930 for the Indian population have not survived.

From the records of the Census Bureau came two National Archives microfilm publications that contain Indian enumerations. One is a census of Shawnees in Kansas Territory in 1857–1858, on roll 2 of M1813, Kansas Territorial Censuses, 1855–1859. Microfilm M1814 is one roll of a 1907 population census of Seminole County, Indian Territory, just prior to Oklahoma statehood.

RECORDS OF TRIBAL INDIANS

Thousands of records about American Indians were processed through the Office of Indian Affairs (OIA), established in 1824 within the War Department and transferred to the Department of the Interior in 1849. The office was created to exercise jurisdiction over Indian matters and became the Bureau of Indian Affairs (BIA) in 1947, still within the Department of the Interior.

Library/Archive Source

Censuses, military and OIA/BIA records, and numerous others concerning American Indians are housed at the National Archives and its regional branches. Many are available for use as transcriptions or on microfilm at the National Archives, its regional branches, and research libraries. To learn about microfilmed records, see *American Indians: A Select Catalog of National Archives Microfilm Publications* in book form or online at the National Archives Web site <www.archives.gov/publications/microfilm_catalogs.html> under "subject catalogs." For newer microfilm publications not yet mentioned in the subject catalogs, go to <www.archives.gov/research_room/genealogy/index.html> and choose "New Microfilm Publications." A number of the publications added in 2000 or later contain Native American records.

Microfilm may be purchased from the National Archives or Scholarly Resources or rented from the Family History Library. (Check the Family History Library catalog for specific availability.) At this writing, to learn which National Archives facilities hold a certain microfilm publication, go to <www.archives.gov/research_room/alic/research_tools/search_microfilm _catalogs.html> and click on "microfilm publications catalog." Type in the *M*, *T*, or other identification number under "enter microfilm ID"; submit your search; click on "display search results"; then click on "full record."

Thousands of American Indians, even some with white or black spouses, continued to live with or near their tribes in the decades following European settlement of North America. For the purpose of identifying federal records about them, these may be divided into two broad categories:

- the southeastern tribes, some of whom were absorbed into the five larger Indian nations, and most of whom were removed to what is now Oklahoma
- tribes who became wards of the federal government, living on reservations throughout the country, some of these also in Oklahoma

THE "FIVE CIVILIZED TRIBES"

In the early nineteenth century before removal, the five largest southeastern tribes—Cherokee, Chickasaw, Choctaw, Creek, and Seminole—lived mostly east of the Mississippi River and south of the Ohio River from Kentucky and western Virginia southward. They were self-governing nations until 1906, just prior to Oklahoma statehood, and maintain a degree of self-government today. Before 1906, each tribal nation had its own agent from the Office of Indian Affairs until the Union Agency was set up in Muskogee about 1874. In the early 1900s, that agency became an area office of the OIA, later BIA.

Among the largest collections of records of the Five Civilized Tribes and others in that region are these:

- National Archives
- Fort Worth, Texas, regional branch of the National Archives <http://www.archives.gov/facilities/tx/fort_worth.html>
- Oklahoma Historical Society in Oklahoma City <www.ok-history.mus.ok.us/>
- Western History Collection at the University of Oklahoma in Norman <http://libraries.ou.edu/depts/westhistory/>

Microfilmed National Archives records dealing with these tribes include, but are not limited to, the micropublications listed below. See also M1011, M234, M595 (for eastern Cherokee, Choctaw, and Seminole) in the following section. Records held and microfilmed by the Fort Worth regional branch of the National Archives were originally designated with the prefix 7RA. Some of the numbers have changed, but the film may still be shown with the old numbers in library catalogs and finding aids.

The four research facilities listed above hold numerous manuscript materials that have not been microfilmed, including census rolls of Indians and freedmen, claims, school records, payment rolls, enrollment files, and land allotment records. In addition, the East Point, Georgia, regional branch of the National Archives holds some eastern Cherokee agency records (1886–1952) and some from the Seminole agency.

The Oklahoma Historical Society in Oklahoma City also holds numerous national/tribal records such as tax lists, censuses, probate and administrative records, and marks and brand registrations. These holdings include records of sixty-six of the sixty-seven tribes that resided in Indian Territory. A portion of the catalog of the Archives and Manuscripts Division is online at <www.ok-history.mus.ok.us/arch/microfilmpage.html>. (At this writing, other online information is being prepared.) These holdings include microfilm from the National Archives, the Fort Worth regional archives, the Tennessee State Library and Archives, and the Western History Collection at the University of Oklahoma.

The University of Oklahoma Western History Collection holds the Cherokee Nation papers, which include censuses and government records of various kinds, records of other tribes, and numerous Indian Pioneer interviews conducted by the WPA in the 1930s. For specific holdings or before a visit to one of these facilities, consult their Web sites or call for a brochure or list of records that could benefit your particular search.

The Dawes Commission Records

Before 1896, these nations had jurisdiction over their own citizenship and over non-Indians who were allowed to live and work in tribal territory. Those non-Indians who did not abide by the rules the tribes established were considered intruders and became the subjects of numerous records.

In 1893 Congress legislated the formation of a commission to "negotiate agreements with the Cherokee, Choctaw, Chickasaw, Creek, and Seminole tribes providing for the dissolution of the tribal governments and the allotment of land to each tribal member."[2] The commission was called the Dawes Commission after its chairman, Senator Henry L. Dawes of Massachusetts. More realistically stated, Congress wanted to persuade the Five Civilized Tribes to

> . . . negotiate themselves out of existence—an essential first step in implementing a policy of allotting land to each individual Indian. Allotment was supposed to

> promote assimilation into the dominant culture, clear the way for converting Indian Territory into a state and satisfy powerful groups seeking opportunities for economic development and profit. However, when the tribal governments refused to cooperate in their own demise, Congress used its legislative power to abolish them and gave the Dawes Commission the almost impossible task of determining who was entitled to a share of land roughly the size of Indiana and worth millions of dollars.[3]

Five years later, Congress gave the Dawes Commission the job of preparing citizenship rolls of the members of each of the Five Civilized Tribes; these rolls would provide the basis for land allotment. Between 1898 and March 1907, the Commission received more than 250,000 applications for tribal membership. Just over 100,000 were accepted. Generally, the enrolled tribal citizens were categorized into these groups, by which researchers find their records:

- Tribal citizen by blood
- Tribal citizen by marriage (intermarried white)
- Minor citizens by blood, enrolled beginning in 1907 (children and youth)
- Newborn citizens by blood, enrolled beginning in 1905
- Freedmen (former black slaves of Indian slaveholders)
- Delaware Indians, granted Cherokee citizenship

The numerous people whose applications were not approved were classified as "Rejected," and their "R" cards and related files often contain a wealth of genealogical information. "D" or "doubtful" applications had to be resolved and moved to either "straight" (accepted) or "R" cards.

Researchers have several ways of viewing the indexes to the "final rolls" of these five Indians nations.

1. National Archives microfilm M1186, *Enrollment Cards for the Five Civilized Tribes, 1898–1914*, roll 1, the index to the final citizenship rolls, described below.
2. Online, National Archives Web site, at this writing: <www.archives.gov/research_room/arc/arc_info/native_americans_final_rolls_index.html>. This is the path: From the National Archives home page, go to "research room," then to "section: genealogy," then to "research topics." Under research topics, click on "Native American records." Scroll down to "Index to the Final Rolls of Citizens and Freedmen of the Five Civilized Tribes in Indian Territory (Dawes)" and click on the "Index to the Final Rolls (Dawes) online." Choose your tribe and category; try different pages to find the alphabetical listing you need. Remember to try spelling variations. For example, we would tend to look for the name Arrington, but the family discussed below was listed under Airington.
3. CD-ROM, Native American Collection (Orem, Utah: GenRef, 1998). If you don't know exactly how the ancestor was listed on the rolls, this option can be frustrating. Broaden the search with few criteria, or use the first two options before going to the CD.
4. Transcribed indexes. One is *Five Civilized Tribes in Indian Territory*, Dianne D. Graves, comp. (Houston, Tex.: G&S Publishers, 1989), transcribed from microfilm T529, roll 2 (1c in the outline below). Another is *Index to the Cherokee Freedmen Enrollment Cards of the Dawes Commission, 1901–1906*, by Jo Ann Curls Page (Bowie, Md.: Heritage Books, 1996). Other books, such as this one, may help you determine that an ancestor may be on the rolls: *1900 Census Index, Choctaw Nation Indian Territory, Oklahoma*, by Gloryann Hankins Young (Wister, Okla.: G.H. Young, 1981).

The approved applications were abstracted onto enrollment or "census" cards. Figure 10-1, below, is census card number 3522, of Benjamin F. Airington of the Choctaw Nation, with information the applicant supplied between 1899 and 1903. During that time, one child in his family died and two others were born, and the birth date of the youngest child was reported. The column for "name of mother" indicates that Airington had been married twice, and he had to provide evidence of both marriages for his enrollment file. His proof of the second marriage is shown in Figure 10-2, on page 360. This document was a bonus for the family's researcher as the marriage was not recorded in the territorial marriage register in the county; the only confirmation of the marriage was in the enrollment file. The second wife, Willie, was a non-citizen, marked I.W. (intermarried white), but even her parents were named. The parent columns show that Airington's father was a non-citizen (non-Indian), but his mother, then deceased, had been a Choctaw citizen in Blue County, where the Airington family also lived. The degree of Indian blood (1/8, 1/4, etc.) listed in the enrollment and other records may or may not be accurate, but the degree accepted at the time of enrollment is considered the final word and cannot be corrected. The process of searching these records is discussed in the following section.

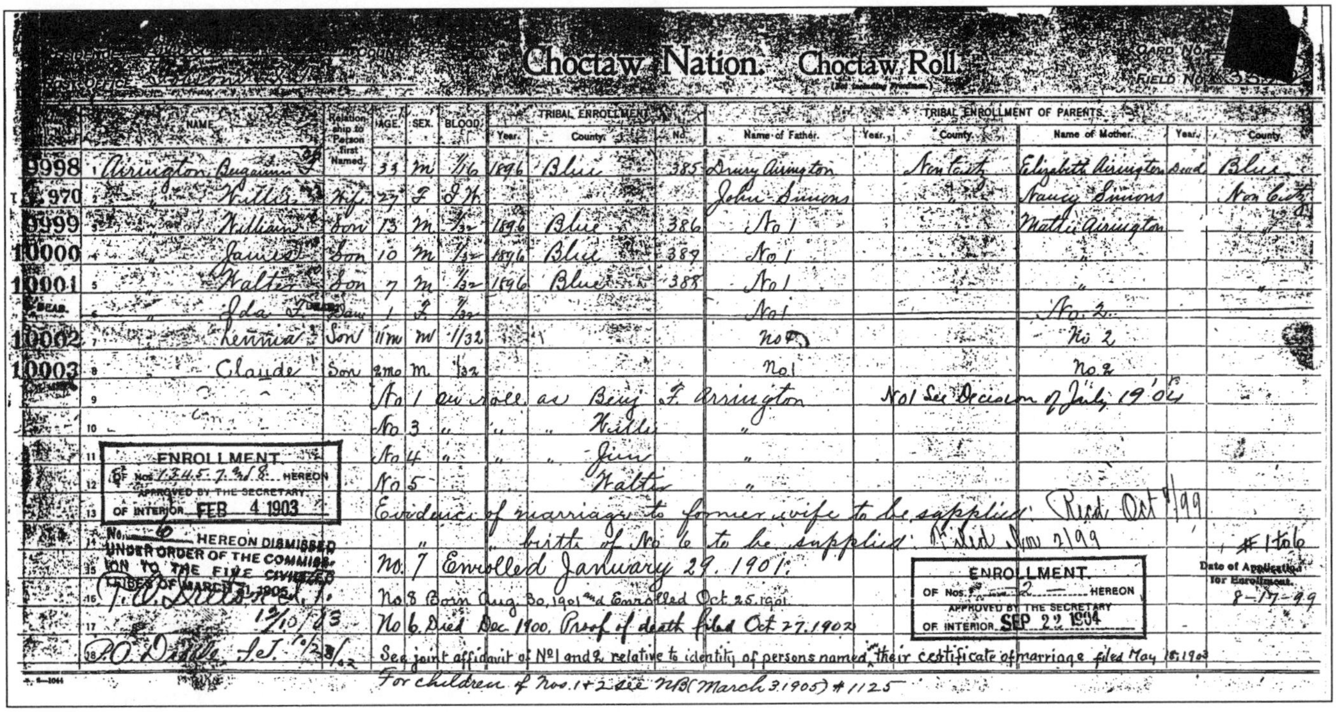
Choctaw Nation. Choctaw Roll.

Dawes' Roll No.		Name	Relationship to Person first Named	Age	Sex	Blood	Year	County	No.	Name of Father	Year	County	Name of Mother	Year	County
9998	1	Airington, Benjamin F.		33	M	1/16	1896	Blue	385	Drury Airington		Non Citz	Elizabeth Airington	dead	Blue
I.W. 970	2	" Willie	Wife	27	F	I.W.				John Simons		"	Nancy Simons		Non Citz
9999	3	" William	Son	13	M	1/32	1896	Blue	386	No 1			Mattie Airington		
10000	4	" James	Son	10	M	1/32	1896	Blue	389	No 1			"		
10001	5	" Walter	Son	7	M	1/32	1896	Blue	388	No 1			"		
DEAD	6	" Ida F.	Dau	1	F	1/32				No 1			No. 2		
10002	7	" Lennie	Son	11mo	M	1/32				No 1			No 2		
10003	8	" Claude	Son	2mo	M	1/32				No 1			No 2		

No 1 on roll as Benj F. Arrington. No 1 See Decision of July 19 '04

No 3 " " Willie "

No 4 " " Jim "

No 5 " " Walter "

Evidence of marriage to former wife to be supplied: Recd Oct 9/99

" birth of No 6 to be supplied: Recd Nov 2/99

No. 7 Enrolled January 29. 1901.

No 8 Born Aug. 30, 1901 and Enrolled Oct. 25. 1901.

No 6 Died Dec 1900. Proof of death filed Oct 27. 1902

See joint affidavit of No 1 and 2 relative to identity of persons named, their certificate of marriage filed May 18, 1903

For children of Nos. 1+2 see NB (March 3. 1905) # 1125

ENROLLMENT OF Nos. 1, 3, 4, 5, 7 and 8 HEREON APPROVED BY THE SECRETARY OF INTERIOR FEB 4 1903

No. 6 HEREON DISMISSED UNDER ORDER OF THE COMMISSION TO THE FIVE CIVILIZED TRIBES OF MARCH 31, 1905

ENROLLMENT OF Nos. 2 HEREON APPROVED BY THE SECRETARY OF INTERIOR SEP 22 1904

#1 to 6 Date of Application for Enrollment. 8-17-99

Figure 10-1 Dawes roll card for Benjamin F. Airington family, Choctaw, card 3522, Enrollment Cards for the Five Civilized Tribes, 1898–1914, NARA microfilm M1186, roll 43.

Microfilmed Records

The following are only some of the microfilm records (M, T, P, and 7RA numbers) available for research on the Five Civilized Tribes. Much of the microfilm is available at Archives I, the Fort Worth and other regional branches, the Oklahoma Historical Society, and the Family History Library; check other public, special, and academic libraries for their holdings. See the Web sites listed on page 358 to learn of additional and newly published microfilm. The list presented here illustrates the enormity and scope of available records; its purpose is to encourage researchers to use these records.

Microfilm Source

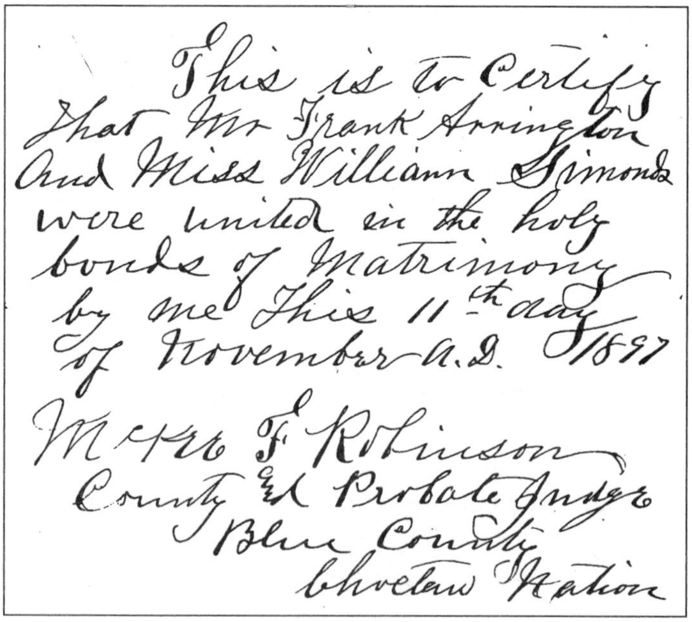
This is to Certify
That Mr Frank Arrington
And Miss Williann Simonds
were united in the holy
bonds of Matrimony
by me This 11th day
of November A.D. 1897
McKee F Robinson
County & Probate Judge
Blue County
Choctaw Nation

Figure 10-2 Airington-Simonds marriage document, enrollment file of Benjamin F. Airington, Choctaw, Dawes roll no. 9998, census card and file 3522, National Archives, Southwest Region, Fort Worth, Texas.

1. **Enrollment records**
   a. Enrollment (census) cards for the Five Civilized Tribes, 1898–1914, the "Dawes roll" (M1186, 93 rolls). The first microfilm roll contains a printed, more or less alphabetical index to the final citizenship rolls, arranged by tribe—Cherokee, then Creek and Seminoles, then Choctaw and Chickasaw. Within each tribe or group of tribes, the index is arranged by category (citizen by blood, minors, newborns, freedmen, etc.) with slight category differences between the tribes. (See the table of contents at the beginning of each tribe's index. The doubtful and rejected applications are not indexed on this roll.) This index is also online at <www.archives.gov/research_room/arc/arc_info/native_americans_final_rolls_index.html>.

   Four steps illustrate the use of this resource.

   Step 1: From the appropriate category of this index, retrieve the name of your enrollee and the roll (enrollment) number. Figure 10-3, on page 361, is from the index for Choctaws by blood, showing the Dawes roll number 9998 for Benjamin F. Airington. Consecutive numbers and names listed after his are those of his children.

   Step 2: Using this Dawes roll number, look at the end of the tribe's index for the printed "final roll," listed numerically by roll number. This list provides name, age, gender, and reported degree of blood for enrollees and their enrollment card, or census card, number. Figure 10-4, on page 362, shows Benjamin Airington's name on the Choctaw final roll. He was age thirty-six, reportedly one-sixteenth Choctaw by blood; he and five sons would be shown together on the Dawes census card #3522. The degree of Indian blood reported on this roll is considered final and not subject to correction. However, the reported degree was not always accurate, so look for other evidence as you research.

   Step 3: Go to the microfilm roll in this series (M1186) that includes your census card number within the pertinent tribe. The census card provides the abstracted information from the family's enrollment applications (see *b* below). See also the errata page with each tribe's final roll. The series also includes Delaware Indians adopted by the Cherokee. A descriptive pamphlet is available from the National Archives. Figure 10-1, on page 359, shows the Dawes roll census card for the

INDEX TO

FINAL ROLL CHOCTAWS BY BLOOD

Name.	Roll No.
Aaron, Sallie	1230
Aaron, Jim	3420
Aaron, Johnson	3451
Aaron, Sarah	3452
Aaron, Moses	3453
Aaron, Annie	3454
Aaron, Selina	3502
Aaron, Nebus	3522
Aaron, Austin	3537
Aaron, Elsie	3538
Aaron, William	3677
Aaron, Lucy	3678
Aaron, Elsie	3679
Aaron, Denison	3680
Aaron, Bekinsie	3681
Aaron, Louina	3682
Aaron, Mary	3683
Aaron, Alex	3684
Aaron, Leana	3685
Aaron, Selea	3686
Aaron, John	3714
Aaron, Sealy	3715
Aaron, Tama	3716
Aaron, Emma	12107
Aaron, Frances	14653
Abels, Henrietta E.	4477
Abels, Margaret L.	4478
Abels, Edward M.	4479
Abels, Lucile Belvin	4480
Able, Etta M.	15458
Able, Maggie	15459
Able, Enos O.	15460
Able, Amos	15461
Achukmatema	9889
Adkins, Tobitha	384
Adkins, Hugh L.	385
Adkins, Lena	386
Adkins, Sarah Jane	387
Adkins, Louis Floyd	388
Adkins, Stella	389
Adkins, Wm. McKinley	390
Adkins, Vivian	391
Adkins, Bettie	392
Ady, Marie Jane	675
Adams, Margaret	7888
Adams, C. H.	7889
Adams, James	8505
Adams, Reuben	8507
Adams, Louina	8508
Adams, Selin	8509
Adams, Jonas	8510
Adams, Rhoda	8511
Adams, Davis	8512
Adams, Abel	8706
Adams, James	8811
Adams, Sallie	8812
Adams, Sarah	8834
Adams, Willy	8882
Adams, Thomas	8909
Adams, Wilburn	9134
Adams, Melvina	9477
Adams, Katie E.	11052
Adams, Willie	11072
Adams, Anna	11075
Adams, Edward B.	12166

Name.	Roll No.
Adams, Arabella F.	13796
Adams, Nanava M.	13797
Adams, Jincy	14119
Adams, John S.	15532
Aduddell, Carl	12499
Agent, Annie G.	14464
Agent, Ruby G.	14465
Agent, Charles C.	14466
Agee, Florence	15275
Agee, Obera	15276
Agee, Zora	15277
Agee, Hester Lee	15278
Agee, Pearl	15279
Ahekatubby, John	1544
Ahekatubby, Simeon	1545
Ahekatubby, Emma	4556
Ahekatubby, Daniel	4557
Ahayotubbe, Leson	8540
Ahayotubbe, Betsy	8541
Ahotubbi,	9926
Ahotubbi, Winnie	9927
Airington, Jackson	550
Airington, Mary Elizabeth	551
Airington, Rosa Valentine	552
Airington, Lilly Ann	553
Airington, Andrew Jackson	554
Airington, Arthur Garvin	555
Airington, John L.	556
Airington, Jesse	557
Airington, Charlie Jackson	558
Airington, Monroe	559
Airington, Luther	560
Airington, Benjamin F.	9998
Airington, William	9999
Airington, James	10000
Airington, Walter	10001
Airington, Lennie	10002
Airington, Claude	10003
Airington, Levi	10155
Airington, Jesse E.	10156
Airington, Eddie A.	10157
Airington, Aldine V.	10158
Airington, Ida A.	10159
Airington, Minnie E.	10160
Airington, Andie E.	10161
Airington, Rufus	10266
Airington, Pearl	10267
Airington, Fred J.	10268
Airington, Dora	10269
Airington, William Florence	10270
Airington, William	11029
Airington, Leroy	11030
Airington, Noah	13576
Airington, Willie Poiee	13575
Airington, Willie Rap	13576
Ainsworth, Martha E.	7323
Ainsworth, James C.	7324
Ainsworth, Thomas D.	7791
Ainsworth, Thomas G.	7792

Figure 10-3 Benjamin F. Airington, Index to Final Rolls, Choctaw by blood, p. 1, Dawes roll no. 9998, in Enrollment Cards for the Five Civilized Tribes, 1898–1914, NARA microfilm M1186, roll 1.

Choctaw family of Benjamin F. Airington.

b. Applications for enrollment of the Commission to the Five Civilized Tribes, 1889–1914 (M1301, 468 rolls), arranged first by tribe, then by category (by blood, intermarriage, minors, freedmen, etc.), and then by census card number from steps 2 and 3 above.

   Step 4: These files contain the documents each individual or family provided during the application process and often contain valuable family history. (Figure 10-2, on page 360, shows confirmation of Airington's second marriage.) Arranged by tribe, the series also includes doubtful and rejected applications. If you don't have ready access to this microfilm, you can order a copy of the application file from the Fort Worth, Texas, branch of the National Archives.

c. Final rolls (Dawes roll) of citizens and freedmen of the Five Civilized Tribes in Indian Territory, 1907 and 1914 (T529, 3 rolls). Includes approved and rejected names; Mississippi Choctaw and Delaware Cherokee; arranged by tribe, category (blood, intermarriage, freedmen), and roll (enrollment) number.

d. Index to Choctaw-Chickasaw "R" (rejected) cards (7RA147).

e. Index to Cherokee "rejected" and "doubtful" Dawes enrollment cards (7RA24).

CD Source

The CD-ROM *Native American Collection* (Orem, Utah: GenRef Inc., 1998), which contains indexes to enrollees, can generate for you a letter with which to order the file.

Figure 10-4 Benjamin F. Airington family, Index and Final Rolls of Citizens and Freedmen, Choctaw, p. 298, Dawes roll no. 9998, census card 3522, in Enrollment Cards for the Five Civilized Tribes, 1898–1914, NARA microfilm M1186, roll 1.

298 INDEX AND FINAL ROLLS OF CITIZENS AND FREEDMEN

No.	Name	Age	Sex	Blood	Census Card No
9950	Lewis, Charles S.	36	M	1-16	3494
9951	Strickland, Arcola	28	F	3-16	3496
9952	Strickland, Florence Edna	3	F	3-32	3496
9953	Strickland, Meadie Blanch	1	F	3-32	3496
9954	Beal, William C.	37	M	1-8	3498
9955	Beal, Mahala	11	F	1-16	3498
9956	Beal, John	8	M	1-16	3498
9957	Beal, Minnie Viola	3	F	1-16	3498
9958	Hughes, Belle	25	F	1-8	3499
9959	Yarborough, Belle	37	F	1-8	3500
9960	Hatchett, Meta B.	19	F	1-16	3500
9961	Yarborough, Emma E.	17	F	1-16	3500
9962	Yarborough, Clarence	13	M	1-16	3500
9963	Yarborough, Eunice	11	F	1-16	3500
9964	Yarborough, John C.	6	M	1-16	3500
9965	Fobb, Joseph	53	M	Full	3501
9966	Fobb, Incy	23	F	Full	3501
9967	Fobb, Pearl	12	F	Full	3501
9968	Fobb, Emma	2	F	Full	3501
9969	Walley, Eliza	51	F	Full	3502
9970	Wilson, Wallace	13	M	Full	3502
9971	Williams, Jefferson	46	M	Full	3503
9972	Williams, Eliza	22	F	Full	3504
9973	Homer, Asa J.	44	M	Full	3506
9974	Homer, Kizzie	48	F	Full	3506
9975	LeFlore, Malena	25	F	Full	3506
9976	Homer, Dana	20	M	Full	3506
9977	Stricken from roll.				
9978	Walley, Johnson	51	M	Full	3508
9979	Walley, Sinie	48	F	Full	3508
9980	Byington, Culberson	35	M	Full	3509
9981	Byington, Sarah	33	F	Full	3509
9982	Byington, Allen	17	M	Full	3509
9983	Byington, David	14	M	Full	3509
9984	Byington, Sampson	12	M	Full	3509
9985	Payton, Mary A.	73	F	3-4	3510
9986	Payton, Noah	31	M	7-8	3510
9987	Payton, Andrew	23	M	7-8	3510
9988	Van Zant, Minnie	20	F	3-8	3513
9989	Van Zant, Henry Alex	3	M	3-16	3513
9990	Clark, Fannie	13	F	1-32	3515
9991	Walley, Sillen	33	F	Full	3516
9992	Walley, Milton	9	M	Full	3516
9993	Walley, Jacob	6	M	Full	3516
9994	Yarbrough, Annie	26	F	1-4	3518
9995	Yarbrough, Steve	13	M	1-8	3518
9996	Yarbrough, LaVere	6	M	1-8	3518
9997	Yarbrough, Julian	3	M	1-8	3518
9998	Airington, Benjamin F.	36	M	1-16	3522
9999	Airington, William	16	M	1-32	3522
10000	Airington, James	13	M	1-32	3522
10001	Airington, Walter	10	M	1-32	3522
10002	Airington, Lennia	3	M	1-32	3522
10003	Airington, Claude	1	M	1-32	3522
10004	Ballew, Ella J.	36	F	1-4	3523
10005	Ballew, Henry C.	13	M	1-8	3523
10006	Ballew, Ella	10	F	1-8	3523
10007	Ballew, Lela B.	6	F	1-8	3523
10008	Gunter, Mary J.	26	F	1-2	3524
10009	Gunter, Emma M.	7	F	1-4	3524
10010	Gunter, Thelma	5	F	1-4	3524
10011	Durant, Jesse	22	M	1-2	3524
10012	Durant, Ora	13	F	1-2	3524
10013	Gunter, Luther W.	3	M	1-4	3524
10014	Jones, Jackson N.	32	M	3-8	3526
10015	Jones, Theresa	8	F	3-16	3526
10016	Jones, Geneva	6	F	3-16	3526
10017	Jones, Brutus Costillo	2	M	3-16	3526
10018	Veach, Sophina	51	F	1-2	3527
10019	Veach, Calvin	23	M	1-4	3527
10020	Seeley, Birdie	21	F	1-4	3527
10021	Veach, Walter	18	M	1-4	3527
10022	Veach, Lottie	15	F	1-4	3527
10023	Veach, Standley	13	M	1-4	3527
10024	Veach, Frances	10	F	1-4	3527
10025	Veach, Columbus	8	M	1-4	3527
10026	Seeley, Gabe Horatio	1	M	1-8	3527
10027	McKinney, Hulda	32	F	1-16	3529
10028	McKinney, George	15	M	1-32	3529
10029	McKinney, Frank	12	M	1-32	3529
10030	McKinney, Elijah	9	M	1-32	3529
10031	McKinney, Lillie E.	7	F	1-32	3529
10032	McKinney, Edward L.	5	M	1-32	3529
10033	McKinney, Maggie	3	F	1-32	3529

No.	Name	Age	Sex	Blood	Census Card No
10034	McKinney, Richard M.	1	M	1-32	3529
10035	Gardner, Alfred W.	54	M	3-4	3530
10036	Harris, Susan	28	F	Full	3537
10037	Emerson, Jackson	8	M	Full	3537
10038	Ingram, Nellie	26	F	1-4	3538
10039	Ingram, Christine O.	3	F	1-8	3538
10040	Ingram, C. T. Bouton	2	M	1-8	3538
10041	Colbert, Clarence	39	M	1-8	3539
10042	Colbert, Lewis C.	16	M	1-16	3539
10043	Colbert, Lena	11	F	1-16	3539
10044	Colbert, Vera	9	F	1-16	3539
10045	Colbert, Clarence, Jr.	7	M	1-16	3539
10046	Colbert, Minnie Belle	2	F	1-16	3539
10047	McClendon, Annie	29	F	7-8	3540
10048	McClendon, Posey	7	M	7-16	3540
10049	McClendon, Eva R.	4	F	7-16	3540
10050	Armstrong, Estella	10	F	7-16	3540
10051	Armstrong, Willie	8	M	7-16	3540
10052	McClendon, Tryphenia	1	F	7-16	3540
10053	Dodson, Mary J.	42	F	Full	3541
10054	Neely, Allen	20	M	1-2	3541
10055	Neely, Joseph	16	M	1-2	3541
10056	Neely, Mary	13	F	1-2	3541
10057	Neely, Ward	12	M	1-2	3541
10058	Dodson, Winnie	2	F	1-2	3541
10059	Nail, Jesse	26	M	1-2	3544
10060	Wechel, Mary E.	20	F	1-4	3544
10061	Hayes, Cornelius	22	M	Full	3545
10062	Hayes, Laurena	21	F	Full	3545
10063	Hayes, Sophia	3	F	Full	3545
10064	Burney, George	26	M	3-4	3546
10065	Crowder, Loran F.	39	M	1-8	3547
10066	Crowder, John H.	6	M	1-16	3547
10067	Crowder, Harvey	1	M	1-16	3547
10068	Stricken from roll.				
10069	Crowder, Thompson	29	M	1-2	3550
10070	Mitchell, Missouri	42	F	1-8	3551
10071	Nail, Edward J.	29	M	1-2	3553
10072	Nail, Robert W.	4	M	1-4	3553
10073	Nail, Rennie	3	F	1-4	3553
10074	Nail, Edward L.	1	M	1-4	3553
10075	Jarrel, Lulu E.	20	F	1-8	3555
10076	Jarrel, Mary Elizebeth	1	F	1-16	3555
10077	Cochneuer, David J.	19	M	1-8	3556
10078	Cochneuer, Nicholas F.	17	M	1-8	3556
10079	Cochneuer, James H.	14	M	1-8	3556
10080	Stricken from roll.				
10081	Cochneuer, Ella E.	9	F	1-8	3556
10082	Cochneuer, Marion McC.	4	M	1-8	3556
10083	Hayes, Watson	23	M	Full	3557
10084	Gardner, Rodolphus C.	48	M	3-8	3559
10085	Gardner, Irena	40	F	3-8	3559
10086	Gardner, Amelia	19	F	3-8	3559
10087	Gardner, Rodolphus C., Jr.	17	M	3-8	3559
10088	Gardner, Sallie A.	15	F	3-8	3559
10089	Gardner, Roscoe C.	13	M	3-8	3559
10090	Gardner, Nora L.	10	F	3-8	3559
10091	Gardner, Walter T.	7	M	3-8	3559
10092	Gardner, Junia E.	6	F	3-8	3559
10093	Gardner, Morgan M.	4	M	3-8	3559
10094	Gardner, Oddie Myrtle	2	F	3-8	3559
10095	Beal, Andrew P.	33	M	1-8	3560
10096	Beal, Mary M.	10	F	1-16	3560
10097	Beal, Martha J.	7	F	1-16	3560
10098	Beal, Charles R.	4	M	1-16	3560
10099	Beal, Hugh L.	2	M	1-16	3560
10100	Beal, John Wesley	1	M	1-16	3560
10101	Duer, Isaac	26	M	1-16	3561
10102	Duer, Thomas William	2	M	1-32	3561
10103	Odell, Gilbert W.	11	M	1-8	3562
10104	Odell, William R.	8	M	1-8	3562
10105	Lauchner, Lela V.	19	F	1-8	3562
10106	Wacome, Burney	24	M	1-2	3563
10107	Latta, Thomas	30	M	1-8	3569
10108	Latta, Alvis S.	6	M	1-16	3569
10109	Durant, Elizabeth	50	F	1-2	3571
10110	Goins, Hampton	22	M	1-2	3571
10111	Goins, Elizabeth	19	F	1-2	3571
10112	Stricken from roll.				
10113	Cochnauer, David W.	31	M	1-2	3576
10114	Cochnauer, Rhoda	28	F	1-2	3576
10115	Cochnauer, Louisa P.	6	F	1-2	3576
10116	Cochnauer, Ethel	2	F	1-2	3576
10117	James, Clayburn W.	31	M	1-2	3585

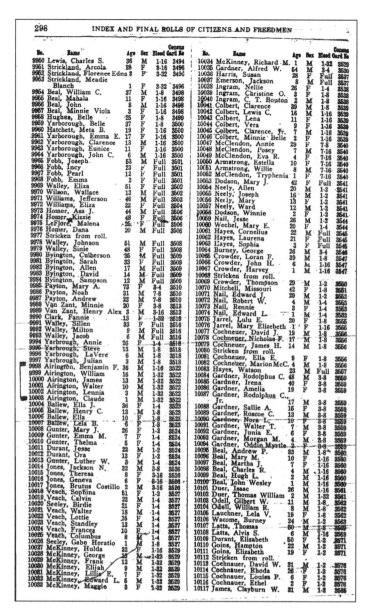

f. Applications from the Bureau of Indian Affairs, Muskogee Area Office, relating to enrollment in the Five Civilized Tribes under the Act of 1896 (M1650, 54 rolls, with index on roll 1). These pertain to Choctaw, Cherokee, some Chickasaw, and a few Creek applicants.

2. **Cherokee and Records Pertaining to All Five Civilized Tribes**

a. Records of the Cherokee Indian Agency in Tennessee, 1801–1835 (M208, 14 rolls). Roll 13 of this publication includes a twelve-page register of persons who wished reservation under the Treaty of 8 July 1817; these were eastern Cherokees, some of whom agreed to move west to Arkansas and others who asked to get during their lifetimes 640 acres of reserved land that would revert to the state on the death or abandonment of the grantee. Though not containing much concrete genealogical information, this register gives the name of the reservee, the number in the family, and a general idea of the family's residence on the rivers of north Alabama, north Georgia, east Tennessee, or western North Carolina in 1817 and 1819. The register has been transcribed in books such as *Cherokee Roots*, by Bob Blakenship (Bowie, Md.: Heritage Books, 1992, reprint of 1978 original); *Cherokee Reservees*, by David K. Hampton (Oklahoma City: Jack Baker Publishing, 1979); and *Cherokee Emigration Rolls 1817–1835*, by Jack D. Baker (Oklahoma City: Jack Baker Publishing, 1977).

b. Register of Cherokee who wished to remain in the east, 1817–1819 (film A21); Cherokee emigration rolls and musters rolls, 1817–1838 (film A23).

c. Cherokee Nation census rolls: 1852 Drennen roll (7RA01; also M685, roll 12). 1867 Tompkins roll of Cherokee citizens and freedmen and 1867 census (7RA04). Freedmen rolls and indexes; includes Wallace roll (7RA51). Revisions to the Wallace Rolls of Cherokee Freedmen and Delaware and Shawnee Cherokees, ca. 1890–1896 (M1833). 1880 census and index (M1875, formerly 7RA07). Cherokee 1880 Census Schedules, Schedules 1–6, Authorized by an Act of the Cherokee National Council of December 3, 1879 (P2072). 1883 census (7RA29). 1883 payment roll (7RA57). 1886 census (7RA58). 1890 census (7RA08 and 7RA60). Old Settler roll, 1895, with index to payment roll, 1896 (T985). 1896 census (7RA19). Index to Cherokee 1896 census, except freedmen (P2136).

Figure 10-5, below, shows Nelson S. [*sic*] and Annie [Sarah A.] Carr and family

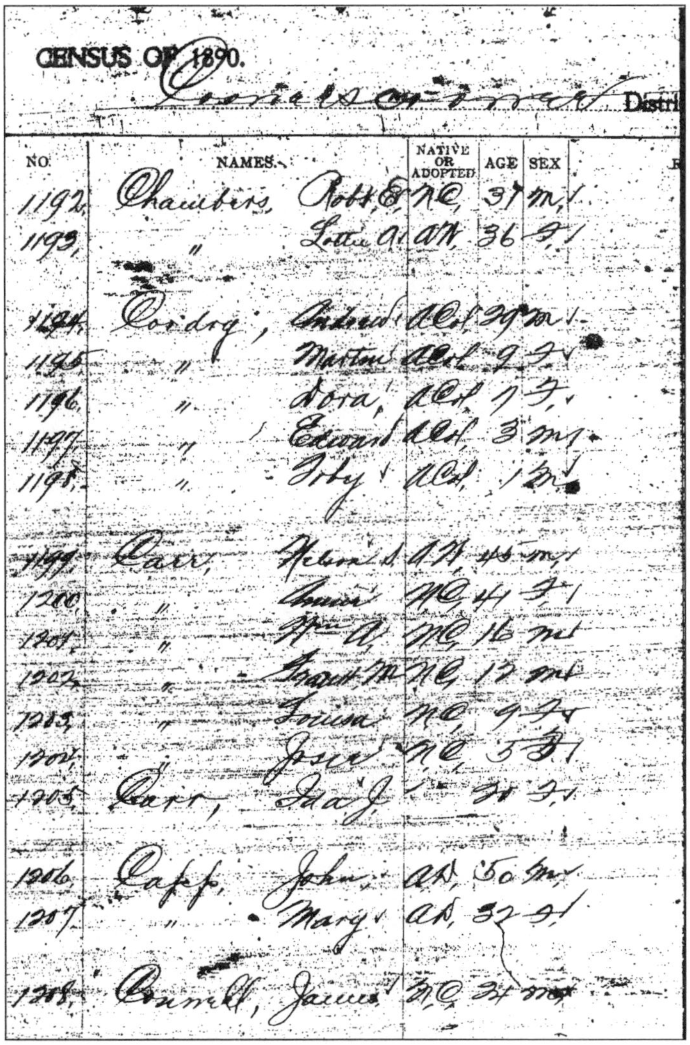
CENSUS OF 1890.
Cooweescoowee District

NO.	NAMES.		NATIVE OR ADOPTED	AGE	SEX
1192	Chambers,	Robt E.	NC	37	m
1193	"	Lottie A.	AW	36	f
1194	Coody,	Andrew	ACI	39	m
1195	"	Martin	ACI	9	f
1196	"	Dora	ACI	7	f
1197	"	Edward	ACI	3	m
1198	"	Toby	ACI	1	m
1199	Carr,	Nelson S.	AW	45	m
1200	"	Annie	NC	41	f
1201	"	Wm A.	NC	16	m
1202	"	Grant M.	NC	12	m
1203	"	Louisa	NC	9	f
1204	"	Josie	NC	5	f
1205	Carr,	Ida J.		20	f
1206	Capp,	John	AW	50	m
1207	"	Mary	AW	32	f
1208	Connell,	James	NC	34	m

Figure 10-5 1890 Census, Cherokee Nation, NARA microfilm 7RA60, roll 1, Cooweescoowee District, p. 53, Nelson Carr family entry.

on the 1890 census of Cooweescoowee District of the Cherokee Nation (7RA60, roll 1); notice the families are arranged more or less alphabetically rather than by neighborhood.

d. Rolls of the Eastern Cherokee: Henderson roll, 1835, with index (T496). 1848 Mullay roll, 1851 Siler roll (7RA06). 1851 Chapman roll (M685). See also *e* and *f* below.

e. Selected letters received by Office of Indian Affairs relating to Cherokee of North Carolina, 1851–1905 (M1059).

f. Eastern Cherokee applications of the U.S. Court of Claims, 1906–1909 (M1104, 348 rolls). Grievances of the Cherokees against the government arising from treaties of 1835, 1836, and 1845 were taken to the Court of Claims, which decided in favor of the eastern Cherokee in 1905. The Department of the Interior had to identify those persons entitled to share in the distribution of the settlement funds. Guion Miller, who compiled this roll, in 1909 reported receiving nearly 46,000 applications, representing about 990,000 persons, of whom about 30,000 were approved. (See the case study later in this chapter.)

   The applications on these microfilm rolls are arranged by file number and show the claimants' names, ages, birthplaces, family members, and other information pertinent to determining their eligibility to share in the court settlement, especially the family's names on previous tribal rolls.

g. Records relating to the enrollment of the Eastern Cherokee, by Guion Miller, 1908–1910 (M685, 12 rolls). In determining eligibility for a share of the settlement funds (in *f* above), Miller used Cherokee rolls and censuses made between 1835 and 1884; thus, the microfilm includes copies of the Chapman (1851, east), Drennen (1851, west), Old Settlers (1851, west), and Hester (1884) rolls that Miller used. Much of this microfilm publication is his final report, summarizing application files in numerical order. Miller's voluminous report details the reasons for accepting or rejecting the applications; testimony includes lengthy reports dealing with Sizemore and Poindexter families and claims of some Creek Indians. Figure 10-6, on page 365, is the first six claims from the Miller report, showing both rejected and admitted claims.

   At this writing, an index to the "Guion Miller roll," including each applicant's name and application file number, is online at <www.archives.gov/research_room/arc/arc_info/native_americans_guion_miller_index.html>.

   See also *Cherokee Blood-(Tsa-la-gi-yi gi-gv): Based on Eastern Cherokee Applications of the U.S. Court of Claims 1906–1909*, by Shirley Hoskins (Chattanooga, Tenn.: the author, 1982) and *Cherokee By Blood: Records of Eastern Cherokee Ancestry in the U.S. Court of Claims, 1906–1910*, 9 vols. to date, Jerry Wright Jordan, comp. (Bowie, Md.: Heritage Books, 1987–).

h. List of claimants and dockets of the Cherokee Citizenship Commission, 1878–1889; list of rejected claimants and persons admitted to citizenship (7RA25). Decisions of U.S. Court on Cherokee citizenship (7RA98).

i. Payroll of the Delaware-Cherokee, 1896, and censuses of the Shawnee-Cherokee, 1896 and 1904 (7RA26). 1867 Delaware-Cherokee list and index (7RA73). Delawares who elected to remove to Indian Territory, 1871; Shawnees admitted to Cherokee citizenship, 1871; and North Carolina Cherokees who removed to Cherokee Nation, 1881 (7RA74). Delaware per capita payroll, 1904 (7RA26).

j. Annuity rolls, 1848–1860 (film NARA35). Cherokee payment rolls: Lipe roll, 1880 (7RA33). 1883 roll (7RA57); 1890 roll (7RA59); Starr roll and index, 1894

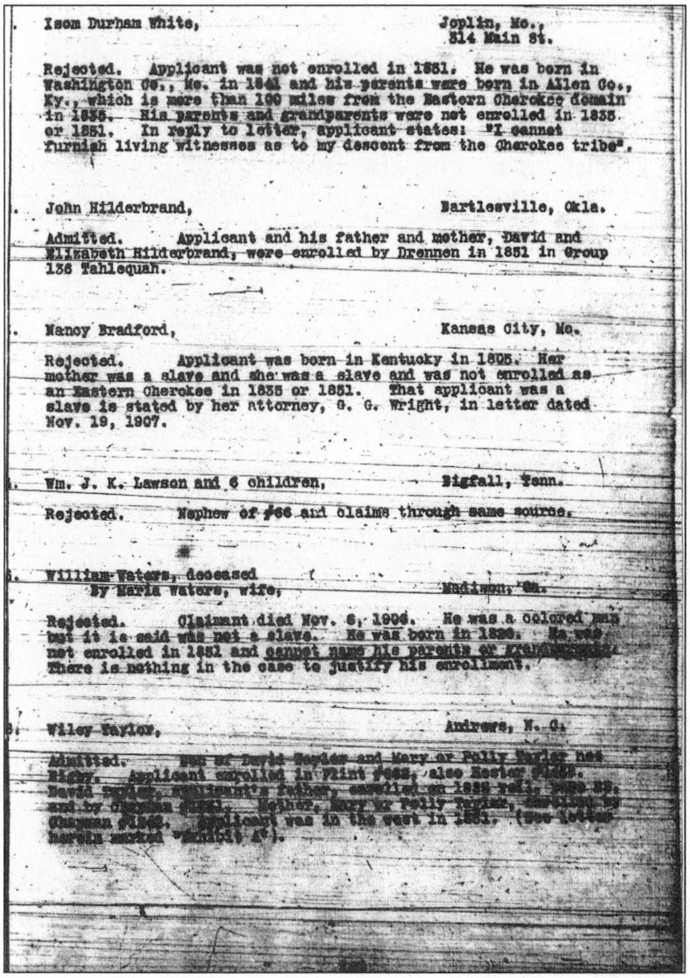

. Isom Durham White, Joplin, Mo., 514 Main St.

Rejected. Applicant was not enrolled in 1851. He was born in Washington Co., Mo. in 1841 and his parents were born in Allen Co., Ky., which is more than 100 miles from the Eastern Cherokee domain in 1835. His parents and grandparents were not enrolled in 1835 or 1851. In reply to letter, applicant states: "I cannot furnish living witnesses as to my descent from the Cherokee tribe".

. John Hilderbrand, Bartlesville, Okla.

Admitted. Applicant and his father and mother, David and Elizabeth Hilderbrand, were enrolled by Drennen in 1851 in Group 136 Tahlequah.

. Nancy Bradford, Kansas City, Mo.

Rejected. Applicant was born in Kentucky in 1825. Her mother was a slave and she was a slave and was not enrolled as an Eastern Cherokee in 1835 or 1851. That applicant was a slave is stated by her attorney, G. G. Wright, in letter dated Nov. 19, 1907.

. Wm. J. K. Lawson and 6 children, Bigfall, Tenn.

Rejected. Nephew of #66 and claims through same source.

. William Waters, deceased
By Maria Waters, wife, Madison, Ga.

Rejected. Claimant died Nov. 6, 1906. He was a colored man but it is said was not a slave. He was born in 1826. He was not enrolled in 1851 and cannot name his parents or grandparents. There is nothing in the case to justify his enrollment.

. Wiley Taylor, Andrews, N. C.

Admitted. [illegible] of David Taylor and Mary or Polly Taylor nee [illegible]. Applicant enrolled in Flint #662, also Hester [illegible]. David Taylor, applicant's father, enrolled on 1835 roll, [illegible] and by Chapman [illegible]. Mother, Mary or Polly Taylor, enrolled by Chapman #1262. Applicant was in the west in 1851. (See letter herein marked "Exhibit A").

Figure 10-6 Claims 1-6, Guion Miller report, p. 3, in General Index to Eastern Cherokee Applications, vol. 1 and 2, in Records Relating to Enrollment of the Eastern Cherokee by Guion Miller, 1908-1910, NARA microfilm M685, roll 1.

(7RA38); Old Settlers payment roll, 1896 (7RA34); 1902 payment to destitute Cherokees and payment to intermarried whites 1909–1910 (7RA80); 1912 per capita payroll (7RA81). Equalization payment rolls, 1910–1915 (7RA82).

k. Cherokee freedmen, various indexes and rolls, 1867–1897 (7RA51). Lists (7RA53, roll 8). 1893 census (7RA54). Cherokee freedmen payment roll, 1897 (A32). See also *The Cherokee Freedmen: From Emancipation to American Citizenship*, by Daniel F. Littlefield Jr. (Westport, Conn.: Greenwood Press, 1978).
l. Intruder cases and indexes, 1901–1909 (7RA53). 1893 census of intruders (7RA55). See also *The Intruders: The Illegal Residents of the Cherokee Nation, 1866–1907*, by Nancy Hope Sober (Ponca City, Okla.: Cherokee Books, 1991).
m. Register of Cherokee students, 1881–1882 (7RA91).
n. Index to Orders for Removal of Restrictions, Five Civilized Tribes, no date (P2097).
o. Rolls and Registers for the Delaware Indians, n.d.; Shawnee Indians, 1871; and Cherokee Indians, 1817, 1866, and 1881 (P2139).
p. Register of Indians in World War I. 1 roll. (P2292, formerly 7RA347).
q. Citizenship case files of the U.S. Court in Indian Territory, 1896–1897 (P2293). Revisions to the Wallace Rolls of Cherokee Freedmen and Delaware and Shawnee Cherokees, ca. 1890–1896 (M1833).

3. Creek

a. Censuses: 1832, Parsons and Abbott roll (T275); Old Settlers roll and payroll, 1857

(7RA326); Payroll, 1857–1859 (7RA23, roll 2); Citizens and freedmen, Dunn roll, 1867, 1869 (7RA44); Census, 1882 (7RA43); Census, 1890, 1895 (7RA12); Colbert roll, 1896, partial (7RA12); Colbert roll census, 1896 (7RA69).

b. Letter Book of the Creek Trading House, 1795–1816 (M4). Records of the Creek Factory of the Office of Indian Trade of the BIA, 1795–1821 (M1334).
c. Annuity rolls and payrolls: 1848–1860 (NARA35); 1858 (7RA23); 1890 (7RA46); 1895 (7RA12, roll 1, and 7RA45, roll 1); Loyal Creek payment roll, 1904 (7RA31).
d. Authenticated tribal roll, 1890 (7RA41).
e. Intruder cases and indexes (7RA53).
f. Citizenship Commission docket book, 1888–1896 (7RA68). Applicants for citizenship, 1896–1900 (7RA42). Northern District citizenship case files, 1897 (7RA388). Dockets A–C of 1896 citizenship cases (7RA70).
g. Selected Records from the Bureau of Indian Affairs, Muskogee Area Office, relating to Jackson Barnett, Creek enrollee 4525, 1900–1946 (P2202).

4. **Choctaw**

a. Records of the Choctaw Trading House, 1803–1824 (T500).
b. List of people who remained in Mississippi (7RA116, roll 1); Armstrong roll, 1831 (film A39); Choctaw emigration lists, 1831–1857 (A40).
c. Index to Choctaw and Chickasaw allotment ledgers, 1902–1907 (7RA153).
d. Choctaws paid by Chickasaws under Treaty of 22 June 1855, payment roll (7RA09). See also *A Complete Roll of All Choctaw Claimants and Their Heirs: Existing under the Treaties between the United States and the Choctaw Nation as far as shown by the Records of the United States and the Choctaw Nation*, Joe. R. Goss, comp. (Conway, Ark.: Oldbuck Press, 1992, reprint of 1889 original).
e. Payrolls: annuity rolls, 1848–1860 (film NARA35); 1893 index to census, payroll, and orphans list (7RA64); Choctaw payment roll, 1893 (7RA65); Index to Choctaw-Chickasaw allotment ledgers, 1899–1907 (7RA153); Townsite index and payroll, 1904 (7RA83); Payroll, 1906 (7RA84); Payroll and index, 1908 (7RA88); Choctaw-Chickasaw annuity roll, 1906–1908 (NARA35); Equalization payroll and index, 1910 (7RA89); Fifty dollar payment roll and index, 1911 (7RA90); Choctaw-Chickasaw equalization rolls, 1912–1924, and annuity rolls, 1925–1927 (NARA35); Index and payroll, 1916 (7RA93); Index and payroll, 1917 (7RA94).
f. Applicants and dockets of Choctaw-Chickasaw citizenship court, 1902–1904 with index (7RA27). Choctaw-Chickasaw Citizenship Court case files, 1902–1904 (M1870, formerly 7RA324).
g. Records of intruders in Choctaw-Chickasaw Nations, 1900–1901, and list of U.S. citizens living unlawfully in Pickens County, Chickasaw Nation (7RA53, roll 8). Indexes to Choctaw intruder cases (7RA53).
h. Census records: 1885 index (7RA62); 1896 census with index (7RA02).
i. Census roll of Choctaw-Chickasaw Freedmen, 1885 (P2128, apparently formerly 7RA63).
j. Census roll of Choctaw-Chickasaw Freedmen, 1896 (P2131, apparently formerly 7RA66).
k. Mississippi Choctaw townsite payroll and index, 1908 (7RA107); 1911 (7RA108).
l. Records relating to identification of Mississippi Choctaw, 1899–1904 (P2219, formerly 7RA116).

m. Records of the Choctaw-Chickasaw citizenship court case files, 1902–1904 (P2291).

5. **Chickasaw** (see also Choctaw)
   a. Records of the Treasury Department, correspondence concerning administration of trust funds for the Chickasaw and others, 1834–1872 (M749).
   b. Annuity rolls, 1848–1860, 1906–1908 (NARA35).
   c. Census roll, 1878, 1897 (7RA21).
   d. List of intruders, not dated (7RA21). Indexes to intruder cases and intruders (7RA53).
   e. Index to townsite fund payroll, 1904 (7RA97). Payroll, 1908 (7RA100). Equalization payment roll, 1910 (7RA101). Chickasaw incompetent payroll, 1903 (7RA96).
   f. Chickasaw Records, 1878–1897: Chickasaw 1878 Annuity; Chickasaw Censuses of 1890, 1896, 1897; Chickasaw 1893 payment; and lists of citizens and intruders in the Chickasaw Nation, no date (P2086, apparently combining 7RA21 with other records for new publication).

6. **Seminole**
   a. Census Roll, 1897; Payment Rolls, 1868, 1895–96, 1895–97; Approved Allotment Schedules for the Seminole Indians, 1901–06 (P2085, apparently formerly 7RA287, 7RA20).
   b. Index and docket of 1896 citizenship cases (7RA70).
   c. Dawes Commission townsite plats, 1899–1905 (7RA18).

RECORDS OF RESERVATION INDIANS

The National Archives holds numerous records relating to American Indian reservations and their inhabitants, although relatively few of the materials pertain to Indians in the eastern United States. (Some of the eastern reservations are under the jurisdiction of state governments.) In addition, the regional branches of the National Archives also hold some Indian records pertinent to reservations, tribes, agencies, and BIA field offices in their region. For example, the Kansas City regional branch holds records of the Consolidated Chippewa Agency and the Winnebago Agency. Contact the regional branches for availability of Indian agency and field office records, which include such materials as censuses, land allotment registers, annuity payment rolls, marriage and vital statistics registers, heirship records, registers of families, student records, school censuses, and records of agency employees. Also contact the state archives or historical society and the special collections departments of public and academic libraries in your research state to identify materials that might help you.

For More Info

A chart that may help you find such records is a table of BIA Indian agencies, schools and other divisions and the National Archives regional branch that holds their records. See *Guide to Genealogical Research in the National Archives of the United States* (Washington, D.C.: National Archives and Records Administration, 2000), pages 163–167.

The microfilm listed below represents a sampling of National Archives publications. Contact the National Archives to order the descriptive pamphlets that are available for many of the publications.

1. **Indian Census Rolls, 1885–1940** (M595, 692 rolls, not including the Five Civilized Tribes)
   Roll by roll listing found in *American Indians: A Select Catalog of National Archives Microfilm Publications* (National Archives, 1998), pages 51–72, or online at the Na-

tional Archives Web site <www.archives.gov/publications/microfilm_catalogs.html> under "subject catalogs." (Check for others in lists of microfilm published after 2000.) These are records submitted by agents or superintendents in compliance with an 1884 law. Not all agencies reported each year. The rolls include schools, seminaries, and only those persons who maintained a formal affiliation with a tribe. The rolls are organized by agency or institution and do not include the Five Civilized Tribes in Indian Territory. They do include Mississippi Choctaw and eastern Cherokee. A descriptive pamphlet is available for this very important resource.

2. **Records of Superintendencies of Indian Affairs**
   Until the 1870s, superintendents were responsible for Indian affairs in a broad area—possibly including numerous tribes—and for the agencies within their jurisdiction. Agents were the government employees assigned to one or more tribes, under the jurisdiction of a superintendent, and, after the 1870s, reporting directly to the Commissioner of Indian Affairs. Agents distributed money and supplies, carried out treaty provisions, and concerned themselves with education within the tribe. By the early 1900s, agents were being called superintendents. The following records include reports, correspondence, and other records.
   a. Records of the Arizona Superintendency, 1863–1873 (M734).
   b. Records of the Central Superintendency, 1813–1878 (M856). Records of many tribes of the central plains.
   c. Records of the Dakota Superintendency, 1861–1870, 1877–1878; of the Wyoming Superintendency, 1870 (M1016).
   d. Records of the Idaho Superintendency, 1863–1870 (M832).
   e. Records of the Michigan Superintendency, 1814–1851 (M1).
   f. Records of the Minnesota Superintendency, 1849–1856 (M842).
   g. Records of the Montana Superintendency, 1867–1873 (M833).
   h. Records of the Nevada Superintendency, 1869–1870 (M837).
   i. Records of the New Mexico Superintendency, 1849–1880 (T21).
   j. Records of the Northern Superintendency, 1851–1876 (M1166).
   k. Records of the Oregon Superintendency, 1848–1873 (M2).
   l. Miscellaneous letters from the Pine Ridge Indian Agency, 1875–1914. (M1229 and M1282).
   m. Miscellaneous letters sent by Pueblo Indian Agency, 1874–1891 (M941; see also M1304).
   n. Records of the Southern Superintendency, 1832–1870; of the Western Superintendency, 1832–1851 (M640).
   o. Records of the Utah Superintendency, 1853–1870 (M834).
   p. Records of the Washington Superintendency, 1853–1874 (M5).
   q. Records of the Wisconsin Superintendency, 1836–1848; of the Green Bay Subagency, 1850 (M951).
   r. Superintendents' annual reports, narrative and statistical, 1907–1938 (M1011). Includes Five Civilized Tribes. All but Roll 1 arranged alphabetically by institution or agency.

3. **Historical sketches of field units** and subject headings used in M18, 1824–1880 (T1105)
4. **Correspondence**
   a. Letters received by Office of Indian Affairs, 1824–1881 (M234). Arranged by

agency or superintendency or by topic, such as annuity goods and emigration, then by registry number. Registers for these letters (M18) give registry number (after mid-1836), name of writer, date written and received, agency or jurisdiction under which it was filed, and summary. Letters sent by Office of Indian Affairs, 1824–1881 (M21). Some indexing by addressee.

b. Letters received by Secretary of War on Indian Affairs, 1800–1823 (M271). Primarily concerning southern Indians and the Seneca in New York. Each year is alphabetical by writer. Letters sent by Secretary of War on Indian Affairs, 1800–1824 (M15, 6 rolls, indexed).
c. Letters received by superintendents of Indian trade, 1806–1824 (T58). Letters sent by superintendents of Indian trade 1807–1823 (M16). Indexed by addressee.
d. Letters received by Indian Division of Department of the Interior, 1849–1880 (M825). Letters sent by the same division, 1849–1903, and indexes through 1897 (M606).
e. Letter Book of the Natchitoches-Sulphur Fork Factory (trading post), 1809–1821 (T1029).
f. Letter Book of the Arkansas Trading House, 1805–1810 (M142).
g. BIA Records created by the Santa Fe Indian School, 1890–1918 (M1473).
h. Correspondence and accounting records of the Puget Sound District Agency, 1854–1861, and Tulalip Agency, 1861–1886 (P2011).
i. Letters received by the Office of Education, Alaska Division, Records of the Bureau of Indian Affairs, 1878–1916 (M1977).

5. **Miscellaneous records and reports**
   a. Records relating to investigations of the Ft. Phil Kearney or Fetterman Massacre, 1866–1867 (M740).
   b. Special files, 1807–1904 (M574). Correspondence, reports, affidavits, etc., primarily relating to many types of claims by individuals or on their behalf. Consult descriptive pamphlet on the series for specifics. See roll list in the *American Indians* select catalog. See also the case study later in this chapter.
   c. Report books, 1838–1885, with copies of letters to Congress, the president, and other government officials about claims, investigations, schools, and other OIA business (M348).
   d. Records relating to the enrollment of Flathead Indians, 1903–1908 (M1350).
   e. Reports of inspection of field jurisdictions, Office of Indian Affairs, 1873–1900 (M1070). Rolls alphabetical by agency, superintendency, or institution.
   f. Osage annuity rolls, 1878–1907 (7RA35).
   g. Chemawa Indian School: Register of students admitted, 1880–1928; descriptive statements of students, 1890–1914; and graduating class rolls, 1885–1921 (P2008, 1 roll).

OTHER RECORDS FOR NATIVE AMERICAN RESEARCH

Apart from the foregoing agency and tribal records, other useful sources for American Indian history and genealogy are standard county, state, and federal records. Genealogists who have traced American Indian ancestry back into and beyond the early nineteenth century often find that the interaction of the Indians with white society or the mixture of Indian and white and/or black blood often helps place the ancestors in the early records of the colonies, territories, and states as they interacted with governments, the military, land offices, trading houses, traders, tribes, and courts. What one author said of the Catawba Indians applies to all: "It should be evident . . . that the ability to trace Catawba genealogy is directly dependent on the extent to which Catawbas came into contact with white society."[4] The following examples illustrate a few such records.

Court records sometimes are helpful in providing genealogical information about individuals. (Chapter eight discusses court records in greater detail.) One such case came before the Ohio Supreme Court in December 1843.[5] Thomas Lane, who lived in Silvercreek, Greene County, Ohio, sent his son John Eldridge Lane and his other two children to school on 25 January 1841. They were not allowed to stay at school because it was said that they were Indian children, not white. The issue in the case was the degree of Indian blood, which was determined to be less than one-half. The court decided in Lane's favor that the children be considered white. The original court records may contain more information than the printed report, including perhaps the names of the other children and the identity of the Indian ancestor(s).

Congressional documents in the *New American State Papers: Indian Affairs* (Volumes 3 and 4: Northwest; Volumes 6–13: Southeast) and the Gales and Seaton (1834) *American State Papers: Indian Affairs* (two volumes) contain speeches, letters, treaties, and information on Indian agencies and agents, trade and traders, land, annuities, and expenses related to Indian affairs. (See chapter eight for more on these records.) In December 1817, Congress received for consideration treaties with several Indian tribes, including the Shawanee [*sic*], Ottawa, Seneca, and Wyandots. Among the provisions were agreements for land grants in Ohio for various named chiefs and other individuals. Part of this list is shown in Figure 10-7, on page 371. As shown in this example, many of the Congressional records help place specific individuals in a given place at a given time. However, this document also contains genealogical information:

- Sarah Williams, earlier captured by the Indians, married a half-blood Wyandot named Isaac Williams, now deceased, and had two children, Joseph Williams and Rachael Williams, now Rachael Nugent.
- Catharine Walker was a Wyandot woman whose son John R. Walker had been wounded in the service of the U.S. at the battle of Mauguagon in 1812.

Online links to other Native American records, rolls, and history are available through the National Archives Web site at <www.archives.gov/research_room/alic/reference _desk/native_american_links.html>. One of the links is to Cyndi's List <www.cyndislist.com>. Another is to a Native American genealogy site at <www.accessgenealogy.com/native/> with a number of records transcriptions and links to state sites and tribal contact information. Investigate other online opportunities for American Indian records, such as the Digital Library of Georgia from the University of Georgia at Athens <http://dlg.galileo.usg.edu/>.

MILITARY RECORDS

Federal military records show that American Indians have participated in the military in many capacities over the years. For example, Navajo members of the U.S. Marine Corps provided unique skills as "code talkers" in the Pacific theater during World War II. An interesting article on their service is "Semper Fidelis, Code Talkers," by Adam Jevec, in the National Archives *Prologue* 33 (Winter 2001), also online at <www.archives.gov/publications/prologue/winter _2001_navajo_code_talkers.html>.

ART. 8. At the special request of the said Indians, the United States agree to grant by patent, in fee-simple, to the persons hereinafter mentioned, all of whom are connected with the said Indians by blood or adoption, the tracts of land herein described:

To Elizabeth Whitaker, who was taken prisoner by the Wyandots, and has ever since lived among them, twelve hundred and eighty acres of land on the west side of the Sandusky river, below Croghansville, to be laid off in a square form, as nearly as the meanders of the said river will admit, and to run an equal distance above and below the house in which the said Elizabeth Whitaker now lives.

To Robert Armstrong, who was taken prisoner by the Indians, and has ever since lived among them, and has married a Wyandot woman, one section, to contain six hundred and forty acres of land, on the west side of the Sandusky river, to begin at the place called Camp Ball, and to run up the river, with the meanders thereof, one hundred and sixty poles; and from the beginning, down the river, with the meanders thereof, one hundred and sixty poles; and from the extremity of these lines, west, for quantity.

To the children of the late William McCollock, who was killed in August, 1812, near Mauguagon, and who are quarter-blood Wyandot Indians, one section, to contain six hundred and forty acres of land, on the west side of the Sandusky river, adjoining the lower line of the tract hereby granted to Robert Armstrong, and extending in the same manner with and from the said river.

To John Vanmeter, who was taken prisoner by the Wyandots, and who has ever since lived among them, and has married a Seneca woman, and to his wife's three brothers, Senecas, who now reside on Honey creek, one thousand acres of land, to begin north, forty-five degrees west, one hundred and forty poles from the house in which the said John Vanmeter now lives; and to run thence, south, three hundred and twenty poles; thence, and from the beginning, east, for quantity.

To Sarah Williams, Joseph Williams, and Rachael Nugent, late Rachael Williams, the said Sarah having been taken prisoner by the Indians, and ever since lived amongst them, and being the widow, and the said Joseph and Rachael being the children of the late Isaac Williams, a half-blood Wyandot, one quarter-section of land, to contain one hundred and sixty acres on the east side of the Sandusky river, below Croghansville, and to include their improvements at a place called Negro Point.

To Catharine Walker, a Wyandot woman, and to John R. Walker, her son, who was wounded in the service of the United States at the battle of Mauguagon, in 1812, a section of six hundred and forty acres of land, each, to begin at the northwestern corner of the tract hereby granted to John Vanmeter and his wife's brothers, and to run with the line thereof, south, three hundred and twenty poles; thence, and from the beginning, west, for quantity.

To William Spicer, who was taken prisoner by the Indians, and has ever since lived among them, and has married a Seneca woman, a section of land to contain six hundred and forty acres, beginning on the east bank of the Sandusky river, forty poles below the lower corner of said Spicer's corn field; thence, up the river on the east side, with the meanders thereof, one mile; thence, and from the beginning, east, for quantity.

To Nancy Stewart, daughter of the late Shawanee chief Blue Jacket, one section of land, to contain six hundred and forty acres, on the Great Miami river, below Lewistown, to include her present improvements; three-quarters of the said section to be on the southeast side of the river, and one-quarter on the northwest side thereof.

Figure 10-7 *American State Papers: Documents, Legislative and Executive, of the Congress of the United States.* Class II: Indian Affairs, 1789-1827 (Washington, D.C.: Gales and Seaton, 1832-1861), 2:149 (1817).

Some Indians allied themselves with the Confederate cause during the Civil War. Microfilmed Civil War records pertaining to these American Indians include the following; the first three are compiled service records:

- M266, Confederate soldiers who served in organizations from the state of Georgia, rolls 578–579, Cherokee Legion.
- M269, Confederate soldiers who served in organizations from Mississippi, roll 7, First Choctaw Battalion, Cavalry.
- M258, Confederate soldiers who served in organizations raised directly by the Confederate government. Rolls 77–91 are units of Cherokee, Choctaw, Chickasaw, Creek, Osage, and Seminole soldiers. Contents of each roll are described in the National Archives select catalog *American Indians* and on the Web site <www.archives.gov/publications/microfilm_catalogs.html>, under "subject catalogs."
- M836, Confederate states army casualties, roll 3, Newtonia, Missouri (1862), Choctaw and Chickasaw regiments, Bryan's Battalion of Cherokees; roll 7, Indian Territory (1862), Creek and Cherokee regiments.
- M861, compiled records showing service of military units in Confederate organizations. Roll 74 contains information on the Indian units.

See Also

Compiled service records, pension records, and other evidence of service are discussed in chapter six.

Other Native Americans scouted for and fought with United States forces before, during, and after the Civil War. The indexes to military pensions indicate a significant number who participated in the "Old Wars," Mexican War, Civil War, and Indian wars. These are some of the National Archives microfilm dealing with their military service:

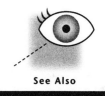

- M594, compiled service records of military units in volunteer Union (Civil War) organizations. Roll 225 includes Indian Home Guards.

- M233, registers of enlistments in the U.S. Army, 1798–1914. Roll 70—Indian Scouts, 1866–1877; roll 71—Indian Scouts, 1878–1914.
- P2292, formerly 7RA347, Register of Indians in World War I, 1 roll. Not a nationwide list.
- M1829, compiled military service records of Major Uriah Blue's detachment of Chickasaw Indians in the War of 1812.
- M1830, compiled military service records of Major McIntosh's company of Creek Indians in the War of 1812, 1 roll.
- M1785, index to pension application files of remarried widows based on service in the Civil War and later wars and in the Regular Army after the Civil War, 7 rolls.
- M1784, index to pension application files of remarried widows based on service in the War of 1812, Indian Wars, Mexican War, and Regular Army before 1861, 1 roll. This includes Indian widows, especially those whose husbands had served as scouts for the army.

See also books and articles about Indian involvement in the military. Examples include

- *The American Revolution in Indian Country: Crisis and Diversity in Native American Communities*, by Colin G. Calloway. New York: Cambridge University Press, 1995. Throughout the American frontier, Indians fought on both sides of the conflict but, on the whole, preferred to stay neutral.
- *The Confederate Cherokees: John Drew's Regiment of Mounted Rifles*, by W. Craig Gaines. Baton Rouge: Louisiana State University Press, 1989.
- *Guide to Genealogical Research in the National Archives of the United States*. Washington, D.C.: National Archives and Records Administration, 2000. Pages 213–215.
- *Indians in the War: Burial of a Brave*, by the U.S. Bureau of Indian Affairs. Chicago: U.S. Department of the Interior, Office of Indian Affairs, 1945.
- *Indices of Choctaw and Chickasaw Confederate Soldiers*, Monty Olsen, transcriber. Calera, Okla.: Bryan County Heritage Association, 1996.
- *The Iroquois in the American Revolution*, by Barbara Graymont. Syracuse, N.Y.: Syracuse University Press, 1972. United by blood and language, the Iroquois were organized as the Six Nations or Six Nations Confederacy, including the Mohawks, Senecas, Onondagas, Oneidas, Cayugas, and Tuscaroras, living in the New York-Ontario region at the time of the American Revolution. Both the Loyalists (Tories) and the Americans (Whigs) sought help from the Iroquois. The Mohawks, Cayugas, Senecas, and most of the Onondagas sided with the British. The Oneidas and most of the Tuscaroras aided the Americans. By the end of the war, the ancient unity was shattered.
- *The Iroquois in the Civil War: From Battlefield to Reservation*, by Laurence M. Hauptman. Syracuse, N.Y.: Syracuse University Press, 1993.
- *Men of Color at the Battle of Monmouth, June 28, 1778: The Role of African Americans and Native Americans at Monmouth . . .*, by Richard S. Walling. Hightown, N.J.: Longstreet House, 1994.

Case Study

Case Study: Private Isaac Ah-pah-kee

Military pension files vary in the amount of information they provide; you cannot know what is there until you look. The file of Isaac Ah-pah-kee provides an amazing amount of information about the veteran, his friends, and his family, as summarized here.[6]

On the ninth of June 1864, Isaac Ah-pah-kee was a healthy eighteen-year-old, a hunter and farmer of the Menominee reservation in Shawano County, Wisconsin. That day, he enlisted as a private for three years' service in Captain James W. Hitchcock's Company K of the 37th Wisconsin Volunteers (Infantry). His service to the Grand Army of the Republic began in the last year of the war.

His company arrived in the vicinity of Petersburg, Virginia, about July 23. According to the assistant adjutant general, during battle about August 19, (July 20 according to Isaac, July 30 by another report) an exploding shell injured Isaac's right hand with wounds severe enough that the surgeon had to amputate his ring and middle fingers to the knuckles and part of his forefinger. Afterward, he was unable to close his hand because the fingers were stiff. Isaac recalled that he received treatment at a hospital at Cedar Point, about five miles from Petersburg, for three days and then a hospital just northwest of Washington City, where he was discharged and sent home in July 1864. The adjutant general's office reported that Isaac was present for duty in February, March, and April 1865 and was mustered out, with an honorable discharge, on 27 July 1865. (Was 1865 a clerical error? How can they explain the February to April muster rolls?)

Reminder

Expect discrepancies in records such as these. (1) The pension file reports dates as each participant estimated them. (2) Clerks spelled names as well as they could when transliterating Indian names into English syllables.

About ten years after the war, in May 1875 or 1876, Isaac married at about age twenty-nine; his wife later claimed it was 1875. She clarified the lack of a marriage record, saying that marriages were not recorded on the reservation at that time. When she and Isaac met, she believed she was thirteen and he, about thirty-one. Regardless of his actual age, he was considerably older than his bride. She was Catherine Moses, born to Menominee parents at or near Keshena on the Menominee reservation in 1858, 1863, or, as she later reported, November 1864. The priest who married Isaac and Catherine was a traveling priest who came to Keshena occasionally and held services for the Catholic Indians.

In the 1920s, the St. Michael's parish priest generated a marriage certificate with the date 10 May 1876 and with the bride's name as Catherine Moses and Isaac's transliterated name as Isaac Parkins. The witnesses were Anthony Wanpachick(?) and Sepachon Moses.

Filing for a Pension

Just before Christmas of 1875, Isaac went before the clerk of the circuit court of Shawano County to apply for an invalid's pension, being "greatly disabled" by his wartime injuries. His friends Edward She-she-quin and Mitchel Oshawano-mah-taw witnessed his mark and his testimony. The following June, Isaac testified that none of the officers of his regiment could be found to substantiate his testimony as none lived in his part of the state and his captain had left the state shortly after the close of the war. A fellow Company K veteran, Private Joseph Pahyahwausitt, stepped in to support Isaac's story.

Moving with typical bureaucratic speed, the adjutant general's office acknowledged receipt of Isaac's pension application eight months after he signed it. That office then requested a hospital report on Isaac's case (gunshot wound to the right hand). The surgeon general's office, in October 1877, could not corroborate either version of the events as the regimental records were not on file, and they could find no record of the Cedar Point hospital.

This lack of records to verify Isaac's testimony caused another delay in processing his application. In March 1878, fifteen months after the process began, another private from Company K, Wah-sha-kah-ka-mick Peter, "having been present at the time," affirmed Isaac's version of the story before the Indian Agent at Keshena, with William N. Rogers and John W. Satterlee as witnesses. The adjutant general's office then searched the available records for evidence of the affiant's story and reported that "Robert" Wah-sha-kah-ka-mick of Company K was present for duty in July and August 1864, but the name of Wah-sha-kah-ka-mick-Peter did not appear on rolls of Company K. After several years of these back-and-forth proceedings, the pension office approved Isaac's pension.

Filing for a Pension Increase

By 1886, Isaac's pension was six dollars a month, but he was no longer able to work. He went before the Indian agent, Thomas Jennings, to apply for a pension increase due to a "sprained back." His friends and fellow Company K veterans, John Shawano-pe-nas (age forty-four) and Charles Ah-pah-to-ka-sick (age forty), declared they had known Isaac for thirty years, lived near him, and knew him to be sound and well when he enlisted. Since the war, Charles had worked with Isaac in the lumber woods and through one haying. At that time, Isaac was able to do only "three-quarters work," earning thirty dollars a month, while Charles earned thirty-five dollars. The difference in wages, he believed was due to Isaac's disability. John, being a close neighbor, saw Isaac often, heard him complain of his back, and knew he could not stand straight. Once he was confined to bed for most of a year and, when up, had to use a cane and could not work. About seven years after the first "attack," Isaac suffered a similar attack that confined him to bed all winter, and by 1886 was troubled constantly with this problem.

Both witnesses believed the injury occurred while Isaac was in the service. They explained that during the battle at Petersburg, their company had captured an earthwork but were driven out afterwards by the rebels on 30 July 1864. As they retreated, Isaac jumped or fell into a trench and, in doing so, hurt his back. He had suffered from this injury since the war, and the disability had grown worse with time. The surgeon, J.S. Williams, who examined Isaac in April 1887, found tenderness in the spine and a slight lateral curvature of the spine in the middle dorsal region of the back, which he felt was about two inches out of line. (Figure 10-8, on page 375, shows Dr. Williams's drawing of the injury.) He found Isaac to be of average intellect but speaking very poor English. Perhaps language difficulties explained his slow and hesitating speech. At six feet tall and 140 pounds, he was anemic and had a very rapid heart beat. The doctor agreed that the worsening back condition made him unable to work and that he could find no cause for the disease other than an injury.

In checking the testimony of the witnesses, the pension office within the War Department could not find John Shaw-wah-ne-pe-nass and Charles Hah-pah-to-ka-sic on the rolls but did not find them on the absent rolls, either. At the end of 1891, after checking the unit records, they confirmed that Company K, on the July 30 in question, was in an assault on the enemy's works near Petersburg. After considerable delay, Isaac's pension increased to eight dollars a month.

The Department of the Interior, Pension Bureau, requested further information from Isaac in 1898 and 1899. He answered the questionnaire, naming his only wife as Katherine Ahpahkee-Ka-tish, whom he married about 1873. Although the couple had lost an infant in 1898, the three living children in February 1899 were Michael Ahpahkee, born 13 May 1877; George Ahpahkee, born 29 March 1884; and Elizabeth Ahpahkee, born 21 January 1893. Whoever furnished these birth dates from the church register apparently confused the four Elizabeths born to the couple. According to the register, the second Elizabeth, born on 21 January 1893, died four days after her birth; the third Elizabeth, born 20 January 1894, was supposedly the one still living. (The first Elizabeth lived 1880–1889. With the third Elizabeth still alive in 1899, a fourth Elizabeth was born and died on the day of her birth in April 1899. Probably the name repetition reflected baptismal names.)

In answer to further questions, in June 1899, Isaac's friends John Shawanopenas, now sixty-two, and Louis Mashaquette, age fifty-six, affirmed before the deputy clerk of the

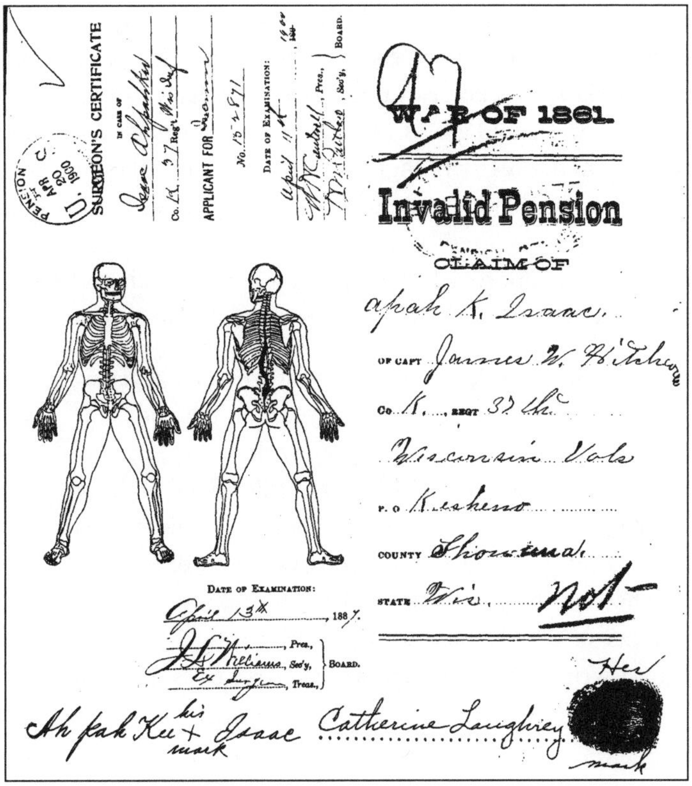

Figure 10-8 Composite of items from the Civil War pension files of Isaac Ah-pah-kee and his widow, Catherine Ah-pah-kee Shunion Laughrey. It includes the 1887 and 1900 physicians' reports that show Isaac's injuries, his mark, and Catherine's fingerprint mark.

circuit court of Shawano County that Isaac had suffered at least eight years with eczema, had weakness in the knee joints that caused him difficulty in walking, and was troubled increasingly with sore eyes, to the extent that he was blind in his right eye and had only partial sight in the left. They considered him three-quarters disabled from earning a living and declared that "his disabilities are not due to vicious habits."

When three doctors examined him in April 1900, they confirmed the disabilities reported by his friends, including "no evidence of vicious habits," and added weakness in both arms due to rheumatism, pain in the chest, difficulty in breathing, and haziness of vision in the left eye with evidence of cataract. He had gained weight to 170 pounds but at about age fifty-four was in rapidly failing health. He died about 23 January 1902.

The Widow's Pension

Isaac and Catherine were communicants of the Catholic Church at Keshena where their children's births and deaths were recorded. In the twenty-five or twenty-six years of their marriage, the couple had sixteen children—about one every eighteen months. Even in a time of high infant mortality, the Ah-pah-kee family experienced more than its share of loss. Five infants died within a week of birth; four others, before their first birthday; three more, before or just after their second birthday. The first of the four Elizabeths lived almost to her ninth birthday; the third Elizabeth lived at least that long.

Soon after Isaac's death, Catherine applied for a widow's pension. Two longtime friends and neighbors, David Istoca (age seventy-five) and Frank Maskewit (age sixty-five), confirmed that they had been present at the marriage of Isaac Ahpahkee and Catherine Shawanokesic in 1875, that neither had been previously married, and that the widow had not remarried since Isaac's death. As of March 1902, she had one living child under the age of sixteen: Elizabeth Ahpahkee, born on 20 January 1894, as shown in the church records.

According to a copy of the church records supplied with the pension request, the sons Michael (age twenty-five) and George (age eighteen) were also living. At that time, Catherine owned a log house valued at fifty dollars, two ponies valued at forty dollars, a sleigh and a wagon valued at thirty dollars, and household goods valued at about thirty dollars. Her house was on tribal land on the Menominee reservation; thus she owned no real estate. She had no means of support other than manual labor and rations issued to her as a poor and destitute member of the tribe.

Although her pension application was approved, her situation was complicated by a letter of complaint written on 20 March 1903 to the War Department, Pension Office:

> Sir—I thought I would write you few words to tell you about when I was trying to get my pension papers that you put me back and I am going to tell about the widow of Icea Apakea that she is got a man there staying with her as husband & she is still getting pension money right along[.] I should think you ought to stay her getting that pension as long as she is marry another man[.] this is what I am going to tell you & please let me know if this letter reach you & I would like to have put her some whers so she can think what big mistake she done. I know that man stayed with her or married her just before she got her pension. I am James Washonahquette I write this letter because Icae Apakea is my own brother.

Off Again, On Again

Catherine's pension terminated officially when she married James Shunion. Originally they were married by a justice of the peace and remarried in the church at the time of James's baptism on 25 October 1909 at Little Oconto, on the part of the Menominee reservation that extended into Oconto County. However, James died four days later, on October 29. After his death, or at least in 1910, Catherine apparently lived on the Oconto County part of the reservation with her son Michae[l] "Puhkun" (close to Pahkee or Parkin) and his family that included a son named Isac. The census listed her there as Catherine, widowed mother of the head of household, age forty-seven (suggesting a birth date of 1863), a full-blood Menominee, speaking only the Menominee language, having been married twice and having borne fifteen [*sic*] children, of whom only two were living.[7] (Figure 10-9, on page 377, shows this census.)

On 28 September 1910, a justice of the peace at Marinette, Wisconsin, united Catherine in marriage to a three-quarter-blood Menominee man, James C. Laughrey, about ten years her junior, who worked as a laborer in the "lumber woods." They lived on the reservation at the time of the 1920 census.[8] Catherine again became a widow when James died, 17 December 1920, as the result of an operation at St. Joseph Hospital in Milwaukee.

Notes

Under several laws of Congress, especially 1916 and 1920, remarried widows who had lost their pensions upon remarriage and had again become widows could resume their places on the pension roll. Thus, Catherine Laughrey began the application process again, providing proof of all three marriages and the deaths of her second and third husbands. One complicating factor was the fact that several records transliterated Isaac Ahpahkee's surname to Parkins. The Pension Board's Board of Review wanted to know whether Isaac was ever known as Parkins, whether Catherine had ever been divorced, how many times she had actually been married, whether her later husbands had ever served in the military, and whether there was truth in "some slight indication that she lived with Shuneon prior to the date she married him."

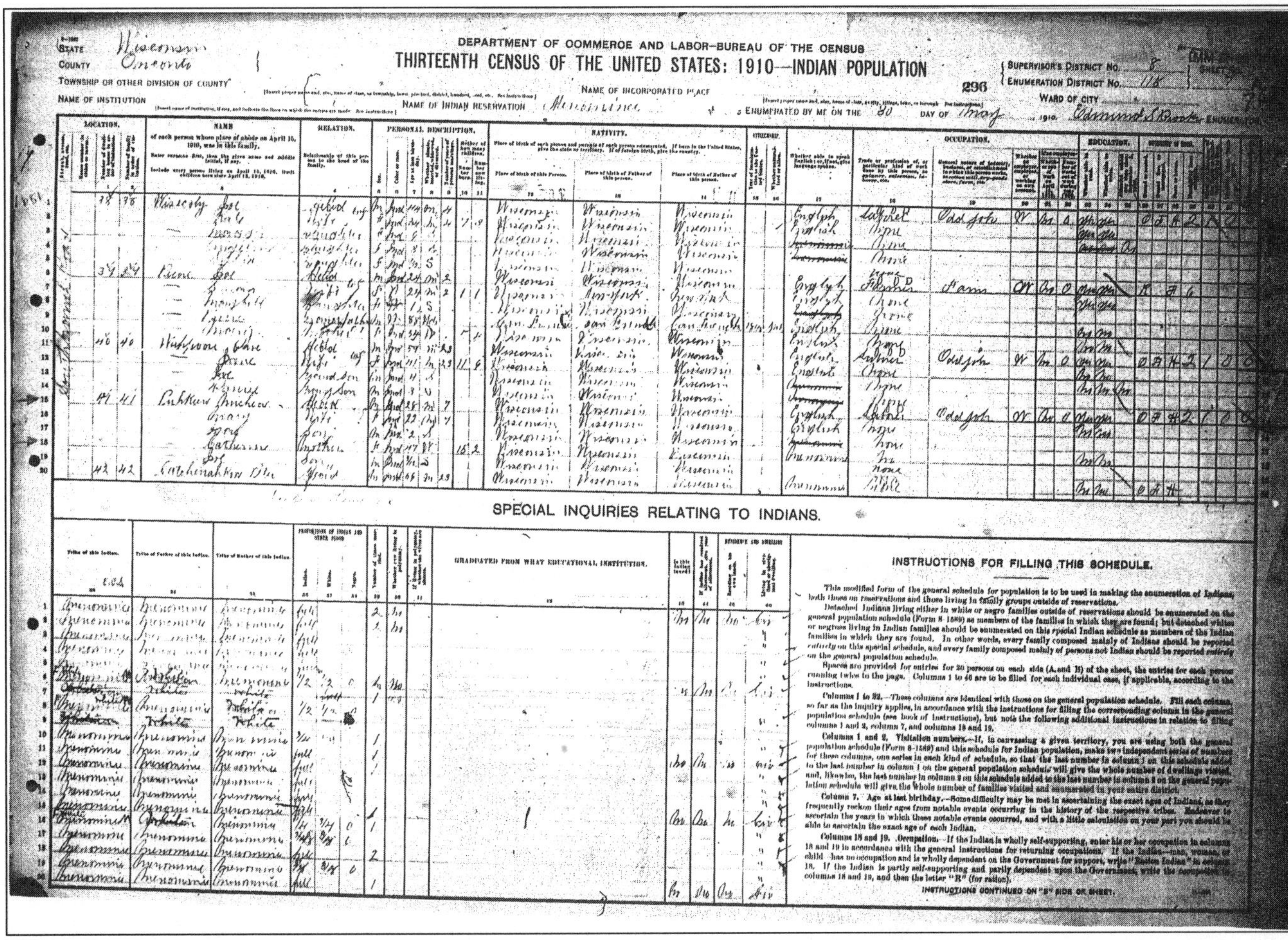

Figure 10-9 U.S. Census of 1910, roll 1729, Oconto County, Wisconsin, Menominee Reservation, Indian Schedule, e.d. 115, sheet 7A, line 15, household of Michael Puhkun.

Thus, at Keshena in October 1923, with the aid of the interpreter Mitchell Waukau, who was also the only witness present, special examiner W.B. Uppercue took a lengthy deposition from Catherine. According to his report, she was "solely illiterate and her statement was taken with great difficulty." At this time, the widow was supporting herself with money she received from doing "Indian fancy work, that is beading and so forth." Catherine affirmed that she lived with each of her three (and only three) husbands to the date of death and without divorce and vowed that she did not assume marital relations with Jim Shunion before her ceremonial marriage to him. She reported that Isaac was never known by a name other than Ah-pah-kee, although the English pronunciation and spelling of that name is Parkins.

Catherine reported her maiden name as Moses and her father's name as Mitchell Moses. She never knew her mother's maiden name or her mother, who died when Catherine was an infant. Catherine's two sisters, Louise Bijou and Cecilia McPherson had died by 1923; she had one cousin, Louie Warden of Keshena. She clarified that Isaac had died at South Branch on the part of the reservation in Oconto County. However, because the agency house was at Keshena and they called any place within several miles of it by the name Keshena, she had reported earlier that Isaac died at Keshena. Catherine claimed that she married Jim Shunion in March 1902, before which time she lived alone with her three children; she named witnesses who had attended the marriage ceremony and could confirm her story. She and Shunion had a son named William, born in 1903, who lived only three months. Of the sixteen children she and Isaac had had, only the eldest, Mitchell on the deposition but Michael in the church record, was living in 1923. Her cousin, Louie Warden, was the only one she knew of who knew Isaac before their marriage; she knew nothing of his life before she met him but believed he had not been married before he married her.

After Catherine's deposition, the interpreter, who was also the chief of police on the reservation, affirmed that he had known Catherine "as long as I am able to remember. We have always lived close neighbors here on the reservation, and I have known practically every move she had made." He confirmed her deposition as correct information and added, "The claimant is a woman of the best type of moral character." The same day, John V. Satterlee, now age seventy-one, also testified on Catherine's behalf, giving the same answers she had given and saying he had known Catherine since she was a child and had "known of most everything she ever did, I guess. . . . [she] has always been a woman of excellent moral character."

The special examiner searched the Shawano County records and found no evidence of other marriages or any divorce for Catherine, under any of her five surnames, between 1876 and 1923. Her place on the pension roll was finally restored.

Epilogue

An anonymous letter of complaint was added to Catherine's pension file in January 1924. Written to the pension commissioner, it alleged what the writer considered misconduct which violated pension policy, but apparently the pension office took no action on it.

> Dear Sir: I wish to depose a fault in regard to a Widow investing her pension money, for luxury, Catherine Lawghery her former name, Mrs. Catherine Pawkey. She drawed her pension two or three months ago, she bought an automobile from Jno Pop, in Shawano furthermore turns over her monthly pension to pay the balance or the installments she goes by her son's name another thing about her present disposition She's keeping courtship from several men, a party found some money hid nearby her house which was put there for her from a sweetheart that's the way she has money but wouldn't pay her hiring for the providing of wood all fall I close to
>
> Yours Respectfully
>
> P.S. If there is any doubtness about this, the Goverment [*sic*] can have his man to watch and would soon find out the fact a whistle is a signal the old lady pops out of her house I suppose there is a poor show inside, because her Son stays with her.

The widow Catherine Laughrey was under a doctor's care for several weeks before she died at St. Joseph's Indian Hospital in Keshena village on 8 October 1936; her death certificate reported her age as seventy-eight. By her reckoning, she would have been almost seventy-two. An unidentified family member was the informant, naming Catherine's parents as Jno. Shawanokesic and Theresa (maiden name unknown). One must ask whether Moses was a Christian surname assumed upon baptism.

The story of these two ordinary, poor, and illiterate individuals could not be told without the pension file, much of which was generated in the government's effort to confirm what the couple reported. Research into other agency and reservation records, tribal and federal censuses, pension payment records, and county and church records may yet enhance and enlarge their story.

PRE-FEDERAL AND COLONIAL RECORDS

Prior to the American Revolution, contact with American Indians was the concern of the governments mostly of Spain, France, Great Britain, and the North American colonies. Records relating to trade, missions, exploration, armies, and colonial settlements are found in the archives of these European countries and the original U.S. states. In addition, some colonial period records relating to Indians are in the microfilmed *Papers of the Continental Congress, 1774–1789* in research libraries. Most of these records are historical and governmental rather than genealogical, although lineage information (a father's name or a mother-son relationship) occasionally is tucked into such records.

Research Tip

If your American Indian genealogy leads you to the eighteenth century, investigate colonial and county records in the original states. Look in library catalogs for published histories and records of the pre-federal period and ask about special collections of Native American materials in academic and public libraries in the area where a specific tribe lived. Consult guides to manuscript collections in state and academic archives and libraries. These efforts sometimes yield information not contained in government records.

Two examples illustrate genealogical information that is sometimes available in early records. The region of northern Mexico and the Big Bend area of Texas surrounding the junction of the Rio Grande with the Rio Conchos was known to the Spaniards as La Junta de los Rios del Norte y Conchos. West Texan Henrique Rede Madrid translated a Spanish report that contains early census records of the area in his *Expedition to La Junta de los Rios, 1747–1748: Captain Commander Joseph de Ydoiaga's Report to the Viceroy of New Spain* (Austin, Tex.: Texas Historical Commission, Office of the State Archaeologist, Special Report 33, 1992). As he traveled, Ydoiaga took censuses in the La Junta region, recording names of heads of household (with marital status and number of children), unmarried women, and bachelors, noting Christian baptism for some. The residents were Indians as well as persons of mixed Indian and Spanish ancestry. Maps in the book help identify the location of the villages, some of which correspond to communities in the same location today.

A second example is in the Archives of the Big Bend at Sul Ross State University in Alpine, Texas: presidio and church records from the La Junta region. Although the presidio and church were on the south side of the Rio Grande, they served the north (or Texas) side as well. The same scenario occurred up and down the Rio Grande and along what is now the entire U.S.–Mexico border. The La Junta church records, 1775–1857, from present Ojinaga in Mexico, contain baptism and marriage registrations. The baptism records give the name of the child, the baptism date, sometimes the age of the child at the time of baptism, parents' names and place of origin, and sometimes godparents' names. Between 1807 and the 1820s, a number of Apache children were baptized there. Soldiers at the presidio had to petition the commanding officer for permission to marry local women, and the records often reflect names of parents of both bride and groom. Selected records have been published in "Settlement and Settlers at La Junta de los Rios, 1759–1822," by Oakah L. Jones, in *The Journal of Big Bend Studies* (Alpine, Tex.: Sul Ross State University) 3 (January 1991): 43–70. Such records are wonderful when researchers can tie into them, but working back from the twentieth century to the late eighteenth is the challenge. The farther back in time the American Indian ancestry extends (on either side of the current border), the more scarce are the records that tie a lineage together.

Case Study

CASE STUDY: IDENTIFYING THE CHEROKEE PROGENITORS OF HILLIARD ROGERS

Cherokee researcher Marjorie Lowe is a great-granddaughter of Sarah Ann "Annie" Rogers, who married Nelson F. Carr on 25 August 1867.[9] Marjorie grew up knowing her connection to Sarah Carr; the Dawes roll and later documents confirm the line of descent. As a child, with her grandmother Jennie (Carr) Johnson, Marjorie visited the grave site of Sarah's father, Hilliard Rogers. As an adult and a genealogist, she wanted to know more about Hilliard's Cherokee ancestry and, thus, her own. Using a combination of cluster genealogy, clues from published sources, and original documents, she was able to discover several additional generations.

What Did She Know About Hilliard Rogers?

1. The Carr family's Dawes roll census card and the corresponding file identified Sarah A. Carr's parents as Hilliard and Martha Rogers.[10]
2. Based on his age when he died, Hilliard Rogers was born 26 March 1819, reportedly a son of John and Tiana (Foster) Rogers. Sarah Carr's 1900, 1910, and 1920 federal census enumerations and her brother's 1900 enumeration reported Hilliard's birth in Georgia; he was born probably in the Cherokee Nation.[11]
3. Hilliard married Martha Ann "Patsy" Fields probably in 1841 in the Cherokee Nation, Indian Territory. Based on her age at death, her birth date was 6 March 1825.[12]
4. Hilliard died 5 September 1870, in what was then Cooweescoowee District, Cherokee Nation, Indian Territory. He was buried beside his wife in the Gilstrap Cemetery near present Bartlesville in what is now Washington County, Oklahoma. His wife predeceased him on 18 January 1870.[13]

Confirmation of Hilliard's Parents

A source closer in time to Hilliard than the book of tombstone inscriptions was Emmet Starr's notes on Cherokee lineages, published in 1921. Starr also reported Hilliard Rogers and his nine siblings as children of John and Tiana (Foster) Rogers.[14]

In June 1906, to satisfy decrees of the Court of Claims in favor of the Eastern Cherokees, Congress authorized payment to these Cherokees for the improvements they had made on their lands and were forced to leave behind when they were removed to Oklahoma in the 1830s. Guion Miller was given the task of determining the roll of eligible recipients for the settlement money. Applicants had to be Eastern and Western Cherokees who were alive at the time of the 1835–1836 and 1845 treaties and were members of the Eastern Cherokee tribe or their descendants. As a qualified claimant because of her parents' tribal affiliation, Sarah Ann (Rogers) Carr applied for her share of the distribution. Her 1907 application file contained much valuable family history:[15]

- The supplemental application for her five adult children—all enrolled Cherokees—to share in the distribution listed her six surviving children who were alive as of 30 June 1906, the cut-off date, with their birth dates and the married names of three daughters.
- Sarah's application reported that she was born on 3 November 1848 in the Delaware District of the Cherokee Nation, Indian Territory. Her residence in September 1906 was three miles north of Bartlesville, Indian Territory. Her husband, Nelson F. Carr, was then sixty-two years old.
- Her parents were Hillard [*sic*] and Martha "Patsy" (Fields) Rogers, born in Georgia and Tennessee, respectively. Their death dates were the same as reported in the cemetery book already cited.

- Sarah listed all nine children born to Hillard and Patsy, with birth and death dates as known. She and her younger brother William G. Rogers were the only two of the siblings to survive childhood. The last child, who was born in 1870 and died in February 1870, survived his mother by only a few weeks; these dates suggest Patsy may have died as a result of childbirth.
- Sarah also named all known siblings of Hillard and Patsy, along with residences or death dates. Hillard's siblings matched the list later published in Emmet Starr's Cherokee history.
- The notary taking the information recorded Sarah's paternal grandparents as John and *Dianna* Rogers, her maternal grandparents as John/Jack and Elizabeth Fields. This information supported the Rogers parents' names given in the Starr history—John and *Tiana*. When asked about degree of Indian blood, Sarah reported that John Rogers was a white man; Dianna Rogers was Cherokee by blood. John Fields was Cherokee by blood, and Elizabeth Fields was a white woman.
- In 1851 her parents were living in Delaware District of the Cherokee Nation, Indian Territory. She and her parents were enrolled at Fort Gibson in 1851, were on all other rolls of the Cherokee Nation, and "participated in all annuities and lands since 1851."

Attached to the Miller report is a typed transcription of the Chapman and Drennen rolls of 1851. Indeed, the Drennen roll showed, in the Delaware District of the Cherokee Nation, the household of Hilliard Rogers, including his wife, Martha, and children Uniza, Sarah [later Carr], and John.[16]

Investigating Tiana Rogers

With the clues from the Miller roll application that Hilliard Rogers's mother was Cherokee, research turned to Tiana/Dianna Rogers. Much research is possible with microfilmed records, but sometimes the links and confirmations lie in manuscript sources available only on location. In this case, Marjorie had heard about a document that named Tiana and her father in relation to some property. Under the circumstances, the document probably would not have been a will, and because the Cherokee owned land as a tribe rather than as individuals, the property would not have been land.

On a visit to the National Archives in Washington, DC, Marjorie questioned a staff member, who led her to the Cherokee Valuations in Georgia, a set of documents consisting of multiple manuscript volumes and unbound papers. Because these records are not indexed, it was necessary to look through the files one at a time. Well into the search, Marjorie spotted the name of Tiana Rodgers in a document of one James Foster.

In September 1837, through an interpreter, Foster requested that the improvements he had made on his farm be transferred to *his daughter Tiana Rodgers*, "as it was her just right and property," valued at $497.50.[17] The farm was in the Salaquoyah Creek area of Cass (later renamed Bartow) County, Georgia. The document describes the property in detail, providing a good picture of Foster's farm and probably Tiana's former home: a hewed-log dwelling house eighteen feet square with a plank floor and roof, another dwelling sixteen feet square, a separate kitchen sixteen feet square with a plank floor, a split-timber smokehouse of the same size, a stable made of round logs (twenty feet square), four apple trees, twenty-seven peach trees, a half-acre horse lot, and nine acres of improved (cultivated) land. (Figure 10-10, on page 382, shows the document which provided Tiana's father's name.)

Figure 10-10 Valuation No. 244 of James Foster, 1837, Cherokee Valuations, Cass County, Georgia, Record Group 75, Records of the Bureau of Indian Affairs, National Archives building, Washington.

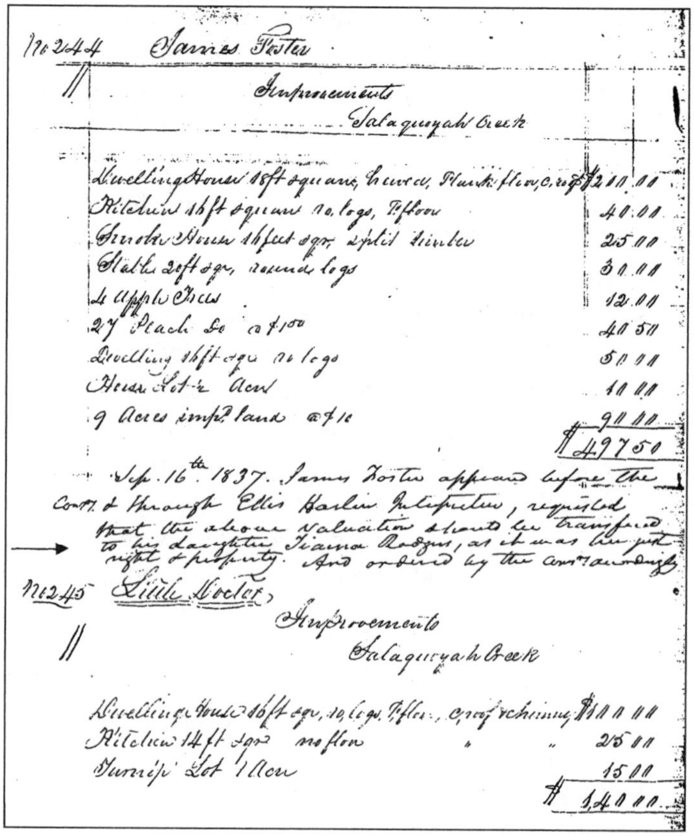
No 244 James Foster

Improvements

Salaquayah Creek

Dwelling House 18 ft square, hewed, Plank floor, c.	$200.00
Kitchen 16 ft square rd. logs, floor	40.00
Smoke House 16 feet sqr, split timber	25.00
Stable 20 ft sqr, round logs	30.00
4 Apple Trees	12.00
27 Peach do @ $1.50	40.50
Dwelling 16 ft sqr rd logs	50.00
House Lot ½ Acre	10.00
9 Acres impd land @ $10	90.00
	$497.50

Sep. 16th 1837. James Foster appeared before the Comrs & through Ellis Harlin Interpreter, requested that the above valuation should be transferred to his daughter Tiana Rodgers, as it was her just right & property. And ordered by the Comrs accordingly

No 245 Little Doctor,

Improvements

Salaquayah Creek

Dwelling House 16 ft sqr, rd logs, floor, chimney	$100.00
Kitchen 14 ft sqr no floor	25.00
Turnip Lot 1 Acre	15.00
	$140.00

Investigating James Foster

Considering that Hilliard Rogers was born in 1819, possibly the eldest child of his parents, it is clear that his mother, Tiana, was born probably within a few years before or after 1800, perhaps no later than 1805.[18] Her father, James Foster, therefore was born possibly no later than 1780–1785. The farther back in time genealogists research, the more extant records for all ethnic groups in the United States generally dwindle. Thus, the choices for research narrow, and the genealogist must learn about and focus on what is available for any given location and any particular ethnic group. **Especially when looking for female ancestors in this period, study often must focus on the husband and other members of the family cluster.**

Research Tip

In this effort, Marjorie Lowe learned about a source pertinent to the early-nineteenth-century Cherokee Nation in an article in *Chronicles of Oklahoma.* This led her to the National Archives microfilm of letters to the Cherokee Agency to look for further evidence of James Foster, Tiana's father.

She finally found an affidavit dated 23 April 1845, with information from one Looney Hicks. He said he

> was well acquainted with James Foster, the Father of Ti-ha-na, the wife of John Rogers, commonly called and known as 'Little John Rogers,' that knowing the character and circumstances of said James Foster, who having in the Old Cherokee Nation two or three sets of children by three several women, the two first wives he did not live with at the time I knew him but was living with the third wife, that he [Hicks] never knew of John Rogers acquiring or attaining any land or farm throug[h] or by his wife from her Father, or through any gift or lega[cy] that I

> believe I should have known from my opportunities and public report, as the several properties of man & wife are usually known and understood by the public in our Nation and that said property as was surrendered to the United States by said Rogers and valued and appraised by the Commissioners as his would have been valued appraised and registered as her property and not that of John Rogers, they having liv[ed] together several years and had several children by said Rogers, whose interest she would [have] kept in said land had it been her property. That Jeremiah Horn, now of Caney Creek in this Nation married a Cousin of said Rogers wife in the Old Cherokee Nation, who were very intimate together.[19]

Besides another confirmation of Tiana Rogers as James Foster's daughter and John Rogers's wife, this document provided an important clue: Jeremiah Horn married a cousin of Tiana.

However, in the same file was an undated statement of one Elizabeth Candy, wife of George Candy, the judge who took her deposition. Elizabeth affirmed that she

> knew John Rogers commonly called Little John Rogers, whose wife is my own Cousin and who now resides at or near Stoney Creek in this Nation—the said John Rogers enrolled himself to immigrate to Arkansas and surrendered his Land to the United States and afterwards removed with two of his children to the Cherokee Nation west, his wife refusing to go, and afterward he returned not long afterward back to the Old Nation East and purchased a Place where he and his said wife and Family lived—and sometime afterwards he sickened and died in the said Old Nation East.[20]

One Clue Leads to Another

The clue of Tiana's cousin marrying a Jeremiah Horn has yet to lead to new discoveries. However, the other cousin, Elizabeth Candy, may have provided a breakthrough on which research continues.

Another Cherokee researcher, George Morrison Bell Sr., compiled a genealogy of Bell and related families from the Cherokee Nation east.[21] He reported that his great-great-great-grandparents were John Adair (born about 1753) and Mrs. Ga-ho-ga Foster, a full-blood Cherokee of the Deer Clan, who was born in the Cherokee Nation in Georgia and who had been married to a Foster, given name unknown. With Adair, Ga-ho-ga had five children, one of whom was Charlotte Adair, who married John Bell Jr. about 1805 in Bartow (then Cass) County, Georgia. John Bell had been born in 1782. These dates would place John and Charlotte in about the same generation as James Foster, born by the early 1780s.

Charlotte and John Bell had ten children, the second of whom was Elizabeth Hughes Bell who married George Washington Candy. Elizabeth was born about 1807 near New Echota in what became Bartow County, Georgia. By her affidavit, Elizabeth, wife of George Candy, was the cousin of Tiana (Foster) Rogers, born by 1805. If they were cousins of similar ages, their parents likely were siblings. Elizabeth's mother was Charlotte Adair; Tiana's father was James Foster. Thus, were Charlotte Adair and James Foster siblings? Since Charlotte's mother was reported as Ga-ho-ga, a Foster wife before marrying Adair, it appears that Charlotte Adair and James Foster were half-siblings, both the children of Ga-ho-ga. The Bell genealogy also supplied another clue by reporting that Ga-ho-ga had a sister named Dorcas, who married Young Charles Gordon Duncan.

Emmet Starr's history supports some of these relationships, and Marjorie Lowe continues to search for confirmation of what Bell and Starr have reported. It is exciting that part of

Sarah Ann (Rogers) Carr's family history is now known as far back as James Foster, her great-grandfather. Ga-ho-ga Foster Adair may yet prove to be the next root on Sarah's family tree.

FOR FURTHER REFERENCE

Libraries hold numerous books on the history and culture of specific American Indian tribes or those living in certain regions or states. They also hold atlases and encyclopedias on American Indians and bibliographies compiled on specific tribes. Consult online library catalogs for your topic of special interest; if your local public or academic library does not have what you need, consult a librarian for help with interlibrary loan. Also consult PERSI and online databases to which your local library may subscribe to learn about books, articles, dissertations, and other materials for your research. Visit the National Archives Web site periodically to learn about new micropublications and to find articles pertinent to American Indian research. Try links from Cyndi's List <www.cyndislist.com> to Web sites on Native American history, culture, and genealogy.

In addition to the books and articles listed below, dealing with genealogy and special collections, many records of the Cherokee and other tribes have been abstracted or transcribed. These include various rolls, censuses, newspapers, and vital records. Consult library catalogs for specific titles.

Tip

When consulting the Family History Library catalog online, use the subject "Indians of North America" to identify numerous materials on Indian records, history, and biography. To determine availability of materials in a particular state, use a "place search" with the name of the state and look for subheadings such as "Native races" and tribal names. Some of the materials listed in this catalog are available on loan through a Family History Center; some are available only at the library in Salt Lake City. Other libraries, as well, may hold the same or similar titles.

American Indian Genealogy

Titles about American Indian genealogy and general study include the following sampling:

"Alaska's Native Population: Sources for Genealogical and Historical Research," by Gretchen L. Lake and David A. Hales. *National Genealogical Society Quarterly* 83 (December 1995): 277–292.

"American-Indian Genealogical Research in the Midwest: Resources and Perspectives," by Stewart Rafert. *National Genealogical Society Quarterly* 76 (September 1988): 212–224.

The American Indians: Answers to 101 Questions, by the U.S. Bureau of Indian Affairs. Washington, D.C.: Government Printing Office, 1974. Answers on legal status, Bureau of Indian Affairs, land, economic status, education, law and order, reservations, health, etc.

Are You in There Grandpa?: Beginning Black Indian Genealogy, by Gloria L. Smith. Tucson, Ariz.: the author, 1994.

Bibliography of the Catawba, by Thomas J. Blumer. Metuchen, N.J.: Scarecrow Press, 1987.

Black Indian Genealogy Research, by Angela Y. Walton-Raji. Bowie, Md.: Heritage Books, 1993. Focuses on the Five Civilized Tribes.

Catawba Indian Genealogy, by Ian M. Watson. Geneseo, N.Y.: Department of Anthropology, State University of New York at Geneseo, 1995.

Ethnic Genealogy: A Research Guide, Jessie Carney Smith, ed. Westport, Conn.: Greenwood Press, 1983. Chapter 7, "American Indian Records and Research," by Jimmy B. Parker, dealing mostly with reservation Indians. Extensive bibliography.

Exploring Your Cherokee Ancestry, by Tom Mooney. Tahlequah, Okla.: Cherokee National Historical Society, 1990.

"Federal Indian Policy: Cherokee Enrollment, 1891–1907," by Kent Carter. *Prologue* 23 (1991): 25–38.

"Federal Indian Policy: The Dawes Commission, 1887–1898," by Kent Carter. *Prologue* 22 (Winter 1990): 339–349.

"Federal Records for Southeastern Indian Research, 1774–1931," by Rachal M. Lennon. *National Genealogical Society Quarterly* 86 (December 1998): 247–270.

A Genealogist's Guide to Discovering Your Immigrant & Ethnic Ancestors, by Sharon DeBartolo Carmack. Cincinnati: Betterway Books, 2000. Pages 145–153.

Guide to Sources of Indian Genealogy, by Charles Butler Barr. Independence, Mo.: the author, 1989.

Handbook of North American Indians, 17 vols. William C. Sturdevant, gen. ed. Washington, D.C.: Smithsonian Institution, 1978–1996.

How to Research American Indian Blood Lines: A Manual on Indian Genealogical Research, by Cecelia Svinth Carpenter. Orting, Wash.: Heritage Quest, 1987.

"Native American Genealogical Research," by Curt B. Witcher. *Indiana Genealogist* 6, no. 4 (1995): 151ff.

"Native American Genealogy Research in Indiana," by M. Teresa Baer. *The Hoosier Genealogist* 40, no. 2 (2000): 73ff.

The Native American: Records That Establish Individual and Family Identity, by E. Kay Kirkham. Salt Lake City: Church of Jesus Christ of Latter-day Saints, 1980. Family History Library microfiche 6070663.

Navajo Bibliography: With Subject Index, David M. Brugge, J. Lee Correll, and Editha L. Watson, comps. Window Rock, Ariz.: Arizona Parks and Recreation Dept., 1969.

"Negro-Indian Relationships in the Southeast," by Laurence Foster. Ph.D. diss., University of Pennsylvania, 1935. Reprint, New York: AMS Press, 1978.

"Questionable Honor: An Analysis of the 1835 Cherokee Census ('Henderson Roll')," by Lathel F. Duffield. *National Genealogical Society Quarterly* 90 (September 2002): 224–235.

"A Seventeenth-Century Native American Family: William of Sudbury and His Four Sons," by Richard W. Cogley. *The New England Historical and Genealogical Register* 153 (April 1999): 173–179.

Tracing Ancestors Among the Five Civilized Tribes: Southeastern Indians Prior to Removal, by Rachal Mills Lennon. Baltimore: Genealogical Publishing Co., 2002. Includes historical background and an extensive bibliography.

Guides to Special Collections

The following are examples of the many guides and catalogs that have been published. Some descriptive guides to manuscript collections are now online on the Web sites of the institutions holding the materials.

American Indian Archival Material: A Guide to Holdings in the Southeast, by Ron Chepesiuk and Arnold Shankman. Westport, Conn.: Greenwood Press, 1982. Repositories by state with descriptions of holdings.

American Indian Resource Materials in the Western History Collections, University of Oklahoma, Donald L. DeWitt, ed. Norman: University of Oklahoma Press, 1990.

American Indians: A Select Catalog of National Archives Microfilm Publications, Washington, D.C.: National Archives Trust Fund Board, 1998. Roll-by-roll listings to help you order or use the film; a must for a personal library when researching American Indians.

The Archives: A Guide to the National Archives Field Branches, by Loretto Dennis Szucs and Sandra Hargreaves Luebking. Salt Lake City: Ancestry, 1988.

Cartographic Records in the National Archives of the United States Relating to American Indians, Laura E. Kelsay, comp. Washington, D.C.: National Archives and Records Service, 1974, Reference Information Paper No. 71.

Cartographic Records of the Bureau of Indian Affairs, Laura E. Kelsay, comp. Washington, D.C.: National Archives and Records Service, 1977. National Archives Special List 13.

Dictionary Catalog of the Edward E. Ayer Collection of Americana and American Indians in the Newberry Library, 16 vols., by the Newberry Library of Chicago. Boston: G.K. Hall, 1961.

See Also

See chapter eight for more on the U.S. Serial Set.

Guide to American Indian Documents in the Congressional Serial Set, 1817–1899, by Steven L. Johnson. New York: Clearwater Publishing Co., 1977.

Guide to American Indian Resource Materials in Great Plains Repositories, Joseph C. Svoboda, comp. Lincoln: Center for Great Plains Studies, University of Nebraska-Lincoln, 1983.

Guide to Catholic Indian Mission and School Records in Mid-West Repositories, by Philip C. Bantin with Mark G. Thiel. Milwaukee: Marquette University Libraries, Department of Special Collections and University Archives, 1984.

A Guide to Cherokee Documents in the Northeastern United States, by Paul Kutsche. Metuchen, N.J.: Scarecrow Press, 1986. No. 7 in Native American Bibliography Series.

Guide to Records in the National Archives of the United States Relating to American Indians, by Edward E. Hill. Washington, D.C.: National Archives Trust Fund Board, 1984.

Introductory Guide to Indian-Related Records, to 1876, in the North Carolina State Archives, by Donna Spindel (Raleigh, N.C.: North Carolina Division of Archives and History, 1977).

Immigration and Naturalization

Immigration to what is now the United States has taken place for at least fifteen thousand years, for American Indians were immigrants too. However, written records of immigrants cover only about five hundred years, with the bulk of these after the mid-eighteenth century. Naturalization, on the other hand, is a relatively recent development, for the most part dating from the late eighteenth century. The two processes often affected the same ancestors and therefore are discussed in tandem in this chapter, but they do not always go hand in hand. Many immigrants have made their homes in the United States without becoming citizens.

When the Internet was young, this message appeared on an e-mail list; the surname has been changed to protect the guilty: "If anyone is doing research on the name [Brian], let me know. I've never seen it out there. I will assume it's Irish. I looked for it on the UK/Ireland web page and there was nothing." Sadly, too many people try to start their genealogy or their immigrant genealogy in this way—surfing the Internet or library books for anything containing their surname. Genealogists cannot reconstruct accurate family history by surfing for surnames and their origins; confirming one's lineage must come through studying specific people. **Whether trying to identify immigrant ancestors or tracing them after identifying them, genealogists need to follow these guidelines:**

Step By Step

1. Begin with yourself and research one generation at a time, without skipping a generation. Confirm each generation's link to the previous one by using legitimate sources, including family and public records such as those discussed throughout this book. Record each specific source along with the information it provides.

2. During this process, you may discover family traditions, family documents, or public records that identify an immigrant ancestor. Family oral tradition often contains truth but may also become a genealogist's trap, so let facts guide your research.

Warning

3. **Caution: Resist the temptation to jump the border or the water and begin researching a surname or a supposed immigrant in a supposed country of origin before you have the facts necessary to make your effort successful.**

4. When you feel you have identified a specific immigrant ancestor, study that person in depth in the records of the adopted country. These records may include published immigrant lists and family histories but must include contemporary documents relevant to the immi-

grant's time and place—federal and state census records, vital and marriage records, other county or city records, institutional records, city directories, newspapers, obituaries, naturalization papers, land and military records, passport applications, original passenger arrival records, etc. In these sources look for key information about the person's origin: birth or baptism date, specific birthplace or home parish, original name, parents' and siblings' names, immigration date and port of arrival in the adopted country. This information greatly aids your research in the records of the native country and helps confirm that you are researching the correct ancestor.

Citing Sources

For information on citing sources, see Croom's *Unpuzzling Your Past*, 4th ed., *The Sleuth Book for Genealogists*, and the endnotes of this book.

5. If you do not find enough of the necessary information on the immigrant, study his or her spouse, children, and siblings in the adopted country, using the records listed above. Studying the extended family, friends, neighbors, co-workers, and other associates may provide information on the immigrant.

6. When you feel you have enough confirmed information on the immigrant's origin, begin the "foreign" phase of your research in libraries, online, and in the thousands of microfilmed records available through the Family History Library. Guides to research in many countries are available in libraries, from book publishers and booksellers, and from the Family History Library. Much of this research can be done without going abroad. This way, when you plan a trip to the original homeland, you will be able to sightsee, visit newly-discovered cousins, stand on the correct ancestral ground, and appreciate the correct ancestors.

COLONIAL IMMIGRANTS

From the colonial period, relatively few immigrant arrival records exist, for there was no uniform or widespread registration. If your immigrant(s) came to North America in or before the eighteenth century, you may or may not identify conclusively a place of arrival or origin. Likewise, in some families, it is difficult to isolate the immigrant(s). In such cases, we must research whatever still exists of records contemporary with the ancestor(s) in their colonial place(s) of residence to try to determine the earliest recorded evidence of family members. Contemporary records vary with each state, including those states that were colonies of Britain, France, Spain, Sweden, or Holland. Evidence of early residents may come from land grants and surveyor records, deeds and bills of sale, militia rolls, marriage or burial records, tombstones, tax and tithable lists, church records of many kinds, New England town and vital records, livestock marks and brands, county or local court minutes, lists of civil and church officials, local censuses, and records of the colonial government, usually found at the state archives or in libraries as published abstracts or transcriptions. Some letters, diaries, and personal papers of colonial immigrants exist in special collections in archives and libraries.

Books and articles on research in each state and its colonial past, as well as documented histories, will give you ideas of what records are available. Consult library catalogs for these, and check the Family History Library catalog for records available on microfilm.

Most of the seventeenth-century and early eighteenth-century immigrants to the Atlantic coast were from the British Isles. France predominated in what became the Louisiana and Great Lakes regions; Spain, in what became the Southwest and early Florida. Some departure records from Europe exist but are not always readily available for research. Some have been abstracted, published, and indexed and are available in research libraries.

Warning

However, **if you do not know a place of origin, trying to work from Europe forward to the colonies (or to later immigrants as well) can be an exercise in futility.** It is usually inefficient and unproductive to begin, for example, with fifteenth-century evidence of a surname in Europe and try to connect to known seventeenth- or eighteenth-century

North American colonists. The effort may give you information on where the surname existed at a given time, but the European population was mobile, too, and surnames were not always constant or standardized until the seventeenth and eighteenth centuries. In addition, many of the compiled family histories purporting to trace colonists to a homeland or hometown are undocumented and full of errors. Even in New England, where the better church and vital records exist, a number of people had the same name, and more than a few early compilers made errors in sorting them out and connecting family groups.

Sometimes, we cannot determine the immigrants in a given lineage or their specific place of origin. In these cases, we must be content to study these ancestors through the vehicle of social history in their adopted land. After all, all lineages eventually come to a halt, usually before we want them to, and some, sooner than others. (Yes, lay aside thoughts of descent from King Arthur, Julius Caesar, and Adam and Eve.)

Pennsylvania. At various times, the original thirteen colonies required foreign—non-British—newcomers to swear allegiance to the English crown, as in eighteenth-century Pennsylvania. In the absence of official passenger lists, these written oaths are evidence of arrival in the colony. The Pennsylvania State Archives houses a large set of Philadelphia arrival records that cover almost a century and are published as *Pennsylvania German Pioneers: A Publication of the Original Lists of Arrivals in the Port of Philadelphia From 1727 to 1808*, 3 vols., by Ralph Beaver Strassburger, William John Hinke, ed. (Norristown, Penn.: Pennsylvania German Society, 1934; reprint of vols. 1 and 3 by Genealogical Publishing Co., Baltimore, 1966). For example, volume 1, list number 156C is dated 12 September 1750: "Foreigners on ship Priscilla, Capt. William Wilson, from Rotterdam and Cowes did this day take and subscribe the usual oaths." The list contains seventy-four names representing 210 passengers.

Virginia. The database of Virginia land patents is available on microfilm, in the *Cavaliers and Pioneers* series of abstracts, and online at <www.lva.lib.va.us/whatwehave/land/index.htm>. It includes colonial and post-Revolution patents. The colonial patents include land granted by (1) the English government and (2) Thomas Lord Fairfax in the Northern Neck. The surviving records, dating from 1624, provide evidence of numerous seventeenth-century settlers, but genealogists must be cautious in interpreting the data.

Until the early 1700s, most patents were issued under the headright system. The crown allowed persons who paid their own passage to the colony to obtain fifty acres of land plus fifty acres for each additional person whose way they paid. For example, in November 1651, Henry Soane received 297 acres in James City County for transporting six persons: himself and five others named Soane: Henry Jr., Judeth Sr., Judeth Jr., John, and Eliza. Likely, this was a family group. However, the record does not confirm that the family immigrated in November 1651. Headright claims could be held for months or years before being used, or they could be transferred to another person, or assignee. The records do not indicate when Henry Soane arrived or how long he may have held his headright claims.

When Daniell Coleman and Samuel Williams received six hundred acres in 1703 for transporting twelve individuals, all of different surnames, the patentees Coleman and Williams were not counted as headrights. Thus, it appears they were not new arrivals, but researchers cannot know

- whether they had paid the passage for these headrights or acquired the rights from someone else
- whether they were acquainted with the headrights (the twelve transported persons)
- when the headrights arrived in the colony
- whether the headrights were new immigrants or settlers returning from abroad
- where any of the headrights lived in 1703

The records indicate that the patentees and the headrights were in Virginia by the date of the patent. Headrights included persons of all classes: gentry, nobility, yeomanry, merchants, students, indentured servants, relatives of patentees, family servants, and sometimes Negroes.

Another Virginia source of origin for some men is the French and Indian War militia muster rolls, payrolls, and size rolls, easily accessible in transcribed form in Lloyd DeWitt Bockstruck's *Virginia's Colonial Soldiers* (Baltimore: Genealogical Publishing Co., 1988), especially between pages 53 and 126. Many of the rolls provide only the names of men in each company, but even a name and date can be helpful clues. Other rolls give the date and place of enlistment; age; height; occupation; description; and residence and/or origin, whether a North American colony or European country. Most of those born outside the colonies were from England, Ireland, or Scotland; a few came from Wales, Prussia, Holland, or Germany. The rolls were not made for the purpose of identifying immigrants and do not indicate when the men arrived. They do show each man was in Virginia by the date of enlistment. For example, a sawyer from Ireland, William Strain enlisted in Frederick County, in May 1755; he was age forty-nine, almost five feet six inches tall, bowlegged, and had a red face and sandy hair (page 105). Edward Breadsell, eighteen and of fair complexion, was a jack-of-all-trades from England (page 98). Upon enlistment in 1753, Abraham Mashaw was age thirty, five feet four inches tall, had a small face, and was a gentleman of Swiss birth who "stoops much" (page 81).

For Further Reference: Colonial Immigration and History

Numerous histories of the colonial period and of specific colonies contain immigration information and name some early immigrants. Look for these in periodical indexes, library catalogs, and WorldCat. Also check library catalogs for books such as the following:

- *Albion's Seed: Four British Folkways in America*, by David Hackett Fischer. New York: Oxford University Press, 1989. Cultural history of the colonial period.
- *The Bristol Registers of Servants Sent to Foreign Plantations, 1654–1686*, by Peter Wilson Coldham. Baltimore: Genealogical Publishing Co., 1988.
- *Cavaliers and Pioneers: Abstracts of Virginia Land Patents and Grants, 1632–1800*, Nell Marion Nugent, comp. Vol. 1, reprint of 1934 original. Baltimore: Genealogical Publishing Co., 1983. Vols. 2–3, published by Virginia State Library, 1977–1979. Vols. 4–7, edited by Dennis Ray Hudgins. Richmond: Virginia Genealogical Society, 1994–1999. Supplement of Northern Neck grants, 1690–1692. Richmond: Virginia State Library, 1980.
- *Child Apprentices in America From Christ's Hospital, London, 1617–1778*, by Peter Wilson Coldham. Baltimore: Genealogical Publishing Co., 1990.
- *Coming Over: Migration and Communication Between England and New England in the Seventeenth Century*, by David Cressy. New York: Cambridge University Press, 1987.
- *A Compilation of Original Lists of Protestant Immigrants to South Carolina, 1763–1773*, by Janie Revil. Baltimore: Genealogical Publishing Co., 1968. Reprint of 1939 original.
- *The Complete Book of Emigrants, 1607–1660* (published 1988); *The Complete Book of Emigrants, 1661–1699* (1990); *The Complete Book of Emigrants, 1700–1750* (1992); *The Complete Book of Emigrants, 1751–1776* (1993); *The Complete Book of Emigrants in Bondage, 1614–1775* (1998), all by Peter Wilson Coldham. Baltimore: Genealogical Publishing Co., publication year in parentheses.
- *Directory of Scots Banished to the American Plantations, 1650–1775*, by David Dobson. Baltimore: Genealogical Publishing Co., 1983.

- *The Early Settlers of Maryland: An Index to Names of Immigrants Compiled From Records of Land Patents, 1633–1680, in the Hall of Records, Annapolis, Maryland*, Gust Skordas, comp. Baltimore: Genealogical Publishing Co., 1968. Also *A Supplement to The Early Settlers of Maryland: Comprising 8,680 Entries Correcting Omissions and Errors in Gust Skordas The Early Settlers of Maryland*, by Carson Gibb. Annapolis: Maryland State Archives, 1997.
- *Emigrants From England to the American Colonies, 1773–1776*, rev. ed., by Peter Wilson Coldham. Baltimore: Genealogical Publishing Co., 1998.
- *Emigrants in Chains: A Social History of Forced Emigration to the Americas of Felons, Destitute Children, Political and Religious Non-Conformists, Vagabonds, Beggars and Other Undesirables, 1607–1776*, by Peter Wilson Coldham. Baltimore: Genealogical Publishing Co., 1992.
- *Emigrants to Pennsylvania, 1641–1819*, Michael Tepper, ed. Baltimore: Genealogical Publishing Co., 1975. Passenger lists from the *Pennsylvania Magazine of History and Biography*.
- *Genealogical Encyclopedia of the Colonial Americas: A Complete Digest of the Records of All the Countries of the Western Hemisphere*, by Christina K. Schaefer. Baltimore: Genealogical Publishing Co., 1998. Helps identify records of the colonial period.
- *The Georgia Dutch: From the Rhine and Danube to the Savannah, 1733–1783*, by George Fenwick Jones. Athens: University of Georgia Press, 1992. History of German-speaking colonists.
- *The Highland Scots of North Carolina, 1732–1776*, by Duane Gilbert Meyer. Chapel Hill: University of North Carolina Press, 1961. History.
- *Immigrants to the Middle Colonies*, Michael Tepper, ed. Baltimore: Genealogical Publishing Co., 1978. Passenger lists from the *New York Genealogical and Biographical Record*.
- *Migration and the Origins of the English Atlantic World*, by Alison Games. Cambridge, Mass.: Harvard University Press, 1999. History.
- *New Sweden on the Delaware: 1638–1655*, by C.A. Weslager. Wilmington, Del.: Middle Atlantic Press, 1988.
- *The Palatine Families of New York: A Study of the German Immigrants Who Arrived in Colonial New York in 1710*, by Henry Z Jones Jr. Universal City, Calif.: H.Z Jones, 1985. Also *More Palatine Families: Some Immigrants to the Middle Colonies, 1717–1776, and Their European Origins, Plus New Discoveries on German Families Who Arrived in Colonial New York in 1710*, by Henry Z Jones Jr., 1991.
- *The Peopling of a World: Selected Articles on Immigration and Settlement Patterns in British North America*, by Peter Charles Hoffer. New York: Garland Publishing Co., 1988. History.
- *The Scotch-Irish: A Social History*, by James G. Leyburn. Chapel Hill: The University of North Carolina Press, 1962. History focusing on seventeenth and eighteenth centuries.
- *Settlers of Maryland*, 5 vols., by Peter Wilson Coldham. Baltimore: Genealogical Publishing Co., 1996. Volumes contain abstracts of early land records; continuation of Skordas's *Early Settlers of Maryland*, listed above. Covers 1679–1783.

POST-REVOLUTION ARRIVAL RECORDS

Except for some baggage and cargo lists or "manifests," few passenger arrival records were kept until federal law required them in 1819. The first mandatory lists were made by ship captains for the collector of customs at the first port where an arriving ship stopped—the first "port of entry." For a time, quarterly reports from the customs officials went to the State Department, which then reported to Congress. Some of these can be found in Congressional documents. These customs passenger lists were kept throughout much of the nineteenth century. Later lists were made under the authority of the Immigration and Naturalization Service (INS), which became the Bureau of Citizenship and Immigration in 2003.

The largest ports of entry for many years were New York, Philadelphia, Baltimore, Boston, and New Orleans, although numerous smaller ports also had incoming passengers, both newcomers and returning citizens. Some immigrants returned to their homeland on business or to escort family members to America.

Important

The passenger manifests varied from time to time but usually included the passenger's name and age, citizenship, and destination. Each list usually showed the name of the ship and captain, the port from which the ship embarked on its voyage to the United States, and the date of arrival at the port. Although the ship may have continued its journey to other U.S. ports, the captain filed the manifest at the first stop. Thus, the names of passengers who disembarked in Galveston, Texas, may be on New Orleans passenger lists if their ship docked in Louisiana first.

One kind of customhouse record was the slave manifest. These lists identify the vessel and date of arrival as well as the name (usually given name only), age, and sex of slaves and the name and address of the consignee or slaveholder. The National Archives has some of these records in Record Group 36, Records of the U.S. Customs Service, for Philadelphia (1790–1840), New Orleans (1819–1852), Mobile (1822–1860), and Savannah (1801–1860). New Orleans lists are available on microfilm from Scholarly Resources (microfilm S3348). For most researchers, they are minimally useful in tracing slave ancestry. However, as with so many other resources, what is not useful for one researcher may be a gold mine for another.

Using Passenger Lists

Existing passenger lists are not centralized in a few convenient repositories. However, publication has made thousands of them accessible to researchers. Also, a number of bibliographies of passenger lists have been published. One of the most helpful tools in immigration research, and a good place to start, is P. William Filby's *Passenger and Immigration Lists Index* [PILI]: *A Guide to Published Arrival Records of . . . Passengers Who Came to the United States and Canada in the Seventeenth, Eighteenth, and Nineteenth Centuries* (Detroit: Gale Research, 1981–). This multi-volume bibliography and index now includes more than two million names from published passenger lists, naturalization records, and claims for headrights. Besides the name of the immigrant, each entry gives age, place and year of arrival, sometimes family members accompanying the immigrant, and the source and page number of the information. For example, John Dick was forty-six when he came into Georgia in 1775 with his wife, Mary (thirty-three), his daughter, Jane (twelve), and a child, Grizel (four). The "Bibliography of Sources Indexed" in each volume identifies the source of each entry so that researchers can find the source and any other details given there, such as the ship name or place of naturalization.

Tip

Naturalization, though a separate process, is an indication of immigration from another country.

The companion *Passenger and Immigration Lists Bibliography, 1538–1900* annotates over 2,550 published sources of the information in PILI. This bibliography also aids researchers by indexing ethnic groups, destinations and arrival ports, and states. For example, under Vermont in the index is an entry for nineteenth-century naturalizations in Franklin County, with the source where this information can be found. The sources in the *Passenger and Immigration Lists Bibliography* have the same code numbers that they have in PILI.

Original passenger lists can be tedious and frustrating to examine because many are not indexed and many are incomplete. One source of arrival information that people enjoy using is the database of arrivals at the port of Galveston, Texas, 1836–1921; the database is accessible at the Texas Seaport Museum in Galveston or online at <www.tsm-elissa.org/immigration-main.htm>. As the major Gulf port of entry west of New Orleans, Galveston received thousands of immigrants bound for Texas and much of the central portion of the nation. The records in the database have come from the National Archives, the Texas State Archives, other contemporary documents, and records contributed by descendants of arriving immigrants. By typing into the system the surnames of interest, visitors can find name, arrival date, country of origin (or embarkation), and destination of more than 115,000 immigrants.

Between 1892 and 1924, more than twenty-two million ship passengers arrived at Ellis Island and the Port of New York. The huge Ellis Island database is online at <www.ellisislandrecords.org>. From this site, you can see and order copies of the passenger manifest and sometimes view a picture of the ship. The online database was a volunteer project in which hundreds of people participated and for which they had to use the microfilm of the originals that no longer exist. Some of the microfilmed passenger lists from various ports of entry, not just Ellis Island, contain pages that are dark and thus difficult to see clearly, and the handwriting was not usually the U.S. schoolroom model for legibility. (European clerks wrote the names on the lists before the ships embarked for America; stylistic and individual differences occurred.) Thus database volunteers worked with less-than-ideal materials to read foreign names in "foreign" handwriting. These circumstances account for some of the spelling variations researchers find in the database, and these variations do not mean "our name was changed at Ellis Island."

Internet Source

Helpful tips and tools for searching the Ellis Island online database are available at <http://stevemorse.org>.

If your research leads you to believe your ancestors came through Ellis Island during the years covered in the database and not through one of the numerous other ports of entry, search the database using the name you believe to be correct, or try only the surname, or try a woman's maiden name, or try the name of a relative, such as a sibling or a child of the immigrant. If the family group came together, you may find the group by looking for different individuals. You can enter other criteria to narrow the search or use only one or two to broaden the search. If you don't find the ancestor(s) using the database, consider the microfilmed indexes, available at research libraries or through a Family History Center. Especially the Soundex indexes allow you to scroll, scan, and cross-reference, looking for relatives you have already identified.

A number of microfilmed passenger lists are indexed, some by Soundex code and some alphabetically. Figure 11-1, on page 394, illustrates two Soundex cards for passengers arriving in Baltimore. Four-year-old Fadwiga Krause traveled with her family from Germany, but no specific former residence was indicated. They arrived in Baltimore on 26 August 1891 and planned to travel to Michigan. Carl Suck was a U.S. citizen and farmer returning from abroad, apparently to Baltimore, where he arrived in October 1868. Depending on the information supplied on the passenger manifest, which varied from time to time and place to place, some of the indexes (in fact, abstracts) supply more information than others. The later the manifest, usually the more information it contains on each passenger, including specific birthplace, the name of a relative or friend in the United States the immigrant planned to join, and last permanent residence.

Figure 11-2, on page 395, is the page of the passenger manifest that listed young Fadwiga Krause and her family. Her Soundex card identifies the ship, port of entry, and date of arrival, along with a code number at the top of the card: "RR-42-3-141." This information

Figure 11-1 Index to Passenger Lists of Vessels Arriving at Baltimore, Maryland, 1820–1891, NARA microfilm M327, rolls 78 (K620) and 131 (S200).

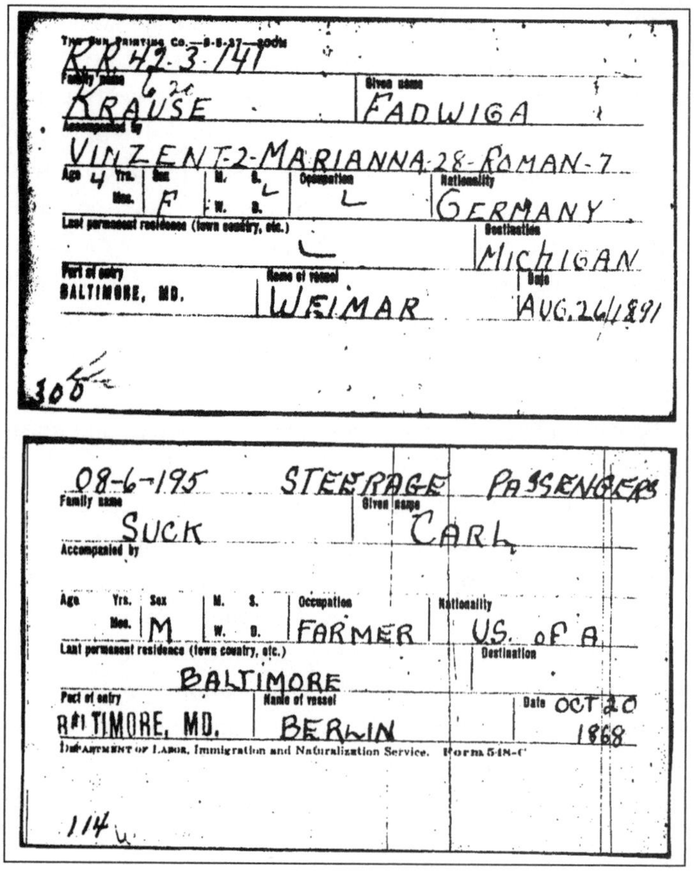
RR-42-3-141
Family name: KRAUSE — Given name: FADWIGA
Accompanied by: VINZENT-2-MARIANNA-28-ROMAN-7
Age: 4 Yrs. — Sex: F — Nationality: GERMANY
Destination: MICHIGAN
Port of entry: BALTIMORE, MD. — Name of vessel: WEIMAR — Date: AUG. 26/1891
308

08-6-195 STEERAGE PASSENGERS
Family name: SUCK — Given name: CARL
Accompanied by:
Age / Yrs. / Mos. — Sex: M — Occupation: FARMER — Nationality: US. of A.
Last permanent residence (town country, etc.): BALTIMORE
Destination:
Port of entry: BALTIMORE, MD. — Name of vessel: BERLIN — Date: OCT 20 1868
Department of Labor, Immigration and Naturalization Service. Form 548-C
114

led first to the microfilm of arrivals for the port of Baltimore (M255) that included the appropriate date (August 1891, on roll 50). The manifests are usually in chronological order on the roll. Showing the date 26 August 1891, the manifest for the ship *Weimar* was labeled "RR-42." On page 3, passenger number 141 was young Fadwiga.

The form for the *Weimar* manifest asked only a few questions: name; age in years, or months for infants; sex; calling (occupation); country of citizenship; intended destination; date and cause of death for any passenger who died during the crossing; location of compartment or space on board; number of pieces of baggage; and whether a person was transient or in transit, or intending a protracted sojourn. If a passenger was denied entry or detained, the manifest may give a reason.

The manifest shows the Krauses had two pieces of baggage and had the same destination as several other passengers listed on the same page. Groups of relatives and friends sometimes traveled together and lived near each other in their new home. Research can move in at least two directions: (1) Studying relatives and neighbors may help identify arrival and origin information for immigrant ancestors, and (2) studying arrival records may provide clues to relatives or friends.

For More Info

For more on researching immigration and naturalization, see Sharon DeBartolo Carmack's *A Genealogist's Guide to Discovering Your Immigrant & Ethnic Ancestors* (Cincinnati: Betterway Books, 2000).

Finding Evidence of Immigration and Origin

Evidence of arrival or origin is found in many kinds of records, including newspaper lists of arriving passengers, voter registration lists, militia muster rolls, military records, World War I draft registration cards, family Bibles, church and vital records, federal land patents and homestead records, obituaries, and census records. In reading obituaries, notice any directive such as "Belfast papers please copy." This announcement, even for cities in Canada

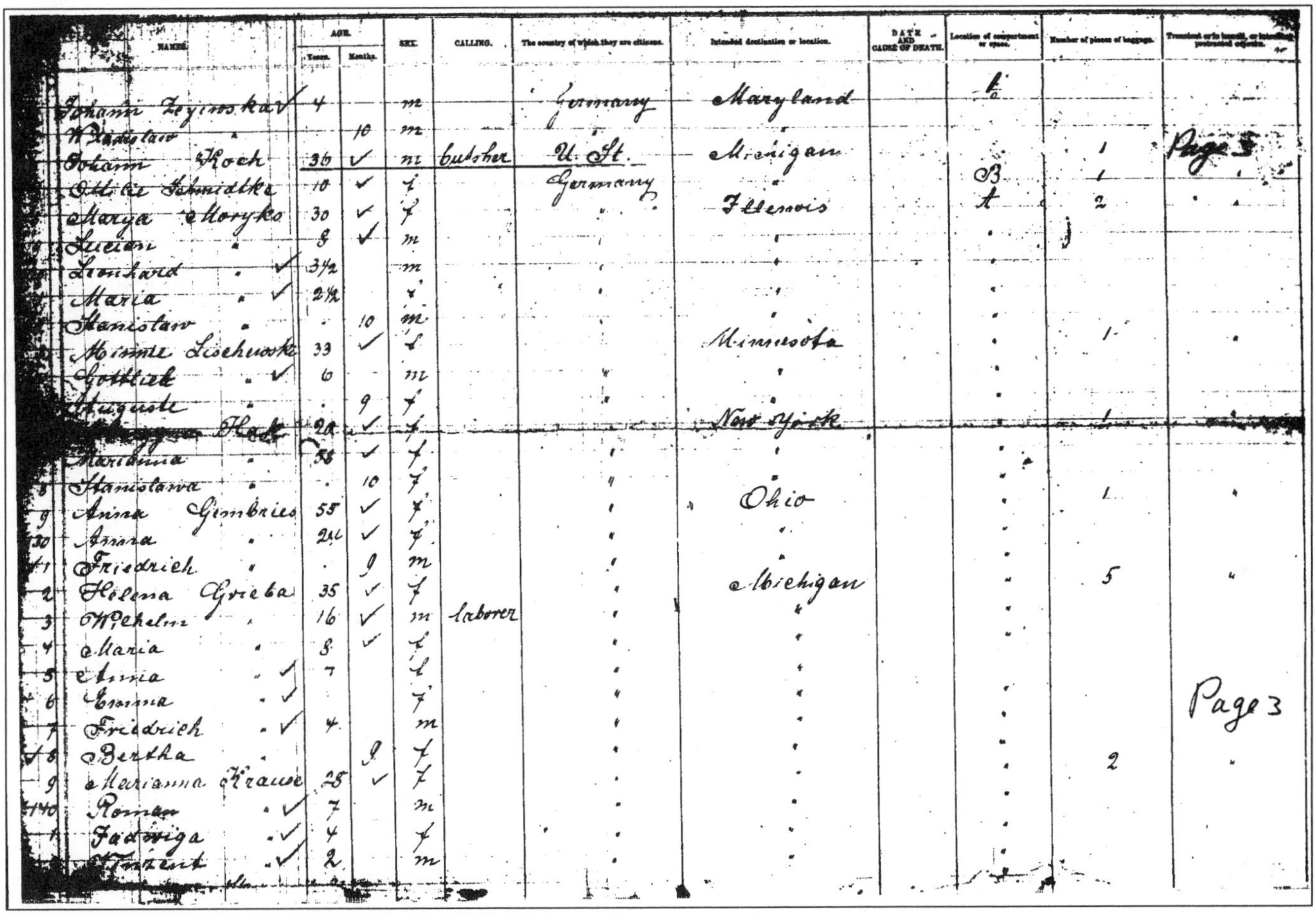

NAMES	AGE Years	AGE Months	SEX	CALLING	The country of which they are citizens	Intended destination or location	Date and cause of death	Location of compartment or space	Number of pieces of baggage	Transient, in-transit or intending protracted sojourn
Johann Zeyinskar [illegible]	4		m		Germany	Maryland				
Wladislaw		10	m							
Johann Koch	36		m	butcher	U. St.	Michigan			1	
Ottilie Schmidtke	10		f		Germany			B.	1	
Marya Moryko	30		f			Illinois		A	2	
Lucian	8		m							
Leonhard	3½		m							
Maria	2½		f							
Stanislaw		10	m							
Minnie Lischwski [illegible]	33		f			Minnesota			1	
Gottlieb	6		m							
Auguste		9	f							
[illegible]	24		f			New York			1	
Marianna	58		f							
Stanislawa		10	f							
Anna Gimbries	55		f			Ohio			1	
Anna	24		f							
Friedrich		9	m							
Helena Grieba	35		f			Michigan			5	
Wilhelm	16		m	laborer						
Maria	8		f							
Anna	7		f							
Emma			f							
Friedrich	4		m							
Bertha		9	f						2	
Marianna Krause	28		f							
Roman	7		m							
Jadwiga	4		f							
Vinzent	2		m							

Figure 11-2 Passenger Lists of . . . Baltimore, Maryland, 1820–1891, NARA microfilm M255, roll 50, *S.S. Weimar*, 26 August 1891, manifest RR42, p. 3, passengers 139–142.

and the United States, has a reason behind it. Usually it suggests a former residence where friends and family remained.

Federal censuses from 1850 forward and some state censuses asked for the birthplace of each person. The 1900 through 1930 censuses ask the year of immigration and whether the person was a naturalized citizen. As with any source of information, details may be omitted, incomplete, or incorrect, but sometimes they provide a needed clue. Studying a person's extended family—spouse, siblings, children, in-laws, cousins, aunts and uncles—may help identify a time of arrival or place of origin. If studying the family doesn't provide answers, make a list of associates (the cluster) and friends. Often immigrants lived, worshipped, socialized, and did business with and were buried among people whose origins were similar to theirs. Several examples illustrate the diversity of evidence available.

In Elizabeth City, New Jersey, in 1920, the census takers varied the detail with which they recorded birthplaces. Numerous immigrant residents were from Ireland, Poland, Russia, Germany, and Italy. However, Marshall Street homeowner Richard Maxwell, age sixty-two, was born in Saxony, as were his parents. His wife, Roberta, and her parents were natives of Bavaria. Although whoever talked with the census taker did not know the couple's year(s) of immigration or their citizenship status, the information on place of origin, if correct, at least narrows the field to regions. In the same enumeration district, shoemaker Tony Drysine and his wife, Angelina, both natives of Palermo (Sicily), Italy, immigrated in

ARRIVAL RECORDS REVEAL A FAMILY CLUSTER

The search for the immigration record of my father, Patrick Conlon, led eventually to the Soundex index to the St. Albans, Vermont, arrival lists and to the discovery of other family members and a large amount of new clues for research.[1] (New names and relationships are shown here in italics, but almost everything was new information.) My father had told me he was born in England and had a sister named Nora. Family tradition was that his father, now known to be Michael Conlon, had departed for the Gold Rush in the Yukon shortly after arriving in Canada. The U.S. arrival records furnish a larger picture, beginning with the arrival in Quebec of at least three or four family members on 21 June 1907 on the ship *Empress Britain*.

According to his U.S. arrival record, Michael Conlon, age forty-six, a cotton weaver by trade, was born in Burnley, Lancashire, England, where his nearest relative was a *brother, John*. Michael was five feet one and one-half inches tall, with fair complexion, and weighed 135 pounds. He planned to settle permanently in the United States and was headed for Lawrence, Massachusetts, on 26 December 1908 when he attempted to enter the United States from Montreal, where he had been living. A week later he was debarred from entering the country, after three days observation, due to chronic alcoholism with tremors and defective memory that the officials felt would adversely affect his ability to earn a living. He was labeled "L.P.C.," or "likely public charge." After being turned away, did he really go to the Yukon or return to Montreal and his family?

Six months later, in June 1909, Michael's wife, Mary, and five-year-old son, Patrick, entered from Montreal, giving their most recent address as the home of *Patrick's uncle, Thomas Smith*, 44 Ellis Street, Middleton (near Montreal). The record gave Patrick's birthplace as Burnley, Lancashire. He and his mother wished to live permanently in the United States and were traveling to New Bedford, Massachusetts to join his *sister, Nora Phipps*, who lived at 24 Salisbury Street.

Three months later, in September 1909, twelve-year-old *Norman Conlon, son of Michael* and thus brother of Patrick, entered at St. Albans, Vermont. His birthplace was listed, probably incorrectly, as Montreal; his last residence was his father's residence at 851 East Notre Dame Street in Montreal. (A twelve-year-old would not likely have been living alone after his mother emigrated. Had Michael stayed in Montreal instead of going to the Yukon? Had Norman stayed with Michael or Uncle Thomas? Was the stated Montreal address the family's residence before Michael attempted to enter the United States? Did Michael eventually go west?) Like Mary and Patrick, Norman too was headed for 24 Salisbury Street, New Bedford, Massachusetts, to the home of his *brother-in-law, William Phipps*, who had paid for the boy's passage.

As so often happens in genealogy, each answer prompts new questions, but now there is a family cluster to study in trying to answer the questions. *A.G. Conlon*

1901; he was naturalized in 1907. Some of their neighbors were born in Dublin, Ireland, and Manchester, England.

Passport applications of naturalized citizens may show both immigration and naturalization information. One application with helpful information is the 1876 San Francisco passport application of Henry Petit, born in France (nothing more specific given) on 6 August 1850, who was planning to travel abroad with *his mother, widow Matilda Petit*; the application showed evidence of his 1873 naturalization in San Francisco. His naturalization papers, censuses, and other California records that named him or his mother could help narrow their arrival date(s), port(s) of entry, and other possible residences in the United States. Sometimes, researchers identify naturalization papers before arrival records; sometimes, the process is reversed. In Figure 11-3, below, the passport application of Richard Hayn, while giving no immigration information, provides his birth date, birthplace, and the court where he was naturalized in 1868.

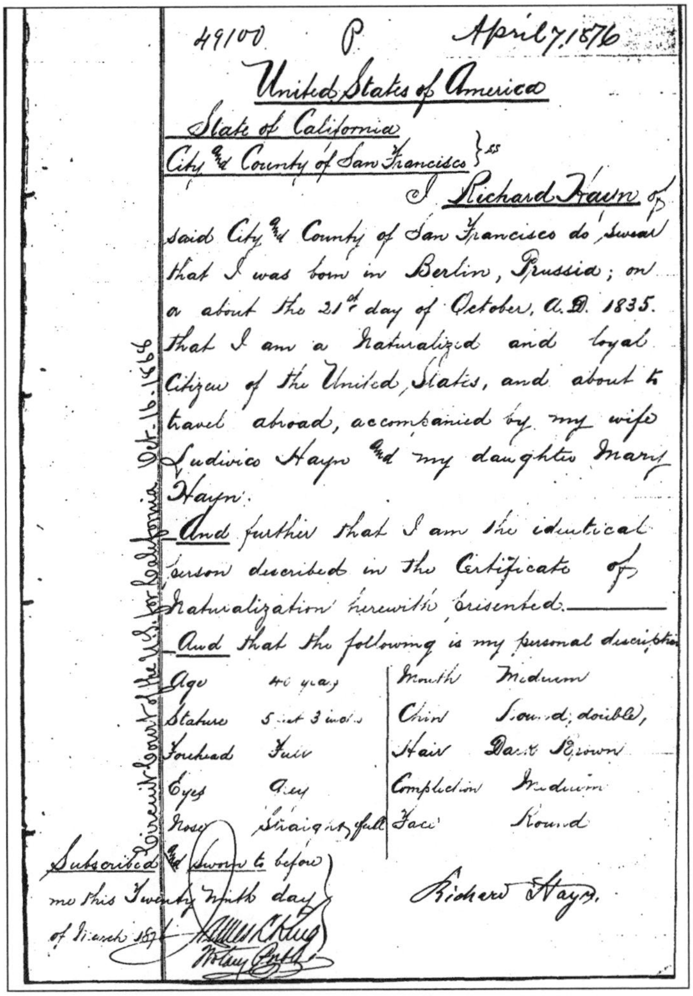

49100 P. April 7, 1876

United States of America
State of California
City & County of San Francisco } ss

I, Richard Hayn of said City & County of San Francisco do swear that I was born in Berlin, Prussia; on or about the 21st day of October, A.D. 1835. That I am a Naturalized and loyal Citizen of the United States, and about to travel abroad, accompanied by my wife Ludwica Hayn and my daughter Mary Hayn.

And further that I am the identical person described in the Certificate of Naturalization herewith presented.

And that the following is my personal description

Age	40 years	Mouth	Medium
Stature	5 feet 3 inches	Chin	Round; double
Forehead	Full	Hair	Dark Brown
Eyes	Gray	Complexion	Medium
Nose	Straight, full	Face	Round

Subscribed and sworn to before me this Twenty Ninth day of March 1876

Notary Public

Richard Hayn.

Circuit Court of the U.S. for California Oct. 16, 1868

Figure 11-3 Passport application of Richard Hayn, #49100, Passport Applications, 1795–1905, NARA microfilm M1372, roll 212, March-April 1876, Vol. 465, FHL microfilm 1432731.

The Emigrant Savings Bank of New York City, opened in 1850, began as a project of the Irish Emigrant Society and still serves customers. Its surviving historical records are part of the Manuscripts and Archives Division at the Humanities and Social Sciences Library of the New York Public Library; the records are also available on microfilm from Scholarly Resources and in some research libraries, including Clayton Library in Houston. In the aftermath of the great Irish famine, the society and Irish residents of the United States sent money to Irish families in need and helped others emigrate from Ireland to the United States. Thus, Irish men and women in the greater New York area, both U.S.-born and immigrants, were the majority of account holders, but depositors also included people born in Canada, Germany, Great Britain, Italy, and other countries as well as residents of New Jersey, Connecticut, Massachusetts, and other states. During the Civil War, a number of soldiers opened accounts.

The records include some Irish Emigrant Society records, index books to account holders, account ledgers, and real estate books, which pertain to people who borrowed money from the bank to buy homes. However, **the most genealogical information occurs in the Test Books and in the Transfer, Signature, and Test Books.** Many entries included immigration information and/or birthplace; some provided the mother's or wife's maiden name, names of children or siblings, and beneficiary choice in case of death. Many signed the test book with a mark; others, with their signature.

Important

Several examples demonstrate the information that researchers may find in these records.

- Phillip Hughes opened account number 43242 on 14 October 1864; resided at 99 Ninth Avenue; was a boilermaker; was born in 1841 in County Tyrone, Ireland; arrived in the U.S. on 8 June 1861 on the *Florence Nightingale*; was single and the son of Philip Hughes (deceased) and Rose McNally. (Test Book No. 4)
- Michael Devine signed his mark to open account number 43239 on 14 October 1864. His occupation was tailor, but he was residing with the 69th New York Volunteers. He was born in 1826 at Castle Island, County Kerry, Ireland. His family included wife, Eliza (maiden name not given), and four children: Mary Ann, John, Michael, and Eliza. No immigration information given. (Test Book No. 4)
- Mary M. Skiffington opened account number 40271 in April 1864; resided at 211 Forty-seventh between Eighth and Ninth; worked as a teacher; was born in 1841 in New York City; was single and the daughter of Bernard Skiffington (deceased) and Ann McDonnell. (Test Book No. 4)
- Elisa O'Connor of 312 Hicks in Brooklyn opened account number 40190 in April 1864; was born in the city of Cork in 1812; arrived in the United States in 1844 on the *Ashburton*; was a housekeeper, the widow of Michael O'Connor, and mother of three children (unnamed). (Test Book No. 4)

Notes

Abstracts are used with permission from Emigrant Savings Bank Records, Manuscripts and Archives Division, The New York Public Library, Astor, Lenox and Tilden Foundations.

National Archives Passenger List Publications

The following are passenger lists and indexes microfilmed through 2002 and available for use at research libraries, including the National Archives and the regional branches (each has film pertaining to its region). You can rent microfilm from the Family History Library, using their catalog to identify roll numbers you need. You can purchase microfilm from the National Archives or Scholarly Resources. The National Archives roll lists for many of these microfilm publications are in *Immigrant and Passenger Arrivals: A Select Catalog of National Archives Microfilm Publications*, 2d ed. (Washington, D.C.: National Archives, 1991), and in the online version of the catalog at <www.archives.gov/publications/microfilm_catalogs/immigrant/immigrant_passenger_arrivals.html>. New microfilm publications through 2002 are included in the list below. For titles and M, T, P, or A publication numbers of newer microfilm publications, see the National Archives Web site at <www.archives.gov/research_room/genealogy/index.html>; scroll to and click on "New Microfilm Publications."

Contact the National Archives or a regional branch for roll lists of new publications not yet in a catalog; provide the title and the publication M, T, P, or A number. If you identify a passenger list you need and do not have access to the microfilm, you can order a copy of the original from the National Archives, using form NATF-81, Ship Passenger Arrival Records. You can request the form from <www.archives.gov/global_pages/inquire_form.html>.

The passenger lists are arranged chronologically. The indexes are generally alphabetical or by Soundex code. (See chapter two for an explanation of Soundex.) Note that some of the lists include crew members on the vessels. If the passengers you seek are not listed on the manifests of the port through which you believe they entered, try the lists of other ports in the region.

1. **Alabama**
   a. Index to passenger lists, 1890–1924 (T517).
   b. Supplement index for M575 (M334).
   c. Passengers arriving at Mobile, 1832–1852 (M575, roll 4).
2. **Alaska**
   a. Alphabetical index of alien arrivals at Eagle, Hyder, Hetchikan, Nome, and Skagway, Alaska, 1906–1946 (M2016).
   b. Lists of aliens arriving at Skagway (White Pass), Alaska, 1906–1934 (M2017).
   c. Lists of aliens arriving at Eagle, Alaska, 1910–1938 (M2018).
3. **Arizona**
   a. Aliens arriving at Aros Ranch, Douglas, Lochiel, Naco, and Nogales, 1906–1910 (A3365).
   b. Alien arrivals at Douglas, 1906–1955 (M1760); at Douglas, 1908–1952 (M1759); at San Luis, 1929–1952 (M1504).
   c. Index and manifests of alien arrivals at Nogales, 1905–1952 (M1769); at Sasabe/San Fernando, 1919–1952 (M1850).
4. **Atlantic, Gulf, and Great Lakes Ports** (see also state names)
   a. Supplemental index to M575 (M334).
   b. Copies of passenger lists, 1820–1873 (M575).
   c. Index to passenger lists of vessels arriving at ports in Alabama, Florida, Georgia, South Carolina, 1890–1924 (T517).
5. **Baltimore, Maryland**
   a. Index (Soundex) to federal passenger lists, 1820–1897 (M327). Index to passenger lists submitted to city under 1833 state law, 1833–1866 (M326), included as part of the passenger lists, 1820–1891 (M255).
   b. Quarterly abstracts of passenger lists, 1820–1866 (M596).
   c. Index (Soundex) to passenger lists, 1897–1952 (T520).
   d. Passenger lists, 1891–1909 (T844).
   e. Passenger lists, 1954–1957 (M1477).
   f. See also "Maryland."
6. **Boston, Massachusetts**
   a. Index to passenger lists, 1848–1891 (M265).
   b. Index to lists, 1902–1906 (T521). Index, 1906–1920 (T617). Book indexes, 1899–1940 (T790).
   c. Passenger lists, 1820–1891 (M277).
   d. Passenger lists, 1891–1943 (T843).
   e. Crew lists of vessels arriving 1917–1943 (T938); may include some Maine, New Hampshire, and Rhode Island arrivals.
   f. See also "Massachusetts."
7. **California**
   a. Index to passenger arrivals at San Diego, ca. 1904–ca. 1952 (M1761).
   b. Manifests of aliens arriving at various California locations, twentieth century (M2030).
   c. Index to passengers arriving at San Pedro/Wilmington/Los Angeles, 1907–1936 (M1763); passenger lists for same ports, 1907–1948 (M1764).

   d. Passenger and crew lists of arrivals at Ventura, 1929–1956 (A3363).
   e. Manifests of alien arrivals at San Ysidro, 1908–1952 (M1767).
   f. Record of persons held for Boards of Special Inquiry at San Pedro, 1930–1936 (M1852).
   g. See also "San Francisco, California."

8. **Connecticut**
   a. Supplemental index for M575, in 8.b-8.g (M334).
   b. Copies of passenger lists, Bridgeport, 1870 (M575, roll 1).
   c. Copies of passenger lists, Fairfield, 1820–1821 (M575, roll 2).
   d. Copies of passenger lists, Hartford, 1837 (M575, roll 4).
   e. Copies of passenger lists, New Haven, 1820–1873 (M575, roll 5).
   f. Copies of passenger lists, New London, 1820–1847 (M575, roll 6).
   g. Copies of passenger lists, Saybrook, 1820 (M575, roll 16).
   h. Passenger and crew lists of vessels (1929–1959) and airplanes (1946–1959) arriving at Bridgeport, Groton, Hartford, New Haven, and New London (M1320).
9. **Delaware**
   a. Supplemental index to M575 (M334).
   b. Copies of passenger lists, Wilmington, 1820–1848 (M575, roll 16).
10. **Detroit** (see "Michigan")
11. **District of Columbia**
   a. Supplemental index to M575 (M334).
   b. Copies of lists, Georgetown, DC (M575, roll 4).
   c. See also "Baltimore, Maryland" (M1477, T520).
12. **Florida**
   a. Supplemental index to M575 (12.b) (M334).
   b. Copies of passenger lists, St. Augustine, 1821–1870; St. Johns, 1865 (M575, roll 16).
   c. Passenger lists, Tampa, 1898–1945 (M1844).
   d. Index to passenger lists, 1890–1924 (T517).
   e. Passenger lists of vessels arriving at Knights Key, 1908–1912 (A3371).
   f. Passenger lists of vessels arriving at various Florida ports, 1904–1942 (M1842).
   g. Passenger lists of citizens and aliens arriving at and departing from Pensacola, about 1924–1948 (M2021).
   h. See also "Key West, Florida."
13. **Galveston, Texas**
   a. Supplemental index to M575 (M334).
   b. Copies of passenger lists, 1846–1871 (M575, roll 3).
   c. Index, 1896–1906 (M1357); index, 1906–1951 (M1358).
   d. Lists, 1896–1951 (M1359), including arrivals at Houston, Brownsville, Port Arthur, Sabine, and Texas City; lists for 1871–1896 are missing; may include some arrivals in Louisiana.
   e. See also "Texas."
14. **Georgia**
   a. Index to passenger lists, 1890–1924 (T517).
   b. Supplemental index to M575 (M334).
   c. Copies of passenger lists, Darien, 1823–1825 (M575, roll 2).
   d. See also "Savannah, Georgia."
15. **Gloucester, Massachusetts**
   a. Copies of passenger lists, 1820–1870 (M575); see supplemental index (M334).

b. Crew lists, 1918–1943 (T941).
c. See also "Massachusetts."

16. **Idaho** (see "St. Albans District, Vermont.")
17. **Illinois.** (see "St. Albans District, Vermont.")
18. **Key West, Florida**
    a. Passenger lists of vessels arriving, 1898–1945 (T940).
    b. Copies of passenger lists, 1837–1868 (M575); see supplemental index (M334).
    c. See also "Florida."
19. **Louisiana** (see "New Orleans, Louisiana.")
20. **Maine**
    a. Alphabetical manifest cards of alien arrivals at Calais, ca. 1906–1952 (M2042).
    b. Alphabetical manifest cards of alien arrivals at Jackman, ca. 1909–1953 (M2046).
    c. Alphabetical manifest cards of alien and citizen arrivals at Fort Fairfield, ca. 1909–1953 (M2064).
    d. Alphabetical manifest cards of alien arrivals at Van Buren, ca. 1906–1952 (M2065).
    e. Alphabetical manifest cards of alien arrivals at Vanceboro, ca. 1906–1952 (M2071).
    f. Supplemental index to M575 (M334).
    g. Copies of passenger lists, Bangor, 1848; Bath, 1825–1867; Belfast, 1820–1851 (M575, roll 1).
    h. Copies of passenger lists, Frenchman's Bay, 1821–1827 (M575, roll 2).
    i. Copies of passenger lists, Kennebunk, 1820–1842 (M575, roll 4).
    j. Copies of passenger lists, Passamaquoddy, 1820–1844 (M575, roll 7) and 1845–1859 (M575, roll 8).
    k. Copies of passenger lists, Penobscot, 1851 (M575, roll 8).
    l. Copies of passenger lists, Waldoboro, 1820–1833, and Yarmouth, 1820 (M575, roll 16).
    m. See also "Portland, Maine," "St. Albans District, Vermont," and "Boston, Massachusetts."
21. **Maryland**
    a. Supplemental index to M575 (M334).
    b. Copies of passenger lists, Annapolis, 1849 (M575, roll 1).
    c. Copies of passenger lists, Havre de Grace, 1820 (M575, roll 4).
    d. See also "Baltimore, Maryland."
22. **Massachusetts**
    a. Supplemental index to M575 (M334).
    b. Copies of passenger lists, Barnstable, 1820–1826 (M575, roll 1).
    c. Copies of passenger lists, Dighton, 1820–1836; Edgartown, 1820–1870; Fall River, 1837–1865 (M575, roll 2).
    d. Copies of passenger lists, Hingham, 1852; Marblehead, 1820–1849 (M575, roll 4).
    e. Copies of passenger lists, Nantucket, 1820–1862; Newburyport, 1821–1839 (M575, roll 5).
    f. Copies of passenger lists, Plymouth, 1821–1844 (M575, roll 8).
    g. Copies of passenger lists, Salem, 1865–1866 (M575, roll 16).
    h. See also "Boston, Massachusetts," "Gloucester, Massachusetts," and "New Bedford, Massachusetts."
23. **Michigan**
    a. Card manifests (alphabetical) of persons entering through Detroit, 1906–1954 (M1478); may include some Ohio arrivals.

b. Passenger and alien crew lists of vessels arriving at Detroit, 1946–1957 (M1479); may include some Ohio arrivals.
c. See also "St. Albans District, Vermont."

24. **Minnesota** (see "St. Albans District, Vermont.")
25. **Mississippi**
    a. Index to passengers arriving at Gulfport, 1904–1954, and at Pascagoula, 1903–1935 (T523).
    b. Alien crew lists of vessels arriving at Pascagoula, 1903–1935 (M2027).
26. **Montana** (see "St. Albans District, Vermont.")
27. **New Bedford, Massachusetts**
    a. Supplemental index to M575 (M334).
    b. Copies of passenger lists, 1826–1852 (M575, roll 5).
    c. Index, 1902–1954 (T522).
    d. Passenger lists, 1902–1942 (T944).
    e. Crew lists on vessels arriving 1917–1943 (T942).
    f. See also "Massachusetts."
28. **New Hampshire**
    a. Supplemental index to M575 (M334).
    b. Copies of passenger lists, Portsmouth, 1820–1861 (M575, roll 15).
    c. See also "St. Albans District, Vermont."
29. **New Jersey**
    a. Supplemental index to M575 (M334).
    b. Copies of passenger lists, Cape May, 1828 (M575, roll 1).
    c. Copies of passenger lists, Little Egg Harbor, 1831 (M575, roll 4).
    d. Copies of passenger lists, Newark, 1836 (M575, roll 5).
    e. Copies of passenger lists, Perth Amboy, 1820–1832 (M575, roll 8).
    f. See also "Philadelphia, Pennsylvania."
30. **New Mexico**
    a. Manifests of alien arrivals at Columbus, 1917–1954 (A3370).
31. **New Orleans, Louisiana**
    a. Customs Service passenger lists, 1813–1866 (V116). Roll 1 includes partial index, 1839–1861.
    b. Quarterly abstracts of lists, 1820–1875 (M272). Chronological.
    c. Index to passenger lists before 1900 (T527).
    d. Lists, 1820–1902 (M259).
    e. WPA transcript of passenger arrivals, 1813–1849 (M2009).
    f. Index to passenger lists, 1900–1952 (T618).
    g. Passenger and crew lists, 1910–1945 (T905).
    h. Crew lists on vessels arriving 1910–1945 (T939).
    i. See also "Galveston, Texas."
32. **New York** (state)
    a. Alphabetical card manifests of alien arrivals at Alexandria Bay, Cape Vincent, Champlain, Clayton, Fort Covington, Mooers, Rouses Point, Thousand Island Bridge, and Trout River, 1929–1956 (M1481).
    b. Soundex card manifests of alien and citizen arrivals at Hogansburg, Malone, Morristown, Nyando, Ogdensburg, Rooseveltown, and Waddington, 1929–1956 (M1482).

c. Manifests of alien arrivals at Buffalo, Lewiston, Niagara Falls, and Rochester, 1902–1954 (M1480).
d. Supplemental index to M575 (M334).
e. Copies of passenger lists, Oswegatchie, 1821–1823 (M575, roll 6).
f. Copies of passenger lists, Rochester, 1866, and Sag Harbor, 1829–1834 (M575, roll 16).
g. See also "New York City" and "St. Albans District, Vermont."

33. **New York City**
a. Index to passenger lists, 1820–1846 (M261).
b. Index to passenger lists, 1897–1902 (T519).
c. Index (Soundex) to lists, 1902–1943 (T621).
d. Index (Soundex) to passenger lists, 1944–1948 (M1417).
e. Book indexes to passenger lists, 1906–1942, grouped by year and shipping line (T612).
f. Lists, 1820–1897 (M237).
g. Passenger and crew lists, 1897–1957 (T715; 8,892 rolls).
h. See also "New York (state)."

34. **North Carolina**
a. Supplemental index to M575 (M334).
b. Copies of passenger lists, Beaufort, 1865 (M575, roll 1).
c. Copies of passenger lists, Edenton, 1820 (M575, roll 2).
d. Copies of passenger lists, New Berne, 1820–1865 (M575, roll 5).
e. Copies of passenger lists, Plymouth, 1820–1840 (M575, roll 8).
f. Copies of passenger lists, Washington, 1820–1848 (M575, roll 16).
g. Check also passengers arriving in Baltimore, Maryland, and Norfolk, Virginia.

35. **North Dakota** (see "St. Albans District, Vermont.")

36. **Ohio**
a. Supplemental index to M575 (M334).
b. Copies of passenger lists, Sandusky, 1820 (M575, roll 16).
c. See also "St. Albans District, Vermont" and "Michigan."

37. **Philadelphia, Pennsylvania**
a. Index to passenger lists, 1800–1906 (M360).
b. Index (Soundex) to passenger lists 1883–1948 (T526).
c. Book indexes, 1906–1926 (T791).
d. Lists, 1800–1882 (M425).
e. Lists, 1883–1945 (T840).
f. Any of these may include New Jersey arrivals.

38. **Portland, Maine**
a. Supplemental index to passenger lists for Portland and Falmouth, 1820–1868 (M334).
b. Copies of passenger lists, 1820–1868, Portland and Falmouth (M575, rolls 9–14).
c. Index to passenger lists, 1893–1954 (T524).
d. Book indexes, 1907–1930 (T793).
e. Lists, 1893–1943 (T1151).
f. See also "Maine."

39. **Providence, Rhode Island**
a. Supplemental index to M575 (M334).
b. Copies of passenger lists, Providence, 1820–1867 (M575, rolls 15-16).
c. Index to passengers, 1911–1954 (T518).

d. Book indexes, 1911–1934 (T792).
e. Lists, 1911–1943 (T1188).
f. See also "Rhode Island" and "Boston, Massachusetts."

40. **Rhode Island**
   a. Supplemental index to M575 (M334).
   b. Copies of passenger lists, Bristol and Warren, 1820–1871 (M575, roll 1).
   c. Copies of passenger lists, Newport, 1820–1857 (M575, roll 6).
   d. See also "Providence, Rhode Island."
41. **St. Albans District, Vermont**
   a. Soundex index to Canadian border entries through St. Albans District, 1895–1924 (M1461); includes various border crossings, including Chicago, Detroit, and locations in Maine, Michigan, Minnesota, New Hampshire, New York, North Dakota, Ohio, and Washington.
   b. Alphabetical index to Canadian border entries through small ports in Vermont, 1895–1924 (M1462). Includes Vermont towns of Norton, Island Pond, Beecher Falls, Highgate Springs, Swanton, Alburg, Richford, St. Albans, and Canaan.
   c. Soundex index to entries into St. Albans, Vermont, through Canadian Pacific and Atlantic ports, 1924–1952 (M1463). Includes entries into Idaho, Maine, Michigan, Minnesota, Montana, New York, North Dakota, Ohio, Vermont, Washington (state), ports on the Great Lakes and through Canadian cities and provinces along the entire border.
   d. Manifests of passengers arriving in the St. Albans, Vermont, district through Canadian Pacific and Atlantic ports, 1895–1954 (M1464).
   e. Manifests of passengers arriving in the St. Albans, Vermont, district through Canadian Pacific ports, 1929–1949 (M1465).
   f. See also "Detroit, Michigan," "Maine," "New York (state)," and other locations along the Canadian border.

See Also

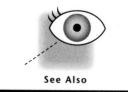

See "By Way of Canada: U.S. Records of Immigration Across the U.S.-Canadian Border, 1895–1954 (St. Albans Lists)," by Marian L. Smith, in *Prologue*, fall 2000, online at <www.archives.gov/publications/prologue/genealogy_notes.html#natur>.

42. **San Francisco, California**
   a. Index to passenger lists, 1893–1934 (M1389).
   b. Lists, 1893–1953 (M1410); may include arrivals at Eureka and Los Angeles.
   c. Passenger and crew lists, 1954–1957 (M1411).
   d. Customs passenger lists, 1903–1918 (M1412).
   e. Registers of Chinese laborers arriving at San Francisco, 1882–1888 (M1413).
   f. Lists of Chinese passengers arriving at San Francisco, 1888–1914 (M1414).
   g. Lists of Chinese applying for admission to U.S. through San Francisco, 1903–1947 (M1476).
   h. Alien crew lists on vessels arriving, 1896–1921 (M1436); crew lists, 1905–1954 (M1416).
   i. Passengers on vessels arriving from Hawaii, 1902–1907 (M1440).
   j. Passengers on vessels arriving from insular possessions, 1907–1911 (M1438).
   k. Citizen and alien arrivals by aircraft, 1936–1946 (A3361).
   l. See also "California."
43. **Savannah, Georgia**
   a. Supplemental index to M575 (M334).
   b. Copies of passenger lists, 1820–1868 (M575, roll 16).
   c. Passenger lists, 1906–1945 (T943).
   d. See also "Georgia."
44. **Seattle and Other Washington Ports**

a. Lists of Chinese arriving 1882–1916 (M1364).
b. Passenger lists, 1890–1957 (M1383) and 1949–1954 (M1398).
c. Crew lists on vessels arriving 1903–1917 (M1399).
d. Certificates of head tax paid by aliens arriving from foreign contiguous territory, 1917–1924 (M1365).
e. Passenger lists of vessels arriving at Seattle from insular possession, 1908–1917 (M1485).
f. Customs passenger lists of vessels arriving at Port Townsend and Tacoma, 1894–1909 (M1484).
g. Passenger and crew lists of airplanes arriving at Seattle, 1947–1954 (M1386).
h. See also "St. Albans District, Vermont."

45. **South Carolina**
a. Index to passenger lists, 1890–1924 (T517).
b. Supplemental index to M575 (M334).
c. Copies of passenger lists, Charleston, 1820–1828 (M575, roll 2).
d. Copies of passenger lists, Port Royal, 1865 (M575, roll 15).
e. Passenger lists of vessels arriving at Georgetown, 1923–1939 (M1842).

46. **Texas**
a. Lists of aliens arriving at Brownsville, Del Rio, Eagle Pass, El Paso, Laredo, Presidio, Rio Grande City, and Roma, 1903–1909 (A3365).
b. Manifests of aliens granted temporary admission at Laredo, 1929–1955 (M1772).
c. Manifests of arrivals at Brownsville, 1905–1953 (M1502).
d. Indexes of vessels arriving at Brownsville, 1935–1955 (M1514).
e. See also "Galveston, Texas."

47. **Vermont** (see "St. Albans District, Vermont.")

48. **Virginia**
a. Supplemental index to M575 (M334).
b. Copies of passenger lists, Alexandria, 1820–1865 (M575, roll 1).
c. Copies of passenger lists, East River, 1830 (M575, roll 2).
d. Copies of passenger lists, Hampton, 1820–1821 (M575, roll 4).
e. Copies of passenger lists, Norfolk and Portsmouth, 1820–1857 (M575, roll 6).
f. Copies of passenger lists, Petersburg, 1820–1821 (M575, roll 8).
g. Copies of passenger lists, Richmond, 1820–1844 (M575, roll 16).
h. Check also Baltimore passenger lists on T844.

49. **Washington** (state) (see "Seattle and Other Washington Ports.")

50. **Wisconsin**
a. Crew lists of vessels arriving at Ashland, Kenosha, Marinette, Sheboygan, Sturgeon Bay, and Washburn, 1926–1956 (M2044).
b. Crew lists of vessels arriving at Manitowoc, 1925–1956 (M2045).
c. Crew lists of vessels arriving at Ashland (and possibly Green Bay and Milwaukee), 1922–1954 (M2005).

NATURALIZATION

Naturalization is the process by which immigrants become citizens of an adopted country. During the colonial period in British North America, each colony established its own procedure for naturalizing foreigners as citizens of that colony. State and county records reflect these actions. Because British subjects coming to the colonies, of course, were not foreigners, no naturalization process was needed.

After the founding of the U.S. government, Congress devised a two-step procedure that remained basically the same until 1941, when the first step was dropped. That first step was a declaration of one's intention to become a citizen, or filing of "first papers," followed usually two to seven years later, depending on the prevailing law, by a petition for naturalization. Any court of record (federal, state, or county) had the authority to accept and approve or reject the documents, and each court kept its own records of the proceedings. (Thus, no centralized repository contains these records.) After 1906, federal circuit courts (abolished in 1911) or district courts usually handled the proceedings, but many went through state and county courts. Records may be found in volumes labeled as declarations of intent, civil court minutes, oaths of allegiance, certificates of naturalization, or naturalization minutes.

Reminder

Of course, immigrants were not required to apply for citizenship, and many never did so. Some filed only the declaration and never completed the process. The immigrant could file the declaration at any time, and many took that step within the first several years after their arrival. The second step, the petition for naturalization, could be filed usually after five years' residence in the country and one year of residence in the state. However, an 1862 law allowed foreign-born, honorably-discharged veterans of the U.S. Army to apply for citizenship without filing the declaration of intention; the residency requirement was set at one year. An 1894 law gave the same privilege to navy and Marine Corps veterans who had served five years. Subsequent laws provided similar privileges to later veterans.

Since women could not vote in most states before the twentieth century and had limited legal rights, few women saw the need to apply for citizenship. Those who did usually were widows or single women. Between 1907 and 1922, U.S. women who married alien men, even in the United States, lost their U.S. citizenship. Between 1855 and 1922, immigrant women who married U.S. citizens acquired U.S. citizenship, as did their foreign-born minor children. Foreign-born women and minor children also gained "derivative" citizenship when the alien husband/father was naturalized. After 1922, women had to file for their own citizenship.

Between 1824 and 1906, foreign-born children who resided in the United States at least five years before turning twenty-three could declare their intention to become a citizen and petition for naturalization at the same time. One young man who acquired citizenship in this way was Frederick N.G. Nordberg, a native of Sweden and resident of San Francisco. When he applied for citizenship before the U.S. Circuit Court for the Northern District of California on 10 July 1900, he was twenty-three and had resided in the United States since 1893, when he immigrated at age sixteen. He had met the legal requirements and was admitted to citizenship the same day.

Notes

The INS was renamed as part of the government's reorganization in the creation of The Department of Homeland Security in 2002.

For more detail on the complex issue of women's citizenship, see "Women and Naturalization, ca. 1802–1940," by Marian L. Smith, in *Prologue 30* (summer 1998): 146–153. At this writing, the article in two parts is also available online at the National Archives Web site: <www.archives.gov/publicatons/prologue/summer_1998_women_and_naturalization_1.html> and <www.archives/gov/publications/prologue/summer_1998_women_and_naturalization_2.html>. Another article, "This Month in Immigration History: March 1790," capsules the U.S. naturalization laws and, at present, is on the Web site of the Bureau of Citizenship and Immigration Services, formerly the Immigration and Naturalization Service: <www.immigration.gov/graphics/aboutus/history/mar1790.htm>. See also the article "Naturalizations Since 1907." *INS Reporter* 26 (Winter 1977–1978): 41–46 and online at <www.immigration.gov/graphics/aboutus/history/since07.htm>.

Naturalization Records

Records of naturalization are scattered throughout the files of hundreds of courts. Many county and state courts still hold their own records, and clerks can direct researchers to the appropriate volumes and files. Court records not still held by the court can often be found in state archives or historical societies. The county records inventories conducted by the WPA in the 1930s may also help locate these proceedings. Federal court records are usually housed in the National Archives regional branch that services the state where the court is located. (See Appendix A.) The regional branches can answer more specific questions about their holdings.

When you know which court an ancestor visited to file the declaration of intent or petition for naturalization and know the location of the records of that court, your search is considerably shortened. Candidates for citizenship did not have to file all their documents in the same court, but petitions sometimes gave supporting evidence of where the declaration was filed.

If you do not know which court(s) an ancestor used, you may still be able to narrow the choices. It is often helpful to determine from census or other records an approximate date of naturalization or identify where the immigrant was living during the first five to fifteen years after arrival in this country.

Records that immigrants created in the United States may also help. For example, the 1870 census used column 19 to designate male *citizens* age twenty-one or older. The 1900–1930 censuses all asked whether each adult male was naturalized or alien, and the 1920 and 1930 forms asked for the year of naturalization. (The 1900–1910 censuses asked for the year of immigration.) Knowing how long a person had been in the country helps narrow your search. Look for church or organization membership records; voter registrations, such as the Great Registers of Voters in California or Arizona; some marriage records, which also may name parents; state census records taken between the federal decennial censuses; military pension records and World War I draft registration cards; federal land-entry case files at the National Archives, especially for those persons who acquired land under the Preemption Act of 1841 or the Homestead Act of 1862; death certificates and interment records; obituaries and newspaper articles, especially in ethnic newspapers; and passport applications.

Passport applications of naturalized citizens usually include the date and place of naturalization. Figure 11-3, on page 397, illustrates the 1876 passport application for San Francisco resident, Richard Hayn. His application reported his birth in Berlin (then Prussia) on 21 October 1835 and his naturalization in the U.S. Circuit Court for California, 16 October 1868. Although providing no immigration information, the document named his wife, Ludivico [*sic*], and their daughter, Mary.

Although immigrants had several choices of courts to use, many localities concentrated their naturalization proceedings in one or two courts, and many courts used separate volumes for these records. Of course, if the family kept the certificate of naturalization issued to the new citizen, that document can furnish the name of the court where the proceedings took place.

If your immigrant ancestor was naturalized after 1906, a copy of the file was sent to the Bureau of Immigration and Naturalization, later called the INS and now the BCIS. You can request a copy of form G-639, available from the Bureau of Citizenship and Immigration Services Web site <www.immigration.gov/graphics/formsfee/forms/files/g-639.pdf>. The instructions say to file your request with the BCIS office nearest you. You may also be able to send it to the Bureau of Citizenship and Immigration Services, Freedom of Information, 425 I Street, Washington, DC 20536.

Until 1941, to begin the process of naturalization, an immigrant usually filed the "first papers," a declaration of intention to become a citizen. Some nineteenth-century declarations give only basic information about the applicant. The following is a transcription of the 1887 declaration for Desire Hautekiet. Italics indicate what the clerk wrote on a preprinted form:[2]

> District Court of the United States For the Southern District of California.
>
> Southern District of California, ss.
>
> I, *Desire Hautekiet*, do declare on oath, that it is bona fide my intention to become a citizen of the United States of America, and to renounce forever all allegiance and fidelity to any foreign prince, potentate, state or sovereignty whatever, and particularly to *Leopold II King of Belgium* of whom I am now a subject.
>
> Sworn to and subscribe this *1st* day of *August 1887*, before me, *E.H. Owen*, clerk of the District Court of the United States for the Southern Dist. of California.
>
> [Signed]: *Désiré Hautekiet*

Other documents, especially after 1906, contained more detail about the applicant. An interesting declaration from the U.S. Circuit Court for the Southern District of California in Los Angeles was the 1906 attempt of Los Angeles resident Antonio Regina, a twenty-nine-year-old musician and a native of Ferrantino, Potenza, Italy, who reportedly emigrated from Naples, Italy, to New York, arriving on 22 February 1904. His application was "cancelled by reason of the inability of said Antonio to give the name of the vessel upon which he came to the United States."[3]

Figure 11-4, on page 409, is a detailed record for David Redit, filed in the U.S. Circuit Court for the Southern District of California at Los Angeles. In addition to physical description, age, and occupation (mechanical engineer), the declaration reports the applicant's

- birth on 11 September 1849 in Bury Saint Edmunds, Suffolk County, England
- last foreign residence as Downham Market, Norfolk, England
- implied emigration from England to Canada
- emigration from Toronto to Detroit on 28 October 1896 on the Central Pacific Railroad between the two cities

When applicants for naturalization had completed their residency requirement, they could apply or petition for citizenship. As in the declaration process, courts kept records in their individual ways. For a while, the U.S. Circuit Court for the Northern District of California noted applications for naturalization as line items in a register book that gave the basic facts of each case, including the petitioner's name, age, residence, birthplace, witnesses, and classification, or the process under which he was filing his petition. The following are several examples from that record (Family History Library microfilm 0940177):

- Alan Owen, age thirty, native of England and resident of San Francisco, petitioned for naturalization and was admitted on 11 August 1900, having filed his declaration of intention in the Superior Court for the County of Santa Barbara on 26 February 1892. (He filed his declaration and petition in the same state but not the same court.)

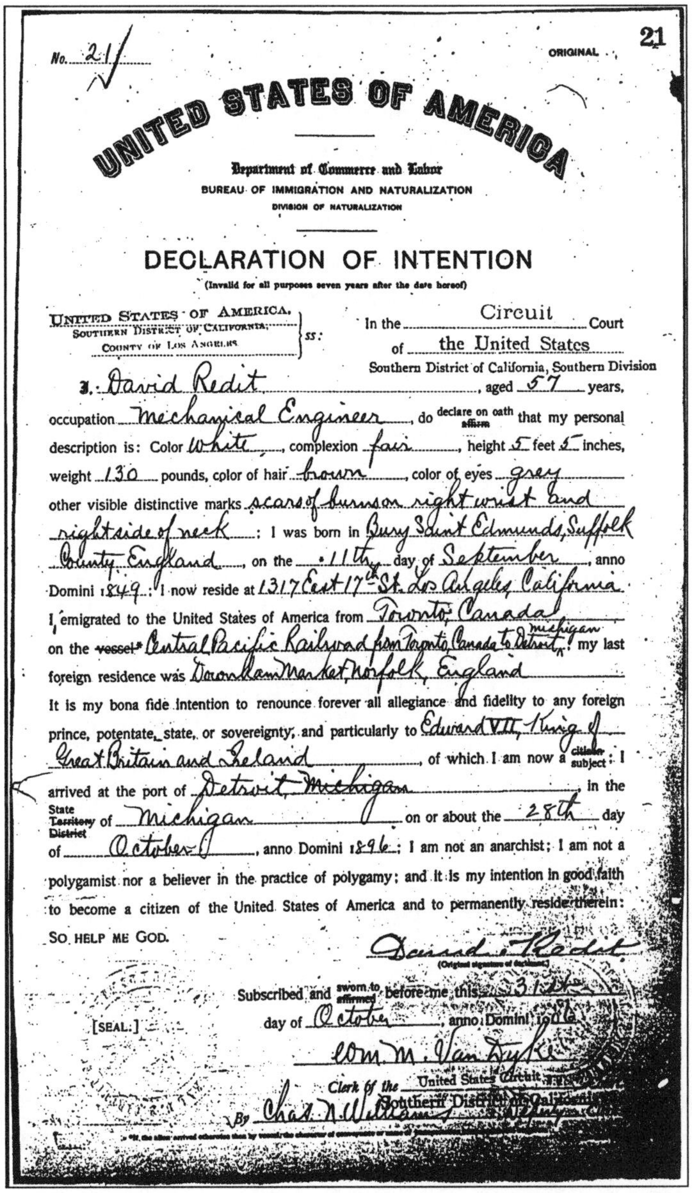

No. 21 ORIGINAL 21

UNITED STATES OF AMERICA

Department of Commerce and Labor

BUREAU OF IMMIGRATION AND NATURALIZATION

DIVISION OF NATURALIZATION

DECLARATION OF INTENTION

(Invalid for all purposes seven years after the date hereof)

UNITED STATES OF AMERICA, SOUTHERN DISTRICT OF CALIFORNIA, COUNTY OF LOS ANGELES } ss: In the Circuit Court of the United States Southern District of California, Southern Division

I, David Redit, aged 57 years, occupation Mechanical Engineer, do declare on oath that my personal description is: Color White, complexion fair, height 5 feet 5 inches, weight 130 pounds, color of hair brown, color of eyes grey other visible distinctive marks scars of burns on right wrist and right side of neck; I was born in Bury Saint Edmunds, Suffolk County England, on the 11th day of September, anno Domini 1849; I now reside at 1317 East 17th St. Los Angeles California. I emigrated to the United States of America from Toronto, Canada on the Central Pacific Railroad from Toronto, Canada to Detroit, michigan; my last foreign residence was Downham Market Norfolk, England. It is my bona fide intention to renounce forever all allegiance and fidelity to any foreign prince, potentate, state, or sovereignty, and particularly to Edward VII, King of Great Britain and Ireland, of which I am now a subject; I arrived at the port of Detroit, Michigan, in the State of Michigan on or about the 28th day of October, anno Domini 1896; I am not an anarchist; I am not a polygamist nor a believer in the practice of polygamy; and it is my intention in good faith to become a citizen of the United States of America and to permanently reside therein: SO HELP ME GOD.

David Redit
(Original signature of declarant.)

Subscribed and sworn to before me this 31st day of October, anno Domini 1906

[SEAL.]

Wm. M. Van Dyke
Clerk of the United States Circuit Court, Southern District of California.
By Chas. N. Williams, Deputy Clerk.

Figure 11-4 Declaration of David Redit, 31 October 1906, p. 21, Declarations of Intention for the U.S. Southern District of California, FHL microfilm 1491530, item 2.

- William Kailin, age thirty-three, native of Switzerland and resident of San Francisco, petitioned and was admitted on 12 March 1901, having filed his declaration of intention on 21 August 1888 in the District Court of Polk County, Iowa. (He filed his declaration and petition in different states as he moved west.)
- Alex Ivar Walstrom, age twenty-nine, born in Sweden and living in San Francisco, petitioned for and was granted citizenship on 1 May 1900 by virtue of U.S. Navy service. He enlisted on 6 January 1897 at Mare Island. He served on the *Independence* and the *Monterey* and was discharged from the U.S.S. *Solace* at Yokohama, Japan, on 20 February 1900.

The 1855 naturalization record shown in Figure 11-8, on page 424, gives very little information about the applicant. By contrast, a more recent petition for naturalization, dated 9 August 1907, contains much more genealogical information. The applicant was Sidney Augustus Marsh, a retail lumber dealer of Wharton, Texas, who sailed from Antwerp, Belgium, in August 1889, arrived at New York thereafter on a ship whose name he did not remember, and was in Texas by December 1889. His petition, filed with the state district court of Wharton County, Texas, gives this additional information:[4]

> Born 7 September 1865, London, England. Wife Silvia Jane (Moody) Marsh, born in Dover, England. Seven living children: (1) Mabel, born 2 December 1887, London, (2) Dora, born 19 June 1889, London, (3) Lucille, born 19 December 1894, Wharton, Texas, (4) Estelle, born 19 July 1896, Wharton, (5) Dulce, born 19 February 1898, Wharton, (6) Henry, born 13 October 1902, Wharton, (7) Audry, born 26 November 1903, Wharton. Declaration of intention filed 29 March 1892, Wharton.

The affidavits on his character and residence were signed by J.P. Taylor, a local rice farmer, and Tom Brooks, a Wharton merchant. Marsh swore his oath of allegiance and was admitted to citizenship 5 December 1907.

Finding Naturalization Records

Microfilm Source

The following microfilm publications are some of the naturalization records—often filmed from the originals held at National Archives regional branches—available at the National Archives and the applicable regional branches. The microfilm may be purchased from the National Archives or Scholarly Resources, and many titles are available for rent from the Family History Library. Many research libraries also have microfilm pertinent to their state or region. This microfilm represents mostly records from federal courts, but many naturalizations are recorded in state and county courts from which some have been microfilmed. Check the Family History Library catalog and other research libraries for microfilmed, abstracted, or transcribed records and indexes.

1. **General.** *American Naturalization Processes and Procedures 1790–1985*, by John J. Newman. Indianapolis: Indiana Historical Society, 1985.
2. **General.** *Guide to Naturalization Records of the United States*, by Christina K. Schaefer. Baltimore: Genealogical Publishing Co., 1997.
3. **General.** *Laws Relating to Immigration and Nationality, 1798–1962, and Directories of Courts Having Naturalization Jurisdiction, 1908–1963* (M2033).
4. **Alabama.** *Declarations of Intention, Huntsville, 1875–1894*, from the U.S. Circuit Court, Alabama, Northern District, from originals in the East Point, Georgia, branch of the National Archives; film available from the Family History Library. See also "Southeastern United States."
5. **Alaska.** *Indexes to Naturalization Records of U.S. District Court for the District and Territory of Alaska, 1900–1929* (M1241). *Naturalization Records of the U.S. District Courts for the State of Alaska, 1900–1924* (M1539). *Indexes to Naturalization Records of the U.S. District Court for the District, Territory, and State of Alaska (Third Division), 1903–1991* (M1788).
6. **Arizona.** *Naturalization Records of the U.S. District Court for the Territory of Arizona* (M1615). *Naturalization Records of the U.S. District Court for the District of Arizona* (M1616).
7. **Arkansas.** *Index to Naturalization Records in Arkansas, 1809–1906*, prepared by Immigration and Naturalization Records Indexing Project of the WPA; film available from the Family History Library. The NARA regional branch in Fort Worth, Texas, holds mostly post-1906 naturalization records from the U.S. District Courts for the eastern and western districts of Arkansas, some of which are on microfilm; a holdings list is available from Fort Worth.

8. **California.** *Selected Indexes to Naturalization Records of the U.S. District and Circuit Courts, Northern District of California, 1852–1928* (T1220). *Index to Naturalization in the U.S. District Court for the Northern District of California, 1852–ca. 1989* (M1744). *Index to Naturalization Records of the U.S. District for the Southern District of California, Central Division, Los Angeles, 1887–1937* (M1607). *Naturalization Index Cards of the U.S. District Court for the Southern District of California, Central Division, Los Angeles, 1915–1976* (M1525). *Naturalization Records of the U.S. District Court for the Southern District of California, Central Division, Los Angeles, 1887–1940* (M1524).
9. **Colorado.** *Naturalization Records Created by the U.S. District Court in Colorado, 1877–1952* (M1192).
10. **Connecticut.** *Naturalization Record Books, 1842–1903*, declarations of intent and petitions for naturalization, and *Naturalization Record Books, 1893–1906*, petitions of naturalization, from the U.S. District Court, Connecticut District, from originals held at the Federal Records Center, Waltham, Massachusetts; film available from Family History Library. See also "New England."
11. **Delaware.** *Index to Naturalization Petitions for the U.S. Circuit Court, 1795–1911, and the U.S. District Court, 1795–1928, for the District of Delaware* (M1649). *Naturalization Petitions of the U.S. District and Circuit Courts for the District of Delaware, 1795–1930* (M1644). *Naturalization Records, 1795–1932*, from the U.S. District Court in Delaware, from originals held at the Philadelphia branch of the National Archives; film available from the Family History Library.
12. **District of Columbia.** *Index to Naturalization Records of the U.S. Supreme Court for the District of Columbia, 1802–1909* (M1827).
13. **Florida.** See "Southeastern United States."
14. **Georgia.** *Naturalization Records, 1790–1940*, from the U.S. District Court, Georgia, Southern District; from original records at the U.S. Courthouse, Savannah. *Naturalization Certificate Stubs, 1907–1926*, from the U.S. District Court, Georgia, Northern District, Atlanta; from original records at the East Point, Georgia, branch of the National Archives.
15. **Hawaii.** *Index to Naturalizations of the US District Court for the District of Hawaii, 1900–1976* (M2074).
16. **Illinois.** Numerous records have been filmed from the U.S. Circuit Court and U.S. District Courts in Illinois; check the Family History Library catalog for details. Examples include these: *Naturalization Records, 1906–1932*, from the U.S. District Court, Illinois, Eastern District; *Naturalization Records, 1856–1931*, from the U.S. District Court for the Southern District of Illinois, Springfield; *Naturalization Records, 1856–1903*, from the U.S. Circuit Court for the Southern District of Illinois; and *Oaths of Allegiance, 1872–1906*, from the U.S. Circuit Court for the Northern District of Illinois. All of these and others are film of originals held at the Chicago branch of the National Archives and available from the Family History Library. *Soundex Index to Naturalization Petitions for U.S. District & Circuit Courts, Northern District of Illinois, and Immigration and Naturalization Service, District 9, 1840–1950*, apparently prepared by the WPA; this district also extended into neighboring portions of Indiana, Iowa, and Wisconsin.
17. **Indiana.** *An Index to Indiana Naturalization Records Found in Various Order Books of the Ninety-Two Local Courts Prior to 1907*, by John J. Newman. Indianapolis, Ind.: Indiana Historical Society, 1981. See also courts of the Northern District of Illinois.

18. **Iowa.** *Declarations of Intention and Miscellaneous Papers, 1849–1888*, from the U.S. District Court for the Eastern Division of Iowa; *General Index to Declaration of Intention and Petitions, 1909–1948; Declaration of Intention, 1917–1936; Petitions, 1909–1936*, from the U.S. District Court for the Central Division of Iowa. These and other microfilm publications are from the originals at the Kansas City, Missouri, branch of the National Archives and available through the Family History Library. See also courts of the Northern District of Illinois.
19. **Kansas.** *Index to Naturalizations, 1856–1897; Declarations of Intention, 1862–1897*, from the U.S. District Court for Kansas; *Declarations of Intention, 1908–1942; Naturalizations, 1865–1984*, from the U.S. District Court for Kansas, First Division. These and other microfilm publications are from the originals at the Kansas City, Missouri, branch of the National Archives and available through the Family History Library.
20. **Kentucky.** See "Southeastern United States."
21. **Louisiana.** *Proofs of Citizenship Used to Apply for Seamen's Protection Certificates for the Port of New Orleans, Louisiana, 1800, 1802, 1804–1807, 1809–1812, 1814–1816, 1818–1819, 1821, 1850–1851, 1855, 1857* (M1826). *Naturalization Records, 1906–1932*, from the U.S. District Court for the Eastern District of Louisiana, from the court clerk's office in New Orleans; these and several other microfilm publications are available from the Family History Library. The NARA regional branch at Fort Worth, Texas, holds mostly post-1906 naturalization records for the U.S. District Courts for the western and eastern districts of Louisiana, Record Group 21. From Record Group 85, the branch holds an index to naturalizations in Louisiana, 1831–1906. Contact the branch for a holdings list.
22. **Maine.** See "New England."
23. **Maryland.** *Index to Naturalization Petitions to the U.S. Circuit and District Courts for Maryland, 1797–1951* (M1168). *Naturalization Petitions of the US District Court for the District of Maryland, 1906–1930* (M1640).
24. **Massachusetts.** *Index to Naturalization Petitions and Records of the U.S. District Court, 1906–1966, and the U.S. Circuit Court, 1906–1911*, (M1545). *Petitions and Records of Naturalization of the U.S. District Court and Circuit Courts of the District of Massachusetts, 1906–1929* (M1368). See also "New England."
25. **Michigan.** *Naturalization Records, 1887–1915*, from the U.S. District Court for the Western District of Michigan, Northern Division; *Naturalization Records, 1970–1930*, from the U.S. District Court for the Western District of Michigan, Southern Division; *Declarations of Intention, 1911–1930*, for the U.S. District Court for the Eastern District of Michigan; these and other microfilm publications of the original records at the Chicago branch of the National Archives are available through the Family History Library.
26. **Minnesota.** *Naturalizations, 1875–1911; Declarations of Intention, 1875–1911*, from the U.S. Circuit Court for Minnesota, Third Division; *Declarations of Intention, 1872–1955; Naturalizations, 1859–1954*, for the U.S. District Court of Minnesota, primarily the Third Division; *Declarations of Intention, 1906–1962*, for the U.S. District Court for Minnesota, Fourth Division (Minneapolis); *Naturalizations, 1897–1911*, from the U.S. Circuit Court for Minnesota, Sixth Division; these and other microfilm publications from the originals at the Kansas City, Missouri, branch of the National Archives are available through the Family History Library.
27. **Mississippi.** See "Southeastern United States."
28. **Missouri.** *Declarations of Intention, 1895–1985*, from the U.S. District Court for

Missouri, Southern Division; *Declarations of Intention, 1849–1911*, from the U.S. Circuit Court for the Eastern Judicial District of Missouri, Eastern Division (St. Louis); *Declarations of Intention, 1892–1936*, for the U.S. District Court for the Western District of Missouri, Western Division (Kansas City); *Naturalization Petitions, 1909–1929*, from the U.S. District Court for the Western District of Missouri, Western Division (Kansas City); *Naturalization Petitions and Records, 1911–1937; Citizenship Petitions, 1930–1936; Naturalization Certificate Stubs, 1916–1927*, from the U.S. District Court for Missouri, Southern Division; these and other microfilm publications of the original records in the National Archives branch in Kansas City, Missouri, are available through the Family History Center.

29. **Montana.** *Indexes to Naturalization Records of the Montana Territorial and Federal Courts, 1869–1929* (M1236). *Naturalization Records of the U.S. District Courts for the State of Montana, 1891–1929* (M1538).
30. **Nebraska.** *Declarations of Intention, 1876–1943*, from the U.S. District Court for Nebraska, Omaha Division; *Declarations of Intention and Military Petitions for Naturalizations, 1867–1909*, from the U.S. Circuit Court for Nebraska; *Naturalization Petitions, 1868–1906*, from the U.S. Circuit Court for Nebraska; these and other microfilm publications from the originals at the Kansas City, Missouri, branch of the National Archives are available from the Family History Center.
31. **Nevada.** Consult federal, state, and local courts and archives in the state.
32. **New England.** *Index to New England Naturalization Petitions, 1791–1906* (M1299), Soundex index to court documents in Connecticut, Maine, Massachusetts, New Hampshire, Rhode Island, and Vermont.
33. **New Hampshire.** See "New England."
34. **New Jersey.** *Naturalization Records, 1832–1847, 1852, 1856–1858, 1861–1862*, from the New Jersey Court of Chancery, microfilm available from the Family History Library. See also *Guide to Naturalization Records in New Jersey*, prepared by the New Jersey Historical Records Program, WPA (Newark: Historical Records Program, 1941).
35. **New Mexico.** See *Over 1,400 Naturalization Records for Various Courts of New Mexico: 1882–1917, Denver Federal Archives*. Lakewood, Colo.: Foothills Genealogical Society of Colorado, 1988.
36. **New York.** *Index to Naturalization Petitions of the United States District Court for the Eastern District of New York, 1865–1957* (M1164). *Index (Soundex) to Naturalization Petitions Filed in Federal, State, and Local Courts in New York, New York, Including New York, Kings, Queens, and Richmond Counties, 1792–1906* (M1674). *Alphabetical Index to Declarations of Intention of the U.S. District Court for the Southern District of New York, 1917–1950* (M1675). *Alphabetical Index to Petitions for Naturalization of the U.S. District Court for the Southern District of New York, 1824–1941* (M1676). *Alphabetical Index to Petitions for Naturalization of the U.S. District Court for the Western District of New York, 1906–1966* (M1677).
37. **North Carolina.** See "Southeastern United States."
38. **North Dakota.** *Declarations of Intention, 1890–1924*, from the U.S. Circuit Court for North Dakota, Southeastern Division, from originals held by the court in Fargo; *Declarations of Intention, 1891–1906*, for the U.S. Circuit Court for North Dakota, Northwestern Division, from originals held at the court in Devil's Lake; *Naturalization Records 1906–1924*, from the U.S. District Court for North Dakota, Southeastern Division, from original records held by the court at Fargo; these and other similar publications are available from the Family History Library.

39. **Ohio.** *Record of Declarations of Intention at Dayton, 1916–1935*, from the U.S. District Court for the Southern District of Ohio (Dayton); *Naturalization Service Petitions and Records at Columbus, 1918–1931*, from the U.S. District Court for the Southern District of Ohio (Columbus); these and other similar publications are available from the Family History Library.
40. **Oklahoma.** The NARA regional branch at Fort Worth holds naturalization records, both pre- and post-1906, from the U.S. District Courts for Indian Territory and for the eastern and western districts of the state of Oklahoma; the branch has microfilmed some records. Contact Fort Worth for a holdings list. Also consult federal, state, and county courts in the state.
41. **Oregon.** *Index to the Naturalization Records of the U.S. District Court for Oregon, 1859–1956* (M1242). *Naturalization Records for the U.S. District Court for the District of Oregon, 1859–1941* (M1540).
42. **Pennsylvania.** *Indexes to Registers and Registers of Declarations of Intention and Petitions for Naturalization of the U.S. District and Circuit Courts for the Western District of Pennsylvania, 1820–1906* (M1208). Also *Indexes to Naturalization Petitions to the U.S. Circuit and District Courts for the Eastern District of Pennsylvania, 1795–1951* (M1248).
43. **Puerto Rico.** *Declaraciones de Naturalización, 1899–1900*, from the Archivo General de Puerto Rico, San Juan.
44. **Rhode Island.** *Military Petitions for Naturalization (Newport County), 1902–1918*, from the Superior Court of Newport County, from originals at the Rhode Island Judicial Records Center, Pawtucket. See also "New England."
45. **South Carolina.** *Record of Admissions to Citizenship, District of South Carolina, 1790–1906* (M1183). See also "Southeastern United States."
46. **South Dakota.** *Declarations of Intention, 1851–1911*, from the U.S. District Court for North Dakota [*sic*], Second Judicial District; *Declarations of Intention, 1891–1906*, from the U.S. Circuit Court for South Dakota; *Naturalization Records, 1904–1906; Petitions and Records, 1906–1928*, from the U.S. District Court for South Dakota; these and other similar records from the Kansas City, Missouri, branch of the National Archives are available through the Family History Library.
47. **Southeastern United States.** *Declarations of Intentions, Naturalizations, and Petitions, 1855–1960*, from U.S. District Court, Southern District of Alabama, with jurisdiction over Alabama, Florida, Georgia, Kentucky, Mississippi, North Carolina, South Carolina, Tennessee; these films of originals at the East Point, Georgia, branch of the National Archives are available from the Family History Library. See also *Naturalization Records of District Courts in the Southeast, 1790–1958* (M1547).
48. **Tennessee.** See "Southeastern United States."
49. **Texas.** The NARA regional branch at Fort Worth holds (a) naturalization records of the U.S. District Courts for the northern, southern, eastern, and western districts of Texas, some of which the branch has microfilmed and (b) a partial index to Texas naturalizations, 1846–1939. Contact the branch for a list of holdings. See also the records of the federal, state, and county courts within the state.
50. **Utah.** *Naturalization Records, 1896–1932*, from records of the U.S. District Court for Utah in Salt Lake City; *Naturalization Records, 1851–1936; Indexes, 1858–1980*, from the U.S. District Court for Utah Territory, Third Judicial District, and the U.S. District Court for Salt Lake County, from records held by the court in Salt Lake City; these and similar records are available from the Family History Library.

51. **Vermont.** See "New England."
52. **Virginia.** *Naturalization Petitions and Declarations, 1867–1912*, from the U.S. Circuit Court for the Eastern District of Virginia; *Naturalization Records, 1910–1929*, from the U.S. District Court for the Western District of Virginia; *Naturalization Records, 1909–1929*, from the U.S. District Court for the Eastern District of Virginia; these and similar records held by the Philadelphia branch of the National Archives are available from the Family History Library.
53. **Washington.** *Indexes to Naturalization Records of the U.S. District Court for Western Washington, Northern Division (Seattle), 1890–1952* (M1232). *Indexes to Naturalization Records of King County Territorial and Superior Courts, 1864–1889, and 1906–1928* (M1233). Index to the same, Thurston County, 1850–1974 (M1234). Index to the same, Snohomish County, 1876–1974 (M1235). Index to the same, Pierce County, 1853–1923 (M1238). *Index to Naturalization Records of the U.S. District Court, Western District of Washington, Southern Division (Tacoma), 1890–1953* (M1237). *Naturalization Records of the U.S. District Court for the Eastern District of Washington, 1890–1972* (M1541). *Naturalization Records of the U.S. District Court for the Western District of Washington, 1890–1957* (M1542). *Naturalization Records of the Superior Courts for King, Pierce, Thurston, and Snohomish Counties, Washington, 1850–1974* (M1543).
54. **West Virginia.** *Naturalization Petitions of the U.S. District Court for the Northern District of West Virginia, Wheeling, 1856–1867* (M1643). *Declarations of Intention, 1908–1938*, from the U.S. District Court for the Northern District of West Virginia (at Elkins), available through the Family History Library; *Naturalization Records, 1844–1875*, from the U.S. District Court for the Northern District of West Virginia, from originals at the National Archives Records Center, Philadelphia and available on microfilm from the Family History Library.
55. **Wisconsin.** *Naturalization Records, 1840–1900*, from the Wisconsin Supreme Court, from originals at the State Historical Society of Wisconsin in Madison and available through the Family History Library.
56. **Wyoming.** Consult federal, state, and county courts within the state.

NAME CHANGES

Numerous examples exist of immigrants or their descendants who chose to change their names by translating, anglicizing, or simplifying the original or by choosing a different name, usually several years after arrival in their adopted land or even a generation later. **These changes did not occur during the immigration process.** The translations occurred later when Verdi became Green, Koenig became King, and Le Blanc became White. Anglicizing may have been simply a matter of a spelling change based on the way people pronounced the name or the way English-speaking recorders happened to write it down. In this way, for example, the German Rhine sometimes was recorded as Ryan. Such examples, of course, tell the genealogist that finding an ancestor recorded as Michael Ryan does not automatically give the researcher Irish roots.

Important

Simplification of the name so that it was easier for Americans to pronounce and spell also has numerous examples: Heidt to Hite; Tighe to Tie; O'Donnell to Donald or Donaldson; Morganari to Morgan; and Preuss to Price.

The following four families have preserved their immigrants' stories, and those traditions may be the only evidence of the name changes that were made. Like thousands of others, they do not seem to have gone through any official channels in assuming their new identity.

1. Jimmy Dalla's family came to the United States about 1909 from the Austrian Tyrol, now part of Italy. Their surname was Dalla Valla. As early as 1911, newspaper accounts were using the name in its original form and in the shortened form, Dalla, which the family gradually adopted.
2. Bill Brohaugh's immigrant family were Olsens from an area in Norway called Brohaug. They found so many Olsens already in their new home that they began distinguishing themselves as the Olsens from Brohaug. Eventually, they dropped Olsen altogether and became Brohaugh.
3. Steve DeAlmeida's immigrant ancestors were Carl and Anna Alice (Gunnison) Gumerson, from Goteborg, Sweden. When the widow Gumerson married the Portuguese Manuel DeAlmeida in the United States in 1884, her son Carl Edward simply assumed his stepfather's surname. Thus a Swede got a Portuguese surname.
4. Naturalization was another process during which some names changed. At least according to his story, the young Greek Spiridon Kalivospheris immigrated from Sparta in the first decade of the twentieth century and later told his son Jerry how his name was changed. When the traveling judge came through Marion, Ohio, in 1910 and naturalized three new citizens, two from Germany and one from Greece, he changed all three names on the spot. Young Spiridon was told his new name would be Spiro Kaler, and so he remained. When his younger brothers joined him in the United States, he made them change their names to Kaler as well.

The card index to the naturalization records of the U.S. District Court for the Northern District of California illustrate a number of names changes, including minor ones—Placido Melchiori changing his name to Placid Melchior in 1941. However, descendants may be surprised to find more major changes, as in 1942 when Moishe Mednikov, a resident of Cleveland, Ohio, was naturalized in California as Maurice Albert Meldon.

Some names changed through court action, and court records can help identify those cases. Some immigrants or their descendants used the state legislatures for name changes. Two examples come from the Laws of Delaware, Private Acts of 1899, when Joseph F. Zinieuries changed his name to Joseph F. Emory and Michael Ostrowsky shortened his name to Michael Ostro. The New York legislature on 27 March 1848 enabled Johan Hinnerich August von Rethwisch to become John Washington. If his descendants do not have family records that show his original name, the legislative record gives them a pleasant surprise.

Which Name Is Correct?

Name changes were not always a conscious decision of the individual or family, nor was spelling always consistent. People fairly new to genealogy often ask, "My great-grandfather's death certificate says his mother's maiden name was Anders; his brother's death certificate says the name was Andrews; her obituary says it was Andress. How do I know which was correct? Is the name Scottish?" The answer sometimes surprises the questioner:

- Expect spelling variations of any name in records created by or about ancestors, especially prior to the mid-twentieth century. Standardized spelling is a relatively recent phenomenon. When speaking with our ancestors, clerks wrote what they heard and often spelled phonetically. If ancestors spoke with a thick regional accent or if English was not their native tongue, clerks may not have understood them accurately.

- Different family members may have used different spellings, consciously or not. This does not necessarily signal a rift or illiteracy in the family. Sometimes it was simply personal preference; sometimes it was easier to conform to the way the community spelled the name than to cling to a difficult spelling or correct everyone's usage.
- The important point is not one of identifying one correct spelling but of finding the correct ancestors in the records we research. Thus, study your ancestors one generation at a time in many different kinds of records. Using given names of the family cluster and building on clues from legitimate sources, you can usually determine whether you are working with the correct family. Once you have identified the immigrant(s) of this family, thorough research may give you clues to their specific origin.
- If you can find records containing the signatures of various family members, you may be able to determine (1) what each person considered the surname to be and (2) whether a variant spelling occurred throughout the family during a certain time period.

ETHNIC GENEALOGICAL AND HISTORICAL SOCIETIES

Numerous ethnic historical and genealogical societies exist in the United States and Canada for descendants and researchers of immigrant ancestors. Below are a few examples. You may identify others through the *Encyclopedia of Associations*, online via Cyndi's List <www.cyndislist.com>, and in books and articles about ethnic genealogy.

- Federation of Genealogical Societies, P.O. Box 200940, Austin, TX 78720-0940. Phone: (888) FGS-1500. General Information, e-mail: fgs-office@fgs.org. Web site: <www.fgs.org>. For information on member societies, including those with ethnic focus: <www.familyhistory.com/societyhall/main.asp>.
- American-French Genealogical Society, 78 Earle St., Woonsocket, RI 02895.
- Czech Heritage Society of Texas, Library and Archives, 4117 Willowbend Dr., Houston, TX 77025. Phone: (866) 293-2443, Web site: <www.czechheritage.org>.
- Federation of East European Family History Societies, P.O. Box 510898, Salt Lake City, UT 84151-0898. From Web site <www.feefhs.org>, see "Ethnic, Religious, National Index" for links to numerous societies in the United States and Canada.
- Germanic Genealogy Society, P.O. Box 16312, St. Paul, MN 55116-0312. Web site: <www.mtn.org/branches/german.html>.
- The Hispanic Genealogical Society of New York, Murray Hill Station, P.O. Box 818, New York, NY 10156-0818. Web site: <www.hispanicgenealogy.com>.
- Italian Genealogical Society of America, P.O. Box 3572, Peabody, MA 01961-3572. Web site: <www.italianroots.com>.
- Palatines to America (German Immigrants to America), 611 East Weber Road, Columbus, OH 43211-1097. Web site: <www.palam.org>. Chapters currently in Colorado, Illinois, Indiana, New York, Ohio, Pennsylvania, and West Virginia.
- Polish Genealogical Society of America, 984 Milwaukee Ave., Chicago, IL 60622. E-mail: PGSAmerica@aol.com; Website: <www.pgsa.org>.
- The Vesterheim Genealogical Center and Naeseth Library, division of Norwegian-American Museum, 415 Main St., Madison, WI 53703-3116. Phone: (608) 255-2224. Norwegian-American Museum, 523 W. Water St., P.O. Box 379, Decorah, IA 52101. Phone: (563) 382-9681. E-mail: vesterheim@vesterheim.org. Web site: <www.vesterheim.org>.

Case Study

Please read the endnotes for this case study, beginning on page 445.

CASE STUDY: GRANDPA'S HOOEY

Charlie Gardes's grandfather from New Orleans always said the Gardes family came from France, but actually he was feeding his grandchildren a bunch of hooey. As Charlie says, "Hooey is fun in your childhood but utterly useless when you start into genealogy."[5] As an adult, when the genealogy bug bit him, he set as one goal to find the European origin of his surname immigrant. He began looking for anything and everything French with the name Gardes on it and found the exercise a disastrous waste of time. Before long, he realized he had to begin with himself and work back one generation at a time. In the process, he discovered that Monsieur Great-great-grandfather Immigrant from France was actually Herr Great-great-grandfather Immigrant from Germany. Was Grandpa's hooey simply an assumption of French origin because of deep New Orleans roots, or was it intentional? Charlie knew something was not right and vowed to uncover the real story.

In his research, Charlie learned that Herr Immigrant was Henri Gardes[6] (*geboren* Hinrich Gärdes, as discovered late in the research); his only child, Henry Washburn Gardes. Family lore, of which there was precious little, told that Henri was an incredibly successful businessman who became quite wealthy; tradition said little of Henry W.

Henry Washburn Gardes

Living family members had no "Aunt Mabel's attic" in which to find a treasure of family papers. Charlie's Aunt Weesie (Esther Louise Gardes) remembered, from her childhood, her two aunts talking about family, but in French whenever they knew their niece was listening. She recalled two tidbits in English that gave Charlie a focus after very limited success with census records: Henry W. was (1) absent from his family for a period in the 1890s and (2) buried in Arlington National Cemetery. Mulling things over in the shower one night, Charlie realized these clues suggested military service, possibly in the Spanish-American War, and therefore he needed to turn to military records.

After months and dollars spent trying to get copies of all Henry W.'s military service records, Charlie was informed that the National Archives had no more documents, and he was referred to the Veterans Administration. Since Henry W.'s widow lived to 1957 and the pension file was a relatively recent twentieth-century document, Henry W.'s Veterans Administration pension file—250 pages of gold dust—came from that administration, not from the National Archives.[7]

Extracting information from the documents, which were not filed in chronological order of events, Charlie created a time line of Henry W.'s life. In a nutshell, Henry W. was born on 5 July 1860 in Washington, Hempstead County, Arkansas and

> . . . saw a great deal of the United States and the world, considering the epoch in which he lived. . . . In fact, for any time period, he led an exciting life. By the time he was forty years old, he had lived in rural Arkansas, rural New York, and New Orleans; attended boarding schools in both New York and Connecticut, and college in Connecticut; enlisted in the military in California (twice); sailed the Pacific Ocean as part of the Asiatic Squadron of the U.S. Navy; and moved to the northern Virginia/Washington, DC area where he remained the last thirty-six years of his life. He lived during an exciting era of history. . . . [He] fought in the Spanish-American War, including three battle engagements, and served in an administrative position during "the World War" (WWI) when he was in his late fifties. He graduated from an Ivy League school [Yale] and served as a coal passer on a naval warship. He was an adult during the industrial revolution

> when the electric light, telephone, motor car, airplane, and radio were not only invented but became part of everyday life.[8] [He died 7 March 1937.]

Although Henry W. was born shortly after the 1860 census, his pension file at least indicated where the family was for that census. Besides giving a detailed description of Henry W.'s army service (1894–1896) and naval service (1896–1899), schooling, and residences, the pension file also furnished the first surprise about Henry W.'s parentage: Henri Gardes, born in *Germany*, and Geraldine Delaide[9] Washburn of Hounsfield, Jefferson County, New York. How they met in Arkansas, where they married, is still a mystery, but family lore was that Geraldine, at age nineteen, was a schoolteacher in Arkansas. The couple married on or about 5 September 1859.[10] Geraldine died in New Orleans of yellow fever when her son was only six, and he was sent to live with her parents in New York.[11]

The Search for Herr Immigrant Begins

While Henry W. was in school in the east, in the military, and in the employment of the federal government in Washington, DC, his father, Henri, was actively making money in New Orleans. Henri Gardes died on 2 August 1913 at age eighty-one and was buried in New Orleans adjacent his wife, Geraldine, in the Fireman's Charitable and Benevolent Association Cemetery, later called Cypress Grove Cemetery.[12]

With voluminous biographical material on Henry W. Gardes and a few enticing clues on his father, it was time to return to the immigrant and the original goal of finding his origin. The search involved looking for Henri in city directories, private club and public business records, and even telegram ledgers from one place Henri had lived. Everything about Henri's origin said only "Germany." The 1910 census was a mess, apparently answered by someone who didn't know the family; the 1860 census had given nothing but their names. Henri's whereabouts between 1860 and 1910 were not clear; he seemed to be a moving target, with the record keepers always missing him.

Even the obituary requested by mail from the New Orleans Public Library covered only a few lines and yielded little. However, the short obituary was not the only announcement of his death in the paper; it was the only one supplied in answer to the long-distance request. Another descendant of Henri found a much longer article in the same issue as the short one.[13] It named companies with which Henri had been associated during his prominence in the business and social life of New Orleans. It also named Henri's birthplace: Bremen, Germany. Henri had arrived at the port of New York in 1847, reportedly in the company of an unnamed uncle. After working in New York for several years, Henri had been a partner in a mercantile house in Washington, Arkansas, and was reportedly in the Confederate quartermaster department during the Civil War. The war service turned out to be either incorrect knowledge on the part of the person providing the information to the newspaper—perhaps his socially prominent second wife and widow—or an attempt to embroider Henri's role in the war. Research determined that he was actually a civilian employee of the Confederate hospital in Arkansas, doing what he apparently did best—accounting and finance.

Why didn't Henri's great-great-grandson stop here and head for Bremen birth or baptism records? He didn't have a precise birth date or parents' names that would confirm the correct family in German records. How would he have known whether he had found the correct infant and family without this additional information? Instead, **he chose to continue learning all he could about Henri in his adopted country.**

Research Tip

In New Orleans after the war, Henri was connected with an important wholesale grocery firm; was in Houston, Texas, in the mid-1880s to help form a bank, which became Texas

Commerce Bank, currently Chase Manhattan Bank; and organized the American National Bank in New Orleans. By the 1890s, he was at the zenith of his career and "prominently connected with the most influential banks of the time. Adversity set in, however, and the disastrous reverses met by the institutions with which Mr. Gardes was connected caused the retirement into private life of the one time financier."[14]

The Reason for Grandpa's Hooey

Adversity usually makes the news: It sells newspapers. It also attracts genealogists who want to know everything they can learn about their ancestors. Henri's genealogist decided to investigate, using the newspaper's name index that the WPA had created. Henri's index entries led to a few minor stories, but his American National Bank was the key to a heretofore hidden chapter of Henri's life.

The bank had closed on 6 August 1896, and its demise and resulting troubles even made the front page of *The New York Times*, whose index Charlie decided to explore based on intuition. The obituary had said Henri came into and worked in New York; family lore said he had been there. The obituary also suggested his connections with prominent banks of the time, and that association included New York bankers.

On 29 August 1896, *The New York Times* headline read "Bank Officials in Trouble. Charged with Making False Reports of Their Institution." That day, the federal marshal had arrested the four directors of the American National Bank and charged them "with signing false statements of the bank's condition. These showed the bank to be all right just prior to its collapse two weeks ago." The previous evening the marshal had arrested the bank's president, Gardes, and cashier Girault. They allegedly had used bank funds to buy its stock, made large loans and false reports, and certified a check on an overdrawn account—all evidence of mismanagement.[15]

As embarrassing as this event surely was for these six families "of high social position," it alerted Henri's great-great-grandson to look for court records. Perhaps in court Henri would have had to state his name, birth date and birthplace, and other information of value in the search for his origin. Next to the New Orleans Public Library is the Louisiana Supreme Court Building, with a law library. The quickest resource to check there was the *Federal Reporter* of appellate cases, in case there had been an appeal after the initial trial. The appeal revealed where to find Henri in the 1900 census: the Ohio State Penitentiary. (See Figure 11-5, on page 421.)

The census enumerated Henri and his cashier Walter W. Girault on consecutive lines. Henri's birth date was reportedly November 1831; thus he was sixty-eight on census day. He reported having been married for twenty-five years and having been in the United States for fifty-three years, since 1847; he was a German-born naturalized U.S. citizen.[16] Again, his genealogist didn't drop everything to try to locate naturalization papers. Where would he look? New York? It's a large place. Arkansas? New Orleans? Or somewhere in between? He needed more information, and he had to satisfy his curiosity about Henri's state of affairs.

How did Henri arrive at this stage of his life? Charlie ordered the appeal file, which contained the trial documents, from the National Archives Fort Worth branch, which holds the files of the U.S. Fifth Circuit, which includes New Orleans. Nearly four thousand pages of typed court documents detailed the trial's stages, which began on 11 March 1897 with a federal grand jury's 136-count indictment, 605 pages long. Based on Section 5209 of the Revised Statutes of the United States, the charges against Walter W. Girault, Henry Gardes, and Thomas H. Underwood involved thirty-two acts of embezzlement and eight acts of false entries.[17] The first trial lasted from March 29 to April 15, with much testimony gener-

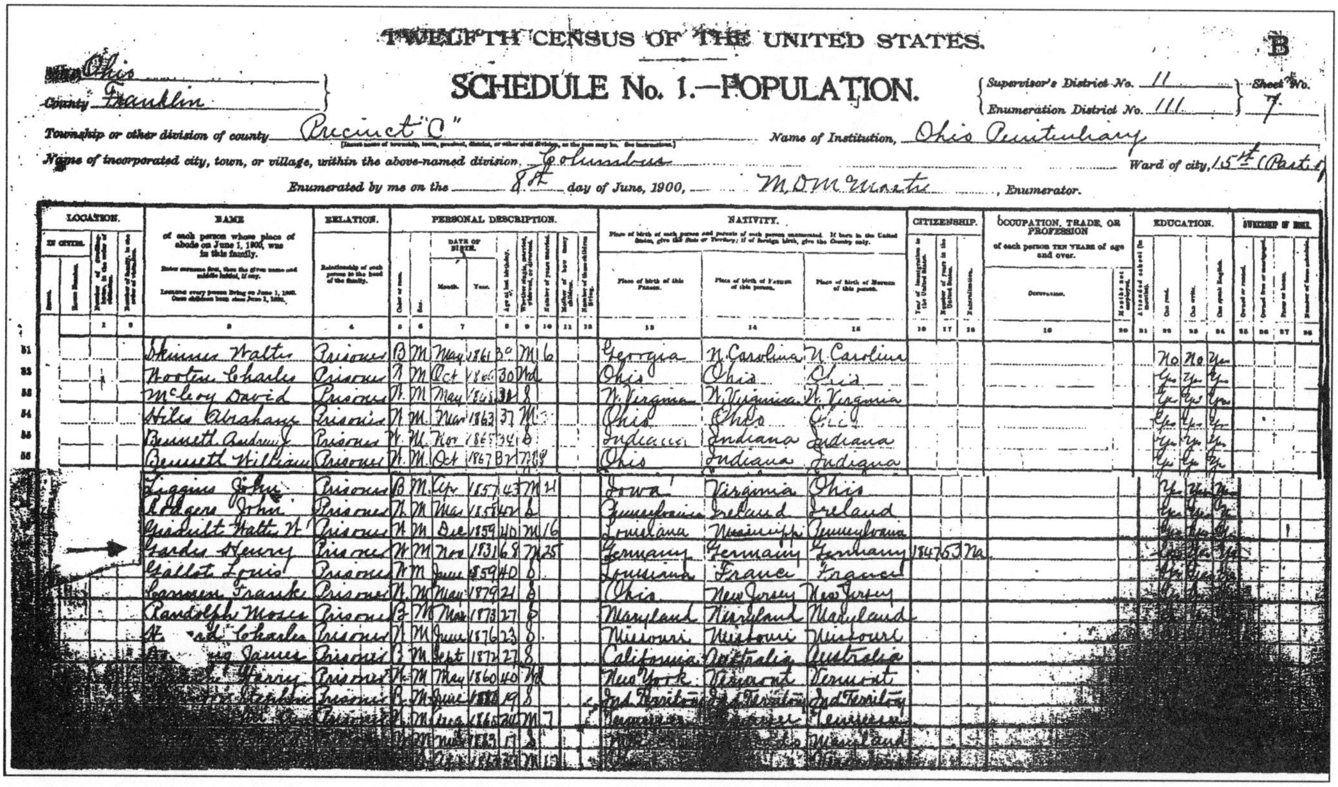

TWELFTH CENSUS OF THE UNITED STATES.

SCHEDULE No. 1.—POPULATION.

State: Ohio. County: Franklin. Supervisor's District No. 11. Enumeration District No. 111. Sheet No. 7 B.

Township or other division of county: Precinct "C". Name of Institution: Ohio Penitentiary.

Name of incorporated city, town, or village, within the above-named division: Columbus. Ward of city: 15th (Part of)

Enumerated by me on the 8th day of June, 1900, M. D. McMaster, Enumerator.

Name	Relation	Color	Sex	Month	Year	Age	Marital	Years married	Birthplace	Father's birthplace	Mother's birthplace	Year of immigration	Years in U.S.	Naturalization
Skinner Walter	Prisoner	B	M	May	1861	39	M	16	Georgia	N. Carolina	N. Carolina			
Wooten Charles	Prisoner	W	M	Oct	1869	30	Wd		Ohio	Ohio	Ohio			
McCoy David	Prisoner	W	M	May	1865	35	S		W. Virginia	W. Virginia	W. Virginia			
Hiles Abraham	Prisoner	W	M	Mar	1863	37	M		Ohio	Ohio	Ohio			
Bennett Andrew	Prisoner	W	M	Nov	1865	34	S		Indiana	Indiana	Indiana			
Bennett William	Prisoner	W	M	Oct	1867	32	S		Ohio	Indiana	Indiana			
Liggins John	Prisoner	B	M	Sep	1857	42	M	21	Iowa	Virginia	Ohio			
Rodgers John	Prisoner	W	M	Mar	1855	45	S		Pennsylvania	Ireland	Ireland			
Girault Walter H	Prisoner	W	M	Dec	1859	40	M	16	Louisiana	Mississippi	Pennsylvania			
Gardes Henry	Prisoner	W	M	Nov	1831	68	M	25	Germany	Germany	Germany	1847	53	Na
Gallot Louis	Prisoner	W	M	June	1859	40	S		Louisiana	France	France			
Cannon Frank	Prisoner	W	M	May	1879	21	S		Ohio	New Jersey	New Jersey			
Randolph Moses	Prisoner	B	M	Mar	1873	27	S		Maryland	Maryland	Maryland			
[illegible] Charles	Prisoner	W	M	June	1876	23	S		Missouri	Missouri	Missouri			
[illegible] James	Prisoner	B	M	Sept	1872	27	S		California	Australia	Australia			
[illegible] Henry	Prisoner	W	M	May	1860	40	Wd		New York	Vermont	Vermont			
[illegible]	Prisoner	[illegible]	M	June	[illegible]	[illegible]	S		Ind. Territory	Ind. Territory	Ind. Territory			
[illegible]	Prisoner	[illegible]	M	Aug	[illegible]	[illegible]	M	7	[illegible]	[illegible]	Tennessee			
[illegible]	[illegible]	[illegible]	M	[illegible]	[illegible]	[illegible]	S		[illegible]	[illegible]	Maryland			

Figure 11-5 U.S. Census of 1900, roll 1269, Franklin County, Ohio, Columbus, e.d. 111, sheet 7B, line 87, Henry Gardes.

ated over the operation and intent of the firm of T.H. Underwood & Company, of which Girault, Gardes, and Underwood were sole owners. The company's relationship to the American National Bank was key to the prosecution's case, which demonstrated that the defendants had transferred monies and credit of the bank to Underwood & Co. on numerous occasions. The defense, on the other hand, revealed that the only purpose for that company was to prop up the value of the bank's stock and accept its losses in order to remain solvent during a time, especially 1893, when severe economic conditions in the country caused numerous banks to fail. The defendants had mortgaged personal assets to fund Underwood & Co. and transferred credits and other assets to the bank to help it remain solvent and maintain public confidence. The jury had much to think about, including intricate banking and accounting practices.

The first trial ended abruptly and to everyone's surprise on April 15 when two court-appointed doctors reported that one of the jurors had become too ill to serve and the judge declared a mistrial for lack of a full twelve-man jury. The second trial began on 17 May 1897, one month after the stricken juror died. For both trials, the courtroom was filled each day with members of New Orleans elite society, the banking community, former employees of the bank, and family members of the accused. Among Henri Gardes's faithful were his second wife, Hersilie Philomene (Bienvenue) Gardes, and her sister, Micael (Bienvenue) Wiltz, widow of the late governor of Louisiana. Although Henry W. Gardes was away, serving in the navy, his wife and children may well have been living with Hersilie or Micael, as Henry W. had married Micael Wiltz's daughter Lucie.[18] Thus, Lucie may also have attended the trial.

The second trial ended near midnight on Saturday, 12 June 1897, after the jury had deliberated on the complex issues for only a little over four hours before reaching a unanimous verdict. They found T.H. Underwood not guilty and Gardes and Girault guilty but did not specify which charges were the basis of the conviction. On July 2, the judge sentenced the two remaining defendants to eight years of hard labor for each of the 136 counts on the original indictment, with the sentences to run concurrently at the Ohio Penitentiary in Columbus, Ohio, which housed numerous federal prisoners. The sentencing resulted in shrieks and screams from those in attendance.

> The cries of Mrs. Hersilie B. Gardes, wife of the sixty-five-year-old long-time New Orleans financier and merchant, were heard the loudest as she ran from her seat behind the defendants and threw herself at the foot of the Judge's bench sobbing and screaming as her husband was taken into custody and led to the Orleans Parish Central Jail. Mrs. Gardes had to be escorted from the court room by officials on the orders of Judge Parlagne. Repeated demands by the Judge for order to be restored were not complied with, and he ended the trial to clear the courtroom.[19]

The defendants spent a month in jail while their families accumulated the bond money; their attorney filed appeals in November 1897. The appellate hearing was held on the following April 19, when the Fifth Circuit Court of Appeals rejected several hundred pages of defense motions.[20] On May 24, the court denied a second appeal; the defendants were taken into custody and transported to Ohio.

The penitentiary was the residence for about two thousand inmates and was the largest prison in the world at the time.[21] Henri and his friend Girault were assigned to "Bankers' Row," where one of their "neighbors" was William Sidney Porter, the North Carolina-born Texan known to modern readers as the short-story writer O. Henry. He was serving five years for embezzlement.[22] Figure 11-6, below, is a post-card photograph of Ohio's Banker's Row, showing the four-foot by seven-foot cells.

Figure 11-6 Banker's Row, Ohio Penitentiary, Columbus, Ohio.

The register of prisoners described Henri as a banker, age sixty-six, a native of Germany; he was five feet, six and three-quarter inches tall, and he had frank slate blue eyes. His hair and beard were gray; his complexion, medium dark. He wore size eight boots and size seven and one-eighth hat. He had a tattoo on the front left forearm: a "Heart, Anchor and 'H.G.' inside of heart." The rear of that arm held a six-pointed star tattoo. His habits were considered "intemperate" and his education, good. His nearest relative was his wife, Mrs. H.B.

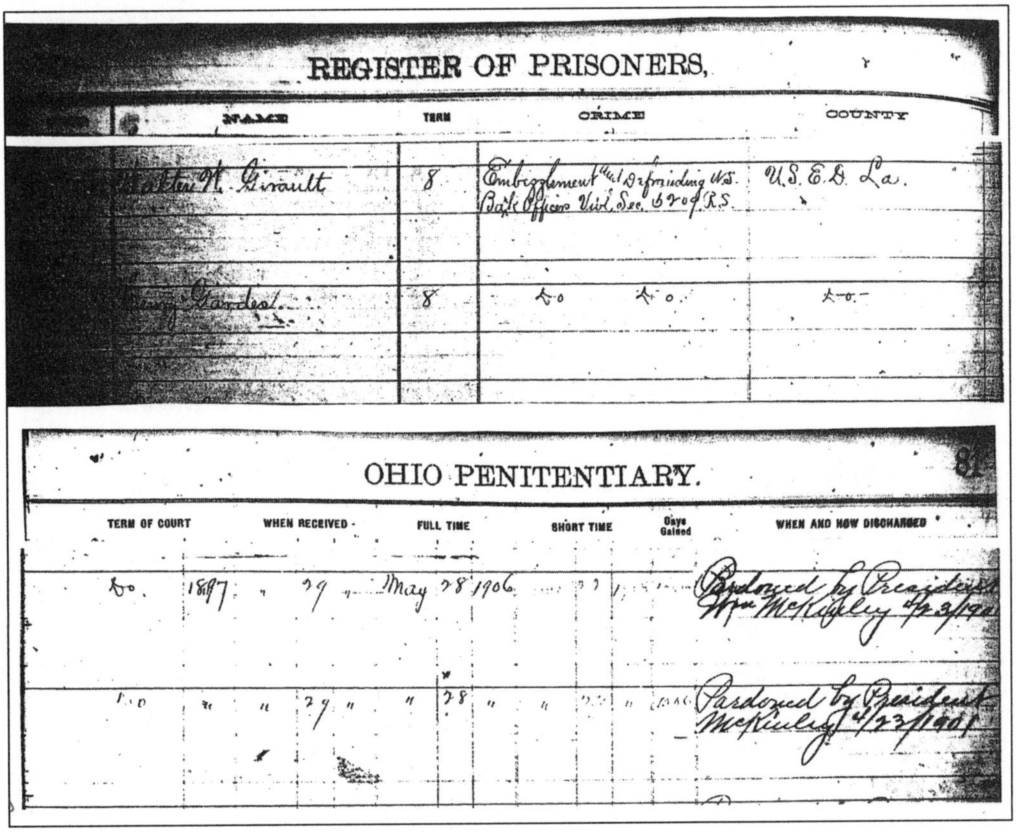

REGISTER OF PRISONERS,

NAME	TERM	CRIME	COUNTY
Walter H. Girault	8	Embezzlement and Defrauding U.S. Bank Officers Viol. Sec. 5209 R.S.	U.S. E.D. La.
Henry Gardes	8	do do	do.

OHIO PENITENTIARY. 81

TERM OF COURT	WHEN RECEIVED	FULL TIME	SHORT TIME	Days Gained	WHEN AND HOW DISCHARGED
do.	1897 " 29 "	May 28 1906	" "	"	Pardoned by President Wm McKinley 4/23/1901
do	" " 29 "	" 28 "	" "	"	Pardoned by President McKinley 4/23/1901

Figure 11-7 Record of prisoners 30781 and 30782, Girault and Gardes, Ohio Penitentiary, Register 21 (April 1898–March 1900), p. 80–85, FHL microfilm 0928458.

Gardes, of 926 Esplanade Ave., New Orleans. He and Girault were serving eight years for "Embezzlement and Defrauding U.S. Bank Officers." They arrived at the prison on 29 May 1897, with terms to expire on 28 May 1906.[23] Although they appealed to the Supreme Court, the high court chose not to hear their case. However, as Figure 11-7 (above) shows, they were pardoned by President William McKinley on 23 April 1901,[24] less than five months before McKinley's assassination. They had served almost half their sentence time and returned to New Orleans.

Back to the Search for Origin

This chapter in Henri's life was far from dull, but it left his genealogist no closer to discovering Henri's origin, other than "Bremen, Germany," or his naturalization. Charlie read about U.S. passport applications containing naturalization information on citizens who planned to travel abroad. Would such a record exist for Henri? Indeed, these records showed a passport application dated 27 April 1871 for H. Gardes of New Orleans. The signature of the applicant matched that of Henri Gardes on other New Orleans records. The application again gave Bremen, Germany, as his birthplace but also provided two pieces of critical information: (1) He had been naturalized in the Court of Common Pleas for the City and County of New York on 15 July 1855, and (2) he was born on or about 6 November 1831 in Bremen, Germany.[25]

The master index of New York naturalizations provided the volume and file number necessary for getting a copy of the naturalization record.[26] In that document, dated 13 July 1855, Henri renounced his allegiance to the Free City of Bremen.[27] (Figure 11-8, on page 424, shows this record.) The record gave no information about Henri's immigration and arrival in the United States. No declaration of intent has been located, and the language of the naturalization suggests Henri filed no "first papers."

The prison records and obituary had given Henri's second wife's name: Hersilie Philomene Bienvenue. It was time to find that marriage record to complete the basic data on Herr Immigrant. Indeed, the 1875 marriage license named Henri's parents as Hinrich Gardes and Metta Winters.[28]

Important

Now with a birth date, birthplace, and parents' names, Charlie began the search for a birth record in Henri's native land. The birth year and birthplace were consistent in all the records found to this point for Henri. The first step was searching the Bremen city directories 1821–1841, ten years on either side of Henri's birth, but they mentioned no Gardes. The second step was the Bremen civil birth registers, 1820–1850, which showed no Gardes birth. Both the microfilm of the city directories and the vital records were available through the Family History Library. Henri's genealogist began to wonder whether Henri was also playing with hooey.

Charlie decided to scour the city directories a second time and found in the back of city directories of the time a list of small towns near and outside the city limits of Bremen. Then he remembered that Henri's naturalization papers had named the "Free City of Bremen." This stall in the search made him realize he needed a lesson in the geography, history, and politics of Bremen and environs. Online research reminded him that Bremen had been a member of the Hanseatic League, a loose confederation of medieval cities organized for trade and mutual protection. As were some of the others, Bremen was and remained an independent city, virtually a city-state made up of the main city and more than twenty surrounding towns and villages. Among these, mentioned in the nineteenth-century city

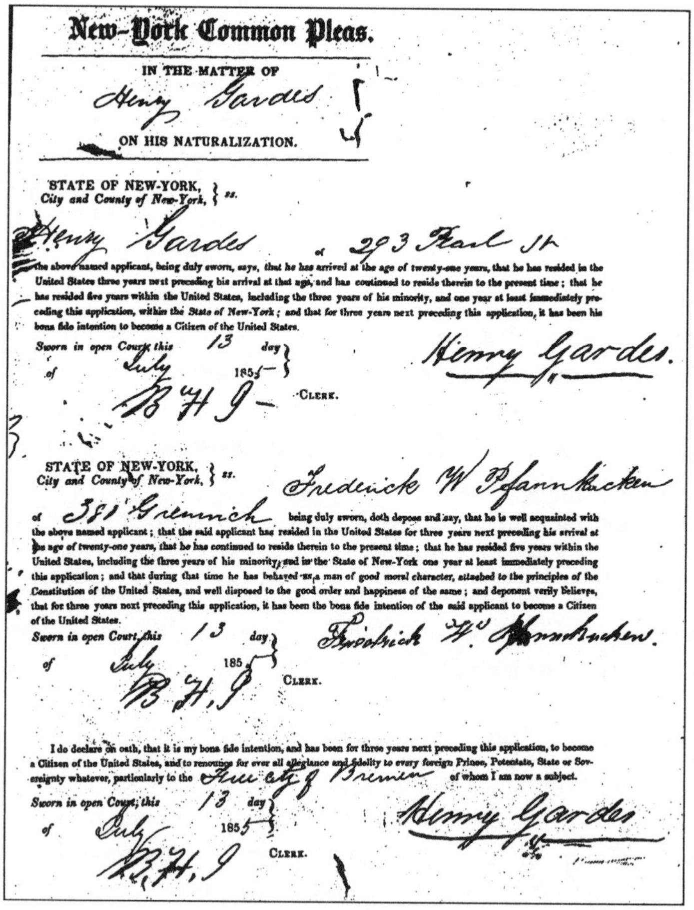

New-York Common Pleas.

IN THE MATTER OF

Henry Gardes

ON HIS NATURALIZATION.

STATE OF NEW-YORK, City and County of New-York, } ss.

Henry Gardes of 293 Pearl St the above named applicant, being duly sworn, says, that he has arrived at the age of twenty-one years, that he has resided in the United States three years next preceding his arrival at that age, and has continued to reside therein to the present time; that he has resided five years within the United States, including the three years of his minority, and one year at least immediately preceding this application, within the State of New-York; and that for three years next preceding this application, it has been his bona fide intention to become a Citizen of the United States.

Sworn in open Court this 13 day of July 1855 } Henry Gardes.

B H J — Clerk.

STATE OF NEW-YORK, City and County of New-York, } ss. Frederick W Pfannkucken of 381 Greenwich being duly sworn, doth depose and say, that he is well acquainted with the above named applicant; that the said applicant has resided in the United States for three years next preceding his arrival at the age of twenty-one years, that he has continued to reside therein to the present time; that he has resided five years within the United States, including the three years of his minority, and in the State of New-York one year at least immediately preceding this application; and that during that time he has behaved as a man of good moral character, attached to the principles of the Constitution of the United States, and well disposed to the good order and happiness of the same; and deponent verily believes, that for three years next preceding this application, it has been the bona fide intention of the said applicant to become a Citizen of the United States.

Sworn in open Court, this 13 day of July 1855 } Friedrich W. Pfannkuchen.

B H J Clerk.

I do declare on oath, that it is my bona fide intention, and has been for three years next preceding this application, to become a Citizen of the United States, and to renounce for ever all allegiance and fidelity to every foreign Prince, Potentate, State or Sovereignty whatever, particularly to the Free city of Bremen of whom I am now a subject.

Sworn in open Court, this 13 day of July 1855 } Henry Gardes

B H J Clerk.

Figure 11-8 Naturalization of Henry Gardes, file 252, 13 July 1855, Bundle 143C, New York Court of Common Pleas, FHL microfilm 0964149.

directories, was the town of Vegesack, where one Gardes lived in the 1840s. Perhaps his presence indicated that other Gardes families were in the neighborhood.

Back in the CD-ROM version of the Family History Library catalog, under Bremen, Charlie noticed vital records for the rural areas of Bremen, listing more than twenty villages. He ordered the microfilm rolls for these rural villages and began scrolling through each one for 1831. The sixteenth village on the list was Grambke, and the microfilm contained births (*geburten*) for Grambke and neighboring Mittelsbüren for 1814 to 1832. Phantastich! In an outlying *dorf*, a "bump in the road" kind of village called Burg, Hinrich Gärdes was born on 5 November 1831, the son of Hinrich Gärdes and Metta (*geboren*) Winters,[29] the same names as Henri's second marriage record had reported. (The birth date on the birth record was slightly different from the November 6 reported on Henri's passport application.) Burg and Grambke were next to each other; Grambke had the civil registration office because it was the larger of the two. Figure 11-9, below, shows this long-sought ancestral record.

The search had spread over almost five years, with two trips to New Orleans, more than one hundred rolls of microfilm from Salt Lake City, and well over four thousand pages of documents acquired by mail. It was successful because of a determined and thinking genealogist who researched one generation at a time, kept an open mind, documented what he found, followed up on new clues, combined history and geography with the basic vital records of genealogy, and worked with sources contemporary with the ancestors. (Even in today's cyber world, most of the research for Henry Gardes could not have been done online.) More significant to Charlie's success was that he tried to learn all he could about the focus ancestor and acquired specific confirming information (birth date, birthplace, and parents' names) before delving into German records.

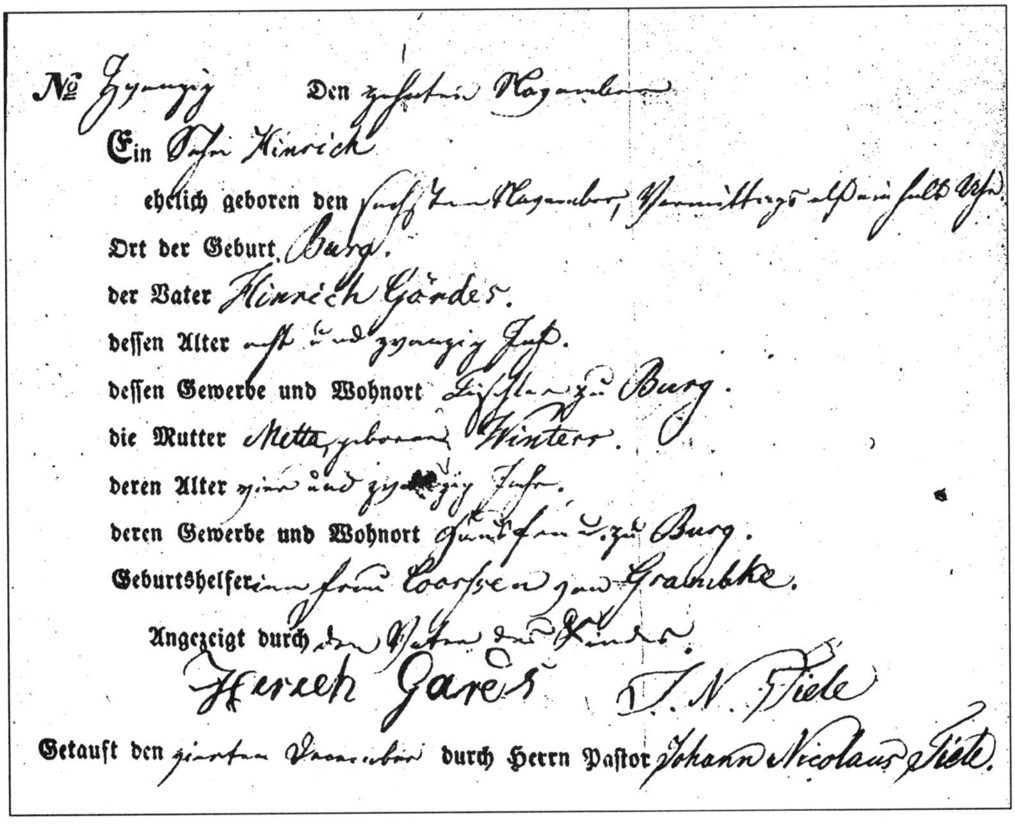
№ [illegible] Den [illegible]
Ein [illegible] Hinrich
ehelich geboren den [illegible]
Ort der Geburt Burg.
der Vater Hinrich Gärdes.
dessen Alter [illegible]
dessen Gewerbe und Wohnort [illegible] Burg.
die Mutter Metta [illegible] Winters.
deren Alter [illegible]
deren Gewerbe und Wohnort [illegible] Burg.
Geburtshelfer [illegible] Grambke.
Angezeigt durch [illegible]
Hinrich Gardes J. N. Tiele
Getauft den [illegible] durch Herrn Pastor Johann Nicolaus Tiele.

Figure 11-9 Birth record for Hinrich Gärdes, 6 November 1831, Zivilstandsregister, 1814–1832, Grambke, Bremen, Germany, FHL microfilm 0953065. A translation appears on p. 426.

TRANSLATION OF HENRY GARDES BIRTH RECORD

NO.: Twenty THIS: Tenth November
A: Son Hinrich
LEGITIMATE BIRTH THIS: Fifth November in the morning half past eleven.

Note: This date conflicts with his passport, which reads "on or about the sixth day of November."

PLACE OF BIRTH: Burg
THE FATHER: Hinrich Gördes [*sic*]
HIS AGE: Eight and twenty years
HIS TRADE AND PLACE OF RESIDENCE: Carpenter, Burg
THE MOTHER: Metta born Winters
HER AGE: Four and twenty years
HER TRADE AND PLACE OF RESIDENCE: Housewife, Burg
MIDWIFE: Frau Coorsen of Grambke
INDICATED BY THE FATHER OF THE CHILD:
Hinrich Gardes (signature) J.N. Tiele (signature)
BAPTIZED THIS: Fourth December BY THE PASTOR: Johann Nicolaus Tiele

The success of this research also illustrates the point that ancestors who are moving targets are not necessarily brick walls. The problem may simply be that the researcher has not yet looked in the right place—either the right locale or the right kind of document—and, as this book has emphasized, you never know until you look.

FOR FURTHER REFERENCE: IMMIGRATION AND NATURALIZATION

Numerous books and articles deal with immigration and naturalization. Some are genealogy books dedicated to specific ethnic groups; some present history. Others are valuable reference tools. For articles on these subjects, check library catalogs; PERSI; the National Archives *Prologue*, especially on the National Archives Web site; and the major genealogical journals. The following books are merely examples of the helpful materials available to researchers. They are given here to whet your appetite.

General Reference and Genealogy

Acadian-Cajun Genealogy: Step by Step, by Timothy Hebert. Lafayette, La.: Center for Louisiana Studies, University of Southwestern Louisiana, 1993.

American Immigration, 2d ed., by Maldwyn Allen Jones. Chicago: The University of Chicago Press, 1992. History, timeline, bibliography.

American Naturalization Processes and Procedures, 1790–1985, by John J. Newman. Indianapolis: Indiana Historical Society, 1985.

American Passenger Arrival Records: A Guide to the Records of Immigrants Arriving at American Ports by Sail and Steam, by Michael Tepper. Baltimore: Genealogical Publishing Co., 1988. Excellent background for understanding and locating the records.

Beginning Franco-American Genealogy, by Dennis M. Boudreau. Pawtucket, R.I.: American-French Genealogical Society, 1986. Mostly New England, Acadian, and Canadian genealogy, with some on France.

Discovering Your Jewish Ancestors, by Barbara Krasner-Khait. North Salt Lake, Utah: Heritage Quest, 2001.

Encyclopedic Directory of Ethnic Organizations in the United States, by Lubomyr R. Wynar. Littleton, Colo.: Libraries Unlimited Inc., 1975.

Genealogical Research in England's Public Record Office: A Guide for North Americans, 2d ed., by Judith Prowse Reid and Simon Fowler. Baltimore: Genealogical Publishing Co., 2000.

A Genealogist's Guide to Discovering Your English Ancestors, by Paul Milner and Linda Jonas. Cincinnati: Betterway Books, 2000.

A Genealogist's Guide to Discovering Your Germanic Ancestors, by S. Chris Anderson and Ernest Thode. Cincinnati: Betterway Books, 2000.

A Genealogist's Guide to Discovering Your Immigrant & Ethnic Ancestors, by Sharon DeBartolo Carmack. Cincinnati: Betterway Books, 2000.

A Genealogist's Guide to Discovering Your Irish Ancestors, by Dwight A. Radford and Kyle J. Betit. Cincinnati: Betterway Books, 2001.

A Genealogist's Guide to Discovering Your Italian Ancestors, by Lynn Nelson. Cincinnati: Betterway Books, 1997.

A Genealogist's Guide to Discovering Your Scottish Ancestors, by Linda Jonas and Paul Milner. Cincinnati: Betterway Books, 2002.

Genealogy for Armenians, by Nephi K. Kezerian and LaPreal J. Kezerian. North Salt Lake, Utah: Heritage Quest, 2000.

Harvard Encyclopedia of American Ethnic Groups, Stephen Thernstrom, ed. Cambridge, Mass.: Belknap Press of Harvard University Press, 1980 or latest edition.

Hispanic American Genealogical Sourcebook, Paula K. Byers, ed. Detroit: Gale Research, 1995.

Immigrant and Passenger Arrivals: A Select Catalog of National Archives Microfilm Publications. 2d ed. Washington, D.C.: National Archives Trust Fund Board, 1991.

The Immigrant Experience: An Annotated Bibliography, by Paul D. Mageli. Pasadena, Calif.: Salem Press, 1991. Part of Magill Bibliographies.

Immigration and Ethnicity: A Guide to Information Sources, John D. Buenker et al., eds. Detroit: Gale Research, 1977. Includes lists of centers, repositories, societies, journals.

Irish and Scotch-Irish Ancestral Research: A Guide to the Genealogical Records, Methods, and Sources in Ireland, by Margaret D. Falley. Baltimore: Genealogical Publishing Co., 1988.

Irish Records: Sources for Family and Local History, rev. ed., by James G. Ryan. Salt Lake City: Ancestry, 1997.

Italian Genealogical Records: How to Use Italian Civil, Ecclesiastical, & Other Records in Family History Research, by Trafford R. Cole. Salt Lake City: Ancestry, 1995.

Naturalization Laws (1918–1972), Gilman G. Udell, comp. Washington, D.C.: Government Printing Office, 1972.

Norwegian Research Guide, by Linda M. Herrick and Wendy K. Uncapher. Janesville, Wis.: Origins, 2001.

Polish Roots-Korzenie Polskie, by Rosemary A. Chorzempa. Baltimore: Genealogical Publishing Co., 1993.

Romanians in the United States and Canada, by Vladimir F. Wertsman. North Salt Lake, Utah: Heritage Quest, 2002.

Second Stages in Researching Welsh Ancestry, by John Rowlands et al. Baltimore: Genealogical Publishing Co., 1999.

They Became Americans: Finding Naturalization Records and Ethnic Origins, by Loretto Dennis Szucs. Salt Lake City: Ancestry, 1998.

They Came in Ships: A Guide to Finding Your Immigrant Ancestor's Arrival Record, rev. ed., by John Philip Colletta. Salt Lake City: Ancestry, 1993.

Tracing Your Scottish Ancestry, 2d ed., by Kathleen B. Cory. Baltimore: Genealogical Publishing Co., 1996.

Welsh Family History: A Guide to Research, 2d ed., by John Rowlands and Sheila Rowlands. Baltimore: Genealogical Publishing Co., 1999.

Your Scottish Ancestry: A Guide for North Americans, by Sherry Irvine. Salt Lake City: Ancestry, 1997.

Research Tools

The Alsace Emigration Book, 2 vols., Cornelia Schrader-Muggenthaler, comp. Apollo, Penn.: Closson Press, 1989 (vol. 1), 1991 (vol. 2). Compiled from records of people leaving or passing through Alsace, with name, approximate birth and emigration year, and birthplace.

The Baden Emigration Book, Cornelia Schrader-Muggenthaler, comp. Apollo, Penn.: Closson Press, 1992. Compiled from records of people leaving or passing through Baden and Alsace in the eighteenth and nineteenth centuries, with name, approximate birth and emigration year, and birthplace.

Bonded Passengers to America, 9 vols. in 3, by Peter Wilson Coldham. Baltimore: Genealogical Publishing Co., 1983. Includes two earlier volumes, *English Convicts in Colonial America*. New Orleans: Polyanthos Press, 1974, 1976.

Czech Immigration Passenger Lists, 9 vols. Leo Baca, comp. Hallettsville, Tex.: Old Homestead Publishing Co., 1983–. Ports of Baltimore, Galveston, New York, New Orleans; varying dates between 1834 and 1906.

Dutch Immigrants in U.S. Ship Passenger Manifests, 1820–1880: An Alphabetical Listing by Household Heads and Independent Persons, 2 vols., Robert P. Swierenga, comp. Wilmington, Del.: Scholarly Resources, 1983.

Emigrants From England, 1773–1776, by Gerald Fothergill. Boston: New England Historic Genealogical Society, 1913. Reprint, Baltimore: Genealogical Publishing Co., 1977.

The Famine Immigrants: Lists of Irish Immigrants Arriving at the Port of New York, 1846–1851, 7 vols., Ira A. Glazier and Michael Tepper, eds. Baltimore: Genealogical Publishing Co., 1983–1986.

Germans to America: Lists of Passengers Arriving at U.S. Ports, Ira A. Glazier and P. William Filby, eds. Wilmington, Del.: Scholarly Resources, 1988–. Sixty-seven volumes by 2002. Volume 1 begins with 1 January 1850; volume 67 goes through June 1897.

Germans to America. Series II: Lists of Passengers Arriving at U.S. Ports in the 1840s, Ira A. Glazier, ed., with foreword by P. William Filby. Wilmington, Del.: Scholarly Resources, 2002–. First four vols. cover 1840–1847.

Hamilton County, Ohio Citizenship Record Abstracts, 1837–1916, by Lois E. Hughes. Bowie, Md.: Heritage Books, 1991. Covers more than twenty-five thousand people.

Italians to America: Lists of Passengers Arriving at U.S. Ports, 1880–1899, Ira A. Glazier and P. William Filby, eds. Wilmington, Del.: Scholarly Resources, 1992–. Volumes 1–4 cover New York, 1880–1890.

New World Immigrants: A Consolidation of Ship Passenger Lists and Associated Data from Periodical Literature, 2 vols., Michael Tepper, ed. Baltimore: Genealogical Publishing Co., 1979.

Passenger and Immigration Lists Bibliography, 1538–1900, 2d ed., P. William Filby, ed. Detroit: Gale Research, 1988. Entries list over twenty-five hundred published passenger and naturalization lists. Companion to *Index* listed below.

Passenger and Immigration Lists Index: A Guide to Published Arrival Records of about 500,000 Passengers Who Came to the United States and Canada in the Seventeenth, Eighteenth, and Nineteenth Centuries, 3 vols., P. William Filby, ed. Detroit: Gale Research, 1981. Indexes published passenger, naturalization, and other immigration records. Cumulative supplements, 1982–1985, 1986–1990, 1991–1995, 1996–2000; supplements 2001, 2002, 2003. Valuable reference source. Over two million names indexed. Preliminary edition, 1980.

Passenger Arrivals at the Port of Baltimore, 1820–1834: From Customs Passenger Lists, Michael Tepper, ed. Baltimore: Genealogical Publishing Co., 1982.

Passengers and Ships Prior to 1684, Walter L. Sheppard, comp. Baltimore: Genealogical Publishing Co., 1970. Early Pennsylvania.

Pennsylvania German Pioneers: A Publication of the Original Lists of Arrivals in the Port of Philadelphia From 1727 to 1808, 3 vols., by Ralph Beaver Strassburger, William John Hinke, ed. Norristown, Penn: Pennsylvania German Society, 1934. Reprint of Vols. 1 and 3. Baltimore: Genealogical Publishing Co., 1966.

Port Arrivals and Immigrants to the City of Boston, 1715–1716 and 1762–1769, William H. Whitmore, comp. Baltimore: Genealogical Publishing Co., 1973.

San Francisco Ship Passenger Lists, by Louis J. Rasmussen. Baltimore: Genealogical Publishing Co., 1978.

Swedish Passenger Arrivals in New York, 1820–1850, by Nils W. Olsson. Chicago: Swedish Pioneer Historical Society, 1967.

The Swiss Emigration Book, vol. 1, by Cornelia Schrader-Muggenthaler, comp. Apollo, Penn.: Closson Press, 1993. Compiled from emigrant and passport records of people leaving from or passing through Switzerland, with name, approximate birth and emigration year, and birthplace.

National Archives and Regional Branches

National Archives and Records Administration
700 Pennsylvania Ave. NW
Washington, DC 20408
Phone: (800) 234-8861 or (301) 713-6800
E-mail: inquire@nara.gov

National Archives II
8601 Adelphi Rd.
College Park, MD 20740-6001
Phone: (800) 234-8861
E-mail: inquire@arch2.nara.gov

National Archives home page: <www.archives.gov>

National Archives—information on nationwide facilities, including regional branches and presidential libraries, holdings, research at each facility, hours, and directions to each location: <www.archives.gov/facilities/index.html>

Regional Branches of the National Archives

Alaska

National Archives, Pacific Alaska Region (Anchorage)
654 W. Third Ave., Anchorage, AK 99501-2145
Phone: (907) 271-2441
Serving Alaska.

California

National Archives, Pacific Region
24000 Avila Rd., Laguna Niguel, CA 92677-3497 or
P.O. Box 6719, Laguna Niguel, CA 92607-6719
Phone: (949) 360-2641
Serving Arizona; southern California; Clark County, Nevada.

National Archives, Pacific Sierra Region
1000 Commodore Dr., San Bruno, CA 94066-2350
Phone: (650) 876-9001; genealogy and general inquiries: (650) 876-9009
Serving northern California, Hawaii, Nevada except for Clark County, American Samoa, Pacific Trust Territories.

Colorado

National Archives, Rocky Mountain Region
Bldg. 48, Denver Federal Center
P.O. Box 25307, Denver, CO 80225-0307
Phone: (303) 236-0806
Serving Colorado, Montana, New Mexico, North Dakota, South Dakota, Utah, Wyoming.

District of Columbia

Washington National Records Center
4205 Suitland Rd., Suitland, MD 20746-8001
For information, visit the Web site:
<www.archives.gov/facilities/md/suitland.html>

Georgia

National Archives, Southeast Region
1557 St. Joseph Ave., East Point, GA 30344-2593
Phone: (404) 763-7474
Serving Alabama, Florida, Georgia, Kentucky, Mississippi, North Carolina, South Carolina, Tennessee.

Illinois

National Archives, Great Lakes Region (Chicago)
7358 S. Pulaski Rd., Chicago, IL 60629-5898
Phone: (773) 581-7816
Serving Illinois, Indiana, Michigan, Minnesota, Ohio, Wisconsin.

Massachusetts

National Archives, Northeast Region (Boston)
Murphy Federal Center, 380 Trapelo Rd., Waltham, MA 02452-6399
Phone: (781) 647-8104
Serving Connecticut, Maine, Massachusetts, New Hampshire, Rhode Island, Vermont.

National Archives, Northeast Region (Pittsfield)
10 Conte Dr., Pittsfield, MA 01201-8230
Phone: (413) 445-6885
A microfilm reading room, serving primarily the Northeast but with census, military, and other records with national coverage.

Missouri

National Archives, Central Plains Region (Kansas City)
2312 E. Bannister Rd., Kansas City, MO 64131-3011
Phone: (816) 926-6920
Serving Iowa, Kansas, Missouri, Nebraska.

National Archives, Central Plains Region (Lee's Summit)
200 Space Center Dr., Lee's Summit, MO 64064-1182
Phone: (816) 823-6272
Serving Department of Veterans Affairs; agencies and courts in New Jersey, New York, Puerto Rico, U.S. Virgin Islands.

New York

National Archives, Northeast Region (New York City)
201 Varick St., New York, NY 10014-4811
Phone: (212) 337-1300
Serving New Jersey, New York, Puerto Rico, U.S. Virgin Islands.

Ohio

National Archives, Great Lakes Region (Dayton)
3150 Springboro Rd., Dayton, OH 45439-1883
Phone: (937) 225-2852
Serving Indiana, Michigan, Ohio.

Pennsylvania

National Archives, Mid Atlantic Region (Center City Philadelphia)
900 Market St., Philadelphia, PA 19107-4292
Phone: (215) 597-3000
Serving Delaware, Maryland, Pennsylvania, Virginia, West Virginia. Genealogical records are at this facility.

National Archives, Mid Atlantic Region (Northeast Philadelphia)
14700 Townsend Rd., Philadelphia, PA 19154-1096
Phone: (215) 671-9027
Serving Delaware, Maryland, Pennsylvania, Virginia, West Virginia.

Texas

National Archives, Southwest Region
501 W. Felix St., Bldg. 1, P.O. Box 6216, Fort Worth, TX 76115-0216
Phone: (817) 334-5515; genealogy/family history: (817) 334-5525
Serving Arkansas, Louisiana, Oklahoma, Texas.

Washington

National Archives, Pacific Alaska Region (Seattle)
6125 Sand Point Way NE, Seattle, WA 98115-7999
Phone: (206) 526-6501
Serving Idaho, Oregon, Washington.

States and Territories in 1861

An important factor in successful genealogical research is the availability of records in ancestral locales. However, in studying ancestors' lives in any location, researchers should also investigate social, political, economic, military, and legal history. This effort may encompass American history and culture, state and local history, and ethnic studies. Reference materials and the laws of the states are often available in public, academic, special, and law libraries.

Legal history is sometimes complex, especially on the issue of slavery and emancipation. Colonial, state, territorial, and national governments regulated the lives of both slaves and free blacks, some laws reaching into the early seventeenth century. These laws not only affected the lives of ancestors, both black and white, but also may have generated records of use to genealogists and historians. In an effort to answer some frequently asked questions, this appendix capsules statehood and abolition history for U.S. states and territories, focusing on the nation as of 1861, the beginning of the Civil War.

Free States

In the 1790 and 1800 censuses, slaves were enumerated in all the original thirteen states except Massachusetts. The Ordinance of 1787 had prohibited slavery in the Northwest Territory (north of the Ohio River and east of the Mississippi River), but slaves did live in some of these areas as well.

The following states were considered free of slavery when the Civil War began:

California—admitted as a free state by the Compromise of 1850.‡

Connecticut—original state; in 1784, state legislature enacted gradual abolition of slavery, with provisions for all blacks born after 1 March 1784 to be free at age twenty-five; legislature enacted several other laws, the last one in 1797, providing that black children born in the state would be slaves only until the age of twenty-one; slaves were enumerated in the state, 1790–1840; in 1848, state legislature abolished slavery.

Illinois—slavery prohibited by the Ordinance of 1787 and by its constitution at the time of statehood, 1818; became a territory, 1809; slaves enumerated, 1800–1840.

Indiana—slavery prohibited by the Ordinance of 1787 and by its constitution at the time of statehood, 1816; became a territory, 1800; slaves enumerated, 1800–1840.

Iowa—slavery prohibited by Missouri Compromise,+ 1820; became a territory, 1838; sixteen slaves enumerated, 1840; admitted as a free state, 1846.

Kansas—originally considered free by the Missouri Compromise+; given the right of popular sovereignty* when it was organized as a territory by the Kansas-Nebraska Act, 1854; two slaves enumerated in 1860; admitted as free state, January 1861.

Maine—free by virtue of being part of Massachusetts in 1780; admitted as free state, 1820.

Massachusetts—original state; slavery virtually gone by the end of 1776; state's Chief Judge William Cushing, 1783, made a statement (at the end of a case but not as a judicial decision) that the state constitution of 1780 had abolished slavery by granting rights and privileges incompatible with the existence of slavery; state constitution's

For More Info

See *A Century of Population Growth* in the source list (p. 437), for more statistics from the censuses.

bill of rights declares "all men are born free and equal" and "every subject is entitled to liberty"; one slave enumerated in 1830; no others enumerated from 1790 to 1860.

Michigan—slavery prohibited by the Ordinance of 1787; became a territory, 1805; slaves enumerated in 1810 and 1830 (in 1830, most of these were reported in the Wisconsin census); admitted as a free state, 1837.

Minnesota—area east of Mississippi River implied free by Ordinance of 1787 and the rest, considered free by the Missouri Compromise, 1820+; became a territory, 1849; admitted as a free state, 1858.

New Hampshire—original state; common interpretation of the bill of rights of the state constitution of 1784 was that the clause "All men are born equally free and independent" meant just that; some in the state inferred that all born after the constitution went into effect were free, and slaves born before it would remain slaves (see Belknap, Skinner, and Supreme Court of New Hampshire in source list starting on page 437); 157 slaves enumerated in 1790, 8 in 1800, 3 in 1830, 1 in 1840; no legislative act or judicial decision initiated abolition of slavery in the state, and no specific date marks freedom of slaves in the state.

New Jersey—original state; legislative act of 1804 declared all persons born of slave parents in the state after 4 July 1804 to be free, males upon reaching age twenty-five, females at age twenty-one; gradual abolition enacted, 1846, with all slaves made apprentices for life and their children being free at birth; slaves enumerated in censuses, 1790–1860, with eighteen "apprentices for life" listed in 1860; thirteenth amendment** to the U.S. Constitution, 1865, freed any remaining slaves.

New York—original state; 1788 state law provided for freedom for all slaves illegally imported into the state; gradual abolition enacted 1799, whereby children born of slave parents after 4 July 1799 were to be freed, males upon reaching age twenty-eight, females upon reaching age twenty-five; by legislative act, 1817, all Negroes born before 4 July 1799 would be free as of 4 July 1827 and those born between 1799 and 1827 would be indentured servants until reaching the ages specified in the 1799 law; slaves enumerated, 1790–1840.

Ohio—slavery prohibited by the Ordinance of 1787 and by state constitution, 1802, prior to statehood in 1803; six slaves enumerated in 1830, three in 1840.

Oregon—organized as free territory, 1848; admitted as a free state, 1859.

Pennsylvania—original state; gradual abolition enacted, March 1780, with (1) children born of slave mothers in Pennsylvania after enactment of the law to be free at age twenty-eight and (2) persons already held as slaves at the time of the law would continue to be slaves; slaves enumerated, 1790–1840.

Rhode Island—original state; gradual abolition enacted, 1784, whereby (1) all children born of slave mothers after 1 May 1784 would be free and (2) to defray cost of supporting these children, they could be bound out, males to the age of twenty-one, females to the age of eighteen; law changed in 1785: instead of their hometown supporting them, this responsibility shifted to the mother's master; slaves enumerated, 1790–1840.

Vermont—slavery abolished in state constitution, 1777, when Vermont declared itself independent and separate from England, New York, and New Hampshire; in 1786, state legislature reiterated that all former slaves had been liberated by the state constitution; no slaves enumerated in federal censuses; statehood, 1791.

Wisconsin—slavery prohibited by Ordinance of 1787; some slaves enumerated, 1830 and 1840; admitted as free state, 1848.

Territories

Congress enacted abolition of slavery in the territories, without compensation to slaveholders, in June 1862. Territories created during the Civil War included Arizona (1863), Idaho (1863), and Montana (1864). Other future western states were included in the territories listed above. Alaska and Hawaii were not U.S. territory in 1861.

Colorado Territory—created as a free territory, February 1861; no slaves enumerated in 1860; statehood, 1876.

Dakota Territory—created in March 1861; no slaves enumerated in 1860; statehood as North Dakota and South Dakota, 1889.

Nebraska Territory—slavery prohibited by Missouri Compromise,+ 1820; created as a territory, 1854, by the Kansas-Nebraska Act, with the right of popular sovereignty*; fifteen slaves enumerated in 1860; statehood, 1867.

Nevada Territory—created in March 1861; no slaves enumerated in 1860; statehood, October 1864.

New Mexico Territory—created in September 1850, with no restriction on slavery‡; slaves enumerated in 1860; statehood, 1912.

Oklahoma/Indian Territory—unorganized Indian territory in 1861; 1860 slave schedule is at the end of the Arkansas slave schedule under "Indian Lands West of Arkansas"; territory created, 1890; statehood, 1907.

Utah Territory—created in September 1850, with no restriction on slavery‡; slaves reported in 1850 (twenty-six) and 1860 (twenty-nine); statehood, 1896.

Washington Territory—created in 1853; no slaves enumerated, 1860; statehood, 1889.

Slaveholding Areas

Following South Carolina's lead in December 1860, ten other slave states seceded from the United States in the first half of 1861 to form the Confederate States of America. War broke out at Fort Sumter, South Carolina, on 12 April 1861.

President Abraham Lincoln's Emancipation Proclamation of 1 January 1863 declared all slaves free in regions still in rebellion—the Confederate states—with the exception of the areas occupied by Union military forces: Tennessee and portions of Virginia and Louisiana. In effect, the U.S. government could not immediately enforce the proclamation because it applied only to the areas over which the government had no control.

However, word of the proclamation eventually spread throughout the Confederacy. Anniversary celebrations in some areas occurred on January 1 of succeeding years. In other areas, freedmen celebrated the anniversary of the day the proclamation was announced, such as 19 June 1865 in Texas. The proclamation did not affect the slaveholding states in the Union: Delaware, Kentucky, Maryland, Missouri, and New Jersey.

Technically, slavery ended in the South with the ratification of the thirteenth amendment to the Constitution in December 1865.

When the war broke out, the following were slaveholding jurisdictions:

Alabama—territory organized, 1817; slaves enumerated from 1800 (as Washington County, Mississippi) through 1860; statehood, 1819.

Arkansas—territory organized, 1819, with no restriction on slavery; slaves enumerated from 1810 (in the unorganized area called Louisiana territory) through 1860; admitted as a slave state, 1836.

Delaware—original state; slaves enumerated, 1790–1860; remained in the Union during the Civil War; did not ratify the thirteenth amendment,** but slavery there was abolished when the amendment was declared ratified in December 1865.

District of Columbia—created out of Maryland, in use as seat of government by late 1800; slaves enumerated, 1800–1860; Congress abolished slavery in the district, with compensation to owners, in April 1862.

Florida—acquired in 1819; territory organized, 1822; slaves enumerated, 1830–1860; admitted as slave state, 1846.

Georgia—original state; slaves enumerated 1790–1860.

Kentucky—admitted as state, 1792; slaves enumerated, 1790–1860; considered a border state in the Civil War; remained in the Union; did not ratify thirteenth amendment,** but slavery there was abolished when the amendment went into effect, December 1865.

Louisiana—acquired in Louisiana Purchase, 1803; organized as Orleans Territory, 1804; statehood, 1812; slaves enumerated 1800–1860.

Maryland—original state; slaves enumerated, 1790–1860; considered a border state during the Civil War; remained in the Union; the state's constitutional convention of 1864 changed an article of the state's Bill of Rights to abolish slavery; new constitution narrowly approved by voters in October and went into effect 1 November 1864.

Mississippi—territory organized, 1798; statehood, 1817; slaves enumerated, 1800–1860.

Missouri—territory organized, 1812; admitted as slave state, 1821, as result of the Missouri Compromise+ of 1820; considered a border state during Civil War; remained in the Union; an ordinance of a state convention, 11 January 1865, provided immediate emancipation.

North Carolina—original state; slaves enumerated, 1790–1860.

South Carolina—original state; slaves enumerated, 1790–1860.

Tennessee—statehood, 1796; slaves enumerated, 1790–1860.

Texas—Spanish and Mexican territory until 1836; republic, 1836–1845; admitted as slave state, 1845; slaves enumerated in censuses, 1850–1860.

Virginia—original state; slaves enumerated, 1790–1860.

West Virginia—part of Virginia before being admitted as free state, 1863; state constitution of 1863 provided for gradual emancipation, one requirement for admission as a new state.

Notes

+The Missouri Compromise, 1820, banned slavery in the lands of the Louisiana Purchase that lay north of 36° 30′ latitude, the northern boundary of Arkansas. Louisiana was already a slave state, and Arkansas Territory had been organized in 1819 with no restriction on slavery. The compromise allowed Missouri to enter the Union as a slave state and Maine, as a free state. The Kansas-Nebraska Act of 1854, in effect, repealed the Missouri Compromise by allowing the practice of popular sovereignty* in the territories.

‡Compromise of 1850—Five measures Congress enacted in September 1850 after months of debate and compromise: (1) admitting California as a free state; (2) Texas relinquishing claim to New Mexico, and Congress establishing New Mexico Territory with no restriction on slavery and allowing for popular sovereignty there (see *) on the issue of slavery; (3) organizing Utah Territory with the same provisions concerning slavery; (4) abolishing the slave trade in the District of Columbia as of 1851; and (5) tightening the federal fugitive slave law.

*Popular sovereignty—The idea that the people of the territory should decide by popular vote whether the territory should be free or allow slavery; incorporated in the Compromise of 1850 and the Kansas-Nebraska Act of 1854.

**Thirteenth amendment to the U.S. Constitution—Prohibited slavery in the United States; proposed 1 February 1865; declared in force 18 December 1865. The following former Confederate states ratified the amendment as a requirement to readmission into the Union but were counted as legitimate and active states in the ratification process, prior to their readmission: Alabama, Arkansas, Georgia, Louisiana, North Carolina, South Carolina, Tennessee, Virginia. The remaining Southern states—Florida, Mississippi, Texas—ratified the amendment later as a prerequisite to readmission.

Sources

A Century of Population Growth, From the First Census of the United States to the Twelfth, 1790–1900. Washington, D.C.: Government Printing Office, 1909. Reprint, Orting, Wash.: Heritage Quest Press, 1989. Especially p. 132–133 (slave population in each state, 1790–1860), 274–275.

Arnold, Samuel Greene. *History of the State of Rhode Island and Providence Plantations*. 2 vols. New York: D. Appleton & Co., 1860. 2:503, 506.

Belknap, Jeremy. *The History of New Hampshire*. 3 vols. Reprint of 1792 edition. New York: Arno Press, 1972. III:280–282.

Cunningham, Valerie. "The First Blacks of Portsmouth." Part 2. *Historical New Hampshire* 44 (winter, 1989). Reprinted online. SeacoastNH.com. 1997. <www.seacoastnh.com/blackhistory/blacks2.html>. Accessed 30 November 2001.

Daniell, Jere R. *Experiment in Republicanism: New Hampshire Politics and the American Revolution, 1741–1794*. Cambridge, Mass.: Harvard University Press, 1970. Page 179.

Dodson, Howard, Christopher Moore, and Roberta Yancy. *The Black New Yorkers*. New York: John Wiley and Sons, 2000. Especially p. 52, 56–57.

Ellis, David M., James A. Frost, Harold C. Syrett, and Harry J. Carman. *A History of New York State*. Rev. ed. Ithaca, N.Y.: Cornell University Press, 1967. Especially p. 186.

Flick, Alexander C., ed. *History of the State of New York*. 10 vols. Empire State Historical Publication XVIII, 1934. Port Washington, Long Island, N.Y.: Ira J. Friedman, Inc., 1962. Especially p. 328.

Futhey, J. Smith, and Gilbert Cope. *History of Chester County, Pennsylvania*. Philadelphia: Louis H. Everts, 1881. Facsimile reprint. Chester County Historical Society, 1996. Especially p. 423–427; also describes the slave registration process set out in two 1780 laws and applicable records of Chester County.

Hodges, Graham Russell. *Slavery and Freedom in the Rural North: African-Americans in Monmouth County, New Jersey, 1665–1865*. Madison, N.J.: Madison House, 1997. Especially p. 129, 134, 149, 175.

King, David Thomas. "The End of Slavery in Massachusetts." In *Historic U.S. Court Cases 1690–1990: An Encyclopedia*, edited by John W. Johnson. New York: Garland Publishing Co., 1992. Pages 339–341. King asserts, p. 341, that the failure of the slaveholder, Jennison, in the several cases against Quock Walker "discouraged other owners from contesting legal efforts of slaves to gain freedom and thus in effect signaled the end of slavery in Massachusetts."

Litwack, Leon F. *North of Slavery: The Negro in the Free States, 1790–1860*. Chicago: The University of Chicago Press, 1961. Especially p. 3, 7, 9.

Long, Luman H., ed. *The World Almanac and Book of Facts 1970*. New York: Newspaper Enterprise Association, 1969. Chronological List of Territories, p. 32.

Ludlum, David M. *Social Ferment in Vermont, 1791–1850*. New York: AMS Press, 1939. Reprint, 1966. Especially p. 4, 6, 134.

March, David D. *The History of Missouri*. 4 vols. New York: Lewis Historical Publishing Co., 1967. Especially p. 950–961, 998–1000.

Morris, Richard B., and Henry Steele Commager, eds. *Encyclopedia of American History*. Updated and rev. ed. New York: Harper & Row, 1965. Especially p. 211, 543–545.

Morse, Jarvis Means. *A Neglected Period of Connecticut's History*. New Haven: Yale University Press, 1933. Especially p. 193, 203.

Pennsylvania Act of 1 March 1780 for Gradual Abolition of Slavery. Online. <www.yale.edu/lawweb/avalon/states/statutes/penn01.htm>. Accessed 30 November 2001.

Randall, J.G., and David Donald. *The Civil War and Reconstruction*. 2d ed. Boston: D.C. Heath and Co., 1961. Especially p. 4–5 (created from 1850 and 1860 census statistics), 372–373, 380–381, 385, 395.

Roth, David M. *Connecticut: A Bicentennial History*. New York: W.W. Norton & Co., 1979. Especially p. 126.

Scarf, J. Thomas. *History of Maryland From the Earliest Period to the Present Day*. 3 vols. Reprint of 1879 original. Hatboro, Penn.: Tradition Press, 1967. 3:583, 596–597.

Skinner, Harland C. "Slavery and Abolition in New Hampshire." Master's thesis, University of New Hampshire, 1948. The date of abolition of slavery in New Hampshire is difficult to determine. "[S]lavery gradually ceased to exist in New Hampshire and what references are given in the New Hampshire laws are merely an official confirmation of this fact. The Revolution had a greater influence in freeing the slaves than the constitution of 1784." (p. 74–75)

Supreme Court of New Hampshire. "Opinion of the Justices of the Supreme Judicial Court." 41 N.H. 553. 1861. *LexisNexis Academic Universe*. 1 December 2001. On 26 June 1861, the state legislature asked the state supreme court for an opinion on the constitutionality of an act passed 26 June 1857, "to secure freedom and the rights of citizenship to persons in this State." The court felt the constitutionality of the act had never been questioned, nor did it change existing law or conflict with U.S. law or constitution. The third section of the law made it a felony to hold any person as a slave in the state; the exception was an officer of the United States or other person acting in the execution of a legal process, i.e., dealing with fugitive slaves. The 1857 law did not initiate abolition of slavery in the state, as some sources report, but it and the court affirmed what was already in practice.

Endnotes

About the Citations:

The Family History Library in Salt Lake City is called by its acronym, FHL.

The National Archives and Records Administration in Washington, DC, is called simply National Archives.

M and T numbers refer to National Archives microfilm publications.

In citing census records from 1880 forward, *enumeration district* is abbreviated *e.d.*

All census records are the population schedules unless otherwise indicated.

Chapter 2

1 Account of compensation due assistant marshals of the United States, Territory of Michigan, 1830 census, National Archives microfilm T1224, *Descriptions of Census Enumeration Districts, 1830–1950*, roll 1, pages unnumbered, under Michigan Territory.

2 Department of Commerce and Labor, Bureau of the Census, *A Century of Population Growth, From the First Census of the United States to the Twelfth, 1790–1900* (Washington, D.C.: Government Printing Office, 1909; reprint, Orting, Wash.: Heritage Quest Press, 1989), 43.

3 Ibid., 45.

4 Ibid., 45, 46.

5 E-mail to author from National Archives staff at General Mailbox NWCC1, 25 November 2002, with information that the embassies were indeed included with consular service personnel in 1920 and 1930.

6 Ibid., with information that known schedules for 1930 apparently do not include overseas military installations or that such enumerations no longer exist; conversation with Dave Pemberton, Census Bureau historian, 14 January 2003, indicating that shipboard census reports (SCR) and military census reports (MCR) were made and overseas U.S. population was enumerated; apparently these schedules have not been located.

7 E-mail from Rebecca Daniels, Alaska State Archives, to author, 12 November 2002, stating they do not have any federal decennial censuses for Alaska before 1900 and do not have evidence that any were taken.

Chapter 4

1 "Jersey City, Hudson County, New Jersey," Part 1, The New England and the Middle States, *Report on the Social Statistics of Cities*, H. Misc. Doc. 42, part 16 [18] (47th Cong., 2d sess.) serial 2148 Washington, D.C.: Government Printing Office, 1886), 701.

2 Ibid., "Burlington, Chittenden County, Vermont," 82.

3 Records of Clemens Memorial Chapel, Houston, Texas, later Episcopal Church of the Good Shepherd, Book 2:82, 102, 110; Book 1:309; Marriages, 1925–1933; records held at St. Andrews Episcopal Church, 1819 Heights Blvd., Houston, 1993.

4 Records of the Bolivar, Tennessee, Presbyterian Church, transcribed by Louise J. McAnulty, 1969, and read at her home by the author, July 1972.

5 Churchill Gibson Chamberlayne, transcriber, *The Vestry Book and Register of Bristol*

Parish, Virginia, 1720–1789 (Richmond, Va.: the transcriber, 1898), 184, 193, 191, 145, 206.

6 Brent H. Holcomb and Elmer O. Parker, comps., *Early Records of Fishing Creek Presbyterian Church, Chester County, South Carolina, 1799–1859* (Bowie, Md.: Heritage Books, 1991), facsimile reprint of original session records, 83–86.

7 Minutes of Salem Baptist Church monthly conferences, Monroe County, Alabama, photocopies of original manuscript records, at Monroe County Museum, Monroeville, August 1997.

8 Theta Chapter report, by Ethel G. Clark, *The Adelphean of Alpha Delta Pi* 5 (December 1911): 51.

9 Isabella Morrison Hartley, wife of John Packer Jr., was born 29 October 1811 according to her tombstone in Eglington Cemetery, Clarksboro, New Jersey; marriage record of Isabella Hartley and John Packer Jr., 17 March 1836, in H. Stanley Craig, *Gloucester County, New Jersey, Marriage Records* (Woodbury, N.J.: Gloucester County Historical Society, 1976, reprint of 1930 original), 144.

10 Letter to author from Mrs. Marie M. Barnett, Librarian, Grand Lodge of Virginia, Richmond, Virginia, 31 January 1992.

Chapter 7

1 Richard B. Morris and Henry Steele Commager, eds., *Encyclopedia of American History* (New York: Harper and Row, 1965), 616.

2 Ibid., 614.

3 *Fanning's Illustrated Gazetteer of the United States, . . .* (New York: Ensign, Bridgman, & Fanning, 1855; reprint, Bowie, Md.: Heritage Books, 1990), 45.

4 Ibid., 107, paraphrased.

Chapter 8

1 Death certificate of James Proctor Knott, 18 June 1911, Marion County, Kentucky, certificate 15955, Bureau of Vital Statistics, State Board of Health, Frankfort, Kentucky.

2 U.S. Census of 1850, roll 419, Scotland County, Missouri, p. 115, family 20, household of Jacob Clapper, showing James P. Nott [*sic*] with the family.

3 U.S. Census of 1870, roll 485, Marion County, Kentucky, p. 43, family 57, household of James B. Chapman, in which Sallie R. Knott (Proctor Knott's wife) was "at home."

Chapter 9

1 Carter G. Woodson, *Free Negro Owners of Slaves in the United States in 1830* (Washington, D.C.: Association for the Study of Negro Life and History, 1925).

2 Dorothy Williams Potter, *Passports of Southeastern Pioneers, 1770–1823* (Baltimore: Genealogical Publishing Co., 1982), 151-152.

3 Ibid., 295.

4 Juliet E.K. Walker, "Pioneer Slave Entrepreneurship—Patterns, Processes, and Perspectives: The Case of the Slave Free Frank on the Kentucky Pennyroyal, 1795–1819," *The Journal of Negro History* 68 (Summer 1983): 289–308.

5 Edwin S. Redkey, "They Are Invincible," *Civil War Times Illustrated* 28 (1989): 32–37.

6 U.S. Census of 1900, roll 1641, Guadalupe County, Texas, e.d. 64, sheet 2 (household of William McGarity), e.d. 69, sheet 1 (household of Charley McGarity), e.d. 69, sheet 11 (household of John McGarity); U.S. Census of 1910, roll 1558, Guadalupe County, Texas, e.d. 52, sheet 12 (household of William McGarity), e.d. 58, sheet 11 (household

of John McGarity); U.S. Census of 1920, roll 1810, Guadalupe County, Texas, e.d. 152, sheet 7, family 131 (household of Charlie McGarity), e.d. 148, sheet 3B, family 57, (household of John McGarity) and family 56 (household of Jason McGarity), e.d. 140, sheet 13A, family 272 (household of William W. McGarity); the Guadalupe County 1930 census is very faded and difficult to read; these families have not yet been located in that record. My appreciation to Franklin Carter Smith who shared in the research of this case study.

7 U.S. Census of 1880, roll 1306, Gonzales County, Texas, e.d. 70, sheet 42–43, family 425 (household of Jason McGarity), sheet 43, family 429 (household of Eliza McGarity).

8 U.S. Census of 1870, roll 1587, Gonzales County, Texas, p. 476, family 25 (household of Nancy McGarity), family 27 (household of Jason McGarity).

9 Gonzales County, Texas, Tax Rolls, 1837–1880, microfilm, listed year by year in rough alphabetical order; Guadalupe County, Texas, Tax Rolls, 1888–1902, microfilm, year by year, usually alphabetical.

10 The 1880 census, previously cited, listed Jason as black; the 1870 census mistakenly listed him and his family as white; in 1900, mulatto was not a racial category on the census; in 1910 and 1920, Jason's son William McGarity was reported as mulatto, as was John's son Jason in 1920.

11 U.S. Census of 1870, Gonzales County, Texas, p. 476, family 24, household of C. McGarity, physician; U.S. Census of 1880, Gonzales County, Texas, e.d. 70, sheet 43, family 43, household of Clemons McGarity, M.D.

12 U.S. Census of 1860, roll 1295, free schedule, Gonzales County, Texas, p. 72, household of C. McGarity; U.S. Census of 1860, roll 1310, slave schedule, Gonzales County, Texas, p. 41B, sheet 3, column 1, slaveholder C. McGarity.

13 U.S. Census of 1850, roll 379, free schedule, Panola County, Mississippi, p. 348, family 605, household of C. McGarity; U.S. Census of 1850, roll 388, slave schedule, Panola County, Mississippi, no McGarity shown.

14 Panola County, Mississippi, Combination Tax Rolls, 1837–1845, Personal Tax Rolls, 1852, 1855, 1856 (some years missing), microfilm; the Mississippi tax rolls cited herein were microfilmed from the records of the Mississippi Auditor of Public Accounts, Record Group 29.

15 Ibid.; John H. McGarrity/McGaherty appears only on the combination tax rolls, 1840–1845.

16 Censuses of 1860–1900 consistently reported Dr. McGarity's age as 39, 49, 59, and 79; U.S. Census of 1900, roll 1653, LaSalle County, Texas, e.d. 138, sheet 2, family 30, household of Clemons McGarity, reporting his father as James Clemons McGarity, physician, age 79, born December 1820 in South Carolina.

17 U.S. Census of 1860, free schedule, Gonzales County, Texas, p. 73, family 43, household of Clemons McGarity, age 23; family 44, household of William McGarity, age 25; U.S. Census of 1860, slave schedule, Gonzales County, Texas, no entries in John's name.

18 U.S. Census of 1850, free schedule, roll 25, Chicot County, Arkansas, p. 183B, household of J.M. [sic] McGarity; U.S. Census of 1850, slave schedule, roll 32, Chicot County, Arkansas, no J.H. or J.M. McGarity shown.

19 Gonzales County, Texas, Tax Rolls, 1837–1880, microfilm.

20 Kathy Bahlman, Jeffrey Bahlman, and Victoria Bahlman, comps., *Slave Transactions, Gonzales County, Texas, 1-25-1839 to 3-11-1855, Based on Deed Records (Bills of*

Sale, Mortgage, Schedule, and Chattel) of Gonzales County, Texas From the Beginning to 1924, computer database print-out, Gonzales County Records Center and Archives, Courthouse Annex, Gonzales, Texas.

21 Marriage record of Clemons McGarity and Blanche V. Abbott, 9 October 1873, Gonzales County Marriage Records, Book B:551, #1761, County Clerk's Office, Courthouse Annex, Gonzales, Texas.

22 Message posted by Joy Shealy, McGarity Family Forum, online <http://genforum.genealogy.com/mcgarity/messages/44.html> accessed 16 April 2002; this message named three sisters, but the referenced will named four.

23 Brent Howard Holcomb, comp., *Union County, South Carolina, Will Abstracts 1787–1849* (Columbia, S.C.: the compiler, 1987), 108; Will and probate file of Clemons McGarity, probate box 12, package 18 (the will also recorded in Will Book B:78–80), Union County, South Carolina, FHL microfilm 0255028.

24 U.S. Census of 1820, roll 121, Union County, South Carolina, p. 142B, household of Clemons Magarity; U.S. Census of 1830, roll 171, Union County, South Carolina, p. 205, line 23, household of Mary McGarity; in 1830, the total number of persons enumerated in the household in 1830 suggest that the enumerator or copier simply failed to mark Mary in her age bracket but counted her in the total; four younger women were enumerated but cannot be identified as daughters without more evidence.

25 Barbara R. Langdon, *South Carolina Marriages, Vol. IV, 1787–1875, Implied in the Miscellaneous Records of South Carolina* (Aiken, S.C.: the author, 1994), 77.

26 U.S. Census of 1820, Union County, South Carolina, p. 145, household of Philip Littlefield; U.S. Census of 1830, roll 176, Gibson County, Tennessee, p. 237, household of Phillip Littlefield; apparently his two older sons were living next door; neither household reported slaves.

27 U.S. Census of 1850, free schedule, Panola County, Mississippi, p. 340, 347, 349, 353, 365; slave schedule, Panola County, p. 161, 185, 187, 203, 205, 267, with duplicate entries on later pages; Flemming [*sic*] Littlefield had two entries, each duplicated later in the schedule, showing 42 and 4 slaves respectively.

28 U.S. Census of 1850, free schedule, Panola County, Mississippi, p. 340, 347, 349, 353, 365; Panola County Combination Tax Rolls 1837–1845, Personal Tax Rolls 1852–1856, microfilm.

29 Gonzales County, Texas, Tax Rolls, 1837–1880, microfilm.

30 Ibid.; Estate of Fleming Littlefield, file 293, Gonzales County Probate Records, County Clerk's Office, Courthouse Annex, Gonzales, Texas.

31 U.S. Census of 1860, slave schedule, Gonzales County, Texas, p. 2.

32 Alice Duggan Gracy, Fleming Littlefield, in *The History of Gonzales County, Texas* (Gonzales, Tex.: Gonzales County Historical Commission, 1986), 395–396.

33 Norma Maxwell, *Phillip Littlefield* (Moscow, Kan.: the author, not dated), 3, at Gonzales County Records Center and Archives, Courthouse Annex, Gonzales, Texas.

34 Holcomb, *Union County, South Carolina, Will Abstracts 1787–1849,* 119–120; Will and probate file of Zachariah Nance, probate box 16, package 15, Union County, South Carolina, FHL microfilm 0130645.

35 Helen Simmons Carey, submitter, "Zachariah Nance Jr. and Sr." on FamilyHistory.com Message Boards, 27 June 2000, online <http://boards.ancestry.com>, for Tippah County, Mississippi, accessed 1 May 2002.

36 U.S. Census of 1850, roll 1310, slave schedule, Gonzales County, Texas, p. 7, slaveholder Charles Hall.

37 U.S. Census of 1860, free schedule, Gonzales County, Texas, Belmont neighborhood, p. 73, family 41, household of D.J. Hall, age 31 and close neighbor of John H. McGarity and Z.N. Littlefield; p. 116, family 290, household of J.M. Hall, age 41; family 291, household of F.B. Hall, age 36.
38 Gonzales County, Texas, Tax Rolls, 1837–1880, microfilm.
39 Estate of Margaret Hall, file 471, Gonzales County Probate Records, County Clerk's Office, Courthouse Annex, Gonzales, Texas.
40 Marriage record of Tennie McGarity and John Bond, Gonzales County Marriage Record Book C:679-680, license #2839, County Clerk's Office, Courthouse Annex, Gonzales, Texas; U.S. Census of 1900, roll 1638, Gonzales County, Texas, e.d. 52, sheet 3, family 49, household of John Bond.
41 U.S. Census of 1850, roll 371, free schedule, DeSoto County, Mississippi, p. 319, family 94, household of F.B. Hall; U.S. Census of 1850, roll 381, free schedule, Tippah County, Mississippi, p. 481, family 1221 (household of Zack Hall) and p. 480, family 1217 (household of Jesse M. Hale); U.S. Census of 1850, roll 371, slave schedule, DeSoto County, Mississippi; U.S. Census of 1850, roll 388, slave schedule, Tippah County and Panola County, Mississippi.
42 Panola County, Mississippi, personal property tax rolls, 1852, (the years between 1845 and 1852, and 1853–1854 are missing), microfilm.
43 U.S. Census of 1840, roll 219, Tippah County, Mississippi, p. 204, line 12, household of Margaret Hall; line 14, household of Jesse M. Hall.
44 Tippah County, Mississippi, tax rolls, 1840s, microfilm, abstract provided by Hall researcher, Cary Hall, e-mail to Emily Croom, 16 May 2002.
45 E-mail from Cary Hall, 16 May 2002; Probate file of Fleming Hall, Abbeville County, South Carolina, probate box 43, package 960, FHL microfilm 0130649.
46 Telephone conversation by Emily Croom with Chancery Court Clerk's Office staff, Huntingdon, Tennessee, 27 August 2002.
47 U.S. Census of 1830, roll 174, Carroll County, Tennessee, p. 175, household of Fleming Hall.
48 Tippah County, Mississippi, Tax Rolls, 1836–1840, microfilm.
49 U.S. Census of 1820, roll 120, Pendleton County, South Carolina, p. 166, household of Fleming Hall.

Chapter Ten

1 *Twenty Censuses: Population and Housing Questions, 1790–1980* (Washington, D.C.: U.S. Department of Commerce, Bureau of the Census, 1979), 22.
2 Introduction to National Archives micropublication M1186, *Enrollment Cards for the Five Civilized Tribes, 1898–1914*, at the beginning of roll 1, remarks written by Kent Carter.
3 Kent Carter, *The Dawes Commission and the Allotment of the Five Civilized Tribes, 1893–1914* (Salt Lake City: Ancestry.com, 1999), ix.
4 Ian Watson, *Catawba Indian Genealogy* (Geneseo, N.Y.: Department of Anthropology, State University of New York at Geneseo, 1995), 89.
5 *Lane v. Baker*, 12 Ohio Supreme Court Reporter 237.
6 Civil War pension file of Isaac Ah-pah-kee (private, Co. K, 37th Wisconsin Volunteers), certificate 152871, and widow's pension file of Catherine Ah-pah-kee/Shunion/Laughrey, certificate 540610, Pension Application Files Based Upon Service in the Civil War and Later, Records of the Veterans Administration, Record Group 15, National Ar-

chives Building, Washington, D.C.

7 U.S. Census of 1910, roll 1729, Oconto County, Wisconsin, Menominee Reservation, Indian Schedule, e.d. 115, sheet 7A, household of Michea? Puhkuw (handwriting somewhat difficult to read).

8 U.S. Census of 1920, roll 2016, Shawano County, Wisconsin, Menominee Indian Reservation, e.d. 122, sheet 16A, household of James Laughrey.

9 John D. Benedict, *Muskogee and Northeastern Oklahoma* (Chicago: S.J. Clarke Publishing Co., 1922), II:128, an article about Sarah's husband, Nelson F. Carr, identifies Sarah's parents and gives the Carrs' marriage date; application of Nelson F. Carr for enrollment in the Cherokee Nation as a citizen by intermarriage, affidavit of 8 January 1907, giving civil marriage date and marriage according to Cherokee law on 17 February 1868, file for Cherokee census card 4206, National Archives, Federal Records Center, Fort Worth, Texas.

10 Dawes roll census card for Sarah A. Carr and family, National Archives microfilm M1186, roll 7, Cherokee census card 4206, naming Sarah's parents; Sarah was called "Annie" in the family but is listed as Sarah A. or Sarah Ann in official records; file for Cherokee census card 4206, National Archives, Federal Records Center, Fort Worth, Texas.

11 Ruby Cranor, *Talking Tombstones: Pioneers of Washington County [Oklahoma]* (Bartlesville, Okla.: the author, 1983), 122, showing age at death and parents' names; birth date figured from Rogers's age at death as shown on the tombstone, copied in the 1970s before the inscription became too eroded to photograph; U.S. Census of 1900, roll 1843, Cherokee Nation, Indian Territory, e.d. 10, sheet 1, family 8, household of Nelson F. Carr, entire household listed as white, including wife, Annie; same roll, e.d. 10, sheet 22, family 7 of Indian schedule at end of e.d., household of William Rodgers [brother of Sarah A. Carr]; U.S. Census of 1910, roll 1275, Washington County, Oklahoma, end of e.d. 252, first page of the Indian schedule, household of Nelson F. Carr and wife, Annie; U.S. Census of 1920, roll 1490, Washington County, Oklahoma, e.d. 271, sheet 10, family 214, household of Nelson F. Carr with wife, Sarah A., listed as Indian.

12 Cranor, *Talking Tombstones*, 122, Martha's tombstone next to her husband's, her birth date figured from her age at death; Benedict, *Muskogee and Northeastern Oklahoma*, II:128, an article about Nelson F. Carr, likely incorporating information gained from the family, states that Hilliard and Martha married when Martha was sixteen.

13 Cranor, *Talking Tombstones*, 122.

14 Emmet Starr, *History of the Cherokee Indians and Their Legends and Folk Lore* (Muskogee, Okla.: Hoffman Printing Co., 1984, reprint of 1921 original), 464.

15 File of Sarah A. (Rogers) Carr (1907), file #617 of the Guion Miller report, National Archives microfilm M1104, roll 70.

16 Drennen roll of 1851, typescript attached to the Guion Miller report, Cherokee Nation, Delaware District, household 937, Hilliard Rogers and family, National Archives microfilm M685, roll 12.

17 Valuation #244 of James Foster, 1837, Cherokee Valuations, then in Cass County, Georgia, Record Group 75, Records of the Bureau of Indian Affairs, National Archives Building, Washington; some of these records are now on microfilm A18, available at Archives I and the Fort Worth, Texas, regional branch.

18 Starr, *History of the Cherokee Indians*, 464, lists Hilliard first among the Rogers children.

19 Affidavit of Looney Hicks, 23 May 1845, before the judge of Skin Bayou District, Cherokee Nation, file 46, frame 873, in Letters to the Cherokee Agency, Special Files of the Office of Indian Affairs, 1807–1904, Record Group 75, Records of the Bureau of Indian Affairs, National Archives microfilm M574, roll 5, copy provided the researcher by the Western History Collection, University of Oklahoma, Norman.

20 Ibid., statement of Elizabeth Candy, to Judge George Candy, Flint District, Cherokee Nation, file 46, frame 859.

21 George Morrison Bell Sr., *Genealogy of Old & New Cherokee Indian Families* (Bartlesville, Okla: the author, 1979), 8–9, 46–47, 96–97.

Chapter Eleven

1 E-mail from A.G. Conlon to Emily Croom, 25 December 2002; *Soundex Index to Canadian Border Entries Through the St. Albans, Vermont, District, 1895–1924*, M1461, roll 91, Soundex code C545, FHL microfilm 1472891.

2 Declaration of intention for Desire Hautekiet, August 1887, District Court of the United States for the Southern District of California, from records held at the National Archives branch in Laguna Niguel, California, FHL microfilm 1491530, item 1, p. 2.

3 Declaration of intention for Antonio Regina, 1906, U.S. Circuit Court for the Southern District of California, Southern Division, in "Declarations of Intention Filed Prior to September 29, 1906," FHL microfilm 1491530, item 2, no. 5, page number illegible.

4 Naturalization petition for Sidney Augustus Marsh, petition no. 4, vol. 1, Petition and Record, 1907–1912, District Court of Wharton County, Texas, Courthouse, Wharton.

5 E-mail from Charlie Gardes to author, 26 May 2002.

6 Charlie assigned the Henri spelling to Herr Immigrant to distinguish him from the son, Henry W., and in keeping with the family tradition of French origin; the senior Henry never used that spelling.

7 Military pension file of Henry Washburn Gardes, Veterans Administration pension file XC-02-423-913, originally filed 22 August 1922, photocopy sent in 1993 from Veterans Administration Archives/Warehouse, Suitland, Maryland, to the Houston, Texas, V.A. office, which furnished a copy to Charles Gardes.

8 Charles A. Gardes Jr., "Henry Washburn Gardes: Research Notes" (Houston, Tex.: the compiler, 1995), Prologue, 1.

9 Card index record for Geraldine Delaide Washburn, in WPA Cemetery Card Index, 1800–1920, for New Orleans, Lousiana, Louisiana State Museum, New Orleans; the only source found so far that identified Geraldine's middle name; all others used only her middle initial, *D*.

10 Marriage license no. 346, Gardes-Washburn, recorded 5 September 1859, Dallas County, Arkansas, Marriage Book B (1854–1895):70, FHL microfilm 0984226.

11 Obituary of Geraldine Gardes, *New Orleans Times-Picayune*, 16 November 1866, p. 4, col. 3; letter from Henry W. Gardes to Commissioner of Pensions, 29 Dec 1922, page 1, in V.A. pension file XC-02-423-913; extract from Henry's Yale biography sent to Charles A. Gardes Jr. by A.W. Gardes Jr., 26 May 1993.

12 Interment record of Henri Gardes, Interment Records of Fireman's Charitable and Benevolent Association Cemetery, WPA Cemetery Card Index, 1800–1920, for New Orleans, Lousiana.

13 "Henry Gardes Dead: Former Banker Dies at Age of Eighty-One," *(New Orleans) Daily Picayune*, 3 August 1913, p. 11, col. 4; short obituary, same issue, p. 8, col. 5.

14 Ibid, p. 11, col. 4.

15 "Bank Officials in Trouble," *The New York Times*, 29 August 1896, p. 1, col. 5.

16 U.S. Census of 1900, roll 1269, Franklin County, Ohio, Columbus, e.d. 111, sheet 7B, line 87.

17 Charles A. Gardes, "Henry Gardes: Chapter Last—07-02-2002—105 Years Ago Today," p. 1, based on the thousands of pages of court documents, *The United States of America v. Walter W. Girault, Henry Gardes, and Thomas H. Underwood*, Cause 2233, Criminal Docket, Fifth Circuit Court of the United States, Eastern District of Louisiana; from the appeals court files of *Gardes v. United States* and *Girault v. Same*, No. 646, Circuit Court of Appeals, U.S. Fifth Circuit, New Orleans, 19 April 1898, identified in 87 F. 172; this section of the case study is based on this Gardes account.

18 Pension file of Henry W. Gardes, V.A. pension file XC-02-423-913, provides marriage date and couple's ages; relationship between Henry's stepmother and wife was known and documented within the family; Henry W. and family were living with his stepmother in 1900.

19 Gardes, "Henry Gardes: Chapter Last," p. 1, from interview with Henry W. Gardes's daughter Hersilie Philomene Gardes (b 1908, still living in 2002), who heard about the incident from family members who were there, probably from her mother, Lucie (Wiltz) Gardes, who may well have attended the trial.

20 *Gardes v. United States* and *Girault v. Same*, Circuit Court of Appeals, U.S. Fifth Circuit, 19 April 1898, No. 646, 87 F. 172.

21 George Cole, "A History of the Ohio Penitentiary from 1850 to 1900" (master's thesis, Ohio State University, 1941).

22 U.S. Census of 1900, Franklin County, Ohio, Columbus, ed. 111, sheet 7A, line 49, William Porter; Record of prisoner 30664, W.S. Porter, Register of Prisoners, Register 21, Ohio Penitentiary, Columbus, Ohio, 1834–1919, p. 26–27, FHL microfilm 0928458.

23 Record of prisoner 30782, Henry Gardes, Register of Prisoners, Register 21 (April 1898–March 1900), Ohio Penitentiary, p. 80–85, FHL microfilm 0928458.

24 Ibid.

25 Passport application of Henry Gardes of New Orleans, no. 11241, *Passport Applications, 1795–1924*, Vol. 373, FHL film 1432672 (apparently from M1372, *Passport Applications, 1795–1905)*.

26 Index entry for Henry Gardes, in index for Fult–Geihsler, New York, Court of Common Pleas, New York County, *Naturalization Records, 1792–1906; Index, 1792–1906*, FHL microfilm 1002058.

27 Naturalization file of Henry Gardes, file 252, 13 July 1855, Bundle 143C, New York Court of Common Pleas, FHL microfilm 0964149.

28 Marriage of Gardes-Bienvenue, 26 May 1875, Orleans Parish Marriages, vol. 5:222, Louisiana State Archives, Baton Rouge, microfilm and certified photocopy.

29 Birth record for Hinrich Gärdes, 5 November 1831, birth no. 20 for 1831 in Zivilstandsregister 1814–1832, Grambke, Bremen, Germany, FHL microfilm 0953065, from Geburts-Register für den Zivilstands-Bezirt Mittelsbüren und Grambke, 1814–1832.

Index